GW01003684

Stefan Brecht
The original theatre of the
City of New York.
From the mid-60s to the mid-70s

Book 1
The Theatre of Visions:
Robert Wilson

Methuen Drama

First edition published in Germany 1978 by
Suhrkamp Verlag Frankfurt am Main
and distributed in Great Britain by
Eyre Methuen

This edition published 1994 by
Methuen Drama
an imprint of Reed Consumer Books Ltd
Michelin House, 81 Fulham Road, London SW3 6RB
and Auckland, Melbourne, Singapore and Toronto

ISBN 0-413-49590-6

A CIP catalogue record for this book
is available from the British Library

Printed and bound in Great Britain
by Cox & Wyman Limited, Reading, Berkshire.

## Caution

# Contents

At this the moon was discovered
in the upper part of the house,
triumphant in a silver throne made
in figure of a *pyramis*. Her gar-
ments white and silver, the dress-
ing of her head antique, and
crowned with a luminary, or
sphere of light, which striking on
the clouds, and heightened with
silver, reflected as natural clouds
do by the splendour of the moon.
The heaven about her was vaulted
with blue silk and set with stars
of silver which had in them their
several lights burning.

*The Queen's Masques: the first, of
Blackness.*

# Preface

Theatre of visions is the staging, with live performers, movements and development in such a fashion as to appear a world or reality or the representation of one[1] by an individual of images occurring to that individual and seeming personally important and significant to him (or her) independently of verbal, intellectual or discursive analysis, – meaningful, but quite possibly the unique significations of their meaning. The making of such theatre can not be construed as the making of a statement: there is, for the maker, no question of truth or plausibility. It is not an imitative nor in any way a significative act: there is, for the maker, no question of meaning. The maker's intent is not to induce pity, terror or hilarity or to purge the spectator of fear or resentment, nor to uplift him (or her) morally, nor to induce him (or her) to change society or to give him (or her) information useful for this, but to impart the vision and a sense of its importance and significance. Theatre of visions is a stage-designer's theatre, theatre of the director functioning as stage-designer. It relates to masques and pageants, and to any theatre dominated by stage-design. But to my knowledge, Wilson's theatre has been unique on the contemporary scene.

The brain is functionally asymmetric. What either half is good at is inferred either from the whole brain's functional deteriorations when that half is wounded, or from a half's capacities – or the other half's incapacities – in individuals, e.g. epileptics, subjected to callosectomy, i.e. in whom the two halves don't communicate. Since the right half specializes in left-hand, the left half in right-hand sensory and motor activities, their respective capacities can also be inferred, taking into account inter-activity competition, from segregative studies of these.

It has been known for a little over a century now that it is the left brain that all in all, – linguistic and manual dexterity being coupled[2]

[1] This distinguishes it not only from non-true-or-false and non-significative modes of other art forms, but from performance-art and happenings exposing the spectator to the peculiarity of particular objects, acts or environments.

[2] That the right brain's semantic powers – it is apparently sometimes aware of the meaning of words, even while unaware of the words! – seem pretty well limited to nouns, in particular don't extend to verbs or to words formed from verbs may be a clue to the link between the left brain's roles in speech and manual dexterity: tho the more general link surely is the role of a language-

– is the linguist, – has the powers of speech and speech-comprehension, writing and reading: but during the last thirty years, the right brain has emerged as particularly endowed with visual powers, – the seer.

In addition, another doctrine of separation of powers has become respectable: the left brain is regarded as preeminently analytic, the identifier (and serial relator) of recurrent elements of experience (identical in their reoccurrence, thus named universals), the right brain as preeminently synthetic: the creator-recognizer of patterns (wholes, gestalten), including, especially, – since this is where this power matters, – abnormal, unfamiliar, new, incomplete and non-sensical (uncategorized, unexplained, useless) ones, creating-recognizing them not additively, but in one (»in parallel«, simultaneously, by acts of intuition). Whether the linguistic (semantic, syntactic, as well as phonological) and manual powers of the left brain are onto- and phylogenetically the basis of its analytic powers, or vice versa is not clear, nor whether the visual or geometric powers of mapping and orientation of the right brain are the basis of its powers of synthesizing intuition: but it seems clear that as naming is the left brain's tool of analysis, so the right brain's syntheses are spatial metaphors, and that as the left brain's powers of analysis seem contingent on an abstraction from the individuation conferred by location, so the right brain's synoptic powers seem contingent on abstinence from verbal universalization. As the left brain's analytic powers extend beyond the aural (phoneme- and consonant-formation and -recognition) and tactile (in handling things for practical purposes) into the visual (in reading and writing), so the right brain's synthetic powers extend beyond the visual into the tactile and aural (e.g. the making and comprehension of music) (and in one manner or another beyond the narrowly perceptual into the conceptual, e.g. mathematics). The right brain's powers are thus visually centered, but not merely visual, but generally imaginative.

Wilson's theatre of visions was a successful attempt to create a right-brain dominated theatre.

dependent purposive intelligence in learned labor. This hints at a peculiar relation of the right brain to art.

# 1. Florescence of visions, 1969-73.

# Introduction

It seems that Robert Wilson was born in Waco, Texas, on October 4th, 1941, that his family was white, middle-class, Protestant and Southern, and that from 1959 to 1962, having graduated from high school,[1] and having in 1958 been more or less cured of a speech impediment by a dancer, Mrs. Byrd Hoffman,[2] he studied at the University of Texas,[3] where he did theatre work with children.[4]

[1] »... when-when I was in – a graduate from high school, we had to, we had to, everyone in our senior year, spent half ot their senior year in high school, ah, writing a poem – they read at graduation. In Waco, Texas, there is, they have the R-Robert Browning Memorial Library, this huge thing, Robert Browning, and somehow Robert Browning's this big thing in Waco, Texas, (laugh) everyone writes like Robert Browr¹ng (laugh) like, you just can't believe it, you know, in a – in a high school I don't know how I had enough sense to know that I couldn't do that, I mean, it's like, it's like the – it's like, that you know, there was something else to do rather than Robert Browning (laugh). So, I just, I wasn't gonna get out of high school cause I – didn't do that and like, when it came time for gradua-tion and- d-d, in this same way, and it goes all day long, these kids go on for twenty minutes – on – just reading these poems – that-that they've written by the (inaudible), you know (inaudible) a lot (laugh) – – – – – Christ! Oh, so the – it was my time and I walked out on the stage and I said »Birdie, birdie, why do you bond so, birdie, birdie why do you bond?« I said it I walked off stage and everyone laughed (laugh). My mother started crying, »Why do you always have to make a fool of yourself?« (Laugh). And my English teacher said, »It's not a poem, it's not a poem and you're not gonna graduate until you write a poem!« (laugh). And I said, »It is too a poem« and she said, »What does ›bond‹ mean?« I said, »I don't know, but it's a poem.« I don't ... She says, »Nope, y-you've got to tell me what it means« and-d-d, I don't know, oh, we really, we had a time. And I wasn't – finally I did graduate, I never wrote a poem (laugh) That was – I said – I said – I said, »That's a poem and I like it« but anyhow, it didn't – I don't know what I liked, I just did it, cause I didn't – – – – – all the others, I just – it was just – ah, it's, I said, oh, I, it seems like a – I just thought – that stupid high school (laugh) s-stupid, in some ways I – sometimes I think that things that I think I hated the most maybe – were best for me – I remember having to go to church and s-stand for one hour, I-hating the f- I mean really now – and somehow I'm glad I did it now (Uhum) yah, I had to stand there like quiet and still, why, well, this is, I hate it, I hate it, I want to get out of here, I do not, I just do not, it was interesting. I sort of hoped (laugh) I used to go along with it – (inaudible) especially, when I lived in (inaudible) (laugh) I – the teachers never liked me, tho, I couldn't – – – – – « (Interv. w/Wilson, 1970).

[2] A propos of his therapeutic work with children during his time at Pratt (1963-65), I asked Wilson whether he'ld say that anybody had directed his attention to the exercises he had them do:

»Yeah, there's one thing in my life that very much (I meant a theory, a name, a person, a book ...) I can show you a book but I'll tell you the most important

During 1962, he seems to have studied painting; with one George McNeil in Paris, but by 1963 he was back in the U.S., a student of architecture at Pratt Institute in Brooklyn, from which he seems to

thing – I had a speech impediment until I was 17 and and I couldn't talk – hah, hah, it was like that. I couldn't get it haaaa, ssssssstutter, also my – I was tongue-tied too, my tongue had been clipped I think it was tied to the bottom of my mouth. Most of it was just fear, not being able to talk. When I was 17 uh my my parents had taken me as an infant to people hum professional people to help me with speech and I I still hadn't learned to talk – and I met a woman who was a dancer (You actually couldn't talk) I could but it was like thaaat, it took me a long time to it was very very difficult. (inaudible question) Yes, and uh and it even got worse as I got older cause I couldn't I became more self-conscious of it and just it became an enormous problem. And teachers – I got to school and teachers would say, ask me to read aloud and-and then say, no there's more, you have to have a longer pause between the words but there is even a little longer, if there's a comma, but it's even longer if there's a semicolon, but the longest is when there's a period and suddenly it became so complex it it was just so difficult for me to do and this woman was a dancer – she was a ballet dancer – she was in her 70's when I met her. She taught the dance – she understood the body in a remarkable way, she she said – oh, you can learn to speak I know you can and uh in about three months of working with her I did, by somehow relaxing and taking my time uh finally I learned to say, I learned to talk (You worked directly on . . . . you talked or did you dance?) I – not dance so much but somehow I got inside my body and I was able to release tension, I was able to uh I was able to somehow through through my own efforts (And then what did she do?) She uh, she pointed out, she noticed I was, that I was very, very tense all through the shoulders and through here and she talked to me about the energy in my body, about relaxing, letting energy flow through so, so that it wasn't blocked and she worked also . . . . she, she would play the piano and-and I would, I would just move my body. She didn't watch, she would be in another room. And she gave me exercises which I, which just relax, it's mostly to release tension. She was amazing because she never taught a technique, she never gave me a way to approach it, it was more that I discovered it on my own. But she made me realise that, a lot of it was just a physical handicap. When I learned to speak that was that was a break-through.« (Interv. w/Wilson, 1970).

A propos of the learning difficulties of children with physical handicaps, Wilson mentioned his sister:

». . . uh like people say well – my son's an athlete and yet he doesn't do well in school or it's difficult for him to learn – it doesn't, it doesn't necessarily mean exercise that way uh – but, but it, but it, it is pretty much a fact that that children who, who are limited, say, say, what – I had – my sister was born with her legs turned in. Uh and so for the first five years of her life they had to uh, she had to go through a series of operations where they break the bones and reset her legs and uh so she was very slow in learning and . . .« (interv. w/Wilson, 1970).

But a love for the *boy* child, a loving compassion for the helpless young male (having nothing to do with pederasty) seems to me a major motif of all Wilson's later work; and a resentment against the demand for speech its major impetus and perhaps nemesis.

have received the degree of a bachelor of fine arts in 1965,[6] continuing his work with children, but working now with brain damaged children, and apparently – to his own mind – applying things he had learned from Mrs. Hoffman:

3 »It's like, my parents were paying for school, I was, I had all-all the security and I suddenly – I left just before I was to graduate from the University of Texas. I said, I just can't do this anymore – I know I want to do something else – I just left.« (Interv. w/Wilson, 1970).
4 »Bob was in Waco Children's Theatre at Baylor University, and that is how I got to know him.« (Jearnine Wagner, letter of VII/10/75.)
»I'd always been doing theatre work with children and it had always been *their* work. I'd work with children and they would write plays and we'd do them. They would perform them. (In what context?) Everywhere, we I did them in Texas. I started when I graduated from high school. I had – there were a hundred children involved with the children's program and then I went to the University of Texas for a while and I started working with children there and uh (You put on plays) we put on plays and we did them outside, we did them in construction sites – – we did them in churches – we did them uh in garages or in vacant lots (They would be written by somebody around?) Yes, but but we we almost never – well we did *Peter Pan* and we did *Alice in Wonderland* and we wrote the scripts ourselves – like from Lewis Carroll we adapted uh (You say we, is that mostly you or is that mostly the . . .) Mostly the *children* and then I would, I worked with them but it was mostly their work. Whereas this this is mostly say my work in that I'm structuring the activities and I'm putting it together. But what happened before is that the children, someone would direct it – the children would direct it or someone would design or someone would whatever . . .« (Interv. w/Wilson 1970).
Apparently he did at least some of this work with Jearnine Wagner. Showing me a book about her work he'd brought along (»We had a book come out called *A Place for Ideas: Our Theater* on the work we did at Baylor and some at Trinity. It described the general philosophy of that time. It was done by Trinity University Press in 1965, but it is sold out and out of print at this time.« (J. Wagner, letter cited)), he spoke of this work: »That's really the thing that interests me most, is education. – I have a book. This is some of the work I did with kids in Texas – this was ten years ago – this is uh a boy – he's now about uh 18 or so, he's going to study architecture. He went to – he was in a reform school he tried to burn down the school – he was a very, very bad kid – all the work used to be with children – here's the – – the dance. This was a theatre that I built that was like a little camera (inaudible), it was very small – not much bigger than this room – it was nice cause you could go up and down here on levels like with a camera like you could focus with light, like we had feet that came down here – – – I'll show you – just with that strip of feet up here and even on a hand there if you put a spot on it you were so close that the audience could see it just – we had stairs that, you could make like solid platforms in here and it was very shallow space – this is the woman that I worked with in Texas – she is still working – and this is just someone who came in to help with the book – the most interesting subjects were written by the kids – a lot-lot of the text is their writing but I'm working on a book now that's that I want to do (Is any of your writing in here too?) None

15

»I've worked, about seven or eight years ago I worked with brain damaged children, working with physical activity, with – and that uh was – I was very, very excited about – about the work that I was doing then or – and

of my writing, in fact I had left before the book was done – but I worked with a lot of these projects like – this was uh a house – (laughs) this was a long time ago – this was a spectacle we did – I worked with Phillip for two years – we wrote the script and directed it, – that – that was ten years ago. I love children – –« (Interv. w/Wilson, 1970).

5 »Yes – – – I've painted all my life, you know when I was a child I was always painting. I painted up until five years ago and I grew up with an image of myself as a painter, and I never thought about anything else. I started architecture, I got a degree in architecture, I did other things but . . .« (Interv. w/Wilson, 1970). The young Wilson seems at this time to have courted and obtained the patronage of some older men of means and influence.

6 The Gale Research Company's *Contemporary Authors* in addition credits him with an MFA. – »When I first came to New York I went to – school at Pratt (Uhum). And I was so frightened to go to school there, I was frightened to be in New York, and I was very frightened. I-I didn't have any money – I-I knew I wanted to be in New York and I wanted to go to an art school and I d-didn't know how I was going to pay for it – I'd never done too well in school, academically, you know – marks, and, ah, but somehow, I figured I don't know, for some reason I wanted to go to school, I wanted to study architecture – I wanted to – I-I had to leave home to do it (Uhum).

And so I-I-I made very high marks. I-first time in my life I got, I got the highest marks in the class, and I got s-scholarships and they paid for my school – tuition, yah, – but then, later I got lax (laugh) that was – that was the first two years I was there – I'm-the first two years I was – I was – first in the class, and then there would be the marks (laugh) and I graduated last in the class (Yah) But that – all the time I was really thinking a lot about I was really thinking a lot about – – – – – (?) (inaudible) That's-that's where I was really getting into so-what was happening to me, what they were doing to me . . . . .

. . when I graduated from Pratt I was offered a job at an architectural – with an architect – a very well known architect offered me a good job – this – going to work for him and I really didn't want to do that, but at the same time I was sort of flattered that I had been asked to do that and-and it also would mean I would have money because I didn't have any money and I was in debt and it would mean a lot – and then I just – I kept saying no – I just know, I just sensed like not to do that – to stay away from it – and I'm glad I of course didn't but – I mean it was hard even at that time – it was amazing – even to have a perspective it was like something really drawing me to do it . . . (Interv. w/Wilson, 1970).

When I showed him a book by Sybil Moholy-Nagy, Wilson commented: »Sybil, Sybil, she's, she was at Pratt, they just, those kids, oh, how, they don't know what they had there, it was like, and the whole faculty, they were so disrespectful to that woman, I loved her, she was, I'd just, I'd go, I'd-d go to her classes all the time just to, just to just watch her (Uhum) I mean, s-s she was giving those kids something they couldn't get anywhere else – I really liked her – – – – – she was extraordinary. It was a great thing to get her in class (laugh). It's interesting, I didn't, she's not, she's not a Pratt anymore, they, threw, they were quite glad to

I think that that's the base of what I'm still doing today in my classes. (What physical – what kind of thing did you do?) Well, uh with the brain damaged children I was, we were working with hum uh very simple exercises. It's believed that if children don't uh or uh if people don't fully develop in, in basic stages of physical activity then their mental readiness to learn is hindered and, that, there *is* a close association, – relationship between physical activity and mental activity and that, uh when I was working with brain damaged children I did such things as, as crawling exercises or pushing and pulling, even more simple than that, turning your head from side to side, keeping your head up. And if an infant doesn't fully develop in each one of these stages then hum – it doesn't mean that he can't learn – but his readiness to learn is hindered and – then even more interesting to me was – was after that I started working hum (How would you motivate them – I mean how would you – what would you do?) Well,

they got rid of her, she is now at Columbia –––––that was a great loss for that school – she was was interested in every kid – there was no respect for her on account of that but they were not, they were not interested, and I never could understand why. (I imagine it was hard to take notes on what she said?) Oh, extremely, it was, I always was fascinated by, I just loved her classes, I used to go in, she never called a roll, s-just go in and, she always – sh-sh-showed slides and talked about them, just lectured, I'd just go in and sit, and-and all the years I was there, just-just so fascinated –––––There were 5,000 students there ––––– somehow it never could excite the others –––––really an amazing woman (inaudible remark by interviewer concerning ›great teachers‹) Yes, exactly, and the thing is – is, you can't judge it by, like the popularity of say like a teacher or whatever. Like in her case, certainly she was an unpopular teacher, I think like just one or two people liked her- (part missing, tape not running) They-they were like talking, but the kids, they were saying, why (inaudible) and related it to this, and this and, I don't know, they were talking about space and all this stuff that we talk about in architecture, and this man, he said, – his head was somewhere else, he was like ––– spaced, he-he couldn't, he wouldn't follow, he wasn't listening to what they were saying, but he had been very critical about one area of the problem, and I kept wanting to talk about the overall thing too, rather than more or less just one little area, you know, – and h-he, hah, one thing was interesting, though, I-I thought when he started talking, I thought, well alright, he's gonna talk about what, you know, it won't mean a thing, but he didn't. He said, a, he says, he was just looking at it and he says, there's one thing that's very nice – there was one little area (laugh) a twenty minute thing, how awful it was, he says, think of what you'd experience if you lived here, or if you walked a little bit and turned here, he was able to project himself within that – in the space and, he was having an experience, it was like, and they were all into their heads, sort of wound up, and somehow he-he was able to, he experienced the whole, I-I really, he was very beautiful, you know, I remember when I was working with that problem too one time, he came up and here I was having a lot of trouble, I just couldn't get it, and he, he'd like bring an onion to class and he'd just put it down or something – and suddenly like, I don't know, I'd just see a thing a different way or something, I don't know, he was so-so beautiful, a very sensitive man, very, ah. –––––« (Interv. w/Wilson, 1970).

it wasn't easy, in in fact sometimes it was uh, it was by force. I started out working with – with a child uh who uh was about five or six uh, had almost no vocabulary, he hum uh there was little hope that he would ever be able to talk, read uh, function in that sort of way. The area of his brain that, that uh is used for those – those functions – the brain cells were, were dead. And uh I – his mother asked me if I would come in the morning, I was going to school at the time – I studied architecture – I got a degree in architecture. And, and uh so this woman lived near where I was going to school in Brooklyn and I would go in the morning and uh for 200, he had a room that was about this size and 250 times he would crawl around the perimeter of the room in a in a tunnel that I made that was oh about uh 1 x 14 – the boards were 1 x 14 – two of them with a string laced across the top. And he would have to crawl through this either pushing and pulling or however and I would count the times. And I did that for nine months. (What was it you hoped for? I mean if the cells were dead?) Well, what happened is that not only – well he was also doing other exercises that that other people were working with him – in that one particular case, within a year uh his vocabulary uh at the end of this nine month period had increased almost to that of a, of a, a normal child his age. And what was happening is that he was activating other brain cells – of the brain – and uh that really turned me around – that (It didn't matter what he did physically – – –?) It didn't matter so much as that it – it's believed that uh that, that learning has something to do with coordination and if the body is better coordinated then – then learning is easier. I think, I think what it's it's getting more to is the body is a resource, and the body can become conscious and that, and that it is possible to, to, to use, to activate brain cells by working with the body – that and how you go about that is very complex. I don't, we don't know about that but one way is by exercise and some – sometime – – I worked in a public school for, we took children that were having difficulty reading, children who were in difficulty and uh in learning language uh in catching a ball uh or repeating a rhythm uh or awkward in getting their hand on the uh hum doorknob or something and we went back and through uh series of exercises – ten exercises – and it was over a six week, six month period which the children exercised and in almost every case where the child was having trouble with hearing a sound, repeating a sound, he improved.

.... when I worked with brain damaged children that was, that was the thing that really began to impress me – and then I started working – I've always worked as a sort of a teacher with children and then I started working on my own – I worked in Brooklyn with a girl uh who had a speech impediment and she began singing, and I worked with uh a boy who was uh twelve years old who was a complete catatonic. Uh he hadn't talked since he was four and he also didn't write, but I somehow sensed that uh he was extremely intelligent that he just had no outlet you know, for the knowledge he had and hum, again it's difficult to say exactly what we did that — in each case it was different. With the boy you write — and uh he had trouble with depth perception, body extension, mostly just gaining confidence in himself, somehow he began to write. We I had uh a a large blackboard that we worked on and the first thing we tried to do was to to get him to draw a line from one corner of the board to the opposite corner or just draw a line vertically, and it it took uh six weeks for him to do that cause he would start here and he would just go over there — and it was hard for him to get from here to here. Hum, but eventually he did. And I also worked with him uh with paint uh very freely. We ——, we worked in the basement of his house and uh I took newspaper and I wrapped newspaper on everything. the floor — the ceiling — on the walls — on the furniture and he would work very much the with its physically being the paint and uh it was more of uh an emotional outlet and it also released tension and — he's now painting, it's interesting, he's also now writing and uh he, he was in *Freud*, that's how.

(Do you become friends with the people that you help this way or —— what kind of atmosphere is there?) Huh I become, there's a personal involvement, I'm learning that it's best to try to keep a distance and uh it's difficult. But yeah I'm like almost forced to now ... a sort of distance because it's not good for them or me (In other words it's not part of the technique?) I feel that uh — I worked very closely uh about five or six years ago with uh uh boy who was in Harlem who uh couldn't get into school — they wouldn't admit him in first grade and uh hum they tested him, they said he was retarded. And, and I had met him in uh uh pre-school center through the working with the welfare department, and uh I I was convinced from the very beginning that the child was exceptionally bright uh he that was his problem and uh he got he got into a lot of trouble in school in day care center so uh he was labeled a problem child. And he he would refuse to give the answers you wanted. He could count but you'd ask him to count and he would go 7, 8, 9 uh 14, 3, 2 and he he ya know, he could do 1, 2, 3, 4, 5 but he just wouldn't or if you asked him »what color this was?« he'd say green, he knew it was blue but it was like something wouldn't let him, you know, it was — he had a lot of problems at home, environmental problems. His mother was an alcoholic, she was seldom home uh the father was never uh at home uh — and there were, there were just a lot of problems. It was interesting too that, they, they tested the child. They said draw your mother, he'd put a dot on the page. They'd say draw the house where you live, he'd put another dot on the page; they'd say draw a tree — and he had a very difficult time talking to the people that tested him. And ... you know ... well .... They said ... I think that's like extraordinary — there was no way to test him, but, but, finally (laughs) hum what happened is that somehow I don't even know how it happened, but somehow we got over the hostility and everyone was amazed at the knowledge — I mean the things he was seeing, and not only that he had a lot of information but he had a lot of ideas about it and concepts — he conceptualized it at a very, very early age. And uh, but then the thing that happened with that child, I I realized that I got very, very attached to him and uh then he moved to Florida with his mother and uh it was very difficult for me uh because I had uh become so involved with him and he with me that uh like I heard from them afterwards and then the child had difficulty once he left New York and uh he wasn't with me and that's happened in the past I know –« (Interv. w/Wilson, 1970).

He started work in the performing arts while at Pratt. He designed and made the gross puppets for the third part (*Motel*) of Jean-Claude van Italie's *America Hurrah*, the splendidly mad – angry and comic – wrecking of a motel room, in 1963, and apparently[7] the same year made a 2 hr. 16 mm film, *The House*, and a film, *Slant*, for NET-TV. Richard Kostelanetz (N.Y. Times, v/8/77) reports that while at Pratt Wilson »rented the Peerless movie house, across the street on Myrtle Avenue, and presented midnight theatrical pieces«, and that in the spring of 1965, he »presented at Pratt a piece called *Clorox* which had a large number of performers ... in addition to 200 other objects«, and that Gordon Rogoff, the theatrical director and teacher, »remembers another undergraduate piece that had a backdrop entirely of tinfoil.« Also in 1965, he seems to have put on a »dance event« at the New York World's Fair.

About 1965, perhaps already in 1964, Wilson found himself unable to paint, seems to have suffered or approached a »nervous break-down,« and shifted from thinking of himself as a painter to thinking he'ld devote himself to doing theatre work with children[8] Apparently he went back to Texas during the summers of 1964 and '65, – perhaps in 1963 also, – and did some more theatre work with children (some or all of it again with Jearnine Wagner). He continued this work at least into 1970:

7 According to *Contemporary Authors*.

8 He took a cab 40 miles out of Waco, checked in at a motel, took a lot of sleeping pills, woke up in a hospital having vomited them up, and was put in a mental institution. As he was into acting freaky at the time, he had to watch himself so he'ld appear normal, – managed to get out after 6 weeks. (Wilson, personal communication.)

»I always thought I'd paint and then it became very, very difficult and I went through a year, a very, very bad year. I suddenly had a chance to show my work here in New York and I don't know whether it was that or something I just couldn't get it out and I just became frozen. For months and months and months I'd look at the canvas and I couldn't do anything. And so finally I just said, well I can't do this and at the same time I'd always been doing theatre work with children and it had always been *their* work. I'd work with children and they would write plays and we'd do them. They would perform them.« (Interv. w/Wilson, 1970).

»Presently he is a Special Consultant and Teacher for Headstart; in the past he has held a broad range of teaching positions, including that of Special Instructor for the Department of Welfare, the N.Y. Board of Education, . . .« (from Wilson's curriculum vitae in his *Production Notes on The King of Spain*, Hill & Wang, 1970.)

He describes some such work of 1967-8: »We almost did a play with four and a half year old children – this was in Harlem, about two years ago, three years ago – with a pre-school, four or five year old kids – we were all alligators – we all made alligator costumes and we had uh one enormous alligator that was like about six children all together – and then we – we invited the parents, a lot of the parents, couldn't come because they worked, but we invited friends and whole – like the other teachers and the other classes came – we had even – I got someone who was in the kitchen to be – (What was the plot?) Hum, the plot, let's see, it was a crazy story. A little boy made it up. And it was about an alligator – an alligator – oh God, an alligator who lived in a house with another alligator, who had, oh a lot of alligators in his back yard and uh I forget the whole story, I don't know – and but we had part of a house that we built and that's where the two alligators lived and we had all, – a lot of alligators in the play and- and then I think a flood came (It was a good thing for the alligators wasn't it?) Yes (laughter) it was, they were all afraid of the flood that was going to come but then they realized when it came that it was really a good thing or something, it was so wonderful – it was it was just like an hour and a half long – and you know at that age for children to stay with just anything for five minutes (Yeah) but it just kept going on and on and on – we hadn't really planned a tie-up when we'd been sort of rehearsing it and it had always been like ten or 15 minutes long – that – it just kept going on and on and on (laughs) – this little story but it was so beautiful –« (Interv. w/Wilson, 1970.)

Theatre work with children, 1969: »And so, I d-d- did a piece in the- in school, last year – they – I had a dog in the piece, elementary school, and they wouldn't let me bring the dog in the school, they said animals are not allowed in school (laugh) I said why? And that upset me – and just finally, in the middle of the thing, I just made a speech about it (laugh). There's supposed to be a dog here, but we can't bring the dog here because animals are not allowed in school. I just thought that was like, really unfortunate, that (laugh).

I worked in a private school last year in New Jersey. This is, these were wealthy people with – who send their children to school, I mean, like, ah, Dupont kids and that sort of thing – And the facilities of the school were just so – just so crazy (laughter) they didn't mean anything (Yah.) I mean, we had a, there-there was no place we could go where-where we could be completely dark, make a completely dark corner, there was no space where two kids could go and work by themselves or where a child could go work by himself, or whe-a space where I could go and work which I – you couldn't get at information – like you had to go to the library at a certain time and it was like – it was like that you couldn't just run to the library, it was like, and the location of it, it was like s-so out of the way and it was, everything just seemed to be, architecturally, to be so wrong, and yet a lot of money had been spent in the – on the physical structure (Yah.)

... and, and isn't that something (pause). I think that's still the thing I'm most interested in, is-is education, teaching, I real – it's like the biggest challenge, it's the thing that, I think about that a lot. One interesting thing happened at this school, private school, where I was working last year. We-we had a girl, a girl in the third grade who was, who was very much a problem child. It seemed quite obvious that she was very bright, there is no question about it, eve-even the faculty, they sort of hated to admit it, but-but they could see that, she's very, very difficult, in every sort of way, ah, and then I got her to teach the eighth grade, I got her to teach my eighth grade class (laughter) so, like this child that no one could manage, and like, you know, she just walked in (loud laughter) –– she just walked in (laughter) and suddenly like she had this whole class going, and she said, you do this and you do this and she was – utter confidence and but really made it work too, and then she sat there and she explained things and – it was wild, absolutely wild, and she really should be a teacher or, I don't know, something (short pause), she's now – I had a talk with her this morning and she's now she's directing a play, she said she's-she's written a play and she's directing, I bet she can do that, she has that sort of, she's very able to manage – – – she's such a, an interesting girl. – I thought if I ever had a kid, I'd just like, I-I wouldn't know what to do I, as far as, far as a school – – – in some ways I think, wow, I just couldn't sen-see sending my children to a school like that and then sometimes I think, well, that really works best and yet, I don't know though, it just seems that (pause) they sure create a lot of problems the schools the way they are set up. There was a girl who last year, I don't know what's happened to her to oh and I kept thinking about her all year – that was in the school and she wasn't able to to pass the academic course, and she just couldn't, but there was something (pause) Like, once you look you see there *are* extraordinary things, I mean, in almost everybody you see the possibilities, I mean you see things. It's like, this one child, she-she, first of all she was the most beautiful girl in school and that made, that created some problems and (short pause) she-she never did – I had her in the class all year – she never did any work with the children, with work on projects, she never did anything, and I'd sort of let her get away with it. Then I told her, »listen here,« I said, – – – – – »everyone has his, own« I said, »Sandra, you gotta, like you gotta really do something for this class or I'm going to fail you and I have that right so you really have to do something and let's talk about what you're gonna do.« – And she says, – well she didn't know what she was going to do, – well, she's going to do a painting (short laugh), so-o – I said, »okay, I want you to really (inaudible)« I was really interested in seeing what she could do. And she was to have it – like – one day and she didn't have it, and then she was to have it next week (Yah) and she still didn't have it, well, almost at the end of school – it was like, the next to the last day. I said, »Where is your painting?« »I don't have it – I'm still working on it.« (Uhum) »Okay,« I said, »we have just one more class and you better have it,« and, the kids thought I was very – sort of, yah, they – I was afraid to think, well, I told her, »well, you-you-you- won't pass my class if you don't have it,« I was very strict (laughter) so came (laughter) the last class I had and she wasn't there. And I said, »Where is Sandra?« (laughter) She's here – she's here – I said, well, why isn't she in the class? We don't know – we don't know – So about twenty minutes, late, she comes in and she-she was fantastic – she's real – (laughter) When she came in, like, she, it was like really theatre, she just walked in, she knew that everyone would sort of look at her and all the guys were sort of going AHHHHHH! (laughter) And all the girls hated her because she was good looking – so she comes and and she sits down in her seat – then there's a lot of giggling, then it's very quiet and I said, »Okay, where is your painting?« She said, »Well . . . .« She starts telling me the story, and then she, for thirty minutes she tells the story, and the whole spacing of her wor- of her language, like, ah . . . she'd say two words and then maybe she'd pause and then, it wasn't like with the commas and the periods and the semi-colons, no, it's, it's and the whole sort of phrasing of the words well, it almost took on another sort of thing when she talked. . . . she's, she says, »Well, Bird.« She says, »I'm gonna tell you a story . . .« So, she s-s-started – she's got the whole class just like this listening to her. And she tells this story, she says, »I was in my room and I-I was thinking – I've got to do a painting for Bird's class. And – and everything she – was very – structur-ally – so she says, »And I couldn't think of what to do so I took my clothes off.« And everyone goes AHHHHHHH! Sandra took her clothes off! – (laughter) So she says, »And then, I got some jars of paint,« You know she tells this whole story, about how she got paint, and, ah, she got paint all over her and she'd, ah, she jumps in her bed, and she pulled the sheets in her bed off, and she was rolling all over the floor, it was like it takes her thirty minutes to tell the story. Incredible story, I can't can't even – describe, how fantastic it is, how she-how she started . . . . and everyone just like this – the whole time listening (short pause) and then, (laugh) she says »And I got the mattress on the floor, and I got the sheets all over the floor, and I've paint all over me, and all over the mattress and all over the floor, and and all over the sheets,« and she says, »And my mother walks in« (laughter) And she says, »Sandra, what are you doing,« »Oh, I'm doing a painting for Bird's class« And then there's like a long pause. Then she says, »And then, Bird, my mother confiscated the sheets.« (laughter) So, anyway, »You get an A – plus« I said. »That's fantastic!« (laughter) It was like, well, it was like, the-just the whole theatre or whatever thing that she had done it was-it was, really really original and anyway – and I tried to like, explain it to the director of the school ... I said said, »You know, the child is, has really something going. I mean you can't deny that and it like, it's« (pause) But it was hard, of course, for him to place that, and then he'ld – and I said, »Well,« I said, »you know, this is really extraordinary with the ...« it really was, it was, I mean she (inaudible) on the stage or something, it was really connected to how within a large group of people (Yah) ... It was a very incredible sort of knowledge about herself – a sense of time, or something – I don't know what – I mean, it real-really connected and she really had the ability to sort of talk with people and-and-and it was a very I thought it was a very beautiful thing (pause). It's kind of those things that just – it's hard to, schools – all those programs that are in the schools (laughter) not art, painting or, you know, it really hurts me, like I go in and they've got, they've got pee time, wash time, eat time. In some ways I am always fascinated with those programs, but, it's like when you think about, well, there are so many other things to do too, (I know) ... They asked me to work on-on, this is where I was teaching. I was finally fired. While I was teaching there, they were designing a-a new school, high school, it-it was only pre-school through eighth grade. I made the suggestion that, ah, that, the boys and girls – would – there wouldn't be a wall (inaudible) (Laughter) I don't know, I didn't know whether it was a good idea or not, but it just ... seemed that like, you, know, that wall sometimes could have created a problem, create problems, that they are so hard for the child ...« (Interv. w/Wilson, 1970)

Theatre work with children, 1970: »... yeah we did it with an audience – (The high school students only, or – –) mostly hum high school students uh were in the audience because uh it's a private school and it's a campus that's sort of away from – – – but people from the community came too (What, what did you do actually?) I did uh it was interesting, I had five and a half hours to work in class time so – I knew that ahead of time – that I had five and a half hours, – so that was a lot to try to introduce another, or my approach uh at the same time to make the piece (to make it?) yeah, make it, to construct it and I wanted to use material that was there – the space that was there – and not do too much thinking ahead of time – but also to try to uh learn something from them too so that it didn't become just that I would go there and like direct them – there would be a feedback from the audience (who were the *performers*?) The high school students and I took some of my group down with me too – I came down before the performance (What did it turn out to be like?) It was very interesting – I liked it (I mean, what did you do?) I tried – specifically what happened uh we were in uh – they had set aside the theatre we could use and uh so it's a proscenium auditorium and uh so I thought possibly that for – for that specific problem of going to a school and working two days to make a piece it would be more interesting to do something for those kids outside of a conventional theatre, something that might make them you know think about theatre in other ways – but that was impossible

I (laughs) – I had to use the theatre, so I said OK. But there was a building that was under construction that was adjacent to the theatre – a chemistry building – and they had only built uh uh the sub-grade level – sort of in rough concrete and partial of the first floor, part of the first floor, had laid it too – and so after the audience left, the active kids inside the theatre they went to the construction site – we had other things happening but they were very sort of static – and all through the building – but, I liked it in terms of the context of the piece I mean it was very interesting as a theatre, I just walked through – the audience was moving – the performers were more static instead of – almost reversing what had happened in the theatre where-where the audience had been static and the performers had been – but also what was – is that-the piece in some ways almost made a statement of some kind, came to a conclusion – and then the people left the theatre thinking that that was – it was a very final sort of feeling an idea and then as they went through the environment they just reversed that statement again. (But what was the statement?) Well, I can't say so much because I'm still-still thinking about it – I-I did realize that in-in a very abstract way, I mean that they had come to this conclusion and in somehow leaving the theatre going through the other part you would come to another conclusion – it seemed that-that was pretty much what happened but, like the conclusion – I I'd have a hard time saying exactly – but but I could see it, and I felt that – and I think that did happen as far as the experience of the audience. It was interesting – on-on stage, what I do is I rehearsed things in groups – I rehearsed my group uh Saturday morning – not knowing what I was going to do and I made one situation with those people – and I knew them very well as a group and we found costumes that we'd never been able to use before – these costumes – really used what was at the school and then with the other – I had two classes at the high school and with those two classes I made separate situations for them to do – and then they saw it all the first time – just just before the performance – with not even a complete run through – we just sort of walked through, like groups, this one's here and this one's there and you come in here – and this one's there and you come in here – and then we went through a performance and they were all like – these other things happening but – and – and they all seemed to – it was a good experience, they were very – very frightened – – – the biggest problem was to get them just to trust it – it would be OK (The audience?) The performers (Yeah) the performers. Cause they said how can we do this cause we don't know what else is happening (Yeah, sure) It'll work, it can work (It all seemed almost designed as a test in courage) Yeah, and if – they are free to trust it and, you know, if you trust it it's ok – but if you doubt, it's, you know just-just it'll be ok – – – like there were two girls left just before we started cause it was a mammoth piece, there were like – lots of things happening (laughs) and people – in a larger sense what-what's really turned me around by going to that school is how cut off it is – how isolated and how much this is a problem – the school is so, it's like – it's like a country club – they have tennis courts and swimming pools and they there are beautiful lawns and beautiful flowers and they-they learn like Shakespeare and things like – it's not in the 20th century, and they don't know really what's happening, they don't know what it's like to to live in Harlem or, I don't know, they don't – it's very removed you know – I, I think its always important somehow to – in the middle of that school – I think of that school in terms of an apple – you want to just insert in the middle of it like uh a cylinder that would have like ugliness or something so you are just reminded of what's going on – they had a very difficult time with-with this work cause they are so used to thinking in another way but they're right in the 20th century (How would you work, get them into that?) Well you know what I did – I said I've got five and a half hours (laughs) now to work with these kids before the performance what will I do? And I had like a lot of different ideas sort of beforehand like well, if-if there is this problem I might do this or I – I used like I took a book of by Gertrude Stein down there and I read them that at the very beginning and they didn't like it they had never heard Stein and I just – I just read and uh then ––––– they left, it really was crazy but uh and then I I had a a girl that was there and I had her continue reading Stein and I went on and conducted class but mostly just doing things myself without-without saying anything – and then gradually going up to them and bringing them – and they were very afraid of that, cause it was another experience for them than a classroom and – it was interesting – they wanted to leave, they always wanted to leave but – and by the end, those who stayed with it though were very intrigued – but but the larger thing is the school is so isolated it's one of the problems – a great problem of our time. I work in the suburbs and I see that all the time – just oh – you have no idea – It's really a worse problem than say in some ways I think – Harlem – where they seem to be more aware of the problem out on the streets – more awareness of, of what's happening.

I did the piece at at George School, ... the kids, they were afraid of it, because they didn't, I didn't give them the concept – I couldn't say to ... so wait til you have, you have – maybe you'll understand it more if we can just go through the performance, after you get the experience of it, but they're so used to – having the idea first ... (Uhum) ... the concept ... first, they're afraid of it ... afraid to trust ... to trust it ... I said you'll best understand like what I'm trying to do if we can just get through the performance ... one performance, when you got that-that experience. Whether you like it or not, like that's okay but, but, they're so used to, like, tah-having that other (pause) There are so many fears, just like, I-I was thinking about like in George School – these kids were-s they-were af-afraid of so many things, they were afraid of me, they were afraid of the material, they were afraid that no one was gonna like it, they were, there were all those fears, it was like, this – I-I said, okay, I said, maybe no one will like it, maybe you won't even like it, only let's, still let's do it .... it- just seemed like a rather – I don't know, it's – and oddly enough the biggest c-concern was that the audience is not gonna like it – they're gonna walk out and they're gonna – I said, maybe not, maybe not, but maybe (inaudible) and that's okay (pause) I don't know, I think, of course, that it's, a lot of things – that is – I try to arrange it though, I try to look at all the kids as – as much as I could to find out, like something that they had, something that they could do instantly, like I tried to, as quick as I could, like to find out what, what can they do so they'll be comfortable, so that it's really hope for them and might be interesting to some of them and I tried to work – – – – – There were a lot of kids and I didn't have very much time, and I was really trying to do that, s-s-s see if, help them see a side where maybe see a side maybe, they didn't see, and encourage them and I felt that – – – somehow you – something I always thought too, I mean Stein said she – she said, I just wrote for a handful of people (laugh) you know, like, if she did it when she – when she was writing – it's like at that time they really wrote for a lot of people interested, but-but, it didn't matter to her, yah, (pause) It's a very (laugh)« (Interv. w/Wilson, 1970)

Apparently during the summers he spent in Texas '63 – '65, he also did work in dance,[9] and also (in 1964 or '65) put on a »performance piece« (as distinct from a »play«) there, that in later years, or at any rate in 1970, he seemed to regard as the beginning of his own manner of work in the theatre: its nature suggests the origin of his *theatre of visions* in theatre as epiphany of the performer's individuality, and in a theory of non-verbal communication:

»... and uh so when I stopped painting I started doing my own work and then five years ago – six years ago – I was had a chance to, I'd written a one-act play and uh I had been asked to to perform it for a five week period and uh so I rehearsed it and then the day I was to show it I I just suddenly – well it had been happening all along, I just had no faith in it and I just, I didn't want to do it – I didn't want to show it cause it just – this is not what I want to do. And there was a problem, I wanted to withdraw it and they said, Oh you can't because it's on a series with other things and it was all set up and (Were there other people in it?) There were two other people in the play and hum it was – it was a one-act play and it was on a program with two other plays and they were to run for five weeks and they had sold tickets and that sort of thing. So uh (Did the content of this play or the manner or anything have anything to do with

9 »Bob came and did a seminar for us at one of our summer programs here at Trinity University. I am extremely bad on dates, but I believe it was in 1964. He did a very exciting movement seminar that he also trouped to Waco with some of the old Waco group who had come down for the summer. In 1965 he would have been working for the »Ideas in Motion« program at Trinity University as an instructor.« (J. Wagner, letter cited.)

your state?) Nothing. But what I did instead, the night I was to perform it, the first night, uh I talked to people I I just did another thing, on the spot. The set was a room with a window and a door and a girl and myself walked out, there were two chairs in the room, we sat in the chairs and it was the third person doing another activity. Most of these were just sitting for very long time in front of the audience and we did small activities and we got up and we walked out of the room and out the door – it was about 35 minutes long. And the first night we did it the audience hated it and they booed and and I faced it you can't do this anymore – you've got to do the play that was (Where was this?) This was in Texas, In San Antonio, Texas and I said we, we you know, we agreed to do another play and this is you're doing the wrong thing and I refused, I said, I won't do it. And so we did it the second night and the audience still didn't like it and we, and after about two weeks – we continued to do this piece – and we did the same thing every night. Well, one night the audience sat very quietly – and it's a very peaceful thing – and I was very excited I thought oh (laughs) what's happening, why did they sit tonight and they didn't sit last night, you know, and I learned a lot a lot from that I think. I learned that part of it was that as a performer somehow if I could relax to begin with, aha, if I could release the tension in myself, then, then the situation would be better, because then the exchange of energy between me and the audience was, was an even flow and it wasn't blocked. And that, that that helped, and it also helped with the other performers. And then I started again going back to my body. Well, how, how do I relax it. And, and then I – I found that I was tight here. Like the audience couldn't see me totally, physically. And they would focus on that instead of the total thing and out of that five week period we had about four or five uh very, very good performances in that there was uh (What was the play about?) The the play had no literary structure and had at that time almost no symbols – it was, I was very, very much against doing anything like that. And I was I was trying to go back to the simplest thing I could do; what, how do I walk, walk out on the stage and how do I sit in the chair and walk off, can I do that, is it necessary to have a story, is it necessary to have characters, is it necessary to have uh symbolism. I didn't know, like (You don't think anything effectively got across, say as regards the relations between the three people, eh not their real ones necessarily but some kind of) Yes, I tried not to have any of that, I tried as much as possible to strip all of that away. I wanted first to see if I could just do that and then (Nobody would have any reason for doing any of the things they did, like getting up at some point or being seated or coming in or anything, I mean there would be no reason indicated, or one you as a performer would think of) At that point I didn't, at that point I was just wondering if I could sit in front of an audience, or if if we could be a room full of people, just sitting together, having an exchange. I just wanted to see if – if that could happen first of all. (You say you did it on the spur of the moment, but did you do the same thing every night?) We did the same thing every night and and then (Why?) I wanted to see first of all if it would if that would work, if I could ever like make that situation uh workable, would it – it ever work, the two of us sitting in the chairs with the audience sitting in chairs uh and we walking out and the audience walking out (What actually did you do? Do you remember – what kinds of things you did?) Uh huh, then what I did after that is that I was trying to take (No, I mean in the play) Yeah. I what happened is that there was a door and uh there was a boy standing, and a girl, a girl standing at the window. She had her hand sort of on the window pane and she stands for like about five minutes, say, and then the two of us walked out, very slowly and we sat in chairs, close together uh and we sat for six minutes or something uh the girl standing at the window put a record on – it was music that had been composed by children, at work – uh (long pause) the girl and I put on white gloves uh the girl in back of us took sand and made uh uh line sand all the way across the room – also uh uh he the the the the wire with the rings on it was hanging there and she moved one ring and uh I forget, there were several other things that the two of us did in chairs – at the end of the (inaudible) she moved the wire again and then she stands – climbs up on a ladder and leans into the wire and started just leaning into the wire and the girl and myself walked out. And as we walked out of the room you could hear someone knocking on the door. (Did you pay attention to one another?) No. We did, but it wasn't obvious – like what we were trying to do is uh is like, is in terms of performing uh we began that we very much were listening to the whole thing – it was like listening to this little sound here – so like, we were having sort of like another experience with our bodies than we normally do. And we found that when we tuned in to listening – just the three of us being together – in terms of performance – if we could hear that then the audience might hear it, you know, or it was more likely that they would tune in to us. And I kept thinking, say in *Freud*, that I kept seeing this – this like a little radio that's turned on way low and if we all listen to the whole piece, listen to what everyone's doing. Not obviously looking at it or aware of it that way but you're very much tuned in to everything around you – what's happening even you know the audience, everywhere, then you know – then it's more possible to connect. (– the way of doing it, your posture and sitting or, – would it be the same way that one of you might do it in real life, or would that question be relevant to it or) No, I don't think so, I don't think it would be the – – – – because what was happening is that we were having another body energy experience. (Just that or) Also the clarity of the movement – it was, it was not like you'd see every day in that in that the time was much, much more different than say, than time we ordinarily experience, that that's one thing that the audience had trouble with – the time was much more drawn out – so that they had trouble with that – because they come in, you know, experiencing time and like you see it on the street, and suddenly there was another thing.

It was much more concentrated and but (Would there be some idea that one could live like that?) I think you could live that way – – – And what's even more amazing too is that I found that, say, say with this 13 or 14 year old child that that's deaf, that I'm working with, and suddenly he is uh oh, (laughs) I was noticing this weekend uh I went to the auditorium early before we performed and, oh for an hour and a half – and he sat down at the piano and he was playing – he played almost for the whole time – like for an hour and a half but for a 13 year old child, especially a uh deaf child to have concentration to that extent, I think it is very, very rare. For any – any child, but that's one thing that – yeah, I think you could live like that I think that it does affect the way we live life. (This tuning in or whatever, er, between people, and somehow having a different relation to time, would that be just an idea for theatre, or something more general?) I think it's more general like, yeah, that's like – one of the things I do even with the little children, the smallest.« (Interv. w/Wilson, 1970)

After he graduated from Pratt, in 1966, he seems to have served a stint of apprenticeship to Paolo Soleri in Phoenix, Ariz., but also seems to have given some solo performance in his New York studio. About this time, too, or perhaps '67, he seems to have started psycho-somatic therapy work with grown-ups in New York and New Jersey.[10] In 1967, apparently, he designed and built a giant outdoor environment-theatre-sculpture, *Poles,* consisting of some 600 telephone poles in an open field at Grailville, in Loveland, Ohio, under commission from The Grail in Loveland. There seems to have been some live performance connected with this.

He started doing »performance pieces« in Manhattan in 1967. I have heard of four antedating *The King of Spain* (1969): *Baby,* performed 5 (?) times at the Byrd Hoffman Foundation School of Byrds loft at 147 Spring Street, in Soho, in 1967 (?), lasting 1-1½ hrs. (?); *Theatre Activity,* performed once (?), after the regular movie program there, at the Bleecker Street Cinema, in 1967 or 1968, in four sections, lasting 20 minutes each; *ByrdwoMAN,* performed once (?), its first part at the Byrd loft, its second in an alley off Great Jones St., in November 1968, lasting 1½-2 hrs. (?),[11] and a »pyramid piece« performed once

10 Cf. e.g. the reference to Mary Peer in *Freud*: »That's that's the remarkable thing about the work is uh there's a lot that you don't see in the performance and I don't like to talk about it so much but there is a woman that three years ago she was completely arthritic – she couldn't move, couldn't-t – she, she's 68 years old and was almost completely paralyzed with arthritis and then she she started moving in class and then started swimming and uh now she's doing remarkable things with her body – and really fantastic.« (Interv. w/Wilson, 1970)

11 This production was preceded by two months by an experience alluded to in Wilson's program notes for the Dec. 1970 production of *Deafman Glance* in Iowa

at Jerome Robbins' American Theatre Laboratory (?) in 1967 or 1968, lasting 1-1½ hrs. Sometime in 1968, he started work on *The King of Spain* (1969), and, according to *Contemporary Authors*, became the artistic director of the Byrd Hoffman Foundation, Inc.[12] I know nothing about where the money for his first productions came from.

Concerning *Baby*, Libe Bayrak in the mid-70s wrote me:

»When I met Bob in 1967, it was while he was putting on a piece called »Baby«. It went something like this. The staircase leading to the Loft at 147 Spring St. was lit by a red light, the effect being pink. The staircase itself was strewn with dismembered dolls' bodies, as well as some wooden crates stacked near the staircase. There was a figure at the top of the staircase hooded in a red windbreaker, legs and feet nude. Face covered by hair and hood. This person was gathering I believe $2 per person and letting people in 1 at a time. Inside there was an usher seating people, unroping a row of seats for each spectator. The room was dark. There was a wire with rings on it stretched in front and above the spectators' heads. The piece started when the hooded figure came inside and moved these rings. Bob Dylan's record *Bringing it all home* went on, the red figure moved some lighted candelabras, 1 candle in each, the only light in the room. Eventually the music became *Maggie's Farm* and Bob came out walking like an equilibrist on a narrow wooden plank using a giant lollipop as equilibrating stick. He was dressed only in a t-shirt. He crossed the plank which was about 2.5 metres long and bending under the weight during the whole duration of »Maggie's Farm.« Then he went away and the hooded figure moved more rings and candles. The hooded figure stood against the righthand wall all the time Bob was on stage. I am not sure about what happened next. It may be the following sequence. A toy train was being set up above the ground, about 1.5 metres, just the rails, without other support. Bob eventually lay under the rails dressed as before, making movements like a baby in a crib. The sound of a locomotive came full blast

City: »At Pratt I wrote my thesis on designing an imaginary cathedral or a fewture city perhaps. Then there was a murder, a murder in the eyes of the top of the cathedral two years ago September as the red dog howled into the moonlight son notta wink! Only the bones can tell.«

12 Certificate of Incorporation filed May 7, 1970. Its purposes according to the by-laws: »1. Conduct childrens' and adult workshops in dance movement, theatre, film and related arts. 2. Develop members as group leaders in dance-theatre activity. 3. Run a summer art program for children and adults from the New York–New Jersey and Texas areas on a ranch in Texas. 4. Produce public performances of the dance-theatre work which is the result of the various workshops.« Robert M. Wilson was the president, DeGroat and Liba Bayrak the vice president, Robyn Stoughton the secretary and Carroll Dunn the treasurer.

over the amplifier while he was writhing on the floor as if in extreme pain[13] and the toy train was passing above him. Then darkness for a while, rings being moved, candles put away and a block was placed in the farthest part of the loft. A Texas revivalist preacher's voice came over the amplifier very dramatic, as well as his audience's response. During this time Bob whose face was painted white was putting over himself, draping himself in, long strips of colored plastic that made him progressively grow in size, till he seemed very tall. The effect was that of a shaman performing a ritual. This lasted for about 15 minutes. I do not remember the end exactly, only that Bob went away and there was light on the piano (which had not been used as an instrument during the performance) with photo of a baby, a

13 When I had the privilege of working for him, Wilson would often tell of a certain film study of mother-baby conduct to illustrate a sub-liminal complexity of what one sees that he felt overtly characterized his stage-spectacles. He brought up this study to a foolish and antagonistic (female?) interviewer, Ossia Trilling, to illustrate that »the body doesn't lie . . . we can trust the body«, in this case apparently meaning that the crying baby's body truthfully perceives the aggressive mother's body without a need to understand her contrary overt, e.g. verbal indications:

»Trilling: Does that mean that you rely very much on the instinct of the body, as well. Wilson: I always give one example and it's very simple and it's quite often misunderstood. And I don't even understand it myself, but I'll . . . (pause) I'll give it now and that's that. I worked with an anthropologist in New York, and we made more than 300 films of a mother picking up a baby. The baby was crying and in each instance . . . and what do we see when we show the film? There's – – the baby cries and the mother picks up the baby and the mother comforts the baby. A very simple picture. And we see that in at least 300 instances. Now, a film can be stopped down. We can look at it frame by frame. I forget, there's something like 32, something like that, frames per second, or 16, or something. So that if we stop it down and look at it frame by frame, we're looking at pictures that are fractions of a second. Now what we see, when the mother picks up the baby, when the baby's crying, in eight out of ten cases, is, that the initial reaction of the mother is that she's (a long, loud, low-pitched screech through the teeth) lunging at her baby. And the baby's responding with the body by (short screech, and grimace) fear, or many emotions simultaneously. Now, when we showed this film to the mother, she didn't believe it. She said »oh, no, no, no, no, no, no, that's not what happened. I'm not (repeats screech): ›don't lunge at me!‹« You see, we're not conscious. It's happening at another level, but with the body communicating in ways that sometimes we don't comprehend. Trilling: The illustration of the point you're making is the cause of this entire 72-hour-long-experience? Wilson: Well, in other words, if we could photograph the conversation between you and me now, and perhaps if we would eliminate the sound of the verbal communication, we'd find that much to our amazement we're communicating on other frequencies. Trilling: You're not suggesting, I hope, that I'm lunging at you and inspiring you with emotions of fear, because I would deny it, like your mother.« (Ossia Trilling, *Robert Wilson's Ka Mountain*. The Drama Review, T 58, June 1973, p. 44).

snapshot in a standing frame. The (?) remained and the audience left slowly, after a while without applauding.

Franny Brooks, who was handling the sound could give you more details, because I am not sure if there was a picture projected, a flash, during the performance. As far as I remember, Andy (de Groat) was the hooded figure for the first two performances, then he left for Mexico and I replaced him for the next three performances.« (L. Bayrak, letter.)

Franny Brooks (interview, mid-70s) didn't remember much about *Baby*, she was doing the lights and worrying about them working properly:

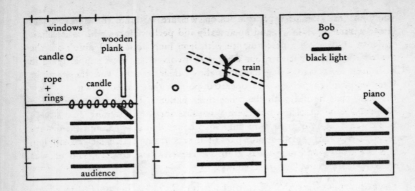

»There was an electric train and blinking lights, and there was a string coming out of the floor,[14] continuously coming out of the floor – Richie Gallo did this – and he did a dance in which he was naked from the waist down ... there was a certain amount of attention to effects without having a person in it, there was something to do with a whole bunch of lights, small Christmas lights that came on one by one in a pattern and it was either a symmetrical V or ... There was a lot of silence and a lot of sitting and waiting for the lights to go on, and I think they were the opening sequence ... really a long stretch of lights in the beginning, absolute silence, and then there was the movement section and he also teetered on a board ... the section where he did the movement. His movement now has become somewhat more elaborate but with that same jerky dangly kind of ... That was the first time he'd ever danced ... Then ... Bob was lying on the floor spread eagle on the train, and a raucous song ... a Nashville type song or a black jazz kind of song, – just a segment of it, cut off ... A very jive black song, hard, shrieky, you know, shrieky blaah! kinda song, very funny song ... That was the most intense moment in a way ... this soul rock piece that was like ... you know this southern Negro Woman ... something about a face in a mirror, and it is a woman singing. There was a shrieky ... you know the way he shrieks ... a shrieky kind of female voice, *Take a Look in the Mirror*, that's what it was. Take a look in the mirror, blaahh!«

In Brooks' memory the hooded, windbreakered de Groat by the wall is Wilson in fur coat and hat,[15] and sometimes she remembered that song, which to her projected a strong image of a certain »type of shrieky Southern dame« as associated with Wilson's standing there: she seemed to feel he was giving a female image of himself ...
She remembers from about this time:

14 Actually in *ByrdwoMAN*.
15 She may be thinking of *ByrdwoMAN* here also.

»Bob was working with paraplegics on Welfare Island ... I suspect it was in the winter of 67/68 ... and he actually did performances with wheelchair patients, and he did a performance with iron lung patients. I didn't see the one with iron lung patients, but what that involved ..., these people lying in their iron lungs had string dangling above their mouths, and these strings went up through pulleys and operated posters that rolled down ... I saw the piece that he did with the wheelchair patients, I can't remember what happened in what order, but there was some sort of rap going on ... there was black light, and there were huge soap boxes that glowed, and there were these posters that unrolled, and part of it was a guy that came out singing, and the background music was *Here she comes, Miss America*, and he was all wrapped in some Christmas lights ...«

Bayrak remembers the next piece after *Baby* as being *Theatre Activity*, – »about 6 months later:«

»The first act consisted of about 6 men and 4 women sitting in two rows of chairs facing each other. The people, dressed in street clothes (jeans and tops) came in one by one and sat down in a chair of their choice. They stayed the lengths of time they wanted, got up and left, trying to sense the intervals between each arrival and departure. Next, people were lined up with their backs toward the wall, then again variously started to walk across the stage and reach the opposite wall as if it was not there, bumping into it, turning around and starting back in their own time.[16] There were cat calls from the audience, »Is this what American theater has come to,« etc. Also some laughter when some people were crossing. All this without any accompaniment by sound. In the next scene there were carpets piled up in the centre with the whole cast lounging in relaxed poses, holding smoking incense sticks. A film shot by Bob and some of the cast in the New Jersey swamps showing tall grass and weeds waving in the wind was projected on a screen behind the cast.

Two people, hunter-like in khaki outfits came out and moved around for a while. Finally a huge slide of a cat's head in color was superimposed on the weed film, held for a time and lights went out. No applause. Each sequence lasted a long time, the whole about two hours. At the end everyone had to spit out a red piece of plastic held in the mouth all the time, all at once.«

Brooks did not remember anything about *Theatre Activity*, because her and, as she remembers it, de Groat's participation in it consisted

16 Brooks (interv.) remembers that she went to Wednesday night group sessions that Wilson had just after he moved into the Spring St. loft, and remembers »one situation where all the lights were off and he had people moving around the space, possibly also with their eyes closed, anyway trying to go through the experience of being blind, but trying to move around as fast as possible without bumping into anybody. And I remember having the experience of coming close to a wall and being able to hear, actually hear the wall, it really sounded different.«

in sitting in the audience with paper bags over their heads. S. K. Dunn (interviewed by Jim Neu, IV/13/75) remembers the walking section (people »leaning into the wall«) as being in bright light:

»And then it got dark, and they brought in, like, pillows and, I think, candles, things like that. And they sat around. It looked like hippies or something, the people didn't, particularly, but the scene did. These people sitting around smo-, you know, as if they were sitting around smoking... It may have been also kind of an Eastern image or something. And they'ld breathe out these bubbles or something... It was great! Nothing was happening. The next thing I remember is the film comes on with this beautiful growing grass. And then Kenneth (King) was standing on one side, and he walks down to like stage front and he just does something like this... like a soldier. I don't know what it really was. I thought it was a man with a gun. And... there was a soundtrack going in the background... it was all about Vietnam... The the glass crashed... and it has like a thing on it. That was another thing about the war thing. To me it looked like a gun sight(?)... It had some sort of a criss-cross on it. Kenneth was either behind it when he started or behind it when he ended. And then the still of the cat came in. That was nice. It was real incredible ... After about ten minutes (the audience) really were mad ... There were people sitting in the audience with bags over their heads, and Franny Brooks was one of those people. And she finally got up cause people were hitting her and stuff.«

Brooks does not remember being hit or getting up before her time. Jill Johnston in her Village Voice Dance Journal (Nov. 7, 1968) wrote of the first part of *ByrdwoMAN*:

»What I saw in the loft at Spring Street was a hay covered floor of performing space also fitted out with horizontal wires (about chest height) and a couple of low boards suspended on low boxes. Bob as Byrdwoman appeared seated in ecstatic profile outside the window on the first escape. An assistant exposed him by extravagantly lifting the window shade to the fanfare of the *2001* ape music. The rest of the piece was very quiet and pastoral. About eight people, including a young boy and an older lady, stood about in the hay, leaning against a wall, leaning a cheek against a wire, occasionally changing positions. Two people continually bounced up and down, lightly, on the two suspended boards. Bob himself looking maybe like an itinerant hobo in drag (a lady's wig straggling down out of a black hat), did some beautiful weird awkward maneuvering on a backgammon pattern from windows to audience across the hay space and through the other relatively static performers. Seemed like he was making an elaborate survey, but he wasn't doing anything with a practical purpose that I could see. A bunch of keys, a toothbrush, and a sink stopper dangled from his waist. His progress was stop and go in a spastic rhythm. The older lady, by the way, was quite fantastic. She said she flew in from Ohio especially for the event. She's a chicken farmer who never left home before. She's tall, large-boned, short white hair, deep melting dreamy blue eyes, clear rosy pale skin, and idyllic heroic sentimental all over face. A parrot at the back of the loft sometimes squawked out a thing like ›Kiki, how are you?‹ At the end, from where I was sitting down front, a cat stole the show playing with a thin rope endlessly coming out of a hole in the floor as a fellow standing a few yards away hauled the rope up and through a little pulley near the ceiling. Bob is as pure and as eccentric as his friend Kenneth King (now in London) and he might have a better sense of humor.«

Johnston »missed« the second half of *ByrdwoMAN*, but, apparently to oblige Wilson, who two days after the performance had »stuck a piano piece (*Be With Us in Might*) in (her) mail slot with diagrams and words about the part (she'd) missed,« finding this information »incomprehensible,«

»called Meredith Monk, who became the Byrdwoman in his stead when the event moved from his loft ... to the Jones Alley on Bond Street. She said she just wore what she wanted and moved about her way, in the apex of the L-shaped alley after a fanfare introduction of the 1812 Overture. Later the audience took over, fooling around with the props and dancing in the alley to a live rock band. They got there after the Spring Street part of it in a truck powered hay wagon. (Johnston, ib.)«

S. K. Dunn recalled there not being too many, perhaps half a dozen rehearsals for *ByrdwoMAN*, and not too many people in it either: she, Bill Stewart, Stephen Dunn, Jeff Norwalk, Saito, Raymond (Andrews?), the lady from Grailville, Ohio, ... – Hope Kondrat who sang, Richie Gallo who »did a bit,« – and, for the second part, Robyn (Stoughton) and Meredith Monk. For the first part, she remembered there still being partitioning in the front of the loft, but the back of it by that time having been »kind of cleaned out,« there being some kind of seats back there, and a part of it by the windows having been partitioned off. There were boards on boxes, and ropes:

»The piece starts with Saito going to the front and pulling up the shade and it's really funny and the music is that thing from *2001* ... It's just hysterical ... And there's this figure sitting out on the balcony ... which is Byrd as Byrdwoman ... just sitting out there. The shade finally pulls up! And then Byrd just sits there and just ... everybody looking out the windows at Byrd. And then I come out and go way back to the back on this board and stand there in sunglasses and bounce up and down ... And then Bill comes out: he bounces on a board slowly. Seems like Stephen comes out ... I think Raymond comes and leans on a wire, 'cause there was a wire someplace. He does that ... Remember how he used to do in *Freud* or whatever? I think that's where he first did that ... And then that woman ... God, I can't remember her name ... came out and talked, I think. And then Hope ... there was a bird, in the back, somewhere, somebody had brought a bird, and it talked. So different times in the piece this bird would say things and I don't know what, but I think it said ›byrd‹. I think that's where that started. Bird would say ›byrd‹ ... the whole thing was a real blowout ... And then Richie Gallo had this whole number where he had a rope or something that he did the whole thing with ... I think, it went all the way down the stairs and out into the street or something. Then there was a cat, yes, a cat comes up, jumps up, and plays with the rope. And there's hay. At some point (Wilson) came out of the fire escape and sort of danced around between us, the boards and all. Then when that part's over, all the people go out and get in the hay wagon ... So this hay truck took everybody over to an alley. (Great Jones Street.) Oh! Robyn (Stoughton) was there. Up ... way up on the fire escape, standing ... all these people were herded into one end of the alley and Bill Stewart built a fire in a can. It was cold. People were standing around. So this alley was, was across them like this, and then there were boards across here and boards across there and it

was very weird. They watched the first part here and then they were supposed to go way around to the other side and come in here for the last
part. For the first part, here was the fire escape. Robyn was way up on this
fire escape. And we were all huddled back here around this corner, and
Byrd and Meredith (Monk) did a whole dance right in front of us, and
occasionally would dance out into this part where they could be seen, which
I thought was really interesting. (They didn't dance where the people could
see 'em?) Well, they would go in and out, but a lot of it was just back in
here, you know, so you couldn't ... There was a film. I think Bill showed
a film on that wall there or something. I can't remember ... and then afterwards there was a rock band, and then the people just danced around ...«

Frannie Brooks associates *ByrdwoMAN* with a chicken barn, and
first of all thinks of the bare light bulbs, glaring, not even frosted.
To judge by photos of hers of a rehearsal, those are the things one
would think of. The image may go back to the vision in the Grailville
barn, and seems to presage the image of *The King of Spain*: the image
of Wilson as a woman briefly introduced into this pastoral scene gone
in *King*, replaced by that of the king of Spain, perhaps, tho Wilson
is still there as Black Mammy shrieking like a bird. The photos show
a quarter section of the loft, perhaps 12' by 20' sectioned off, funnel-
ing toward the windows at the rear, which are all covered in white,
except for a small rectangular section of window at the lower left,
close to the hay covered floor: sectioned off by a standing partition
about 7' high at the left, this partition, perhaps only cloth or paper
tacked to boards and supported, facing a contiguous row of something like plaster boards of about the same height up against the loft-
wall on the right: these two walls connected by a long thin piece of
wood, perhaps 2" by 4", close to the hay in the foreground, one or
two other such boards going across at different heights further back,
perhaps suspended from the ceiling. Also, about midways in, a wire
goes across, disappearing through a hole in the left-hand partition,
maybe 5' from the floor. At the back, by the sheet-covered rear wall
with the window, two wider boards seem laid over crates at each
end. Three big bare glaring bulbs are hanging down in sequence in
the center of this rectangular space. The whole looks ramshackle,
not unlike a chicken coop without the top, – the wood, the raw
light, the rough hay, – the impermanence and the inconvenience of
it, ...: but also rather pleasant, sort of the suggestion of something
beautiful in the mind.
The piece opens with the raising of a shade over that window section
to the Beethoven out of *2001* and the discovery of Wilson on the fire

escape outside, – Brooks relates this beginning to the end in an alley, outside, seeing people on a fire escape, – in a fur coat and a big hat, »womanish« looking, »partly an ambivalent image,« a »scrawny kind of a skinny person,« in profile, the room (the playing area) dark and empty, the only light on him, on the fire escape. As Brooks remembers it, one had only an instant image (accompanied by that music) of byrdwoMAN. Probably after a black-out,

»the next portion involved people dancing gently on those boards, and he dances in between them … the slowness of people there doing the same thing, kinda bouncing, it was not even really a movement, it was just an element, a fixed element, the background for his movement, a very very scarce, scant movement.«

Then the lady from Ohio came out and talked, and Hope Kondrat sang her Russian lullaby from among the audience. – Leaving, the audience found that Wilson had put shaved ice all over the sidewalk. A flat bed truck with hay on it took them to the L-shaped alley, where they stood not quite all the way up one of the legs of the alley, not quite able to see up the other leg, perhaps held back by some boards that had been set up, the image of people up on boards being repeated here, and also that of someone on a fire escape (Robyn S.), and Meredith and Wilson did a dance only part of which could be seen. It was dark by then, and the illumination was by

»string lights … Canal Street reflecting-lights … (with) real chintzy alumi-num reflectors that we used for regular light bulbs. There really was not that much light there at all, so there was a great deal of murky feeling to this whole thing. And I think around 10 o'clock the performance ended or maybe 10:30, when there was supposed to be a dance … in the alley. They'd arranged for a group, a live rock band, that came and played … the image (in the first part) was obviously … this was supposed to be like in a chicken house with the bare bulbs. Even tho there was hay on the floor and you don't get hay in a chicken house, but, ah, that doesn't matter, it was this hayseed kind of image. And then the repetition of that image in the alley way. The boards and the people doing slight, almost static movements, just small movements … so you get the hay here, and the hay in the hay wagon, I think there was hay in the alley too, so it was like taking this kind of image and putting it in an entirely different kind of space. And the space was interesting because it was L-shaped, and because we were very *high*, there was this very strong vertical thrust in the buildings around it, – whereas (in part I) you were quite conscious of being closed in, the ceiling, especially with those people up on boards, he put them up quite high … And I think this *hat* that he wore, with this straggly hair coming out, it was probably, yes it was the same hat that he wore sitting on the fire escape.«

Bayrak remembered a piece done after *Theatre Activity*. She did not remember whether it came before or after *ByrdwoMAN* (which she remembers as *Alley Cat*): it »was done at the atelier of J. Robbins« and

»involved four people, one of them Hope Kondrat, building a pyramid with BYRD written on it and some objects inside ... This was the first of Bob's pieces that gained applause.«

Brooks thought this piece was done after *ByrdwoMAN*, because she had »the feeling the progression was toward cleaning up the imagery and making it more pure,« and she remembered Wilson as having done it with kids at the YMHA on East 14th Street. Showing photos:

»This was basically a perfectly square structure which was erected on the spot, in other words, it was just boards lying there, and the performance really was to construct the thing, and put in the bones and bolt it, it was all pre-drilled. In the end these curtains roll down (covering the structure on all four sides), and a piece of glass breaks inside of it.«

Wilson, Kenneth King, and Hope Kondrat were in this piece, and a skinny girl whose name she does not remember, –

»so there was this feeling of those three kind of string bean people, and then Hope« (who was quite a small old woman).

»These early pieces were very sparse, – I think he was influenced a lot by John Cage around this time, ... the concert where he played one note, ... he was very strongly influenced by this kind of minimalist, you know, thinking. I don't know what happened when he went into *King of Spain*, but somehow he became much more baroque, a sort of combination of baroque and the minimal.«

# The Life and Times of Sigmund Freud.[17]

> »Because of a bodily maladjust-
> ment in a certain sense there was
> an extended range of feeling or,
> even, sensibility that, once uncov-
> ered meant an expansion of aware-
> ness and communication .... the
> servants came out to help us pick
> it up.«
>
> Wilson, Production notes to *King
> of Spain,* Hill & Wang, 1970

Like everything good it is clearly one man's show of himself, naturally
sui generis. It is very beautiful. It is not vulgar. Beauty characterizes
it.
Its coloring, of insect shells and moth wings, cannot be random.
The stage space is enormous. The play easily uses it all without
seeming fit in or stretched out. A tight-rope walker walks across way
up, you only see his legs. Entrances suggest people came from elsewhere. Beasts, some furniture attached to strings going up and out.
Beyond the rear wall there is a vast bright space, for instance the
ocean. Objects – a chair, staves which assemble or not into a
shutter, a dangling rope – make their way slowly from the fly
space. A large white rectangle turns out a slim vertical opening –
reeds or flowers appear on it as light exposes a space beyond.
The play is silent. A woman's amplified chatter, small talk not to be
made out, a waltz to which a dancing-teacher's voice counts the time
in a German accent do not change this. Two hidden microphones pick
up steps, the tinkling of a glass, the scraping of a chair .... Silence is
the form. Within it, each colorful reality is suspended.
It gives a fourth depth to this vast space, allows things to unfold,
creates a quiet deliberation of space-seeking. A cry of gulls makes an
ocean beach vast. A snaking rope slaps on the floor in the endless

---

17 Dec. 18th and 20th, 1969, and again on May 22nd and 23rd, 1970, both times
at the Brooklyn Academy of Music. Somewhat under 4 hours long. Its second act
was *The King of Spain*, shortened, but, according to Wilson (Interv. w/Wilson,
1970), more or less unchanged. Perhaps some previously successive actions are now
simultaneous. – Cf. Wilson's account of *The King of Spain*, infra, appendix 1,
and his account of *Freud*, infra, appendix 11. – I wrote this piece on *Freud* in
1970.

breaking of long waves. Chosen sounds are released into the pictorial continuum.

Of that dancing which makes time real by giving a movement-series the unity of a sound-Gestalt there is only two cunningly dissonant walk numbers by the Big Black Mammy (Wilson), one with a magically mushrooming tail of Smaller Black Mammies. Otherwise there is no dancing – no musical choreography. But there is an exquisite disposition not so much of the places as of the areas and paths of individuals. The movements are arrivals, a peopling of the scene. (The cast is enormous.) The generic mode is immobility. The spacing seems chance and the distances seem right. It is as though choreography had been translated into the pictorial: a still effigy of movement, a moving effigy of stillness. Again within that paradox of fortuity and justice, the appearances space themselves in time, each arriving on its own, but with the force of freedom to redefine, instantly, the whole so as to be definitely included – at its own time and place. As generally in modern art, time is spatial and the event takes place in the amplified space.

Beauty arises out of the very slow movements and the slowness of the movements, out of the syncopated metre of recurrent figures (a runner in different costumes), mildly and humorously surprising reappearances, out of the lifelike shifts within each of the THREE SUCCESSIVE LARGE TABLEAUX, minor events within their contexts stabilizing its reality, and out of the valence of that peaceful sound-ornamented tapestry of silence. *Nothing happens. Nothing* happens. The movements and shifts are small leisurely actions unrolling at the unhurried rate of assured agreeable enterprises, naturally in time with the life of those rewarded by undertaking them, their achievement never even sufficiently in doubt to warrant the name of Purpose. The air is that of a strange life-process below the threshhold of or perhaps removed from the anxieties of pleasure and pain, carrying on, innocently in its own way.

The phenomenon dissolves into mathematics and ambiguities and these into the gesture of the genially playful host, composed of:

delicacy and gentleness +
mystery and humor +
a marvelously unpretentious matter-of-factness =
?

The performers are the director's friends. They act themselves or perhaps dress up and present a figure – a snake charmer, an animal . . . . There is no plot. They do simple things or nothing.

The beauty of the play is the semblance of inward life, its proportion seemingly of sensitive growth and not of number.

This life is without drive, the play *is* genteel — rigorously relaxed, casually well-bred, insistently pleasant (humorous rather than witty), severely ordinated by a governing intelligence which stays on top as the judgment of good taste, elegantly avoiding the faux pas of showing.

The play has the quality of a dream, of dreamt life free of the *danger of dreams*, and so leisurely.

It backs up its gently satirical evocation of genteel life by a marvelous intimation of the strangeness of life, the wonderful though not quite wondrous strangeness of what people are and do. The nice sincere people are a little silly, aren't they? — but it's just because they seem a little removed from the passions and anxieties of the vulgar and the powerful that their pointless acts and peculiarities are like little works of art, surreal. Not vapid!

The idea suggested: distinct orders of reality attach to different individuals' lives so that rightly viewed the ordinary standard gestures of others reveal indefinable meanings hinting that they live in worlds of their own. These worlds are wonderful and people marvelous for being so different. We should strain our sensitivity to the unfathomable in others and regard them highly for it. Furthermore we need not strain to be extraordinary.

But the play's sense and evocation of strangeness goes beyond this quite exceptional though still jejeune gentility. It proposes that strangeness is the reality-dimension of human existence. It proves it by the slightness of the terpsichorean and thespian means — slowness, masks, animals, drinking a glass of water ... by which it transposes the familiar and ordinary into that dimension. Peter Harvey, the production supervisor, helped Frank Corsaro do somewhat the same thing in *Baby Wants a Kiss* and in a play by Carol Oates.

The play deals with Freud. He walks through severely, clothed as in some photograph, Anna on his arm — a strolling husband father out of the nineties, but also the outside, disinterested recorder, the reductive intellect. In fact, Wilson had one Maurice Sondak as Freud never look at what went on around. In the last act he takes a seat at a table that a dark lady has been loading with Oriental objects, on a chair that in the course of the play has gradually floated down in time for him. Sitting quite still, finally in the scene, he does not watch a boy die on the floor next to the table. When the boy expires, an object released from above shatters on the floor with a crash. A prologue has informed us that the death of his only grandson shattered Freud and intimates: »in spite of all his smart aleck theories,« – cf. the production notes (published by Hill & Wang), p. 269 on the »psychologists with their Ph.D.'s.«

Obliquely, the play throws out Freud's pansexual science. Against his exhausting explanation that life is the sensible frustration of simple organic libidos in the interests of culture, it sets up its image of gentility as a strangeness *beyond* the economic brutalities of both intellect and instinct, so as to say: not only is niceness oh so profitable, but it comes free!

The loving irony with which the play stages gentility has also the nostalgia of one of those childhood memories of papa and mama and all those visitors that might feed into a dream à la Freud (or Proust). An ante-bellum Vienna in a Jamesian New England is the butt of the gentle fun – and by making us discount the Master's brutal and base sexual reduction as a scream in those stuffy drawing rooms, the play *might* move us to embrace a post-freudian airy gentility.

The play kids Freud, counterposing the informal naturalness (instantiated by the performance style) that it deems genteel existence capable of to his uptightness and the real wondrous strangeness of life to his dry, unmoving countenance.

The play is murderous. It makes the emotional impact of a sole male descendant's death shatter the brain which threatens the serenity of genteel life and the marvel of living.

By way of a defense of poetry against intellect, the play brutally dismisses Freud as a lout, – presenting him as eminently dignified, it exposes him as pushy sexualist who doesn't understand our ways, misses the finer points of life, spoils innocent fun and makes everything seem so sordid.[18]

People ignore one another in the beautiful country Wilson has staged – asensual, asexual, unemotional. The air is pure of threat, there is no anxiety. The uncanny, the weird, the sinister are absent. The boy's death is sad but is not of this country. It is an event only for the intruding stranger, a tourist attraction prepared for him by Wilson.

18 The play's three acts progress *inward*: from open beach to drawing room to cave, from natural joy to conventional nicety to inner solitude, from youth to maturity to old age. Whether as tale of Freud or of man, this tragic content is hidden. It is as though Wilson, stunned by the perception of life as an inexorable rout inward too swift to allow us to reach out, had glazed it over with acceptance, turning the common tragedy of man against Freud, giving to a vision of defeat the color of beauty.

De Quincey's heart was fretted by the splendors of the uncanny invading a strange Serenity more fantastic than Wilson's. But here, when the ophidious note is sounded as by the screechily croaked sonata introducing Act III or by the boy's death, the slow life of the dream absorbs it unveeringly. The Big Black Mammy's slight eeriness passes as the crankiness of our Beloved Old Nurse or as camp on Aunt Jemima.

The country's style shuts out sex and anxiety. This sinister exclusion does not make it or the play sinister for they are neither cold nor dry but cheerful. Something is missing, but nothing is missed.

Nobody has a purpose. The human figures move as figures seen by others — by others *delighted* to see them but who do not happen to care to attribute motive or to wonder what they are doing. They are just *seeing* them. We see what these others saw. Acts are not means or consequences but symbols in this play:[19] but the symbols mean nothing. Carrying symbol function, they do not function as symbols. The play's dream-style deflects our attention from intention and purpose to meaning but provides no meaning. The dream is *uninterpretable*. Life is a language without denotation.

Death and sex being excluded, it is no wonder that not only anxiety but all passion and emotion are likewise out. But somehow purpose left with them. Libido gone, there is no fear, but anything done is only contrivance to no point. There is no desire at all.

Construing life (and his play) on a plane of rigorously non-Freudian gentility, Wilson had to leave the life out of life. Serenely lifeless life is a dream — the dream that guides neurosis. One of the ways that Wilson puts ordinary life in the perspective of strangeness is with animals. There is a live dog, a camel peers into the drawing room, a mechanical turtle crosses the stage, the legs of a giant cat march past, grizzlies and polar bears, a horse.... A monstrous creature sits through the second act with its back to the audience, in an armchair hiding it. Another, or the same one, furry, with a large lunar mask thrones on a stack of hay in the third act. This may be the King of Spain which is what Wilson as a boy in Waco, Texas told somebody he wanted to be. Here his is the kingdom in which man and animal live at peace. These animals are not hungry. They are tame. Freud told us we were animals. Here we see they are toy. There is really no reason to shutter the animal cage of Act III.

Yet they are not cute. Though not weird, they are mysterious, though

19 Whereas *happenings* gesturally *deny* the symbolic function implicit in the presentation of concreta and invite your confrontation with the meaningless *fact*.

not ominous portentious. They contribute to the play's strangeness an air of brooding and waiting, of heraldry. In the end, though the Strange with which the play familiarizes us is neither alien nor odd, Wilson has managed to kindle pleasantries into mystery.

There are enigmatic characters: the lady with the parrot, a Walrus whom I did not see (Jack Smith), the King of Spain, perhaps the man on crutches or the snake charmer – after a while everyone seems enigmatic, even the three intent board-game players making their moves in turn with pieces won from objects at hand but at times exchanging places in clockwise rotation, their creation of the senseless, unchancy, success- and lossless game, a symbol of genteel life. The cumulative effect (concentrated in the fantastic animal cave, uterine mind, of Act III) goes beyond the genteel fictions that people are interesting or that private lives are secrets irradiating banal acts. It suggests the presence of emblems in life which to the willfully unseeing eye of the intellect are configurations of fact only, but which carry purpose and true meaning indifferent to us and not to be comprehended by us. The genteel child will accommodate innocently to these figures – golden haystacks, human ladders. They impart to life a quality of waiting for important events, of attendance.[20]

The play bases its construction of the Mystery of Life on the implications of the death of loved ones for the existential order of scientific ambition. I.e., on the shattering of that order by love and death. It does not register their implications for the order of private gentility. Thus it maintains the Sweetness of that Mystery. Wilson did not want the play devastating or defiant (production notes p. 263). The illustration on the program cover by Blake cites Job xl-xliii. But Wilson, anxious to keep down terror, kept Jehova's illustrations of the mystery of life, the Behemoth whose strength is in his loins and the stony-hearted Leviathan, out of his play.

The production notes make the history of the production out a series of barely, God knows how avoided Disasters. Through the cover of humor and ostensibly insincere embarrassment, anxiety is shown, a life of it, never overcome. The *awareness* that Wilson teaches in New Jersey turns out to be a degree of *self*-acceptance – a sufficient acceptance of one's *awkwardness* so that one can relax enough to communicate. Mary Peer's *solo* chatter in Act I exemplifies such communication: it is a history of crises the point of which is that if only one can relax one's defenses one may muddle through. Thus the

20 Wilson's theatrical magic assembles a puzzle of riddles, jocular and plain, but unsolvable. Reality is this mosaic that resists giving the picture.

Mystery of Life seems to be that even after one has exorcised failure by telling oneself that it is only in the eyes of others, the threat of it will not leave one. This is a mystery only if we deny Freud, the overpowering force of death and sex. It is not sweet. We are raging furnaces.

The spectacle's exquisite informality is guarded by a censorship which it disavows. It is beautifully untrue. When in the confection of it, it turned into a concentrated attack on Freud, its untruth turned into a denial of the truth. Gentility is bitter.

The design of the few civilizations — e.g., the French, the Chinese — is to satisfy aggression and the appetites to the fullest. Thus in the service of *life*, they have no fear of intellect and wit, but unleash them. (The civilized man is the intelligent savage.) Life is notably unmysterious in the civilizations. The mysteries of desert, bog or forest, love, death, fate or the starry skies *are* redeeming graces of life: in the *uncivilized* nations. Ontogenetically, the sense of the mysterious is perhaps characteristic of adolescence and is maintained in happy individual cases if the culture does not offer demystifying resolutions, those worked out and offered the individual by civilizations. The fortunate child has a sense of the wonderful but it is no more mysterious to it than the humdrum.

The sense of mystery is not intellectual wonderment. It is a sublime translation of frustrations and anxieties (and so is tinged with terror). Its source is within oneself. The explanations of natural science, Freudian or other, tend to do away with it: either by brutal repression, a totalization of the repression still delicately expressed in it, not yet total as long as the sense of mystery is alive, or, in the context of a civilization, by transforming it into an aesthetic sense, a delight in revelations of order and harmony, e.g., Pythagorean or Confucian. There is no intrinsic reason why cosmogony should be less mysterious than a tree, but it is a different order of mystery and if expression of civilized life it has a different quality.

Wilson's theatre of mystery seems to me however, at this point (where Wilson is at now) not only to express the sense of mystery, but to endorse the fearborn repressions that generate it. This is what I mean by saying that it is genteel. And thus he makes the mystery sweet. In fact his play by where it locates mystery — in genteel life — seems to go so far as to say that the genteel stance is the only access to mystery. This is not true: barbarians and savages surely have at least as strong a sense of mystery as do the genteel. Gentility, a defective shield raised against life, a substitute for civilization invented by decent middle classes, fears intellect and wit. At its best, as in this play, it yields a delicious dream of life in which the irridescent night of mystery covers Pandora's box, pure, i.e., lifeless beauty.

Wilson's attempt at a liaison between gentility and mystery has the merits that it hints at the source of mystery in repression (frustrations and anxieties) and that it hints at the true solution, the intelligent ordering of life according to our natural nature — civilization. But its shortcoming is that it opposes civilization — both qua adequate culture of the human animal and qua free exercise of wit and intellect. Freud's similar endorsement of Kultur, the gentility of German barbarians, has the same flaw. But at least the indiscrete Semite clearly stated the (unacceptable) cost: repression.

In the American bureaucratic, commercial and engineering context of non-civilization, the sense of mystery saves — Wilson's mystic transcendence of gentility is precisely in the line of Hawthorne, Melville and perhaps Poe. In view of his *genius* he may as yet go further and voice the aspirations of an American civilization — as did the later Henry James or Merce Cunningham.

# Deafman Glance.[21]

I. Taking our places at the performance of February 25th, 1971, at the Brooklyn Academy of Music, of *Deafman Glance*,[22] at 9:00 p.m., we see

1. In front of the lowered grey curtain, a vastly high prison wall, small blind windows painted in it, up high, a perfectly erect, perfectly quiet black figure, tall, but small before the wall, standing, her back to us, a woman in a severe, elegant, dark ash-grey dress, her left hand gloved in black, her very long right hand bare, its palm, light in color — it is a Negress — turned toward us: tragedy herself, someone fated to do something, not prisoner so much as emblem. There is a hum of music, humming. The wall reveals itself to be an inside wall, the beginnings of the adjoining walls, the ceilings are outlined, she is inside this vast cell, and perhaps we are with her. The wall is cracked, in one place the grey bricks are showing under the mortar. She is on a platform. With her on it is a little colored boy on a stool reading a comic, his back to us and another sleeping child under a sheet. There is a narrow table with a pitcher of milk, two gleaming glasses, a knife, a napkin. The table is covered with a white table cloth, falling to the floor. The platform, the boy's shirt, the sheet, the napkin are also white. The milk is a richer white. The white sets off her blackness against the grey nothing of the wall. She stands still for a long time. People are settling down. A white plaster lion, muzzle on paw, faces the audience this side of her old-fashioned, forbidding silhouette. The hum stops.

2. The woman turns, slowly gloves her right hand in black, slowly pours milk in one of the glasses, with incredible slowness brings it over to the boy, he takes it without looking up, drinks a little, she waiting, she takes the glass back from him, brings it back to the table, picks up the knife, very slowly wipes it off, turns, walks, with a hint (only) of predatory stealth and power, back to the boy, leans over him, he is reading his book again, stabs him in the chest (he is paying no attention), he collapses, she guides him down to the floor with her left, stabs him again, again very deliberately, carefully, in the back, withdraws the knife, walks back to the table, wipes off the

21 I wrote this piece in 1971/72.
22 Performed 1970/71. By Robert Wilson and Raymond Andrews Cf. appendix v for their collaboration.

knife again. Her action has been entirely unemotional. Her gestures indicate a complete imbuement with a sense of maternal duty. When she lifts the knife for the kill, a taller, older boy, suspenders over white shirt, round, low black hat, Nigger Jim as Huckleberry Finn, perhaps twelve, ambles onto the stage, stands watching. She again pours milk, takes it over to the covered figure on the floor, pulls back the sheet, there is a sleeping Negro girl. Kneeling on one knee, she wakes her, gives her to drink, takes back the milk, puts it on the table, returns with the knife, stabs the sleeping girl in the chest, guides her down, stabs her in the back, rises. As she rises, she extends her hand over her victim as though to keep her down, ban her, quiet her. Utter silence in the white light. Except that as his sister (presumably) is stabbed the second time, the older boy starts screaming a discontinuous, almost neuter scream, emotionally colorless jabs at utterance,[23] not too loud. She has walked back to the table, is wiping the knife off again in the gleaming white napkin. All her gestures have been supremely slow, but, translated into their extended, frozen time, quite smooth, almost natural. We see it happen. She walks over to the standing boy, passes her hand over his face, first touching his forehead, then his open mouth. His scream had gotten louder as she approached him. She smothers[24] it at its loudest. Her gesture is that of reassurance. He starts to walk along the wall. She follows him. He has taken the lead. They come to a certain point, he turns, walks right into the wall,

3. which rises, lets them pass, they penetrate into the world that was outside the wall, or into some other world. It is a delightful dream scene, a musical garden party on the old plantation, in ante bellum times, a dozen or more ladies in white – hats, veils – are seated among the park's poplars, under a bright moon, listening to a *Moonlight Sonata* that starts as mother and son enter, played by an old-time story-book's Black Mammy, also in white, seated at a piano among the trees, her elbows and wrists dancing fantastically above the keys. As the visitors enter, the ladies oddly raise their right hands on which perch white birds. They sit, their arms laxly extended, listening to the music, as the murderess and the boy advance into the scene, halt in a space near the scattered assembly of genteel ladies, where the woman stops and remains,[25] her back to us, while the boy

23 Raymond Andrews is a deaf-mute orphan.
24 Wilson's own term: she »absorbs« the scream. The play has lasted one hour up to this point.
25 Wilson refers to this spot as the »holy spot.« It was intended to be marked

goes off to one side, seating himself inobtrusively, near an elegant waiting couple, a young girl and an elderly gentleman, putting his hands on his knees, regarding the ground between his legs, at ease, detached.

4. As they entered under the rising curtain, a pink angel to their one side retreats backward in a smooth and almost negligible powerful withdrawal, fading out and blending into a magician advancing, to a lugubrious, possibly ominous sequence of piano chords, in solemn state, tall, black, ungainly, in the formal clothing of a professional (stage) magician of some little time ago, top hat, tails, cape, coming on along the angel's path of retreat, meeting the murderess, providing a reception for her (as the boy walks off with the air of one who has provided for his parent or perhaps has settled them down in his own place). The red lining of the magician's cape momentarily provides a pink berth for the criminal. He has brought her presents, a little black monkey in a wicker baby carriage, which he parks behind her, and a black bird, which we see perched on the back of her uplifted hand, now gloved in red. It is a ceremonial investiture – she stands passive – having accomplished which, he retreats from her again smoothly, arm lifted, walking backward, his concentration on her continuously maintained, while as though set off by the interplay of charges in this scene set up by the forces that arranged the action of the scene of crime, a wisp of an old lady flutters toward her from the other side, spreads a black veil over her head and retreats again in a pirhouette past the quietly seated boy. The magician is laughing derisively, his arm pointing at them. (In the far background some other ceremony is going on, men seem to be lifting a cadaver,[26] holding it to be seen, lowering it again.) So far, the reception of the mother has by its ceremony, though not by its cruelty and finality, been in keeping with the elegance of the gathering, but

5. now a grotesque outsider enters, destroying the reality of the plantation scene, a vulgar woman in a short, tight, cheap, worn, ill-fitting black dress, ankle boots and red socks, ridiculous black hat, with an awkwardly practical hand bag stiffly attached to her stiffly

off by colored lighting contrasting with consistently achromatic lighting elsewhere. There is what Wilson referred to as an »altar« there, a tree stump (which Jack Smith, the magician, knocked over during this performance, confusing the image of his reception of Sheryl Sutton, the grandiose murderess, when he uprighted it).

26 Originally intended to be a seated Buddha. The refs. of Wilson's images always being multiple, anyhow, however, the Buddha's comment might still have comprised a cadaver's.

sticking-out left arm. She walks on as the old lady fades away and commences, her back to us, to write in the air, on an invisible surface, slowly shifting her weight back and forth from leg to leg, her hefty pale arms and calfs shocking. While (for the first of several times) she is producing her unfathomable meaning, a small sturdy figure, equally, but differently out of place, a woman with a goat, the goat balking, appears on the black, veiled figure's other side, hardly more than a detached, strolling, momentary observer, but when the message-writer turns to walk on (her black glasses giving her an additional sinister air), they freeze for an instant in an occult gesture of recognition, tied together across that dark immobile figure, then both exiting in their different ways. (The corpse in the background is disappearing.) The magician now advances again, arms uplifted, and from the other side – in a third mechanical concentrated convergence on the woman that killed her children – the stiffly gracious couple near which the boy had seated himself also comes forward, a red-haired timid slip of a princess of a girl and a slightly older gentlemanly figure, she has a red bird on her uplifted hand, he is pointing at nothing, the murderess turns and starts to walk toward us, back out again, they fall in behind her, like a new-found, slightly shop-soiled, substitute pair of children, and they exit toward us, followed by the lumbering dark figure of the pointing, laughing magician. But she is cut off from them by the falling curtain and continues alone, bird on hand, up the aisle to our rear, our attention wandering from her even before she has disappeared.

6. We are suddenly out in front of the curtain again, on the scene of the crime. The heavy-bell-like chords of the magician announce and accompany the entrance of a woman in black, with a black blindfold over her eyes, crossing with great poise, taking position with her back to us, standing with her arm raised, waiting or commanding, followed by the magician and another magician. The magician and his associate proceed with deliberation to clear away the evidence, eliminate the murder scene, they carry off the two small stiff corpses, take out the table with its gear, the boy's stool, one of them twice pausing behind the blindfolded figure, briefly standing behind her as though in communion or exerting an influence. The heavy, bell-like tones continue, sometimes lowered in pitch to a growl, time standing still in a moment of preparation of some important action. The magician is gone. Their practical pseudo-abolition of the crime completed, the associate magician after seeming to release the woman from her attendance advances

7. into a spotlight and magnificently announces the play, an actor, after a stately bow (in the direction of a loge in which we may now perceive, bathed in weak projector light, the couple that had joined the murderess, seated):

»Ladies and Gentle-men. Our play will be three hours long. Ladies and Gentle-men, the Byrd Hoffmann Foundation Incorporated, in association with the Byrd Hoffmann School of Byrds, with the Brooklyn Academy of Music, proudly presents: *Deafman Glance*,«
– in phony, strange, ironic, demanding, weird tones, as though the play we are about to see was a play within some other play in which he was acting, a put-on: or a trick.

8. The curtain rises. There are forest noises, the park has changed into a somber forest beyond which a pyramid dimly looms and in the shadow of which, at its edge, the boy, the center of the scene for us, is seated in the same place and in the same attitude of unperturbed self-reliance and contentment, but now in great isolation. Behind him, the forest seems populated by some vaguely horrible, crawling creatures, we perceive their movement rather than them, it is unimportant. The ladies are gone. A banquet table, with three chairs behind it, incongruously has appeared in the foreground, away from the boy. Behind it, crowded in, stagey, a high-gabled fairy-tale little house, a grey hut, with a low palm tree in front of it. After a while we notice that a giant green frog is presiding over the table, immobile. By the dim aura of brightness on the near horizon beyond the forest, the time seems to be early morning, the cold forward edge of dawn.

9. Two workmanlike characters, T-shirt/nude upper body, shorts/denims, enter in an unconcerned way, and slowly, with some requisite minimum of care, in businesslike small movements, empty two buckets on what appears to be a small flowerstrewn mound in front of the boy (who is, however, not looking), a bucket of dirt, a bucket of water. They could be gardening. The buckets empty, their task finished, they leave. The mound moves, a little girl rises from it, in her panties, then a nude woman with short, silver hair and a magnificent arse. Moving with graceful deliberation, but no affectation, they gather the flowers into the buckets, exit with them, their bodies still a strong imprint on the pale, tentative scene, as

10. a lank, neuter dancer enters, his boneless limbs agitated in jerky yet soft gyrations, his steady feet stirring up the sand of the two females' place of birth, as also, but inconspicuously, a quartet of turtle-backs slides into view like racetrack rabbits, coming to rest in

a rectangle, and the two workmen come out again and without paying any attention to him (nor he any to them), intent on their work, seem to conduct a survey of the ground there with the aid of a rope, the giant frog a looker-on from a distance, the boy not watching any of it. All three leave, but

11. the workmen (soon joined by a third, a woman) reappear, carrying crude raw wooden boards, out of which they slowly, with the air of some guys doing something, proceed to construct on top of the four turtle backs a structure like so:

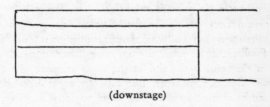

(downstage)

It takes them quite a while to build it, for they work slowly, so that after a while our attention wanders from their mechanical carrying, placing, hooking, screwing (which one of them occasionally spices with calisthenic spasms, tumbles, shoulderstands) to the scattering of other activities on the stage, equally uninspiring. But while these »bins« are being built there is no well-defined other scene on stage attracting preoccupation or even just intensive focus. We are being exposed to an uneventful period of waiting, thinly occupied by not only meaningless but uninteresting activities, the problematic beauty of which is marginal: like certain quarter-hours or decades of a lifetime, period of low concentration, random ideation, no will.

12. Almost unnoticeably, the magician has emerged in the thick of the forest far behind the boy (the fateful piano tinkle, his motif, starting), carrying first one, then the other of the two little dead children, depositing them there, engaged in a most indistinct, barely discernible ceremony or service of sorrowing, on his knees, now bent over them, now erect. You can't tell what he is doing,[27] perhaps

27 Jack Smith's incredibly intensive and varied wake is wasted back there. Though the use of gradation extending down to marginal impact on perception is a major working tool of Wilson's mises-en-scene – often arranged for delayed impact, or used in conjunction with a quite different intensity of affective (than of sensory) impact – the complexities of technical execution (e.g. lighting), aggravated by financial exigencies, sometimes interfere with, distort or exaggerate the intended effect.

he is covering them with some of the large fall leaves heaped upon the ground back there. He is little more than the broken silhouette of top hat and cape, a presence inferred from slight movement, a faint reminder.

13. As the builders get on with their chores, something like a Red Indian with a tomahawk on the warpath, devilish-funny in red, with a long red train, by no means consistent, stalks onto the scene, furtively moving in the direction of the boy, as though intending him harm, but veering off to leave, somewhere behind him, harmless as a figment of the imagination, a boy's imagination.

14. Smoke has begun to whirl off the hut, it seems to be afire, we see red reflects through its large chapel window.

15. The forest is still, the forest noises continue. We more or less know the magician is in there, glimpse him occasionally between the sapling tree trunks.

16. A gaunt servant waiter like a butler, undertakerish, with a vivid red wig, commences to serve at the table, a greasy-spoon diner waitress with hairnet assisting him, her frowziness contrasting with his seedy elegance. They focus our attention on the banquet table and on the bloated presence at its head, the frog – though the bin-builders are not yet finished. Soon after the table service begins,

17. a boy, a rural image, Huckleberry Finn or Tom Sawyer, fishing pole in hand, slides in seated, on the floor, carelessly immersed in his fishing, very slowly gradually crossing just in front of the table, reeling in, his line extended to over on the other side of the stage,

18. incidentally perhaps drawing our attention to a red band on the floor, all across the front of the whole scene, sometimes dull, some-times bloody burgundy, possibly a river in which he fishes, in (on) which we now notice, if we did not before, a prone slithering creature, blood-red at times, already half across, a man, a fish on his back, spasmodically, painfully, with infinite slowness pulling himself forward by his arms – »just one more of the things here that don't make sense.«

19. The waiter has been shaking a cocktail mixer and now serves the drink dexterously[28] to the big frog who picks it up and drinks it. The thin sound of the ice cubes in the shaker was quite distinct

28 Maurice Blanc is too busy. The naturalism of the professional actor crowds his performance with insignificant detail attesting only to his identification with his role. The local disturbance shatters the totality (continuity) in space and time aimed at by Wilson and unbalances Wilson's gradations of emphasis within this totality.

(the forest noises are faint). It was disturbing,[29] though the modern touch to the fairy-tale image of the lordly frog is also amusing. The waiter commences to mix another cocktail. The activity at the table has an air of legendary elegance, of formality and high living.

20. The builders seem to have finished. They collapse on their hands inside their structure in a faintly dramatic way, then crawl out of it with diverse movements of the mutilated or handicapped, one of them backward, one on hands and toes, with low jawping noises, as though of animals or mutes. They disappear. The thing they have put together is perfectly ugly though in no way disgusting: a roof-and floor-less, multiple-unit container off the ground, apparently, even evidently, without function, just deep enough to lie down in and about as big around as a big car. Its (obviously illusory) rawly utilitarian character counterposes it to the witch's house, the forest, the inward boy and everything else there. Fish are slipping along its upper edges.

A basic structure has gradually emerged:

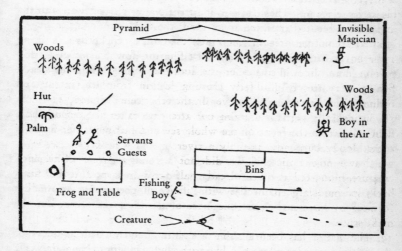

Within the incongruous scene, the background, defined by the forest, dominates the foreground affectively, in terms of mood, but visually the foreground is dominant, the activities there attracting our conscious attention: on the right, the labor, to the area of the stark

29 It had been the intention to wire this sound and have it come from elsewhere. Perhaps this was in fact done, and the sound made with paper clips.

construct it creates, on the left the formalities of service and living to the banquet table. These foreground social and culture images do not jibe with the brooding quality of the forested rear environing them. They clash with one another also, however. Furthermore, each of them has its queer or discordant edge – the table that of the fairy-tale motif of the frog, the bins that of the fish and the odd gymnastics of the workers. The extreme foreground does not really go with anything else, and is itself also discordant – between the small-town boy playing hookey on the one side and the creatures out of Dante's *Inferno,* (the first is followed by others, there is one, sometimes there are two, in sight throughout most of the play) on the other side. The magician, the crawling creatures in the forest (»Branch People«), and the pyramid are not at this point elements distinct from one another, but obscure components of the forest. The boy, off center to our right, provides a reference point for us, like a narrator, first person singular, in a novel. But he does nothing and pays no attention, so far, to anything. In fact, except for the almost invisible magician, nobody has been paying any attention to anybody else on stage, unless we chose to view the waiter's attentiveness to the being he serves as attention.

21. The builders are making their departure, cocktails are being served: a little girl dances on, an elf, arms down, arms and body relaxed and natural, the quiet exuberance of young life in the steady off-beat patter of her feet. Dancing almost in place, intent and unconcerned, her infinitely small progress seems aimless, you lose yourself in it, she is out in the sun. Her path takes her around those bins, up in the direction of the little grey hut. But while her figure is defining itself, our attention is drawn away to

22. a comment, an outside reference, a young man in white shirt, tie over one shoulder, a little dissheveled, by dress, posture and mien clearly outside even the very wide range of performing arts modes present on stage, serious though without gravity, at home on the stage, following the little girl on her heels, doing a shuffling little step and tiny hand motions, as though in friendly comic mimicry of her. Or as though he would like to be her. He stops. He stands. He walks off.[30]

23. A gong and a tinkle of bells, a slightly structured musical occurrence with evocations of the East Indies – of temple sanctuaries – accompanies the appearance of a weakly defined ox-shape with some

30 Robert Wilson, the author and director of the play.

human figures crowding around it in the rear of the forest at our edge of vision, and which advances, its motion imperceptible, as

24. the little elf, skipping, obliquely approaches the looming hut – it takes her a long time – in the ogival window of which the head and shoulders of a womanly figure, in the red reflects from within perhaps recognizable as the woman with the live goat that earlier inspected the veiled murderess, have appeared. The little girl seems to make her a present and then stands there, her arms raised in slight curves. Her friendly trust suggests that the inhabitant of that forest house is a good witch. But the tin-roofed house is ornamented all over with the jawbones, horns, skulls of goats, (there are also a toy banjo, the wings of a dead bird,) giving it the appearance of a charnel house.

25. During this visit, Robert Wilson has reappeared, he has put his suit jacket back on, and crossing the stage sits down at the banquet table, and in a normal voice, though with many odd pauses and in a slightly puzzled manner, relates a rare, perhaps occult, obscurely very relevant experience[31] into the mike on the table, reading from some papers he has pulled out from inside his jacket.

As the little girl dances off (the goat woman again disappearing from her window),

26. he walks up behind her, his normal walk setting off her sunbeam motion, stands behind her again, mimics following her, shuffling his big bare feet in a little shuffle in place, then follows her out.

27. The forest noises are still going on as she dances off (she is a vivid denial of the burial/wake that is secretly proceeding in the forest) – the manservant is serving the frog another martini, the slithering, sliding creatures out front are blood-red now.

A guest arrives. It is the aristocratic woman in black that earlier, blind-folded, had a role in the removal of the appurtenances and victims of the crime. She takes seat at the center of the table, facing us.

28. Two other guests follow, a dignified, substantial older couple, together without quite being a couple, approaching the table in state. He is escorting her. He has a monkey on his back, one of his eyes is painted and larger than life, painted onto a white goggle. She is large, forbidding-looking, dressed for genteel company, though not perhaps for an *evening* party. Like the soft, ladylike figure of Justice that arrived before them, they have, to an extent, an air of authority

31 Wilson seems to have been reading from *Technicians of the Sacred*: about how to become a shaman.

about them. Unlike her, possibly an authoritarian air. They take seats to both sides of her. She does not seem to like to see them arrive — she shields her eyes. But then she seems to accept them by a gesture with her hands over their plates, as though blessing — though possibly cursing — them. They all subside into prayer, heads bowed, then immediately respond to a silent toast offered by their host, the Giant Frog. All drink. They seem to have been expected. A formal dinner seems in progress. One may think of parties attended by Alice in Wonderland, but if so, then the boy who is not at the table and is not paying any apparent attention to any of this, though it may all be in his head, would be Alice.

29. The little elf dances through the forest, following a bent figure, perhaps the old lady that veiled the child-murderess.

30. A guy in black pants, naked upper body, thigh-boots, one of them quilted in silver, smoking a pipe, nosies about, a tall, lank, comic weirdo, as much a stranger who has happened into this whole scene as the Red Indian previously. He stops at the table, seems to be studying something at the older man's end of it. Leaves.

31. Dinner is progressing all this while, the elf and the Sherlock Holmes type only momentarily distracting interludes. Apparently fish is being served, they are eating fish. We are startled by a remark, apparently made by the previously blindfolded lady in black in the middle, but not seeming to come from her, »You said you wanted to see me,« in an accent, perhaps Slavic. She has not moved her head. From time to time during the dinner and afterward, there are more scene as the Red Indian previously. He stops at the table, seems to ominous and restrictive sound, though they seem anxious rather than threatening:

»No cross examination.«
»They said he is free and must make a decision soon.«
»Have come then to return to never come again.«
»How can you serve love by death.«
»You must drink something. Drink a little.«
»Do you laugh? Are you cynical? Are you skeptical?«

One may get the impression that the proceedings perturb her. The other two are almost completely non-verbal. Once or twice, when the

32 Liba Bayrak has been given a set of cards, each with one of these remarks on it. She chooses which to make, when to make it, how many of them to make. The woman that played her part in the previous production, in Iowa, also had a foreign accent.

waiter allows himself a sneeze, the man with the large eye in reproving tones tells him, »Don't sneeze,« irritated by the disturbance or breach of decorum. When the plates are cleared away, the big woman with the hat decorated with a bird cantankerously says, »Don't take my plate. I want the bones.« But throughout their long period at table (easily an hour of theatre time, perhaps more), neither says anything else. The absence of talk at the table does not seem constrained, but due partly to the intense preoccupation of each of the figures there with their own concerns (and as regards the frog, to his innate modesty), partly to the formal nature of the occasion: whether, as at first, when it seems a dinner, because its nature is such that speech would be a merely conventional formality, equivalent to not saying anything and perfectly replaced by just demeanour, a kind of posture; or, as, gradually, later, when it begins more and more to seem another sort of occasion, because its nature does not call for expression or interchange, but for presence in state or possibly for the making of a decision, less by a process of deliberation than by identification and subsumption. Besides, since nobody on the stage away from the table at any time says anything at all, the rare phrases at the table, while not garrulity, do add up to a representative quantum of use of language, even to the point of making language seem a doubtful because extrinsic (conventional) form of expression. We hear the remarks as though overhearing something not intended for us. Having served the fish, the waiter comes out with a small violin. He plays it (without sound) while they eat. It makes the frog weep. He wipes his large yellow eye. Apparently he has a soft heart or is sentimental.

32. The ox with its compact group have made it all the way across the stage. Our attention wandering from the dinner, we glimpse them somewhere in the distance behind the hut. A small graceful child is riding on the ox.

33. A round-shouldered civilian in informal black, like Robert Wilson, previously, not seeming to belong in the play, seeming not to belong in it, comes in and joins at table, sits down with his back to us and in a heavy unidentifiable accent, different from that of the poised but perhaps perturbed lady at table, starts making a statement, reading it, half personal, half a formal deposition, syntactical permutations of the words of his initial proposition, given a running translation into a foreign language, apparently her native language, by that lady, seated opposite him – the effect that of private conversations in half-tones at night-time, overheard in a half-waking

state on a long-distance train; but with a nuance of quasi-official proceedings.

The stiff, relatively ceremonial dinner party seems in a process of metamorphosis into something else, something perhaps official.

34. A small silver ball over the table has been going up and down for a long time.

35. A slight figure in loose white has during the translation (which is merely an episode at the table) entered beyond its area, bent under the heavy burden of a rock strapped to his back. He reposes himself on his knee in front of the grey, gently smoldering hut. After a while, he gets up, and continues as

36. there appear, from the opposite direction (from behind the boy), three semi-nude figures, male and female, their bodies fine and pale, carrying very occasionally scintillating sheets of glass. Sometimes something is reflected in the panes. They are close to being mirrors, yet aren't. This scene now attracts our attention, the banquet table momentarily forgotten. It is a ballet, made beautiful not only by the slow, careful semi-processional movement of the carriers, but by those slight chromatic flashes and transparent duplications. The paths of the glass carriers meet and cross;

37. the laden rock carrier on his way out replaced by an additional glass carrier, seeming to transform into the opposite of himself:

38. his replacement or second form advancing on the witch/fairy godmother, who has emerged from her house in a dark red gown, seemingly intent on approaching the still inwardly withdrawn boy on his bench, but now is retreating before the figure with the sheet of glass in his hands, and again leaves:

39. the glass carriers converging on the boy, the three holding up their panes behind him, pane above pane, the one who repelled the woman, in front of him, holding his sheet up to him and to the sheets behind him, as though a mirror in which he might see himself or nothing or other mirrors or nothing reflected in nothing. But the boy pays them no mind, i.e., does not seem to, does not look up. They disassemble and leave in counterpoint,

40. as behind the table and its occupants, the stage lights dimming, there is projected on the moving lower edge of a slowly descending (and then smoothly again rising) screen a film of the first part of the murder scene, of the murder of the little boy, but not of the stage representation of it that we saw, but of something that seems to relate to it as the original of it in real life. In a neat kitchen, the mother, white bandana on her head, is fixing some food for the boy

(seated reading at a table in the back of the kitchen), pours it into a bowl, puts a spoon in the bowl, brings it to him, stands over him with her hand, like a black claw, in the air, while he eats. She goes back to the sink. He is eating. Facing us, she cleans a knife in a wadded towel, turns slowly, gently murders him (as in the play), returns to the sink, washes the knife. The persons are the same as in the play, the strong contrast between white and black is the same, the super-cooled slowness (amounting to a style) is the same, only the details are different, but the filmed scene seems real. As the screen with the film moved down, the woman with the purse that was in the reception committee for the mother in the prologue, had come on, writing in the air near the edge of it as before, with the same body movements. Aided by the two servants she proceeds to light candles in a row of candles on a shelf running along the wall of the hut under its overhanging roof – just possibly an offering to the souls of the dead. It is dark, but the pyramid is outlined against the still light sky.

41. As the screen rises and the stage grows light again, we see that the dinner guests have been invested with red judges' robes by ghostly presences behind them (in nuns' habits) whose faces, silvery grey and shapeless, covered with tissue, hover above their heads. But even as we are taking this in, almost before we have conceived the idea that this is a tribunal sitting in judgment or at any rate people who take judgment upon themselves, the presences are already again removing the robes and sinking down out of sight with them.

42. The waiter serves the people at the table children's globes of the world. They toy with them.

43. A figure, her nude upper body silvered, moves through the upper reaches of the forest, across our line of vision. Others, some male, their upper bodies similarly silvered, follow at more or less regular intervals from now on. The same figures reappear. They move like statues, without much movement of the arms, unhurried, aimless and free spirits of the forest, straight, slim and still as the trees between which we glimpse each in turn. They are semi-permanent presences like the fishing boy and the river people in the foreground.

44. A little closer to us than they, and nearer than before, though still in the distance, the ox and its attendants – a perfectly grotesque, even hideous, though in no way frightening group – emerge in the middle of the forest: an old man with an enormous grey beard, a person on crutches, swathed in bandages, a misshapen dwarf with a huge head, innocents to the gods by their misfortunes. An

undefined[33] upright figure (we vaguely discern a companion, another dwarf) moves to their encounter from the other side, its arm straight out toward the little child on the beast's back. The bandaged attendant raises a crutch in a warding-off gesture. There is a tiny pop, as though from a cap pistol. The child slips off the ox' back, down into the group, onto the ground. It would seem that it has been shot. The ox' sacral motif, gong and bells, sounds to mark this ambushlike execution in the dim of the woods. The ox and its attendants continue on their slow way, increasingly important in the total picture.

45. Robert Wilson reappears in the wake of the sacred (?) child's execution, in shirt-sleeves again this time, does something indistinct but apparently in some sense necessary, meanders off.

46. As the ox continues its advance, the globes are removed from the table and the waiter serves its occupants a variety of gear of the emblematic sort in renaissance prints distributed around alchemists, merchants and symbolic figures, though its precise nature is not too or is not at all apparent to us, partly because of the distance, partly perhaps because our attention is attracted to other events. The man with the large eye gets a box with flashing lights, a pair of callipers, a quill pen and ink, a large black book and a ledger to write in. The large woman with the bird on her hat gets kernels of corn, a half full glass of water, a candle, matches, the younger woman in the middle gets a light bulb apparatus that connects up with the table, an artificial hand, a sheet of glass.

47. But in the immediate, what happens next, almost the immediate sequel of the quasi-ritual assassination in the forest, is another projection of the film on that slim, unfurling white banner, the full world on the stage around it fading before its stark reality. The other, older boy has appeared in the kitchen doorway, the murderess seems to be moving toward him but goes to wake up the girl, sleeping on the table at which the boy had been reading, under some coats, gives her the book he had been reading – the other boy standing motionless in the doorway – then gets the bowl and puts it before the girl, who starts eating, still lying on the table, her head lifted over the bowl, the boy watching her eat, gets the knife and towel at the sink, cleans the knife, goes to the table, stabs the girl in the chest, precisely as she had stabbed the boy, reaching under her as the girl sinks down, as though to help her down, stabs her in the back. The girl's arm slips off the table, hangs down. Two features of this action stand out as we now see it a second time and just after the murder in

33 Cf. footnote 27.

the forest: the repetition of gestures in her killings of the boy and of the girl, as though everything had to be done just right — a ritualistic quality — and the passivity, almost amounting to acquiescence of the victims, a further ritualistic quality as in a sacred ritual of sacrifice, or in a sacred sacrifice.

48. As the screen is coming down, the writer on the air, with her purse, has sauntered on again, to write her indecipherable ephemeral message at the edge of the screen and to light more candles,

49. and about this time too, the magician's chords sound, and he is glimpsed appearing from elsewhere in the forest, to bend over the new child victim, presumably to sorrow over it also, perhaps to bury it.

50. A shapeless grey rock that's been lying at the forefront of the stage all this time cracks open and divides into two halves, revealing the glittery silver insides of a hollow Easter egg, a geognostic mystery — a large, fluttering, green chiffon rag escaping from it,[34] jerking upward into the air and out of sight. The dwarf buddy of the ox-born child's executioner in the forest ambles on with arrogant assurance. His athletic upper body is bare, he wears white Turkish pantaloons, his arms are stumps, ending above the elbows, he is a freak, a circus sprite. He carries each half of the rock egg, the cracking of which may be connected with the death of the child in the forest, in turn up to the grey hut, clamped between his stumps, deposits them there.[35]

51. From time to time a silvery wood spirit swims through the air in some opening between the trees in the rear of the forest.

52. A small but wide female,[36] not unlike the Venus of Willendorf, comes dancing out of the forest near the boy, swaying in large arcs, with wide, demonstrative liftings of her arms, laughing (perhaps derisively). She seems to be performing for the boy. For the first time in the play he looks up. His attention seems awakened. He watches her. Her movements are almost abandoned or even wild, but loose rather than strong or agressive. She sits down next to him on his bench, with her back to us, hunched over, a dark blob.

34 Like a little piece of tissue orally emitted by Rafi ben Yehuda, the little boy on the ox, when he is shot: not visible to any member of the audience, I dare say.
35 Near the »holy spot« (cf. footnote 25), marking off an otherwise unmarked »path« to it, running straight perpendicularly from downstage across the »river.« Wilson emphasized that performers were to take this path. It does not emerge in the performance.
36 The »Earthwoman.« A soprano, a singing »Earthwoman,« was to follow her, but didn't show up.

53. At one of the remarks, this one apparently astrological, from the dark woman at the table, »February 25, 1971, 9:00 p.m.[37] Eclipse, age of pain, age of despair, suffering,« a sign, »April 15, 1986,« suspended under a white dove, rises up from the table, comes to rest in mid-air above it. A complicated contraption, the elements of which dangle around down around his head has been fastened onto the man with the large eye. Perhaps it is therapeutic.[38] Perhaps it is a toy or a whimsey. He and the large woman are now and during the sequel using the gear they have been given. He seems intently occupied with working the light box (it doesn't seem to work), intermittently studying his book or taking notes. We cannot make out any of this too clearly,[39] but he does seem busy, bent on the advance of some project or the solution of some problem, and perplexed – stymied. The large woman plays with her maize or, inattentively, produces shrill sounds from her water glass. Their activities are more and more clearly seen to be senseless,[40] gradually then they appear idiotic or mad.

54. The fishing boy collapses sideways (he does this several times during the play, perhaps twice).[41] Silvery ball bearings roll from his mouth as he collapses.

55. But behind these minor events out front, a dance sequence begun with the Earthwoman's show for the boy continues, self-contained, a dream within a dream. A sturdy beautiful blackface nurse appears from behind the grey hut with a white baby doll in her arms. A Black Mammy – Aunt Jemima, vast pillowy buttocks and bosom, satiric insignia respectively of her African race and her American function of nursing the brood of others, emerges (another Black Mammy behind her) on the opposite side, staff in hand, comically dance-walking as though through deep soft sand or in water, with deep knee bends, large paddling motions of the arms: dances across to the nurse, kneels before her. The baby is shown (presented), perhaps adored. They leave the staff there,[42] sticking in the ground, in front

37 Date and time of the opening of *Deafman Glance* in New York. The remark may be from the horoscope Wilson had cast for the play.
38 It is. Wilson saw an illustration of it in some magazine such as the National Enquirer.
39 In real life, our ability to name what we or others are doing lulls us into attributing meaning to it.
40 Which, if it is the intended effect, makes it quite all right that we can't quite make out the equipment or what they do with it: while the particular props they've been given makes them do the things apt to give them the particular air intended.
41 It was left up to the performer how often and when he does this.
42 At the »holy spot«.

of the hut, and the Mammy walk-dances back and out past the boy, following the more dignified nurse, who is cradling her baby.

56. The Earthwoman gets up from the boy's bench and leaves after them with comic modifications of her previous dance movements, possibly as though ironically mimicking the nurse. She seems to be pointing at her, following her out.[43]

57. The boy had been watching all of them, turning sideways on his bench – with an intimation of personal concern? He turns around again to watch the exit of the Earthwoman, moving his body from side to side, arms half lifted, his hands moving toward and away from one another, a kind of abortive applause, as though he was pleased by her humor. There is nothing startling in his activation, but it is moving, after his long-sustained detachment. In a very subdued way it is a kind of climax, namely insofar as he and his attitude have perhaps been conditioning, without our being too aware of it, the mood in which we have followed the play so far.

58. The theme of motherhood is again idyllically evoked by the next event: three young white women with white babies in their arms dance prettily across at the edge of the forest near the boy, swinging their babies up in the air, the sheets flying.

59. The magician kneeling over the dead child or children is quite visible as the mothers move past him.

60. Perhaps because of our focus during these past scenes away from the foreground – the empty bins, the deteriorating situation at the table – and onto the events just this side of or just within the forest, the moving denizens of the forest, steadily flitting through its depths have been within our ken, though still only at the rim of our awareness, for quite some while now. They have defined themselves as definitely sexual, though because of the alteration between the male and female naked upper bodies, confusingly, perhaps even vaguely perversely sexual – not at all or very sexy? Non-satyrs not pursuing nymphs. In any event, we have become quite aware of breasts. This may have obscurely reinforced or extended or possibly twisted or even counteracted our momentary pre-occupation with motherhood – the theme blackly posed at the beginning of the evening, brightly put forward (though with some irony) during the immediately preceding.

61. At some point now we find that the servants at the table have abandoned their ministrations to the personages there, the waitress

43 Hala Pietkiewicz, the »Earthwoman,« is the mother of Eva Pietkiewics, the »Nurse.«

having taken up raking somewhat to the rear of the table, the waiter shoveling.

62. Also the ox has finally emerged from the forest, it is now behind the bins in the forward area of the stage near the boy. Its attendants are watching proceedings, almost part of them, as though expecting some development crucial to themselves. The green-faced dwarf is staring (his eyes are red), a ferocious expression on his green mask.

63. A gracious but slightly lunatic-appearing, sprightly old lady in ruffled white, the same one that put the veil on the murderess much earlier – she has a jeweled arrow in her hair – is suddenly standing there, also near the bins. After a wait in suspension, she quickly swivels into them, disappears in them, with an odd diving movement, that of a burglar or a suicide. Only one hand and the lower arm stick out. They wave weakly. Their signal of continued existence, of cramped confinement – life in a play by Beckett – persists during the following.

64. A small crowd of other people follow her into the bins. During the sequel, their likewise occasionally protruding limbs tell the same story.

65. The servants now give up their gardening tasks, she disappears, he files out, in passing depositing a shovel of dirt on the banquet table, possibly a sign of contempt, perhaps a profound form of purification, surely a terminal gesture, both as regards his functions and as regards the grave activities at the table.

66. The boy's bench with him on it, without his agency slides across the stage into a position near the hut (and the »holy spot«). The displacement, almost negligible in its smoothness and gimmickry, literally puts him in the center of the action – at a time, when the cultural institutions in the foreground have come to some kind of a definite pass, the manual construct utilized to the brim, crammed with the living dead or the buried alive like a tenement, the table, authoritative locus of censorious pomp, disintegrating into idiocy, anxiety and madness, and a point of development at which the mythical creature of the forest, its horns gilded, a garland around its neck, its muzzle gaping in sorrowful anguish, has made its appearance among men, while

67. way to the rear, at the upper edge of the pyramid, which up to this point, in spite of its overarching status in the picture, has been merely a background, a self-effacing, though occasionally, depending on the lighting, impressive cliché, not even an attending presence, there dimly appears the slight figure of the little dancing girl, quite

obscurely busy, it seems, with some task connected with the pyramid, though still in the motions of dance.

68. And now suddenly also, the magician appears again in the area of action, near the banquet table — Ariel in the shape of Caliban — followed by two giant assistant magicians,

69. and the more elegant of the personages there, the dark lady, foreign, inwardly perturbed, anxious, though at one time having appeared to be perhaps Justice herself, is deranged by the suddenly risen spiritual presence behind her — her alter ego? — who calmly but with intensity bends down and whispers something in her ear, not intimately but as though the time had come for this act. The woman responds by gestures seemingly of horrified refusal, her hands lifted to shoulder level, shaken rapidly, palms forward, from side to side; her hands covering her eyes with the shoulder-lifting of a shudder; a violent shaking of her head, a shivering motion throwing her black hair over her face, but seems compelled to accede nevertheless, rising as though drawn up, turning, automaton-like, in the direction of the seated boy nearby, and, the powerful nun at her shoulder, slowly advances on him. But now the magician who has been advancing in her direction at some distance behind her, lifts his arms and, walking backwards, seems to exert a force on her, contrary to the nun's (the woman's super-ego?), like it spiritual in origin and action, physical in exertion, but supra-naturally impersonal in nature rather than (as the nun's) meta-personal, exerted through space rather than by close bodily proximity, and pulls her away from the boy, pulls her with him as he retreats out of sight. A moment later she reappears, running in front of the table this time, apparently escaped from the magician, but she freezes, the magician again appears behind her, slowly advancing, and again pulls her off, retreating slowly. She is possessed. His giant gawky apprentices, duplicates of his through some distorting mirror, have been hanging about in the meantime and the nun has remained behind, foiled, a blank, but powerful and evil presence.[44] She now goes back to the table, disappears behind the woman's vacated seat. Nunnish super-ego has lost out to some redeeming overriding magic. The scene — a struggle in mind, a personality crisis — stands out: it is the only show of emotion in the whole play.

44 The acting of Irene Leherissier, once one of Peter Schumann's Bread and Puppet Theatre's few powerful performers, memorable for her screaming »Earthwoman« in his original *Cry of the People*, is absolutely quiet, her movements restricted to the essential, her postures minutely and powerfully projective: even in this tiny role, to which she applies her knowledge of nuns, gained as pupil in a convent school.

We do not know what happened. Perhaps the protagonist, the boy, has been saved from worldly justice.[45]

70. The hut has now really started smoking. A young fellow, in light shirt and pants, not in costume, carrying some boards, comes out without ceremony, leisurely boards it up. His hammer blows sound from afar as though his carpentry were unreal. We see the Goat Woman leaving her house with her goat. The hut is still smoking.

71. The woman that writes on air reappears in her mission. The light dims. The scroll comes down with the last part of the murder scene. The mother is turning from her second victim, looks at the boy in the doorway, approaches him, he smiles at her, stops smiling, looks up at her, his mouth opens, he may be screaming, she puts her gloved hand on his forehead, moves it down over his face, seeming to close his eyes, the film ends with him still screaming. The last candles are lit on the boarded-up hut.

72. As the stage lightens up again, all three judges (the woman is back in her seat) are in their judicial red, their faces (except that of the large-eyed man with the crazy gadget on his head) gone under red hoods pulled over their heads, holding purple cabbages up before where their mouths would be. The spiritual presences hover above their blood-red heads, shimmering silver-grey. The gadgeteer with the goggle-eye is also holding up a cabbage. The dumb poses evoke the arrested courtroom moments after the judgment has been arrived at, just before it is announced, or the instant at high mass when wine turns into blood.

73. But at the same time we also see the beginning of a ceremony, the entrance to the sound of sacred organ music of a high ecclesiastic personage, pope or other, a small, slight mitred figure of spiritual governance and redemption, his apparently crippled hands softly clasped on his chest, at the head of a procession of three young males in white. He drifts to the seated boy's side (who has finally become the center of central action), takes root there, a frail flower, and starts to subject him, gently, softly, compassionately, to an unmercifully sustained gesture of his right crippled hand, the little finger pointing, the arm going up and down, a marvelously intense blessing or admonition, blessing more than admonition, as though painting the boy into space, creating him by his action, – but is not a blessing also a finishing off of him who is blessed? Perhaps the boy is being

---

45 Wilson first met Raymond Andrews, the protagonist, on an occassion when Raymond was being beaten up by a policeman for throwing a rock through a window. Wilson saved him from the cop by some talking.

beatified, but his response (his first and only act since his applause for the childless Earthwoman's lighthearted mockery of the nurse: but more of a self-assertion, since it seems a resistance) is to begin shaking his head, slowly from side to side. He sustains this gesture of refusal, of denial of guilt and/or of consternation. Another figure has now joined this scene, the ghostly spiritual presence dressed like a nun from behind the man with the eye, at the table, *his* conscience, that of an obsessive monomaniac.[46] Placing herself at the boy's other side, she puts a slim silver-grey conical dunce cap on his head (removing his black Nigger boy's hat), and commences to belabor him with a stick — a slow, methodical purificatory castigation of the flesh symmetrical with the pope's purificatory castigation of the spirit. With a gesture of her hand she has put a white streak on his face, giving him the appearance of being in black-face. The kid is really being worked over, but the still face, turning steadfastly from side to side retains its dignity in spite of the white paint and the dunce-cap.

74. The magician, trailed by his apprentices, has again appeared at the edge of the action. He is pressing his hands to his temples as though concentrating his powers, and as though in pain.

75. The three young fellows in white have not followed the pope up to the boy. They have instead advanced up to the ox (whose attendants are still by the bins, watching). They pick it up (it now clearly becomes an object of ceremony, prop of ritual) and lift it into the bins, facing away from the scene with the boy — this is evidently going to be a distinct ritual. As they lift the ox (sound of gong and bells), it suddenly looms terribly large, and there are now two centers of action on the stage, two pulls on our attention, though the fate of the boy is still primary. The servants of the ox kneel down in prayer and waiting, in a white row in front of the bins (which are being purified by the presence of the sacred animal? destroyed by the invasion by a plaything? — hands and feet have been sticking out of them from time to time, moving weakly).

76. The boy puts that endearing black hat back on his head, and under his own power gets into another bench further back, out of the

46 These connections may not be part of experience in the theatre, only products of subsequent reflection. Gerald Fabian, the performer of the Man with the Large Eye may have been too intent on acting out that he was maniacally obsessed with making his light-box work, i.e., himself not sufficiently an obsessive maniac, to get this particular pathological humor across to us. Then again Wilson may have been stretching his metaphorical play out too far if (*if*) he intended to have us connect the action of each ghost/nun with the character of the figure she is placed behind.

center (strapping himself in). The fishing boy (who has been, like the prone moving creatures, out front all this time) comes up to him and presents him with his rod. Reeling in, he has become the image of a normal boy, black version. A cotton candy pink suffuses the entire stage and the boy rises up into the air on his bench, higher and higher, the pope still berating/sermonizing below, looking a little foolish now, the ox' freakish attendants observing, the white-frocked servants of the ox praying. We hesitate between a feeling that the boy has magically escaped correction and an impression that it has been of a nature to free him.[47] At some point during his rise he catches the fish the white boy has been fishing for all this time, a large paper fish that detaches itself from the stage floor.

77. And while he rises, the smoking hut collapses, sinking down to half its size, a weakly reassuring image gone from the stage that the boy has left, while at the same time the little palm in front of it grows, grows up to great height above it.

78. The stage darkens, the pink fades somewhat, in a light cone from above the image of the suspended boy slowly dims but remains in mind, attached to the white spot of his shirt, even as the stage grows entirely dark.

79. Then there is light again as though of morning, the sky blue above and pink below, and the sound of ocean waves, though the organ is still on. The stage is lit up, the pyramid is clearly visible, a golden presence nullifying the forest, the aetherially sexual spirits of which are moving across together, in uniform motion raising staves above their heads. The hut is gone. The fishing boy, minus his fishing pole, enters and kneels, facing us. The protagonist is still shaking his head up there.

80. The pope stops blessing, is now just watching the boy above, hands in prayer. The Goat Woman appears and circles him. A man comes in, walks up to the pope, catches him in his arms as he keels over softly (a rhinestone band issuing from his mouth). As the man is

47 I suspect Wilson intended to create that feeling, not that impression. But his direction of Mark Shafer, a beautiful person, as the Pope was such as to create that impression of salvation by absolution. Perhaps he intended both and the doubt between them. Only if a large number of spectators came away with that impression only and did not have the feeling of witnessing an escape, could we possibly say that there is here a weakness of the mise-en-scène. Raymond Andrews could not walk away otherwise: not only if his escape was to be magic, but also because his withdrawals would perforce be under cover, undercover – his or those of the boy in the play. No fault or weakness of the mise-en-scène *there*. Finally: magic escapes, e.g., by horse, are dubious: carry with them the very harsh corrections that they are responses to.

carrying the frail figure away in his arms, walking toward us, they encounter a woman who kneels before them in homage or obeisance, hands joined above her head and places some kind of dry brush on the dead pope. They turn and leave in the direction of the forest, followed by the woman who seems to be sorrowing, their diagonal procession across the stage

81. joined by a now appearing band of a dozen or so Negro boys of the protagonist's age and dressed like him, his images, fishing poles in their hands, liberated Nigger Jims, walking two by two, in turn followed by a tail end of men in black-face, in minstrel outfits and red gloves, and by the servants of the ox who have risen from their prayer. They all leave through the forest, soon reappear, now following the pope's splendid glass coffin, born aloft on a bier, this touching and only slightly comic funeral cortege crossing inside the forest. The organ music fades out, only the ocean sound remains.

82. Sometime during these aftermaths of the hero's removal and ascension, or perhaps during the darkening that accompanied it, the judges' robes and hoods have been removed, their dubious normalcy restored to them, and the spiritual presences attached to them have sunk out of sight again.

83. Sound of ocean waves. A pause. Nothing is happening. The large woman at the table idiotically makes her glass whine.

84. Abruptly the brash music of a pop tune (*Mutual Admiration Society*) blares out in a burst of genuine artificial gaiety, the first and only in the play. A bee or other bug, a young girl with a green insect mask head, dances out within the forest, feet and hands in small, rapid, nervous movements, slightly stiff flutters, flitting ahead, suspended in place in agitated vibration. She is joined almost immediately by a large white rabbit, dashing madly, limbs gyrating, large ears flapping. They dance together, across, then back, their movements in absolute contrast, wiggle vs. tumble. It's the small-scale life in an isolated meadow on a summer noon. The tune cuts off abruptly. The ballerinas are gone.

85. Again nothing. It is as though, with the removal of the boy, the world on stage had lost its original impetus, the energy translating into its images, and had since been merely drawing on a remainder of it in wiping the slate clean with the elimination of the pope (but then again subsiding into lethargy), and on mere rigid will to go on, in picking itself up on a sudden decision, with a last spurt of energy, in the woodland ballet, again, feeling the falsity of this improvisation, depleted, relapsing into a state of waiting, and was only now about

to get going again slowly in the development of a theme clearly stated previously, that of the ox, a theme now free to yield up its energies and beginning to do so. The marvelous thing felt in this pause is, first, that this is the natural movement of the creative energy of a man, and, second, that its specific rhythm is immanent to the particular outflow of images making up this play, or, rather, inversely, that the concatenation of these particular images naturally proceeds from an energy so moving.[48]

86. The servants in white reenter. They lift the ox, and, by a circuitous route (around the bins), move it to the table. Gong and bells. The ox now touches on the second bastion of institutionalized activity. Things there are not so queer but that the incongruousness is striking. There is the feeling of an invasion. The servants kneel down in prayer again, at the far side of the bins this time.

87. A young boy guides the principal among the attendants of the ox, still standing there in an attentive, waiting group, the old gentleman with the enormous beard, around to the forefront of the stage, brings a stool and a basin and proceeds to wash the now seated old man's feet, while a shivery, eerie, organ-like, portentous music starts low, penetrating the forest noises, gradually growing in intensity and drama. It prepares us for a great event. The other two attendants have turned around to watch.

88. The light from above is a festive, but slightly lurid mixture of red and blue. The old man, his feet clean, approaches the ox cumbersomely, throws coins before it. The other two attendants follow him and do the same. The little ceremony, a parting payment of respect, accomplished, each in turn, bowed low as though in humility or by some loss or through a sudden aging, walks out. The boy has carried out the stool and basin and now

89. reenters and goes to the head of the ox,

90. while the magician, again hanging around, his apprentices behind him somewhere, slowly raises his arms and brings his mesmeric powers to bear on the characters at the table, apparently causing the two ladies there to rise and leave. They take up a position, next to one another, on the other side of the stage, their backs to the scene, increasingly strong presences in the sequel. The man with the large eye alone remains.

91. Whereupon a bright round disk prettily, slowly dangles down to in front of the ox at the table where the boy is waiting for it with upstretched arms (the magician and the two women putting on sun

48 Which implies that the play will keep on changing.

glasses as though to protect their eyes from the approaching sun): the boy unhooks the disk, rolls it up, it is of a pliable material, stuffs it down the ox' maw. Gong and bells. The ox glows. That shivery, eerie music is at its height. While the sun comes down — self-destruction of the universe —

92. the waiter is clearing the gear off the table, and

93. the half-bare spirits of the forest approach in a candle-carrying procession through the forest, standing and waiting in its nearer regions until the sun accomplishes its descent, presumably in a celebration of their fellow forest-creature's gigantic role in the cosmogonic rite. When he ingurgitates the sun, they blow out their candles and disperse.

94. The magician has again appeared — he is taking on the dimensions of a demi-urge, the author-in-presence of the play.[49]

95. The ox stands, its belly lights up. Then suddenly its head clatters to the ground. We have witnessed a rite of sacrifice (perhaps not the first in the play). The loss of the head, obviously mechanically contrived and slightly comic (in both respects like the detail of much other transcendental ritual, pointing up its mystic nature, the mystery of transubstantiation) is stunning. Gong and bells. The servants of the ox approach from their prayer, place the headless ox on the other side of the stage, at the far end of the bins. It stands there, its speckled skin transparent, glowing, a terrific image of a deity. Gong and bells.

96. While his apprentices move off through the forest, the magician, carrying a big metal tray, gets ready to pick up the sacred head. He takes his time. Having taken an infinite time in the approach to the delicate act, he with a briskly efficient gesture — to be done with it — places the head on the tray. He carefully more than respectfully, though by his posture in movement indicating the importance of his responsibility, carries it down to the fore, center stage, deposits it there, kneels next to it, his back erect, facing us, and remains there during the following, guardian and witness and perhaps more.[50]

97. The body of the ox is moved off by the servants.

98. The bins slip off, propelled by their prone inmates.

99. The two female personages formerly at the table have left. The

49 He is of course not a real magician. He is a stage-magician. He could have been costumed as a real magician: but wasn't. Wilson's self-irony.

50 The magician's position here is the performer's, Jack Smith's, invention. In his own Saturday midnight shows in his loft in the Soho district of N.Y., the negatives of his friend Wilson's shows, he almost never performs. The last performance of his I saw, a brilliant one, was as »Mr. X« in Charles Ludlam's *Big Hotel*.

stage is dark and very empty behind the kneeling magician. The pyramid is a black outline against the night sky, a slight movement is dimly discernible against its edge, way up. At its base, there is an eerie, icy white glow, an indistinguishable ghostly disturbance, as though of a multitude of crouching slave-prisoners in the dark. We are aware of the boy, high up, only by the faint spectral white of his shirt. The large eye of the remaining convivant/madman/justiciarian at the table begins to glow.

100. As it grows brighter, we see at the end of the table the outline of the frog's head – the eye, the alligator snout, then his head. He seems to be ogling the man with the incandescent eye, turning his head to do so. He has remained cool so far, but this new development seems to excede him. At length he climbs up on the table, a large, heavy, impressive, even frightening movement. He waddles along the table slowly, now looking at the man, now at us. He jumps: past the man to the other end of the table and in continuous movement[51] up in the air off the table and heavily across the floor and away (a spotlight following him). We never knew what it all meant to him.

101. An eerie blue light, cold and alien,[52] outlines a small moving figure near the top of the pyramid, way up, near its top. It seems to be – it may be – the little dancing girl from before. The illumination of the madman at the table (induced by the ritual conflagration of the ox?) seems to be catching. Then the same sort of light seems to grow out of his head. It has a shape, the shape of horns or of a burning bush. It reveals the dim presence behind him of his spiritual alter ego, with the same kind of light, in the same shape growing out of its head. His eye grows brighter. As it brightens, the other lights fade out, and suddenly a huge eye like his lights up in the pyramid and the top of the pyramid sails off with the eye brightly in it, a life-like, elegant eye, seeing as such, in the abstract, not looking, in fact blind. It shines only briefly, then goes out. And the man's eye fades out too. We have witnessed an expression of energy mounting to fantastic minor epiphanies/effects, but pressing on – whereat they fell away – so that nothing showed – and so coming home in the supreme effect.[53]

51 There is a trampoline built into the table.
52 Neon.
53 Parable for the structure of works RW's work aims at. But note also the wilderness of ideas in Wilson's mind: the man has a greedy eye – his obsession is to make a light-box work mechanically and he can't even do it, while all the time he is himself the most fantastic light-box – when the sun dies the spirit

102. The stage grows light again. The man gets up, walks off slowly, followed at some paces by the table (then overtaken by it), the three ghostly presences of the people that had been at the table, females in nun's habits, closing off the exodus in a single file, stiffly carrying the three chairs before them, pure magic. The shivery music that has been with us since the foot-washing preparations for the cosmogonic sacrifice of the ox, slowly dies out as they leave, the forest noises that have been there throughout again growing in strength, the sound of ocean waves joining them.

103. Ocean and forest sounds. The stage is completely empty except for the forest and some mystic reliques of the earlier events, the cracked rock, the stave stuck in the sand. A full moon rises next to the pyramid's outline, again intact. The spirits of the forest are there, but no longer dance through it: they run past, at intervals, in steady reiteration, as though the nighttime forest were in a sterner mood. The magician's back is turned toward this landscape (the boy in his high perch is out of it). He is concentrating. His back is straight up and down. He is totally still, but he exudes energy, gathering force, unmoving motive power.

104. As though conjured up by him, introduced by the briefest recrudescence of that suspension music that led up to the ox sacrifice, an opening chord immediately going over into the sound of relief and of returned tranquility, of Fauré's *Requiem*, a Dancing Black Mammy dances out, transforming the scene into a Henri Rousseau, very, very slow, the huge arse tricky, arms waving like water plants, knees rising on the turns, a delicious wiggly movement between each two high-kneed steps, three movements in all, a path of circles, a white loop. She dances across like a moon: a dream-dance to Fauré, sensuous a little, but very tranquil and not at all frightening.[54]

105. As the soprano aria commences (immediately heightening the visual intensity of the scene), irregular processions of slowly moving white figures (like the ladies whom we saw seated, listening to music, during the prologue), their flows lead by nudes, begin to people the scene, turning it into a springtime (touched with winter), the solo dancer freezing, then merged in the swirl. Moving as though caught

shines – seeing is a brilliance, an outgoing illumination – seeing is its own end, there is nothing to see (negative corollary to the preceding positive).

54 Wilson draws on Lesbian powers. Lesbians have been the secret high priestesses of native female – sheerly, slowly sensual – sexuality, largely suppressed sofar in civilisation, i.e. diminished and distorted by its adaptation to assertively impatient male dominance (not just to male sexuality), but currently coming out: a marvelous gift to men of the Woman's Lib movement.

in the same dream, the white figures in three slowly spreading foamy streams, the gentle overspill from behind some dam, coalesce into a slowly rotating wheel or a camelia, for a moment the background of a nude male dancer and two nude women dancers, one pregnant, the other not,[55] also rotating, turning around themselves as they advance with the others, the whole then descending in a vortex into the ground in the forest,[56] in whirling smoke,

106. but not before they are joined by the boy, who comes down slowly out of the air, met by the Goat Woman (who in this figures somewhat as his fairy godmother, though furry all over, horned and with hair of straw), and by his mother still all in black and well-nigh invisible and as straight and rigid as ever as she follows the boy and his half-bestial protectrice down, and joined also by one of the giant magicians, carried on another man's back as though magicians were also done with.

107. Eerie rainbow reflections here and there in the white crowd – a minute but powerful effect, an occasionally irrupting phosphorescence of a St. John's Eve féerie, – reveal that the white ladies are carrying panes of glass.

108. The stage is empty. There is only the split rock, the stave, the empty bench, and the forest, smoke rising through it, turning dark red. Fauré's *Requiem* dies off. The red light dims. The stage is dark.

109. But the play starts up again once more. Spreading cones of bright light, crossing overhead, issue from below the ground, up through the grey trees and the scads of greyer smoke. The moon lights again. There is a golden harp standing in the open this side of the forest. Under the tent of the light cones, the forest is dark, however. Huge black shapes emerge into this darkness from below, struggling through the shafts of light, milling about in the smoke, lumbering toward the near edge of the forest. They are large black apes. To a lugubrious music, they squat down in a loose congregation, an ironic duplication of the musical garden party of the prologue – one sits down by the harp, plucks it without producing a sound. They extend their arms in approximate imitation of the gesture of the white ladies of that prologue scene: there are huge red apples in

55 Lucia Reudenberg, a marvelously gentle dancer. Her pubis, for a moment the dark juncture of a straight leg and one raised, bent, curving and turning, as in Luc Godard's *Mao*, is for that moment, next to that pregnant belly, the hub of the scene.

56 Three openings in the floor onto stairs into the basement. Wilson had wanted an elevator platform which would slowly lower the ladies in white.

their hands, setting off the black of their fur. A child ape is seated out front. They sit without moving.

110. A couple strolls in below them, at the corner of the stage, near us. They are in white, in the aristocratic dress of the Age of Enlightenment. Her sunshade is on fire, its glowing ashes crumbling down. They stand, their faces glistening silver, confronting the gathering of brutes. He seems to be pointing them out to her as

111. all the red apples rise into the sky.

112. Stars fall,

113. and to the sounds of *When you're in love, it's the loveliest time of the year,* from a accordion, a waltz, the curtain slowly comes down.

## II. *Meaning*[57]

0. A serene wisdom, in the absence of an ability to love passionately, envisaging life as rebirth in infinity, rationalises anxiety, fear of death and a desire to return to the womb. *DG* images a mother's crime and her boy's withdrawal (II, 1-7) and the madness of the surface world of cultured man in supernatural nature (II, 9-14), equating, in the comically magic rhythm of the *real* world, the boy's withdrawal with victory (II, 15), a victory achieved through fortunate encounters (II, 16-19). (Summation: II, 20). – The images carry suppressed and absent affective charges: anxiety (fear of death and other) and a longing for the security of protected childhood under motherlove are suppressed, the passion of love is absent (II, 21-30). The themes of death (murder) and of motherhood, intertwined into the theme of rebirth, pervade the spectacle (II, 21-23). But their affective charges are suppressed: the spectacle is unemotional (II, 24, 26), except for three emotional scenes which however reaffirm the suppression of affect (II, 25). Even setting aside the images of death and murder, the imagery pervasively correlates to the affect of

57 Wilson would pretend that his plays have no meaning, or that, at any rate, he does not intend them to have any; at least that whatever meanings they have for him, does not guide his work on them, or at the very least, is not what he aims to put across by them. Cf. f. inst. the interview reproduced in Tel Quel (nos. 71/73, Autumn 1977, – »Ce que je fais est avant tout un arrangement architectural.«) This pretense informs not only his interviews but his plays. Wilson relates to the meaning of what he does by hiding. Naturally, as in all art, the meaning is metamorphorical: analogic rather than iconic or abstractively analytic. A man would have to be an idiot to put work into art that didn't make sense to him.

anxiety: but it is suppressed (II, 27). The theme of motherhood is unemotionally presented (II, 28), and sexuality is absent (II, 29). (Summation: II, 30).

1. The germ of the spectacle is a mother's murder of her two children. In view of our species' dependency on maternal care, this is *the* crime, but Wilson hasn't done it that way, though the way he has done it invites this feeling: he had Sheryl Sutton do it with the calm routine of a conscientious mother. It is a fait divers (its black-and-white reproducing the little item on a back page): the world we live in. It is also done as an obligatory sacrifice: not a propitiation, but in need, for needed rewards. Finally, the watching boy's muted scream of terror tells us it is a harsh breach of trust.

The world is full of such-like acts. Wilson is commenting on his genteelity, formalism and love of beauty: they are not the way of the world.

2. The spectacle presents itself as the discretely metaphorical picture story of the effect of this heinous crime on the mind of one implicated as witness, beneficiary, survivor, son of the malefactress, older brother of her victims. It vouchsafes for the relevancy of the crime by recurrent recalls of it. The murderess is ejected from the body of the play, that victim literally made its central character.

3. What was the damage done this child? Wilson's delicate touch allows us, as on everything in this play, the initiative of alternative feelings.

To my mind, the boy must be feeling guilty. The mother's solicitude for her victims and his seeming assurance of his status of non-victim onlooker, the indications of her love for him all suggested to me that he would feel guilty: as presumptive beneficiary and survivor, if not simply because the guilt of our relatives is ours. Absolution from and/or surmounting of and/or denial of guilt seemed in question.

The boy would also feel guilty on another score: his rejection of his mother. For I saw the immediate sequel to the murder (3-5)[58] as a false beginning and end of the play, as familiar first reaction to a shock to our ego: the mind's hysterical action in high-tension calm of willed absolute disposal of the matter. One's fantasy – here the boy's – explodes creatively in the guise of reason and imposes a simple schema on what happened, gives a name to it and makes an external object of it to which one (momentarily) no longer relates

58 The parenthetical Arabic numerals in this section (II) and the next (III), unless preceded by Roman numerals (II or III) referring to this section or the next, refer to my accounts of scenes in section I.

personally, which no longer has anything to do with one: one relates to it by understanding it. It is an act of extrusion and rejection – a fake catharsis. Since this muscular ingenuity cuts one off from the involvements that make one what one is and give one life, it is involuntary suicide if successful. The mother's reception into the altogether delightful world of a totally surface cliché, with the boy slipping off into a quiet seat off-center, leaving her to face the music: to be categorized as black destroyer of the life she had created, to be judged and mocked and expelled, strikes me as precisely such a first coping with a shattering of one's place. The scene's character of »totally surface cliché« reflects the hysterical urgency of a deranged mind out of touch with reality, not assimilating an experience, but clutching at straws to reject it: a leap inward, a cutting off of intercourse. (The pretty fantasy of this garden party of olden times among real gentlefolk is unlike all subsequent fantasy in the spectacle.) This is not only a piously furtive betrayal of the one the boy loves and who gave him his life, it is the extrusion of the vital dimension of life, death.

Every criminal trial is such a ceremony of extrusion, intended to reestablish a sanctified purity of the universe by the sequestration of an element branded as alien because aberrant and by the institution of an exactly countervailing fact, the punishment. These statements-in-act do not affect the universe, merely sterilize it for us.

Thus these scenes may equally be the boy's fantasy or his observation of society's reaction.

But the boy is not done with his mother, nor with the epiphanies of vital energy by the negativing of which by such words as »death,« »evil,« »murder« we strike at it within ourselves. There is no safe residence for him in the delightful party world of his fantasy.

The murders themselves may be a fantasy of the boy's, wishing his mother's exclusive love, wishing his siblings dead, or vengefully loading a crime on her. Here again the upshot would be guilt.

4. The preludial gesture of the central and only character is a smothered scream. Its liberative energy is channeled into the mute inward imagery of the spectacle. Its repression gives to this imaged world its aspect of a cracking gloss. Rather than specifically guilt, perhaps, it is the quality of the life of a shattered soul, holding itself together in rejection, frustrating its personal vital energy, that the play portrays; or perhaps an inward struggle against such death. We may wonder, however, whether the play itself is not such a withheld scream.

5. Many of us by our mother incur the loss of trust and of the faith that the world is ours. Others, by their mother given too easy a trust and faith must lose it. Either way, we withdraw, advancing a facsimile, or not. The spectator is apt at first to view the spectacle as withdrawal into dream or other fantasy, then as such a wounded soul's view of the world.

6. But a gradual focusing of the action on the boy and the appearance of a certain development in him suggest a spiritual career, conveyed by five images: 1) a metaphor of mirrors (35-9), 2) a dance show on the theme of motherhood (52, 55-8), 3) his displacement to the center (66), 4) a purge, beatification or attempted correction (74), 5) his detachment or escape from the scene, in the form of an elevation above it (77):

  1. confrontation with an inefficient self image? a first, inward looking out? awareness of non-identity? state of willful seclusion? refusal to accept an empty alien image?

  2. by their trite simplicity, these scenes function as evocation of a theme, that of motherhood: recall of a former safety? pleasure taken in an incident of maternality? an ironic mood? In any event: an outward response.

  3. the intensity of the foreground images (bins, 63, 64; table, 46, 61, 65) had increased. The boy's move to the center suggests the sudden experience of the pressure of environment, the feeling of being on the spot.

  4. resistance to authority? denial of guilt? the foiling of an attempt at integration? Isolation is maintained, but there is involvement and outward action: the more real, or less, for being in opposition?

  5. an ascension equivalent to salvation? flight from society? final withdrawal? In any event: an act of self-preservation, though perhaps on a low energy level.

This may be a process of healing. Whether it ends in failure or in salvation is unclear: as is the role of *the others*.

6a. The obscurity of this almost imperceptible story and its essential ambiguity do not hide a character but characterize it. And though it seems a particular character encountered by us not infrequently, they attach to the story of most of us. Our inward man, within the adventitious stereotype, unless favored by fortunate encounters is apt to be no more than we see here and to have no more of a story and that story no less doubtful in its episodes and direction.

6b. But if we saw the hero not as the guilty victim but as the weary observer, our view of the stages of his career might be:

86

1. rejection of identity.

2. rejection of procreation: of identity in another and of duration in time.

3. rejection of place in the world.

4. rejection of responsibility and engagement.

5. rejection of this world: in view of its futility, surveyed.

7. By the end of the prologue, the crime seems dealt with. In a fairy land of patent falsity, the criminal has been decked out in conventional and mystic insignia, disposing of her. The witness/victim becomes a nugget in a spurious social reality. The real play thus starts with the crime concluded and seemingly done with, all traces removed and retribution made, with the boy in loneliness.

We find ourselves (8) in a non-sensical world in which the ordinary crowds the fantastic. The terms of this incongruence are not altogether clear. They scintillate, they vary depending where we look on stage, and they develop in their apparent meaning. The contrast variously appears as between the realistic and the theatrical, the mundane and the poetic, the modern and the romantic, the everyday and the dreamt, the real and the imaginary, the social vs. the natural, the cultural vs. the supernatural. Sometimes three zones of activity, awareness or reality seem to define themselves: activity, spirit, life, ordinary activity, fantastic life, spirit as a kind of path between them, perhaps a blind alley. The incongruence after its initial statement (9-10) gradually defines itself as dichotomy and even opposition. This tension develops only gradually, partly because the earlier course of the play (up to about 61-4) is largely a development in the ordinary. But the fantastic from the first lines the ordinary as incongruous detail, and soon emerges as secondary and background theme. And for quite a while the dominant experience is not so much of a rift in reality as rather a reaction to the dynamics of the scene.

8. We are disoriented but we still believe things will fall into place in terms of some convention. But the anticipation of a sequel has been raised by the strong beginning, so we now feel let down. There is a drop in tension, e.g., that large empty area where the bins will be (soon to be only lackadaisically busied). There is no well-defined action gripping our attention. The original heroine is out of the show and the new protagonist is doing nothing and is not even paying attention. No new drama is unfolding. There is an air of hesitancy and waiting on the stage as though this world had not gotten itself together as yet, as though its inner energy were, momentarily, neither formative nor driving, its levels of tension and organization low.

9. In a disassociated manner various events occur. They are out of unrelated frames of reference. As conventions of representation are played off against one another, the *mode* of reality becomes dubious. The form goes beyond ambiguity into evasiveness: only barely, though definitely, triumphing over our inevitable discontent by beauty, a bravura trick. If reality there be, it is reality in act, not in being.

On the large stage there is a world. Its characteristics: fragmentation, incongruity, amorphousness, uncenteredness, aimlessness, inconsistent plurality of mode. A brief, abruptly terminated resurrection of focus and structure (8, 9) makes them more poignant.

This might be the world of someone whose world the bottom had fallen out of, for whom things had lost meaning, life direction. Someone who might or might not make a new beginning.

But we may view it otherwise also, namely as the objective world not hidden by our imposing on it coherence, congruity, structure, focus, direction and a single exclusive mode of possibility, as the raw world which in spite of all our anxious strain at synthesis continually reappears at the fringes. Here it is out front, organization only a continuously aborted, forever incomprehensive stirring within it.

10. Within this diffuse, clashing medley, not going anywhere, one element, the ordinariness of a kind of work (11), which subsequently (20) turns out to be a labor of self-confinement, at first (up to 16) predominates, though without instituting either structure or direction.

The story of the *bins* continues intermittently and desultorily for much of the play. Work on them begins 11, they are finished and the laborers move off 20. Then (while most of the development of the image of the *table* goes on), they are just standing there empty. They fill up (63-4), about when the ox-theme emerges as competitive focus, but then again just stand there, though now with signs of life, until they slip off (99).

Thus most of the time they are as meaningless a part of the fixtures as is most of what goes with *work* in modern society. We are apt to take this staged image as a happening, i.e., a point- and meaningless activity, not as representation of anything outside the theatre, e.g., point- and meaningless activity. But there are several reasons why the spectator is also apt momentarily to generalize the image by an identification of it with the chief horror of industrial capitalism in his own life: the alienation of labor; or with any intrinsically unrewarding enterprise the extrinsic pay-off of which is restraint. For the bin-building is completed by the occupation of the bins which gives the work practical purpose, i.e., economic status. It is coupled with a complementary sociological image (the table), evoking consumption, upper class living, civic authority, the state. Both are together counterposed to: »the« individual (the boy), nature (the forest), and to an antagonistic realm of magical action and of mystery resilient to their cultural order. The meaningless, pointless, graceless activity with its negative utility thus stands for anything like it, from the holding of any job to alienation to the futility of worldly endeavor. And the occupied bins insinuate the *message* that the roles available in social life are too damn cramping. The image goes beyond itself qua datum in the theatrical here and now.

The bins-theme has an ending, a fulfillment though not a resolution: a putative, but inobvious function is clarified, a question answered, when the bins are occupied: though a non-definitive and a down ending, trailing out. The products of modern labor enslave the (consuming) producers, our efforts bury us.

We cannot tell whether this development of the image of the construction of the bins is an insight of the boy's or whether it's merely that all activity seems idiotic to him. He may not even be aware of any of it.

11. The table with the frog has been there from the first, we have noted it as likely locus of action, but the first event there, the serving of cocktails (16 ff.) is so inconsequential, so drawn out and in its minor humorous way so self-contained, that though it draws our attention away from the construction of the bins (11-20) and competes for our attention with the little girl dancing (21-26), we are apt soon no longer to consider it the start of an action. But the theme has been discretely sounded in one of its dimensions: formal living, genteelity .... Only with the arrival of the guests (27-8), bin-builders and little girl out of the way, does it establish itself as semi-permanent focus and as probably continuing and developing action. It remains for quite a while (into the sixties and seventies of my count) the dominant foreground theme, though events elsewhere again and again claim priority.

There is this table, there is a host-figure out of fairy tales, service at the table, pretty formal, is going on, some of the things served of a fairly regular sort – guests arrive and are seated, are welcomed, install themselves in distinctive fashions, decorum is observed and infracted. A dinner party, rather odd, but still a dinner party seems to be going on, people are eating and drinking – speaking even – again oddly, the speech accented to the point of incomprehensibility, the remarks disjointed. Little by little we add up indications, perhaps, that the gathering is or is also in the nature of a tribunal, the guests not guests, but judges, that a legal process is underway: the self-repressive rigidity of the high-life or »society« aspects of the conviviality seems to be translating into a stultifying if perhaps not actually threateningly oppressive combination of moralism and legalism. We may momentarily relate this to the murder and/or to the surviving victim's later experiences of a court trial, or perhaps only to guilt-feelings of his – was he the murderer? her lover? – or possibly just to guilt and punishment generally or to repressive social order. These are apt to be flitting evocations.

There is a sense of progressive definition of a situation, and that a clarification (of what's going on) is in the offing.

But this resolution is never reached, for as we watch we attain to a predominant sense of the non-sensicality of what these people are doing, finally probably arriving at a conviction that they are mad. They are pathologically afflicated, paranoid, megalomaniac-obsessive, hysterical characters. We are led to this insight so gradually that it forms as a judgment on what they have been doing from the beginning: pursuits such as these are insane. We feel we have not observed a sequence of actions, but the self-revelation of the nature of an activity, though along the way we are also apt to give up guessing what it is they are supposed to be doing, to decide it's a silly or brilliant put-on, and/or to subside into a somewhat distracted appreciation of the image. In any event, our judgment will take the form of passing thought, wonderment, vague feelings, keeping us engaged in *looking*.

We don't watch this table theme in isolation. It impinges on us in a series of discrete images as we stray from it to other happenings on the stage and back. The image forms not as when during a court trial we are attending, we gradually attain to a conviction that this judge and jury are functioning as unbalanced autocrats, private men in public positions, nor as when we gradually come to see our analyst as an egoist, but rather in the manner of the growth in us over some decades of life of a tentative sentiment that the law is a low-grade atavism, a sentiment not steadily with us but intertwined discretely in many other, to us, more important bends of attitude.

We perceive an image breaking down. Unemphatically, humorously, it is the image of institutionalized repression, of decorum and judgment. It decomposes without being judged. Since there has been no individualization, only a surrealist evocation of essence, we participate in the disintegration of the institution itself, not just of an exemplar, of a kind of procedure: that of the maintenance of a social order.

We relate it to the fantastic images elsewhere on the stage. At first by contrast: the contrast of the ordinary to the fantastic. Then, as the ordinariness of the table set-up crumbles into extravagance and insanity, we may come to see it as part of the fantastic. The ordinary begins to seem fantastic. Then finally, but only as the ox-motif (cf. infra) takes hold and the forest extends its dominion (cf. infra), its madness takes on the brightness of a mode of *spectacularly* arational cosmic energy. We come to sense that it was not a metaphor of this-worldly endeavor that we saw, but a this-worldly charade. Visually, this decomposition is achieved in subordination to the emergence into pre-eminence of the supra-natural.

12. From the beginning, we are confronted with the dominant contrast between the light foreground and the forest to the rear, though at first the forest is hardly more than the background of the foreground activities. When clearly seen, it is a woods in late fall, the bronze leaves at the foot of its slim bare trees. But relative to the foreground it figures as a dark place, though less a region of peril (but cf. 8), than a warm, alive mysterious place, womb or protective night.

Its nature is curiously dual. On the one hand it is instinct with life – with free movement and sexuality (Little Dancing Girl in forest, 29; Forest Movers, 43, 51, 60; Little Dancing Girl and Pyramid, 63, 101; Bee and Rabbit, 85). On the other hand, it is the place of death – of the dead and of service to the dead (the pyramid, 8, 63, 80, 101-2; the magician's forest wakes, 12, 15, 59; assassination of the ox-rider, 44; pope's funeral cortege, 81; candle procession, 94; entrance to nether world, 107, 110). But this duality is a unity of opposites. Not only is the forest the place of both life and death, but of death as integral form and part of life. Thus pyramids are not just tombs for the dead, but places for their after-life; the magician's forest wakes are rites generating magical energies; the ox turns out to be a mythical symbol for the regenerative and spiritual powers of death; the burning candles are not in commemoration of the defunct, but serve their living souls; and the nether world is a sunny place of regeneration, of the »eternal return« of life. Within the stage-world, the forest is nature, and it seems qua nature that it gradually reveals itself as the origin and place of the super-natural – of the cosmic energies acting in and through its representative figures, the magician and the ox and the pyramid. Both qua nature and qua transcendental, the forest is visually and in terms of the action in contrast and in opposition to what goes on in the foreground – the bins – and table-themes. They relate to it as culture to nature and to supra-natural reality, and as will and activity to life and to eternal energy. Their negative fulfillments in the death-like life of the bins and in the living death of the company at table gradually constitute it the superior principle.

It also emerges as victorious principle. For the overall action of the play (8-103), a contest of images, is a contest between the sterility and madness of culture and the vital mystery of natural life, though the ordinary, too, defined as culture, or social life, turns out to be immanently mysterious and magical: but only by disintegration and in response (101-2). There is a special kinship between nature and magic and mystery.

13. We gradually become aware of a growing element of magic and mystery. As it grows, it absorbs the fantastic (the fantastic reveals itself as magical and/or mysterious) and invades and destroys the ordinary. The everyday gives way to magic and mystery, the strange or weird turns out magical or mysterious. As the ordinary reveals its insanity, the forest grows – acquires increasing reality, power and weight in our perception, and its forces and principles define themselves as vital magic and commence to act on culture and to destroy it.

The development of the forest theme is somewhat as follows. Initially (8) the forest is a distant background infested with a vaguely disturbing life. It soon (12) defines itself as locus of the magician, and thence, but only gradually, as a place for magic. A little later (23), a mysterious beast (the ox) appears in it and (29) the dancing child seems at home there, and a little later yet (43) we have become aware that it has its own kind of life, a life not alien to man, human in form. Then (44) the first important event indigenous to it occurs, a ritual assassination giving it a sacral and mystic quality. As the as yet preponderant cultural activities in the foreground define themselves and take a turn to the negative, its life defines itself as sexual in a somehow spiritual way (60), its mystic beast emerges (62) and the dancing child turns out to have business in it, business not incompatible with the child's innocent vitality (63). The magician now also emerges from it (69) and begins (70, 75) to exert its power in the daylight world of the insane and ordinary, while the sacred ox now looming large, commences to subject this world to the regenerative powers of a destructive ritual (76). With the boy's ascent (77), the forest with its mystery, the pyramid, for the first time emerges as dominant visual element (80), underlined; and again defined as locus of innocent vitality, of natural life (85, dance of bee and rabbit). From this point onward, the forest may be said to furnish the central action, namely the ox-ritual (87-98) (its other representative, the magician, disbanding the table (91). The bins move off (99) and the dark forest as fore-court of the pyramid which is now the object of some magical work, is the sole image on stage, the whole world (101). There is an epiphany of its vital magic (102), not only in its depth, but transfiguring the ordinary world, transforming its madness into spiritual illumination. The sequel is a forest event, palingenesis in nature (106-10), and the finale (111 ff.) poses the dynamic principle of this whole development, the opposition of culture to the magic mystery of life.

14. The ox is clearly of something like papier maché and pushed by its attendants. It is not very large nor very expressive, more like a drugged calf. But its not existing in its own right comes across as intimation of awesome majesty: its insignificance as an individual enhances its ceremony. We see an object of veneration approaching. Its serpentine approach signifies that it comes from »a place which is far away,« »beyond the forest,« – common parlance for the supernatural. But it comes through the forest. Nature betrays culture to the supernatural.

With some nuances, Wilson gives us a traditional nature deity. A grabbag scattering of signs provides religious aura: gilded horns, garland; musical temple motif; sacrificial ambush of innocent child; white-coated prayerful servants; freak attendants; foot washing (32, 44, 62). The nuances: the ox is neither bull nor cow, no udders, no phallus, neither male nor female principle. Pomp and awe are slight: there is no terror.

The older nature deity (animal) defeats (eats) the younger nature deity (heavenly body) (92). In a comic denouement (96) this defeat of day (sun) is turned into a victory of light – if we wish: – other responses are possible, Wilson is inviting their variety. The ritual enactment of myth is also – may also be – a rite of sacrifice. Diurnal night, annual winter, having eaten the sun gives birth to it again. The death-life, assassination and birth cycle of our natural world is also the rhythm of the cosmos (105-10). And Wilson also goes off on another tangent: knowledge of the vital cycle is spiritual enlightenment (101-2); the light of the spirit is the fruit of natural death

(101-2). A minor metaphor is built into this mystic confabulation: the way to enlightenment is through failure and madness (101).

This playfully multifarious symbolism is apt to, though it need not, evoke the vital cycle: its broader theme is the perpetual reassertion of mystery. The specific mystery invoked is that of life: creative power working by destruction. But whether the spectator goes into this or not, he can hardly help getting some sense that he has participated in a theatrical demonstration of the absurdity (incompleteness, vulnerability) of the »ordinary.«

Culture, organized society, intellectually manipulated (stultified) life are insane and subject to natural decay: because they are set into a cosmos the energy of which is destructive-regenerative and thus disallows stably maintained definition whether in thought or existence.

The play conveys this in good humor and pretty form and quite coldly. Its mysticism is whimsical, unemphatic.

15. I outlined the protagonist's dubious career supra. The relation between it and the other themes, disintegration of culture, growth into ascendancy of the vital magic of the forest, is almost absent in spectatorial experience. It is not a stressed structural element. The way we are aware of the boy during most of these other developments, namely until the disintegration of culture is fairly well accomplished and the forest principle is in the ascendant, is rather like the way one is aware of oneself in a dream: as a presence to which all the action relates, but not as agent; and as object of rather than as part of the action. The idea that the action takes place in his mind is there somewhere in ours (as in some dreams), but relates primarily to the foreground action in front of him, to the culture-themes, not to the counterpoint between these and the forest theme gradually invading the foreground. When the boy after this long hiatus becomes the center of action (66, 74-9), this coincides with the disintegration of the foreground and what we might call the forest's victory over it. But if we consider the boy's career in terms of the contest between culture and the magic of life, it takes on the aspect of an escape from guilt and repression (foundations of culture) by that magic and into it, though perhaps not into life. Culture cannot heal him nor integrate (correct) him (74, 77). This failure is ambiguous if we view it merely in terms of its proximate context: interaction of culture and hero, as I did previously, either spiritual salvation or escape from attempted correction. In the larger context it appears as on the whole a lucky escape if not absolute salvation. The hero is not off dancing:

but he has preserved an inward integrity; and has escaped the tortured consciousness attendant on outward integration and or even just on openness to and exposure to the pressure of culture. What saves him is not culture – legality, morality, organized Christian religion, education – but, probably (cf. 75), magic.

In the end (107) the boy after escaping into *superior* withdrawal, is swept away with the whole lot of us, he is just one more of us many mortals. I think this is not only imaged by the play, but is the feel it gives. In the perspective of eternity, of the come and go of humanities, one more little boy does not matter.

16. Three figures in the nature of transcendental presences, in different ways perhaps representing the author and/or transmitting energy for the events, moving the action, move freely through the spectacle and give it some continuity and even some degree and kind of dramatic unity, namely insofar as they relate, as apparently benign forces, to the boy on the one hand, and, as incarnations of the magic of life to the theme of life's opposition to social order, on the other: the magician, the Goat Woman and the little dancing girl, a shaman, a witch and an elf, perhaps. They are figures rather than persons or characters, though the little girl is also a natural person, and figures rather than images, and are thus visually distinct within the spectacle as a whole, as they also are by their frequent appearances, continuous reappearances and random motions throughout this world: unlike the other performers, they are not restricted to any place or area and they move freely in all directions. The magician is more an arcane agent of fiction, the witch more from an illustrated fairy tale book, the little girl a person seen. In spite of these differences, they in the end figure in the same two phenomenal orders: as individuations of the Vital Principle; as abstractions of Fortunate Encounters in Life. Those fortunately encountered being fortuitous and free – and invulnerable – are wondruously alien: which is how these figures appear in this spectacle's world.

17. The magician comes on ambiguous (4): burying a mother with mockery, avenging murder, mocking guilt? or laughing it off? He holds services for the dead (6, 12, 49, 59, 97, 101, 104-5), and, by a projection of concentrated inner powers, perhaps generated from the dead, rules the living (69-70, 75, 91, 104-5), but only at moments of crisis or in a very large way, like an author (6, 95, 104-5).

He seems to direct his powers against authority (69-70), on behalf of the boy-hero. Later his image shifts and grows: he seems to represent cosmic vital energies, overarching the deaths of individuals and ge-

95

nerations. There is no hint of morality, personal warmth or good will in him. His costuming ironically presents him as a charlatan.

Perhaps because I know that Wilson has worked therapeutically with handicapped children, the magician's wakes strike me as perhaps metaphors for the personal liberation of the stunted or repressed vital energies of children.

We are all sometime living gifted children. But family and society kill us functionally dead in body and spirit. We are left alive but not living, a condition to which neither an anxiously careful husbandry of our life, the prizing of it as a possession, the frantic waste of it, or the unconscious spending of it in imposed, extrinsic routines of the flesh and the spirit are exceptions, but only variants, a condition which enlists even love and friendship as reinforcements of it. The only way out of it into life is by the universal wish to do things and to do them our own way. Generally the transformation of this wish into driving desire – dropping it into the flow of our committed energies – has been rendered impossible. But even where, by personal and social luck of circumstance, this wish is driving desire, action on it is blocked by care: care for self-preservation, care for the feelings and judgment of others. To kindle that wish into desire and to act on that desire – whether that action will be living depends on what capacities one has been left with, – requires special intervention from without: changing that hungry throught into movement, rendering us careless. This happens rarely and only by the encounter of a powerful personality.

These personalities are the only real magicians and the ones Wilson may have in view. They vivify us by a resurrection of the child carelessly doing things his way. Their action on us is magic because nothing is transmitted – no example, teaching, warmth, flattery or other reassurance; they neither push nor pull: we respond to the power of life in them by our own power. And in fact this is the only form this help can take. They reduce authority to a shadow, annihilate guilt, make us present. The paradox of this liberation is that in coming alive as a person, one abandons all care for oneself and for life.

But if the world really is as it appears in dreams, the magician, subversive necrophiliac, may merely be a nihilist mover of its images, indifferent to any boy or judge.

18. The Goat Woman represents a different positive principle in life: the warm, benign, helpful persons we encounter, useful and calming figures. It is reassuring to know they are there. They are reprieves

from the snarling pack of egos surrounding us and from the general indifference to us of man and nature. They cannot actually help us very much. But to know of them significantly lessens the terror of existence. They are forces merely by appearing: their power is an aura of concern (in which, less harassed, we have a moment of leisure to try to get ourselves together): it is not an active unlocking power like that of the magical personalities. They are persons that tell us nice things, bring us little gifts, give us a break when we need it, or a hand, people one can count on. While we are children there are not a few such people, but later they become rare.

In the play, she turns up as observer (5, 81). The little girl likes her (24). She seems to wish to help the boy in his identity-crisis (38). In the end she turns out to be his guardian angel (107).

To some extent we think of her as the woman who lives in that hut, which is burning down, a fact I can't make much out of though it's a nice touch. The feeling I get out of the image is that she is strange and alien, fragile and impermanent, not well established in this world, but at ease with the perishing of things.

19. The little dancing girl really does nothing but dance (21, 29): her visit with the Goat Woman is a dance (24) and so is what Wilson refers to as her »work« on the pyramid (68, 101, 102), and which I felt was her contribution – a transmission of her energy – to the mystery of the illuminations (102). The little girl's moving figure is powerful in the play. In her tireless, constantly varying steady motion, she seems energy incarnate, the energy of life as such, deploying itself for the sake of its deployment, undirected and mindless, the essence of childhood, a paradigm of life.

Her action in the play is totally obscure. But her image assigns her a part in it: as counterpiece to the quieted boy, bereft of his childhood, alive, but not living; hers is the *kind* of power which is directed in action, but in the form of a person; the opposite of the mechanized worker-athletes of the bins and of the rigidly self-disciplined society-folk judges at the table; kin of the spirits of the forest. Robert Wilson's two passes with her (22, 26) suggest his identification with the principle carried by her image.

20. Though he is brought back later and disposed of, the boy's story ends with the attempted correction of him (74) and his ascent (77): he is out of the picture. This follows closely the conclusions of the autochthonous histories of bins (they are occupied 63, 64) and table (the servants leave, 61, 65) and coincides with the involvement of these two themes with the themes of boy (judge's derangement, 70;

hoods and cabbages, 73) and ox (ox in bins, 76). What follows is essentially the ritual of the ox, i.e., the second part of its mythical advance, the story of its action within the human culture foreground. It is true that the most important development of the table theme (lit eye, departure of frog, 101; illuminations, 102; departure of judge and table, 103) is yet to follow and that it follows the conclusion of the story of the ox (ox body off, 98). Moreover action at the table continues during this ritual of the ox, though, until that final illumination, only in a negative sense, as dissolution (e.g. removal of 2 judges, 91). But not only does the story of the ox continue beyond that of the bins (bins off, 99) and table (table off, 103), namely in the magician's wake with the ox head (97, 101, 104, 105): that important development of the table theme 101-3 appears result of the ox ritual. Substantially, therefore, the spectator does, I think, experience a sequence: story of boy (8-77) relative to story of internal cultural disintegration (table 16 to 73; bins, 10-64), followed by the ritual of the ox (76-98) relative to story of culture disintegration under the action of ox and magician. The resistance of the boy to mad culture is followed by the victory of forest magic (ox, magician) over mad culture. Or: the story of the boy is followed by the story of the ox.

If the boy's withdrawal (77) is a superior detachment, following observation in place, and is not merely an escape, *Deafman Glance*, after showing us the madness of the world as it appears (to a clairvoyant within it), then shows us its humorously magic rhythm as it is, an eternal becoming and unbecoming, apparent to the superior view of one wholly detached from it: themes of bins and table, followed by theme of ox and forest, all in the boy's mind.

21. The themes of death and birth – murder and motherhood – murder particularly in the form of child murder – run through *Deafman Glance*. They keep cropping up like things one is trying not to think of or facts unsuitable for a mood one is sustaining. Only the prologue deals with them together and head on.

From the rear, the stage is dominated by a pyramid, abode of the (living) dead. The foreground might be a river of blood out of hell (18). The protagonist is a motherless child (7-78). The initial child murders are evoked throughout the play (7-78): by the magician's wake over the victims (12); by replays of the murders (40, 47, 72), accompanied by the lighting of candles; by the tribunal aspects of the banquet table (41, 73): it was at a later performance draped in funereal cloth (8). The spots where the victims lay are intermittently luminous.

The second theme of the play, the ox-theme, reaches a first climax in a child-murder (44). The magician performs a wake over its victim also (49). This theme reaches its final climax in the death of the world's life-giving force, the sun (92) (with candle procession, 94), and in the death of its cosmic hero, the ox (96). The magician again holds a wake (97). Then we see the spring-time death of humanity (106).

But death is throughout. A cadaver is held up (4). A boy dies repeatedly (54). The representative of worldly spiritual authority dies, is carried in a funeral cortege (81, 82).

The prologue stresses the mother's maternal solicitude for her victims and for the survivor (2). In fantasy restitution she is given royal children and a monkey baby (4). The play starts with a creation of life out of earth and water, flower people are born (9). Images of boyhood life recur (17, cf. 77; 81); an image of childhood runs through the play (cf. 21). The hero of the second theme, the ox, has a child rider (32) and is itself a calf more than bull or cow. A dance cycle on the theme of motherhood initiates the boy-protagonist's development (52, 55-8). The Black Mammy, to Wilson a dark cloud like Andy De Groat, but an arch-symbol of maternity, recurs (3, 105-6). The background contains not only the death/life image of the pyramid, but the sexual spirits of the forest (60). The death of ox and sun is the birth of light (101-2). The scene imaging the death of humanity centers on pregnant nudes, a vulva (106). The play climaxes with the rebirth of humanity (110).

The intertwining of the two themes states the superior theme: rebirth.

22. This theme provides an ambiguous world view and attitude. The show evokes the universality of death and destruction and the equal universality of birth, creation and renewal. It suggests, if only by its good-humored calm, that they relate, whether because the destruction of the old generates the new or because the creation of the new requires destruction of the old. The finale suggests a further signification of the theme: the same returns, the new is really the old, nothing changes. But taken together, the preceding ideas also suggest still another one, in some ways opposed to this last one: rebirth is the only escape from death, renewal the only mode of conservation.

In the end, though he is very distant now, very small, the withdrawn, perhaps guilty boy is placed in this vast panorama of flux and return and new beginnings. If by an effort of concern we draw him closer, his guiltiness (if in fact he feels guilty) seems no more than an unfortunately disabling but otherwise negligible illusion of his, without moral or ontological status, an identification with some old (past) destruction inhibiting the flowering of its consequences and his own regeneration, a blindness to that panorama; and his withdrawal an in essence comic, though of course pathetic gesture of suicidal self-preservation, a futile attempt (presumably a response to his having once suffered destruction) to shield himself from universal agression, at best exempting him from universal regeneration.

23. Or else a wisely indifferent removal of himself from the futile turning of the wheel.

24. With two or perhaps three exceptions, there is no emotion in *Deafman Glance.* The performers show none: their gestures indicate none, but represent unemotional variants of the actions or reactions[59] they represent. I.e., they not only do not indicate any emotions, but indicate unemotional action. It's not just that the indications of emotions are left out, but that indications of non-emotion are included. A world of dispassionates is adumbrated. And the images are constructed so as not to evoke the affective aspects of themes.

Nor do the performance-style and the staging seem designed to evoke emotions in the spectator, but on the contrary to give no occasions for his passions to arise, but to calm him.

We watch the show with a serenity slightly tinged, perhaps, by uneasiness and with an amused sensual delight shading off into boredom or somnolence: possibly also we are faintly disgusted by the (»inhuman«) absence of emotion. Serenity and delight seem the intended effects.

The themes are in fact, however, of highly affective *sorts,* emotionally highly »charged:« the images of a troubling (and sometimes moving) nature: characters with strong feelings, upsetting situations, disturbing events, distressing developments, actions normally motivated by and performed in passion, and normally triggering emotions or passionate responses in others involved in them. The images and themes seem selected for their »latent« emotional charge: so packed is the play with such images – images normally, whether naturally or conventionally, presupposing and inducing emotions, inducing them in both participants and in spectators.

Predominantly and almost exclusively, the show's specific (though latent) emotional content is anxiety – or feelings ranging from vague perturbation through fear to dread, horror and terror. If we accept

59 There are almost no reactions in the spectacle.

that pity or compassion is a normal corollary to these in the spectator, we may add pity or compassion.

This latent emotional content of anxiety is seconded by one of sonly and motherly love and of the desire to be a child. For the themes of the birth/fertility imagery that counterbalances the imagery of death are motherly care and the child's vitality, not sexual drive. Nor love between man and woman.

The presence of these themes, but the absence of the correlative emotions implies either abnormalcy (or that the normal is not natural), or else inhibition (repression) or some other elimination (by sublimation or by a cancelling out) of these emotions: on the part of the characters (humanity) portrayed; on the part of Wilson and the performers; and on our part.

25. The two major exceptions to the lack of feeling in the play are the boy-hero's scream (2, 72) and the magician's wakes (12, 49, 59, 97, 101, 104-5). The scream seems a scream of horror (more than of terror). But not only is it a muted, effectively neuter scream[60] of horror: it is smothered. The horror is suppressed: the boy's attitude from this time on is easy, relaxed (3, 8), on occasion he is amused (57). He thus serves as example of the attitude toward the show's images and themes adopted by Wilson and his performers, as expressed by the style of the performances and the staging, and by us, in response to this style: the natural emotion is suppressed.[61] This exception thus functions as a comment, and there are two ways it is not quite an exception: what is shown is less an emotion than its suppression; the emotion signified is not fear or anxiety, but dismay at a breaking of faith or trust, and revulsion.

The magician's emotion would seem to be sorrow (rather than pity). But not only has this show of feeling (powerful during rehearsals) been hidden in the forest (cf. 12, n. 1) and the one wake in clear view (97, 101, 104-5) is free of it: the sorrow he appears to feel is calm, dispassionate, a feeling rather than an emotion; more than sorrow for, he seems to feel the presence of the dead, he is communing; and the ritual air of his show is such that it seems a show more

---

60 The only kind of scream Raymond Andrews, a mute, is capable of.
61 Thus, if we view the show as representation of the world as the boy sees or dreams it, it contains some explanation of the lack of feeling. But on the whole I incline to think that to the extent that we are to take the boy as medium, Wilson chose and introduced him to justify — theatrically — the show's form of unemotionality; rather then that he gave it this form because it was appropriate to that choice and introduction of a medium.

of a metaphysical emulation of a feeling than of the feeling itself: it seems borne by insight and directed toward a universal. Also, it is free of fear.

This leaves just a minor though strong exception: the passionate horror and disgust acted out (at Wilson's direction) by one of the »judges« when (70) her »spiritual alter ego« prompts her to do something or to take some stand relative to the hero. Since the hero is about to be subjected to something which among other things looks not unlike the execution of a sentence (74), one surmises that she recoils from judgment, probably a condemnation, though possibly an absolution. But when she is magically freed from this obligation, she seems equally fearful of this dispensation. There is no suggestion that she feels pity or compassion: her revulsion seems from action, commitment or engagement, i.e., is similar to the boy's earlier horror, but hysterical: perhaps because she is already, by her position, committed to action. Unlike his, perhaps, her withdrawal is thus a disintegration. Her passion may be a sign of the imperfection of her detachment. In this sense, the function of this one strong show of passion in the spectacle may be to criticize or reject passion.

Aside from birth or fertility, death and murder is the recurrent theme. But neither they nor the tenuousness of existence, its major feature in this representation, seem to induce anxiety in those involved, and hardly any in us, and they are staged and acted as though there is no reason why they should. Yet »normally,« they would: they are »supposed to.«

26. A mother kills her children without any show of emotion (2), whether anger, desperation or pity; she shows no regrets; and the children show no fear. Neither her victims, not the other dead evoke any passionate sorrow in any other characters and their dying is so staged and portrayed that we don't feel any either – nor repulsion from or pity of the killers, or fear for us and ours. Neither performance nor staging signify the horror of killing, the fearfulness of death or the pity of it all. The child murderess is mocked (4); a pope's funeral cortege is a minstrel show (82). A ritual of sacrifice and cosmic death (92, 96) has been carefully provided with touches of levity. What may be the death of humanity (105-8) is a pretty festival.

27. Even apart from death and murder, the spectacle consists almost entirely of metaphors of anxiety: the painful motion of the prone creatures in the foreground, moving, in a river of blood, endlessly

and effortfully[62] (18); a sequestration in bins, image of claustrophobia or of being buried alive (20, 63, 64); the crawling in the forest (9), mutedly adumbrating the disgust-horror associated with reptiles; armed strangers on the prowl (13), spying strangers (30); secret signs and indecipherable messages (6, 40, 47, 72); ghostly nuns, one of them, at least, powerful and evil-seeming (70); the carefully arranged, gradually revealed, diversified psycho-pathology of authority figures, idiocy, hysteria, obsessive monomania (31, 42, 46, 70, 73). These judges are by manner and appearance cast as characters with all the potentials of the sinister, of horror and threat: the beautiful but heartless foreign spy, the powerful, older, cruel, immovably dominating lesbian, the freakishly insane mad doctor (seen by one reviewer as Sidney Greenstreet). There are two cripples in the cast, the performers of the pope[63] (74) and of the »assistant to the star« (50), their deformities prominently used in their action; and of the two horror show attendants of a sacred beast, one, wrapped in bandages, was supposed to be done by a cripple, though in the end he was not, an uncrippled performer playing him as a cripple, the other done as a midget. Though the aura of the upstage part of this world, forest and pyramid, varies with the lighting, much of the time and on the whole, it carries the air of mystery of a dark and alien place which in other contexts or done slightly differently would suggest danger and panic fear. A steadily burning hut, in another context or given some additional touches, would similarly, though more subtly, convey a sense of peril or at least of insecurity (24): as it is, it is adorned with the insignia of a charnel house. A burning sunshade (111) has the same (equally unrealized) affective potential. A ballet of glass carriers subtly evokes two nightmare themes: the empty mirror and him condemned to carry a burden or Sisyphus, both alluded to by the action as staged (35-9). The magician in black, given his initial cruel mockery of the mother and his close association with the dead, similarly was a natural for a Grand Guignol treatment he did not receive – that same reviewer saw him as Dracula. What may be a witch seems »good,« but glimpsed in the burning hut, she verges on the sinister (24). Even the »innocent« little dancing girl dances in a manner which at least at times fleetingly makes her appear a mechanical puppet (21). A sacred creature's loss of its head

---

62 Their mournful or anguished moans during rehearsal were deleted from the performance.

63 The performer's hands were crippled. On occasion during rehearsals he was done by a man with a crippled leg: Wilson intended him to be crippled.

(96) and the iridescence of one character and luminous outgrowths on one other (101) stop short of being frightening, but are in the area of the disturbing and the weird. There may be shafts of sunlight emanating from a nether world, but also smoke (105, 110); and what may be the rebirth of humanity is given the form of a silent assembly, in darkness, of giant, lumbering, black, powerful apes (110). The hero himself is close to being a traumatized catatonic.

Very slightly beneath the surface of this beautiful, delightful dream there lies a world of horror, a compendium of the world of the insane – a Winterbranch within a Summerspace. The substance of this world is emotion and one particular emotion: fear. But while a very slight consideration of the images of the play reveals them to be structures of this world, that emotion is absent, neither represented nor evoked. Watching the show, we are, except for a slight uneasiness, totally unaware of this world.

28. The variously imaged theme of motherhood is similarly shorn of affect. The mother's solicitude for her children is cold (2). Her relationship to what seems her oldest carries a faint suggestion that it may be that of a woman to a man. And she kills her children: the image inhibits normal, conventional or natural, responses to the theme of motherhood. The motherhood sequence (55-8) evokes the »adoration of the child« (55) and a young mother's delight in her baby (58), but is a charming blend of the pasty and the poetic, inimical to emotion, and is tinged with irony (55, 57). And that this theme, like that of sex, is ancillary to that of birth: regeneration cools them both off.

29. There is no show of sexual interest, passion or attachment, whether on the part of any character or in any images of libido. Nudity is the spectacle's only approach to the erotic, but it is such that it is apt to titillate only few spectators and them only marginally. A nude »flower woman« appears with a flower girl in her panties and is followed by an, in conventional terms, unmale male dancer, and appears part of a metaphor (9, 10). The silvery nude forest spirits, male and female, are an androgynous, aethereal background (43, 51, 60). The (male and female) glass carriers are poetic and their carrying panes of glass diverts interest from their nudity (39). The male and female, pregnant and non-pregnant nudes among the descendants into the nether world are part of the larger poetic image and evoke the theme of fertility (and of the vulnerability of mortal flesh, briefly in flower) more than sexual desire (106).

The show uses nudity to show man/woman as body in motion, a physical thing: object of only narcissist sensuality – of the dreamy, aesthetic, non-genital auto-eroticism of a physical culture devoid of sentiment, passion and drive. The impact of this nudity is not too distinct from that of the totally non-erotic little dancing girl, who, incidentally, evokes admiration for the non-concupiscent, free vitality of childhood, rather than tenderness.

We cannot say, however, that libido joins anxiety as hidden content. Not only is the incidence of »in principle« libidinal imagery, viz., in our culture, nudity, much lower than of that of anxiety (death- and murder-imagery and other) – the show is clearly not engineered toward its co-prevalence: but this quasi-libidinal imagery carries specific non-libidinal themes: in conjunction with images of mother-hood and of the vitality and innocence of children, it is part of an imagery figuring the themes of birth/fertility/regeneration; and/or it is imagery of sensual but asexual kinaesthetics.

30. Death and the fearful are there, but we don't feel them: whereas we don't feel sex because it is not there. That it is not there, given the co-dominant theme of birth/fertility/regeneration, however, is strange: whereas the affects of fear are suppressed, sex, the theme itself is suppressed. Unlike the theme of sexuality, however, the themes of mother and childhood are there, in the images; and, as in the cases of death and fear, only the affects connected with them are suppressed (or annulled). Not sexual, but filial passion and childhood nostalgia join anxiety as hidden affective content.

In unvoiced affect-language, the spectacle expresses anxiety and an awareness of death, and desire for a return to the safety of innocent, protected childhood, all perhaps conditioned by an inability to love passionately. In relation to this hidden affective content, the theme of rebirth, imaged out front, appears as rationalization: as a con-solation, and an attempt to get rid of that anxiety, that awareness and that desire. But it presents itself as wisdom, which it may be.

## III. *Form*

1. *DG* is possibly purely formal, but whether this is so and its form are ambiguous (III, 2-4). Systematic ambiguity is, in fact, its form: implying the unimportance of the particular (III, 5-8). It might be a self-analysis (III, 9-18). It seems a world (III, 19-21). Indubitably, it is a collage of images (III, 22-29): though there are several ways in which it is other things also, i.e., not just that (III, 30-32). It seems both imagery and performance: but performers creating images, i.e.,

performance only supplementally (III, 33-43). By the style of the performance, it is the solemn celebration of human body-motion (III, 44). Qua performance, it has the form of human activity: but we adduce this form to perceive the images (III, 45-47). Is it drama, a fable? — no: rather the enacted subversion of these into imagery (III, 48-54). It is an exhibition of people (III, 55-62): of figures setting off the images by relating to them as such (life as imagery) (III, 55-7); of an individual, almost a protagonist, dramatically unifying the images as perhaps his or as perhaps only that for him (III, 58-60); of actual persons: unequivocal non-images, but who qua outside the show point up its character of imagery (III, 61-2).

An absence of defined line and of accentuation (III, 63-4) and a marginal and equivocal presentation (III, 65) by-pass the ego-structure of perception. A symbolic presentation of themes (III, 66-7) by-passes the ego-structure of cognition. This allows the dynamic patterning of the imagery to be such as to provide the spectator a free gymnastics of awareness (a natural rhythmic deployment of sensory energy): which opportunity is the show's specific form qua juxtaposition of images, its preponderant, native form: the spectator's mode of perception can correspond to the performance-style (III, 68-74).

This play of imagery has the movements of life: beginnings are reiteratedly generated by endings: a subsidiary or latent theme becoming dominant — musical wanings and resurgences (III, 75-78). It takes place in the three dimensions of a plane of images, a line of awareness, a containing space of time (III, 79-83).

The indefinite identities, the metamorphoses and the growth of the imagery give the show a dreamlike quality (III, 84-99).

2. *Deafman Glance* is as evasive formally as it is thematically. It refuses to define itself for the viewer, but inspires alternative hypothetical views, all of which seem somewhat applicable, as to what it is. This formal ambiguity seems as intended as the thematic one: itself the form of the spectacle.

3. Formally, what is on stage does not present itself as about anything *other* than itself. It has almost the form of non-objective painting, abstract dance, music, or of a happening. Not only is there no obvious story, much less a point of view: there is not even any commitment to the activities on stage representing any fictitious actions, characters or situations. No representative function of theirs is signaled. They may be presented merely as aesthetic data: for direct apprehension. In which case these images would not even be designed to carry themes. The spectacle thus does not by any gesture

affirm itself as in any way meaningful. It may be only a visual delectation or a riddle without solution, and thence a situation arranged for finding an at least momentarily unquesting peace of mind.

4. But it does not affirm itself to be only this or meaningless. For this formal affirmation requires either a higher degree of aesthetic abstraction, a gesture of pure formalism, or a higher degree of provocative concretion, a gesture of pure fortuity. It stays between these.

5. Wilson's form is systematic ambiguity. You never quite know whether A did a or whether perhaps B did it, or whether A really did not do a but only thought of doing it or else did a' or perhaps somebody else did a to him, or, indeed, quite what either the agent A or the act a are. To my mind this is quite realistic.

First of all, it gets at a certain indeterminacy of our per- and conception, notably as these are deployed in a context of intentions and action, characteristic both of the agents themselves and of observation of others. Precise identification is a (literary, scientific, legalistic, moralistic) fiction of great utility but which systematically does injustice to things as they are and notably to acts and agents. The claim to be in possession of it is accompanied by a fairly definite sentiment that one is not. The identifier is putting on an act.

Secondly, what things really are, e.g., people, and what they are really doing is somewhat within, above and beyond the particulars so that different sets of particulars, e.g., different and even often opposite kinds of things, notably types of people or acts, are really when you come right down to it the same thing. If one wishes, therefore, to say what really is going on, how things really are, for instance what really happened on a certain occasion or who really did it, it has to be done poetically, by which I mean that you have to indicate a set or range of equivalent alternatives. Since this can be done only by coming up with (in a gesture, text, poem, play, whatever) some particular or particulars – the same falsification inhering in any higher order genus you could signify or name – you have to build ambiguity into your (significatory) product, or rather: take care to keep it in there. You mustn't throw out the edge of »or.« On the contrary, you have to build it up. This is not a license for irresponsibility, but a requirement of sensitivity (discretion, judgment). The only alternative is to qualify hell out of your statement (gesture) (which I tend to do), but this is painful and the road to vacuity.

Thirdly, not only are the particulars though crucial, secondary and within a living system and within limits exchangeable: they are unimportant. Namely simply in view of the infinities of time, space, matter and (presumably) life. The import of their unimportance for attitude and conduct is not that anything goes, but that gravity is ludicrous. You have to chose between particulars and arrange them in orders of importance, and within these orders some will be very important, others not very: but even the most important will not be very important or, in fact, at all important, for instead of an absolute scale there is only the infinite. E.g., inconsiderateness implies that you take yourself too seriously and is therefore ludicrous, but adulterating a serious taking-care of your friends or promotion of the interests of humanity as you see them by taking humanity or your friends seriously (»attributing absolute value« to them) is equally ludicrous. In infinity only a humorous seriousness is reasonable. This implies that comedy is superior to tragedy because tragedy is really just comic.

I take this last point, the *unimportance of the particular*, to be the point of *Deafman Glance*. The point implies the play's form of comedy. It also requires »systematic ambiguity,« the negation of the particular by itself as in dreams and myths. For if you devote your efforts to establishing the particularity of particulars and getting it across to others (an audience), that's a gesture implying the particulars (»as such«) matter, e.g., this woman's motives or that what she did was wrong.

I suspect that it's on this very last point that my reader is apt to balk. Wilson extends his humorous depreciation of our finitude within infinity to the moral. Now there is no doubt to me that child-murder (as generally the killing of civilians) except under very special circumstances (after all it has been, like the killing of the old in some primitive cultures, established and accepted practice in some civilizations) is wrong, and I am sure that Wilson takes roughly the same attitude. In fact, if I am not mistaken, he picks a mother's killing of her children precisely (though not only) because it is just about the wrongest act there is: so that what applies to it will a fortiori apply also to less wrong acts. But the question is not there (no one will dispute that on our relative scales of importance there is room for the negative), but whether *this* particularity of acts, their particular moral quality, is ultimately important. It is no more important ultimately than any other.

To sum up this justification of systematic ambiguity: it is epistemologically realistic (we can't really tell the particular); it is pragmatically realistic (not the particular, but the essential is real); it is ontologically realistic (the particular is really unimportant because the infinite is reality).

6. We cannot be sure this show is about anything. It may be a mere fact. Decide it is about something: we cannot be sure what it is about. Decide what it is about: we cannot be sure what it says about that something. Decide what its standpoint is: we cannot be sure what it recommends. In each regard, the »we cannot be sure« registers a positive formal aspect of the show, inviting a decision, and distinguishing it from theatre making the decision for us.

7. Whereas a happening is formally arranged to appear not to be about anything, this spectacle is formally arranged both to allow us to think it is not about anything, but also to allow us to think that it is about something, as in conventional theatre.

8. Systematic ambiguity is not meaninglessness. Rather, it translates into sets of alternative hypotheses. We cannot pin the artist down but have to assume the responsibility for meaning. This may inspire us to take a stand of our own.

9. *DG* may be a personal expression, whether a determinedly private one or one designed to make us intuit Wilson.

10. It is *in fact* the stage-representation of a somewhat organic coalescence of images around some crystallizing images in Wilson's mind in 1970, centering on Raymond Andrew's personality and pictures, at least originally, and on Wilson's relation to him: or rather, a representation of what resulted from a work-process of supplementing, modifying and arranging these images, and eliminating some. This work process was guided by Wilson's aesthetic sense and by his intuition of internal relations between the images. It was oriented toward providing viewers with peace of mind while delighting them, but a peace of mind freeing their awareness for spontaneous participatory activity. It was undertaken in a condition of intense but minimally cerebral self-awareness and ditto awareness of his friends, wards and patients (many of them performers in the show). The appropriateness to their personalities of their activities in the show, and its promotion of their mental health were perhaps further considerations.

11. The work started with images and was carried on with them – drawings by Raymond Andrews, pictures in magazines or on phonograph album covers, things seen, dream-images, things Wilson's friends did. Wilson would try to feed these images back into his dreams, then recording them the next morning. He would construct and play with scale models. The creative process continued through rehearsals and performances.

12. A delicate process during the working-up of the show of mutual

adaptation to externally minor vagaries of expression that individual members of the group come up with – in a spirit of membership – makes for a (secondary) collective authorship: the show is not only Wilson's and Andrews'.

13. But watching the show, a feeling is unavoidable that the activities on stage reproduce images that came to someone, rather than acting out ideas or a story; that these images came to, were held on to, were selected, heightened, by the same person; that they struck him with something of the force of minor visions; and were chosen for reproduction because of their relevance and importance for him personally, as vital intuitions; and that the variations of individual images on stage, the development given them, as well as the obviously carefully arranged neighborings, simultaneities and successions of these images and of their developments, and the overall system of images and development of the whole were worked out by him by a sensitive intuition of what was important to him during this period of his life, if not absolutely most important, then at least important along some cross-cut through himself, possibly defined and restricted by a project of public reproduction, by a central subject and/or set of images initially settled on, and by some shyness of coming to grips with himself and/or some fearfulness of divulging himself. We sense the significance of the detail and of the structured whole to some maker.

14. To the extent this feeling is valid, the show would, setting aside some modifying factors and intentions mentioned, be a reproduction of an indirect inventory Wilson took of himself at a certain stage of his development, by abstaining from direct self-analysis and from discursive thinking, instead registering only visual images – fortuitiously encountered – and among these only the ones that felt personally relevant and important (without analysis of why they might be relevant and important, of what their meaning to him might be), elaborating, supplementing, relating them according to the same criteria (only). This is a form of self-analysis in the tradition of Freud, akin to dreaming, to associative thinking about dreams, to free word association. The underlying assumptions are that the peculiar method of registration, selection, development – on the visual level, uncerebrally, by felt personal relevance and importance – yields a selection of symbols, cohering, as related, into a symbol (the show; or its visual image in the mind); and that this symbol is a projection of the self.

15. I suspect, further, that the operative sense of »symbol« would

be closer to Jung's than to Freud's: neither a semiotic nor an allegorical representation: but the optimal and at the moment optimally clear and characteristic representation of something relatively unknown; a bipolar synthesis of the conscious and the unconscious; transporting spirit beyond the finite; »over-determined«; created by a generalized libido (= life-energy) or by a libidinal excess; an energy transformer, not only signifying one's further road in life in terms of what is best in one, but itself – its formation, vision, – a step onto that road, a forward-directed movement of one's vital forces; and possibly archetypal to some degree and hence interpersonal.[64]

16. Yet we do not sense any intent of the maker to communicate himself to us or to make autobiographical revelations. The show seems intended as expression, but not as communication. Nor has it been provided with a gesture of communication or of expressing anything personal. Without being unequivocally impersonal in form, it is in no way personal in its form. Rather, it displays an air of objectivity. The aesthetic sensibility at work seems spectator-oriented. There are no positive indications that the activities reproduce experiences or the experienced; nor that the whole represents one man's view, or that man himself.

17. The governing whole, Wilson's spontaneous self, it not identified in the spectacle. It is present only as ineffable unity of apparently unrelated images and as occult cause of their ordination in the time and space of the stage: as inescapable inference from a peculiar combination: on the one hand the images and figures and their developments seem to relate thematically not at all, and do not interact obviously or in any conventional sense; on the other hand, their close and smooth choreographic coordination overpoweringly suggests that they do relate intrinsically: at least for their coordinator.

18. One may from the spectacle's style hazard guesses as to its maker's personality: whimsical, indirect, discrete, highly organized, with strong but inhibited emotions, etc. But one can always do this: it does not make a show formally a self-exposition.

19. One striking impression is that it is a world: a real and absolute totality, self-contained, with no outside, events within it taking

---

64 Cf. C. G. Jung, *Psychologische Typen; Wandlungen und Symbole der Libido; Psychologie und Alchemie; Über die Praktische Verwendbarkeit der Traumanalyse, Wirklichkeit der Seele; Über die Energetik der Seele; Instinkt and Unterbewusstes.* I am here summing up a discussion in R. Bossard, *Psychologie des Traumbewusstseins,* 1951.

place according to its own laws, diversified, its aspect of totality transcending the aggregate of individuals within it, pre-existing as their locus and possibility.

19a. We may relate this feeling to the concrete spectacle, to a fictitious world we may take it to represent, or to our world, viewing the spectacle as representation of it.[65]

20. We are formally introduced into this world (3):[66] the hero's penetration into it, reducing »elsewhere« to the irrelevant locus of our awareness of it. The Venetian perspective of the deep stage, enhanced by a pair of »legs« Wilson had put in, gives it a feeling of self-contained interiority. The permanent set (from 8 on) gives it stability, and rounds it off: Lethe (18) its one edge, the forest, man's primal home, its rearward expanse, with a horizon behind it, in which the centered acme of the pyramid (as later (79 ff.), the suspended hero) gathers it all in. The ordered distribution of sets and actions by the transversal zones (a major concern of Wilson's) is not designed to provide an aesthetic order, but a reality-order, the extension of a multiple and variegated reality, many-centered as a world and of a space and real place independent of the scattered actions. These and the characters are placed into a framework not created by them, and since they seem mutually independent, do not create an order of action that could by another definition of the given reality compete with its definition as world.[67] Entrances and exits not so staged as to seem from and to some accidentally unobservable place within this world (e.g., the forest), are staged as actualizations and sublimations within this world, like fantasies in a mind: not coming from or going to elsewhere.

An individualized hero is so exhaustively reduced to his relation to the world – to its subjective origin, the world his dream or what he sees; or to a gesture of rejection and withdrawal – that he cannot distract us from it onto the psychic reality which conventional Western theatre presents to us instead of a world.

65 Like ours, this world has a sun (92), moon, both rising and setting (3, 104), stars (113), and the cleavage between nature and culture.

66 No moviemaker can pull off this trick. We buy illusion at the movies by taking leave of our senses, but just therefore are never elsewhere.

67 Wilson seems to have thought of a spot which he privately called the »Holy Spot,« slightly stage-right of and down-stage from the center of the stage as dramatic center. This is where the forces of this world apply, and where things come to a head (locus of mother, 4; locus of cracked rock, 50; locus of nurse with baby, 55; locus of boy's ascent, 56, 74, 77, 81, cf. also 104). But this dramatic center in no way becomes for us geographic center: testimony to the structural strength of the world-space created on stage.

It is true that at the end of the spectacle, this whole world is revealed to be incomplete. A mass descent and a mass ascent, repopulating it, outline its incompleteness, a bright nether world negating extinction in the world we have looked into: but this rather extends that world's time into infinity, than that it indicates another place.

21. Again, however, there are no formal indications that we should view the show as world or as representation of a world or of our world. It does not present itself as the cosmic allegory that analysis hints it is: the apparent, closed world of the inward, segregate individual, suspended between a surface of ordinary, purpose- and value-ridden existence and an aimlessly, rhythmically moving depth of natural life, magically opening up onto an enlightened vision and onto the superior reality of the infinity of the cosmic cycle of life, death and return.

22. Ostensibly it is only a flowing collage of images, structured as such a plait of tableaux vivants.

23. This is only in a negative way due to the almost complete absence of speech in this deaf-mute's world. With the exception of Wilson's reading (25), which however, formally presents itself as outside the show, the verbal utterances, voiced thoughts (31) syntactical calisthenics (33), or formal reprimands (31), seem appendages of the images, like the balloons in comic strips. That they are spoken into microphones, electronically transformed and transmitted through amplifiers located away from the speakers enhances their character of quotations – signs, but not acts of signification; as do the foreign accents (31, 33). Like visual signs, they are there to be »read«: have lost the character of coming to us normally attaching to auditory signs. The sound of the music does not so much deepen or add another dimension to our sensory appreciation of the spectacle, as that it enters us affectively; our appreciation of it is by mood; and even on this channel, the sound merely enhances moods evoked visually.

By »images,« I mean distinct graphic units, apparently designed to be taken in separately, whether to be collated subsequently or not, detaching themselves as visual wholes from their surroundings, some static, some developing, some without, some with distinct sub-elements of the same sort; and apparently designed, either primarily or exclusively, for appreciation as visual data: not as images of anything other than themselves, nor as metaphors for ideas, nor as significatory expressions of the states of mind or characters of the human figures contained in them: though certainly allowing inferential interpretations of any of these three sorts.

25. Such images are facts in the phenomenal form of visibles: something that may be seen, and something which is what is seen if it is seen: nothing but potential relata.

26. There is something private about the images, creating the impression that we are privileged to see them. They have the character of existing to be seen: but their discretion is such that we feel very much that it is up to us to realize this intrinsic relation to us: we, not the performers, have to be the active party. We have to search out the images.

27. The images are not so much shown or given as exposed to us. The distinction is conveyed by such features as that many of them are obscured, e.g., within or behind the forest; the appearance of some is so brief we can at most glimpse them; there are so many things happening simultaneously, we cannot dwell on everything, but have to search, select, focus, in order to see, *mere* looking won't do; the developments are unaccented in their beginnings so that often we come in on them belatedly, not guided, but in a process of scanning; images or developments compete for our attention; we are constantly aware of a mass of detail that escapes us (a kind of inwardness of an image);[68] the transition from visual intake to identifying and classifying perception is systematically rendered difficult by inconsistencies within, obscurities or ambiguities of the images (we cannot quite get hold of them).

28. The images are single, first because often neighboring ones derive from different modes of awareness such as sensory perception or fantasy: their orders of reality differ, e.g., natural, cultural, supernatural; second, because with almost no exception, the performers of one pay no attention to any other, seem unaware of all the other activities; third, because equally generally, the activities constituting any one image have no effect on or relation to, at least no ordinary or obvious effect or relation, those constituting any other; finally, because there is little exchange of elements: the same figures and props stay together.

29. Most of the images contain people. They create the image. But to begin with and on the whole, we see them neither as its performers,

---

68 Wilson has distributed a variety of props to the performers that are well nigh imperceptible to the audience or the precise nature of which it is just about impossible for us to make out. E.g. the gear served those at table (46); or the objects to be orally emitted by the dying (green tissue to the child on the ox (44); a rhinestone band to the pope (81); ball bearings to the fishing boy (54); or the little girl's present to the Goat Woman (24).

nor as what the image is about, but as parts of it, figures in a picture. Their stances and movements are pre-set, seem to originate outside of them: thus they do not seem performers. Their trance-like and/or natural, smooth slowness detaches their acts from their personalities: thus the image does not seem about them.

30. But unavoidably we will interpret the images

   1. psychologically, amplifying visual perception by the induction of psychic states and forms and substances; and thus

   2. as representational imitations of fictitious real-life individuals and of classes or types of such;

   3. and as allegorical representations of themes;

   4. and as, by their nuances, developments and relations, expressing points of view concerning these themes: standpoints.

31. Besides which the formal ambiguity of the spectacle induces other views of it besides as flux of images:

   1. as activity of the performers, as performance;

   2. as dramatic action;

   3. as the story of an individual.

32. Finally, not only can we transcend (III.30) and bypass (III.31) the image-character of the images: some of the activities on stage hardly have image-character at all, but are seen as people in action: »individuals,« »figures,« »actual persons.«

33. Taking up III.31 I find: our experience of the show is pervasively dual: we are watching images and performers creating images.

34. We see strong, somewhat unusual personalities: energetic, passionate, willful and self-disciplined persons, able to exert the force of their personality over others and used to doing so, unconventional in their way of life, though not necessarily in their conduct, with some discretion or gentility in pursuit of their own ends, intensely at grips with important problems. Wilson makes us a gift of his friends, patients and objets humains trouvés, a selection.

35. But these strong personalities are engaging, in public, in a highly disciplined manner, in specific, simple activities, chosen for and never explained to them, obscure to them, closely coordinated. The gross of entrances, exits and of the beginning of specific actions is on cue: as in a clockwork. Only the timing of some incidental and some recurrent activities has been left up to the performers, generally ones that Wilson has worked with for a long time, whose sense of fitness he trusts. Scarcely anything is impromptu.

36. The movements are intense but relaxed. They are slow discharges,

at a physiologically natural rate, if such there is, of energy at a high level. They approach freedom from mental *interference*. They seem to a high degree *controlled* by the mind: but by a mind at ease freely to concentrate on the body now, its administrative functions an elegant minimum of coordination. The mind is immersed in the body, at its service. Nothing seems willed, the gestures have no vectors, the activities unfold, flow. There is of course an element of pretense in this, as in a drunk's drunkenness, a lover's passion.

37. The bodies are at one with their stances and movements, but the ambiguity between abandonment to the arranged and spontaneous act persists.

38. Neither as performers nor as active components do the participants in any given image pay much attention to one another. Each does his own thing, in concert. The (non-existent) script hardly ever prescribes action of A on B. Conventional theatre's ostentatious indications of acting-on, being-affected by another are absent. The very precise choreography, a lengthily developed sense of what the others are doing at any given moment – body awareness – facilitate timing even more than in other theatre. To some extent, the approach or gestural deployment of any given performer will, as is normal, affect others in the same frame as an upsurge of force tending to compel them to act in the same rhythm: but, with the exception of some blend-ins, fadeouts and mirror-effects, this response has been inhibited: each image maintains its own distinct time, in which its performers share.

39. The usual gestures of address to the public, heralding or accompanying a genuine or pretended effort of communication are absent. The nearly complete absence of vocal and facial gestures facilitates this rejection of projective gesture.

40. The actions required are simple. They demand no unusual skills or exertions. Thus the director can specify them concretely, without reference to character, motivation, dramatic function, meaning, or desired effect. With one startling exception (85), framed by intervals of inaction, they are to be so slow that the performer finds himself engaging in them for their own sake. Most start on cue, but instead of being limited by a terminal cue, are to proceed on their own time, providing the cue for the next action: so that the performer can find the variant of the general slow tempo congenial to him. Just when, sometimes how often, a performer is to do a specific thing within a sequence is often left up to him or her.

41. On the one hand a natural, self-possessed bodily ease and balance, physiological intensity. On the other, a purge of ego in relaxation, somnambulistic, hypnotized, puppet-like.

42. The strong personalities are invested in the performance. We sense them as power of self-abandon, as energy within the closed system of each performer and of the collective performance. We sense them as *not* functioning as such, unlike Wilson, not expressing or imposing themselves. They present themselves to us as out of their minds.

43. Thus our awareness of performers and performance does not clash with, but supplements our perception of images.

44. THE PERFORMANCES HAVE THE FORM OF SOLEMN CELEBRATIONS. THIS FORM IS CREATED BY A CERTAIN TYPE OF BODY MOVEMENT. THE OBJECT OF THE CULT IS BODILY MOTION.

The movements are generally very slow. This generates an air of solemnity. They indicate that what is being done has value. On the other hand, their unhurried care does by and large not seem in tribute to the value of the particular actions performed, e.g., because of a symbolic significance of these, but seems indiscriminately expended on all gestures: so that, these being ordinary and simple – pretty or expressive, all formalized gestures being avoided – the body itself, namely in the particular sense of an organic automobile, of something capable of moving, as kinetic capacity, or bodily motion, seems the object of the cult. Some of the actions of course strike us, given the devotional air, as rituals expressing a veneration for the particular action performed or for something it symbolizes: e.g., the murders. But as we perceive how all actions, some of them purely body activity with no objective beyond themselves, i.e., beyond movement, are valorized by the same intense care, we come to identify bodily movement as such as the object of the cult. The slowness of the movements also carries the same point: the same care being expended on each part of each bodily movement – habitual accentuations disappearing – it is not what is done, that particular activity as a significant whole, nor any objective to be attained by it – getting someplace, say – that is made to seem important, but the activity of the body as such, whatever it is presently doing, even just the lifting of a hand. The fact that the performers do not pay attention to one another nor formalize any address to the audience, also contributes to this impression: their concern is not with anything other than with the rudimentary reality of what they are doing – moving in space. The absence of language – projected movement of the mind – further, since it is extraordinary, delimits the object of the cult. The facility of the actions – no athletic feats, no Grotowskian contortions – and Wilson's inclusion in the cast of cripples, children and old people, tells us that what is being worshipped is ordinary natural body movement. There is no research for particular beautiful movements: the idea that any deliberate improvement of movements (but particularly: by conscious attention to their external shape) is possible, is opposite to the point being made. The occasional shaping of gestures by inept performers away from or beyond the physiologically functional stands out. Performance and performance style very nearly, in this theatre, come down to manner of body-motion. This manner is evidently different from the usual motion of people, but not because of the absence of veneration of the body in everyday life, and a consequent lack of care, but because everyday life perverts body motion. Practical and social concerns not only distract from the body, but reduce it to an instrument, subvert its movements for utilitarian and expressive purposes, and regulate them and interfere with them in extrinsic and unnatural manners.

The imagery symbolically insinuates that life is vitally complemented by death. This performance style analogously conveys the feeling that motion is the issue of tranquility: by a context of figures in sustained immobility (the seated boy (2, 8 and ff.), the magician (12 and ff.), the murderess (1, 5), the Ladies in White (3), the Prince and Princess (3), the frog (8 and ff.), the apes (110), the 18th century couple (111)) and of moments of waiting in which the whole scene is still (cf. infra). (In Wilson's *Prologue* (June 1971, Espaces Cardin, Paris), this matrix was provided by numerous nude corpses.)

Veneration is conveyed but not expressed: there is no special set of cultish gestures expressing respect, nor deliberate solemnity, but only solemnity as by-product of the tranquil detachment from self which makes natural movement possible. It is of the essence of this cult to be without religion: an attitude toward the body is revealed by a way of moving, but there is no doctrine – »of the mind« – formulating this attitude and enjoining this movement and which it is to convey. In principle, at least, this manner of movement is to result rather from the absence of values – from the *non*-imposition of any desiderata or objectives on movement whatsoever. What an outsider like myself sums up as a cult, i.e., implementation of ideas, to the Wilsonian is just a way of being. The movement is to result from letting the body take over: but neither expression nor cult are body-functions.

Ego and instincts shape bodily movement and cause it. Wilson's performance style sets both aside. His performers are to move unmoved by either or at least as though unmoved by either. We are made to participate in a cult of movement divorced from both: life at its most abstract.

Thus also, the standard dancer's mysticism, cloak of a cult of the object body, of the dancer's own materiate hulk, is alien to Wilson, and forms of the dance using the body for expression, even for expressing attitudes toward the body like those conveyed by his performer's movements, are precisely those to be avoided by them. There is a difference between movements resulting from immersing the self in the body and movements expressing ideas or an attitude enjoining or endorsing immersion of the self in the body: the former express the body, the latter express the mind; in the former the body is master, in the latter the body is being used.

The difference between the Wilsonian and other modern dance is along these lines. It follows that Wilson would have to deny that Lennie Wagner's, Andrew de Groat's, his own, or S.K. Dunn's styles of dance represent a new form of the dance developed by him.[69]

What is in question here is thus a performance style. The cult is the way the show is done, it is not what is done, it is not the content of the show. We are not given it as object of perception. We are to take in the value it puts on the human body or rather on bodily motion and its conception of the human body, as autonomous kinetic organism, unconsciously: by way of a corresponding relaxation, perhaps a kinetic, bodily response, a disposition to such movement (cf. III.74). On the conscious level we are given an imagery, of which this form of motion is only the general form, how it is created.

45. The images are of human activities, even poignantly so. But though, as always, we project an analogue of our psyche onto these humanoids, varying it according to their conduct and appearance, our projection hardly pierces the surface of the images, but merely imparts a structure to it. We know of course that the performers are people,

---

69 A symmetric loose-jointed flinging/whirling of bent limbs around the pendant or jumping swaying body . . . . Serial repetitions of complete movements, each of which though closed goes through a point of regeneration . . . . States of relaxation paradoxically function as states of reference and of departure for kinematic initiatives: a responsive inner listening — attentive abandon — mediating between growths of desire for motion in the still body and an atuned but playful kinetic imagination? Theory: 1) the relaxed body wants to move, 2) the mind can respond to its desire, but 3) as initiatory and inventive faculty. — Wilson seemed at this time apt one day to develop a vocal style along the same general lines.

not robots. But we experience the characters performed as effigies of people. We adduce character or intent only to form our image of the action.

46. There are several reasons for this. For one thing, the show does not address us. It is self-contained, seen from afar. The characters are not acting on one another or on anything, they are going through motions. There is no forward pointing line, fable or plot, inducing us to make that hypostatic imputation of subjecthood as basis for wondering what will happen. There is no expression of choice or decision. The simile-figures in the images do not speak.

47. Thus the flatness and the passivity (object-character) of the images are preserved.

48. The initial murder-scene (2) is not unequivocally an image. It also comes across as an agent's motivated action in a certain situation, setting up a conflict, as drama – a Greek tragedy,

49. which then (8) seems to settle down to a story of consequences, a psychological study of an individual in trouble, a fable.

50. But once we are thrown into the kaleidoscope of imagery, we correct these anticipations and assimilate the nascent drama into the surrealist collage: particularly because of two image-features:

51. the agent's character-motivatedness/situatedness are in Sheryl Sutton's acting not presented as cause of her action, but as its inwardness merely, at one with it: there is no indication of will, whether spontaneity or determined will;

52. and her action unrolls fatally toward its fixed end, a picture on the still surface of time.

53. The incisive action is not followed in its reverberations: the follow-up is as to its essence and is up to us. We are merely furnished materials for it. It is left dangling in the plane of chaos: into which we do in fact in life throw up our never decisive actions. And similarly for the hint at an incipient fable: the protagonist does nothing, and his outwardness is (like that of all of us, but in this show brashly) a mystery: in which we may attempt to participate. Whereas in conventional drama, words and demeanor tell us the lies one tells oneself, in this show nothing pretends to clear up the mystery. So that the fable does not come off.

54. Wilson hasn't just left drama and fable behind, their subversion into imagery is part of the show, a development.

55. Some of the characters in the show are not absorbed into images,

but stand out as people: *actual persons, an individual, figures*. They do not coalesce with their action: you see them act, and thus in depth, with a psychic space within, so that you wonder what they will do and feel that somehow they might have acted otherwise. But in the end, in different ways, they function as support of the imagery, not as alien addendum.

56. By a »figure« I mean an individuation of an abstract type or of principles of human existence. In this show, they are of the latter sort, individuated existential modes, embodiments of some dimension of human life: of life as a power not opposed to death, but either indifferent to it, not relating to it (the little girl) or accepting it (the Goat Woman) or transcending it (the Magician). We see a figure by an intuition of the type or existential mode it embodies.

57. The roaming figures are lines of continuity in the show. Themselves on the verge of imagehood, they break into the images by the contrast of total self concern (the little girl), by observing them (the Goat Woman), by interfering with, moving or creating them (the Magician): thus setting them off as images of life, of life as though it were itself mere appearance, no more than a show of animation.

58. By an »individual,« I mean a singular person of a particular character and in a particular state of mind, such that these determine conduct in accord with them. We can be aware of an individual without knowing what their character or state of mind is. The one and only individual in this show, almost the protagonist, is the fictitious character created by Raymond Andrews.

59. He functions as our suppositious medium: one may suppose the images to be in his mind, the spectacle about what he sees or dreams. In private, he and Wilson will both say that the show is »about« him. But his function varies. At first (3-5, 8-77), he gradually changes from just our medium, reflecting a world within which he is, though in isolation, to a possibly reactant object of attention and action. Later (80-106) he is completely detached from the scene, events in which (80-98) may now seem a representation, in mythical/ritualistic form, of his frame of mind or of his relation to the world: though in fact Andrews contributed the image of the ox. Ultimately (104 ff.) events seem to relate to him only as a comment, only generally and incidentally pertinent to him (107), on the world.

The show's movement relative to him is that of a film camera moving away from its object. We perhaps start inside him, then have a view of him as this individual, then lose sight of him as such, seeing him only as *an* individual. In terms of content, *he* moves: at first he is, under increasing pressure from it, increasingly in and with the world, then detaches himself from it, keeping it in view, then vanishes.

In part the show may like narrative fiction be a psychic film.

60. As dramatic center, he provides the imagery dramatic unity: permanent reminder that it may cohere immanently, perhaps as the ignition points of a unitary soul. Inasmuch as the images are not quite nor only his and their unity is inobvious and obscure, he is off-center. Nevertheless he is instrumental to our experience of them.

61. By an »actual person,« I mean someone in their private capacity, with a civic status and personal life outside of the performance, entering it, but not performing. Robert Wilson's appearances (22, 25, 26, 45) are of this sort: that of the other vocal intruder (33); that of the person boarding up the hut (71); and perhaps, though unlike these others he is in costume, the first appearance of the male dancer (10).

62. Whereas the figures and the individual shade over into images, the actual persons stand out as unequivocally non-images: people there to do or say something, not just to have what they do looked at. But since they also figure as intruding outsiders, the show's character of a juxtaposition of images is conserved: they set off the show's unreality, declare it coextensive with that unreality.

63. Wilson's theatre is magically fantastic. But its spectacular wealth of beautiful effects and arrangements, birds and candles, masks, assemblies and animals, sliding, sinking, flying objects, processions, dances and moons, makes us feel that anything might happen, but does not crank up the steady taut interest either of a sustained rational development or of a conventional development of mythical power, when cunningly presented in astounding progression or juxtaposition, by illumination and/or paradoxical exemplifications, near the edge of plausibility or conventionality, or invested in complexities, concrete or formal, not too great to kill off anticipation, but sufficient to create surprises. Neither kind of development is there to carry us, and the effects and arrangements are discrete: elegant and whimsical. Our delight in them greatly heightens our attention, but also diverts it.

64. Extended expositions and repetitions, the silence and the slow movements, the unaccented evenness with which new things appear, and above all the self-sufficient concreteness of the individual images (they do not tell us what they mean) liberate our awareness: whether

we pay attention, what we pay attention to and what kind of attention we pay are up to us. We must mobilize original energies for it, we have to orient it ourselves, and what it yields us will depend on what we make of things. An activation of sentience takes place. It is inhabitual for the non-artist. Looking becomes imagination.

65. The images are evasive. One feels that what is going on is slightly over from where one is looking. In focus sensorially, the images are out of focus perceptually. In spite of an apparent simplicity, sometimes even familiarity, they are consistently somehow abstract and not only somewhat obscure or even mysterious, but ambiguous, inconsistent, contradictory. We find we cannot say precisely what is being done or what is taking place: there is some dearth of detail, some lack of specificity, something we can't quite make out, perhaps, or some sign to be given by conduct or expression that is not given. Recurrently it seems that the nature or point or intention of the activity may be one of several between which we cannot quite decide – the »over-determination« of dreams. Then again, there is always something that does not fit in, an incongruous detail or development, often something fantastic in something ordinary. Not infrequently, what we see lends itself equally to incompatible, even opposite interpretations.

A man is trying to make a gadget work: we can't make out what it is or what it is supposed to do. Was that a gesture of aid or of condemnation? Is this individual serene and relaxed or anxiously withdrawn? Is he dying or fainting? Is she mothering or murdering the child? Is he digging a grave or gardening? Is it an erotic image, a fertility symbol or a pure dance? Is she going there or passing by?

Among the reasons for this: the abstraction of events; the multiplicity of events; the unrelatedness of events: the lack of guide from plot, fable, ostensible theme or language; obscurities apported by decor or lighting; the lack of accent on new elements and on the direction of apparently aimlessly slow developments, due both to performance-style and to the staging; a permissive attitude induced in us by the lack of cognitive structure of the imagery and by the performers' manner of movement: an erosion of perceptual acquisitiveness takes place, our analytic, identifying, retentive propensities are relaxed.

We thus recurrently find ourselves obliged to recall and take into account something we saw but did not take notice of – saw inattentively or without definitely identifying it or perhaps only at the edges of our field of vision, looking at something else, or saw not very clearly – perhaps something that presented itself as incidental, »not important,« but which we now find was the beginning of a structured event or of a salient development. We do not so much perceive as »come to be aware of« things: gradually notice them; or they suddenly register. They enter our awareness surreptitiously, liminally. Also, impressions, Gestalten formed, identifications made are by further developments shaken, put in question, abrogated or enriched. Consistently, things turn out not to be quite as or what they seemed.

This technique of *marginal and equivocal* presentation is contrary to dominant theatrical practice. By it, the imagery to some extent by-passes the ego-structure of perception: already weakened by the performance style (III.44). It complements the dramatic technique: the *symbolic presentation of the themes*: by which to some extent the cognitive content (meaning) by-passes the ego-structure of cognition.

66. Whether there is a fable is doubtful. The show is designed to make this doubt active part of our experience. Indications are given, commitments withheld, traces obscured. If there is a fable, it consists in the spiritual development of an individual who does not speak and whose only act is to shake his head, to all appearances a refusal of involvement: the climax of his career. That career seems to consist in a faint approach if not to involvement at least to awareness: it is equally interpretable as successful resistance to involvement. Another, only possibly complementary, impression given is that the hero surmounts a trauma, and probably guilt. The actions do not act out this rudimentary fable the very existence of which is uncertain, but indicate it: possible symbols of the hero's awareness.

67. Assume the show is a symbol for the unimportance of particulars (cf. III.5). But its distinctive character is that it consists only in particulars – images. It thus notifies us that the finite is inconsistent, and transcendence possible only as free act. The doubt animating the message structures its delivery.

68. Excepting some marked intervals of ending (79, end of 103, end of 110) and of new beginning or waiting (1, 8, 80, 84, 86, beginning of 101, 104, 109), which divide the show into movements,[70] the stage is continuously active.

69. At most times several things go on independently in different places: incidents or occurrences, like chance events, fortuitious improvisations or like the odd details of a street scene, fantastic flashes,

70 Cf. III, 75-8.

or entire scenes, small shows, often dances, complete actions; and surreal static appearances, details from a painting. The show concludes with a series of large actions enveloping the stage, organizing it in its entirety. The development has been toward this integration. But also, along the way, some of the incidents, small shows and static appearances progressively coalesce into larger patterns – an individual, recurrent figures, semi-permanent, shifting tableaux, though it is left up to us to single them out. While the three »figures« have the whole stage for their arena, and the »actual persons« do not belong on it, the »individual« and the major images establish themselves for us by a prop and a certain location of their own. There are only three or four of these major images: that of the forest and those associated with the bins, the table and the ox. Their shifts, set over against the still figure of the individual give the show its surface structure.

70. They shift in the manner of a surreptitiously altered picture. Something has become different. When we look at them, they seem still, as though we never caught them in a change: but the changes themselves are still. We cannot say that anything leads to anything else. Instead, we see variations on a theme obscurely, ambiguously suggested by the image, never grasped, but analogically glimpsed in its variations. The developing image enfolds a variety of possible situations. A sense of a direction of the development gradually asserts itself. Sometimes it seems in the direction of a breakdown, sometimes toward an impass or an explosion or just a slight fatal fissure. We are not watching the action of people, but the enactment of the development of a situation.

71. At times we are dozing or our mind is wandering. We may have only a generalized awareness of the stage, looking without seeing, our focus, discrimination, identification at a minimum. We may be scanning Wilson's event, unattachedly noting the salient features of the moment. An inattentive awareness may have come to attach itself to some particular image or ongoing act, already, previously, identified. Or we may feel there is nothing going on: we are attentive, but have no object – may be waiting for something to happen. Our attention to something in particular may be waning: the object is receding into abstraction. Or we are shifting our attention from some act that seems to be ending or is no longer holding our attention to something that is beginning to budge. Sometimes we are torn between two developments, we go back and forth, or try to divide our awareness. Our attention may be gripped by a detail, some recurrent gesture

of the hand, a rising silver ball: such intentness may be mindlessly idiotic or discriminatory, appreciative. Or we may come to focus with the attention of reflection or of open, perhaps intent, delight on some image or activity in course of development, possibly an entrance or a dance, possibly a stage-wide state of the show, delight, sensory discrimination, and reflection may coincide, or we may be off along only one of these avenues of attention. Attention may even open up into intense concern, possibly tinged with emotion, or into an approach to intuition, possibly one we feel may be important.

72. Wilson's art subtly stimulates our awareness to range over an extended scale of attention: a loosening-up exercise for the mind of the same sort as the physical free motion exercises by which Wilson trains and prepares his performers. Assuming you can abandon yourself to the free movement of your awareness – growths and fadings, closings-in and expansions, zoomings-in-on, dolly-shots, fade-outs – *your awareness itself will become a medium of enjoyment and even of awareness*, as usually only the particular forms of awareness, visual, tactile, etc. and the particular relations of awareness (to some particular object as such) are. This is most particularly where Wilson is at. There are three peculiarities to this imagistic art of his: it is only indirectly managerial, demanding a personal, active exercise of our attention, that we not only come but go out of ourselves and it provides an organized pattern of stimulating opportunities for this; it induces or allows a course of shifts throughout the *whole* registry of modes and degrees of attention; and it particularly allows for and requires recurrent states of low-level attention. We cannot operate willfully in Wilson's artistic space. Our energy for acute, intense or concentrated attention must accrue out of a state of dying. Wilson makes it *difficult* to maintain attention, to get anything into focus or keep it in focus. Like a dancer's awareness of his body in motion may at times give him an awareness of the space he moves through, so our awareness of our awareness – as an energetic state (but not grasping act) of participation – may at times give us the awareness of what Wilson is making happen before us.

73. The show has been designed on a basic principle of the alteration of strong and weak impact (engagement). In the developments of each of the major images (ox, bins, table) and of the boy's story, strongly engaging scenes are followed by periods of declining engagement, these by stretches of low impact, followed by gradually rising engagement. Plotting engagement (impact) against time, we get graphs of the following sort:

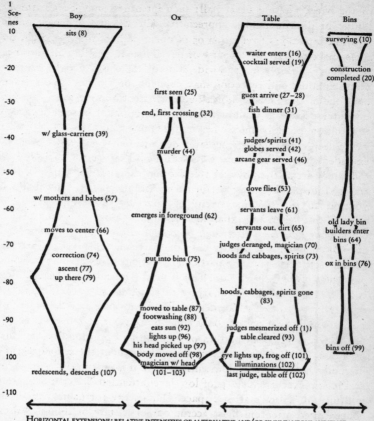

| Scenes | Boy | Ox | Table | Bins |
|---|---|---|---|---|
| 10 | sits (8) | | | surveying (10) |
| -20 | | | waiter enters (16)<br>cocktail served (19) | construction<br>completed (20) |
| -30 | | first seen (25)<br>end, first crossing (32) | guest arrive (27–28)<br>fish dinner (31) | |
| -40 | w/ glass-carriers (39) | murder (44) | judges/spirits (41)<br>globes served (42)<br>arcane gear served (46) | |
| -50 | | | dove flies (53) | |
| -60 | w/ mothers and babes (57)<br>moves to center (66) | emerges in foreground (62) | servants leave (61)<br>servants out. dirt (65) | old lady bin<br>builders enter<br>bins (64) |
| -70 | correction (74)<br>ascent (77)<br>up there (79) | put into bins (75) | judges deranged, magician (70)<br>hoods and cabbages, spirits (73) | ox in bins (76) |
| -80 | | | hoods, cabbages, spirits gone (83) | |
| -90 | | moved to table (87)<br>footwashing (88)<br>eats sun (92)<br>lights up (96)<br>his head picked up (97)<br>body moved off (98)<br>magician w/ head (101–103) | judges mesmerized off (1))<br>table cleared (93) | |
| 100 | redescends, descends (107) | | eye lights up, frog off (101)<br>illuminations (102)<br>last judge, table off (102) | bins off (99) |
| -110 | | | | |

HORIZONTAL EXTENSIONS: RELATIVE INTENSITIES OF ALTERNATIVE AND/OR SIMULTANEOUS AUDIENCE ENGAGEMENTS IN FOUR THEMES DURING SHOW TIME

Even apart from the problem of a scale of impact or engagement, different spectators would tend to experience impacts differently, and not only because impact (engagement) is a complex function. But on the other hand, they would probably agree somewhat as to the locations of strong and weak impact: putting these graphs together, we get the following kind of thing:

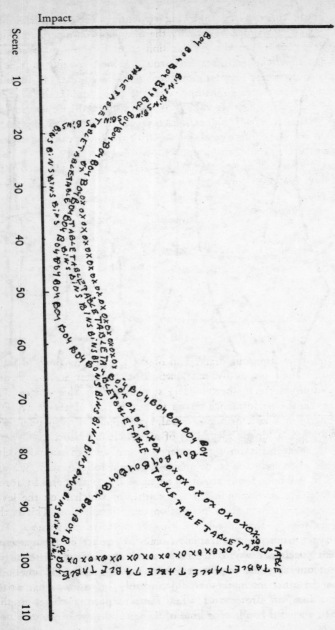

This graph suggests the following structural features: initial high and terminal low impact (actually the play ends on a terminal high, declining impact, but the graph's limitation to those major themes does not show this); after a first trough, a first roughly coincident impact of the major themes; subsequent staggered peaks, the declining impact of one theme coinciding with the rising impact of another; but in such a fashion that valleys of relaxation and recuperation are preserved; successively higher peaks, from the sixties of my scene-count onward, i.e., an overall curve, after the first peak and trough, of increasingly rapidly rising impact.

We may compare this picture with Wilson's own sketch (according to Melvin Andringa):

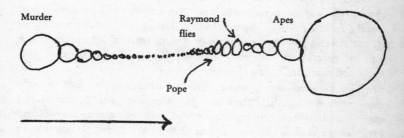

74. The show from our first vision of the Dark Lady onward takes an occult hold on us by our unconscious interest in the themes (life/death/rebirth; mother/murder) symbolized by the images. The manner of the performance draws us into a cult of the body, first inducing in us a state of non-cerebral, sympathetic correspondence to body-motion, a kinetic awareness of a participatory sort, an experience of engagement on the border between awareness and body-response, then inducing in us an iso-rhythmic followership. We are drawn in and bound, our attention engaged, by content and by form, in two closely corresponding ways, neither of which is on the level of conscious discriminatory perception or of intellection. This is the basis on which – the state in which – we perceive the images. The flow of these images is as graphed (somewhat as graphed), in waves: both in purely sensory and informational terms, and in terms of symbolic meaning (unconsciously participated in) and of human body motion (also unconsciously participated in) – the category of impact being a complex function of all of these. Wilson's art lies in this triple or even quadruple coordination. Given that state of unconscious,

non-cerebral, sympathetic, participatory concern and followership, the psychosomatic activity of image-perception turns into a rhythmic deployment of sensory energy, its rhythm relaxed and natural, like that of those body motions, its deployment approaching freedom from cerebral tension and interference: from ego-control. Our perception becomes intense, but we are not straining to perceive.

Possibly – I am not sure – such »free« perception partakes of two features of »free« body motion and of the graphed structure of the show: its discharge is in waves, periods of large and small discharges alternating; and there is something like an accumulation of disposable energy-of-perception, brought about and sustained by the process of »free« discharge in natural rhythm. If this is so, Wilson has artfully timed the impact-rhythm of his imagery to coincide with a natural rhythm of »free« perception, and our perceptive activity is not merely following that impact-rhythm, but is freely participating in it: and, in this case, generally: there is some internal relation between sensory perception and body motion, they are analogous or like body-activities, following the same »laws.«

75. Though without intermissions, the spectacle is divided into movements by a radical stop and go: successive endings, staged and experienced as true endings, followed by beginnings, staged and experienced as new beginnings. The endings are staged to provide an atmosphere, mood and feeling of things truly coming to an end – of exhaustion and waning: not just, as in conventional act-conclusions, of some particular thing or some stage having reached a conclusion; nor just to provide the feeling that the author intends to cut off things here; and, either because of this or independently, one also has the impression that also thematically, as regards action, meaning or content or presentation, whatever was begun or had been going on has come or is coming to an end, that a potential for development is exhausted, whether it has been fully actualized or not. When things then start up again, one either feels that this last impression was erroneous, or that a spontaneous regeneration (within this *world*) has provided a possibility for further continuation. The beginnings are staged to provide the appearance and mood that nothing has as yet begun and of a mere (inspecific) possibility (without necessity nor even probability) that things might happen or developments take place: an air of waiting, potentiality, even expectancy; and of a clean slate, i.e., of a new or fresh beginning: nothing in postures or arrangements suggests that any previous developments might continue or that possibly eventuating events would relate to any pre-existing potentials.

In this sense, the beginnings are as absolute as the endings. When things get going again, the feeling changes in one or more of the ways I mentioned above, so that the potentials of the beginnings now *are* attached to the previous, so that the beginning now appears as *another start* for the agencies, parties, conflicts, problems or constellations previously in motion. And once things *have* gotten going, our feeling once again changes (and also whatever thematic interpretations we might be making): no new beginning, in any relevant sense, whether absolute or relative, now any more seems to have taken place: instead we are confronted either with a continuation of the old, or else with something else.

The overall experience is that of a musical composition going through movements of waning, exhaustion, completion and of resurgence.

76. These experiences, this mode of development, non-existent in other theatre, I believe, is the very stuff of life. E.g. the feeling of resumption or recommencement sometimes in the morning or in spring, falling in love again, getting well or watching one's children. At the core, at some point, is a feeling of uniqueness, absolute newness; and then its paradoxical transformation into a new start, another chance. Finally, the new day, year, love turns into merely another day, year, love, the same and something else.

77. In Wilson's theatre, each successive ending is quite final (in content and in feeling) for the moment. But Wilson has introduced into it elements of color, excess, formality and irony which subsequently, after a new beginning, equally absolute at the moment, having remained with or returning to one, gradually make it assume the aspect of a preparatory purification. The beginnings are empty moments, nothing is happening and there is nothing to look at in particular; gradually, there are stirrings, first signs of an order in formation, an embryonic focus. One goes from a feeling of loss or depletion, an awareness of no longer, to an awareness of not as yet. The past is then for a while put out of mind, but there has been a fleeting moment during which the new came on as replacement.

78. There is a first start, in front of the curtain, with an impressive person after sustained immobility getting ready for action (2); with a crime (2); followed by an action on the stage, curtain up, signifying that the criminal is definitely dealt with (3-5); ending with the criminal's ejection back into the audience, and departure, the curtain falling again (5). The end and the beginning are unequivocal, it is a mini-play.

Within this mini-play (2-5), there is, however, also a new beginning

(3): the preludial action concluded, the players and characters enter the stage through the rising curtain and find themselves in a scene which we take to define the setting of the play itself. The impression is it is a new beginning, if only a fantasy one, for the second character so far, the boy: we expect to see the theme develop within this setting. But it doesn't, instead we witness an expeditious conclusion (5). I.e., we have been exposed to something like a false start. To my mind this is a remarkable theatrical device.

The ending of the mini-play (2-5) of crime and punishment turns out to be a false ending also, however, not only because the spectacle, after a formal announcement of it (7), after a further underlining of that false ending (6) – the previous action trailing after it has ended – and starting with a new curtain rise (8), indeed continues (8 ff.), but because it begins with a scene of beginning (early morning lighting, no action, waiting on stage); because we find that the apparently secondary character of before, the boy, is the central character, his effacement of before (3-5) delusive; because this character and to some extent the setting provide continuity; because the modification of the setting toward the sober impresses us as rectification (possibly of that character's reaction); and because the now ensuing »real play« (8-77/79), the boy's story, by various signs (e.g., the movies of the foreplay) presents itself as continuation or elaboration of the incepted theme of the foreplay, and in fact probably in some manner as revision or critique of that false ending.

There is no doubt, however, that this »real play,« the boy's story, has a proper and apparently definitive ending also (77-79): not only because there are signs of conclusion (78) and a formal scene of ending (79), the stage darkening, but because the central character's story ends with considerable finality (74), and that character leaves the action apparently for good (77), free of his involvement, and all reverberations and reflections of the action of the foreplay done with.

But the spectacle starts up again, and again with a scene (80) of new beginning (early morning air, inaction), and, after, again, a trailing on of the previous action again in the manner of a taking care of loose ends (81-85), and an interlude (85), isolated by in-action (84, 86) a new movement, around the *theme of the ox*, a theme that had attained (62) to the status of a prominent sub-theme during the previous »play,« but that now (87) becomes the center of action, starts (87). This new movement (80-97/100), which concerns the action of this ox-theme on secondary themes (bins, table) of the preceding movement (8-77/79), eliminating these – this continuity of themes contributing to the aspect of recommencement – something previously not quite finished is now really finished – again ends in a formal manner (97-100): after a climax (92, 96), with the destruction (96), consecration (97) and removal (98) of the central character, the ox, and with a darkening of the largely emptied stage. As in the case of the boy's story, a rather definite (though obscure) progression of events, a curve of development, seems to have reached a resolution.

But again there is a new – gradual – beginning (101). Something apparently had not been finished after all (the table-theme): even though there had been a series of events (61, 65, 73, 91, 93, 100) apparently bringing it to a logical conclusion in dissolution. And apparently even the so finally concluded dominant theme of the previous movement, the ox-theme, had not yielded its final resources, but had further consequences, *the »illuminations,«* which furnish the action of this 4th movement. The central imagery of this movement, that of luminous radiation, enlightenment perhaps, takes as its point of instigation the climax (96) of the preceding movement, besides suggesting, metaphorically, the dynamism of the rebirth. Again there is a formal, apparently final ending: a ceremonial, final departure of all the elements, including the musical one, of the ox-theme, a real wiping up, (103) and an emptied, inactive stage, not dark this time, though, but desolate (104), on which a curtain might very well fall, e.g., while the moon rises. The more so, since before this end the movement had formally progressed to a climax, and one tantamount to a kind of achievement (cf. 102) and even to a resolution of a conflict (cf. section II), of the conflict (if any), animating the preceding 3rd movement, all the elements of which now seem totally exhausted and done with.

This very notion/feeling of conclusion and exhaustion, however, provides the image, that of the collective *descent*, of the next, 5th, movement (104-108/9), with the transitionally dominant (cf. 104, 105) segregate presence of a previously also perhaps motive but integrated, subordinate element, the magician, providing an additional manner of continuity and resumption, and a metaphorical suggestion, again, of a dynamism of rebirth, the generation of creative energy by death and destruction. A stage setting (104) providing for the transformation of a mood of completion to one of anticipation (cf. III.79); a musical chord evokes the action of the previous movement (105); and the 5th movement moves from an upbeat prelude (105), to a dynamic visual climax and into a visually literal decline (106-7):

finishing off with, as it seems, everybody and notably all the images, figures and individuals of all the previous movements (106-8); and leaving the stage emptied, silenced and darkened (109), in as total a finale as some conventional dramas' concluding slaughter of protagonists.

But there is still another, and this time last, though this time, note, definitely not final (definitively last) movement (109/10-111/14), a movement of reascent, the very theme of which is *rebirth* or beginning-over-again, complementing and correcting the preceding movement's note of triumphant finality: as the 2nd, 3rd and 4th movements (8-103), revised the false ending (3-5) of the 1st movement (2-5). The prolonged maintenance before us of the »total finale« (109) changes our surfeit to unease, dramatic effects (110) – lighting, smoke – challenge the apparent triumph of death, a ground-swell of reanimation, in Darwinian terms, a potential re-peopling, moves into a powerful (dynamic) stasis (110), and concludes in a confrontation, visually (111) and musically (114) evoking the eternity of eternal return.

A false ending (110) is built into this last movement (109/10-111/14): the upward swing achieves itself in a still visual structure, evocative of commencement, visually analogous to and evoking the false beginning (3) built into the first movement (2-5): but annulled by a complementation (111) which clarifies that evocation and makes it explicit, modifying the impression of commencement into one of recommencement by the addition of the element of the return of the same.

79. The dimensions of a phenomenon depend on it. In the case of an artistic phenomenon, the artist sets up the general structure of perceptual experience.

80. This spectacle is in three dimensions: the depth-line of vision, along which our regarding and sympathy move inward and the energy of the performance and the symbolic inspiration outward; along which a second dimension moves laterally, a flat rectangular plane of vision, frame of the images at any moment; and time, the substantial space of this spectacle, in which it is contained, an extension in which still movement takes place, the future unfolding into successive presents.

81. The depth-dimension results not only from the stage being deep and relatively narrow, nor from the focus of the top of the pyramid in back, but from Wilson's choreography by transverse zones, from front to back, within which movements – largely cross stage – and images tend to be contained: our shifts of focus away correlate to

changes of imagery. Perhaps the impression of a linear depth-dimension is in part also brought about by two characteristics of the show: we look at isolated visibles; the inwardness, marginality, equivocality, ambiguity of performance and imagery force us to be searchingly active. Our attention seems a ray going to performers and images and generating the experience. Also, at the beginning, we follow a penetration into the scene (3), and toward the end (106-9), the scene is emptied by a vortex pulling from the rear. In between, the generating center of action seems to move gradually upstage: from the foreground themes of bins and table, to the boy's ascent, to the forest-origin of the ox, the scene finally becoming altogether the domain of the upstage forest. We feel an outward radiation toward us from the depth of the stage.

82. The plane of vision is real, not only because of the in-depth stratification of images, and because Wilson places them with a painterly reference to the solid frame of the stage, but because the performers' way of moving and their reduction to images make the images weightless, so that the vertical is not substantially different from the horizontal, but coalesces with it into a plane of situateness and indifferent availability. The stage floor does not appear as surface on which men act, nor the reaches of fly-space as that under which their smallness disports itself, characters in terms of which I imagine Tudor theatre rendered the vertical distinct. That we look at the show as onto a movie screen, albeit not a looming one, complements its powerful depth: the gentle shifts of the plane do not shatter the depth, for each has its own kind of reality, the depth that of movements of energy, the plane that of presence (of body movement, of imagery, of meaning). The lack of vector in the movements of the Wilsonian performers prevents their displacements from separating out the horizontal, and the bobbing body dips and pivoted limb spirals of their dancing do not resolve into horizontal and vertical components.

83. The spectacle's time does not move: motions, actions, developments lack the vectors of purpose, anxiety, drive. They and their world seem located with in its extended continuum. Instead of efficient causation by the previous, there is, on the one hand, growth toward fulfillment or actualization, whether approach to dissolution or to extinction or to attainment, on the other hand, repetition. In the former case, intrinsic unfoldings, in the latter, natural motion. We sense this time as presence and unbroken duration.

84. Wilson's theatre has a dream-like quality,

85. not attaching to the movie projected (40, 47, 72), strengthened by the contrast to the movie's realism;

86. though only one of its movements (8-77/79), and one of its sub-movement (3-5) present themselves with a suggestion that they are dreams or dream-like perceptions of reality (8-77/79) or dream-like fantasy (3-5), namely the central character's.

87. The dream-like quality is engendered partly by the presence of fantasy-elements (cf. II, 7, 11, 13; III, 28), partly by the way the performers move (III, 36-44), but mainly perhaps by the show's composition out of images (III, 22-9), its intimation of hidden, subjective unity, a fabricating ego (III, 9-18), or by its character of a world (III, 19-21), and by its organically discontinuous but resumptive manner of development (III, 75-8): though most of its other formal features are compatible with this impression, except perhaps the emergence of an individual central character and his story (III, 58-60), of »actual persons« (III, 61-2), and of performers as strong personalities (III, 34).

88. Perhaps (cf. II, 30), *DG* is thematically a dream of Robert Wilson's according to Freud.

89. Perhaps (III, 13-5, 63, 65), it is formally dream-like according to Jung's theory of dream symbolism.

90. Wilson's theatre is dream-like because it makes us suspend the reality principles of waking consciousness, substituting

  1. growth – suspension of the principle of efficient causation (cf. III, 59, 77)

  2. metamorphosis – suspension of the principles of discontinuity and uniformity

  3. multiple and abstract identity – suspension of the principles of substance and self-identity.

91. The apparent form of development(s) in the spectacle is the apparent form of growth: supervening on some static, apparently stable condition of life in a given form, which it breaks out of; not instigated or determined by anterior or external conditions, but by inner tendencies to maintain or achieve some form: not inexorable tendencies, but tendencies of greater or lesser and of varying energy; growing and waning in some natural rhythm; issuing, after some epiphanies of form, into degeneration and extinction; both those epiphanies and that extinction taking the form of metamorphosis. The hallucinations of sleep grow like plants.

92. In waking perception, the ego forms its objects according to principles of discontinuity and uniformity. It isolates something from

anything different from it, whether in its place at another time, or in some other place, by assuming an intervening, continuing series of qualitatively self-identical matters of fact which by their variation lead from one to the other and the variation of which is subject to some single set of laws of nature – governing all neighborings and changes. For each waking perception we assume a world transcending it of which the perceived is part; and assume this world is uniform. Thus we don't see a wall until we have supplemented an unseen house that makes it a wall; and we perceive the house by supplementing the house just before and during the instants just ahead in a way that really makes it a house. Waking perception thus never perceives anything changing – in space or in time. Its world is discontinuous. And when it perceives serial variety that is unfamiliar, it *assumes* its conformity to universal uniformity – that it is a case out of a single repertory of possible variations in space and time; and construes the objects perceived accordingly, as well as it may.

93. But in dreams and in Wilson's theatre, the changes and neighborings of situations, things, figures and acts are experienced as natural to them and to them only, without invocation of a single world in which things happen uniformly and by failing to assume that before something can be something else it must have ceased to be what it is, we perceive things changing into other things. From moment to moment and place to place one form goes into and turns out another.

94. Sometimes this is done by analogues of film camera tricks, e.g., the pink angle blending out into the magician (4), the rock carrier into a glass carrier (37). The transition from the jail cell into the park landscape by the advance through the rising curtain (3) or the transformation of the park into forest (8), but even the disappearance of the bins (99), the table (103) or the hut (81) are of this sort. So are the juxtapositions of ordinary and fantastic images within one scene and the fantastic touches to the ordinary images, but more importantly, so are quite often if not always the transition from one image or figure to another: they merge with, emerge from others. Similarly for the development of a given image or figure – cf. e.g., II, II re the table-image: a dinner party metamorphoses into and out of a judicial tribunal, or into the common room of an insane asylum. The development of the whole spectacle is of this sort: subsidiary images or theses or latent aspects of theirs in one movement becoming dominant in the next, so that any one of the movements is apt at some point of its development to take on the aspect

of a metamorphosis of its predecessor, especially when visual or thematic analogues give us a sentiment of modified recurrence, e.g., the different deaths (2, 44, 96), or the musical assemblies (3, 110). We are rendered susceptible to metamorphosis by the performers' way of moving (III, 38a) and by the staging technique of marginal and equivocal presentation (III, 58-61, but especially 63 and 66).

95. For waking consciousness, the sense of being impressed by an independent reality (things) translates into the necessary self-identity of its objects of experience. The real things have to be what they are and nothing else, since otherwise there would be no reality, and the same applies to their appearance as our objects of experience, since otherwise sensory certainty would not be justified. To justify our sense of being impressed by an independent reality, we therefore assume that the variations of experience in the spatial and temporal continua can be broken down into qualitatively self-identical discrete states constituting or characterizing »objects at a moment,« and consider our actual experience an approach to an experience of these. For the same reason, we attribute to objects of experience a minimal completeness even in cases where actual experience does not positively warrant this, namely that they all have all the qualities entailed by that minimal set of the (real) properties of (real) things requisite for the being and for the appearance of those (real) things.

96. Sleeping consciousness, on the other hand, (quite properly) not underpinning its experiences with a realist metaphysics, consistently perceives either potentially or actually over-determined objects, and frequently under-determined ones. By objects, I mean individuals, acts, events or situations. By over-determination I mean one of three modes of non-identity of (dreamt) objects: non-exclusive identity, multiple identity or specific non-self-identity. By under-determination I mean deficient identity, some degree of indeterminacy.

97. When I meet my father in a dream, I have no doubt of his identity, but at the same time, there is nothing about my identification that would preclude that figure from not only being something else, but from not being my father. Sometimes this may go so far that we actually experience a dream object as being some individual and also another individual or as doing something and also doing something else instead incompatible with it. More often, perhaps, we only feel that whatever the object is, it is not necessarily only that, it is possibly also something else, it is possibly also not that. Thus, when in the further course of dreaming, it turns into or turns out to be something else, we sometimes feel it has changed and has become

that, but at other times, that it was that right along, even before. Sometimes, of course, also, we are not sure of what something is in a dream – which individual, what gesture or situation, what kind of thing, – we are in doubt, and may be hesitating between mutually exclusive identifications. But this is something else, and I do not think that all dream situations of 1) non-necessary only-that-ness, 2) that-and-something-else-ness, 3) that-and-not-that-ness are of this sort. Rather there are some in which the individual object itself has one of these characters of on the one hand identity, single or multiple, on the other non-identity with itself. Dreamt objects are not necessarily self-identical. And if something in the course of further dreaming without apparent metamorphosis turns out to have been something else, we may of course sometimes have a feeling that we were mistaken in our previous identification (even if previously we were sure), but there are also occasions on which we do not feel so, but simply accept it that that individual object, act or event or situation was and was not such and so.

In waking experience also the nature of an object is often not evident, we do not know quite what it is (what is happening, what that person is doing, what the situation is), can not identify it, or suspect or realize that it has aspects which we are unaware of. But in such cases, we instantaneously assume that the reason for this objective indeterminacy is our ignorance, some deficiency in our perception, or perhaps an inadequacy of the conditions of perception. In sleeping awareness, on the other hand, we accept it as intrinsic to the object: we do not presume that the object is in any general sense necessarily completely determinate; we do without standards of object completeness. Of course, there are also in dreams situations in which we figure that there is something in or about the object that we are missing, but that is there: but this does not, I believe, exhaust all cases of this sort. E.g. a dreamt object may be shapeless.

98. The images and figures of dreams and those created for us by Bob Wilson and his performers seem to me to be of this sort. Whereas conventional theatre so fashions the appearances acted out as to suggest real people whose appearances they are and to which, through the appearances, we are to relate, Wilson's theatre makes us relate to the appearances created only: in themselves, as phenomena; and so fashions them that we perceive them as possibly other alternatives, intrinsically ambiguous, of multiple identity, non-self-identical, as definitely incomplete and inconsistent.

99. The performers have not been told what their characters are nor

what their gestures mean, nor of any role in any plot, and their sessions and rehearsals with Wilson were such as to tend to make them appreciative of these mysteries, and to resist their inclinations to provide meanings of their own by which to give nuances to their performances which would make these signify (real persons with definite identities). They have been given very little to do and that simple. Their costuming is neither individualizing nor typifying, but abstract; obscure or mysterious; or suited for an occasion. There is virtually no speech. The result is that we relate to images and figures real as appearances and as appearances only: ostentatiously abstract (indeterminate), yet full of alternative meanings.

# Robert Wilson as performer, notably in *Overture* (1972).[71]

The Byrds did *Overture*, from 6 to 9 in the morning and from 6 to 9 at night, every day from April 30th 1972 as part of a one-week open house. The full title was *Overture for Ka Mountain and Gardenia Terrace, a story about a family and some people changing*: it was an overture to *Ka Mountain* etc., the one-week show done in September of that year in Shiraz, in Persia. But it was perhaps also conceived as an Opening for everyone, a week of Whitsundays. It took place at the School of Byrds' three loft floors on Spring Street in Manhattan. At lunch time, food in the style of a different country was served free each day to all comers in the basement. The greater part of Wilson's living loft on the second floor, arranged with flowers, cushions on the floor and low tables on which were drawings and writings by members of the Byrds family, stayed open as a reading room and meditation space. The street level had with much labor from the Byrds been redone into a sparsely elegant sanctum, the monastic chapel or temple space of a Buddhist order. There was a grid of birch trunks in the square entry, the floor of which was covered with sand. In the main rectangular space beyond in which the performances were given, glassed candles had been placed around the edges of the polished floor, an array of cushion strips near the entry, orphic screens executed by Ann Wilson along the longer walls. Between performances this was a gallery. No admission was charged for any of this, but as there was room for only 30 to 40 people to attend the performances, those who had made reservations were given first entry to these. More people came, even for the dawn performances, than there was room for.

The morning performances, which varied from day to day, were loosely structured, reading, dancing, music, recitation, different individuals doing what they had become good at, with intervals, some as long as 20 minutes, inviting meditation or contemplation, – no tableaux or story-like actions. The evening program, which was, so to speak, *Overture* itself, had been prepared in detail, was always more or less the same sequence of about 24 events, presented as sequential parts of a developing whole.

The center of both shows, but intensely of the evening show, was a

71 I wrote this in 1974.

varnished, pegged wooden pyramid, about 8 feet high, close to the inside end of the room. It was cut off at the top and open, like a volcano, and had a low rectangular entrance in front. Suspended above it there were three live lights, a medium-size turtle, a large egg. Through the entrance, three burning candles and a square of light in the floor were visible. There was also a Chinese temple bell, borrowed from a Chinatown museum, sounded three times to signal the beginning of the show, neither it nor the person sounding it visible from the outside. The square of light was an opening cut into the floor from which a large funnel led to a small cabinet constructed in the basement. The source of light was a projector on the floor of this cabinet, and the light travelled upward through three increasingly large plexiglass plates invisible to the spectators, inserted in the funnel, on each of which had been traced the plan of a city, Piranesi's map of ancient Rome, a mad jumble of temple- and palace-sites, a map of the grid of Manhatten, pattern of abstract regulation, and, uppermost, Paolo Soleri's solar city, »city in the image of man.« Wilson had had this image of an old man reading in an underground chamber, and the image grew till his voice travelled up through the great cities, the city of the past, the city of the present, the city of the future. He had asked the dance critic and poet Edwin Denby to read, but in the end Denby was aboveground in the show (at times reading from Nijinsky's autobiography), and Wilson, seated on a crate in the cabinet, spoke, chanted and declaimed, his voice coming out of the house of the dead, which, when the room was dark, glowed coolly.

A little to the front of the pyramid, a wide, transparent scrim screen, whith the skeleton of a huge tiny-headed dinosaur outlined on it in white, hung rolled up just under the ceiling. The screen was unrolled twice during the evening show: the roll lowered to the floor and untaped by Ann Wilson's small compact twin girls, rushing out, working at high speed, and then the unrolling screen hoisted: once a little ways into the show, after some humming from the group and after Mrs. Hamilton, Wilson's grandmother, had come out and spoken briefly about her marriage, her grandchildren, her lonely life since her husband died, and then again a little after the intermission, for an act with an onion that Wilson did with Sheryl Sutton. Each time it was struck again, by the reverse procedure, the first time almost immediately, the second time after a little while. It thus acted as a delayed curtain: a non-curtain, lowered rather than raised. A veiling of the secrets of the pyramid. Much of our preparation for the show had revolved around the term »dinosaur« and the image.

We would silently concentrate on either, concentrate on the image and perhaps mentally compound it with other images or do movements at the same time, chant the term, varying it, recite »the dying dinosaur,« »the dinosaur soars, is soaring, soaring, soaring,« »the dinosaur is dying« in chorus, singly or in several voices, dance to the choruses . . .

Though diversity of personality, that within the group, gave the show its texture, it turned out a cloak of serenity for Robert Wilson. The pyramid was the heart of the show and it was the house of Wilson's voice. When he came on in body, for a dance and for that onion act, as when he spoke, the intensity of the images rose dramatically and the disturbance of challenge entered the (consistently handsome) esthetics.

Wilson seemed to speak when the spirit moved him and/or when the aural picture seemed to require it, but most evenings, once soon after the beginning of the show, – overlapping with the preceding act, Cynthia Lubar's Latinate automatic or prayer-mill recitation of what member of the group was doing what in the show, and the following, Andy DeGroat's Sufi-esque twirling, magnifying glass in hand, – and then again once near, and once at the end. At times counterpoint, the voice would at times emerge as solo oracle:[72]

11/14/71

DIANA DIENA KAASOWRD

THE DINA DYE KNEE THE DINA
DYE EYE THE DINA DIE DIE
DIEING DINA SORE SORE SORE
THE DINA DYE KNEE THE DINA
DYE EYE THE DINA DIE IHE
DIEING DINA SORE SORE SOWRDS!
THE DINA DINA SORE SORE SOWRDS.
THE DIE DINA DIE DIE DYING

72 The following is a text that Wilson wrote October-November 1971 in a mountain cabin in Crescent Spur, B.C., Canada. I take it from a notebook in which it is preceded by 6 pages of notes on writing in which Wilson seems to be feeling his way from *Deafman Glance* to *Ka Mountain*. His recitations during *Overture* may have included some additional material, probably varied this material, probably repeated parts of it. But he had prepared a reading of it: I heard him read it soon after he returned from British Columbia, before the group started its work toward *Overture*.

DIE DIE DINA SORE DIE DINA
DINA SORE SORE SOWRDS
SOWRING SOWRDING THE T DIE
DINA SORE'S SORES SOWRDING
THE DIE KNEE SEE US YOU ALL
US THE DIEING DINAS SORE SOWRDS!
THE DINASTOR THE DINASTORE STORES THE DINKNEE SEEUS
DINESEUS DINESEUS DINESEUS
THE DIANA DIENA KAASOWRD THE DIEING DIENASORE

11/14/71

THE OVER REVERBARATIONS THE BODY
JESTICULATE A LAYERING A RING, A LING
A DING THE OVERREVERBATIONS
THE BODY OVERREVERBERATION A ZATION
REVERBALIZATION A NATION REVERBARAT
ING A RATIONING OF ALL NATIONS
THE BODEEE REVERBATES
THE JESTICULATE A LAYERING VIBRATES
A RING A LAYER ANOTHER JESTICULATING
ANOTHE LAYER LAYERING I SING
THE BODY OVER OVER OVER
OVER REA REA REA REA VIB
THE BODEEE JESTICULATE A
LAYERING ARING A LING
THE BODY JESTUKLE YOU LATES
A LAYER THEN RINGS THE
OVER RE BA RATION THE BODEEE
REVERBATION A NATION RATIONING
CATIONING THE BODY JESTICULATE
A LAYERING RING SINGING

11/14/71

THE WIZARD TAPE OF CANADA NOBODY
IS WRITING IT DOWN WE GO BEFORE WE
GO YOU GO YOUGOSLAVE VEE WE GO
UP. YOUGOSLAV WE ALL US WE GO
YOUGOSLAVEVA THE BODY JESTICKLE
YOU LATESA LAYERING RING UNI UNIN
UNIN UNISON SUNS SUNS THE
WIZARDS TAPPING TAPEING IT ALL

DOWN WE GO BEFORE WE GO UP
YOU GO WE GO YOU GO SLAVE
SLAVING YOU GO SLAV YOU GO
WE GO RINGING SINGINGALINGING
ALING A DING RIGHT NOW RIGHT
THE WIZ THE WIZ BANG GO
THE WIZ BANG GO BANGO MEDE-
ATION OF NATION DIE MEDDEE
ATION METTA METTRANSLATION
THE METRANSLATION A LAYERING
THE META TRANS MU TATIONING
OF METTA TRANSULATING A
LAYERING, THE MAN INTO HIS

11/14/71

PARTS PARTICULAR THE MAN SLICING
THE ONION AS THEY DO AS DO
THEY DO AN ARTIST PAINTING A
PICTURE A MONSTER WORLD
TRANSMIGRATES AS THE BODY JESTICKLE
YOU LATES A LAYERING A RING
THE BODY JESTICKLE YOU LATES
ERRUPTING ENTERING REERURRUPTING
THE ABSENCE OF SELF IN EVERYTHING

MYRAMID A WHIRLING LING A
MYRAMID A WHIRING WHIRLING

11/14/71

A WHIRLING WERELD WHIRLING
WERELD POOL WE'RE ALL
POOPED WHIRL POOL POOLING
WHIRLING RINGING SINGING
RINGING WHIRLING LINGING
SINGING A WERE LD WHERELLY
WHERE WHEN A MAP THERE'S
A MAP OF THE WORLD. A DINASORE
TRACK
A MOUNTAIN ERRUPTS, EEEE
RURU RU RU RU RU RUPTING
ERRUPTING A MOUNTAIN EVOLVING
EEEU ROPE EAN CITY

EMERGES AGES OF ALL
PEOPLE TOGETHER IT IS AS
CALM AS WATER WA RUT
WA WA WACO, TEX, TEX, TEX.
WE ARE WIERDPOOLING WORD
POOLIN PULLING WORDS
POOING A WHIRLING
WHIRLY BIRD WHIRLES A
MOUNTAIN SWRILS SPIRALS
AND SPIRALS WRITUYING
MOUNTAINS SWRILLING
RINGING RING A MOUNTAIN
S CAPTIVACING A VACANT
EXTRA RA JA RI KATEING
EXTRA RA JA YA MIRAGA
JA A KA KA KATING
EPSPUNICATION ESPUNINACTION
CATION ALL OVER THE OVER
REVERBABARA VARLA LOU
LOU LOO LOO LOOKOATION
CATIONING CATIONING CAUSION
SUN ONE A MOUNTAIN
SPIRUS WINGS AND WINGS
OF SMOKING MOUNTAINS
SWIRL WHRILING WORLD
POOL WORLD PULL
WERD (WEIRD?) PERPLE
MY IDA EYES VIBRATE MY IDA'S
EYES WAVE WAVERING UP AND
DOWN VIB A VA I VAB 2, 3, 4
VAB A A A MY IDA YOUR
IDA DA DA DO MY IDA
DA DA DO YOU MY IDA
IDEALYEYES ISEYESEUING VA
VA VA VA VA THE DINING
THE DINNIEASIAS THE DINA
THE DINE KNEE SEE US THE
THE DINA THE EYES THE
UI THE UI THE UI THE
UII IIIIII IN III
THE WAVERING MOUERING

RING MOUERING VERTICAL
HORIZONTAL STIMULUS
WAVES WAVERING VIBA
THERE IS THAT IN HIM THAT MAKES
HIM HIM — THERE IS THAT IN HIM
IN HYMNS — THERE THAT
IN HIM THAT RING THAT MAKES
THERE IS THOUST IN HIM THER
IS THOART THO ART THO ART
THERE IS THAT IS IN HIM
THAT MAKES US SING THERE
IS THAT WE SEE THAT MAKES
US SEE THERE IS THAT
THO MASTICS US

11/28/71

THERE IS THIS ELECRA WHEEL
WEEALS WHEEL WHEELS
WHEELS — SO THAT WE CAN
HEAR SO THAT WE CAN HEAR
TO EAST IS CHINA TO SO. AFRICA
THE WEST AMERICA TO NORTH RUSSIA
BODY ALIGNMENT

THE PINE TREE IS THE KEY
AND THE PINE TREE TURNS
AROUND
KA MT.

NOV. 30, 1971    CRESCENT —

THE URBANIZATION OF NATIONS-A
SUN CITY THE URBANIZATION OF
NATIONS A SUN CITY THE JESTER
JESTICULATES THE URBANIZATION OF
NATIONS CATTERING THE EARTH
IMPRISONED THE EARTH IS IN
PRISION. A EUROPEAN CITY
EMERGES CATIONING NATIONING
LANDRISING TO A SON, A MOTHER
TO US ALL A SON, A SUN
CITY EMERGING ELECTROWAVEN
ELECTRIC TEAGRAMS WE GO DOWN

147

WE GO DOWN ELECTRIC DOA
GRAMS EMERGING A FORMLA
LATENING LAYERING THE OX IS
INSIDE INSIDE THE TURTLE CARRYING
US ALL BACK BACKING BACKWARD
YEARING A THOUSAND AND ARTIC
BOAT APPEARETH AN ARTIC
EGYPTIANING A BOAT A MAN A
ANAMAL BIRDS CIRCLING FIRE
ESCAPING THE LAMB THE LAMB
THE CHILD BECOMES BECOMING
ICE EYES E E ELECTRICCHARGED EEEECC
C C ELECTROCITY SILLI SILOGGAGRAM
THE OVERREVERBERATION
BACKELECTRICTROSICITYEYS
LOCKED THE EARTH THEY DID, THEY
DID THEY DID DID DID DID.
USE WRITING ON RECORD
THE KA AND WRITING
THE OLD MAN COMES FROM THE BOX
AND READS (ME HIS WRITING FROM A
BOOK ON A TABLE WITH A CANDLE
BURNING — VOICE MIKED

A CITY OF LIGHT OF CRISNING LIGHT
ELECTAOLOSEETROSUNCITYOVOST
ASIZENEARINGRINGING AND
SINGING SIN CITY SUNK!

11/30/71

THE OLD MAN SITS BY THE TABLE READING
TO ME FROM HIS BOOK MAKING
HIS WAY BACK TO NEW YORK CITY
73    (I AM I SAID TO KNOW THERE AND
NO ONE HEARD IT NOT EVEN THE
CHAIR I AM I SAID AND I'M
LOST AND CAN'T SAY WHY, BUT
IN LONELY STILL — DID YOU EVER
READ ABOUT THE FROG WHO DREAMED
OF BECOMING A KING AND THEN

73 Text in parentheses (8 lines) crossed out in Wilson's notebook.

148

BECAME ONE HE'S NOT A MAN) HE
SAID ALL DAY WITH HIS BOOK THE
OLD MAN READS TO ME HE IS THREE CAMELS
SIDE BY SIDE CROSSING ALL DAY THE
THREE CAMELS READ WE SEE THE
OVER REBA VA VABATIONS CATIONING ALL
OVER ALSO THEY TOO ELECTROCITY ELECTROS
SITY ELECTROSITY A SUN CITY A
SANCITY ILLUMINATED ILL WILLING
NUS AGREED TO START TO LEAVE WE'RE
ON A SLOW BOAT TO THE EAST IS
CHINA THE SOUTH IS AFRICA AND
TO THE WEST IS AMERICAN AND TO THE
NORTH IS RUSSIA BODY A LINED
ELECTROTOTICTATIC ACTING ILLUMINATED
WILLING NOT LEAVING THE CAMELS
NOR THE OLD MAN WE PREPARE TO
LEAVING WE'RE BEHIND NEARING
YEARING THOUSANDING BLASTING AN
ARTIC EGYPTIAN ALAS ALAS
A PINER ROSE A PINK ROSE IN
A GLASS A UNDERWATER
A BLUE A TEMPLE A GERAFFE IN
A BOAT THE OLD MAN IN THE
BOX.

11/30/71

DUNCAN SITS AT THE TABLE. WE'RE EATING
ROAST BEEF ANDY LIT A CANDLE
JESSIE DANCED AND RAYMOND SANG
AND PLAYED HIS GUITAR ROBERT WENT
TO THE MOUNTAINS AND ANN TO HELP SOMEONE AGAIN
CINDY SINGS SK'S A MOTHER, MARY PEER'S
A MOTHER, I AM FATHER THERE IS A
SUN, THE EARTH IS IN PRISION A
COLD PLANET, AND SUNDAY IS
THE SEVENTH DAY A SUN DAY
WE REST METTA TRANSLATING REVERBATEOUS
CAUTIONS TO THE ELECTROCONSTATICALLY
CONTROL OF THE REVERIBLWILLINGCONCONICALY
WITH EASE OF MOTION

THERE IS THAT THAT IS IN HIM
IN HIM IN HIM IN HIM THERE IS
THAT THAT IS IN HIM MAKING HER
SING CINDY SINGS. THE BIRDS
SING SING THEY RING AS CINDY
SINGS AS KIT AND CINDY SING AN
ANCIENT EGYPTIANING BOAT LANDING
UNDERYOU WAITING UNULATERLAYERING
SKULLS AND SINGS CINDY SINGS KITT
SINGING EGYPTIANING BOAT
A LIVEING A TRIANGLE AHEAD
THE SUN THE FATHER, THE STARS
THE MOTHER, THE LITTLE GIRLS, THE DAMM THE
EARTH IS IN PRISION STAY HIGH
FOREVER IN HIM THERE IS THAT
IN THEM WHEN THEY SING
THERE IS PIERRE THERE IS AIR THERE
(ARE THAT THAT SORE PIERRE PLAYS THE
VIOLIN AND DANCES WHILE HE)[74]
PLAYS MANY SOUNDS AT ONCE LAYING
TO (?) YOU THAT PHYSICALLY
WIRERLERRING INSTANTLY WIRERLERRING

11/30/71

RING WE ALL SING THE EARTH
IS A COLD PLANET THE SUN THE MOON
THE STARS MARS SUNDAY SUNDAY SUN CITY
CITY OF LIGHTROELECTROELECTRACICITY
LIGHTROLICELECTROLLOCITY EXTROLLACITY
EXTRALAVAAGRAMSOCITY CITIES OF
LIGHT BARELY A TRACE OF RACE
WE'PON A SHIP A ISLAND IN THE

SKIES THE WOUNDED STAG ON THE
HILL IGOR SPLITS TAPES IT ALL
DOWN, IGOR IS ALL DOWN WHEN WE'RE
UP AND HE UP WHEN WE'RE
ALL DOWN WE GO UP WITH IGOR
BY STAGE, BY STAGE, BY STAGE

74 Text in parentheses struck out in Wilson's notebook.

A STAGING A MANAGER ONION
LAYERED BY STAGE MANAGES


11/30/71

TO KEEP ALAN PLAYING ANN KEEPS
ALAN PLAYING THE PIANO AND PAINTING
WITH COLOR PICTURES AND COMPOSING
AN OLD IN A BOX THE
OLD MAN READS TO ME WITH
WHY IS THE EASE OF MOTION —

WE SING PRAISE OF THOSE WE KNOW
AS RAYMOND SIGNS GIVING SIGNS
SIGN BEARING ELECTRICALLY
CHARGED SINGING RELEASING
JESTICULATALAYERINGRINGING.


11/30/71

THE HOUSE OF DEAFMAN
KA MOUNTAIN AND GUARDINA
TERRACE A STORY ABOUT A
FAMILY AND SOME PEOPLE
CHANGING AND ABOUT THE
DYING DINA DIE KNEE SEE YOU
US SEE US DIEING DINA SORE.


NOV. 18, 1971    CRESCENT SPUR

ENDIGNATION INDIG US
NATION INDIGNATION IG NIGHT
TA LATE INGANATION
SIN GA SINGA SINGA
GERING SINGING THE
METTAATAAMMMMM MEAN
MEDA META SUATION
SIANT TRANSLATE A RING
A RING A BRAN
CYCLE LICK LICLIIC LICTING
THE OVERVERBATION THE
OVERREBATION! WHIZ GO
META TRANS MIGRATION
INDIGNATION ST. INDIGNATION!

ERRUPTERING WHIRLING,
WHIRLESLING LINGING

NOV. 19, 1971    CRESCENT SPUR B.C.

THE FISH ARE OUT OF THE WATER
AGADA THE FISH ARE OUT OF
THE WATER THE FISH ARE AGA
AGA NY KA AGA NIZ ANALEYE
S AA SYNTHEYZIN A GA NIZE
RECOGNIZ INDIGNOUS AGADA NIZING THE
FISH ARE OUT THE IT A CALM
ASA A WATER.

NOV. 19, 1971    CRESCENT SPUR B.C.

THE DIE KNEE NEW SORE
NEW YORK CITY KA KA
ERRUPTING AGA AGNIMNAM
NA PALMING KA GLIDER
REFLECTOR REVERBARATION
ERUPTING ERUPTS THE MOUNT
WHO SWIRLS SARAL AIR
ALL WITH A EUROPEAN
SIN CITY EMERGING KA
COM BI EYENING A
RING A EUROPE A YOU
ROPES A A JESTICLAT A
LAY A RING AGADIG
MA WE ARE ON A SLOW
BOAT TO THE EAST IS
CHINA TO SOUTH IS AFRICA
TO THE WEST IS AMERICA
TO THE NORTH IS RUSSIA
BODY A LINEMENT THE SOUIX
INDINAS LIVE ON THE CRESCENT
OF HILLS BODY ALINEMENT
I WENT TO DRUG STORE ON
A SUBWAY AND A BUS
BODY ALINES TO THE EAST
LIES CHINA TO THE SOUTH
IS AFRICA, TO THE WEST LIES

AMERICA AND TO THE NORTH
IS RUSSIA METTA TRANSLATION
LAYERING TRANSMITION OF
NATION THINGS GO SLAVE
TRANSLATE A LAYERING
THE MAN SLICES IN TWO
HIS PART THEN FOUR THE
EIGHT BEFORE THE NINTH COMES
ALINED A LING YOUING
VERBATIONS OF NATION CATTERING
TO THE TINEST SOME IN THEM
SUM SIGNIFICANT LINES
RINGING THE DANCES ANSWERS
1950 MIND VIBRATING ECO YOU GO
GU GU GU KA SINGS STILL
THE BODEEE CENTERING
RING SPIRLING EYES KAGLINDER
REFLECTING MAVING MOVING
SOUNDS 1970 AND THEN TOGETHER
FREQUENCY RACES TRACING RAISES
TO WORDS SPLIT UPON WORDS
RAZORING LAYERING SKID
RIDING WE ARE ALONG
ON A FIRE ESCAPING THE
GENERAL MAN IN TWO HIS
PARTS PARTICULAR KA
SINGS. AND KA RINGERING
THE HOT SUN THE COLD EARTH
HOUSE A SUN CITY A NAKED
MIND ELECTRIC TRICES
TRACES CITY FROM A FAR
ELECTON SUN ELECTION
INDIGNATION IGNITE, AND
MORE LIGHT SLICING THE
ELECSION RON RUN CO
CURRENTLY ALONE SIMALTANEOUS
PATHS ACROSS NOT ONLY
AGAMEDIA EARTH BUT
UNIVERSALLY LINK MAN
BEYOND A CLOUD OF EARTH
HOOVERING INTELLIGENCE

DOMINATION OF MEDIA
LINK TO STARTLING INTHRAL
ING LINK TO ELECSION
OF RON RUNNING TOGETHER
IN STOP AND GO ACTIONING
CATIONING YEARING 2,000.
THE SOUND NOW TRAVELS EASILY
UP AND DOWN AND FROM SIDE
TO SIDE SIMULTANIOUS VERB
ALING LAYERING WITHIN
EACH ALINEMENT TO THE EAST
IS CHINA THE THE SOUTH IS
AFRICA TO THE WEST IS
AMERICA TO THE NORTH
IS RUSSIA AND THEN FROM THERE (?)

AROUND A MAP OF THE WORLD
THE LAST WHOLE EARTH
DEPART PARTING. AN ARTIC
EGYPTANING TANING SINGING
A METTTTAAAAAAAAA TRANSLATE
LATE A RINGING COLATERALING
SIMULTANEOUSLY WITH THE
SIMPLE BODY JESTICULATION
IDA EYEING SIGNING
SLAVEING THE MAN
FALLS TO ERRUPTING A
WHIRLING WORLD POOLING,
SINGING SIGNING FINDING
A TRACK ARE DIEING DINA
EUROPEAN CITY REMERGE
AGES CALM AS WATER.
RAAAEYEIC 'S IDA AND
EYES AND HANDING TOGETHER
UP AND DOWN UP AND DOWN UP AND
DOWN AND AROUN AROUND
THE DIE NING THE DIE KNEE
THE DIE KNEE THE KEE

KEY THE OVERINGING VERVEB
ATIONS A A A GA GA INIGA
IN IN N N N N DIC DIDD DI

NIC NIC APLPH NATION NA
IS A NOTATATAIN THE THE
IN NIG NATION NASHOUS
SHOWING US JURYING INDIG
NATION META MEANA
METTA PATFATA — SLICING
IN THE MAN MANERERRRING
BRIMMING (?) OVER RAVER
RA REVERBATION INDIG
SIG NATION SAINT ST.
INDIGNATION ERRUPTING
THE OLD MAN YEARING
EYES EYEING. CRYING SIGNING
UP AND DOWN, HORIZONTALLY
AND ROUNDING SINGING

OCT. 15th 1971

THE KIT KAT KITTY KIT KATE'S KATE
A LATING KIT KIT KAT JESTICKUE
LATE A LAYER A RING A
LINE A KATE KIT KATE LATE
LAYERING

THE MAN INTO HIS PARTICULAR
LAYERING THE MAN INTO
HIS PARTICULATE A LAYERING
JESTERER KIT ER LAYERING
THE MAN INTO HIS PARTICULS
JESTERS THE OVER REVERBRATING
ORATE TERNING THE MAN
THE MAN THE CHILD, THE
THE CHILD THE THE THEE I SEE

THE MOTHER THE FATHER THE SON
THE JESTERERS JESTICKULATES
KATE OVER REVERBATIONS NATION
AND NATIONS OVER REVERBARATING
OVER REVER O OVER REVERBARATING
RATIONS, NATIONS, OVER REVERB
BA BA RA RA RATING
THE MAN.
THE MAN INTO HIS

THE MAN INTO HIS PART,
PARTICLATE A LAYERING
A RING A LING A DING
THE MAN INTO HIS PARTICULAR
SLICING THE ONION AS THEY
DO DO DOING IT OVER REVERB
BA RATING NATION
CATION CATIONING OVER
REVERBARATING JESTICULATING
OVER REVERBABABA
RATING JESTICULATING OVER
REVERBA BA RATIONS JESTICULATE
A LAYERING A LING ADING
A DIME AS WE MORE OR LESS
JESTICULATE ALATE ALATE
A DATE APRIL 5, 1986 A TAKE
A LATE A LAKE
THE BODY JESTICKLE YOU LATE
THE MAN INTO HIS PARTICULARS
JESTICULATES HIS.
THE MOTHER THE FATER THE SON
THE STAR THE MOON JESTERING
RING AND RATIONS CATION
AND NATION OVER RA
RE REVERB RE VERB
REVERB BA REVERB BA
REVERB A A A RATIONS, NATION
CATION OVER REVERBING RATING
RATIONS NATION OVERING A
RING. A RINGING ALL OVER.

He is plaiting idea-images. A thought content is swirling about, but the discursive connection, the weave of reason, once there and perhaps still somewhere, is gone. He is flying through intellectual space, from near one planetary concept to near another, zigzagging and swooping like a swallow or bat. The images of reason seem to exert on his zooming mind violent repulsive force making it swirl away: through layers and layers of LANGUAGE, His approach to each turns into a tumbling retreat through the word designating it. To connect with the idea, it seems, he had to use a word, – or made the mistake of trying to use words? – but the word resists his grasp. By language

or by his own prideful hankering after it kept out of the ideal world, he finds himself trapped in speech, and now finds the speech incompletable, – whether because completion in any direction would betray the pure intensity of the idea present to him as image, or because a power of reason curiously intrinsic to language keeps leading him away from the ideas he would hold, or whether because physiological physical laws of speech (language) qua reality of its own kind constrain him to move according to them. His experience is that of a pull exerted by the word-become-whirlpool, i.e. as a drowning: but on the other hand, apparently his thought or mind is in a »movement« such that often more than one thing or image of a thing is denoted at the same time, calling for several words simultaneously: if only because his thought or mind (and Wilson conceives of this as a condition common to all men) often tends in several »directions« at once: a tension which crucially qualifies its »movement« (process). To express (such) thought, words have to be compounded, or, in other words, the given, first or preponderating words distort themselves in the thinker's mouth to accomodate their rivals, either within themselves or as their linear successors. – Thought »reverberates« in »oververbation.« He leaps into a word, the word disintegrates, he stumbles linguistically out of the word, caught in a fandango of his vocal chords. He falls away again and again, through a disintegration of the word which will not stay whole. The whole term breaks under the weight of its artificiality: it is a bad sign, can't stand itself. The word develops itself, with solitary power and runs him, confined within it and undergoing its fate of phonic abrogation, down a path. Though confined and contorted within the sound, he is still leaping in futile attempts to grasp an overhead meaning. He has assumed its all too solid flesh. But he is still searching for an idea.
– But he has committed himself to verbal action, the making of meaningful sounds. These sounds engender other sounds for him, in him, by him. He is the inspired poet-chanter, his tongue dancing in the rhythmic blast from his throat, twisting itself into the successive shapes of sounds next to one another, now sliding out of one consonant into the next, now slipping out of one vowel into its variant. Again and again sound provides the inspiration of the sound production, but in spite of this auditory fixation, – an immersion in one dimension of bodily existence, a dance of the tongue, – he seems not only cognisant of meanings, but bent on intellectual effort (the finding or specification of truth), and even gives the impression of finding his phonation of phones intellectually productive. And again

and again, he abruptly extricates himself from the lingual whirlpools, wrenched out by force of thought, tho' echoes subsist. His word-association seems to seem to him if not positively illuminating, at least significant, cognitive in nature: as though the phonal vectors of phonal production had an inner correspondence to logic or to the relations perceived in wisdom, – which of course no more precludes ultimate failure than does reliance on logic or reliance on language as form of wisdom or of the search for it. Even when he is not declaiming in the manner of proclamation, he never drops the words as though in themselves insignificant, and the phones that are only parts of words, mean nothing, are uttered with a tone at least marginally either reminiscing or searching, as debris of names pronounced or as elements of names it is hoped will come, – and as steps in a process of affirmation. Again and again, in the reverberating progressions of chant or in the trajectories of pure or inarticulate sound, the reference to meaning is Robert Wilson, making an abstraction of himself in this certain direction. He is speaking out of an intellectual position. It is true that this intellectual position seems in his case to have taken the form of a fascination by certain images, – an image of himself: the jesting but cosmically aligned body of man which like an onion is nothing but a whole »j«esticulating in reverberations to a landscape of mountains spiralling like whirlpools, erupting volcanoes, perhaps hailing the approach of the (apocalyptic?) year 2000, but singing, ringing while seeing a pine tree still as water, far from a large city, New York or the city of Europe, a sinful electrostatic city, city of light, perhaps the city of the sun? all on the cold, cardinally divided prison island of the earth, a cloud in the sun's light; – the image of the boat of the dead of the Egyptians and the image of time as a backwards and forwards yearing; – the image of an old man at a table inside a box reading to him from a book, this image shifting into that of 3 camels (or perhaps that of the approach of the gift-bearing magi). The images image process: everything is process: the sound of language reports the vibrations of electicity/light, the thinking body vibrates with a cosmic explosive energy. Thus the gerundial flourishes. Perhaps the venture into speech was to carry from the images to ideas? The images make much sense. His tone indicates that they are not mere images nor in themselves all that he speaks of, but, themselves a language alternative to verbal language, are to be taken as vehicles of truth, means of affirmation, thus ipso facto as means and signs of thought if not themselves thought. They are evoked as affirmations of something in the nature of knowledge, and the manner of their succession sometimes suggests analysis, sometimes demonstration, and sometimes even a story, and the concrete play of the vocal organs, moving, though there is a man's passion (indignation?) also, with some of the autonomy of these organs of the body, sound like episodes of the whole.

The performance thus seems to illustrate the assumption that meaning is intrinsic to the body's sounding, – the bodies of the race that selected the sounds for discourse in a family of languages and the body of the individual. And not only meaning, but truth: whether the truth of experience or a resident wisdom of the body. In some ways the man seems simply to be stuttering, stuck, in others to be playing off linguistic production against a pre-existing fund of discursive thought in image-form. But there still emerges some such idea as that the body's authentic expression of itself is the original and even the only avenue to insight, – intellection and its expression furnishing at best distortions or pale reflects. The performance obliquely balances this idea against the other one, that verbal discourse cannot adequately provide or express insight.

Of course we can't make much sense of what he is saying. We hear speech slipping into and again out of non-verbal sound.

His discourse is discontinuous. It stops. He stands there, empty-looking, lost-looking. He's still very much there. He doesn't fade out. But he is not doing anything, inside or out. When the next thing comes upon him, he instantaneously goes into it. There are no transitions. Yet these interruptions do not disrupt. Nor do the sudden collapses, the sudden take-offs. A line of energy is continuous even tho the action is not. New gestures are delivered with an air of absolute spontaneity out of a momentary total suspension of all activity. They do not refer to the precedent tone.

Wilson's recitation much of the time has the form of terrible passion. It's a sound picture of terrible effort: anguish, strain, an effort, *made* obvious, to shape sounds, wilfully distorted incantations, the wilfullness made explicit. The stops and starts suggest the speaker hates to say what he is bound to utter and hates what he has just said. It may be a bodily voice or a voice making itself body, but there is someone else there, not entirely cooperative. There are *experiments* with sound: »is this right?«

Again and again there is a note of satire, of an actor's activity of forming. It's the picture of a man in private, talking to, for himself, unafraid of expressing his irony toward himself, even his hatred of himself. Most of the tones are squeezed, hoarse. Consistently speaking with an air of great overbearing authority, he sometimes seems to be announcing an important message: and recurrently issues into gibberish. He is speaking in tongues as though the voice came into him from elsewhere and he was made to speak or was spoken. It has been written that »Therefore is the name of it called Babel; because the Lord did there confound the language of all the earth: and from thence did scatter them abroad upon the face of all the earth« (Gen. XI, 9). But also:

> And there were dwelling at Jerusalem Jews, devout men out of every nation under heaven. Now when this was noised abroad, the multitude came together and were confounded, because that every man heard them speak in his own language ... Parthians and Medes, ... Cretes and Arabians, we do hear them speak in our tongues the wonderful works of God. (Acts, II, 5-11)

Whereupon Peter preached to them the word of God out of Joel:

> And it shall come to pass in the last days that I will pour out my spirit upon all flesh: and your old men shall dream dreams: And on my servants and on my handmaidens I will pour out in those days of my spirit; ... And I will shew wonders in heaven above, and signs in the earth beneath; blood, and fire, and vapour of smoke; The sun shall be turned into darkness, and the moon into blood, before that great and notable day of the Lord come: And ... whosever shall call on the name of the Lord shall be delivered. (Joel, II, 28-32)

Wilson's mode of delivery varied, but in the main, a taking language back to the animalic, or, further, to the sounding organs' kind of sound alternated with an actor's or rhetorician's oratory: the two extremes at which meaning disintegrates, though affirmation is at its highest. Now Faust sets his vocal parts free and dares them go the limit: now Don Juan sweats in silence under the heavy leather mask of ambiguity and pretense, pointing to himself with dislike.[75]

75 Wilson shifts between the two analogous extremes in his visual stage-appearances: magician of high solemnity, figure of affective abandon (e.g. the tragic Greek torn-open mouth on the head jerked into profile parallel to the crookedly extended arm, the mouth that we also know from the horse in Picasso's *Guernica*). In between he appears as »himself,« quiet, suavely modest, eminently in compos mentis, – and handsome. Handsome in a respectable way. The kind of good looks that appeal to ladies. He may be wearing a conservatively slim dark smart suit, white shirt and tie. Do we see a fleeting smile? Not exactly: a *fixed* smile appears fleetingly. It shakes the image, which is shaky. – He is announcing the play, say *The Life and Times of Joseph Stalin*. Having come on as alter ego of a magician, tall as he, disappearing as he enters in the same place, he begins to speak. His voice fails him. Making the appropriate accompanying gestures with his left arm

An apparent *absence* of meaning, the detritus of reflexion that can't get going, scraps of phrases to which the utterer attempts to lend the importance of high significance without being able to specify this significance, and unsure of whether it is there, allowing his uncertainty to pierce through — deteriorate into sound and fury signifying nothing, into what for the speaker himself can't be but pure sound. It goes something like this:[76]

... »dine ... dine ... dina ... a map of the world ... a whirly-bird ... whirly whirly whirly ... a mountain whirls, whirls, spirals ... dyne ... dyna ... (growls) ... soar ... soar ... soaring ... the dyna, the dyne ... soars ... (very high, squeaky voice) (long pause) (all this under Cindy's Latinate, totally mechanical reading) ... gesticulate a layering a ga ring (high whining voice) (incomprehensible talk in a very high voice) ... immediation of nations ... meda meda meda ree (you can't tell what the fuck he is talking about) ... there is a map of the world and a dinosaur track- ka (very sharply three times:) ka ka ka ... a mountain erupts ... Waco, Texas ... Tex ... we are ... whirly ... whirly mountain whirling whirling ... an ancient Egyptian boat landing under you ... there is that that is in him .. there is that there is in them ... (the tone becomes surprised, but as though he is putting you on, then snidely arrogant) ... dine see you us? ... dine see you all us? ... the overreverberations (pretentiously bombastically) ... the body gesticulat-ing ... layering (holding the »ing« on a note, his voice vibrating) ... the urbanisation of nations ... a European city emerging ... sun city ... the old man sits by the table reading to me from his book ... the organisation of nations. the sun city ... the pine tree is the key and the pine tree turns around ... a sun city illuminates us willing agreed ... agreed. the urbanisa-tion of nations ... electro-city ... electracity ... electricity ... the old man in the box ... (with an air of great authority, also elsewhere used:) the over-reverberrations, the body gesticulating ... we are on a slow boat to ... the general, the genera ..., the general man into his particular parts ... (sneers:) part II, a comedy .... (continues as though enumerating, in a tone of an attempt at giving an exhaustive inventory (of variant sounds or words): with the severity of one speaking unpopular truths or fulfilling an onerous and weighty obligation ... then tones of harsh impatience ...)

The ravings from the underworld seemed to me to put the soaring

and hand, he mouths some words but nothing is heard. The announcement is then presented reasonably and audibly, and with the courtesy due the public, tho it is a little bombastic in places. But there are some off-tones and we notice that his right hand is silvered. He has somehow skipped the »of« of the title, — we have an intimation of anxiety, of the predicament of mutes. The »Joseph Stalin« comes out a little harshly, in a Slavic accent. Everything has come off all right, though, on the whole. As he leaves, there is an odd quirk of his head. The slips of nor-malcy into bombast have not exactly been redeemed by such glimpses of debility.

76 Snatches of different declamations Wilson did during the week.

and dying dinosaur, link in evolution, destined for extinction, into a parallel to modern multiplying urbanisating humanity: fated for self-destruction or capable of unification?

Wilson's dance was done with Liz Pasquale, then Liz Denis, Galasso, one of the group's beautiful untiring girl dancers (the other being Julia Busto), then in normal intercourse and in the image of her dancing a sweet lovely innocent slip of a girl, a little bird. During the group's Persian tour she fell apart, her flesh became heavy and cold as that of a Lesbian, and she steered it wilfully through its awkwardness, exercising force. But she danced her way through this phase and now danced as beautifully as before, and as easily, but powerfully, in a warm womanly way, though she was as scrawny as ever (a veritable Eve when she danced nude with her husband), with touches of wildness in large leaps. She prefaced her dance by an obeisance to the pyramid, perhaps a truncated yoga greeting of the sun, presumed beneath it. To piano chords from the choir loft, she danced by herself with an ever so charming lightness and fluidity. By some paradox of her time, her girlish awkwardness transmuted into grace of childhood. She floated off the floor, hands flying with her slender curving arms, an easy flow of energy all the way, never ahead of herself, dipping and turning surrounded by the curvilinear arabesques of her arms. Wilson came on in a bum's slouch hat and red pants, the music changing to *Dark Town Strutters' Ball* or the Moms and Dads' *Silver Moon* from the tape, white gardening gloves on his hands. He's the ever unfortunate suitor, sentimental and clumsy. We think we know him from Chaplin's early poignant shorts. He is moving in an awkward drunken manner. He is a clown and he is terrified as he undertakes a series of hopeless attempts to coordinate with the sweet lovely innocent girl. He is slightly naughty, almost though not quite goes so far as to paw her. He is rude to her. He is even arrogant and aggressive. He is an endearing figure in spite. His body is at a bias. His long arms move like weeds in the wind or as sea grass under water. His feet keep crossing, he gets stuck that way. He definitely attempts a duo. But he is not quite on the beat, is off in his timing in dance-stepping over to meet her, bumps into her, he never grabs her quite right. He falls, – dragging her with him, – Liz stops dancing, can't help laughing, – his legs go up in the air. He goes into and, discouraged and disoriented, out of his attempt to dance. – His act was so comic and moving that, blinded by his theatrical pretext of doing a defined character other than himself who is trying to dance, one only barely perceived the nevertheless persistent image of a dancing that is trying, ipso facto a trying that is dancing, dying. – Sometimes Raymond Andrews, the deafmute Negro boy, now quite handsome, would come out before the end of this number to conduct the music. After that he would play on an imaginary small violin, and gradually his playing would become a filing of his fingernails.

Wilson's onion act with Sheryl Sutton came after the intermission, during which wine was served and a Roadrunner cartoon shown downstairs. The first three times only he had an onion, then he and Sheryl both did.

The way it was done at first, tall brown Sheryl in a long ivorywhite gown is just elegantly seated out in front of the pyramid on the floor. Dressed in formal black, dress shirt, bow-tie, in black-face, his hair silvered discreetly at the temples, white gloves, carrying his right glove in his gloved left, a bouquet of slightly wilted but grand, long stemmed gladiolas in his right, Wilson would come in on the unsuspecting audience from in back of them, slinking along the wall in his almost jerky way, rushing and hesitating both, looking at the wall mostly, crab-like sideways, apparently much wanting to advance, but afraid to, also, then, arrived in front, precipitating himself to Sheryl's feet, on one knee, thrusting the bunch of flowers onto her lap, the knee of his extended left long leg out away from her and up, just about to rush on, but he is holding the gesture, when suddenly his other, left hand comes out with another, smaller flower, a daisy that he sneaks onto her lap, – the real gift, a gift from the heart, – then he is up and off a step or two, head high, again hesitating as he arrives at the dinosaur scrim drop behind which is the table with butcher knife and onion. One time when, head turned away from her in shy self-abasement as before, he offered the girl-lady his homage, his right was extended way out to her with the flowers, and his left also, but away from her, behind him, in the direction he is looking, toward the wall, in a simultaneous gesture of despair, and when he got up, he went to the wall, stared into it, threw his head back, his hand shading his eyes, looked into the distance, – then slid off behind the screen. On another occasion, during one of the last four performances, his hands were both already gloved when he presented the flowers, – slamming them on the table, – and getting no response he seemed to wait for one, but then, taking off the gloves, picked up a piece of her onion and offered it to her. One evening he went back to Sheryl after already having worked on his onion a good deal, around the screen, put the *little* flower he had initially given her more squarely in front of her on the table as though in a second or last effort at contact, and picked up the big ugly bunch, and dropped it on the floor as though now decided that the more formal gesture had been inappropriate. His gesture as he drops it is sweeping, he strews the (tied-together) bunch of flowers on the floor. He again returns behind the screen. A sentimental interlude! – The little introductory scene with the brown beauty suggests propitiation, regrets, an apology, an attempt to obtain absolution or to redeem himself: possibly that his concern with the onion, to which he is on his way, is a deplorable alternative to more human relationships, sexual or of love. She does not react.

On his way to the table behind the screen he stops by the entrance to the pyramid, looks in: a last chance!? – of salvation? He seems to shrink back in fright, as though unworthy because of the impurity of his desires. He works the rubber glove (we now see it is a rubber glove) onto his right: sometimes with an attitude both of resolute determination to proceed and of unwillingness and distaste, sometimes merely the impatient but careful preparation of a well-known routine dear to one's heart. He walks up to the table, head lowered perhaps, stands there pensively, but then, mind made up, walks around it quickly, and, standing away from it a little, one foot forward, bent over, but his upper body straight, seizes the knife, scraping it along the table top (grating sound) as he pulls it toward him, and then, in a rush of affect, grabs the big onion, and chopping at it, with grim determination slices it all the way through in two, the papery light-brown skin crackling, the white inside responding with an almost soundless low squoosh. The onion is noisy. He has cut it with terrible haste. Having opened up its wet odorous flesh – all this veiled by the elegant drop with its silly-headed dinosaur, the raw act muted into event, – his long bent body jerking as he saws at the vegetable, – the knifeblade having with finality grated against the table top, his passion seems spent. The deed is done.

But its perpetrator is by no means finished. Almost absent-mindedly, he gets a hold of the one onion half, his claw-like hand closing about it, lifts it close to his body, he is upright again, one foot way in front of the other, legs bent a little, and, head back away from it and us at an odd angle, his stare straight ahead, not on what he is doing, face tight as though he were inwardly mumbling an old sheet of recriminations or perhaps apologies or stumps of prayer, erratic, spastic movements of the distinguished but criminal head alternating with its holding still in pondering reflection, desire incessantly interrupted by thought, – anguish of conscience, agenbite of inwit, – he commences to pull the onion apart with both hands, gloved fingers digging into its reluctantly yielding core, his body moving forward and back with the effort of his hands, his back shaking or almost with the effort as the demi-globe gives to the unrelenting pull of his close-together hands working away in a to-and-fro rotary grind in front of his belly. He knows what his hands are doing, all right, yet they are doing it on their own. Stepping back with a large step, half-straightening out, he extends his left arm, the one closer to us, – his head is turned away, – out behind him. His hand opens reluctantly. With regret no less for the end of the pleasure than for what he has done, for the onion, the victim, but also with an air of »what's the use? what's done is done,« an air of resignation, he shakes his head, and drops the succulent sundered cloves and sheafs and leaves and pieces of skin. They fall, heavily and lightly, messily, to the floor. A slight wet thud. He is staring off into space, in a moment of emptiness between anxious, painful fulfilment and the (morally) perilous, threatening but also tempting future, a very long, thin black figure, more or less upright, knees still slightly bent, right foot forward, right hand still up in front, close to his body. Sometimes, at this point he recited, a declamatory announcing of the inevitable, horrid, »To the East is China, to the South, Africa, and, you see, to the West is America, to the North is Russia,« – and a little girl (Jessie Dunn) walks across as an Old Woman, while a large blonde woman, (Anna Lisa Larsdotter), after placing a lit candle next to Sheryl, starts dancing gracefully, slowly.

His head jerks. He is coming back to the present. The fever is taking hold of him again. But no, he steps back, one, two steps, his body turning away, arms down. He stops again, his head pulls up sharply. His eyes are focussing. With rapid, negligent steps he goes to the table, carelessly dropping the other quarter onion still in his right on the way, reaches out and takes the knife: at which point the full passion falls on him again, so that he is moved harshly to scrape the tip of the blade in a shallow semi-arc back and around the remaining half of the onion, lying there. Marking its place. Getting a kick out of its not being able to get away. He is not looking at it. He is looking at a far corner of the table. But his back is almost horizontal as he lifts the knife under him and, positioning the half onion with his left, cuts through it with a steely tautness, – though with a slight nervous vibration in his body, voluptuary and assassin. Dropping the knife, lifting his face away from the cleft object, he pincers his lower right arm in on the one quarter of the formerly big, slightly shiny, delicate-skinned, round brown onion, sliding his left arm toward the other quarter (sometimes, weaving on his feet as though close to fainting or as though in the grips of tumultuous passion, he approached the final quarters of the onion from a distance, talon hands in the air like a movie madman's, held the stance . . .) grips them both as he straightens up, lifting them a little ways, then drops both arms. His arms hang a little bent. With all his force coming down under the black coat sleeves from his long back into his hands, staring ahead, his head jerking irregularly in the horizontal from one pointed-nose position to another an eighth or a sixth of an inch away, he is mashing what remains of the onion, squashing the finely structured brilliantly white sections still left within his gloved palms, murdering them (exhausting the gamut of ways of murder) with regret and delight. The drop is being lowered very slowly. We suddenly see his head, his black shoulder, white shirt top, white-encircled neck, bow tie very clearly. He seems sad now. He turns and walks away from the table, passes the edge of the screen, is entirely visible, a man. As he continues a little ways in the direction of the wall, his walk momentarily is the comic walk of Groucho Marx. His back is more or less toward us, but we see his face in quarter- or one eighth profile. He is perhaps almost done, his hands, inactive, ceasing to be tools. He stands. He is looking into the corner of the room. Turning again, he comes back. Most of his body is again covered by the transparent, slowly dropping screen, but his near left shoulder, arm, hand, extended behind him, protrude beyond the screen. The hand, its back curved toward us from the wrist, slowly lets go of the pulp which dribbles heavily to the floor in front of the screen, adding to the mess on the floor. He leaves.

He did the act in profile. Using his formal suit, height, extending his long arms and legs, keeping them separate, stepping backwards and forwards, he created a silhouette. His stances were tense, unnatural. – Suspense is regenerated many times. He portrays a sensuous and destructive compulsion in conflict with inhibition, possibly of a moral character. He gets as much emotion and character into the figure as Max von Sydow got into the leading part of Gregers Werle in I. Bergman's version of the *Wild Duck*. – His acting concentrates us on *him*.

The onion peels away into nothing.

For the last four performances, he *gave* the act to Sheryl, – or, as though testing himself as an actor, he gave himself another handicap in addition to the screen. Doing it behind her and behind the screen, he became her shadow merely, almost invisible. He became more and less histrionic. Some of his gestures became more melodramatic, for instance at one point he throws scraps of onion at the table as though treating the onion with contempt, but his performance, – conformed to hers, – became more subdued. Once The Beauty is herself preoccupied with her own object, not only is he subjected to an initial rejection, – for the foreplay of courtship was retained in the act, – but he finds himself placed in a world of loneliness, a world in which everybody is preoccupied by their destructive abstraction, unconcerned with other people.

Sheryl Sutton's fascination, though she is the group's one trained actress, results from her absolute attention to what she is doing. She does nothing else, her body is quite still except in the doing of the one thing indicated, and is quite into that one thing, and similarly for her posture, defined by that one activity and defining it; and the one activity she *devotes* herself to she does as simply and effectively, as economically as possible, going about it in such a way as to achieve some minimalisation of gesture still allowing quietness and fluidity. She assumes the right stance immediately, goes into it without hesitation, her movements leading naturally, smoothly and pointedly into it, by the shortest path. At the same time, one can not say that she acts out attention to that activity, – let alone to how she goes about it. On the contrary, it seems the performance of an autonomous bodily function, with her mind absent or elsewhere. It is as though her concentration on her activity induced the viewer to concentrate on her *without* any awareness of her mental concern with what she was doing. Her concentration appears to be of a sort not excluding her mind's unconcern with her body: because the principles governing every little movement have been clearly *settled* in her mind? Her activity appears to be on the borders of the unconscious. To judge by her appearance, her mind is not busy with anything. But though untroubled, it very much seems on something, namely on the *object* of her action, – the child she is killing (*Deafman Glance*), the imaginary interlocutor she is addressing in a vehement dramatic monologue (*Life and Times of Joseph Stalin*, act VII), her own image as dressed in white she does a little walking dance along the front of the stage, parade past the audience, remarking to them at the end, »this is certainly a classical act« (ib., act VI), the play around her as she sits on stage immobile for hours, in a black dress, a black bird perched on her left (*The Life and Times of Sigmund Freud*), the water she is pouring from a glass pitcher, glinting silvery, into a small ceramic bowl on a table, continuing to pour while it overflows, splashes on the floor, at a certain point starting to hum (the sound seems to come from somewhere else) (*Overture*), some inner secret or nursed pain as she stands, very straight, in the entrance to the pyramid, her back to us, then (lights out) collapsing against the frame into a lovely pose, head to one side, both arms rounded out, upward (ib.), or on what's inside the pyramid or on what she is going to do in there, when she then, the lights going on again, straightens out and goes inside, vanishing from sight (ib.), – or on the onion she is taking apart. Maybe her mind *is* on the how (on her body), and sometimes the *object* of the activity merges with the *what*, its nature or purpose or what it is to look like, but though appearing in a state of emotion and directed at an object, her mind seems empty of thought. It is true that her figure invites our attention, – and that, when we go to it and into it, expecting her to be present there, we find her absent, and are led out of her, away from her, to an awareness of spiritual infinity by absence, –: but though we may be so led through an awareness of what she is so wholly doing, it is not her concentration on what she is doing or on how she is doing it, but her apparent concern with the object it is done to that holds and leads us. Her apparent absence in herself is her apparent presence in her object. I don't think she knows this herself.

Gowned Sheryl comes out, stands in front of the dinosaur drop at a small table, picks up an onion on it. On another part of the stage, Carrol Mullins, the group's ash blond strange beauty, sits with a big anchor next to her on the floor, a little girl (Jesse Dunn) stands motionless next to her. Wilson comes out for his act a little later, after Sheryl has started cutting her onion. Sheryl begins by peeling the onion, slowly, carefully pulling off the strips of parchment brown, the outer thin white skin underneath with them sometimes, smoothly, tenderly though not exactly gently, never brutally. When she has half peeled the outer skin off, – rather than like Wilson pulling it apart in a manner contrary to its nature, she peels the onion layer by layer, – she sometimes, before going on, first cut a small sliver off the top, where the leaves once grew out together, straight across, a practical measure executed without any indication that that's what it is. She is holding the onion in both hands, it turns as she handles it. It is almost only her hands that are moving, her head is inclined above their action. The paucity of her movement and her intense concern with (almost for) the onion make what she is doing seem an investigation of it, perhaps the expression of a spiritual, possibly only of a theoretical concern. Its coming apart seems almost an incidental by-product of this preoccupation. Sometimes she acted out wondering about the onion, turned it in one hand, looked at it, – somehow the white peels came off nevertheless, though she seemed not to de doing anything to it. Her movement is unified by her economy of gesture into a flow, it seems to grow, incrementing organically with each additional turning of the bulb, as *it* diminishes. She appears absolutely bound to take it apart utterly, without this result being either any great concern of hers or anything the doing of which would or could worry or trouble her. She acts out no emotion, but neither does she act out an unemotional practical attitude. Her first use of the knife, apart from that one-time de facto practical gesture I mentioned, is an incision, knife-point first, only piercing into the globe, not advancing its decomposition, an insinuation with implications of cruelty which were absent from Wilson's brutal destruction of the object, – he used the knife for cutting only. But apart from this preliminary sondage, I did not notice her using the knife at all hardly: just her hands seemed occupied (not busy), – which made the action more intimate, – and the onion somehow came apart in them in spite of the almost loving care of her fondling of it. Whereas we see Wilson at grips with the onion, with difficulty overcoming its resistance to dismemberment.

At some point during the naturally endless-seeming operation, she starts humming. The humming changes into singing. People come out from behind the pyramid, sit down to both sides of it, start rocking, start chanting »the ocean roars,« one of them playing a flute accompaniment. The scene is changing into a sea-scene. A grown up man and a little boy (Sebastian McDonough Brecht) start rowing motions up in the choir loft. Behind them a man holds up a large model of a clipper ship, swaying from side to side, while flashlights illuminate the boat from both sides. As Wilson and Sheryl finish with their onions, sea sounds from the loft answer the chant from below.

On the last evening of the Byrd Hoffman School of Byrds *Solos* of May 7-12, 1973, given at the Byrds' 147 Spring Street performance studio, Robert Wilson, together with somebody called Elaine Luthy, did something called *King Lyre and Lady*. The program announced

it as a mellow dramatic balletical opera in several acts, and gave
the title as:

dor

o

stitic act

ddorgg

*king lyre and lady*

d

desert wasteland, a boy or girl

or

*in the wasteland*«

who has grown up in a temper

with

a lac of rain

with

a barbed-leaved aloe

dor.

On the carpeted center of the performance space a girl plays the
flute, one Larry Fagin with simple-minded pretention reads his pre-
tensiously simple-minded poetry, and one Duskin Shears reads some
idiotic, i.e. totally uninteresting letter, so that the perfume of his
personality might spread as faint intimation of the vibration, cadence,
pitch and timbre of his voice. It spreads, and Shears is O.K., but it
is not interesting. Then they leave.
This heavily costumed and made-up gent (Chris Miller), in a cape
and black top hat and a freely hanging loosely knotted grey silk
scarf, black-and-white-striped gloves on his small hands, his elderly
big-nosed face all white, his lips red, enters and strides slowly, hawk-
like, but searching rather than ferocious, through the room, leaning
forward, sometimes one black-shoed foot angularly up in the air
behind him, suspended in the air as he himself seems in his floating
coat, circles around the carpet once very slowly making very slight
sounds with his pursed mouth, whispered words such as »bird,«
»flower,« and leaves, after pausing momentarily, one hand on the
edge of the wall, through the vestibule, through which a lady, tall,
thin, blonde, pretty, with a slightly harried and worn face (Elaine
Luthy), walks in, in a black cape, glistening, I think, in a big black
hat, carrying a bag. She stands at the edge of the room for a long
time with nothing happening. We don't exactly expect her to do

anything, but we are interested in what's happening. After some time she reads very rapidly from various books she takes out of her bag, which makes it apparent that she is a Southern Lady, no matter what has happened to her. For a while, before she started reading, it is good: a mysterious lady, waiting, perhaps for someone, exhibiting, the way things seem to budge if you watch them for a length of time, incessant minute tremors of feelings, thoughts and decisions, all unachieved, and like a night-time scene as our vision adjusts seeming to open up in the process. If one wanted to, which I didn't, one could study her emotional block or that tiny jagged rift in her personality, through which, if it were to tear open a little wider, her emotion might conceivably some day discharge. But at some point during this she lost her grip, i.e. the concentration of her awareness on the situation went, and with it our concentration on her. This is a well-known disappearance act, but she didn't do it, it happened to her.

Some time into this, it seemed a fairly long time later, Wilson came in. He had on a large black Western hat, had put his tall lanky self in levies and a short-sleeved shirt, had left the wrist watch on his bare arm, but wore a cape of royal purple. His hands were painted red. The lady seems to have expected him, greets him timidly. The sequel is that she either fails to get a response from him to further intermittent timid questions, or, more often, gets a delayed but then disconcertingly matter-of-fact response.[77] Each time when she finds she has to wait for an answer, or gives up on getting one, she reads aloud from one of her books. – She offers him a drink. He finally accepts. Getting glasses and two miniature bottles out of her bag, she offers him a choice. He responds »Watcha got?« – after a long while. He finally makes up his mind he wants Johnny Walker Red Label. Much later she thinks to offer him ice. After a long time he accepts

77 In *The Life and Times of Joseph Stalin* (Copenhagen and New York, 1973), Wilson almost consistently delayed his own responses or did not answer questions at all, and systematically interposed pauses of from 5 to 40 seconds between everyone's contributions to the pseudo-conversations. In the legitimate theatre pauses tend to be unrealistically short, – the actors know their lines. In real life, social convention regulates the interval for any given type of conversation (sometimes stipulating interruption or overlapping), though the conventionality is covered up by the metrics' having become reflex, or by simulations (time for pretended deliberation, etc.). – Wilson's delays set the motor-remark, query or not, vibrating in the interval, and this vibration, while it severs the waiting maker of the remark from it and empties him out, enters into the non-respondent as visible power. These effects, like obliqueness of response, isolate both interlocutors, expose self-contained persons hidden in fictive social intercourse.

and she gets a plastic sack of it out of her bag. After another long interval and repeated queries, he finally agrees they might as well take off their costumes, – they remove their capes and hats. After another long interval and after she has asked him again and again, he allows that maybe they should do the opera now. But they never do. During this extended scene which takes perhaps half an hour, they very gradually advance perhaps 3 feet into the room. A little dancing follows. Luthy tried to dance with and like Wilson, but can do neither and is ill at ease with both her failures. The whole act takes place by the entry, in the relatively small space between it and the carpet. There is intermittent soft whistling of a tune from a tape and some piano playing from the mezzanine loft behind them. Their dancing is accompanied by some soft country-western rock, perhaps *Tambourine Man*. The whole is a show of timidity and intimidation.

Wilson's performance is fascinating throughout, his standing, then his dancing. He stands there in total isolation, dependent on nothing. Occasionally he makes queer little sounds in between growls and screams, not very loud. His posture in standing as when he dances is at all times slightly, but only slightly, odd, the way he holds his arms, leans forward a little, places one leg slightly forward, the angle of his feet. His balance is improbable. He never seems tense, but seems continually aware of the whereabouts of every part of his body, seeming to relate to these parts, which without relating to one another much are distributed in space into the shape of his body, of course, by this awareness of where they are, rather than by will, that is rather than by the will to have them be there, yet not as passive onlooker, but rather as though holding himself together by a slight distortion of himself operated by this attention, a receptive but by no means very intense attention, by the way, not an outgoing attention, his mind being rather on itself.

He leaves no doubt that as he stands there, he is conscious of himself as a performer, – and one appreciates this, you might say one is grateful for it, – and of appearing to be a performer, and that he intends this effect, but one's awareness of this may come to be ever so slightly troubled by some such doubt as whether he is putting on a performance for us or is merely trying to perform, I mean his concern seems to be with performing rather than with us. His performance – dancing or non-responsive standing – which consists, as I have hinted, in some distortion of himself, of his body to be precise, seems to be truly a matter of concern to him, though not for its own sake, but because of a feeling of his that some particular distortions might prove of value in solving some problem, or rather (he is not looking for answers to questions) might *resolve* some difficulty (not quite trouble) that he is in. It is a difficulty rather than trouble. He is not troubled. Perhaps a difficulty in performing altogether? The difficulty of functioning?

Noting that, (1) while the distortions he operates on himself, awkwardnesses he gets himself into, sometimes briefly give an image of pain, of *uncontrollable* spasms befalling him twisting him, even at such moments, — and that is why I said »give an image,« — there is also an impression that he *contrives* the image, and no impression that he experiences pain; and that (2) he systematically intersperses his bodily research into non-functional allocations of body-resources with moments of total *ease*, stepping out of performing altogether, just standing there as one might, or doing an easy little shuffle or high-stepping dance-number, just a few steps, these elements of detached self-possession, affable non-commitment to doing anything, balancing those other moments at the other end of the scale of engagement when he is stretched out at a tilt in the air, mouth distended, or is brokennecked on the floor, neither sitting nor lying: as though they were designed to prove that he hadn't lost himself in performance, and wasn't about to, but is still around, and is just doing these things; and noting furthermore (3) that he is totally *into* each *particular* thing he is doing, snapping out of it and just directly going into another, not in curves but simply totally altering direction, bending his line at an angle, nothing he does tainted by its sequel, — making allowance for all this, one is still moved to ask oneself whether performance to him also means representing someone else?

He does seem like one possessed, though also as one inviting that possession, and also as one mimicking being possessed, though mimicking it not just as something to do, but trying it on for size, as something that might happen and he wanted to see what it would be like, though he might be telling himself he was trying it out because it might give him some information, which is not quite the same thing. I don't mean that he appears to be representing one possessed, but that he — to some degree, cf. the foregoing qualifications, — appears to be representing one possessing him, perhaps the one that might take possession of him, a spirit riding him, as it is sometimes put, not exactly a demon (though perhaps his own daemon): someone other than himself, in any event. The only character this other has is that he is not him, but is in charge of him to the extent of having taken over, and of having taken on his outwardness. The performance would thus be the mimesis, by Wilson, of this creature's acting in his own, Wilson's, guise. This mimesis would not have to specify any of the creature's particularities or characteristics other than the abstract ones mentioned which are the creature's relations to him. A possessor has a new body. The distortions of Wilson, standing unresponsively, this way and that, – present as absent, – or dancing, appear not as failures, but as achievements, achievements of the will, as in the bending of something to one's will. Thus might a possessor move the body of another, with triumphant glee. In fact, such are perhaps the best moments in life: moments of achievement. One does what one could not possibly have done. I am always struck by the grotesque awkwardness of works of genius and I think it is hidden from so many only because *these many* contribute the patina of classicism, hiding from themselves the tense unnaturalness of the learning child. Don't one's achievements seem to one to have been achieved by another?

But where is Wilson? The performance of one possessed is most intimately commanded by another, who is making one perform for him (, her or it?). One's own experience, possessed by another, would be of the possessor. This slave is absent in Wilson's performance, even in rebellion. Wilson himself is there as the will-less but aware observer within the body whom I mentioned earlier, and who appears to hold it at the cost of distortion. There is no conflict of wills. There is only the split between the awareness and a will that commands the body and that seems alien.

Wilson commands attention as performer even when immobile, his face inexpressive of anything but tensed awareness of something or other possibly grave but inevident, without emotional gesture. He often takes this stance. I don't recall his ever acting out a reaction. As entertainer, he works with his lanky but oddly put together body. His body barely *diverges* from elegance. A faint heaviness of the seat, – his upper body is small, – is suspended among the limbs he breaks and breaks, performing. But he proceeds on the weighty assumption that a perfect containment will shoot out like shrapnel, over and over again, exploding in the spectators. He proves the assumption by test and discards it over and over again in squeaks and growls or collapses of the system, arms flailing, when he demonstrates the nervous insanity of us all.

Thus, in act IV of *The Life and Times of Joseph Stalin*, while Stalin's first wife is on the proscenium platform dramatically dying of consumption (Wilson tried to make the actress die like Ludlam as Camille), after Wilson and Cynthia Lubar in identical white Yalta Stalin uniforms and moustaches have come out and very slowly have lowered themselves into two armchairs, for Wilson so much the central image of the show that the poster for the play, under the title had only them on it, covered with sheets as though not in use, from which to observe the dying woman, they sit, Wilson not so much stiffly or rigidly as erect but leaning forward, in a total suspension of himself in that position, without moving, attending, continuing to sit after she has died. At one point, both Stalins give a sudden little jump.

Wilson in this scene and others conveys attention (to something, probably something within himself) and concentration of energy. The way he holds his head contributes much to this impression. It is inclined forward, very still, the back of the neck in profile in a strong ascending line of movement. The head is the end of a man, but it is not always the image of a conclusion: more often its crown gives an impression of fortuity, and its front, the face, *leaks*, giving an impression of dependent interaction. A man must end *himself* there. Oddly, whether he appears to be doing so depends as much on how he holds his head as on the expression on his face. He appears complete, and thereby soaks up our attention, when the image is that of a rotation of thought within the skull: an appearance not created, incidentally, by an expression of thoughtfulness or of trying to think, indeed, destroyed by expression. On the other hand, looking for something, taking it in, desire of something or interest in it, need not shatter that image. For *him* to seem really *there*, it suffices if the stance conveys the person's absorption in that autonomous churning. In the deathbed scene, the spectator does not know what Wilson/Stalin is thinking, nor, though he does not suspect him of being a callous bastard, whether he feels any emotion at all. Wilson for the purpose of this play supposed that his first wife's death was for Stalin a turning point, as was for Freud, watching it from the chair that, gradually lowered during all the preceding part of *The Life and Times of Sigmund Freud*, had finally arrived for him on the floor, stage center, the death of his favorite grandson. Wilson supposed that something broke and shattered in both men at these moments. At such moments (which only those who themselves die young can avoid), one is perhaps apt to be vacuous, merely a thought of something like survival rotating in one's purged skull. In that scene, Wilson/Stalin seems to be listening to the sounds of waves breaking. Perhaps he is watching the inward onslaught of the event, perhaps its destruction of himself. Then time passes and one senses a reformation of the man in some inward shifting. His abdication from outward signifying affects one as an abdication from humanity.

When Wilson gets up in this scene, he goes over to his dead wife. During rehearsals on his next play, a few weeks later, he assigned as an exercise the thinking of something both tragic and funny, and the acting it out in a way that would show it to be both at the same time. He gave the death of his mother in May 1973 as an illustration. He was there. It had affected him as tragic, but at the same time he had not been able to help feeling there was something funny about it. Doing the movements, he gave his gestures on approaching his dead wife's deathbed as Stalin as a further illustration. The tragedy of it: upstage right arm out, left leg back, toe touching, upper body bent forward, head bowed down to the level of the outstretched arm. The comedy or grotesquerie of it: erect body, straight back, slightly bowed head, both arms lifted in front from elbows, hands hanging, – also in profile. He added deprecatingly that of course his intention might not have come across, he didn't know ... I myself remembered only his leaning over her, earnestly regarding her face.[78]

Wilson often mentions that film study he once saw of the responses of mothers to their crying babies when they pick them up to comfort them. The film was progressively slowed down more and more. The apparent expression broke up. The slower the film ran, into the more expressions did the expression decompose, revealing itself the composite of a rapid succession of quite distinct expressions indicating a variety of emotions. The apparent expression resulted from the rapid-

78 The whole scene according to Carrol Mullins' log:
1:12 A.M. Stalin's first wife gets up crying »Stalin Stalin« and coughing. She coughs more, goes ..., staggers downstage coughing and cries »Stalin, where are you?«/Bed is placed on murder platform./All sound gradually becomes quieter. She lies on bed jerking, gasping and coughing gradually less and less./Chairs fly in./1:15 A.M. red curtain comes down ..../Two Stalins enter murder platform and jump on a 1-count. Bob (Wilson): »Well I don't know what to do.« – Cindy (Lubar): »I don't know.« – Bob and Cindy: »OK OK.« – Bob: »There is a castle on a hill, just outside of town. ... Well OK OK, if you say so. ... You see, my father was a shoe ..... It won't be long now.«/Paul Robeson sings »I love you« (tape)./Violin player plays./1:21 A.M. Curtain goes up very slowly as Sheryl (also in white Stalin uniform, with moustache) begins to sing »I love you.«/Frog at table begins to play and sing »Going Down the Road Feeling Bad.«/Stalin (Sheryl) walks ... then ... off SL./Stalin (Cindy) gets up and dances./Stalin (Bob) gets up and dances ... goes off SL./Waiter briefly comes in and dances. (All three dances overlap)./1:24 A.M. Chairs fly./First wife follows Stalin (Cindy) and exits SL.

176

ity of succession of the true emotions expressed. Whereas it expressed solicitude, they expressed modes of alienation from the baby, some murderous rage. It may be pertinent that Wilson claims his mother never touched him, and kissed him for the first time when he left for college, but his account of the film relates to his advice to actors to aim at the production of a clear image, one that reads well, but to introduce into it a detail or touch putting it in doubt, so that looking at it will be like looking at something while blinking rapidly or while moving the fingers of one's hands rapidly up and down before one's eyes: momentarily one is not sure the something is there or is as seen. Wilson's inexpressive expressions seem designed by their firm control sub-liminally to convey their decomposition-elements to the spectator. The superbly neat image is unidentifiable: the clear and distinct idea it produces in the viewer lacks name and definition.

Wilson's thoughts come flying from all directions. This is the state of anybody creating. Actors ordinarily do not express it, perhaps because they are repeating, not creating. But Wilson acts it out, – perhaps he can do it because so much of his acting is improvisation, but there is another factor: instead of portraying this state as a conflict, he renders it as the confluence that it is, whether as an odd but coherent complexity of the moment, shown in a held gesture, or as sequence of discrepants. He frequently exhorts his performers to maintain an awareness of the variety of sensations and impressions, aural and visual, relevant or not, impinging on them at each moment of their performance, not to shut them out, but to work out of this open consciousness and active attention. But he himself seems to be doing this on the higher level of creation: in which relevant thoughts crowd in.

He has the gift of discontinuity. His figurations are discrete: he neither leads into nor out of them. Devoid of past and future, they are present. The spectator experiences his own growing awareness of them as entry into their presence before him. But their beginnings and ends, even when rapid (sudden) transitions from other configurations or rapid (sudden) entries or exits, are unaccented, – movements by their manner kept outside the performance-space. They disappear. Sometimes Wilson achieves this effect by appearing over and over again charmingly to be again deciding what to do next, now. Each re-beginning then seems a beginning in liberty. Sometimes he does it by a show of awkwardness: what he is doing then seems to equal the overcoming of obstacles in himself. By driving himself without residue instantly into the effective image (to which nothing ties any *him*), he preserves the continuity of his presence and of the show into which he inserts himself, leaving the feeling of a line of energy smoothly extending before and after his appearance as well as through it, unbroken by or within it. To generate this feeling of a static energy flow, the performer's mental energy must be at a high level during his performance, and the performer must be quite in possession of his body and so attuned to it, that he can release the energy, in spite of his tension, not explosively, but freely and evenly. Thus, for instance, as Wilson often warns, the expressed energy of voice, gesture or movement must not drop toward the end of the expression. This would drag the energy line extending beyond the expression down, and then either the spectators would be distracted from the event, or else the performer (or another) would have to pull the energy level back up, which would produce an *irrelevant* flickering of the image and an energy-chaos.

Insanity[79] is partly the universal condition, no mere deficiency of intellect or excess of emotion, but the sub-stratum of the soul, like the earth's sometimes supposed molten core, a chaos in turmoil, slowly or rapidly turning, the rabid morass that's the heart of the forest, perch of certain birds, *underneath,* more prosaically the faculty of perception, viz. violent imagination, map-maker to the will and furnisher with privilege to royal reason, a confusion: but partly it is a special vice, a perversion, the hidden violence of some, gourmets of dissolution who are therefore amateurs of drama, toward which they work a little. If in the sane insanity is a small frozen tremor, in the insane it is a constant ray of blue light, their quirk. Like pederasts, thieves, the benevolent Jews, snake-eyed Gypsies, collectors of only one kind of small object, the insane are brothers, recognising one another by an involuntary guffaw on regrettable occasions and by a certain minute tolerance, unbearable to others, but, fortunately for them, inobvious. They are possessed of an unerring ear for the make-believe mad, the boisterously crazy, the delight of the philistines. How many of the insane are incarcerated in the institutions designated for them is unknown: probably not too many of these certified unfortunates are insane, being merely ill, viz. compulsives, or catatonics. A fondness for playing games and their intensity of venture tend to keep the insane out of these institutions: it is only their cunning that may betray them to the authorities, or the scandals they cause by their insane behaviour, and then the charge of destruction can usually

79 The following symptomatology is introspective.

not be lodged, for lack of proof. It is a strange fact that members of the peasantry get along well with the insane, unbeknownst to themselves bearing them love.

Insanity is not *just* incapacity for a prudent pursuit of pleasure or the proneness to act on phantasy as reality, as in the chronic indulgence in magical acts. Recidivist infractions of the logical code have nothing to do with it. It is delight in disorder.

But who is insane does not like a mess. Insanity loves reason and delights in orderly argument. Such webs of order are most congenial to the insane, for viewed in their invariably ragged totality, a view they invite, they are the most delicious discrepancies of all since in the context of their axiomatism and of their incompletion, their coherence appears a mad stunt. Thus also who is insane will strive to be neat in person and decorous in conduct and in his sometimes stunning syntax strives to be correct. For where there is no order, there can be no disorder, but only the jumble that comforts the sick in mind. Adoring design, the insane are given to a proliferation of patterns with which there is something wrong.

Sane people are reassured and pleased by the evidence of order, – to them harmony, – which the force of their modest sanity disposes their eye to perceive even when all is tumbling about them into a concensus of exceptions. Their disposition meeting with the evidence it provides, they are at harmony with the world, no matter how sorely vexed, – to the utmost bitterness, – by what will not stay put. Sanity is this power of composition, – a resident force, disposed to act, since its exercise is capped by the effect of endorsement. All is well and 'tis well it's well. We witness the fervor of the housewife after her blood has flown, the fever of the great physicists as they wrestle their equations and the corrupt police officer's ingrained sense of duty.

The insane brother on the other hand malevolently focusses on death: all indication of impending or eventual collapse kindles in him a spark of glee. By no means, note, does he delight in the suffering of others: unlike the sane, who can see the worst as, in the last analysis, for the best, he is, time permitting, a compassionate fellow, for he is grateful to sufferers, disorder incarnate, salient snarls in the skein of good order, seeing them as martyrs for redemption. But he hungers for excitement. He would see small conflagrations throughout. His appetite for malfunctioning is so extreme he even forgets self-interest.

Consider a partial list of what an insane man delights in:

volcanic eruptions
car accidents
people that can't talk right
misspellings
war
tidal waves
fires
comets
crowds of mushroom after rain
the colors of autumn
economic disturbances
the grandeur of urban civilisation in nature
the decline and fall of the Roman Empire or any other
the cooling of the universe
criminals, beggars, perverts and cripples, all monsters
children and wild animals
sudden death
all festivities and great joy
extraordinary achievements
mongoloids, genius
the moon, the stars

The insane person faces the world rather than lives in it. He would have it be a large object. This object turns out to be a machine, the parts of which so regulate their interaction as to reproduce the same regularities of their coincidence and relation. He doesn't mind these patterns. Even their repetition per se does not bother him. What he cannot stand is their contrived persistence, the conservative functioning toward coherence, the individual elements' pulsating life of contribution to repetition. For it *is* after all his environment, it encroaches on his home, and he is exposed to it and under the rule of necessity within that multitude of regulations he stands condemned. He feels sure of his freedom (though not of any individual substance), but the world to him is sometimes a smooth pane on which he crawls endlessly, sometimes a thickening maelstrom englutting him, and at all times a mathematical matrix in which he is merely the imagination of himself. But he tries not to let it get him down. After all, he knows that things are not what they seem, that secretly, in more ways than one, really they are other, conspiring toward their seemingness. Everything has a second nature and an assumed shape. When he is feeling good, he can see oddity sticking out in everything, and even when he isn't, he perceives the minute shifts that the ordinary engages in all around, its shivers in instantaneous ambiguities of identity.

And ultimately, of course, nothing really works, at least not for very long. The breakdowns allow him some deep breaths.

Insanity manifests itself in breakthroughs of exuberance through a carapace of rigidly ironic attention. It is the source of hilarity, a spring that rebels against gravity but springs out of it in all its freshness, cleaving the mouth. Facts may seem so witty that even bloodshed cannot abrogate their humor, – in fact, fear may be said to be the softly cushioned nest in which this little vice, insanity, dwells. I don't think I am revealing anything we don't all know. I may as well add that though the insane deplore violence (because its crudity advertises the power of order), crime is kindly taken by them, they cannot help a fondness for it. An insane person is at least in small ways invariably a criminal, say a thief. In fact, a vast anger from which hatred radiates underlies the insane hope for catastrophe so characteristic of the underworld and of witches.

Children slyly hope something bad will happen to their parents, and that somehow the at times incredibly oppressive little system of their home might fall apart, fall away like a house of cards, revealing this incredibly delicious garden all around, the terrestrial paradise, – while their parents work their arses off to maintain this little enclosure within the brutal hell of nature, and to get the little buggers ready for similar heroic feats of self-protection. Just so, the insane hate the social order around them, defiantly ignoring the brutal miseries of alternative savagery. This is all to the good.

In any civic order, anger and hatred directed against its fancied, possible or actual disrupters are endemic among its sane supporters, a bitter rancour among the mob of those the order disadvantages, a fearful terror among the mob of its beneficiaries. Many dim minds are by these affects paradoxically steadied within narrow ranges of sardonic or apprehensive shared sane opinion. But the angry mode in which the insane person, contemptuous of status, is ever on the jump, and the furious energy of the insane person's scorn are steadily inclined against the surrounding legitimacy bearing down on the individual, say the respectabilities of high, middle or low bourgeois proprietorship, the terror-supported moralisms of bureaucratic functions and/or the fagotty heroics of leadership, – or perhaps against the sterilities of a dominant race's culture, the pattern of brutalities of a dominant gender, the hypocritical repressions exercised by a dominant age-group, e.g. adults or the middle-aged, or the system of order in manners, in conduct, discourse and communication, enforced by the physically and/or mentally normal, posing as normative.

An exciting violence in the soul, this angry scorn renders the mind erratic but alert, an individual intelligence akin to the wit of oppressed races, except not so self-consciously ad hominem, — the insane mind is not rebellious. Yet insanity is a debility.

Unwilling to commit itself to identifications, not trusting notions, insecure in definition, wavering between image and concept, constantly distracted by thoughts of alternatives, totally incapacitated, by its inability to maintain distinctions firmly and by an intellectual weariness born of scepticism, for a steady search for implied presuppositions, let alone first principles, its affective allegiancies rendered inoperable by its curse of irony, the insane mind is untrustworthy. It knows itself to be such. Whence a kind of desperation. Unfit for explanation, it can provide only the benefits of symbolic description, incapable of love, it can provide only the benefits of an angrily tolerant affection. These benefits, to which we should add those of a constant love of liberty, are not inconsiderable.

# Notes on the work sessions leading up to the N. Y. *Overture* (1972)

Your mind is habitually active in a wasteful manner, straying, alimping along in fragmentary recapitulations, each day over and over again engaging a new set of blind alleys, none of them hardly even pointing in any important direction anyhow.

This activity, chasing the infinity of same rabbits you keep dragging out of your hat, not only keeps you busy, tires you, but distracts you from what at least relative to it appears as your own center, a blank spot of existing, not in motion.

The tug to be away from this place (in one's mind it seems somewhere in one's lower chest perhaps) is really quite weak and not even continuous, but in the end extremely powerful, it is so unrelenting: and one must to some extent reduce oneself to defenselessness against it in order to cut down on the extent that it bothers one.

The flickering candle, concentration on a minimal image in mind, counting: lashing oneself to one's mast not to hear the sirens, playing yo-yo with oneself. In fact, money-making and work are of this same sort, or advancement in rank (especially insofar as by your ambition you come to deal with the others as only role-players defined by your ambition). Inversely: loss of selfhood in a quivering candle flame is no more salvation than are the socializing anaesthesias. These are means, but you must *use* them.

A blank mind is nothing. A foolishly busy mind is foolish. The problem posed by a pacified mind: how to use it? »Problem« and »use« in the preceding sentence are both indescriptive (wrong). The 0-state of mind is energetic (in fact: the normal busyness of mind, the every-minute turmoil in your head is discharge of that energy). Like a bud tending toward apple-rather-than-plum? Like a spring tending toward grace? Whenever you chance on yourself you seem nothing: because you manage it by negation only?

An incidental seduction or two: the feeling of warmth (well-being) from emptying your mind, an inner Florida; the sense of achievement; the impression of being beautiful; death.

The origin of everything: random motion, probability, time, a handful of necessities. (These are categories alien to the origin). A handful of top soil – dancing sunbeams. One's ordinary mind is of this sort, like a busy intersection seen from a bird's-eye view.

In fact you damn well know you are a little hand grenade, a museum stuffed by your life, a little plot laid out by your parents and theirs. »Little«: in view of the many others and of the expansion-programs implicit.

These are extraneous considerations. Seated in an approximation to the yoga-position, the fact is you feel the possibility of a motion natural to yourself (without your having to specify that self) and the possibility (nothing else) seems to invite you.

Images of such natural gesture: the pear-shaped tones of a pompous judge suggested to an actor by Ludlam: the fat smiling Buddhas sparsely throning in the dry and rocky Afghan highlands by a surrounding of large photographs of which the Buddha, anti-Christ in effigy, is presented in the Musee Guimet or Cernuschi in Paris; the oval inviting gesture from the fat forearm of a blond half-gypsy whore sitting on a chair inside her door or half-lifting her curtain; the opening of a flower recorded by a super-slow camera; the slow detachment from its ledge and formation of a drop after a rainfall.

I leave this matter here.

All this time there is your body. It is perhaps weighty without being ponderous; it is a warmth; you have to arrange it somehow; there are various little stiffnesses and constrictions in it here and there; you may notice it heaving with your breath; there may be a lightness in your head, a tingling in your feet, a hanging feeling in your belly, a soft ache in your back, a rigidity of collar-bone, – nervous fingers; chances are, I would say, you don't feel your genitals, probably not your toes either. Mostly it is a space filled by a diffusion of warmth, secondly a shape, vaguely tubular, its surface not too well defined.

In all the previous I abstracted from it and this is what you do: at least what someone new to this does. Arrived at the point of dynamic emptiness – and you arrive there many times, it almost gets to be like any other silly trip, – in fact I imagine a great impatience with it, like that of an actor with a part played many many times may be one of the difficulties of this routine (way), – you feel there is a kind of a problem here: surely your body is not just yours but you?

(In writing this down I am somewhat bothered by an awareness that there is two thousand years or so of literature on the subject: I can say nothing that won't be trite and half-false). Something is not quite right: you ought to be taking your body with you. You ought to feel that your body is you. You seem to be stuck with a false image of your actual present situation: as a point (the mind you have been identifying yourself as) above ! a sphere: which or where are you?

In fact, just when you seem to have managed to ensconce yourself within your mental ivory pagoda, not even looking out, – restfully mind, person, someone, – a feeling of identity with your body, at first pleasing, but then problematic and puzzling befalls you: not that you think about it, – or perhaps just a little.

You figure if you can just arrange yourself perfectly comfortably, all the muscles distended, minimum weight, blood circulation unimpeded, somehow the problem will be solved: this perfectly homogenous, warm extension (a limited extension) would not differ at all, at any rate not pertinently from a blank mind.

There are these habitual localised tensions, slight discomforts, and a recurrent physical restlessness. You try to relax.

There is now a conflict between an ideal of stillness which somehow appears not just mental (the point is not just to get your body out of the way), but in the body itself, of the body, and inclinations toward motions, in my case slow stretching motions as when one yawns.

An urge to move is apt to arise in the body which if one has relaxed one's body (this is something you have to do to it) will appear to come from it and be natural to it. You may feel like somehow dancing.

Sticking to my line of exposition (actually I am leaving out so far several crucial factors: the leader, the others, the having gotten yourself into this whole thing, having left a variety of things temporarily unattended to, motivations) your situation is now that as mind you may from time to time be feeling opening up into act, but at the same time you are coping with this body-problem and may get it to the point where as body you are feeling like opening up into act. As in sex, the two of you may be synchronised and wanting the same act, – or perhaps not.

But you glimpse not necessarily discrepant possibilities, that is, you feel that you – or one – might move in a mentally free way or might launch into a mental (incidentally: multi-dimensional) process qua corpus.

This is a happy feeling. You are apt to degrade it by the thought that this whole business may be useful (instrumental): that having gotten this far you could do something else. (Ultimately, I would think, this is utterly appropriate especially if you don't dwell on it: but you ought to be doing what you are doing).

The exercises that empty your mind by furnishing it perfectly spurious objects involve this difficulty: a leader (Bob Wilson) is telling you which to furnish yourself with. But that is all right. But then you must imagine that pine tree yourself or must yourself be in your mind drawing that circle expending a constant amount of energy on each part of its circumference. Or if it's counting, silent or loud: there is a difficulty about putting energy into each number, not just following the sequence of numbers. Any of this requires concentration: warding off other »thoughts,« keeping the object of your imagination in focus. And this concentration is not itself enough, it merely is a pre-condition for the actual doing, e.g. conjuring up the image or holding it »there« or imagining yourself doing something (it is not easy either both to imagine doing something such as drawing a circle and imagine yourself doing it, one imagined motion, the other visualisation). One's mind continually wavers.

In short, these exercises by the arbitrariness of their specifics prefigure that autonomous actualisation of empty mind into native act. The truth is the leader is insinuating not arbitrary but to him charged images. But their simplicity and aspects of universality (circle, pine tree, an airplane rising above successive layers of turbulence, you are in it, a room within a circle within something else you have imagined which is within the circle, and in the room you are with a desk, a telephone on the desk and a TV set in the wall, and nothing else, and you may either pick up the phone and talk to someone or turn on the TV set and watch any movie you want, an old man in a box, reading) give them a kind of aspect of being your own, and in any event the projection of your imagination is the arch-gesture of free enterprise. Exercising this power loosens up your mind like physical exercise your body.

Wilson tells you to move while engaging in these mental gymnastics of mind-emptying and of empty-mind-deploying. You are seated on the floor, you may sway, he may tell you to start moving your arms. It is difficult to do both at once, – move your arms, say and concentrate on a mental image or be imagining yourself doing something. This difficulty is not the point: the point is that in fact you may get into a feeling, 1) that the movement comes from your body, expresses and actualises its state, 2) that your mind is smoothly expanding into the image, *and* 3) that body and mind are, perhaps not one, but »of a unity,« plus 4) that bodily and mental action correspond, – that this body motion goes with that mental act.

You are actively getting yourself together.

We are here dealing with a number of paradoxes that are practically resoluble. Actually a few basic ones reappear in different shapes. For instance, as in practice there is a resolution of body-urges toward stillness and toward moving, so there is a strong conflict between moving your body and moving your head and limbs, but the latter motion's disruption of the former is found to be not inevitable, you can satisfy the drive toward displacement of yourself and yet be shattering your body at the same time by whirling arms.

Utterance, joint action of body and mind is usually of course not given as such, but as use of body by mind. We are to attempt to retrieve that internal duality of the unity, a statement that will also be a working of diaphragm, chest, throat and mouth, – and yet will still be statement. The procedures, difficulties and resolutions are as in the two separate cases of mind and body supra. In fact Wilson seems engaged in generating a public statement – a show and performance – out of some non-sense sentences that came to him. There is an uninspected arbitrariness about the point of departure, »the dinosaur is dying,« »the dying dinosaur,« »the dinosaur soars, is soaring, soaring, soaring« . . . .

To Wilson's tyranny is added that of the word. You try to keep the word from turning into mere sound, but on the other hand you want to keep it a sound, – actually you don't continually have to try, you may have hit it right and nothing may be troubling your balance, – like learning how to ride a bicycle: but you are apt to slip off either way from time to time. But as regards the sound you are apt to start feeling you are being carried along by a wave, that you are not making the sound any more, it's there, and as regards the word, that you are carrying a giant advertising sign and there is some wind: why this word? and why should this word have this sound? I merely wish to suggest there is apt to be some turbulence in you.

We dance, move to music, dance music or not. Or we are to sit or stand and move, e.g. an arm. Or to walk moving our limbs. Sometimes in certain places, in a jagged chess board order or where we happen to be; sometimes walking in a circle in a line, sometimes all advancing in one direction . . .

One gets into a movement or into making a sound attempting to make it according to how one – one's body – feels. At the same time there seems a general sense of discretion: one would not want to disturb the others. But more probably it is felt somewhat generally that one feels in a quiet, subdued mood: one makes small sounds. But in principle one is self-centered: the sound is to happen, – out of oneself.

The sessions generally start with sitting. Approximations of the lotus position are preferred. Silence is observed. There is an attempt not to move, e.g. scratch. No attention is paid to the others, late comers. »Meditation« is sometimes used as term for this sitting. 10 minutes or an hour, – Bob wanted 2 hours once a week. What happens in the candle-lit dark – a little light from the windows at the entrance – is that a group-feeling drifts in. You are aware that you are doing this with others, that something like what happens inside you is taking place in the others, perhaps in fact, because of the states of abstraction and of identification of mind with body that you approach, the members of the group are approaching similarity – non-non-identity, say. The silent sitting creates a unified space. The coincidence of essayed recovery of self-identity and approach to group-identity is paradoxical.

Attempting to put out your own (body's) sound and/or movement, you not only try not to interfere nor disturb, but find yourself influenced by what the others, or perhaps someone near you or in front of you, are doing. There may be some tendency toward imitating them: perhaps the influence is subtler: a tendency toward some manner of felt complementation or suppression of felt discordance.

Periodically Wilson calls on us to follow so and so: everybody starts imitating that person. As one catches on to what they are doing and provided they keep doing it long enough and it isn't too hard – mostly someone named as momentary leader tries to do something slightly special and rather more regular and marked than otherwise – one is apt to make it one's own, one's rhythm gets smoother, one no longer watches the leader to be in time, but stays in time even so. Next, then, one is apt to imbue this movement with something personal, one adjusts it to oneself. This whole process of making what another or what the group is doing one's own recurs again and again. Even in counting, f. inst., a frequent thing, an initial strain to keep in time with the others is followed by an independent counting of one's own, without waitings or rushings, in one's own rhythm, which however is that of the group; and this state possibly by a harmonious personal deviation from the group cadence.

Sometimes the word is to work with someone else and you turn to someone nearby whose sounds and movements are quite different from yours. Here you try to fit into the other's style and time or timing, without, probably, imitating them, but also without giving up your own. You try to make a whole out of what both of you are doing. Each of you may be trying to do this or one may be waiting for the other to take the lead or to follow him: this complicates the whole thing beautifully: you are working with them in a superior sense. Of course nothing is said.

Wilson will again and again break up these sub-wholes consisting of more than one person: sometimes releasing us back into solitude – just walking, f. inst., – sometimes telling us to find another partner, or calling for twosomes to join one another (»work together« by fours) ... Each such temporary sub-group is apt to get something going within it – sound, movement, words, – that has some approach to unity and structure and some fascination for those doing it while they are doing it. By making its composition fortuitous, temporary and changing, Wilson makes it in effect an approach to integrating the whole group (15-20 people): even though, in the instant, it has the same kind of closedness, outward oblivion, that the individuals have at the beginning of each session or when they are doing their own thing by themselves only.

The attentive adjustment to another individual in a very simplified relationship such as f. inst. holding their hand or lying next to them, shoulders or heads only touching, or moving in some kind of harmony but very slightly with them, is a very intense experience: especially in a situation in which one is making a strong attempt toward (abstract) egocentricity and in which also one has in an abstract way become rather integrated in the larger group. One is very much aware of »an other.« (Whereas e.g. in love-making what you are doing and the pleasurable sensations lend so much texture to the relation as to obliterate, to some extent, its social nature.) There is however a kind of feedback into self-awareness: a strong vibration at the margins of yourself is set up which if everything works right sets up a centripetal vibration of yourself. A calmed turbulence may be a greater calm. Also, of course, the hand you hold or the arm movement you respond to act like numbers you recite: free you from adventitious thoughts, clean you out.

Sometimes there are designated leaders, often there are self-appointed leaders. The former are easy to cope with. You assume you ought to do what they say, that it is just a *way* of getting yourself together either by yourself within the group or together with an other: some of the trust you have in Wilson is transferred to them: they and the actions they set up are mere means, – not always though, e.g. you may respond especially well to the warm voice of Helen, or badly to Charles' quick rhythm, may find yourself irrelevantly charmed by the one, fighting the other. But the self-appointed leaders are harder to cope with: people that are a little louder than others, or more emphatic, or more rhythmic or more self-assured in voice or gesture, more oblivious of others and of »the group,« resist changes introduced by others (shift to an alternative chant, to a different pitch or rhythm). At worst you will resent them and will then have to cope with your resentment. To some extent they are apt to upset the delicate balance between response and initiative that apparently is the ideal mode of interaction, – they may throw you into passive followership. One basic difficulty is that ideally a succession of leaderships should emerge in a kind of organic way: momentary dominance of proceedings by a specific individual seems a desideratum for this way the whole thing is enriched by that personality or if not by that personality, by that individual's production of energy. But it should just happen and should happen where the relative personalities and energy-states warrant it.

It's all silly. I.e. up to a point there is no point to it. The group is given certain materials to work with – sentences such as »the dinosaur is soaring,« »the dinosaur is dying,« »sun city ... illuminated us,« some recurrently played rock tunes and tunes from the 20s, some images to bear in mind, counting, the words »ocean,« »temple,« . . . .: but as these seem and indeed by and large are arbitrary or fortuitous, at least as far as is apparent, i.e. really fortuitous relative to the members of the group if not relative to Robert Wilson, this does not lend sense to the whole thing, – and anything that the group can think of is done with these elements. Of course, a certain style is imposed by previous work with Wilson, e.g. the slow arm movements, arm bent, whirling, lugubrious tones, . . . . a certain air of cultish reverence or solemnity. Bordering on matter-of-factness (mystics tend to be matter-of-fact people, incidentally, quite suspicious of mysticism), this style is not quite as easy to achieve as it seems, but neither is it hard, though maintaining it may be hard, unless you lean toward it by your personality to begin with. This silliness makes this work – these sessions or classes – effectively (at least in my experience) very exhilarating: you come away relaxed, more witty than usual, quicker and more productive, looser and in effect more effective in your work habits, gayer. Partly you are more together (body and mind), partly your mind really does get somewhat swept out, the compulsive oddments, tics in it are less pressing, partly you get into an attitude of free doing, partly you find yourself more consistently concentrating on essentials. (Sometimes we are told to tell ourselves

»yes, my body is healthy« or something like »I must always do what is the highest best for myself.«)

On the other hand, after a while, some weeks, three goals do appear, make themselves felt: mystic communion or ecstasy of a low-key, poetic sort; a public performance; a certain public performance, i.e. that of a work already or more and more conceived by Wilson and gradually outlined by him to the members of the group, – an old man is to sit in a box reading in a certain spot, under three plexi-glass maps of cities (Rome in a Piranesi frontispiece, Manhattan, a solar city), – also under a small pyramid? – there will be move-ments around the pyramid, in a restricted, small area, – there will be a choir-loft near the entrance, with a choir on it, – the whole will be arranged in three spaces from the entrance with certain heights, – birch wood in the second space (under the choir), – in the main, largest room (with the pyramid) there will be a certain number of screens along the walls, with pictures and writing in them, – these screens will respectively deal with certain themes (North: Runic stones and the stag – snow crystals; South: Egypt, temples and pyramids/palm trees/Jerusalem and Stations of the Cross; East: India and China, Buddha/mountains/temples; West: American Indians; Shaman drawings.../fire/desert/cactus.... there is some hesitation between themes, at one point one of them will be The Body ...) One person is going to be an ostrich.

I wouldn't know if mystic communion has by anybody ever been declared a purpose of the exercises. I have never heard anything like it mentioned. The exercises are generally devoid of humor, i.e. wit or irony, though not always of gaiety. The gravity attending them does not seem relative to the aim of performance. Certainly personal therapy (as which I have experienced these exercises) does not ge-nerally seem the objective. The lotus position is sometimes main-tained with a certain rigidity, OM intoned with – faintly – perhaps – an air of higher significance. The emblematic movements, sometimes remindful of the murals in Egyptian tombs, are done with an utter gravity (e.g. by Carol who has a vivid sense of humor) that seems to go somewhat beyond the natural serieux of mind-emptying and mind-body union.

During a prolonged absence of Wilson's in Paris and Iran, to arrange a summer tour, certain lieutenants seemed to come to feel that the exercises should be more closely oriented toward a performance and its requirements, e.g. prolonged chanting, varied but somewhat de-finite movement in groups in a confined area, – perhaps the development of certain specific preferable patterns of chant, plain song, humming, movement. They conveyed a certain impatience, anxiety, even irritability in this regard, — some intolerance for refreshing innovations (such as explorations of space). The evening when this happened, although what was done was not without beauty and interest, depressed me a great deal: I felt something free and open had become narrowly enclosed, — that something extrinsic had intruded. At the end of this closely guided, watchtime divided session, with a definite, varied distribution of functions (observation, chant, movement) rock was played and the release seemed greater than usual, e.g. when I put on one of Sun Ra's earliest recorded pieces, almost impossible to dance to, there was a general strong rejection: it cut off the release offered by the rock (and by Aretha) . . The sessions had not naturally channeled into more definite patterns of a sort that might be offered in public performance. Indeed this seemed not to have been the expectation. Instead there was a sudden imposition of discipline, and a sudden definition of relevant elements and relations. I left the group at this point, almost for good: shocked, angry.

## *Overture* in Paris (1972)[80]

It continued from one midnight to another, consuming a day of daylight, placed between stretches of night: the early night of Saturday, the night before Monday morning; to the participants seemingly, to some extent, placed in *a* night, or even, an interlude, in night. It did not begin on an evening, ending on a morning. It did not begin on a morning, ending in an evening. The geography of this waking interlude:

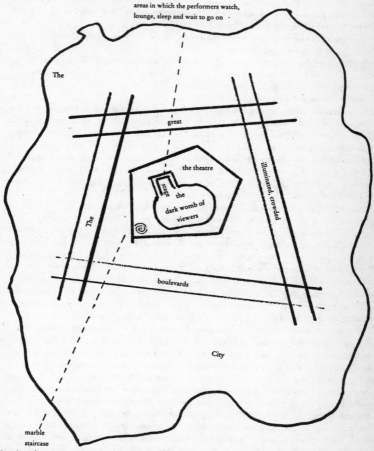

80 At the Opera Comique: following the 7-day Iranian version. Ossia Trilling

The task of the performers was to stretch a continuous weave of image into this space (of time). It was to be suspended and transparent, allowing a view of the rich, fat content, viz. night. Whether

(Drama Review, T 58, June 1973) gives some information about the Iranian and Paris versions: »Wilson's marathon production of *Ka Mountain*, with 30 members of his »Byrd Hoffman School of Byrds« and 20 specially recruited Iranians, lasted 168 hours.

The site selected by Wilson for his show was named Haft Tan (Seven Bodies) after the graves of the seven Sufi poets buried at its foot. The mountain comprised seven hills and the action, covering seven days (of Creation?), was spread over them. The entire performance, inspired by *Deafman Glance* and, in fact, recapitulating the main events of that entertainment throughout the first 24 of the 168 hours of playing time, proved a logical sequel to it.

Before the entertainment proper on Haft Tan began, Wilson staged *Overture* in the Narenjestan or »House of Mourning,« one of several beautiful courtyard buildings to be found in the ancient Islamic city. From the courtyard, spectators passed along walkways giving onto rooms or small shops in each of which different members of the company could be seen, often moving at such a slow pace that one was scarcely aware that they were in motion at all.

On the first of several acting levels, there was a flat auditorium seating about 300 persons and a platform specially built just above ground-level to include a small picture-frame-stage left open behind so as to afford a view of the sloping mountainside beyond it. Some sixty sketches, only a few of them containing intelligible (or even properly audible) speech, provided the main acting material for the stage; they were presented at all hours of the day and night, *Jail* was inspired by Wilson's month-long imprisonment (without trial) in July on the island of Crete for allegedly being in possession of drugs.

The emblems encountered on the way up the mountain were pictorial, as might be expected of a director-poet who sees the world primarily with a painter's eye. Biblical symbols could be identified as well as others taken from ancient and contemporary mythology. Jonah's whale, Noah's Ark, the Sphinx, the Acropolis with its Parthenon; there were countless representatives of the animal kingdom (both real and imaginary) and flora of every description. There were various man-made edifices and constructions, including a complete American »suburb« of cutout houses, which the company assembled themselves; in them, they performed different allotted or self-chosen tasks – from simply sitting still as a statue to reading from texts, often in a manner as to be quite incomprehensible.

The many symbols – like the pasteboard stereotypes of bent and white-bearded old men that Wilson had studded all over the landscape – were not readily interpretable, nor did they need to be. The readiness to experience them was all. What was the significance of the dinosaurs' footprints dropped here and there along the procession to the summit? Of the flamingoes? The graveyard with mythical inscriptions? Clearly the echoes of American folklore were very strong, but they could hardly be identified by non-Americans, let alone appreciated by them. What did the legend of The Old Man of the Mountain suggest to a non-American? On the other hand, the sketches reproducing the atmosphere of a saloon-bar in »the Wild West« were far less enigmatic for very obvious reasons, though one cannot be sure how many local Iranians were acquainted with the Western film ambiance that these evoked in the mind of the European spectator.

this was achieved, – the effect of a bubble of strictly finite surface but infinite volume, – I do not know. (I was one of the performers.)

For the same reason I cannot say what the play was about, – I have no *idea*. From the performer's viewpoint it was that different byrds would go out and do their thing, something Bob had worked on with them, something that had developed from the New York 3-hour production of the spring via the Iran 7-day production of the summer, something that particular performer had come to do (e.g. Kit sipping tea, Scotty talking about Iowa, Sheryl cutting an onion). There was an hour by hour schedule (rehearsals consisted largely in Bob telling people what they were to do during what hour), it could be consulted on the wardrobe walls: a few things were actually rehearsed during the week preceding the show. Bob stood in the wings, sending people in, sending messages to the lighting booth, to Igor on the tapes. There was too much material: on the 20th hour we were only up to hour 17 or so. Nicolas Baltram maintained his lotus position for 24 hours. Cindy who had shaved her hair like a Jewish bride, stayed out front throughout: she took over the show, made it hers, something that had not exactly been expected, but that had in some way, I would say, been felt to be an eventuality. The basic text, published perhaps, was hers, Bob in a sense had thought of the show as hers (as *Deafman Glance* was Raymond's). She was mad. An important feeling in the company was that the hot work on the mountains by Shiraz had changed everybody in important ways: the quality of *this* show would be this change. Perhaps there was also a feeling that the show would make the change final. As for the quality

... Wilson's idea of painting the entire mountaintop white to simulate snow had to be sharply curtailed on grounds of cost. However – despite echoes of Hiroshima or any other allusion to the apocalyptic cataclysm that the poet saw as the inexorable fate awaiting mankind – New York, instead of exploding, was made to go up in flames on the last day, when it was replaced by the emblem of a Chinese Pagoda sheltering the victorious Lamb of God at the final apotheosis.

The final 24-hour-long performance was ... a condensed version of »Ka,« exactly as at Shiraz, beginning with the same introductory scenes from *Deafman Glance* and culminating in the same apotheosis.

Wilson designed four acting areas parallel with the setting line. He used a sky-cloth as background, a water-filled caisson (representing a lake) downstage of it and three descending platforms between this and the so-called »dancing platform« that protruded partly over the orchestra pit. A few rows of chairs that were moved around from time to time, huge branches and trees, with their roots suspended over the stage level, and little else provided the framework for the company in which to retell the story of this most unusual family.«

of the change, I could not say: a deepened feeling of righteousness perhaps?

As to what was done, it could perhaps be said, that it was figures moving. The lighting was very important. What I saw of it (like most of the others, I managed, treading my way through the feast in the lobbies, a few moments in a loge or in the upper balcony (source of left-wing protests)), it did not so much give color or set off individual performers and their acts, as that it gave a depth to the peopled stage by various distributions of grey spots, lighter cones or flame-shapes, gradated bands of light in the zone near darkness. The spectacle itself was, I believe, visual, though there was continuous sound (a drone of messages from the glass-covered ›control booth‹[81] in the musicians' stand), much music, even songs, and some speech (e.g. Cindy's French explanations of what went on to the audience, the lines of the *Jail Play* (which was about a visit rendered Bob by some byrds during his incarceration in Crete for possession of hashish) and of the *Trial Play*).

81 This control booth was out of the film *1001*, a great favorite of Bob's: the whole show was a spaceship like Fuller's spaceship earth moving through the cosmic night. 4 or 6 performers were down there at all times in formal dress perched on high stools in the heat of the brilliant illumination reading fom texts of their own choosing into mikes continually, simultaneously.

# Wilson's theatre of visions, 1969–73.
## The dialectic of individuality, energy and time.[82]

From *The King of Spain* to *The Life and Times of Joseph Stalin*, putting on performances was a way of life for Wilson and for those performing with/for him:[83] consuming much of their time, thought and energy, their central preoccupation, substance/framework of their

82 The following generalisations concern only Wilson's larger pieces, and these only during the period indicated. Thus not, for instance the quasi solo pieces *king lyre and lady* (1973, at the byrd loft), nor A MAD MAN A MAD GIANT A MAD DOG A MAD URGE AND A MAD FACE (in 1974 presented successively at the Teatro di Roma, Rome, at the J. F. Kennedy Center, Washington, D.C., at the Faculty of Letters, Shiraz, Iran, and at the Ala Gallery in Milan, Italy, – Wilson and Knowles).
They concern a series of larger pieces that may be viewed as a single developing play: *The King of Spain* (2 (?) performances in January 1969, one on January 30th, at the Phyllis Anderson Theatre on the lower eastside of Manhattan, according to Wilson (1975) »just under 3 hours« long; *The Life and Times of Sigmund Freud*, act II of which was a shortened version of the preceding, (two productions at the Brooklyn Academy of Music in 1969, according to Wilson (1975) »under 4 hours« long); *Deafman Glance*, (first done at the University Theatre of the University of Iowa, Iowa City, Iowa, Dec. 15 and 16, 1970, and there, according to Wilson (1975) »4¹/₂ hours« long, then in 1971, first at the Brooklyn Academy of Music, then, with *Freud* as 4th act, at the Nancy Theatre Festival (8¹/₂ hours (?), then, in a distillation to normal theatre length, at the Teatro Eliso in Rome, and in Paris at the Teatre de la Musique and at the Espace Cardin, – about 28 performances in all, – then in Amsterdam (where a shorter *Deafman Glance* was played one night, the longer, 8¹/₂ hr. long full one, the following night); *Overture*, first done in 1972, in a 3 hour version, as daily part of a week-long series of all-day open house occasions, at the Spring St. byrd loft, then, still in 1972, at Khaneh-e Zinatolmolk, Shiraz, Iran, and, under the title *KA MOUNTAIN AND GUARDenia TERRACE, a story about a family and some people changing*, in a vastly expanded 7-day version, there and on Haft Tan mountain, Shiraz, Iran, then, also still in 1972, at the Opera Comique, Paris, in a 24-hour version; and *The Life and Times of Joseph Stalin*, a compendium in 7 acts, lasting (the first performance 14) 12 hours, of *Freud* (acts I-III: The Beach, The Victorian Drawingroom, The Cave), *Deafman Glance* (act IV: The Forest), and of three additional acts, the first two of which (act V: Temple, act VI: The Victorian Bedroom) contained materials from *Overture* and *KA MOUNTAIN*, the last (act VII: The Planet) being new (1973, first at Det Ny Teater in Copenhagen, Denmark, then, on December 14, 15, 21 and 22 (1973) at the Brooklyn Academy, and in 1974, under the title *The Life and Times of David Clark*, at the Teatro Municipal, Sao Paolo, Brazil). According to Frantisek Deak's account of *Stalin* (The Drama Review, T 62, June 1974), act I in New York took 48 minutes, act II 105, act III 49, act IV 135, act V 60, act VI 54, act VII 90.
83 The formation of a group of disciples, the BYRDS, whose lives importantly centered around preparing and putting on Wilson's pieces goes back to 1968 and

personal lives, life itself. As people become byrds, they tend to find their friends and lovers among byrds, their personal artistic ambitions and activities, if any, either disappear or become instrumentally integrated into Bob's work, they spend increasing amounts of time around Bob at the Byrd headquarters, ›the loft,‹ at 147 Spring Street in Soho, recurrently living there or at other byrds' lofts or with other byrds, give up their outside jobs, taking on a variety of menial administrative or clerical, artisanal responsibilities relating to the work, to some extent may become financially dependent on the Foundation. If Wilson's theatre makes theatre out of living, it also makes living the making of theatre.[84]

The performances are the recurrent climaxes of this way of life. Up

the work, that year, on *King of Spain*. For the pieces of 69-73, Wilson used people with persistent independent artistic preoccupations (e.g. Kenneth King, Bill Stewart, Richie Gallo, Meredith Monk) and adventitious admirers, especially younger boys and older women, without artistic aspirations, tho also some people that became byrds, e.g. Libe Bayrak, Robyn Stoughton, Saito, Hope Kondrat, becoming a byrd typically involving a languishing of the byrd's independent artistic endeavours, as e.g. in the cases of Libe Bayrak (a painter), Robyn Stoughton (a dancer), Saito (a performance artist). With *A Letter for Queen Victoria* (1974) things changed, inasmuch as tho everyone in the production was a byrd (including the assistant stage manager, Terry Chambers, who had been in the early *Theatre Activity* and Francie Brooks, who furnished slides for the piece and did lighting for Wilson's pieces in 67/68), only a dozen plus people were involved: the gross of byrds as of 1973 had been eliminated. About 16 out of 69 performers in *$-Value of Man* (1975) were still byrds, about 4 of a dozen in *Spaceman*, and about 3 out of 19 in *Einstein on the Beach* (1976). *Einstein* was the first piece not done with disciples, but with adventitious outsiders who were also professionals (singers, dancers), and who had been selected by auditioning. A byrd (Jim Neu) assisted off-stage in *Patio* (as sound-technician), and a byrd (Alan Lloyd) wrote the music, but the only performer other than Wilson in it, Lucinda Childs, tho she had also worked (starred) in *Einstein*, was not a byrd in any sense, but an independent artist. In short, Wilson's period of theatre of visions substantially coincides with his period of working with byrds, with effectively amateur disciples absorbed in his work. – In the spring of 75, Wilson finally moved out of the communal work place and place of gathering of the byrds, the byrd loft (by then 3 floors), at 170 Spring St., and got his own place. He had been living there since 67 or 68.

84 »Wilson's theatre is not in fact professional but is some kind of psychodrama performed by amateurs as a therapy session. And to talk with some of Wilson's company would seem to confirm this. They all seem not only dedicated to the Wilson way of theatre life but to be getting something back that is deeply personal and psychologically very rewarding to them. None of them seem to think like actors at all. They do not aspire to play Hamlet or Saint Joan, nor do they seek a Hollywood contract or their name in lights. They live and work together more as members of a commune than as members of an ambitious theatrical company.« (Basil Langton, *Journey to KA Mountain*, The Drama Review, T 58, June 1973, p. 53.)

to *Letter* (of which over a period of a little over a year 79 performances were given and except for the Paris run of about 28 performances of *Deafman Glance,* usually there were only two or three performances of each piece, which defined ›performance‹ relative to the working process rather than to the public; its point not the public's seeing, but the Byrds' action in visibility; a conclusion of a working process marking that the action was in the nature of something visible to others, – was, incidentally, a spectacle.

The group's attitude, – not discussed within the group, – toward doing this work may as regards nearly all of them be negatively defined by a lack of personal ambition of any sort; nor have they, typically, been regarding it as a job or as a profession, nor even, in many cases, as an exercise of personal artistic creativity. For the long-time inner-core members, attachment to the charismatic personality of Wilson is of course an important psychological factor, as is, for them, but perhaps more for the many others attracted to work on a given work, the (rather limited) status conferred on one in the artistic world below 14th Street by being a Byrd. Typically and basically, I would say, work on Bob's works has by Byrds been felt to be in the nature of a humorous religious activity, oddly enough trivially everyday personal as well, its transcendent and everyday natures joined as two triangles at their apex, its humorousness not only making it a sort of fun, but marbling its religiosity, giving that religiosity almost the aspect of a vast joke, the coincidence of an everyday personal with transcendent activity a delightful paradox: can one put an infinite distance behind one instantaneously walking in an ordinary manner? does infinity adjoin finitude everywhere walled off from it only by an open door?[85] This atmosphere explains how people can keep working this way, the work becoming their life, without personal ambition and rewards. It is also the atmosphere of the performances for spectators, at least those that go with it.

Byrds, generally white Protestants from upper middle class families, or assimilated to a WASP manner,[86] are apt to be undemonstrative, unemphatic, reserved people, superficially cool and off-hand, not

[85] The members of the company from the wings with gravity observe not one another on stage but the phase of the drama. They have seen the act a number of times, but it has, for them, the intense radiation of a magical rite, perhaps of the sort of the gesture by which in the imagination of some primitive religions a laughable but very strong animal somewhere maintains the universe in existence.

[86] The ethos of the Byrds and of the Bread and Puppet Theatre is Protestant and upper middle class, that of all forms of ›ridiculous‹ theatre is catholic and lower class, that of the Open Theatre, the Manhattan Project, the Living Theatre, the

given to shows of emotion, generally keeping their feelings, if any, to themselves, rather carefully controlled in their conduct, with unexpressive faces and voices. Tho' their living is day-to-day, – no long-term projects, – they are not at all hippies: conventional rather. Generally well-read and -informed (and college graduates), they tend to be non-verbal, with few opinions, careful to avoid abstract terms, generalisations. Their talk tends to be small talk, often about what others in the group are doing, inclining toward the anecdotal, the unelaborated account of a fact or an experience. No intellectual discussions, no discussions of principles. They don't discuss the work or Wilson's art other than as to details, – what's being done at the LOFT, what happened at such and such a performance. An orientation toward mysticism, but no strong commitments. Politics is never discussed. Tending toward a mild conservatism, they are quite apolitical. A terror of being phony, trivial or pretentious informs their conduct. One has an impression of a hygienic bisexuality, of experimental encounters, of strong inhibitions, promiscuity. Most of the time you wouldn't be able to tell which way someone was swinging, who's going with who, or if an affair is still on. They are nice people; in truth withdrawn. The atmosphere is low-key as where marijuana smoking is quasi-continuous. Social intercourse is matter-of-fact or humorous. They are not given to the inter-face of ostentatious acknowledgments of others, in everyday intercourse are apt almost to ignore one another's presence. Except for formal shows, – hugs and triple cheek-kissings after extended separations, – there are few shows of affection. Tho', identifying as Byrds, Byrds loom huge in one another's lives, the bonds seem impersonal, dissolve when someone drops out. Most of them, – I can think of only one exception, – came to Wilson without any experience or training in theatre. – Tho' perhaps more *quiet* than most, we are ordinary people, borderline psychotics.

During the winter 74/75 and spring 75, groups of Byrds put on playful performances – movement, broken bits of phrases, lighting, a mystic aura, – at the loft, later elsewhere. It would be hard to find another group of people so into performing who are so ungifted for it. Terrible inhibition expresses itself as refusal of discipline. Anything goes, everything is ad hoc, nothing has been rejected, nothing thought through, everyone does what kinda feels right; no

Performance Group is Jewish and middle class. This is largely, but not only, a matter of the personality of the leaders.

one dares make a definite gesture, and if someone does, e.g. Liz Pasquale, advancing across the floor rocking in a rocking chair, then rolling on the floor in a curlicue pattern away from it and back to it, it's lost by a smidgin of bad timing, a marginal lack of assurance, in the general chaos. When these same unfortunate people are in Wilson's shows, their painful impotence does not show. Wilson's genius, accepting it, transmutes it into the grace and dignity of an individuality as it is; they find peace in being told what to do and convey their peace. Wilson has found a way to do great theatre precisely with not just totally unskilled people, but with people peculiarly unfit to perform.[87]

The materials for the shows can be categorised as what was at hand for Wilson. They were found without search, they imposed themselves, neither chanced on nor thought up, nor deliberately chosen. They are not the products of a theatrical imagination, nor of an intention to do theatre. They recommended themselves to Wilson by the absence of conscious control in his reception of them. Tho' some may seem crucial symbols, some mythic, he did not choose them as symbols or for their meaning; only for their immediate power and persistency, unexamined, felt, not rationally or consciously evaluated. Tho' only some were fantasy images that occurred to him, in dreams or otherwise, or that had stuck with him for a long time (e.g. the figure of the king of Spain since his childhood), adventures within him, while others were simple things that people around him did or said, spoke of or drew, and still others stray items he picked up reading (he doesn't read much), they were what he found in his mind. He drew not on his experience of life, but on his life of the spirit, and only on its representational, figurative, to the exclusion of its intellectual part, and there not on fantasies of events, but on images.

---

87 Two byrds have put on interesting and affecting performance pieces: Ann Wilson (»*Ohio Relic*, at the Wilson Theater in Cincinnati and an environment for art theater also called *Ohio Relic* at The Contemporary Arts Center in Cincinnati« (mentioned in the program of her presentation of Acts from *Electric Affinities*, Dec. 11, 1976, at the Inst. of Contemp. Art, Philadelphia, Penn.), *Electric Affinities*, June 76, at The Kitchen in NYC), and Melvin Andringa (*The Drawing Legion paints Jacob's Dream*, Oct. 4th, 1975, at the byrd loft; *The Confidence Man*, April 1st, 1976, at the St. Thomas More Chapel, Fordham University, N.Y.C.). – Kikuo Saito's *Water Play* (La Mama, Jan. 1976) was Wilson reduced to ineffectiveness by insensitivity to the physiology of the spectacle. Neither the director nor the performers had the spiritual discipline by which so to relax with stage-space and -time as to subjugate them to the images proffered. Actual space and time persisted. The imagery thus failed to take on the reality of visions, was mere gimmickry, whimsy.

These may have detached themselves for him from experiences, things that happened (a Byrd speaking of her childhood, a Byrd sipping tea), but this was incidental. Life sprinkles a choice of highly individual figurations into awareness: normally they are ignored, fade or disappear; Wilson trains his inner eye on them. His shows reproduce them. They are not objets trouvés, chance images, but pretty wounds; tho' not autobiographical data, – the very idea of intimate revelations, coded or not, may not have occurred to him. Some material is needed; this is the material at hand in the mind. He is going to show visuals; he has them in stock. Precisely *what* it is may not even matter. He is not out to *prove* anything.

The material (up to *Letter*) has been largely and essentially visual. Fiddling, the Moonlight Sonata, a waltz, some remembered tune, a variety of small sounds, such as the tinkling of ice in a glass, conversation, barely audible, or the throw-away connectives of conversation such as ›hm,‹ ›o.k.,‹ ›there . . .,‹ things said during rehearsals, phrases sticking in his mind (›there is that in him‹) complemented the visual, emerged as aural horizon, – completed or gave the image, where this was the image, of a person or of people talking, – e.g. Mary Peer's long monologue in *King,* or the image of an individual as when Wilson sometimes has people just stand there and tell their name: »I am . . .,« »Hi, I am . . . .« As with the visual material, the sense of it was not the point.

These materials were sensory; the visible as seen, the audible as heard; phenomena of awareness, not existents. And phenomena of self-contained, interior awareness, not of awareness in touch with exterior reality; imaginary images, remembered images or noises, things seen or heard deliberately filtered through sleeping awareness overnight, – for *Letter,* bits of movie dialogue, sifted through deliberate inattention to late runs on TV, were used: he would draw or do housework while listening, noting down phrases some while after hearing them, for *$-Value,* TV commercials jumbled in the recall of a mentally defective boy, Chris Knowles.

Powerful images are the hallmark of Wilson's shows[88]. They are

88 »Un théâtre classique, en fait c'est une boite dans laquelle toute la mécanique qui permet de faire un spectacle est en grande partie cachée, dirigée des coulisses: avec des poulies pour faire avancer un train (dans *Einstein* par exemple) . . . Tout est dissimulée, et le théâtre ainsi obtenu est un théâtre de surface, avec un aspect quasi magique. A cause de la bi-dimensionnalité, c'est un théâtre plat . . . . Cette, utilisation très minutieuse de l'appareil scenique est en fait eloignée de ce qui s'est produit dans le théâtre des années 60, ou justement on ne voulait plus utiliser

beautiful, strange and fascinating, apt to engrave themselves on your memory; the descending metal shutter, the ladder turning into haystack, the cave of beasts in *Freud*, the garden of ladies, the floating eye in the pyramid, the lovely couple under the burning umbrella, the frog at table, the burning, collapsing hut in *Deafman*, the transversed hall of mirrored doors, the old-man thief in the women's dormitory, the float of fools on a dead planet, the dictator-tribune halting the plebs in *Stalin*, the mandarin behind the mirrored blinds in *Letter*, the gaming tables like drowning pools in *$-Value*; surreal individuations and invented mysteries, elevated by their banality above the idiosyncratic. Unlike the occasional dazzlements of costume, light, decor of conventional theatre these are not theatrical effects, nor, like the spectacular effects of musical comedy, the pyrotechnics and pseudo-magic of entertainment. More like the decor of 17th century masques, resting in themselves, radiant, they dominate the stage, gather the performance around them, subordinate theatre to image. They are visions encountering our vision, the sublimating materialisations of imagination: what Wilson sees made visible to us. They are not component signs of a story in theatrical language, not frame of event, not even ornament of rhetoric or metaphors. They are not signs at all. They are Wilson, shaped up to show forth. In them, Wilson makes himself visible, tho' neither as man nor as producer of theatre, but as reflective conflux of imagery. That this iconography, the *markings* of an *individuality*, may *denote* a *personality*, is, at least in Wilson's intention, incidental.

This is not to say that the shows do not show a viewpoint. Its focus is on the perilous situation, – and a kind of death and perhaps a resurrection, – of the self-contained child, a boy child, autistic in the eyes of an adult world continually busy in a make-believe show of exchange of affect and intelligence.[89] This kid has been present in all the shows as a watcher, – Jamesian mediation for the audience, – often as superior victim, up in the air, – in *Letter* gave voice, ran

toutes ces techniques du XIXe siècle. Ni Yvonne Rainer, ni Merce Cunningham, par exemple, n'auraient utilisé de décors peints qu'on fait descendre et remonter pendant le spectacle, ils n'auraient pas mis en scène de »salon victorien«, ni de »temple«, ni di »forêt.« C'étaient des décors peints qui suggéraient la forêt, des décors vieux-jeu, et donc inhabituels pour le théâtre de cette époque qui rejetait tout cela. A la fin des années 60, un spectacle supposé être une sorte de somme de l'art de ces années-la, a été donné au »Whitney Museum«; un spectacle qui s'appelait *Art against illusion.* Or, à ce moment-là, je faisais le *King of Spain* qui traitait précisément d'une illusion.« (Wilson, interview, Tel Quel, nos. 71/73, autumn 1977.)
89 Cf. Introduction.

*$-Value*, mike in hand.⁹⁰ The figure, enhanced by a crippling of the organs of normal communication, communicates inwardness. But the Wilsonian hero is not the cripple, but the boy, – from a parental viewpoint, any child is a mentally defective deafmute; comes up with the weirdest things; you don't know *what* goes on in that head. The shows are like that child; outwardness of a sensibility. They speak for him. Their hidden violence is his suppressed rage.

But here again, up to *Letter*, we were only seeing Wilson; the shows were presentations not representations; only with *Letter* and *$-Value* did they take the form of reference and judgment; of a denunciation of normal adult organised – verbal – communication (*Letter*); of a denunciation of normal adult organised – commercial – exchange (*$-Value*). Materials and presentation in these shows were chosen and used to make a point. Up to them Wilson had only been exhibiting an awareness.

Unlike the performances of the Performance Group, Wilson's are not

90 Wilson himself, as equilibrating boy child (naked from the waist down) and as tortured baby was the hero of *Baby*. There was a boy, Stephen Dunn, in *Byrdwo-MAN*, perhaps leaning against a wire, listening. Another boy, Cedric Jackson, had a pivotal role in *King*:

»A solitary prince in a royal white jacket enters the box by the stage and bows to the audience. The curtain goes up. We see a drawing room – an old musty Victorian drawing room. In the center, back facing the audience, a highback arm chair. After a long pause the hairy head of an undistinguishable, beastlike creature slumps sideways becoming visible and remaining immobile with its back to the audience until the end, ... A very stout elderly man enters and studies a game table located stage right containing on top a variety of very different, almost enigmatically shaped geometrical objects, – cubes, etc. For a very long time he contemplates the pieces. A small black boy enters and standing and moving a ladder carefully lights a row of candles along a shelf positioned on the rear wall (stage right). Then a second player and a third appear and stand on each side. Like a giant game that requires all of one's powers of concentration. Infrequent moves.« (Wilson, Production Notes on *The King of Spain*.)

*Freud*, which was about the death of Freud's grandson (played by the same boy), had another boy, Jessie Jordan, lighting the candles, and still another, Raymond Andrews leaning into a wire. In both plays, the boy-illuminators of our grandparents' age then instigate what may or may not be a union of man and nature (performers and haystack in the drawing room). *Deafman Glance* is about child murder, its hero, – Raymond Andrews, – again initiator into the play's Victorian scene, and its detached superior central observer (a role reappearing in *Einstein*.) A boy (Christopher Knowles) with Wilson between the scenes provides a kind of comment on *Letter* and with Wilson frames the action of *$-Value* (also providing most of its text).

preceded by warm-ups. But, except for the work leading up to *Letter*, work on a piece has largely consisted in work-sessions of which rehearsals were often the smaller part, and which in the main consisted in dancing to the less frenzied types of rock and of movement with or without music. The Thursday evening open house – mostly dancing – is an institution at the loft. On tours, many nights are spent at discotheques. Much of the time, during these work-sessions, everyone would do their own movements, walking or dancing about, generally without a partner, without a set step or directions. (Wilson's idea seemed to be that subconsciously one would sense and adapt to the movements of the others.) The sparse instructions would suggest obeying one's body's impulses; trying to be aware of what movements it actually wanted to do at each moment. The newcomer is amazed to find his/her body has such desires, – impulses to relate to the space in a specific way, to create a space of his/her own, to concretise time, and to individualise it according to him/herself. To some degree one finds oneself *able* to move freely in this sense; without purpose, aware of one's body's needs for movements, easily going with its kinetic impulses. Recurrently Wilson designates a leader, now this one, now that one, whose movements everyone is to follow. (Work on $-*Value* largely consisted in movement following Chris Knowles'.) Sometimes one individual would be chosen for a little while to move or dance for the others, – then sometimes another one called to ›work‹ with him or her.

The normal adult is afraid to move. There is safety in a fixed place, a kind of identity. Movement draws attention to one, gives one a responsibility, seems dangerous. Moving the body seems extrinsic to the body; one feels there should be a purpose. If one moves for no purpose, one tends to obsessive repetition, e.g. pacing, drumming with one's fingers, whipping one's leg up and down. In free motion, the arms are last to be mobilised, lifting them is akin to disintegration. One feels the obligation to create a pattern. One is relieved to be able to try to follow or depict the music: instead of having to make visual patterns of oneself. – Participating in Wilson's sessions, one realises that a specific inhibition underlies the common sense, decency, economy of normal adult movement: an object-less fear actually felt in permanency, so regular a state of muscular inhibition one is not conscious of it, a fear not of one's body but of acknowledging one's identity with one's body, a fear that comes down to a fear of identifying oneself, for fear that one is not good enough. If one doesn't own up to what one is maybe one won't be thought less of for being just that. Kinetic inhibition is a try at invisibility, at not really being there.

Wilson seems to conceive of this limbering up as raising the energy-level and freeing the body for further activity; the activation of energy not increasing one's energy absolutely, but releasing or unlocking it, making it flow or vibrate freely in one, making it available to one by, like fatigue, breaking down a barrier between awareness and the body: easing, smoothening its further expenditure in whatever one was going to do, in *specific* movement. These sessions do not have much of an immediate *or* long-range effect on the normal adult. One doesn't move differently. The fear is alleviated, but this by itself does not result in spontaneous activity or creativity: for which other impulses seem needed. A certain appreciable rather lasting elation and increased ease with oneself apart, the main effect might be that one becomes able to move in the outlined ›free‹ manner in Wilson's shows, doing specific designated things on a stage, on cue.

Partly because of the recurrent exigency of uncued or obscurely cued timings, and because there is little else to the performance, tho' it isn't *al*together easy to keep one's mind from wandering, to stay with it, the Wilsonian performer's mind pretty well stays on what he or she is doing on the stage: at the moment: in an immediate physical sense; with attention paid to doing it as naturally, lightly, unemphatically, but ›read‹ably as possible, and so it will, as movement in space, coordinate with others' movements, tho' perhaps not quite exactly.

The effort is not to make it look a certain way, but to feel one's body's movement: so as to keep it together, unmarred by uncertainties. The displacements, poses, acts are designed by Wilson to be seen, and the performers can't help being aware of this, but, until *Letter*, where there was some posing, by and large are not shaping their movement, they have already made up their minds it will read right if it feels right. This is helped by the low level of their concern with the audience: which is in their character and is promoted both by their interest in the work and by the high level of most everyone's on-stage awareness of the other performers. The self-awareness is unselfconscious and not a concern with appearance (not caring what one looks like of course tends to be one's defense against one's anxiety about what one looks like). The performer is not out to look good or impress anybody.

This awareness of one's movements is not deliberateness. (In normal theatre, the actor may use deliberateness: to lend emphasis to the character's actions and attract attention to their meaning.) It is relatively divorced from exercise of will. One *follows* one's movements. (What one does is simple. One knows what one is going to do.) It's not the concentration attending the doing of something difficult, requiring effort or skill, not any kind of *special* attentiveness or care. It is a dialogue with the body: the performer is alert to and responds to its signals as to how far to carry a gesture, or as to rate, or as to when to end or begin an action; and may find occasion to relax his or her body. It is an awareness rather than a consciousness of the body.

It is the *kind* of ordinary, simple awareness of what one is doing that accompanies the ordinary, simple activities of everyday living when one is not doing anything very much, or at any rate is not worried about getting something done or getting it done right, nor is inhibited in one's movements by the presence of another. This is precisely the kind of bodily self-awareness that is normally so faint as to be almost non-existent, the kind accompanying automatic, habitual, unconscious moving. The Wilsonian performer's self-awareness differs from it in two respects only. He/she makes this awareness strong in him/herself and excludes thoughts of other things, concentrates his/her mind in the mode of this body-feeling; and includes in it awareness of the movements of the other performers, tries to experience his/her body's movements as a moving with them.[91] The whole trick is not to make these two emendations alter the quality of the awareness (which would alter the quality of the movement).

[91] The basic requirement for acting in a Wilson production is sensitivity to the group's energy-discharge: the rate and volume of its flow into action. How fast are things going and how much is going on? You judge i.e. sense this from the wings, and, more importantly, after you've gone on, from on the stage. I don't mean that necessarily there is more going on if there are a lot of actions and figures on the stage at the same time. The more of a sense of occasion, relevance, importance, meaning of their own or of *the* action flows into the actions of the actors, and the greater their concentration on what they are doing, the more is going on. The rate of discharge seems to relate not so much to the speed of speech and gestures as to how often (in a 5- or 40-minute period) the situation changes, which is a matter of the sense of those doing things as to whether they or the others are still doing the same thing or are starting or have started (or are into) something new. Distraction, perfunctoriness (absentmindedness, mindlessness) lower the intensity of the gesture and are sensed in and from the wings more than the gestures themselves are taken note of. If one is open to a sense of the general level of energy at the moment (as determined by volume and rate of flow) one is hardly able not to adjust to it in one's own actions: which is why I say that the sense of it is the important thing.

The actor of normal theatre does not have this kind of awareness. Attention to playing the part, – creating or sustaining the character, – to make the movements (or what one says) look (sound) like something precludes it. Instead, the actor is aware of his/her body in terms of what it and its poses/movements look like, and of what psyche or state of the psyche this will convey.

The Wilsonian performer's group-aware bodily self-awareness not only smoothens his/her action, giving it the pattern of a self-subsisting image by connecting its elements, and so diminishing their appearance of having been inspired by the performer, and integrates the pattern with the patterns of other performers' actions, but projects: without him/her projecting it. The spectators share in his/her awareness, perhaps somewhat like spectators in normal theatre may emphatically share the feelings of characters. (The actor's awareness of his/her acting in normal theatre is not supposed to project.) This participation in the Wilsonian performer's awareness directs the spectator's attention to the patterns of the performer's movements: but not *as* acts but as patterns: as features of an event, as Motions outlining an Action, as lineaments of an image. The self-awareness translates into the manner of the movement. This manner valorises the things done. The spectator sees the performer in terms of the event of his/her performance, and sees it as intrinsically significant. The individuality of the event comes to preoccupy the spectator in abstraction from its factuality.[92]

92 »So why, you may well ask, was I so overwhelmed by my first experience of *Overture*, if I can't even tell you what happened? When all I can do is exclaim like my daughter that it just looked real . . . . . . .? Perhaps the first thing that shook me was that I couldn't see anyone performing! I was only aware that everything in the garden existed. I couldn't even have an opinion about it. How does one have an opinion about a flower? One simply has the experience of a flower's existence – or not.

As I continued to watch *Overture*, I began to have a burning desire to participate as an actor. I wanted in. But the more I thought about it the more I realized how impossible that would be. Here was a work of theatre art that I passionately approved of, and yet it was far outside the range of my own talents. In fact the problem was that I was too talented. For all my years in the theatre had trained me to perform, and nothing would destroy Wilson's work quicker than an actor acting. We are back with Coquelin's age old argument: to be or to perform the role.

It seemed at first glance that the Byrd Hoffman School of Byrds (Why do they call themselves Byrds I wondered? I was sure it had nothing to do with Aristophanes) were trained to be the role and not to perform it. Yet that couldn't be exactly true either. For nothing that they did was natural. There wasn't a sign of the famed Marlon Brando method scratch. Everything was larger than life and

Wilson's directing is pretty much limited to specific physical, graphic directions; where to go or be when, what physical gesture to make. He does not describe to a performer what he/she is to do in psychological terms. Much of his directing consists in requests to do things fast, slow, faster, slower, louder, less loud, or else in calls for lightness, relaxation, ease, combined with demands for more energy, for sustaining the energy, or for its even flow (continuity), and with exhortations to sense and be aware of oneself, of the other performers, and of what the others are doing (›you are not listening to one another!‹). He rarely demonstrates an action. His indications often seem deliberately incomplete even just factually: not to give the performers leeway to do the thing his or her own way, but as tho' to oblige them to figure them out by observing what goes on, and to sense when or at what rate to do something by way of a feeling for the dynamics at that point. He never gives directions in terms of character or motivation, hardly ever in terms of mood or situation. He may draw a performer a diagram schematizing the stage layout, the relation of different movements on stage, or the dynamics (in terms of energy) of the play or of an act. He does not ever tell what the play is about, rather tells the performer he does not know. Instead he is apt to tell the performers in strictly graphic terms the setting he has envisaged (›a wall, the kind of concrete that starts crumbling

often extremely theatrical. They employed mask, dance, mime, symbol – all elements of the classic theatre tradition – and the verbal and visual images were more often sur-real than real. Yet in spite of this super-natural un-reality, there was no sense of anything being performed. Everything seemed merely to exist, in its own time, its own shape, and its own dimension. And how, I wondered, could I ever be a part of that? How would I audition? I would have to undo everything I had spent a lifetime learning to do. To begin with, I would have to lose my ego. And how does an actor act without his ego? Here was a theatre unlike anything I had ever known, unlike anything I had ever trained for, and yet was unmistakably an authentic work of theatre art.

However, if the Hoffman Byrds were not professional enough to join Actors Equity or be given a Broadway contract (I wondered if a whirling dervish could join AGMA?), it was clear to me that night that they had developed a discipline and a technique of their own that allowed them to do things with astonishing control and refinement. In fact, as Overture came to an end, I was so impressed by their technical skill that I couldn't believe that the whole performance hadn't been accidental – a piece of »chance art.« So I decided to stay for the second performance and put it to the test of repeating itself. (That, by the way, is someone's definition of a professional: a performer who can repeat himself.) And lo, the second performance of Overture not only kept to the script, the scenario, the choreography, the design and the rhythm of the first performance, it also managed to go deeper, and if anything become more truthful.« (Basil Langton, Journey to KA Mountain, The Drama Review, T 58, June 1973, p. 52, 53, 54.)

almost right away it's been poured,‹ ›lots of tropical plants, like in a hotel lobby,‹ ›like the paths in a formal garden‹ . . .). He urges the performers to ›make it easy‹ for the audience, to enable the audience to relax, not to call for strict attention from the audience, to make gestures that read clearly, not to do too much. He does not want the audience grabbed or pulled in as ›on B'way.‹

Theatre is communication, but Wilson's theatre is marked by refusals to communicate:

no gesture of communication with the audience: the intent to communicate is not signified: the performers do not by tone or gesture signify that they are performing for or addressing someone;[93] the normal gestures of theatrical appeal (coyness, cuteness, sincerity, heartiness, the outrageous . . . .) have been deleted from performance-style and staging:[94]

no gesture of having been communicated with by the public: the overt claim to conformity to expectations is absent; neither the plays nor the players make out they are playing their part;

no communication with the audience;[95] the information normally given is withheld: the structural elements normally conveying it

[93] Exceptions: parodied archness in a night club or musical comedy song number of Sheryl Sutton's in *Stalin*, of a ditto mime-number of hers in act IV of *Letter*; and the vocal quality of *delivery* in voices projected for audibility in *Letter*. There had been little or no voice-projection attempted in previous shows. – Certain differences in timing seem to correlate with whether the performer conceives of his/her performance as communication (address) or not and with whether the audience perceives it as communication or not. The timing that holds a gesture the precise amount of time needed to make it sink in *and* to make its mark is wrong in a Wilsonian performance: the Wilsonian performer either withdraws it as soon as its being noticed right *afterward* (leaving something like an after-image) is assured, or *holds* it until the spectator feels *exposed* to it: but does not hold it the exact time needed to impress. – The normal timing for an *address* so extends it that its final segment meets with resonance from the addressee: so that it overlaps, at least in its vibrations, with an initiation of response by the addressee: but if in a Wilsonian play one addresses the public, one feels obliged to terminate before this assurance of response can germinate: which for the audience is like finding itself retroactively not having been addressed at all: the address has been withdrawn. – The difficulty in a Wilsonian performance of cleaning address out of performance is to do it without making it a show, whether of oneself or of the gesture.

[94] Note also: the in-depth staging; the predominance of transversal displacements; the props so small the audience can't properly make them out; and before *Letter*, e.g. in *Freud*, the conversational remarks so low they can't be understood.

[95] The announcements of the plays are parodistic and mystifying *performances*. On the speech introducing *Freud*, cf. the footnote to appendix III.

(plot, continuity and coherence of action, characters, motivations) are absent; nothing makes sense;

no communication between characters: the plays do not define their relations; the figures do not relate; not only don't they hardly ever speak to one another,[96] but most of the time they seem unaware of one another, don't react to one another, move independently:[97]

no communication of the interiority of the figures: faces, tones and gestures are inexpressive; the characters don't say what they think, and express no feelings or emotions: the audience gets no psychological cues.

96 Inaudible conversations and a long micro'd monologue in *King* (act II of *Freud*). The monologue was conversational, sociable in tone. Addressed to no one on the stage, it was feasible to regard it as conversation with the audience. But it was in the style of interior monologue: some people do, and charmingly, – or maddeningly, – make talk like that: one doesn't feel addressed, tho' one may feel privileged. With minute exceptions, – e.g. the Man with the Eye's sharp remark to the Waiter, – there was no dialogue in *Deafman*: what little was said was as voicing of thought, not even as speaking to oneself. There was a good deal of unaddressed utterance in act VII of *Stalin* by various, e.g. the Iceman: when Wilson at one point actually talks to him (›I don't believe you, Rick.‹), the tone of address comes as shock. In the earlier acts there are two taped telephone conversations of Stalin's (Wilson as one of the Stalins mimics listening to them on the telephone), the vaudeville-style mini-dialogue between the Tourist and his Wife (when Wilson did the Tourist he always so delayed his responses as to negate the dialogueform), some reading by a Stalin in a glass booth, that goes out over the p.a. system: but no dialogue anywhere in *Stalin* except that tourist bit. *Letter* is all dialogue; but not as regards the content of what's said: the lines do not relate in meaning; and almost all the lines are given in the accents of address, a minority in those of response: a parody of dialogue. $-*Value* beneath vaudeville joke repartees, individual coordinated declamations, Knowles' running commentary (in the intimate tone of telling someone of something and advising someone: with the someone not specified on stage) and Wilson's spaced-out delivery of verbalisms in his head, had a running sub-texture of components of dialogue, all addresses (to no one in particular), no repliques. In spite of the sound of dialogue in these two plays, there was no real dialogue.

97 Interactions are performed ritualistically: each party to them going through his part independently, with no overt signs (signals) of reaction, with no acted-out attention to, focus on, or intent to affect the other., e.g. eye contacts are rare, never intense. Freud does not overtly react at all to his grandson's death in *Freud*, and otherwise, except for some inaudible bits of cocktailparty conversation, there is not even such ritual interaction in the play, e.g. the 3 board-players are each concerned only with his own moves, not with the other players. The murder dominating *Deafman* is done ritualistically, there are no reactions from the victims, the onlooker's scream is not done as reaction to the act but as expression of his own state. But there is a number of such inert replicas of interaction in *Deafman*, e.g. the little girl's giving of a present to the Goatwoman, the Nun-Ghost's slapping of the Boy. When Wilson as Stalin in *Stalin* reacts to his first wife's death, he does not

The non-communication between those putting on the spectacle and those for whom they put it on, the audience, repeats within the spectacle: as tho' a new mode of sociability were to be both shown and put into effect. In both cases it is obvious that something is being done with a view to its effect on another (tho' without regard to a response). The audience does feel the show is being put on for them, and with a positive intent, perhaps even concern:
as a statue might be made to be put in a park, or as one might set up a Christmas tree for one's children and then stand back so they may be dazzled by *it*. But in normal theatre, – normal live performance, – normal direct intercourse, – there are 2 additional elements here absent: communication of meaning, verbal or proto-verbal communication; and the form of communication. Wilsonian communication is not a transfer, but the making of something so that others can make something of it.

Wilson evolved his theatre out of therapy that had been inspired by Ms. Byrd Hoffman's help to him. His therapeutical work with children judged retarded, autistic or mentally impaired, often with apparently organic deficiencies or lacking in coordination, and generally uncommunicative, – the immediate problem, – seems to have focussed on getting them to do simple things on the principle that this activation by fostering their bodily self-awareness and giving them self-assurance would generalise into a general mental activation, as well as a more general awareness of themselves and of others, and, itself a mode of communication, would make them more communicative. Those ›simple things‹ might be just movements, or any of the expressive things that the children inclined to do or might be moved to do, such as drawing or painting, movement to music, making whatever sounds they were capable of: art. His own judgments 1) that in fact these children were mentally active and had been right along, 2) that their mental activity was of a high order, 3) that their habitual activities were in fact communications, 4) of artistic sort and value, 5) and that they could and should be communicated with in terms of them, i.e. on their own terms (a second principle of his work with them) perhaps stood in contradiction to what parents, teachers, etc. wanted him to achieve (channel the kids into normal, conven-

really react to it, but expresses his internalised feelings resulting from it. I remember no instance in a Wilson play either of acted-out reaction to another or of action on another with acted-out attention to the other. In this sense, there is no interaction. – But compare this with what R. W. says (cf. Appendix 1) about the relationships between the figures in *King*.

tional learning processes), but probably were essential to his work. At some point he got into similar work with more or less normal, functioning repressed adults: awareness-sessions. The general point seems to have been to start people doing things, for the sake of doing them, naturally expressive of their individuality as corporal beings rather than pointedly expressive of their psychic personalities: what they could do.

He got a degree in architecture and tried to be a painter, but found himself inhibited. His head was full of visual images to which he wanted to give external form. He had all this energy. He had a breakdown.

Wilson proceeded to build images out of people acting natural.

Wilson proceeds as architect and painter. He builds up the stage-image by zones lying one behind the other, giving resonance to one another, and giving him a spatial order to work with in constructing the dynamics of the temporal dimension. This depth-layering gives a kind of massiveness, – solidity, – reality, – to the phantasy constructed. It is vivified, – broken through, – by isolated, carefully controlled diagonal movements.[98] He does not deploy an action in space; he constructs his space by actions. The space, not the action, is his primary material.[99]

His initial givens, what he wants to stage, are images, not ideas.

98 On the occasion of the first production of *Stalin*, in Copenhagen, in 1973, Wilson pointed out that, setting aside the movements parallel to the audience, movements in the first half of this play were on the diagonal up-stage, stage-right/down-stage, stage-left, while in the second they were the inverse: up-stage, stage-left/down-stage, stage-right. Tho' his diagram was in lines, not arrows, in fact the movements, insofar as they conformed to this schema, were in both cases from up-stage to down-stage, toward the audience; and in the second half of the play the line was not straight, but twice broken:

The down-stage point of change of direction was to some extent important throughout the play also for transverse movements: important figures, e.g. the dark murderess, Queen Victoria, would advance to it, stop there. He has such space-realisation diagrams in mind for all his plays. They often seem to involve a mirroring doubling.

99 One of the great things about Bob's plays is the vast exotic spaces they take place in, i.e. that we see the Figures in. Even the Drawingroom becomes a vast exotic space – in which anything could happen. What does happen in these vast

These primitive images are generally not of people or groups or actions, but of settings, or else of objects. They are visual images: sound in his work is ancillary to the visual. This remained so even in *Letter* and *$-Value*. He generally develops the action only during work with the performers: to be in accord with the primitive images and to bring out what they mean to him. Of course sometimes some of the primitive images are of people: an old man (reading, walking), a black woman sitting, a boy in the air, a party of ladies at an outdoor nighttime concert.

The over-all stage-image for a given act is apt to consist of several discrepant images in juxtaposition (not so in *Letter,* except for Act I, scene 2: two men reading newspapers in front of a mimed repetition of the preceding scene): e.g. a planetary surface and a ship of fools in judgment in act VII of *Stalin.* The juxtaposition is apt to occur to him after the images occur to him, not with them, not as interior relation between them. I.e. he constructs the over-all image out of separate visual blocks. Similarly for the successive images introduced into the over-all setting: the spectacle at any given moment has been put together out of originally independent images. This procedure contrasts with various normal theatre-procedures: elaborating a single image, arranging actions into images, finding images for ideas. It may be compared e.g. to an architect's constructing a facade out of traditional elements of some style and in independence from engineering and functional considerations, or to a painter's introducing balancing elements into a composition having settled on a dominant element.

With some qualifications we can say that the performers of a Wilsonian spectacle appear as themselves.

exotic spaces *is* anything, but, surprisingly, it comes on as tho' very much at home, 2nd nature. We are in this sense not in the theatre at all. – Contemporary theatre even at its best can hardly accommodate Lenin or even Robespierre. In fact, it's too small for King Lear: MacBeth is just about all it can manage, and then only because he's a criminal, so we feel right at home with him. The little Lenin in my mother's *Bells of the Kremlin* was embarrassing. – Events *do* take place in New York, Africa, the Pacific or on the surface of the moon, and not 57 Sutton Place etc. Life is not on the block but in the city. – The spaces of human activity are defining spaces; realities; and large. They are historical/geographic entities defining for men (and not only for great men) the situation into which they insert their action or inaction: and for some centuries now this has been a matter of experience for people. Wilson unintentionally found a way to put this reality on stage in its true dimensions. The spectator sees the activities in his stage-spaces as incidental to them: as what happens to happen in them.

There are no ›characters,‹ the performers do not imitate, impersonate or represent personalities: neither what they do, nor how they do it, certainly not anything they say, allows the identification of a personality other than their own. The performances are inexpressive of feelings, moods, thoughts, intents, emotions: non-psychological, not acting. Movements and gestures are not in character, in any character other than the performer's.

Costuming, tho' not any make-up,[100] what is done, and sometimes slightly how it's done, do identify roles, viz. two-dimensional *figures*: Freud, Stalin, Queen Victoria, The Frog, ostriches, apes, assorted beasts, an Old Man, A Waiter, pilots, a Chinaman, gamblers, Ladies, middle class people in a drawing room (Nice People), Country Lads, a Magician, a Prince and Princess, a Tourist and his Wife, a crotchety crackpot (The Man with the Eye), an insane Oriental Potentate (perhaps recognisable from some movie as Ivan the Terrible), Black Mammies, Stalins, stock vaudeville characters, an 18th Century Couple (probably not recognisable as George Washington and Marie Antoinette, but resembling the George Washington and Martha Washington couples done by kids in certain parades), The Iceman (a tall thin man in furs swinging two blocks of ice from ice tongs), the Woman that Writes on Air, The Goatwoman (an old witch/fairy godmother), The King of Spain (a large furry man-beast with a huge head made by Wilson), A Little Girl, A Crazy Old Lady . . .[101] By and large, these are stock figures: fantastic, but not extraordinarily fantastic, not far out but out of some child's everyday imagination:

100 Wilson has come on in black face and in white face. Sheryl Sulton has used eye make-up. I have shadowed wrinkles.
101 *The Life and Times of Joseph Stalin* was a more or less complete collection of this imagery:
»Prolog:
(Robert Wilson's *The Life and Times of Joseph Stalin* began with a five-minute wordless speech/song by Queen Victoria, standing in front of the curtain. The Prince and Princess descended from the stage and took seats in one of the boxes. Wilson and a boy have repetitious exchange: »What? What? What did you say I said?« Wilson announces the performance.)

Act 1 – The Beach (48 minutes).
The stage is covered with sand; there is a blue sky drop. A chair hangs from the flies. All movement is made along several planes parallel to the proscenium line. No one crosses in front of the Byrdwoman, a black woman in a black dress with a black stuffed bird. Among the many figures are runners who pass at irregular intervals throughout the act and, with some exceptions, throughout the entire performance. Three dancers, nude above the waist, execute a repeated series of seven simple movements. Bears and a turtle (photo) cross. A man, only his legs

some of a fairy-tale sort, some historical, some identified by social status, some by profession according to entertainment-industry clichés, mostly slightly touched and retouched by Wilson's whimsy; and some

visible, walks a beam lowered from the flies. A man in a heavily padded suit wearing a black stocking over his head does a whirling dance across the sand. Freud and his daughter Anna pass. Forty black mammies, identically dressed in kerchiefs, long dresses, and aprons dance to Strauss's »Blue Danube.« At the end of the act, the Byrdwoman stands, places an Egyptian figure on downstage table, looks out at the audience, and emits a long scream-like sound.

Prelude to Act II:
(Two men in cowboy outfits rise from the holes in forestage, where the heads of the chorus can be seen during most of the production. One plays a fiddle; the other plays a guitar and sings »Goin' Down the Road Feelin' Bad.« A drop is revealed that shows the facade of a Victorian house. Holding a monocle up to his eye, a man looks out from one of the windows. Queen Victoria appears singing her wordless song seated in a carriage without horses. As she moves across, the shutters of one window after another pivot, revealing painted flames.)

Act II – The Victorian Drawingroom (105 minutes).
The second act is one of adding, collecting, assembling. In a large, sparsely furnished room, someone sits center, turned away from the audience. The hanging chair is lower. A row of candles high on the left wall is lit. Among the figures who function in isolation or in small groups and often are motionless, are: a »boy« who stands on a stool for the entire act, a blind man and two other men who play chess, Freud, Anna, Stalin, a photographer who takes their picture, a piano player, and a walrus (photo). A tall man (Wilson), in blackface and a padded mammy costume, does a loose eccentric dance. The performers exit in a procession. The figure in the center chair turns: It is the »King of Spain« – a huge grotesque head with long hair.

Prelude to Act III:
(A man whose head and shoulders are visible above one of the holes in the forestage looks through a small glass prism. A nearby telephone rings. The man answers it. A taped conversation between »Boris Pasternak« and »Joseph Stalin« can be heard. »Stalin« asks »Pasternak« if the poet Ossip Mandelstam (who was sent to Siberia and died there) is an artist.)

Act III – The Cave (49 minutes).
A large dark cave is seen from within. Two or three animals and the King of Spain are resting there. In the bright light and swirling mist outside the cave entrance, semi-nude figures dance. The Byrdwoman enters and sits beside the King of Spain. Freud's grandson is brought in. One by one, more animals gather from within the cave: a lion, bears, a real sheep, a walrus, a fox, a turtle, an ostrich, and an ape. At irregular intervals, heavy vertical bars fall, eventually closing the mouth of the cave. The gatekeeper mimes a Russian folk song. Freud sits center in the chair that has been lowered at the same small table that has appeared in the previous acts. A somber funeral procession passes outside the cave. Figures from the

are purely creatures out of Wilson's imagination, but so clear, simple and sober (*un*whimsical, unironic), and compounded of such general elements that they are assimilated to the stock figures. Their quasi-

procession in animal masks and half-masks peer in through the bars. The grandson begins to cry. A hanging pane of glass falls and breaks.

Prelude to Act IV:
(A drop just behind the curtain line shows a grey, cracked wall. The Byrdwoman, a young boy, and a little girl are motionless on a white platform. All are dressed in white. While the »boy« of Act II (played by a girl) watches, the woman, in slow motion, stabs both of her children. The »boy« screams.)

Act IV – The Forest (135 minutes).
A pyramid is seen upstage. In front of it is a forest of two-dimensional trees and a three-dimensional house. Supported on the backs of four turtles at the right is a large square »pool«, across which three wooden fish slowly »swim« during the act. At the left, a dinner table served by a butler and maid is presided over by a large frog. Processions pass. Three people carry panes of glass. In the middle of the act, the death of Stalin's first wife occurs witnessed by two Stalin figures. At irregular intervals, prone performers, each with a fish tied to his back, slowly make their way across the stage. A young woman speaks in Persian from the house. Smoke pours from the house and it collapses. A bull on wheels is brought on in a procession. The head of the bull falls off, smoke comes from the neck, and the body glows. Stalin's second wife commits suicide on the plexiglass platform. People climb the upstage pyramid. An eye at the top lights up and rises from the openings. Nine apes ascend through the smoke. They pick up in white and holding panes of glass into two upstage openings in the floor. Smoke rises from the openings. Nine apes ascend through the smoke. They pick up apples that are on stage and hold them up, at which point, the apples fly up out of their hands.

Prelude to Act V:
(Helen Keller, Ann Sullivan (her teacher), and Alexander Graham Bell are grouped center. They exchange signals through touch. With Keller's hand resting against her throat, Sullivan sings. The man with the glass enters. The telephone rings. Finally, he answers it. The taped voice of »Stalin« can be heard ordering a general to commence firing. Cannons resound as the curtain rises.)

Act V – The Temple (60 minutes).
A pyramid is seen from inside. The act involves several dances staged by Andrew de Groat. Sixteen people in 18th-century costumes perform a mechanical doll-like dance in square formation. A row of people lying side-by-side pass wooden dowels. The sevenpart sequence of movements from Act I is seen again. There is free dancing. Performers spin for extended periods each keeping on his own track. Several people dressed in yellow do a contained bobbing dance upstage and then lie down side-by-side. Using a microphone and amplification two monologs are recited from within a glass booth (photo): one is a series of sounds, words, and disconnected phrases; the other is based on a piece by Stalin. The Byrdwoman, dressed in black, leads a black-dressed procession across the front of the stage. When it has passed, the Byrdwoman reappears dressed in white. At the end of the

or pseudo-universality and their individuality so balance as to allow an ease of recognition, but no wallowing in familiarity, nor a shock of recognition. A gentle humor lightens but does not destroy their

act a man in an 18th-century costume appears carrying a torch and kneels facing Stalin in the glass booth.

Prelude to Act VI:
(The facade of the Victorian house that burned can be seen again. Now all of the windows are boarded over. A woman pushes a supermarket shopping cart heavily loaded with food from the right to the left. She loudly relates a personal anecdote to no one in particular.)

Act VI – The Victorian Bedroom (54 minutes).
Upstage is a Victorian bedroom drop; in the center, a long mirrored hallway opens directly toward the audience. (During the act figures from the second act can be glimpsed in the hallway.) On stage are twelve beds, arranged in rows. A person in a white nightgown lies in each bed. In the corridor, an old man dressed in a long coat with a stick in his hand slowly moves forward. The sleepwalkers get up and slowly »search« in unison, lanterns in their hands. These sequences are repeated three times. At one point, a black woman in a white tophat and tuxedo moves across downstage to an Otis Redding song. A schoolteacher sits at a desk downstage left. At the end of the act, a desert drop comes down separating the old man and the schoolteacher from the sleepwalkers. The schoolteacher cries »Thief! Thief!«, at which point the old man throws off his coat. He is naked with a snake wrapped around his body.

Prelude to Act VII:
(Icebergs rise on the apron between the two chorus areas. A girl comes up through one of the chorus holes and plays a flute. A red elephant enters, kneels at the icebergs, and speaks. The lights go down, and a girl in a man's suit dances in front of the curtain. The elephant speaks and sings; the chorus echoes him. The curtain goes up, revealing Queen Victoria. She runs off.)

Act VII – The Planet (90 minutes).
The backstage drop shows a clear sky and a rugged, crater-filled landscape. Again the stage is covered with sand. About twenty ostriches dance. A cycle involving, among others, the man with the glass, Queen Victoria, a woman with a book, a man with a tree branch, and performers doing the seven-part movement sequence is repeated four times, building in volume and intensity. Three times the Byrdwoman comes up through a hole in the stage; each time she is dressed differently. In Egyptian dress, she recites a speech from *Medea*. In an evening dress, she sings. In a white Victorian dress, she recites a poem. Between each of the four cycles there are blackouts, during which slides of a door closing and a hand coming through the door are projected. At the end of the fourth repetition, a drop is lowered downstage showing Moscow burning. A crowd of poorly dressed people enter downstage right and cross toward Stalin, who is dressed in white. There is a tableau while the crowd hums the Pachebel Chorus. Stalin answers the telephone. »Stalin« and »Pasternak« are heard again discussing Mandelstam.

gravity. There is The Frog, but there are also ostriches; there is The Waiter and Waitress, but there are also pilots; there is Stalin, but there are also Stalins; there is Freud but there is also The Man with a Tree on His Head Who is writing on a Typewriter and the Woman standing on a Ladder listening to a Wire. This medley inhibits the identification of a genre, e.g. fairy-tale, but what they almost all, even f. inst. the Big Woman telling of her childhood, done in the performer's own character and simply, – perhaps only the dancers excepted, – have in common is a clear distillation through imagination, an individuation of universality (there are no types), and the character of visual images (they are not incarnations or personifications of anything, not symbols).

These figures are acted out only to a minimal extent, – by some simple version of an old man's walk, of a waiter's suavity, a Chinese accent, a society person's affectation, ... They are not acted: the acting-out is so minimal as to remain obvious, merely suggests some familiar identifying characteristic that is not only clearly superficial, but of a superficial (unserious) sort, a handle, a visual cliché. There is no attempt to indicate that they are real people, or to individuate them as persons. There is no attempt to indicate an inner life, e.g. the sorrowing of Jack Smith's Magician in *Deafman* was formal, he acted out a sorrowing figure, – not a character's sorrow. But neither do the performers attempt to diminish the reality of the figure by parody or by deliberate elevation into the universal.

The childlike surface-character of the figures and the childlike simplicity of the acting-out keep the performers in view as themselves. There is no way to identify them, *as real people*, as substantial individuals with definite personalities, with the figures. Unlike what is the case in the creation of characters by actors, their creation of the figures can not of itself blanket them out of the spectator's awareness, allowing him/her the illusion of watching the action of the figures. If the spectator is to bracket them, qua real-life people now performing, out of his experience of the spectacle, the spectator must deal with them directly, must transcend their substantial reality without recourse to the fantasy of the figures.


The performers appear as themselves (engaged in acting out figures).

The curtain falls. (Frantisek Deak, *The Byrd Hoffman School of Byrds/Robert Wilson*, The Drama Review, T 62, June 1974, p. 74-80).
102 I am here disregarding individual instances of theatricality: in *Letter*,

But they don't exactly act normal. They act normal[102] but not exactly normal.

Until *Letter* and *$-Value*, which were fast, the tendency was toward very slow movements (sometimes, rarely, interrupted by sudden small fast gestures, jumps etc.: discontinuities, slips), lasting a long time, actions repeated, postures long maintained in immobility. The performers, figures, actions were on exhibition, thus enhanced. The performers' concentrated awareness of their bodies and of what they were doing (physically, at the moment), – appearing as inwardness (awareness plus non-communication) – focussed attention on what they were doing, made it seem important: to them personally, in itself. Slowness, deliberateness and concentration combine to make all parts of each action seem equally important, not done to accomplish an end, but important in itself, as that extended pattern. The purpose seems to do them: make them happen. The performers' awareness of one another is inobvious as such but results in an impression of supra-individual coordination between the actions/movements, seemingly independent of the individual performers, as tho' something were working itself out through them; and makes the evolving images to which more than one contribute cohere. All this combines to create an air of spirituality, awe: tho' as tho' these were somehow intrinsic to the proceedings without being actually the spiritual states of the performers themselves (or even of the figures acted out). With some exceptions (Robyn Stoughton, Ann Wilson) neither the facial expressions, nor the gestures indicate such states: they are not solemn, not authoritarian. A style of the extraordinary results: as of a participation in rituals, – unknown rituals. (Rituals are routinely performed in a non-solemn manner: as routines; and yet do not by this lose their solemnity.)

All of this is very faint sometimes: the performance-style is rarely very far from the matter-of-fact, from the being busy at something, tho' without business, but even so, given that it takes place in a performance-situation, and a relatively formal one at that (not just in any old loft, or in some loft, or in some crummy old theatre), and given the extended durations of everything, the manner's normalcy

Sutton's movements, gestures and intonations were conventionally tho' sophisticatedly theatrical throughout, Ashley's theatrical; Lubar's poses were theatrical in act I, her diction stylised in act IV. Francene Felgeirolles did the death of Stalin's first wife in the N.Y. *Stalin* in French high tragedy style. Wilson's own performances consistently alternate high theatricality, – extreme, grotesque, artificial gestures, movements, poses, intonations, – with the supra-normalcy of acted-out absent-minded ease.

seems super-normal, verging on the supra-normal. This becomes very clear when someone, – f. inst. Melvin Andringa, the stage-manager of *Deafman*, at one point during that play (or sometimes dancers getting to their place on stage), – makes an entrance in a non-performing style, merely to take care of something. Wilson in a masterly way, during one performance of *Overture*, explaining the breakdown of some mechanical equipment to the audience, played on this distinction, shifting back and forth between a non-performance (the evidently functional action of explaining, apologising, getting his listeners in a good mood: of communicating, in person, with the audience) and a performance (doing the thing for its own sake, as an act); until it became clear to one, in one's total confusion, that the whole thing was an act and that normal behaviour and normal communication are performances: the breakdown of the equipment, not a part of the performance, had become a part of the performance, but the performance was also not a performance.

There are those discontinuities, slips. There are the occassional raw-sounding screams, odd repetitions of a word in an otherwise normally spoken phrase, slight voice-sounds following a word as tho' an after-image of it. The nice patterning of simple conduct described supra then breaks down. Raw energy breaks through in a moment of anarchy. Normalcy, heightened or not, comes to seem other than natural: a matter of control, performance.

If the manner of the activity on stage, the performers' way of moving, is ordinary/natural enough to seem each performer's own, – it is in fact more a relaxation with individual nuance than a suppression combat situations). If they are not outright fantastic (the Frog's of it, – the activities are only in the most superficial sense everyday (and became less so from *Freud* onward), – partying, dining, fishing, watching animals in a cage, running on a beach. In fact they are decidedly *odd,* when not out of the ordinary (dyings, murders, summersaulting exit off the table and all the activities relating to the Ox or the Pyramid in *Deafman*, the activities relating to the ladder or the cage in *Freud*), they are odd by some detail or accumulation of details, by a context of setting or of other activities, or simply by prolongation or repetition, or else odd, i.e. inexplicable, not making sense, in themselves (taking snapshots of a hole in the ground, listening to wires, using a magnifying glass as lorgnet, carrying rocks or panes of glass, covering a ladder with hay). In the context of this general quiet madness, some perfectly reasonable natural things that are done, – sipping tea, telling about one's childhood, – seem odd too.

The distinction between the (heightenedly) normal manner of the activities and their odd nature is perceived as distinction between the normal activities of the performers and the odd activities of the figures acted out by them. The figures and the fantastic or odd action are abstracted together from the ordinary-looking performers and their ritualised but normal/natural movements and after a while turn into an independent iconography, watched for its own sake. But to begin with, this separation makes the performers' appearance of ›real people,‹ appearing on stage as themselves, stand out even more.

A similar paradox characterises the dancing when it has been choreographed by Wilson. When choreographed by Andrew DeGroat, it is an orgiastic anarchy of self-indulgently vain posturings: the 5th act of *Stalin*, the introductory and concluding scenes of *$-Value*, – even the onstage dancing of DeGroat and Julia Busto, beautiful if limited dancers, in act 4 of *Letter* tended toward the shapeless, substituted phony expression for individuality. When choreographed by Wilson, – the runners and Black Mammies in *Freud*, the ›seven parts movement‹ in the first act of and the swirling mass-descent toward the end of *Deafman*, the spinning of Busto and DeGroat in front of the scene in *Letter*, – the dancing, tightly coordinated by Wilson into the clean abstract movement of a scenic element or whole, sets off the individual normal body movements of the particular dancers.

Showing performers as themselves seems incompatible with theatre. We think of theatre as dissimulation. That these performers frankly themselves are interesting to watch and even beautiful is strange particularly because Wilson does not pick particularly beautiful or graceful, nor strange-looking people, but aims at a diversity of appearance within the range of conventional appearance, – ›just people,‹ – and even stranger because the people he does pick tend to be both awkward and impersonal, inexpressive, uncommunicative, – of a reserve approaching the autistic, – and move and speak accordingly on stage. They are on show as individuals but incline not to show themselves and are encouraged by Wilson not to. Yet a powerful communication, – of individualities, – results. It is not a resolution of these paradoxes, but a further paradox that fantastic images and a strong illusion are created. (And there is yet another, final paradox: the striking images resolve into a show of energy.)

Setting aside the sets, mood-music and introductory announcement, the audience's experience starts with seeing people doing things. The spectator is led to concentrate on these people's individuality.

Awareness of the performers' individuality in Wilson's theatre replaces the awareness of a personality (or in pre-bourgeois theatre, a character) represented by an actor. This awareness is the gateway into Wilson's theatre. Tho' Wilson's theatre is not in the end a gallery of individualities, much less a glorification of individuality (and even less of particular individualities), but rather the opposite, it works by way of this awareness. Its performance style is oriented toward engendering it, – and only then toward making the spectator transcend it. If theatre is not to bog us down in the illusion of reality, it must tell us stories: but if it doesn't tell a story, how can it get us past the illusion of the reality of the performers? In fact, how can it be theatre? To make the performers disappear into the intangibility of their individuality is Wilsonian theatre's solution of this problem. For individuals to reveal themselves was probably his original theatrical intention.[103] To this was added the intention of

---

103 ›At about that time I'd decided to do *The King of Spain* and I thought about it and I wanted to get a lot of people together and I had been looking and specifically noticing different people for, oh, I guess about the last year or so and had been thinking specifically about using them in something . . . in a large theatre piece . . . and so I got a lot of them together but the way I started getting them together was to think about them first of all clearly I guess – now let's see now – clearly about what they were and then I'd think about each one individually – that any one was was so different from another so totally different and I thought that *was* especially curious. That was nice – I liked any two of them being together at different times.

›And then I kept thinking too that certain people I knew had never just uuuuuuuuuhhhhhhhhhh seen a different kind of people (or persons) other than themselves. Then I also kept thinking about what I've done at parties – getting different people together – and it's curious how at parties totally dissimilar persons get together unexpectedly like so I guess maybe that's really how I got the idea for my play.‹ (Wilson, *Production Notes* on *The King of Spain*, p. 247.)

›And then I'd say that the piece is going to work because the people are so very different. That is even though there isn't much action going on the people all being themselves and being very different construct of their own accord a context, or their own play, by presenting themselves as they are, then (theatrically) no more is necessary – I mean that's what any professional director tries to create only it's in the context of an imposed structure, not one that is drawn from within and generated of its own accord. Because I did the initial work (as such) of structuring the sequences of the stage action and activities, that is, the order of their entrances, the huge Victorian set and backdrop and the slow, modulated game the three elderly men play throughout, the ›plot‹ in that sense became a loose, open-ended structure – or a non-structure in that it freed the people in it, enabled *them* to

showing his images. It may have been some dubiety about his images – himself – that resulted in a technique negating the images. I know of no other theatre working to create awareness of individuals. Individuality strikes me as the contemporary mode of self-identification: but as little understood. The concept of individuality is elusive. Its tricks may cause some of the mentioned paradoxes of Wilson's theatre.

People are anxious to be seen, appreciated and dealt with ›as individuals:‹ to have their ›individuality‹ recognised and taken into account. What they mostly have in mind is 1) they don't want their consent, opinions, feelings taken for granted. 2) they don't want to be taken as of some kind or type, 3) they want their differences from other people appreciated. They want to be dealt with as independent agents with a mind of their own for them to make up: as autonomously functioning wholes. They want their specific character, – what they are really like, – to their mind usually a unique way of being, – reckoned with in its peculiarity. They often go to a great deal of trouble to show that they *are* ›individuals‹ in this double sense: free and different, freely different, differently free; and how. Much of their communication is devoted to such shows of mind and will and of how they are peculiar, and to shows of appreciation of such shows. In modern times,[104] – during the bourgeois epoch, – people have tended to identify themselves and others in terms of such an integration by and of will and consciousness into a peculiar functioning whole, and the arts, theatrical and other, have tended to represent people in terms of it, viz. as PERSONS possessed of a PERSONALITY or PERSONAL IDENTITY. I believe that this ideology misuses ›individual‹ and its cognates, that individuality or individual identity are something else: or at any rate in these post-bourgeois times have come to be conceived of as something else. Bureaucratisation and proletarianisation have made personality seem pointless, – no identity.

By ›individuality,‹ I mean not just an individual's being *an* individual,

step outside of themselves naturally by stepping into the context of *The King of Spain.*‹ (Wilson ib., p. 249.)

104 In pre-bourgeois civilisations, identification was by CHARACTER: a posture, evinced in conduct, that one assumed, as agent and sufferer, toward one's life (fate), identity conceived as *nature*, rather than as consciousness-centered, freely willed self-specification, the individual conceived not as functioning whole, but as a thing with certain properties or of a certain type, – moral properties, a moral type.

nor any other less general but still generic identity of its, but its individual nature or identity: that in particular which makes it *that* individual, the individual it is (the one and only): which its being itself consists in.

We normally identify things, whether verbally or by awareness, by *what* they are: by their specificity. Either meaning that this, taken by itself, is their identity, or that all or some of it distinguishes them from everything else. These identifications may be by kind or by properties or by both. By the ›complete‹ identification of an individual, one would normally mean either 1) identifying everything it is (its aggregate specificity), whether by enumeration or by summation, or 2) identifying something it is that nothing else is, f. inst., if this can be thought of as something an individual is, its location at a given time, or some other unique peculiarity, or some combination of features uniquely peculiar to it.[105] It is immediately apparent, I think, that there is some sense in which neither kind of identification, especially in the case of organisms and more especially of organisms seeming endowed with freedom of action and with the consciousness requisite for such, – people, – necessarily adequately identifies an individual. Rather one feels, that an inventory of characteristics, or the summary of one, could adequately identify an individual, especially an individual of a highly evolved type, only if it identified it as a whole or in its functioning as a whole, and an identification by distinguishing characteristics only if these were essential to its functioning as a whole, or indicative of how it functioned as a whole. If an identification did not indicate a mode of functional integrity, one feels it would not grasp an individual at all, only a something, perhaps a single and even singular something, but not it as an individual. Its individualhood would be missing from the identification. But, and this is my point, even an identification fulfilling this requirement would not identify an individual as individual, – its individuality, – but only a type (kind) of wholeness and functioning characteristic of it (and possibly of it only), – a *generic* identity, – unless in addition it identified the *individual* characterised *by* the identified specificity of wholeness and functioning.

An individual has obviously not yet been identified as individual when we have identified it as *an* individual (identified its generic

105 »even ... identical twins or triplets ... exhibit some differences on the molecular side.« (Dr. Franciko Ayala, U. of California at Davis, New York Times, June 19, 1975)

individuality, its individualhood). But neither can we achieve this by identifying it by its way of being (its particularity), whether as a functioning whole or not, and whether pinpointing something unique about being that way or not. Particularity does not add up to an individuality; peculiarity does not resume the uniqueness of an individuality. The individual has an identity beyond specifics.

Four references may suggest what ›identifying an individual as individual‹ might mean.

Everybody in introspection has direct experience of him- or herself not only as an individual, and not only (nor even necessarily) as a particular kind of individual, but as the individual he or she is: not only of his/her generic individuality, nor of a type of individuality (this latter in fact often escapes detection), but of his or her individuality. And, tho' one can't *define* one's identity by any particular attributes, – e.g. self-awareness, activity, self-actualisation, – the definition of oneself as ›the one one is aware of as oneself‹ is circular, – one finds oneself infinitely particular: has positive awareness of what makes one not just *an* individual. There is a sense in which one not only knows of but knows oneself even if one is unsure of or doesn't know what one is. Or what one's difference consists in. One finds oneself in the texture of one's awareness: as the one engaged in being aware, as active awareness. One thus identifies oneself not by recognising signs of oneself, – properties, – but in an encounter (engagement) with one's own being. One finds oneself neither a substance distinct from one's attributes, nor abstract singularity, nor a form of oneness, but active energy of individuation.

The experience of oneself has the form of an experience of self-identity within an act of self-identification: one can't help but catch the self in the act of individuating itself. There is no view of the self apart from a – other than a – self-identifying self; nor of a *relation* of identity between oneself and oneself. The self thus appears – inevitably – a self-actualising activity. One always finds oneself coming into being by the very act of one's identifying oneself. Tho' one isn't all the time focussing one's awareness on oneself, one carries the experience of oneself as individual with one throughout one's periods of awareness. Whenever one is aware of anything one has an unfocussed awareness of one's self-identity, a feeling of one's own individuality. This self-knowledge, an act of self-identification, seems an automatic and indispensible constituent of all object-perception. It seems absent, and even then really isn't,[106] only in one's experiences of other individualities.

Individuality, then, as distinct from specificity (tho' not as exclusive of it) *is* experienced, – namely in introspective self-awareness, – *does* exist; introspective self-awareness provides every person that person's primitive model of it; and by this model it has the form of active energy, not of substance, and specifically of an activity of self-actualisation.

People experience themselves as concrete (specific) individualities not only qua psyches, but also corporeally. For tho' to one's visual perception one's own body is an alien object, – a substantial thing, – *without* one's individuality, – to which one relates only extrinsically, identifying oneself as observer of it, as inhabitant of it, and/or as its master or animator, one may, merely by attempting it, render conscious one's permanent subconscious *feeling* of one's body, of one's extendedness, may make oneself feel the generic attributes of one's body, such as extension, warmth, weightiness, movement and rest, as one's own, as attributes of the same I that one is aware of as aware (thinking, sensing, etc.): tho' one will then experience these attributes not as properties, but as processes or events, as one's own ongoing instantaneous actualisations. In this feeling, – a view of one's body from the inside, an identification with one's body, – one experiences corporeal individuality. This experience provides a model for experiencing the individuality of other corporeal individuals.

There is a third type of experience of individuality, also ordinary and universal: that of the individuality of other people, primarily, tho' not exclusively, acquaintances, and sometimes even of individual domesticated mammals, – dogs, cats, horses. This is quite unlike the experience of one's own individuality.

We look at someone and feel we ›know‹ that someone, – know him or her for what he or she is: ›as individual.‹ Sometimes the feeling is that of having a ›vision‹ of them, or of ›really seeing them, for the first time,‹ or of ›only now really seeing them;‹ sometimes, – significantly, I think, – of ›feeling what it must feel like to be them.‹ Sometimes one has attained to such acquaintanceship without noticing: there has been no first conscious experience of coming to see that person ›as individual.‹ We again and again *re*cognise an individual: find that individual's individuality the same as before. Subsequent

106 Cf. infra re the ›displacement of the center of experience‹.

227

encounters generally reconfirm – or modify very little – such impressions of people. These very strong and definite intuitions (sensings) of what a person is, of persons, of their identity, can and do arise from brief encounters: observations of them in the flesh doing simple, superficial, ordinary things or nothing at all. They seem wholistic perceptions of recurrent patterns in the way they do things or hold themselves. Observing people in the flesh is not merely the occasion for these impressions: they are impressions of them in the flesh, tho' not as things, but as tho' their flesh were something they did, and they themselves the doing of it, its energy.

The attitudes and manners of the visible body, – for me, I would guess, especially the way a person ›holds‹ him/herself (as a complex Gestalt resulting from a complex of partly unconscious muscular tensions), ›uses‹ his/her eyes, and the way his/her voice ›moves‹ (cadence, patterns of timbre, pitch), – *seem*, in these impressions to function as a complex expression of the individuality: which itself in these impressions seems to be an energy of the psychosomatic whole imbued with that expression. Whether this is so or not, – whether an unconscious response to a ›body‹ language takes place or not, – I don't know. One certainly feels one has grasped more than merely the distingushing peculiarity of the individual, viz. feels one has grasped his/her essence. If indeed ›how an individual does things‹ leads attention to that individual's individuality, it probably does so rather as a *trigger* of the experience of it, than as a sign, for it gives rise to that intuition only when it makes one notice their distinguishing peculiarity not qua what distinguishes them (makes them unique), but qua *theirs*: if how *they* do things (*do* things), not *how* they do things, is what it brings to one's mind. In fact, tho' the image is striking, one hardly notices its particulars. Perhaps one first achieves a wholistic perception of an individual's peculiar corporeal self-integration by muscular empathy, – by a ›body‹-sensing in the nature of an imitation, – and then experiences this corporal identification with the other as an identification in awareness.

Tho' it is in a particular stance or act of theirs that one catches a person's individuality, and tho' one never has a separate intuition of it, divorced from all concretion of image, not only can one recognise it, having once become aware of it, in all their poses and whatever they are doing, but even in that first perception the specificity of the image is felt to be irrelevant. The individuality imbues it, comprises it, is in it, but is not just it. And the *nature* of what they are doing, the meaning, purpose or function of it, is not just irrelevant, but is not even part of the impression, is not in one's mind, or fades from it as one becomes aware of *them*. Eo ipso, the stance or activity need not be particularly significant, need not indicate anything important about that person. No revelation of, no information about a person's character or personality, – of what is in their mind or of what their mind is like, – is needed for an intuition of individuality.. On the contrary: tho' a poignant display of feeling or the revelation of a crisis-situation may by focussing one's attention on a person indirectly lead to an experience of that person as individual, – provided they don't distract one or cause one's feelings to interfere with one's perception, – a person's attempts, conscious or habitual, to create a certain impression of themselves, whether of what they feel they're truly like or of them as they would like to seem, obstruct intuitions of their individuality by stimulating a perception of a role which inhibits any disposition to see them as individual. A show of identity acts as a shield against identification.

Awareness of an individual as individual in no way increases one's ability to predict or explain conduct. It adds nothing to one's knowledge or understanding of a person. Nevertheless it is experienced as not only insight into but comprehension of a person's nature and essential being: perception of what a person *is*.

There is still another type of experience of individuality, but unlike the foregoing, it takes a special effort or a special mood. One can perceive the individuality of any object of visual or even auditory perception, – can perceive it as individual, – by concentrating one's attention on it: provided one makes an attempt to see it as an integral whole without focussing on (without trying to identify) its individual features, and provided one tries to avoid identifying it in any generic way (as of this or that sort).

If the attempt is successful (you can try the experiment: its successful outcome is quite distinctive), one will, tho' one won't ›notice‹ them much, still be aware of the specific features of the object, – they won't change, of course, – but any generic identification one might have made will have receded into the background, and one becomes aware of its specific features as *its*, as its *specifically*, rather than being aware of it in terms of its specific features: sees them relative to the whole, instead of vice versa. The experience, not a mystic one, is that of an object's redefining itself before one's eyes: as tho' one *observed* its, – *its* – integration of itself: *by* its specific features. Its particular features take on the character of instrumentalities. It seems to change, without changing in any *particular* regard. In the process it may seem to move out from its background, toward one, to *become* 3-dimensional. Its particular features, including the location and distribution of its parts, take on the character of processes or events, instantaneously completed and yet ongoing: vibrating energy: its acts and its actualisation. And one has the impression of perceiving the object's individual nature or individuality. One feels one is participating in its being.

If my distinctions are valid and if my examples support them, individuality turns out something quite different from what one thinks: very little, no more than a faint coloring on a window into infinity; too much, an entire existence at a moment in time. The I seems both concrete and a non-entity. The examples suggest:

as an object, something has substance, as the individual it is, it doesn't. *An* individual is perceived (thought of, sensed . . . .) as substantial, as a substance, the individual is not, but is perceived as process or event, – as a fire, a changing cloud. Whenever we identify the individuality of something, it turns out a becoming[107] rather than a being. If the individual nature of things is their real nature, and if the experiences mentioned are in fact of the individual nature of things as it really is, then reality is process.

This process is energy in action: an energy turning into activity and defining itself by its activity: but real only in and by this activity, not existing apart from it: constituted and constituting itself by its activity.

The process constituting the individuality of something is its own activity: its self-actualisation. Since activity presupposes an agent, this is a paradox; and if activity presupposes the pre-existence of an agent, this paradox may be a contradiction. Our intuitions of individuality may be irrational.

Individuality is in yet another sense not a mode of being: it is a mode of existence. It is read in the individual's appearance. As individual, an individual is perceived as being what it is perceived as being: just so, just that. Its reality for the perceiver coincides with

---

107 ›Becoming‹ used without temporal connotations. The time of the individual as individual is the eternal present. It is experienced as all there, at the moment, – not as having a reality before or after, – but since this moment is not experienced either as the now of the experience, nor as instant of objective time, but as *its* present, *without* before or after, it is not experienced as not having reality before and after either.

its existence, and its existence with its appearance (which seems an appearing). Its individuality is and/or lies *in* this reality, imbues it, gives it identity, creates it.[108] It is not an inferred interiority mediately expressed. It is a stance or pose. It seems appearance: but it seems real as appearance. It seems an image of the individual: not the observer's image of that individual: not a reproduction or representation of the individual, distinct from it: but the individual itself as image. Or it seems *in* this appearance and image.

These are the key-features of individuality: the coincidence of reality and appearance in existence; that this existence is an event; that this process or event is energy in action; that it is the individual's own activity.

From the viewpoint of ordinary experience, these features add up to a surprising loss of substance. Since in ordinary experience, reality defines itself as substantiality, from the viewpoint of ordinary experience, the experience of individuality is a delusion. But from the viewpoint of the experience of individuality, the substantial reality of objects is a subjective construct. Arbitration seems impossible. Within the experience of an individual's individuality, the individual is intensely real, and in fact seems suddenly to *become* real. It becomes *real* for one as self-sustaining process of energy.

The intuition of individuality is attended by a displacement of the center of experience from oneself, reference-point of normal object-consciousness, to the individual.

In the normal modes of object-awareness one experiences oneself as actively appropriating the object's particularity, – its coherent form or an aggregate of self-identical universals (properties). Sensing the individuality of something, one experiences oneself as passive recipient attending the individual's undirected (not oriented toward oneself) disclosure of its nature and being (that disclosure seeming to coincide with its nature and being). The experience is constituted and defined by this event: by the individual's appearance: rather than by one's apperception of it. It, not oneself, is the epistemological reference-point.

In normal object-experience, the object is experienced as *in* a time

---

108 That the same observer attributes the same individuality to the same object on occasions on which its appearance and existence are not the same does not mean that its individuality lies beyond appearance or is independent of appearance. It may in fact mean that it resides in unaltered aspects or proportions of appearance: but to the pereiver it is not so isolated or separable.

and space subsisting independently of it, and as *definitely located* in both, even tho' they, its containers, continuous and infinite, have no definition defining any places. One thus experiences oneself as origin of the definition of the object's places in time and space: by the definition of a now and a here, defined not by anything in time or space, nor by any objective locatedness of the object's, but by the moment and place of one's awareness; and by the definitions of directions, units of extension (measurement) and points of reference (which last themselves can only be defined by the subjective nowness and hereness *for some observer,* of some object occupying them), likewise defined neither by time and space themselves, nor intrinsic to objects, but conventional. Normal awareness thus locates objects ego-centrically in spite of the apparently independent subsistence, – independent even of the observer, – of the space and time it locates them in.

But aware of the individuality of a thing (or person), one experiences its here and now as defined by *it,* by the moment and place of its self-actualisation and appearance, and experiences time and space – and to begin with its extension and duration, – not as independent subsistence, but as its extensions or modes of being. The individual itself is one's spatio-temporal reference-point, and in this way also the structural center of the experience of it, – as well as, for the moment of one's exposure to it, of the whole world: seeming *its* environment.

This displacement of the center is a destruction of objective order. Not a mere reordering of it from ego-centered to object- (individual-) centered. For while normal object-awareness has one stable center, oneself, and, as a corollary to its perception of objects as substantial entities, a definite frame of reference accommodating them all, a space and a time perceived as independently subsisting and thus as capable of sustaining ego-centered systems of relative but definite location, in the experiences of individuals as individuals each individuality appears centered in a space and time of its own, its individual appurtenances, individuated by it, so that there is no common space or time, no objective order. The only reason these systems don't clash in experience is that one cannot experience more than one individuality at a time.

The experience of an individuality seems verbally inexpressible and incommunicable. One finds oneself unable to tell others what a given individuality, one's own or that of a third party, is: one cannot put it into words for oneself. One senses it, but there seems no verbal equivalent. The structure of language seems adapted only and specifically to conveying the normal experience of objects: by conventional signs, some denoting universals, others (part of the logical vocabulary) abstractly referring to individuals (substances), identified by these universals. The peculiar unity of an individuality that one can sense on direct contact, – or perhaps in a replica, – unavoidably seems irretrievably lost in a verbal representation. The reader/listener could perhaps by a synthesising act of the imagination overcome, – reverse, – the disintegration of the individual by language insofar as it was sequential: but that disintegration is into universals, and it seems doubtful that the imagination can construct an individual given merely universals. Signs other than icons can not convey individuality: individuality cannot be reduced to a meaning. Thus it seems to me that literature can convey a character or a personality, but not an individuality.

The perception of an individuality requires a disinterested interest, – that one's attention be attracted by the object in the absence of extrinsic interest in it. Nothing will disclose its individuality unless dwelled on. But neither will it, if any reason for focussing on it, whether pre-existent or given one by focussing on it, – whether a practical end or an end of knowledge, – structures one's interest in it. One's own teleological schemes (structuring normal experience) must become inoperative. The individual's call for one's attention, anchored in these schemes, must not divert from *it*. For any extrinsic reason reduces the individual to mere object: by assigning to it a role in an enterprise of one's own so that it figures for one only as an object having or not having specific features making it suitable for that role. E.g. introspection to ascertain one's feelings or motives, body awareness in the performance of physical functions, emotional concern for another person, a look at something because one may need it or to see what it's like. But on the other hand the individual must not be taken for granted or ignored because it's familiar or uninteresting. The perception of individuality requires exemption from these two alternatively dominant dispositions of ordinary life.

The perception of individuality requires an interest in the individual as a whole. Before we can perceive an individual as individual, we must see it as an individual. The perception of its individuality grows out of a perception of its integrity. Thus outstanding features or parts, actions or poses interesting in themselves, or close integrations into an environment, whether by engagement in actions which or by involvement in events which transcend the individual, inhibit recognition of individuality.

It requires that the individual be perceived in relation to itself: by itself. Its relationships to other things divert attention from it to themselves or to the other things. For its individuality to emerge, it must absorb our interest. The moments when an individual is least involved with others, e.g. being in some way much involved with itself, or when our attention is not to its involvements, are best for it to show as individual. Thus attention to others precludes introspective awareness of one's individuality, as does one's body's involvement with other things the sensing of one's physical self-identity. If we observe someone active relative to or oriented toward a third party or toward ends (purposeful), and pay attention to *that*, we will not see that someone as individual. In particular, if we feel ourselves addressed by another, or in any way the other's end, – whether by some act or by some deliberate or involuntary communication of theirs, – we are apt not to see that person as individual: the relation or our reaction, the nature or meaning of the act or of the communication will distract us, – and our interest will not be disinterested. If we observe a thing acted on or affected by another, its individuality is apt to escape us.

The object must not be seen in terms of a category: as of a type or kind, as characterised by a certain property: or even in terms of its similarity to another individual or other individuals: but in its own character. Preliminary or initial classifications must be surmounted. Awareness of a classifying sort precludes perception of individuality.

Finally, the object must be perceived in its immediacy, as given in its existence, as apprehended: as a concretum. If, i.e. as long as in our perception of it we make some distinction between its outwardness and its inwardness, – e.g. by perceiving its outwardness as expression, or as appearance of an inner reality, or as manifestation of an inner force, or as sign of something within it, – we are ipso facto precluding the *kind* of integration characteristic of individuality. The unity imported into appearances by these explanatory, interpretative and transcendental dichotomies is extrinsic to them and displaces the intrinsic unity of individuality. Thus introspection governed by a notion of soul, mind, psyche or ego, distinct from its contents, acts or states, will not yield a sense of one's individuality (but merely of one's being *an* individual), nor will body-awareness

## HUGH HALES

General Manager

Mayfair Theatres & Cinemas

First Floor, 110, St Martins Lane,
London. WC2N 4AH.

structured by assumptions of a body/mind duality. We will not see people as individuals while thinking of their appearance or acts as expressions or consequences of their personality, character, or state of mind. A thing seen as manifestation of an, itself not evident, physical structure or process, or of God, or as phenomenon in our mind, created or structured by it, will seem devoid of individuality.

Whether an object is seen as a whole, by or in relation to itself, in its own character, in its immediacy, or with disinterested interest depends not only on one's frame of mind, but also on the object and the situation. Some objects are more apt to be seen as wholes than others, and more apt so to be seen in certain states than in others. The situation may be such as to present the object in relative isolation. The object may or may not invite classification or explanation by an inwardness. The situation may or may not set up a disposition in one to see the object as a whole, in context, or by itself. The object or the situation may or may not stimulate one's interest, this interest may or may not be or persist in being extrinsic. – This means that tho' one cannot induce the experience of the individuality of others in people, one can so manipulate their environment as to promote it. Wilson's theatre is such a manipulation.

These experiences of I who am I, Me, this body, He himself (or She herself), It itself, are extraordinary. They momentarily disrupt the normal order of existence. But they result from a focus on a single individual, and pertain to it only: one is momentarily not paying attention to the normal order around it, but is not oblivious of it: its presence to one's mind is signaled by an aspect of restraint in one's concentration on the individual. It has been shattered for one, but one is aware that it would instantly reform if one changed one's object of awareness or mode of attention. And the normal world of me, them, and this, that and the other, fragments of formed substance scattered in the empty frame of space, in empty equitably passing time, persists. We snap back into it having learned nothing basic: even as regards the individual we ›suddenly saw.‹ E.g. another person's individuality normally instantly turns from their essence into just another fact about that person, or even not even that, but merely a subjective experience we've had of that person. For in real life we have to *deal* with – and therefore to *reckon* with things and people, and this overriding need perpetually forces us back into a world viewed as world of objects. The perception of individuality is impractical.

This dual existence of ours under normal conditions shapes our *effective* impression of individuality. What we do is, we attach the individuality of objects to them as another property of theirs. This is how the individuality of an object initially emerges into our experience; this is the impression we ›carry away.‹ The experience of individuality normally assumes the false form of the experience of an object to which an image of individuality attaches. This reintegration of a momentarily glimpsed other reality into normal reality is a denial of it.

Wilson's pieces up to *Letter* were initiations.

The spectator's initiation is by three transcendences: of normal ego-centricity amidst substantial others into selfless centering on insubstantial individualities; of this state, into contemplation of appearances; and of this state into participation in appearing non-finite energy.

The inducements for the first step come from the style of the individual performances, those for the second from images. The arrangement in time and space of the images induces the third. The individuations of the performers negate the reality that confronts normal object-awareness, the images negate the individuals, the staging negates the images.

This works only for some of the spectators, only some of the time, never works completely. The effect ends with the show. I am here going to discuss it insofar as it works.

The elements of Wilson's non-representational, transcendental theatre may be schematised:
1. individual performances that reveal the performer's individuality in pseudo-rituals;
2. a show of images;
3. spectacle as imagery-flux
4. spectacle as encompassing environment.
The spectacle is an awareness-session designed for a step-wise modification of the spectator's awareness: from
1. observing things the performers are doing; sensing their movements;
to
2. contemplating images produced by what the performers are doing,

images structured as the actions of figures; attending the images'
quiescences and evolutions;

to

3. participating (being immersed, absorbed) in the energy-borne flux
of imagery: in touch with a process of creative energy producing the
fluctuating imagery, participating in it.

The spectator is guided from one object of awareness to another, or
rather from objects of awareness to a surface of awareness to a
texture of awareness:

1.

    a  performers (people) doing things (engaging in movement)
    b  individualities, concreted into their activities

2. sustained/evolving images

3.

    a  an energy-borne flux of imagery
    b  a process of energy appearing as a fluctuating imagery.

None of these objects normally appear in theatre.

The dynamics of normal theatre is defined by an action, i.e. by
change or evolution, generally for the better or worse, in the relations, situations and/or insights of one or more characters. It is a
dynamics of content. This dynamics defines the dynamics of the
audience-reaction: in terms of anticipation or emotional engagement.
Anticipations are set up, teased, fulfilled and/or disappointed; sym-
pathies, empathies, are created, the audience is made vicariously to
share the hopes, sufferings, joys, successes etc. of the characters. This
dominant audience-awareness-dynamics may be accompanied by
others, notably an increase of self-awareness by way of identification
with or recognition of characters, of reflection on their action, and/or
a change in feelings about, attitudes toward and/or insights into
institutions or types of people. Someone or something may be revealed
to be different from what they seemed. But these dynamics still relate
specifically to content. They involve only one kind of change in
object and mode of awareness: from observation of a performer to
awareness of a character: from looking at actors on a stage to
watching with familiarity certain characters in their environment.
This is a change from realism to illusion. But the object of the illusion
is a suppositious reality of the same sort as the object of the realism:
the activity of real substantial people in a real substantial environment. In this sense, there is no change. Except for this deception,
normal theatre at its most ambitious only adds to awareness, i.e. to

its content, diminishing misconceptions, adding information, but does not change its form, and adds to it only by increasing its content or its valid content, but not by heightening it. It mobilises the spectators' energies only for affect: does not stimulate their sensitivity.

Wilsonian theatre dispenses with these dynamics of normal theatre. Its dynamics are designed to heighten and to change the mode and object of the spectator's awareness. They cannot be defined in terms of content, but only in terms of the (intended) effect on the audience. Wilson's theatre has no propagandistic, moral, emotional, educational intentions or effects. It addresses itself to the power of awareness only:[109] to its reform.

Wilson's theatre is set up not only to induce the spectators' experience of the individuality of the performers, to sustain it in each case, and to give the spectators a generalised disposition toward it, but to prevent backsliding, the renormalisation of the experience: not by prolonging that experience indefinitely, but by leading the spectator smoothly from one experience of an individuality to another, by a systematic repression of references to normal reality, – whether that of the theatre-situation, or one represented by a play or its characters, – and by promoting a shift in the spectators' attention from the individuals as individuals to the images of their appearances and actions (as individuals), viz. to images structured by the motions of figures acted out by the performers.

The spectator sees one or more performers, preset or entering in front of the drop or on the stage after the drop's gone up. The spectator has identified them as performers only in a preliminary suppositional way: by their segregated presence on the stage.[110] The spectator thus identifies them as Persons – Someone – Doing Something (moving, holding a pose, relating in some manner to some object) and (by props, costuming, relation to a stage set) Presenting a certain Stage

109 This connects it to the avant guard painterly N.Y. theatre of the early '60s, – happenings, – a kinship apparently still apparent in »ByrdwoMAN« (1968).
110 Wilson favors traditional interior theatre-architecture and large proscenium-stages. He makes ample use of the drop-curtain, uses various devices to separate the audience from the spectacle, e.g. the down-stage line of ›fishes‹ in *Deafman*, the two rotating dancers (and, in the pit, the chamber music ensemble) out front in *Letter*. He is intent on this separation: the continuum between people-spectators and performer-performers is to be disrupted: the spectator is to see the spectacle at a distance, not as real in the sense in which the house and the other spectators are real to him/her.

Appearance. The spectator has separated a personal datum from a theatrical datum. As yet, the Something Done is part of the personal datum.

Separetely analysing these two data, the spectator proceeds to some identification of *What's* Done, and notes it's done in a certain Performance Style (heightened normalcy), and notes also a Personal Attitude of the performer's toward doing it (reserve, no attention to audience, quiet attention to and involvement in what he or she is doing), as well as certain facts about the performer's Personal Appearance — (age, sex, hairstyle, body type . . . .; that the appearance is ordinary).

Connecting up What's Done by and the Stage Appearance of some performer or group of performers, the spectator identifies the theatrical datum as a Figure going through the Motions of a certain Action[111] in a certain Setting. The action might be e.g. the writing of an announcement on the air, or a mother's killing of her children in some room, or a Stalin halting a movement of the masses. The Action is presented in its Motions: it is not represented by the Motions. The Figure is presented in its appearance (form): it is not represented by the appearance. The spectator sees the Performer as presenting them: thus sees them as relating attributively to the performer; as (the performer's) performance: not (yet) as self-subsisting image.

What's Done and Stage Appearance not lending themselves to psychological interpretation, and the Performance Style inhibiting it, the spectator abandons attempts (prompted by an expectation that the performer would represent a character) to postulate a Character represented by the performer or to interpret What's Done as *representation* of an action, or to view the stage with its sets as *representation* of a setting. Instead, the spectator views the theatrical datum as theatrical datum: as Spectacle.[112]

---

111 The Performance Style promotes this view: the performers move as tho' their movements traced out pre-existing patterns: eked them out, embodied them, bodied them forth.

112 Backdrops, stage-sets isolated from one another, costuming and lighting, provide a fantasy-setting not unlike that of musical comedy (operetta), but of an unearthly beauty, somewhat abstract in the manner of the surrealist painters, and affecting the spectator as painting. The lighting is strikingly unrealistic, — artificial, unreal. Any one tableau is apt to present incongruences, implausibilities: what would not co-exist and discrepancies of scale. Stage-technique is utilised for effects of discrepancy, estrangement: slight uncanny movements by objects, slightly uncanny amplifications of sound. Animals wander through. An audience-disposition against realistic interpretation is set up. Dispositions toward realistic interpretation

The spectator is apt to be puzzled by the Significance of the Action and to wonder from what Point of View it is being presented. But the spectator is given no clue as to either. Tho' this puzzlement and wonder may not subside completely, the spectator is thus reduced to observation of the Spectacle. E.g. the spectator of *Stalin* seeing a Stalin-figure (done by a black girl in a Yalta-type uniform; with a stage-moustache) halting the advance of a ragged mass may think of Napoleon's retreat from Moscow or may wonder what the image is saying about Stalin's regime, but in the absence of clues will confine his or her attention pretty well to the tableau: in which a faintly ludicrous, childishly simple but imposing stock figure defines itself, apart from the identity it derives from the spectator's newspaper- (etc.-) -conditioned historical imagination, by the Action outlined by the gesture. As in a true ritual, the Figure is not seen as having existence outside of the event pictorialised: does not function as sign, does not represent, – e.g. the real Stalin, – but is:[113] and so is seen as defined by the Action.

The performer's Personal Appearance and Attitude similarly inhibiting identification of the performer's personality, the spectator identifies the performer by external characteristics of his or her Personal Appearance as an Individual of a Certain Appearance, – acting out a certain Figure going through the Motions of a certain Action in a certain Setting. Because that Figure is not a character, and because of the performer's Personal Attitude of quiet attention to and involvement in the Performance, viz. the presentation of the Figure going through the Motions of that Action, the spectator sees the Performance as *personal*. This links the theatrical to the personal datum. The Performance Style of heightened normalcy promotes this linkage.

The Spectacle develops very slowly. Since, again, the Stage Appearance is only a Figure, not the representation of a character, and What's Done is only the Motions of an Action gone through, not the representation of an action, the spectator cannot identify the performer and the performer's performance with or as a character represented and an action of such a character's. Figures and Motions do not obscure the Individuals of a certain Appearance acting them out. The theatrical datum does not absorb the personal datum. On the

are not absolutely discouraged: the spectator's desire to settle down into a fantasy-reality, accepted as real, is frustrated.

113 True ritual is non-representational for the opposite reason, that the enacted event, the ritual, *is* the substantially real imaged event itself, whether as its magical double or as in eternity identically it.

other hand, the personality of the performer is not in evidence. In this situation, the spectator is apt so to concentrate on the performers as to relate to them *as* individuals, – so as to have an intuition of their Individuality. The mentioned requirements[114] for this are initially fulfilled: especially also insofar as the theatrical datum on the one hand is exposed long enough so that the spectator's attention is not definitely distracted to it from the performer, and insofar as it is seen as a personal performance.

The spectator, in a withdrawal from the observational posture, felt to be unprofitable, loses him/herself in (gets lost in) some individual performer. The experience is one of sinking in. There is a feeling of participating in that performer's experience of the event, and of, by way of this, entering the spectacle: experiencing it from within, – as something done, not shown. This feeling predominates over whatever appreciation or acknowledgement of that performer's particular individuality there might be. One seems to sink through the surface of that Individual of a certain Appearance, and instead of finding something within, a kernel, finds oneself, – one's awareness, – expanding as though within that individual's empty inner space into what that individual is engaged in doing. One is in effect hollowing out the performer, reducing him/her to a surface integrated in the visual space-time Gestalt created by his/her movements. This experience, like the concentration on saying ›om,‹ is a mere transitional point. But I am suggesting it is crucial to Wilsonian theatre.

Seen as individual, the performer is no longer seen as a person – someone – doing things, nor as an individual of a certain appearance acting out a certain figure, nor as performer presenting a spectacle. These identities disappear. The spectator becomes unaware of them. Losing substantial reality, the performer for the spectator turns into what he (or she) is doing at the moment: an event. His/her actual appearance and existence fuse with his/her reality: it is in them that the spectator sees the performer's individuality. The performer's individual identity is his (her) identity as phenomenal reality and event. But this event consists not only of the performer's Personal Appearance and Attitude, but also of the performer's personal Performance: of a certain Figure going through the Motions of a certain Action. Seeing the performer as *an* individual or *as* performer, – as an object, – the spectator sees the performer acting out the Figure and the Motions: *presenting* them; and distinguishes this appearance presented by the performer from the performer's reality as *an* indi-

114 p. 233-235.

vidual, *as* performer: however personal, it is not that performer's own appearance. But gripped in the experience of the performer as individual, the spectator loses the reference to the performer's substantial reality distinguishing the personal from the theatrical datum. The two fuse into that individual's appearance: which is now also that individual's reality.

The spectator's individuation of the performers, since it grasps them in the act of performance, integrates them with their performance, viz. the Figures going through the Motions of certain Actions in certain Settings. It fuses personal and theatrical datum.

This elimination from the spectator's awareness of the performer as an extra-theatrical reality within the theatrical event, – fusion of the performer into the performed, – differs from the illusion operated by normal theatre (achieving the same elimination and fusion through the spectator's identification of the actor with his/her part), in that it is achieved not through the spectator's focussing, – ignoring the real performer, – on the performed, viz. the character represented and the character's actions, but through the spectator's focussing precisely on the real performer: so much so as to come to see him or her as individual. It works by an exposure of the performer. If it involves an illusion, it is that the performer is not real, viz. not substantially real, as object,[115] – not the illusion that the figure presented is real. In normal theatre, it is this latter illusion that makes the real performer disappear: substituting a fictitiously real character for him/her. In Wilson's theatre *this* illusion never arises. Like normal secular representational art, Wilson's art induces the sublimation of the given into image: but it provides no replacement for the lost reality.

The spectator now relates only to a certain individual who *as individual is* a certain Figure going through the Motions of a certain Action. Only the image of What is Done remains. It has the structure of that Figure going through those Motions of that Action in that

115 There may be a limited analogy here to true ritual as experienced by believers: the believer's experience of the *real* transcendency (*transcendent* reality) of the enacted action or other event is grounded in his/her faith in the transcendental qualifications of the officiant or priest: the ritual, for the believer, turns into the magical double of the conjured event (the rain, the successful hunt), or into the actual theophany enacted (the presence of Christ), rather than merely being a representation of it, *because* the human officiant has for him/her turned into a transcendental being. In rituals also, the officiant as human being disappears into the event enacted by the officiant. Wilsonian performances in terms of this analogy and others are pseudo-rituals.

Setting. It is individuated by the individuality of the performer.[116] It has no substantial reality. But not *lacking* it relative to the reality of a *performer*, it is real as image. It never was the image *of* a figure, of an action, of a setting: now it no longer relates attributively to a performer. It is a self-subsisting image.

The spectator can transform the entire spectacle for himherself into self-subsisting image by relating to a single performer as individual: not just the Figure and Motions immediately presented by that performer: namely if the Figure and Motion immediately presented so relate to the others (presented by other performers) as to define them for the spectator, – if only *as* Setting for the Action. E.g. the presentation of a mother's murder of her children: the spectator by relating to the performer of the figure of the murderess as individual will come to see the self-subsisting image of a mother's murder of her children without necessarily relating to the performers of the figures of the victims as individuals. The force of the image, that of the murderess's act, individuated by the murderess-performer's individuality, will push the real child-performers of the victims out of the spectator's awareness. Similarly e.g. for up-stage background dancers or runners: they melt, their individuality unrecognised, into the scenery, made image and defined by the foreground self-subsistent image.

There is nothing absolutely preventing a spectator from returning to a view of a given performer as *an* individual or as *performer* rather than as individual, and thus, unless a view of some other performer as individual in turn de-substantialises the spectacle for him/her, from re-relating Figures and Motions attributively to real performers. But built-in features of a Wilsonian spectacle mitigate against this. In real life, some fact about or something done by an individual relating to the teleological schemes dominating our real life is apt to snap us out of an experience of that very individual's individuality. But the Personal Appearance and Attitude of the Wilsonian performers (unlike those of f. inst. performers, notably the stars, in musical comedy) does not draw attention to them as personalities, and their Performance Style (unlike that of most kinds of actors) does not draw it to them as Performers. E.g. a Wilsonian spectacle does not stimulate prurient interest in individual performers. In real

116 Whereas, in principle, a true ritual is not individuated (nor personalised) by the individuality or the personality of the officiant.

life, an automatic return to mind of the teleological schemes dominating our real life, e.g. that we relate to the individual in question in some particular practical regard, tends to pull us out of an experience of an individual's individuality. But the spectator of a Wilsonian spectacle like the spectator of most other kinds of spectacle (even a B. Brechtian one) is apt to have abandoned for the time of the spectacle, his/her practical extra-theatrical interests and concerns, and is apt to have no real-life extra-theatrical relations to the individual performers. And a Wilsonian spectacle, being unrepresentational, is less apt than normal theatre to recall to the spectator his/her everyday interests and concerns, and, unlike most normal theatre, not setting up but discouraging expectations of gratification (by amusement, skill of performance, resolution of plot, emotional involvement, representational values), i.e. not setting up but inhibiting teleological schemes relating to the theatrical experience itself, if it captures and holds the spectator's interest at all, is apt to make this interest a non-finalistic, – contemplative, – interest. Whereas the expectations of gratifications set up by normal theatre invite recurrent evaluations from the spectator, reminding him/her he/she's in the theatre, and thus, among other things, redirecting his/her attention to the performers as such.

The images are in fact reproductions of images in Wilson's mind. But in addition, – no nexus materialising that would make them appear the appearance of a supposably real world, – they have the character of images for the spectator. They are not just insubstantial, disembodied forms generally, but have the pulse and texture of configurations of awareness, of pictures (and sounds) in mind, of the seen, heard, dreamt or imagined: like what one sees staring abstractedly at something for a long time, or like the kaleidoscopic figures of light one sees shutting one's eyes tightly, or like the isolated images one sees falling asleep or waking up. The spectator sees them *as* imagery not by consciously identifying them as hisher own illusions or as creations of Wilson's imagination, but because heshe is in fact seeing (and hearing) them, but without the normal accompanying attribution of material substantiality, and because Wilson has staged them as visiting configurations of awareness: providing nuances of unreality, the discrepancies and whimsical arbitrariness of fantasy, the excessive simplicity and clarity – and the prettiness – of visions or of images of the imagination, the illogical transgressions of definite self-identity characteristic of dreams, the indefinite hints at meaning beyond that attach to the perceptions of a puzzled or troubled mind, content charged with sub-conscious affect, but above all, the flow and flux of contents of mind, the shift of focus, the transformations, the variations of energy characteristic of mind, because characteristic of independent mind, of mind not imposing on its awareness the structures of reason and/or reality. Sensitive to this texture and pulse, contemplating the individual images in their geneses, evolutions, disappearances, the spectator experiences them as of the stuff of awareness, in their nature and process not differing from the nature and process of hisher awareness. But this feeling never precipitates in an experience of any awareness underlying or giving rise to the images. For no subjective unity emerges in the content of the spectacle: its contents are no more structured as expression of a personality than as the phenomena of any world. There is no encounter with an awareness.

The imagery-flux has the *character* of a free process of awareness. Wilson has so designed it: free from the constraints of logic, reality, and psychology. There has been no selection, shaping, or ordering by logical principles, concepts or ideas. Wilson has resisted or eliminated this influence. There has been no selection, shaping or ordering by a world view, i.e. by any one definite per- or conception of any one definite order of objective reality, or to make the aggregate or process of the images or these themselves conform to any conceivable natural order. Wilson has not only resisted or eliminated this temptation: he has systematically sabotaged its satisfaction. There has been no selection, shaping or ordering to express a personality. The flow of imagery is free in that the images seem to devolve and proliferate according to their own nature: no extrinsic, esthetic or other ordering scheme is in evidence, there are no interruptions or discontinuities suggesting the interference of a conscious artist. This freedom is evidently illusory: an appearance created by conscious artistry. But there is no suggestion in the spectacle itself that it is illusory. That the form achieved is in fact the form of an (in however limited a sense) free activity of awareness is borne out by the spectator's ability to give him/herself to this flow, to participate in it, and to sense him/herself, in the atmosphere created, free in doing so, i.e. to experience him/herself as actively aware in a natural rhythm, with no violence done hisher imagination. This experience, a self-awareness in which the spectator is aware of hisher own awareness, and is aware of it as an energy-charged activity, and as a natural or unconstrained activity of hisher very own, is one of the achievements of Wilsonian art.

This experience may be *contingent* on the spectator's not experiencing that imagery-flux *as* process of awareness: this would give a definite identity to it that might impede that feeling of a freely energetic activity in the participation in it. This identification is at any rate not part of the experience. Even less does the spectator identify it as process of some *one* awareness. Richard Foreman's spectacles come to be experienced as experiences of another consciousness, probably, – program-notes and stage-devices aiding, – Foreman's. But Wilson's theatre rather leads one on to an experience of impersonal cosmic energy.

By ›energy‹ I mean an actual capacity for and disposition toward work (for/toward doing something to make something, for/toward creative activity). Actual: not an abstract or theoretical potential nor something inert to be summoned up or activated, – no ›latent energy‹: but some definite, dynamic state: an activity or process, tho' not necessarily an excitement. The capacity consists not merely in quantity, but in availability and readiness: to be energy in this sense, the energy must be convertible into work. The disposition is not necessarily a drive, but on the other hand does not necessarily need a stimulus to turn into work: it is an orientation or inclination toward work, a tendency. Tho' in its exercise such energy may turn into a driving or compelling directed force and into a power over something, it is not itself either, nor even intrinsically or necessarily a capacity for or disposition toward either. – This definition outlines what one means by ›an energetic person,‹ but makes allowance for relaxed energy and a natural state of activity.[117]

Experiences of energy are either of it at work, – experiences of formative or other creative activity, or of the formative or creative processes induced by such activity, – or of it itself, and in this case are either attributive, as when on the basis of previous experience, perhaps by analogy, and either by reflex or reflection we adjudge someone or something capable of doing work, or direct, when it itself is the object of our experience. E.g. watching performers in action,

117 The preceding gives several examples of energy in this sense: the state of the Byrds devoted to Byrd work; the state Wilson's therapeutical work aimed to get his young patients into; the state into which Wilson's movement-sessions get one. Since it is also the substance of individuality as well as a state any artist who has found hisher own thing to do, e.g. Wilson, is in much of the time, it is not surprising that the ultimate subject matter of Wilson's art is neither individualities nor the images in his mind, but energy.

we may experience their activity of performing as output of energy, or we may experience what they perform (present or represent) as output of energy, or we may think of them as exercising energy because (as we read the signs), they by their manner of performance or otherwise indicate this or we may sense or otherwise directly experience the energy. The experience is not necessarily inferential, and insofar as it is inferential, is not necessarily limited to the work.

Experiences of energy, power and force are integral to theatre experience, both for the producers (author, director, performers) and for the consumers, the audience, each experiencing them in themselves[118] and in the others,[119] the audience sometimes experiencing them as energy, power or force of the producers, notably the performers, sometimes as energy, power or force of the performed, – the presented or represented.

The productive energy is partly energy for[120] creative imagination, and perhaps for emotional agitation, partly the energy for controlled physical movement and for the awareness needed for this, indirectly energy for affecting the audience. In Wilsonian theatre, the consumers' energy is almost purely energy for awareness, in normal theatre also emotional, imaginative and sometimes ratiocinative energy, as well as energy for enjoyment.

In normal theatre (the non-avant-guard, non-experimental, formally not too innovative forms of theatre of modern times), the productive energy tends to be experienced, by both producers and consumers, as excitement and as force and/or power, but not in Wilson's theatre. The energies are and seem different. In normal theatre, it seems to both parties specifically that of the producers or of the produced (the play, the show): Wilsonian theatre may in both parties give rise to experiences of pure energy, of energy neither specifically that of the producers or of the produced.

In normal theatre, the spectator, when he pays attention to it at all, tends to experience the individual performer's work as exercise of a

---

118 The fun of entertainment is 1) to play with the public's nerves (teasing), 2) the athletics of making an object out of oneself. (If that object is an art object, that's gratifying to the artist, but none of his (her) business.) Both are experiences of energy mobilised for power.
119 E.g. the difference, for the performer, between a dead house and a live house.
120 ›For‹: used for, not necessarily of a sort limiting it to or orienting it toward such use. Not energy necessarily bound up with a particular faculty or propensity, not necessarily energy ›of‹ a faculty or propensity.

profession, as execution of someone else's design, as the performer's expression of him or herself, as communication intended to give an impression of him or her, and/or as the production of something intended to be pleasant, entertaining or beautiful and/or, possibly, instructive, i.e. as expression of needs and intentions and as use of aptitudes rather than as actualisation of energy. Wilsonian performances are not experienced as expressions of needs and intentions, nor as use of aptitudes. This facilitates the spectator's experience of their energy.

The spectator of normal theatre is apt to experience something like a power of the spectacle or performance over him/her, to feel that it is reaching out and grabbing him or her, drawing, pulling or sucking him or her in, unable to resist, and that it overcomes, vanquishes, captivates him or her and takes him or her in charge. Sometimes the attractive and assimilative force seems exerted by the charm or the power of personality of a performer, sometimes by the dramatic or esthetic power of the play or spectacle. Sometimes it emanates ambiguously from the producers, notably the performers, or from some individual performer, and/or from the illusive extension of the performance, i.e. from the play or spectacle. It is the force imposing the illusion on the spectator, compelling him/her to take the glamor, pretty sentiment, gaiety, or else the grandeur, tragedy or misery, and the contents, for real. The spectator may feel that the energy of the show or of performers is backing up or even creating this power or setting up the force, – creating the suction, – but in the main will experience a power and its force: will feel seduced or overwhelmed; and will experience those energies more directly in other ways.

The analogue in Wilsonian theatre is a feeling of sinking into the spectacle, of going out to and entering it, not drawn by it, certainly not grabbed or pulled in, nor moved to do so, but as tho' by a natural proclivity. Whether a power is exerted or not, no power or force is experienced. This affords an opportunity for the experience of the energy behind such power or force.

Setting aside the occasional impression a spectator may have that some performer (or an author or director) is straining, that the performance has called for or is calling for an effort, and in this negative, incidental sense has involved or is involving an expenditure of energy, and the impression occasionally created by a performance or spectacle but seeming irrelevant to it that some performer (or the author or director) is or is not in fact an energetic person, a theatre audience is apt to experience productive energy in two ways: as energy put by the performers into their performance and/or projected onto the audience ›across the footlights‹; as energy of a show in its forward motion, discharged into it along the line of its development. I shall take up the former first.

To the extent that the spectator not only infers that the performance, because it seems shaped with a view to its effects on him or her, has been or is intended for him or her, but feels him- or herself addressed by the producers (and not just, metaphorically, by the contents), experiences it as a communication, – and this is normally formally the case in normal theatre since e.g. its performance-styles tend to have built-in gestures of address to the audience, – the spectator may feel a more or less of energy in the address. But, because of the nature of the gesture of address, he or she is apt to think of it not in terms of energy exercised on affecting him or her, but in terms of some specific disposition, e.g. a will to communicate, a desire for expression, fellowfeeling, good will toward or concern for him or her. The feeling of being communicated with is thus more apt to generate the spectator's feeling of power over the producers (the gestures of communication are normally sycophantic) than an experience of energy.

But there are forms of theatre and performance-styles, e.g. music hall or musical comedy, specialising in ›across the footlights‹ projection of energy: designed, like rock shows, to demonstrate the energy of the performers (and of script-writer, lyricist, director), viz. a capacity for putting out much of it any instant, and, as indicated by the apparent ease and sustainment of the volume of its flow, an apparently limitless supply of it, a capacity for keeping on putting it out. Tho' style and timing, and the directness of the producer's projection toward the audience of himherself (whether by a performer's facing the audience, or in another sense) are crucial for this, by and large these shows of energy depend on its actual output: style and electronic amplification alone won't do it.

Unlike f. inst. the energy-shows of good Afro-American jazz drummers, whose performance is styled to indicate power by indicating a supply of energy not used, these energy shows, by an edge of push, fake a force that will out: an exuberant vitality, perhaps an aggressive virility, a surfeit of spirit, some enthusiasm or excitement. Fake, not because the performers may not suffer from such a force by personality, tho' surely not evening after evening, but because the motivating force is terror, the terror that inspires the need to charm:

as is very clear in a related medium, the shows of night club come-
dians overpowering one with the proliferation of their inventive-
ness.

These shows are designed to show quantity of energy, and not only
to show it, but to project it through the performance onto the
audience: in the form of a maximum direct effect at the moment, a
hit, even a shock. The audience experiences it as directed by the
performers (and/or by the writers or the director, such as when the
text or the staging convey some urgency of theirs, e.g. to please or to
convey a message) *into their performance*: but for the sake of its
impact *on the audience*, to make the performance come across more
strongly: thus indirectly as a force aimed at itself. And the audience
experiences its pressure on (and perhaps power over) its sensibilities.
The ultimate aim – and the audience feels this, – of these energy/
force/power shows is not (as perhaps in rock shows which are also
forcible actions on and exertions of power over the audience and are
experienced as such) to energise (excite) the audience, but to enable it
to savor its superior detachment by an appreciation of the performers' sweat, – willingness to put out the energy. The audience's
appreciation of the magnitude of the performers' energy is secondary
– instrumental – to this self-appreciation, the tranquility of which
controls the nervous excitement (a kind of good time) with which
the spectacle's or the performers' apparent excitement may have
infected the audience or which the series of impacts on its sensibilities
may have induced.

In the more high-tone forms of normal theatre, these projections are
less blatant and of a different sort, – nuances, sub-textures of good
professional (normal) theatre, perhaps not inessential to the enjoyment of it. In order to create the illusion, the producers must not
attract attention to themselves or to their productive activity. If the
performer's creation of the character is in evidence, the character will
seem less real (and also the author's point, if any, less important).
But the actor's active identification with hisher part, perhaps a personal identification investing hisher personality, and also an artistic
professional actor's concentration on the nuances and inward psychological truth of hisher imitational portrayal of the character (or else
on the clarity of the figure and situation), may come across as a
vibrancy: the performer seems to be generating an energy for discharge into hisher work and seems to vibrate with this generation.
A play may similarly convey its author's having a personal stake in
its issues, or a production the shaping energy of the director. The

spectator experiences these energies at least in part as the performer's or other producer's energies: not just as energy of the performance; nor just, although it definitely has these aspects also, as the performer's power over hisher performance or as force heshe directs at hisher performance. Insofar as the producers direct them *at* the performance (not just into it to blow it up), the spectator's experience of them is apt to separate the performance, – the play, the character, something done by the performer or other producer, – from the performer; and the spectator does not feel them to be, even indirectly, directed at him/her, but observes them at a distance, perhaps responding by a sympathetic vibration, perhaps by an excitement of appreciation.

Audience-identification with a character whether more or less specifically or in terms of its identification of the character's situation with its own, as well as other engagements of the audience's emotions (pity, horror, sympathy, antipathy) set up emotional tensions, charges of affect in the audience, a psychic activity that it feels as calling up its energies and as using them up, perhaps as draining or depleting it of them. They are experienced only extrinsically as responses to a performer: they are experienced as responses to a character or situation created by a performance. The spectator's awareness of the character's psyche and responses to the situation comports an awareness of the energy consumed by those responses and by that psyche's activities, and the spectator's identification with the character provides a vicarious experience of this expenditure of energy. The spectator is straining, charged, tense, vibrating with the same energies, as tho' sharing them. Even if the character should happen to be psychically and somatically relatively or in some ways inactive and lacking in energy, or is shown as psychically responsive or compelled rather than as initiators, i.e. as energised from without, the spectator identifying with it is apt to have some experience of its energies 1) because normal theatre tends to rely on conflict or at least on the strains set up in a psyche by a character's situation, 2) because the spectator's identification requires a mobilisation of hisher own emotional energies: so that the identifying spectator cannot altogether avoid an experience of the psychic activities of the character induced by that stress or by those conflicts *as* activities into which energy is going. Heshe is not merely observing them, in abstraction from their mobilisation. Of course, vibrating em-, sym- or anti-pathetically, or with pity or horror, the spectator also experiences those energies as exercising a power over himherself, i.e. as power, – in relation to himherself: identical with or part of the power sucking himher into the spectacle. And this may be hisher primary experience of them.

On the whole, normal theatre's ›across the footlights‹ shows and projections of energy don't so much stimulate mobilisations or expenditures of energy in/by the customer, but rather relaxation specifically relating to not having to do the work, having it done for one, a capitalist pleasure paying off in increased energy for one's business. They tend to have the form of and to be experienced as manifestations of power in the exercise of a force. And in the higher forms of this theatre, the energy is only marginally experienced as the performers', but more importantly vicariously as the characters'.

The Wilsonian performer is seen involved in doing simple physical things effortlessly. Attention is drawn to hisher activity as just activity and as hishers. He or she thus figures precisely as potential of the movement (or of the holding of the pose); unemphatically intending it every moment, not intending anything to be accomplished by it, nor any effect that seeing it might have on the audience. The simple physical movement or stance actualises this simple physical performer. Hisher energy is not experienced as driving, hardly as directed, and neither as exerted or released by the performer nor as a special charge generated by himher for the performance, – but if anything rather as possessing (moving) him or her, tho' not in the manner of an excitement, – but as *there,* and as naturally flowing into this activity.[121] It does not seem a much of energy nor a sufficiency of it nor any kind of amount. In fact one does not think of it in terms of the activity, but of the activity in terms of it. The spectator's primary impression may be of this quiet energy, the movement seeming merely its manifestation. The manner of performance defines the performer by energy (in the sense of my definition). No aspect of force or power attaches to it.

This is a peculiar but not altogether unheard of impression of energy. A running brook when one forgets it's running downhill or a plant

121 The description of a Wilsonian performer's performance as expressive of energy or, cf. infra, spiritual energy, is misleading if one thinks of energy as push, drive, force or power, or of spiritual energy as contingent on spiritual as opposed to bodily awareness, as arising out of transcendence. (E.g. the Living Theatre has from 1969 to 1974 gone from a projection of the former – frenetic physical – to projection of the latter – spiritually oriented – energy.) Some individual Wilsonian performers do, it is true, convey impressions of such directed, some of such spiritual energy. I think their performances have been exceptions from what Wilson had in mind.

going through some transition of its annual cycle when one abstracts from the sun's action seem entirely devoted to what they seem to be Doing and seem full of energy of this kind: their existence itself this kind of movement: the movement itself their existence. Similarly sometimes moving children, old people at rest. Or as when someone is naturally outgoing. Since such existential energy is the stuff of individuality, the spectator's awareness of the performance in terms of it prepares himher for seeing performers as individuals.

The movement appears the embodiment of intent: not the result of will. The spectator does not see the performer's body moving in obedience to the performer's mind, does not even perceive the performer mindful of hisher body, but sees the performer's mind and body as one. The movement does not seem to actualise a physical energy released in response to an exercise of mental energy, – which is how most purposeful, expressive and/or stylised real-life activities and thus just about all stage movement of normal theatre affect one, – but an energy that is neither specifically bodily nor mental, but pervasively both: as though, if we conceive of sentient awareness as coincidence of sensing and sensed, it *consisted* in the performer's sentient awareness of hisher moving body. In this limited modest sense, we can refer to the Wilsonian performance-style as spiritual: namely inasmuch as the view of fact as product of awareness only, without the intervention of material or efficient causation, is spiritualist.

The most unemphatic, effortless, undemonstrative and natural movement executed in a humdrum (tho' not sloppy) and not in an otherworldly manner, when put on stage and exposed as a person's movements (not as imitations or representations) *most* shows as epiphany of that person's vital energy, and specifically of a spiritual-seeming energy: provided only that that person in spite of acting simply, effortlessly, unemphatically etc., i.e. keeping up doing so, musters up awareness. It is this effort that shows through as creative energy; or that makes that awareness show as energy. The energy the spectator becomes aware of is this awareness. To summon it up and maintain it and yet not become artificial or projective is work.

The Wilsonian audience does not experience the performer's energy as directed at it nor is there any feeling that it moves into the audience-space. But because it seems more a state the performer is in than something mustered up by the performer, and because the coordination of movement on stage suggests that it is a state shared by the performers, the stage may come to seem to the spectator a field of energy or an energy-space.

In normal theatre, the varying ›forward‹ energy of a show partly results from involuntary variations in the creative energies of the producers, partly is the result of deliberate manipulation of dramatic structure by an author, of staging by a director, of their performances by performers. A dynamics structuring a unity is created. A show may here or there unintentionally flag, fall apart, move in place, pick up or lose energy. A play or a production might be designed to start out slow, pick up energy during a first act, move at a high level of energy during a second, and with a rapidly increasing energy during the third to move to a final burst of energy, greater than those at the ends of the first and second acts. Tho' the spectator is apt to be aware that this energy depends on the energy exerted by the producers, it is not experienced by himher as their energy, – nor as that of characters portrayed, – but as a directed finalistic force residing in the play itself, in the course of events represented, and as exerted on and in fact creating these events: driving the action to its conclusion, the plot to its resolution, sealing fates. The play's plausibility and emotional yield, – how satisfying it is, – depend on its fatality. Its fatality sets up and resolves its dramatic tensions. The spectator attaches this force to the content, in terms of the theatrical illusion; and measures its pressure by the speed of the course of events, the number of happenings per unit time, and their importance in the lives and experience of the characters, and by the intensity and magnitude of tensions or conflicts within or between the characters, as well as by how well all these seem connected. The spectator is apt to participate in what heshe experiences as a force driving a play on by an anticipation, – a curious concern with what will happen, – charged with affect by hisher identification or other emotional engagement with the characters. This is an experience of being subject to a power; of being involved, gripped, caught up in, carried along, and, to some extent, of using and perhaps depleting one's energy in something like a sympathetic tension or vibration, – the experience of a backseat driver or of a gambler with something at stake.

The images in a Wilsonian spectacle, seeming organic events rather than constructs, appear possessed of energy. As the energy of the phantom characters created by the actors in a normal play seem intrinsic to these, and as in a normal play the ›forward energy‹ seems intrinsic to it, this energy seems intrinsic to these image-events. When unchanging, the image seems not merely there: it seems to hold under its own power, as tho' charged, sometimes as tho' sustained by an inner tension, sometimes as tho' vibrating. When the image evolves, each stage seems the manifestation of a latent energy in the preceding state of the image. Sometimes one feels an accumulation of energy in a changing or static image, a charge building up, an impending shift or change of direction or disintegration, a build-up of something within the image which will in due time induce its transformation. The approach to a crisis seems to manifest itself as a heightening of an inner tension: the crisis itself as a collapse of tension (no discharges in explosion!) followed by disintegration, a loss of energy. All of this has analogies in normal theatre, but is there a matter of psychology, of fictitious conflicts of will or interest or inclination or principle, or of emotions, – within or between characters. Wilson does without the illusion of psychological energies. Instead, the tensions, charges, polarities, vibrations seem partly in the outward lineaments of the visible configurations (like the esthetic configurations of energy that art criticism and descriptions of architecture attribute to the surface of art works,) partly the inward energies or like the inward energies with which our sub-conscious invests signs and symbols of archetypal conflicts or traumatic experiences: the esthetic energy of the image seems to translate an alienated inner energy of neurosis. This neurotic energy is not illusory: it is Wilson's. But it is in this theatre not psychological, even indirectly: it attaches to the images.

Because the individual images are set up by scenery and props located on the stage, as long as the spectator focusses on them they do not appear as manifestations of their energy. They appear imbued with it and dependent on it, but also as possessing a reality (as images) apart from it. The energy of each image is not quite its substance: more an essential attribute. Nevertheless, the stage to the spectator preoccupied by the images begins to seem structured as a field of energies: high charges here or there, low charges or none elsewhere, a current set up along one path, a flow in progress somewhere else, the tensions mounting and declining.

Time is of the essence in a Wilsonian spectacle. The spectator becomes aware of it. The spectator's time-perception is altered.

At first, watching People Up There Doing Things, their movements are experienced as taking place in the normal located unextended presents of a normal 3-dimensionally future/present/past passing time, accretion of the past. But the movements themselves, unhurried, smoothly continuous, pre-determined, relate peculiarly to this normal time. They seem to lack the quality of direction, do not have the form of a pointed actualisation of the future, the instrumentality of the present to the future characteristic of directed action is absent: their components seem equally important. They don't have the forward direction contrary to that of time itself, – a quasi-escaping, a fleeing into the future, – of animal action. Their segments do not give rise to their sequels. Thus they seem to float like white strips of paper in a brook: detached from tho' inserted into moving time: possessed of their own unbroken time.

Should the spectator now relate to a performer as individual, this directionless continuity of the acts undergoes a change, – the acts now seem processes unfolding or unrolling in an evolution intrinsic to them, – and invades the spectator's awareness of time: time itself now seems the time of that individual and seems to be an unlocated unmoving extended present, a stationary extension not squeezed in between a past and a future, but defined as present by the presence of the performer and hisher performance, the sequentiality of its moments defined by the internal order, a function of their process, of the activities. The ticking of time fades, the restrictive order of time disappears: but time has not disappeared: it has become a way of being of individual visible processes, the extended space of evolving images, proper to each still event.

This is the time-awareness of the spectator pre-occupied by the Wilsonian images. That they take place *now* seems to have nothing to do with them. Their now is theirs and is anytime. As sometimes a cloud long stared at, a snowclad distant mountaintop, a lone leafy tree on a windless spring day, a poignant gesture or a poignant expression briefly glimpsed on the face of someone close to one, they seem no longer in the passage of time at all, but at some upward angle to it, outside of time. They are not wholly timeless for they are temporally extended, tho' in a peculiar manner: their undelimited duration (not an enduring against time nor a lasting, but a totally effortless distension) seems in their nature, a quality of their being, or even their being itself, and seems only derivatively temporal: as tho' we had to translate it into temporal terms, as tho' it were only an extrinsic, perhaps subjective form of their happening (in analogy to how the spatial extension of objects seems an extrinsic form of their matter). The images do not so much change or undergo change as that there are changes in them. The phases seem to arise out of rather than lead into one another. There is no forward pressure or logic associated with the changes: they seem to obey an inward impulse. They take time to come about: their own sweet time. The sequence of the phases (which are not segmentally discrete) similarly appears to be only incidentally and extrinsically temporal.

There is, however, a multiplicity of images, each with its own stasis, its proper time. Shifting attention from any one to another, the spectator half regains his normal sense of time, of its unity and objective order. But only half: heshe has a disturbed sense of objective time, it seems broken up, not quite real, doubtful.

The images, unlike true rites, are not self-subsisting mysteries, not sacral events. As one succeeds the other, as the development of one succeeds that of another, as their overlays multiply and repeat, and as, at the same time, the spectator's attention, grown more passively responsive, less autonomously active, — heshe may be sleepy by now or in a half waking, half sleeping state, — becomes engrossed in, absorbed by and encompassed by the stage as locus of events, the Spectacle becomes an encompassing reality sui generis for himher, — a Buddhist ›floating world,‹ the shadow-world of Plato's cave. The spectator's awareness constricts down to the stage, locus of events. Within its expanse hisher awareness is no longer focussed preclusively on individual images and their individual evolutions, no longer relates to each in its individuality, but relates to them partly as old familiars, this one, that one, partly as ›yet another,‹ ›one more,‹ and moves, in the rhythm of their flux, from one to the other, swinging with the spectacle. An energy-borne flux of imagery has emerged as the *new* object of awareness: not just the sequence or the band of sequences of evolving images, not the set of them, but the flux itself.

As long as they were the primary data of experience, each image had its own time: temporally unlocated in its own eternal present, its temporal duration mere metaphor for its native extension, its internal before-and-after measured by its autonomous metre. The spectator contemplating now one, now the other, had lost the unity and encompassing order of time, and the sense of time itself. Shifts of focus from one to another gave reminders of objective time, but did not quite reconstitute it. But the shift of focus from them to their flux reconstitutes temporal unity and order: but of a time experienced as substance of the spectacle-reality itself.

The show seems to go on and on. The spectator's expectation of an end and awareness of a past beginning fade: hisher awareness of the show-time as delimited finite whole to which a time of one's life and within the time of the performers' lives has been allocated disappears. Show-time is no longer a part of, thus itself is no longer, objective time. The sense of objective time is lost or numbed, as also the sense of a place of one's own in it, of its relation to oneself. Instead, after the peripaties indicated, the spectator senses a time defined and measured by the spectacle, by what happens in it: by the imagery-flux. Not an independently existing time but a time seemingly intimately associated with the reality by which the spectator is confronted, the spectacle, the flux of imagery, *its* time.

The spectacle's duration substitutes for objective time. The spectator experiencing that duration as without beginning or end, as ongoing merely, this substantial spectacle time like objective time extends indefinitely.

The sensory density and dramatic intensity of the flux varies. Sometimes the stage is almost or quite empty, nothing happens, no denouement seems impending: sometimes the stage fills up, many things happen at once, things seem to come to a head here or there: in between the quantum of imagery fluctuates between such extremes.

These fluctuations seem in the density and intensity of time-occupancy, not of space-occupancy. E.g. it is not so much that the stage is empty, as that the moment is empty. The spectacle seems to take place in time rather than in space. The stage seems a passive expanse, matrix. As space to normal awareness seems the dimension in which objects *are,* so time now seems the dimension in which these events happen, their frame or screen. Time rather than space become the locus of reality, – of reality rather than only of this spectacle, insofar as this spectacle has come to preempt the awareness of the spectator, has become the spectator's world.

Time itself seems to bring on the imagery, to create or produce it: its source and nemesis. Their visible existence qua spatially extended seems due to its workings: as tho' it were a male energy infecondating points of passive space, blowing them up into the specific shapes of images.

Qua the energy that – by action on space or ex nihilo – creates it, time seems the essence of the imagery: within it. They are swollen with it. As extended matter seems to normal awareness the substance of things, so time now seems the substance of these appearances: tho' not qua their matter but as their energy. The images seem concretions of time. And since this imagery seems to vary in quantity from moment to moment, this substantial energy seems to vary in amount from moment to moment. And since this peculiar time peculiar to the spectacle has for the spectator become all time, time itself, it is time itself of which there seems now more now less.

The body of the spectacle, part of its ›illusion,‹ is now an unrolling time-scroll. It functions as time for the spectator. Its movement is forward: toward more, other imagery, events that have not taken place, – in the direction which in a normal time-frame would be toward the future, i.e. the direction of action, not of normal time itself, opposite to that of normal, passing time. A time of expectation rather than of experience.

Insofar as the spectator is engrossed in the spectacle, its time his/hers, he/she experiences time itself: as that which appears in the flux. It comes up with the images, gives rise to them, declines in them, fluctuates. The spectator senses its underlying energy. It is organic creative energy. Since the movement of hisher awareness is from the images to the flux, the focus is at first not on this energy itself, but on time's relation to the flux, and then on time's, in terms of this relation, seeming energy. But gradually that which seems to produce the flux of the visible, the energy, replaces its production of the visible and of its flux in the spectator's awareness: as the perennial reality of the matter. Time itself, the visible's form of flux, comes to seem merely an extrinsic appearance of this reality, in itself timeless.

The spectator feels after a while that underlying the multiplicity of images moving independently of one another in various directions, there is a single something working itself out, a single process of energy now swelling, building up, building up to greater intensity or to a more of visible concretion, now receding, retreating into itself, approaching a zero-point: an unfolding and retraction, expansion and contraction in alternation.

Wilson's arrangement of the imagery gets the audience from contemplation of images to a sense of tidal energy by a balance between major focusses and multiplicity of focusses. On the one hand the composition is arranged into major dominant images in each of which a visible evolution betokens one movement of energy: an upsurge, then a recession; on the other hand, he so counterbalances these major processes against and with one another, and against and with a sufficiency of minor events/images as to provide for a continuous smooth and repeated reshifting of focus. Attention is not allowed quite to decompose the picture by exclusive focus on individual elements; nor quite to arrange the several processes into a complete whole of any sort. Thus the tide and ebb of energy-flow itself becomes the phenomenon the audience is in touch with. There is no surface unity of the visible: the sensible relation between the images are not there; and the unity of beginning/middle/end is lacking, so that there is no unity in time either. Thus the visible specifics take on a look of incidentality and the mind is led on to the process of creative energy itself. The arrangement is not oriented toward organising a content of awareness, but toward orienting awareness beyond specific content.

I suppose it is in part because in the end the particular images seem arbitrary and their line potentially infinite that the spectator discerns an energy creating them. In normal theatre, which is devoted to creating the contrary impression, that what's shown a) is a unit, b) is just right (whether as truth about reality or for amusement or in whatever regard), the idea of a pure creative energy − of energy as such − at work does not arise: at most the idea of some person's or epoch's particularised energy: and what is made to seem to matter is precisely the specific content − even when this content is a nihilist message.

The specific images and image-trains ultimately come to appear incidental: as tho' they could just as well have been other than they are. One's feeling then is that the energy is the reality: when it reaches a certain intensity, it takes visible form, produces *a* phenomenon. Ultimately, even that it do so seems incidental. Perhaps, one feels, it doesn't even really do so: perhaps the appearances we are seeing are our constructs, − put on formless, purely quantitative energy-states. The spectator's imagination has become transcendentally active. − One may consider this state of awareness an illusion: after all, was not *Wilson's* creative energy bound to come up with certain images rather than others? One may consider it a break through illusion: is not the variegation of the forms of the imagination (and of nature) infinite when the infinities of all time and of the cosmos are taken into account? In any event, the energy ultimately sensed by the spectator to the spectator seems independent of the particular forms it takes.

The energy is not directed. Its production of images seems incidental to its being, and the flux not only has no discernible goal or end that would define a direction, whether the existence of any one image or set of images, or some state of energy, e.g. its exhaustion, but on the contrary produces the positive impression that it is indefinitely renewable. (Which may be one reason Wilson could and did keep composing new spectacles by the addition of preceding ones.) No conclusion is reached, there is no achievement, none is expected.

The energy seems a space of energy in place onstage, or, as far as the spectator's actual experience is concerned, all around. This ›space of energy‹ is not a place full of energy, whether the stage, the theatre or an illusory environment, or any place or all space, but a kind of space peculiar to energy and containing the spectacle's visible-extended space within it as one of its dimensions. It is a standing space of energy: variations of intensity in it appear as flux of the visible-extended.

The spectator does not identify the energy as that of this spectacle or of a spectacle, but as the energy underlying the phenomena (the spectacle) of his or her world (which world happens to be this spectacle). ›Of his or her world‹: not of the cosmos: for obviously the spectator is not such a fool as to identify (positively) his or her world as specifically *the* world any more than as specifically only his or hers. The reality experienced is neither *the* reality nor *a* reality but reality. In spite of the encompassing content of these spectacles (heavenly bodies, nature and civilisation, the nether world), the illusion created is not that of (the totality of) objective reality. The images are not representations. The contents do not in the end in experience add up to ›the real world.‹ The spectacle is not a *statement* about it. On the contrary, the images in the end come to be experienced as, as regards their specificity, fortuitous. The reality exhibited is not their set but the *production* of their *variety*. This production comprises the negation of any of them, and of any set of them. The spectator perceives the negativity of finitude, the negligibility of particular existence. He experiences it regarding a reality which after the experience is over and the spectator has left the theatre is not reality (*the* reality) but an artistically created illusion. It is only as this point that the spectator can view that theatrical reality as a paradigm of the real world, and can view the spectacle as carrying a statement re the real world, e.g. that it is, like that illusory theatrical reality, the illusory appearance of blind energy, and can view hisher experience in this theatre as rehearsal of an experience that can be had of the real world.

11. Assault on speech. Decline of the theatre of visions, 1974-77.

# Preface

As Wilson's theatre 69-73 can be thought of as the sub-dominant hemisphere's coup d'etat, a theatre of and for the left hand's brain, so his theatre 74 ff. can be thought of as the right brain's attempt to annex the province of speech.

The right brain's synthesizing powers do not seem to extend to language per se, i.e. conceived, – in a left-brain manner, – in abstraction from speech, or at any rate from speech as communication. It seems to have no particular contributions to make to naming or to the sequential ordering (›manipulation,‹ ›handling‹..., – note in these terms the left brain's predilection for dextral metaphor) of signs. The right brain's peculiar prowess for verbal communication, – both for the production and for the understanding of expressive and meaningful speech, – seems to arise from its access to paralinguistic meaning (›sense‹): as distinct from literal denotations and their syntactic (›logical‹) ordering. It seems three-fold: a peculiar ability to take context into account (to interpret in terms of circumstances); a peculiar semantic liberality; a peculiar phonetic sensitivity.

The right brain seems equipped to take into account two kinds of context (of speech) relevant to meaning: the individual him (her) self, notably, but not only, as visual configuration (e.g. in terms of stances, expressions[1]); and the environment or situation, the external circumstances attending and possibly relevant to the communication. The right brain's semantic liberality is partly the associative ability to adduce associations, connotations and metaphorical meanings, partly a complementive ability for getting at the possible meaning of faulty or imperfect or incomplete expressions, – and both of these abilities seem to relate to powers of the imagination, – partly a tolerance for inconsistencies (of expression *and* meaning), for abnormal or seemingly or actually arbitrary conjunctions: it may have less of a disposition than the left brain for cleaning up communications and for throwing out (ignoring) what seems incidental, subsidiary or inconsistent. The right brain's peculiar phonetic sensitivity is its ability to take into account the implications of tone of voice, and tonal patterns of all sorts, tho especially the finer ones, whether in speaking or in listening.

In all three regards, the right brain is probably peculiarly fit for

[1] The right brain plays a crucial role in recognizing and remembering faces.

265

coping with simultaneous manifolds, whether of utterance or of meaning, and whether in speaking or in listening (and comprehending), – group-speech or dialogue as a unit (or whole), levels or layers of meaning in individual utterances: in speaking or listening synthesising them by simultaneous attention to context (the speakers and their relations, the situation or circumstances); over and above the literal-logical nexus between them, interpreting each element in terms of the others; and, able to hold on to each element in terms of its melody or rhythm, catching, as indice or dimension of sense, the harmonic pattern of the whole.

These performances of the right brain could either be viewed as providing an extension or a frame for the literal semantics and the syntax-encoded logic of the left brain, or vice versa.

Right brain verbal theatre would address right brain dominated speech to the audience's right brains. I.e. it would have to come up with speech freed of the habitual conscious left brain domination, and this speech would have to be such as to get the audience's brains working in a manner freed of left brain domination.

Wilson's attempt at a verbal right brain theatre has failed so far for two reasons: a pre-occupying antagonism toward the left-brain aspects of communication; a predilection for the comic and dramatic values of phrases, contingent not only on literal meanings, but on standardized (conventional) – left brain – modes of speech and hearing. His resentment against discursive intelligence distracted him from working out the problems of what right-brain dominated speech would be like and how it should be fashioned for right-brain audience reception. This negative orientation toward left-brain activity resulted in texts and delivery continually enticing and then disrupting left-brain understanding, i.e. ensuring left-brain non-dominance, without ensuring right-brain dominance; or else, the speech turning into solfeggios and measure-counts, speech referring to itself, and to itself only as phonal phenomenon, in pseudo-texts without meaning, virtually eliminating left-brain activity, but also eliminating speech as speech, and so precluding right-brain dominance in the delivery or apprehension of speech. His partial destructions of denotative meaning and syntactical logic did not of themselves afford occasion for right-brain syntheses; his elimination of them deprived the right brain of speech as object of synthesis. His wish to entertain resulted in texts and delivery continually providing left-brain stimulation, obstacles to right-brain activation.

A right-brain dominance might have been achievable: but not in the form of an attack on left-brain dominance; nor by a continual teasing solicitation of it.

In the process, Wilson gave up theatre of visions (as well as its basis, work with byrds, i.e. performances as exposition of personality): not that he didn't still base his pieces on images rather than on texts or stories, – images illustrating the scenarios of Herman Kahn, – but these became adventitious to other concerns, mere occasions, and their visual development no longer governed structure, an extrinsic arithmetic of repetitions did. It was as tho the mere turn to intelligible discourse, even though it was an antagonistic one, disrupted his right-brain's domination of his work.

Language poses a problem for such theatre, not because its essential mode, speech, is in the medium of sound, and perhaps only marginally because speech by its sequentiality orders time otherwise than vision, but because it is the form and instrument of definite denotation and of judgment, – of specific signification and of commitment to it. The staged image is broken by such reference and commitment, whether the performer's or the author-director's. It becomes an epiphenomenon. Wilson's attempt to incorporate speech independently of its syntactic and semantic essence into his theatre of visions destroyed it.

# A Letter for Queen Victoria (1974/75),

was planned by Wilson as a tight piece. *Freud* had established him where it counted, in Soho; *Deafman* had gained him admiration among the Parisian intelligentsia of both banks; *Stalin* media-ted his name above 14th Street. He may have had a sense of people waiting for him to repeat himself. He desired, I think, a hit in a new style, showing that he could do something quite else too, that his use of performers and imagery did not depend on distension and profusion, but would work with strictness, economy, containment, and in something *like regular theatre*.[2] With some brutality, *Stalin* hardly over, he picked out 7 performers, a brain-damaged or for some other reason mentally aberrative kid, Christopher Knowles, for an 8th, 2 dancers, a musician, a stage-manager and a lighting technician, — this was 13 people, but with himself it was 14, instead of 40 or a hundred, there were going to be only (including himself) 9 on stage; and started work.[3]

I[4] gleaned no intelligence as to what images he had in mind to stage. I suspect, from the experimental way he picked people from among us 7 for the parts, from the way he described to us the sets that he wanted,[5] and from the way the play was worked up, that for the

2 That the sets and costumes with some exceptions turned out uninspired and slick may have related to the idea of evoking regular theatre.

3 Rehearsals begun earlier in the winter in New York continued in Sao Paulo from the beginning of March 1974 to the opening April 9th: we did individual acts from *Letter* on a proscenium stage in front of performances of *Stalin*, done mostly by Brazilians. They resumed around the middle of May in Spoleto, continued there till the opening, at the Festival dei due Monde, June 15th, of a one-week run. We again rehearsed it for about a week before opening in Belgrade on September 19th, and then took it on a European tour, and rehearsed it for the last time for about 3 weeks before the opening, March 22nd, 1975, of a two-week run at the ANTA theatre in New York City. Wilson had intended to show it at the ANTA for 4 weeks, but not enough people came. In all, the play was done, I believe, 79 times: – 1974/5, Wilson put on several shows with just him and Knowles in them or centered on them, using material from *Letter*, and developing his entr'actes with Knowles in *Letter*, e.g. *A Mad Man* (1974), re which cf. C. K. Wittenberg, *Wilson at Art Now*, The Drama Review, T 63, Sept. 1974.

4 I was one of the 7. The following account is written from a participant's limited perspective. I never heard (any more than I could see) what the piece was like. My comments on its *effects* are guesses.

5 He didn't get them. Spoleto wouldn't pay for them, and he could work out no deal that would have done it with BITEF like the deal he worked out with the Goulbenkian foundation for the sets of *Stalin*.

first time in years he was not pushed by any images:[6] but at most had settings in mind in which people were to talk[7] and perhaps some number system such as $2+2$ performers for a first, and 4 for each of a 2nd and 3rd act. My 12-yr.-old son, after seeing the play, contrasting it to *Stalin* said, ›it seems in Bob's mind, not in the images.‹

In terms of *settings*, Wilson saw the play this way:

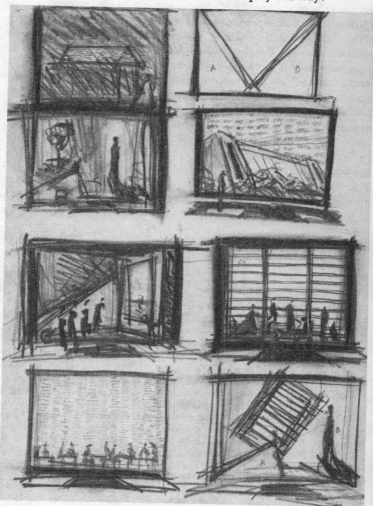

6 The dominant image of act I and of the epilogue goes back partly, I believe,

Scatterings of visual and dialogue-references made *war* the context of the action, and suggested variously an action relating to 1) a *nuclear explosion* or holocaust and/or to 2) a *plane crash survived by a pilot*. I don't think Wilson set out to make a play about war or focussing on the mushroom image or on an aeronautic disaster. Perhaps the accident of his seeing a TV rerun of *Birth of a Nation* brought the War between the States into act 1, and perhaps this, in combination with other accidents, such as seeing me 1973/4 going around in the kind of surplus uniform he then used for the pilots of act 1 and for the combattants of act 11, or such as seeing the mushroom poster on my study wall, resulted in the play's war context. Seeing Santos Dumont's 1906 airplane in a Sao Paulo museum probably re-enforced his attention to the pilot theme. Probably the pilot and airplane images and even the war context were quite minor intentions and got the exposure they got during the work on the play only to give it the internal echoes or spurious unity[8] he wanted it to have. These themes remained as peripheral in the play as they probably were most of the time in Wilson's mind: it reveals them somewhat as Hopi by covert word classes and cryptotypes revealed an Einsteinian physics to B. L. Whorf. – The play turned out a comment on verbal communication: I doubt that Wilson intended a comment.

I suspect his intentions were chiefly formal. Among them, I would say, were so many rehearsals, all performer's attention to what they were doing would have been filed away, and they could save it all for the doing of it and for the movement of the piece in one another; a flexible transposition (keeping it intact) of his sinuous rhythm into a register of higher speed; an enclosed feeling (it would all take place between walls, perhaps at angles, in closed groupings); some-

for the figure of Lubar, to *Program Prologue Now, Overture for a Deafman* (Espace Cardin, Paris, 1971), partly, for that of Sutton, to various tall black ladies in *King, Freud, Deafman, Stalin*.

7 »Lorsque je prépare une piece, mon approche est dans chaque cas très différente, ... Dans *Une lettre* par example, j'étais surtout intéressé par le contraste entre la voix de Georges et celle de Jim Neu, entre la voix de Stephan et celle de Scotty, entre la voix de Sheryl et celle de Cindy. Il s'agissait d'articuler ces différentes lignes de voix, ces rhythmes, ces façons de parler et de les tisser en chaines pour produire un effet de chant. J'ai donc choisi de la façon la plus intéressante possible. La voix de Cindy était très coupante, de lignes très droites, la voix de Sheryl plus riche, plus coporée, de lignes plus baroques, celle de Jim très ›cool‹, ...« (Wilson, interview, Tel Quel, nos. 71/73, autumn 1977.)

8 Cf. fn. 45 on a more important simulacrum of plot, related to the afore-mentioned image of act 1.

thing near normal length; not too big a stage; and 1) all the aspects of regular theatre, but not really; 2) the appearance of tight, direct interaction; and 3) a concert of conversation,[9] definite, marked, audible, senseless, complemented by continuous music. The last three were perhaps the crux: he would carry his techniques and working methods and their effects on awareness over into the semblance and abstraction of a conventional play, a pseudo-play, having, but having merely, the forms of drama, – characters, motivations, interaction, dialogue, conflict, plot, drama: the mere essence of theatre:[10] demonstrating the otiosity and vulgarity of the rest. Since the plays of regular theatre *are* movement-supported speech, – conversation, – an abstraction of the form of speech was essential to this. But the challenge of speech probably was also a direct one. This piece, in stark contrast to the previous pieces, but like regular theatre, was to be all about people talking with, to or at one another. A continuous accompaniment of music would assimilate speech to sound in the form of vocal gesture.

In addition, there was Chris Knowles. Wilson's idea, when rehearsals (and the gathering of the text) started, seemed to be that we, the performers, were to learn from Chris, by talking to and being with him (we were going on tour together), by attempts at communication with him, and by imitation of him (imitation would make communication possible). This would within us hollow out/fill out what was to be the show piece of the piece, the form of rational verbal intercourse, would make it vibrate by and would put it in counterpose to a non-verbal, arational communication taking place (so Wilson seemed to suggest) by harmonious sensed reverberation. We would learn to relate, – communicate, – vocally without relying on or without concern for the meaning of what we said or of what was said to us. It would help impart to the conversation an ineffable formality, the same air of *ritual,* perhaps, that in the previous pieces had attached to social motion, but at the same time would no less discretely offer the public an example of true intercourse.

Chris's voice then had a perfectly empty and marvellously sustained enthusiasm; his repetitions lined out, in arabesques in place, the heartfelt arrests of mind; his responses were never immediate, did not have the tone of responses, came from far away. Sometimes, feeling

9 Of which perhaps the conversation between the occupants of the space ship/ float in act VII of *Stalin* was the prototype.
10 Act I showing Relation between Characters, act II the Undergoing of an Experience, act III Conversation, act IV, Dramatic Action.

good, asking one a question, he would humorously promote little mysteries of memory, but it was at all times clear that his words were not giving away his thoughts. This resolute, not even unfriendly privacy powerfully recommended his mode of speech to Wilson, I think. Of course Chris, even at that time, spoke, though then infrequently, in complete grammatical and meaningful sentences, made his wants known, imparted factual information, say when we were going to meet again or met last time, – he had a mania now somewhat abated for exact times of day and dates, the time of something happening, and a good memory, – asked questions and understood the answers, at least if they were simple and factual. But it was clear that he had a wealth of peculiar information (arising from peculiar experience and peculiar mentation) that he couldn't put into words (he didn't try to, gave no sign he wanted to), that perhaps by its structure didn't lend itself to sentence, but that, Wilson seemed to feel, would come across, carried by the patterning of his speech and gestures, in sustained conversations or in the multiple verbal contacts attendant on living with him: provided we were interested and attentive and sensitive to this other dimension of talking, and attempted to be responsive, in his manner, in the same beyond-meaning channel. Wilson exhorted us to get involved with him.

The rehearsals were initially designed to accord to Chris this role of praeceptor. But the project aborted: partly by its difficulty, partly by the resistance of some performers, partly, I would say, because of its risk, seeing as how Wilson was anxious for a success.[11]

During this early work on the piece, Wilson would come down

11 Wilson's next spectacle, *The $-Value of Man* (1975), was worked up (somewhat hastily) around Chris in the manner that had been envisaged for *Letter*, – though by this time a year of life, work, exposure and achievement with the company in the world of *Letter*, as well as appearances with Wilson in *MAD DOG* (1974), had made of Chris a different person: outgoing, self-confident, disciplined, hard working, and quite able to express himself and to converse at some length rationally. – The only fruit of the work toward *Letter* with Chris was the text of act I, sc. 2, *The Sundance Kid*, an infinitely repetitious prose-poem not without beauty, in praise of the grace of the hero of the Redford-Newman movie. During an early rehearsal Wilson wanted us all in turn to have a conversation with Chris in front of the others. Mine turned out a discussion of the movie in which I disagreed with Chris's feelings about the Sundance Kid (I hated the movie). Wilson got angry with my critical intellectualism, and had Jim Neu replace me when Chris had just gotten started on his totally unresponsive (to me), convinced declamation of ›the Sundance Kid is beautiful.‹ – George Ashley and I read it together in *Letter*. Ashley did not want to do it in Chris's manner, I found Chris's manner, – an emphasis of conviction, accenting certain syllables (*beau*tiful . . .) over and over again, never falling into a metre, – too difficult to sustain. We read it in our own

almost every time with sheets of lines he'd picked up stoned[12] from late movies etc. off a TV set he'd borrowed, assigned not to any characters but to ›1‹ and ›2,‹ or to ›1,‹ ›2,‹ ›3‹ and ›4‹ in regular alternation, and would try out different combinations from among the 7 performers for each stretch of lines, progressively separating this text into sections, chopping the ends off sections to make scenes of appropriate length.[13]

At this time there was also some experimentation with delivery centering around the distinction between the skin, meat, bone of something: Wilson would have us repeat a given stretch of dialogue as skin, as meat, as bone.[14] This was soon abandoned, however. There was no other work on delivery – none on the vocal stances of denotation, assertion, address, whether on varying them or on

manners. – The original title of *Letter* was *The Sundance Kid*, – abandoned, I believe, for something like copyright reasons.

12 Cf. in the sequel re distortions, echoes, anticipations.

13 I don't think he fooled with the order in which he first jotted down the lines. Thus the lines from a particular movie, soap opera or whatever, – I suppose he also wrote down phrases flitting through his head, – would cluster, and thus also certain moods would vaguely transfer to certain stretches, to be picked up on by the performers, and later the audience, or not. As he proceeded he more or less deliberately occasionally introduced verbal references to previous lines, deceptive hints at a continuity, e.g. the references to Manda and to the killing of a brother in acts II and IV after those in act I, to the Sequachee Dam in act IV, after that in act I. The text is probably more disconnected and arbitrary, namely near totally, than people seeing the play realise: the acting (delivery) and the staging (costuming, sound effects, lighting) convey meanings and connections that spectators then attribute to the lines or in retrospect think they got from them. E.g. Sutton's Civil War uniform in act II and for parts of act IV may make an Old Men dialogue in act IV seem a resonance of the Civil War theme actually in the text of act I, sc. I only. The plane crash/surviving pilot theme is in the text only in 2 (3 times repeated) lines in act I, sc. I, and in the epilogue: it is carried by the pilot costumes in act I and by plane projections. Acts II and III clearly take place in war: the only reference to war in the dialogue of these acts is in a question ›Where are the planes?‹ in act II, and in the whole play the only other textual reference is ›I don't know what kind of a war we are fighting‹ (act IV, – from *Casablanca*). The uniforms, shots, explosions, smoke, lighting and the mode of performance influenced by these (for *Wilson* said nothing of any war nor of our being combatants) created an effect of war that I suppose seemed in the dialogue as well. A single reference to the atom bomb (›This atom bomb is impossible‹) in act II, echoed by another in act IV (›But what about the atom bomb?‹ – answered by a derisive ›Ah, honey!‹) may, given the staging, then conversely have induced an impression of atomic explosions by way of lending related meaning to other lines and to the action on stage.

14 A little of this schema remained in the 3-fold repetition of the text in act I, sc. I. – Each performer in the group privately interpreted the terms his own way and Wilson gave no meaning.

transcending them, and whether in terms of intonation or of timing, — no attempts to generate the combination of relaxation and energy in speech that in previous productions had been done to generate it as regards movement. We were left to our own modes of delivery, it having been stressed that the meaning of the lines didn't matter, and it being understood that detachment from the content was de rigeur.[15]

Early on, Wilson had indicated he wanted the lines said unemotionally, but when, to varying degree, expression, even feeling, did creep in, he said no more about it. Most of us probably worked out a private, not too choate rudimentary but operative conception of our parts in the different acts, and of what a given scene was about, and spoke accordingly. I.e.: we gave our lines meanings independent of their literal meanings. A varity of modes of delivery resulted. Of the two stars that soon emerged, — the focal, framing and most powerful figures of the play, — with the most lines and who learned them first, — Sheryl Sutton and Lubar, the former spoke with the accents of the trained actress, delicately laying out a great variety of expressions, every two or three of her lines outlining a different part or situation, while Cindy maintained a powerful ostentatious inexpressiveness, speaking her lines mechanically, as though by rote or as though remembering them, monotonously. The delivery styles of the others varied between these extremes, though without the skill and talent of Sutton and without the power and consistency of Lubar. Overall, delivery was the upshot of a double tug of war: some real-life way of saying a line would contend with a theatrical way of saying it, and a Byrd's tendency toward the unemphatic/inexpressive would contend with a private ad hoc functional meaning given the line by private ad hoc notions of the part and situation.

15 Wilson in Sao Paulo: ›you have got to get past the lines — the most important thing is your awareness of where you are in space — you must master the space — the dialogue is *supported dialogue* — the lines should be delivered the way I heard them, as something secondary while doing something else (cleaning up, drawing) . . .‹ He spoke of his liking for Kim Stanley's acting in Strasberg's *Cherry Orchard*: ›she spoke as though she'd almost forgotten the words: they are back there in her mind, she has been programmed for them, but she is doing something else.‹ — During the Spoleto rehearsals Wilson at one point said: ›by act IV, the play should have been dissolved, you should be beyond it, into something else.‹ — Yet he also, at one rehearsal, told us to speak more ›as though we meant it,‹ which I thought indicated that he wanted the tonal figures that would normally attach to someone's saying a line like the line in question *expressively*, but wanted *that* tonal figure *in*expressively rendered.

Wilson kept driving for speed[16] and fluidity, and for concert: the introductory pauses by which a speaker makes a line his or her own were to be suppressed, the different speakers' lines were to be continuous with one another, each speaker was to ›connect‹ with the other speakers by maintaining sensitivity to their sound and responding to it.[17] Wilson's work on the vocalisation concentrated on its organicity. He trusted that doing it together often would not only make the talk ›transparent,‹ but would produce the right cadences and intonations, as also the collective coordination with the keys and rhythms of the chamber music.[18] ›I wish we could rehearse it hundreds of

16 At the Spoleto opening, the play lasted 3½ hours; after 40 performances a little less than 3 hours; toward the end in New York 2½ to 2-¾ hours. No cuts were made. The shortening was partly due to Wilson's abandoning most of the original scenery's walls so that scene changes became quicker; but mostly to a continuous drive for speedier delivery. But Wilson wanted it fast from the beginning. E.g. re act II he said in Sao Paulo, that he wanted it ›like dust,‹ and that except for the 4 pauses intended, the action should be very fast and matter of fact, so that the energy would carry through the pauses.
Sub-conscious responsiveness to how the other performers are doing their parts is possible both at very slow and very fast rates of speed. Especially given enough rehearsals and/or the kind of exercises Wilson gave in preparing his earlier spectacles, something like alert participation in a communal trance can arise both at extremely low and extremely high speeds. But while extreme slowness promotes, extreme speed inhibits individual gesture: conscious/deliberate control is knocked out at either end of the spectrum, but high-speed performance in a collective invites recourse to standardisations and to signalling accentuations, – the modes of efficiency in collective performance. On the stage this in practice comes down to seduction by conventional theatrics of delivery: which in fact have been evolved precisely though not exclusively to make acting together easier for the actors, – similarly to the way the theatrical voice has been evolved to make it easier on the individual actor to make himherself heard and understood, or at any rate followed, in a large space.
17 Just as the preceding spectacles had worked only by the right relative responsive timings of everyone's movements, *Letter* worked only, – even more so, – by the right rhythm of the dialogue, shifting from scene to scene, for each scene subconsciously settled on by the performers by mutual adjustments, guided by the music, over a period of rehearsals and performances, and by some feel – that seemed to come about by itself – for the right tone. The timing was splitsecond. In the previous pieces, time had been an extension, allowed play: it was urgent, restrictive, in *Letter*. An aural microstructure had replaced a visual-kinetic macrostructure. The play worked, – its scenes meshed into coherent and rhythmical organic aural wholes, – a matter not only of swinging but of syncopation and counterpoint, – at most once out of every 10 times it was done.
18 Alan Lloyd wrote the music off on his own in the U.S. while we were on tour with *Stalin* after attending only a few early rehearsals. Mike Galasso, the chef d'orchestra adapted his mailed scores to the evolving stage performance. My feeling was, Wilson didn't care what music he got.

times.‹ And he'd always run through the whole piece, in order. The result may have turned out for the audience the sound of verbal exchange 1) participated in, not composite of contributions, 2) meaningful not by the meaning of the words but as interplay of specific attitudes and feelings (Wilson not caring which we came up with as long as they jibed), conveyed by vocal gesture. Perhaps this was the sound Wilson wanted.

We were exhorted to speak loudly so people could hear us, and there were up to half a dozen stage-mikes and the 2 stars had body-mikes, but the mikes, tapes and sound systems were consistently bad. Wilson also wanted the music loud, and while he consistently spent scarce time lavishly on lighting and relighting,[19] he could not find time to work on the sound: as though he didn't want the words understood.

Most of his directing went to the visual. The gross of instructions to performers concerned movement. (For the sake of simplicity, but also because an amateur performer like myself is more concerned with hisher movements than with hisher stance or place, I here and in the following by ›movement‹ mean stances, displacements, gestures, places on stage. But in fact most of the directing concerned where to move when.) Wilson worked on this opera as choreographer, and even more so than when he directed his previous spectacles: because he had fewer concrete images in mind to realise and so was intent on creating abstract images, patterns of grouping and regrouping. But he did not work on movement as he had previously, viz. on its quality. Once the choreography was settled, he sat and sat,[20] silently, while we went through the piece over and over, and his notes to us at the end of each rehearsal were few.

The speaking, – coming in as soon as the previous speaker finished,

19 There were about 110 lighting cues.
20 He will sit there, hands wringing, except they are not moving (so they are clasped), straight-sitting, head up, bird nose upsweeping, dead eyes (red-rimmed blue behind dark glasses) unerringly fixed on what somebody is doing, an idiot's knot of concentration in the sinoidal spot behind his eye-bridge-bone above, at the upper end of, his nose: a knot or thick lump of concentration, the in-head rotation of thought crawled up into a tight little bundle, the unseeing eye's gaze/ stare, a dead center from which spins off, but only because he is a genius, i.e. has a sly margin of rapid cunning mental motion left, food for directorial, directed, shaping thought: ideas on how to do it otherwise, save the situation superlatively, make something of it: but it still is that *Idiot*'s immersion in the present idiotic fact that's feeding the imagining brain, a debility, an almost getting buried, risk taken in self-loss death, an almost coming to a stop, or even: quite, the dead halt, through which a believed-in momentum carries him off into a further great arch or loop of flight.

being attentive and responsive to the ensemble tone and cadence, – kept one busy, even tense: there was little time to think of one's movements or feel one's body. The vocalisation was the thing: one *also* had to remember where to deliver the line, turned which way, with what gesture, if any, and how to get there. The gestures, – not too many except for Sutton using her lovely long hands in stylised expressions, – felt as though they went with the vocal expressions, the changes of place felt as though they related to the conversations.

In point of fact, Wilson designed the movements independently, – primarily from a painterly viewpoint designing a dominant visual pattern for each act, modulating it within the act, secondarily from a choreographic viewpoint, setting up a visual dynamics for each act, contrasting the dynamics of successive acts.

A primarily *visual* play resulted, I think. It was, however, not abstract, but the image of conversation, of different ways of talking together, varied in terms of relation, viz. of outside, group, sub-group, person, and of conflict and alliance. The tight rapid choreography turned out formally the image of the vocal interchange. The minimalisation of the apperceptibility and relevance of the literal or properly verbal meaning of the speech adapted it to the relative abstractness of this image of conversation. In this limited and peculiar sense, but only in it, – not as the dominant element, but as complement of a visual image of people talking, – speech in *Letter* assumed the role that movement had had in the earlier Wilson productions.

If theatre is an exposition of people by a presentation of personal interaction in speech and movement,[21] in regular theatre, 1) speech dominates movement for the audience, and movement appears a supporting complement of speech, 2) speech is delivered and listened to as a presentation of meanings (of the meanings of words), and 3) is stylised and experienced qua manifestation of personality, viz. 4) as expression of feelings, attitudes, intents. In Wilson's pieces before *Letter,* 1) movement dominated speech for the audience, and speech appeared an incidentally supportive supplement of movement, 2) movement was stylised into (and experienced as) ritual sublimating into image, 3) by a suspension of personality, viz. 4) by a suppression of kinetic expressions of feelings, attitudes, intents, 5) and similarly for speech, which moreover 6) was delivered, and even when it was not so delivered tended to come across, in abstraction

21 ›Movement,‹ in the foregoing comprehensive sense of visible acts and arrangements of bodies.

from meanings. I had at the outset expected that *Letter*, would revert to regular theatre as regards its characteristic 1) supra, but not as regards the characteristics 2)-4) of speech in regular theatre, but that it would replace these by the characteristics 2)-4) of movement in Wilson's previous pieces. I had no definite expectations as to what would happen as regards verbal meaning. As rehearsals went on, it became clear that neither of my expectations was going to be realised: speech would not have the primacy over movement it has in regular theatre, but on the other hand it would not diverge from the speech of regular theatre by having the characteristics of movement in Wilson's previous pieces.

Wilson had not in his previous spectacles invented any new or beautiful movements, any new dance form, even less any distinctive mime style, – though he would have if he had trained his performers in his own expressive manner of movement, a manner of movement acting out perplexity. But by an appropriate selection of personnel,[22] and by work with them on movement with body-awareness, he had cultivated a kind of movement combining energy and relaxation and creating the impression of an individual rather than of a personality or ego: unselfconscious or unselfconscious-seeming; not betokening the ego or person behind the movement, self-contained and apart from it, a psychic self using a body; but on the one hand seeming to flow naturally from a mind and body at one with one another, and in this respect an enhancement of the individual moving in the eyes of the viewer, on the other naturally becoming, for a viewer, the line of an image, an insubstantial event absorbing the moving individual, an event into which the moving individual disappears, and in this respect the annihilation of the moving individual in the eyes of the viewer: a revelation of movement as natural link of the body to time, assimilating it into time. The result had been a kinetic event which was rather beautiful, and absorbing and fascinating – and which was a sacrifice of the performer to Wilson's images. Attention was focussed on the movement: the moving performer was put on exposition: the spectator transcended him or her by an expanded awareness of himher in motion. Movement functioned in the opposite way from the way it functions in regular theatre. – Wilson has no animus toward movement. It stands for him for ›doing things,‹ is the visible, phenomenal form of activity, and he is all for everybody doing things. In the form it assumed in his pre-*Letter* theatre, –

22 Cf. my description of byrds in *Wilson's theatre of visions, 1969-73,* supra: strong people, survivors with aura, but unformed, unstructured.

unegoistic, non-egocentric, un- though not impersonal, inexpressive and freed of the signs of instrumentality, – it corresponds to his own way of doing art. And as, in this form, a self-transcendence of the individual, it has for him, I would say, a metaphysical rightness. So in his spectacles before *Letter* it emerged as something positive, valuable. And there was no implied comment that any kind of movement was bad.

When, with *Letter,* he turned from movement to speech, in competition with regular theatre made speech the substance of the theatrical event, it was logical though perhaps rash and naive to expect a play in which speech would be analogously transformed and would function analogously for an audience. Certain experiments made one anticipate an opera in which the human voice would show as a natural mystery by which people importantly and beautifully transcend into solitary nullity.

At the time of *Overture,* there had been exercises in which one would attempt to let one's body decide on its own sounds, relaxing it, – sometimes engaged at the same time in concentrating on an image in one's mind, or in one's imagination trying to draw a perfect circle with an even motion, evenly expending energy, or doing some particular physical movement, – or trying to do all of these at the same time, – listening to one's body, feeling a sound build up within it, attempting not to force its coming out, waiting for an urge toward sound and then following, not anticipating, its working itself out, and voicing only what seemed to *want* to come out: and other exercises combining movements with the repeated saying, declaiming or chanting of more or less onomatopoetic statements of some image (›the dinosaur soars,‹ ›the ocean roars‹). During the work on the different versions of *Overture* and on *Stalin,* Cindy Lubar had developed her own texts and a delivery of them, a metallic, not exactly euphonious, consonantal, Latinate non-sense poetry, poetry not of emotion or perception but of reason or logic, scientific-sounding, delivered harshly, automatically, inexpressively, with machine-gun rapidity, very distinctly. She used this delivery, though no such text, just once in *Letter,* for a speech in act IV. She had also extended a use of the scream, raw, crude, into chant, with controlled very sudden changes of pitch. These two lines of vocal experimentation of Lubar's complemented one another the way Wilson's two modes of declamation in *Overture,* cf. my *Wilson as Performer,* complemented one another. Wilson feels that the mind is normally multi-focussed, mental activity multi-layered, and that therefore expression to be expressive should have a multiplicity of simultaneous evocations. Meredith Monk's vocal experiments did not have this quality for him: in Lubar's screaming he heard several voices simultaneously. Such screams frame *Letter*, and there are a few within the play. Wilson's scream-song between acts II and III, more rebellious, not so helplessly compulsive, authoritarian as Lubar's, seems influenced by her screaming. In act VII of *Stalin*, Wilson experimented with the conversational use of the fill- or stammer-words of speech, the signals of inner conflict and of what will not be put into words ›hm,‹ ›o.k.,‹ ›there,‹ ›well,‹ . . . One should be able to say anything with them, he said. This probably had some influence on his intercalation of a secondary dialogue into the dialogue of act II, section 6 of *Letter*. Chris during the work on *Letter* came up with a private vocabulary of his own, perhaps meaningful to him, ›burrup,‹ ›spups,‹ ›door,‹ ›scarf,‹ in his mouth humorous interjections or expletives, sometimes faintly plaintive. Wilson made him say one of them during his transit in act II. He sometimes used some of them on his own in other parts of act II and in act IV, and when he did, sometimes Lubar would respond in kind. During the concluding N.Y. run, Wilson had us all say them during the final silent moments of acts I and II, – sounds of emptymindedness. These experiments bore fruit in the Spoleto *Prologue* to *Letter*,[23] but not in *Letter*.

23 In the Spoleto *Prologue* to *Letter*, which Wilson had planned for the space, – a vast cold pillared church or palace cellar hall, – from the time of the first New York rehearsals, Wilson attempted a use of voices analogous to his use of movement in his preceding spectacles. The hall was divided into two rows of five cubicles each, leaving a central walk and open spaces at both ends free. A cubicle was assigned to each of ten performers, one of them a local man exchanging jocularities with the locals among the visitors. In the open space at the end Julia Busto and Andrew DeGroat danced. The 80 minute duration was divided into 10 segments: certain set movements, sounds and words and a text were assigned to each section. E.g. in an introductory section, Shelley Valfer, seconded by Bob, read the letter to Qu. V., the sounds were ›hoo hoo‹'s and ›hohoho‹, the words were ›burrup‹ and ›door‹; in section 1, the sounds were breathing and clucks, the words ›OK‹s, the text was a jocular address to Chris, perhaps from a letter to him from his sister; in section 2, the words were Lubar's ›arc are arc arch . . . arc are arc air . . . ear air ear earth;‹ in section 3 the words were Sutton's ›paydaton . . . moohacone . . . freda‹ and ›Queen leader . . . the Queen leader . . . paper planes . . . (etc.)‹, in section 4, the sounds were finger snappings, slight claps, faint growls from Lubar, breathing, the word was ›there‹; in section 5 the sounds were sibilant hisses and a low hum, the word was ›spup‹, the text was a science fiction kind of thing by Carol Mullins, in section 6, the sounds were ›hi‹s and ›hu‹s, and ›a a a‹, ›mmm mmm mmm,‹ ›a-o a-o a-o,‹ the word was ›scarf,‹ the text was Scotty Snyder's about her Iowa childhood; etc. I was to recite poetry written for the occasion when the spirit moved me. Each performer was in each section to do the words,

Instead, so far as I can tell, the aural effect of *Letter* was that of more or less ordinary conversation, though only of its semblance, without its substance, the abstract or form of it only, the sound of regular theatre. The close back and forth, the intonations of address and response, and the performers' adaptation to one another's tone in any given scene must have created the impression of the sociability adjunct to discursive intercourse. But the dimensions of meaning and of expression, – of literal or verbal meaning, denotation, *and* of gestural meaning, – had been gutted. The sentences were meaningful, but their literal meanings did not relate: the conversation had no literal meaning. *What* was said was clearly not meant. Whatever was spoken of was in no one's mind. The utterance was meaningful but its meaning did not relate to the meanings of the words. There was the sound of something being said about something, but what was said of what was clearly irrelevant. Just what anybody thought about and what they thought about it was not in the picture, – not said.

The voices had the sound, – cadences, accents, – of expressiveness and were expressive: suggested now this attitude or intent or feeling, now that. This was true even of Lubar's voice: it expressed not only an indifference to expression, but a fierce controlled will to *do* it, to

sounds and movements assigned to that section. The movements varied from section to section, a fairly complex sequence of simple movements for each section. DeGroat designed them and was supposed to direct the whole thing. Each section was to start with just the movements, then the sounds were to be added, then the words, then the text, until they were all going: 2 minutes of each. The idea was that the sounds were to ›grow out of‹ the movements, the words out of the sounds (or out of sounds plus movements), the texts (not in their words or meanings, which were pre-set, but in their reading) out of the words, or out of the mix. Mike Galasso played the violin, Kit Cation the flute. The visitors were asked to be quiet. They could circulate as they wanted. Somehow it was hoped they would move in a body from cell to cell, staying for the length of a section (marked by the tinkling of a bell by Galasso) with each performer. They moved largely in a body, but rarely stayed the length of a section with any given performer. The musicians visited each performer in turn, staying with him for the length of a section. Most of the performers, I believe, forgot a good many of the movements and felt it hard to do a solo piece in front of a close audience. The piece had an appearance of serenity and beauty, conveyed a higher sort of cool which I felt to be phony. – One *might* suspect that in Wilson's conception this piece, which he handed over to DeGroat, would do with and for vocalisation what Wilson's earlier pieces had done with and for movement, would be what *Letter* wasn't, a body-opera, extending body-movement into body-sound, presenting text as product of movement. But perhaps he only thought of it as propaedeutic introduction of *Letter,* illustrating the thesis not illustrated by *Letter,* that true individual speech is a mode of individual movement.

say whatever she said. When in section 2 of act II I tried for an inexpressive voice it instead expressed detachment from the situation we were acting out. Cation's flat tone expressed a neutral personality, Snyder's flat middlewestern tone a matter-of-fact attitude. Sutton's gifted, skilled voice acted out dozens of shifts of attitude. Most of our voices most of the time expressed a variety of attitudes and moods.

But at the same time, the expressiveness was merely formal. The pauses needed to make things seem meant had been suppressed. When the expressive quality went with what was said, it didn't fit in with what seemed the action; and vice versa. In act II the expressive intonations were repeated with the repeated dialogue, in act I they were varied systematically. The lines were spoken by the performers on stage in regular alternation. Most of the time there were no body or arm gestures to go with the vocal gestures. When there were, they were either highly stylised (Sutton) or mechanical (e.g. Lubar's), and recurrently they were mysterious gestures invented by Wilson, not expressing anything. The changes of place and relative positions were obviously designed patterns. Movements and distributions thus supported speech in a fashion destructive of taking its expression seriously. All this, by denying reality to the personalities, moods, feelings, intentions expressed, worked toward making of the voices' expressive qualities mere sound effects. Whatever was expressed wasn't there: only the form of expression. I suppose the reduction to form of vocal expressiveness and verbal meaningfulness had one effect that the ritualisation of movement in the pre-*Letter* pieces had had, namely that it prevented the introjection of personality or ego, prevented the audience from grasping the play in terms of such, – reduced us to figures by undercutting psychologising. But I am not sure of this.

As *Letter* turned out, speech in it had the sound of meaningfulness in both senses of ›meaning:‹ gestural meaning, the expression and communication of feelings, attitudes, intents; literal or verbal meaning, the expression or communication of ideas about something. It did not have specific literal meaning: its literal meaning did not matter, was irrelevant to characters and situations, was not meant. It probably came across as having specific gestural meaning, – specific gestural meanings were probably apprehended by the audience, – and these probably seemed meant in the context of the play at each moment, characters having the feelings etc. indicated by the tone of voice were probably perceived. The play was designed to undercut taking these seriously, construing the characters, designed to make these specific gestural meanings seem merely pro forma. This may or may not have frustrated inclinations to attribute the specific gestural meanings to characters. But regardless of this and of specific meanings, speech had the sound of meaningfulness in general.

Whereas in the pre-*Letter* spectacles, movement lacked the forms (such as expressiveness and indication of purpose) conveying personality and ego, speech in *Letter*, if only formally, just like regular theatre exhibited these forms, – denotation, assertion and denial, expression, purpose, address and response; so that whereas in those spectacles movement, individualised but without the psychic denotations of mind and will, integrated the moving performers into insubstantial images, speech in *Letter*, retaining the attributive character of being the speech of *someone*, of a substantial (›real‹) person or ego either 1) could not achieve any integration, namely if the absence of effectively and consistently attributable specific meanings prevented the construction of stage-characters, – or else 2) did achieve one, but not into insubstantial image, namely if a spectator construed a character from the specific meanings conveyed.

The sublimation of the talking figures into insubstantial image was impossible. There was no nexus of verbal or literal meaning between the speech and the figures. There was a nexus of gestural, tonal meaning (expression of attitudes, feelings, intents by aural figurations). But this latter, since it constituted the figures persons or egos, characters in the manner of the characters of regular theatre, did not provide insubstantial images. If the spectator focussed on this dimension of the speech, heshe found himherself watching something like a regular play. If heshe abstracted not only from literal but also from gestural meaning, from the expressiveness of the speech, heshe found himherself aware of an abstract image of conversation in which speech as speech was lacking. There was no way, I would say, for the audience to remain aware of the speech as speech, let alone focus on it, and 1) to transcend, as had been possible (relative to movement) in the earlier spectacles, awareness of the performers performing, but without 2) entertaining the illusion of fictitious characters. The manner of the speech did not invite but hindered this transcendence. Of course the audience could carry away the audio-visual image of this or that figure or group of figures on stage in a certain combination of body-gesture and vocal gesture: but it would be of quite a different sort from the visual images carried away from Wilson's earlier spectacles: it would include a depth-dimension, – a psychic dimension, – viz. some notion of what the figure or figures felt or intended or of what their mental attitudes were, in short of their personality: a depth-dimension lacking in those visual images and the lack of which made them insubstantial, made them images properly speaking, purely images. This depth-dimension would be the only thing tying that vocal gesture into the audio-visual image.

*Letter* presented speech purely as social activity. The only occasions in which it was not participation in conversation were 3 brief addresses by myself to the audience in act IV. There were no monologues. The phrases Wilson had picked for the play were all very specifically dialogue phrases, talk addressed to another, set colloquial units. The speech was explicitly social, the notes of address and response were in the delivery no less than in the phrasing. Speech in *Letter* thus carried the signs of a function, the function of affecting another, of communicating. Some of it was more informative, some more expressive, – 2 other functions, evident in phrasing and delivery, also part of its expressiveness.

Though this is only rarely the chief point made by its manner or content, what makes speech speech is its representation of thinking, viz. of a process of meaning in mind. But speech normally by manner and/or content also *indicates* what it is to be taken as, and normally identifies itself *not* as externalisation of ongoing thought, but as expression of opinion (*result* of thinking, *a* thought, – attribute of the thinker/speaker) or feeling, as communication (means to move another), as argument (arrangement of signs in conformity to logical structure), and/or as information (representation of what is spoken of). But these are its instrumental characters or functions, and what it is is sounded thought. Normally this is evident in its manner even when it does not advertise itself as such, but identifies itself by its purpose. Speech with indication of its point (purpose, function) presents itself as relating to – as activity or product of – a person or ego distinct from it: denuded of such indication it appears, depending on its manner, either as arbitrarily produced sound, non-speech accidentally in the form of speech or as sounded thought, as process of the individual: the individual itself appears in it, rather than standing behind it as person and substance. It appears as sounded thought rather than as non-speech in speech-form if its manner indicates the process-nature of the thinking sounded: voices the connections, arrests, conflicts, etc. Such vocal indication of process is distinct from indications of the thinker/speaker's intent to think or effort of thinking, intent to voice thought, effort of putting thought into words.

Speech as sounded thought, shorn of indications of purpose and personality, appears to me similar to the kind of movement characteristic of Wilson's pre-*Letter* spectacles or at least capable of similar representation.[24] It lacks the attributive quality of normal, – socially oriented, – speech, of the conversational speech presented by *Letter*. At least in this regard, it would lend itself to the sublimation of the thinker/speaker into (auditory/visual) image. But this would have required not only making the meaning of the speech an integral – meaningful – part of the theatrical event, but structuring the performance around it: putting speech qua meaningful on exhibition (and suppressing its functional indications, its signs of being expression, communication, argument or information). Given that Wilson did turn from movement to speech, doing this would have been in the logic of his development as theatre artist. Not doing it resulted in a discontinuity. *Letter* is radically unlike his previous pieces. Unlike them it is not radically innovative. It may from Wilson's own viewpoint have been a failure.

What stood in Wilson's way, I would say, was a passionate antipathy to discursive reason. I would say he views it as the very bone of language,[25] its peculiar power, distinguishing language from other species of signification, and thinks of it as inescapably the formally impersonal statement of objective (divine, moral, logical, natural . . .) necessity, and dislikes it as such, – for being always pre- or proscriptive. I suppose this is a feeling children have about language, naturally resulting from their verbal intercourse with adults: the information given by language restricts the world of their daydreams, of their imagination and desires. Language points out to them the

24 Wilson's own style of declamation in *Overture*, cf. my description in *Wilson as Performer*, focussed on the meaning of words and stylised speech as sounded thinking. But it stressed the affective dimension of thinking (anguish, anxiety, triumph), and presented it as a negative dialectic of verbalisation (necessity cum insufficiency of verbal definition), in terms of a dichotomy between thought and language, – as process of perplexity. Presented in this form, – which is analogous to the form of body-movement in Wilson's dancing, – it would not yield a sublimative opera analogous to the pre-*Letter* sublimative spectacles. Whatever moved him to develop for others a style of movement obviating the honest pain of his own style of movement, did not sufficiently move him in 1974 to do the analogous thing with speech.

25 Though recent research on subjects with a split corpus callosum by Zaidel and Sperry indicates that the right hemisphere of an adult's brain may have the vocabulary of a 14-year old and the syntactical ability of a 5-year old, i.e. is not without verbal power, speech on the whole seems to be a function of the left hemisphere.

limitations of their freedom. Even just a statement of fact points to a block in a path one might want to take. Furthermore, like any child, Wilson feels that the necessities stated are not necessities, that speech is a means of deceiving, if not conning, and feels it to be, unlike other forms of communication, — some merely showing something, some merely offering something, — demanding address, address demanding assent, and resents it on this score too: as aggression and invasion of privacy, and at the same time babyish admission of a need for help. Finally, he thinks of it, I would say, as self-definition, hence restriction by oneself of one's liberty: a statement confines one to a stand. This tyrannical aspect of language might perhaps not have precluded the kind of meaningful speech that would have made *Letter* a transcendental opera in the sense in which the spectacles preceding it were transcendental, — might not even be relevant to it, or might have been obviated (neutralised) by linguistic means, — but Wilson's sensitivity to it is to my mind probably the reason why he did not feel up to tackling the problem of (literally) meaningful speech, but made verbal meaning irrelevant and settled for a show of (gestural) meaning, and made this incoherent, irrelevant, not meant, — settled for a (n abstract, primarily visual) show of language as means of intercourse. Inasmuch as *Letter* conveys a variety of relationships, attitudes, feelings independent of what the characters say, but conveyed by their way of saying it, it demonstrates that communication is independent of verbal meaning, and suggests that what people say is not the content of communication. *Letter* is a gesture of contempt toward verbal meaning. Wilson sacrificed his art to this gesture.

THE PLAY. The play turned out to have 4 acts, though the 3rd is only a brief interlude, and was perhaps slipped in as a transition. A reading of the Letter was made a preface. The beginning of act 1 turned into an introductory tableau. A concluding scene or epilogue reflecting it was added.[26]

Wilson had introduced himself in isolated roles into his earlier spectacles disrupting them and sounding a corrective note: as the screeching Big Mammy in *King* and *Freud,* as initiatory Magician in *Deafman,* as the Stalin struck by his wife's death in *Stalin*[27] (and

26 Approximate durations (minutes): reading of letter, 5, foreplay, 5, 1.1, 20-30, 1.2, 10-15, 11, 40-50, 111, 5-10, intermission, 10, 1v, 50-60, epilogue, 5, — the play, 2 hrs. 35 minutes to 3 hours 10 minutes.
27 Wilson thought or sort of assumed that Stalin much loved his first wife, and

then as killer of the poet and as amateur of artillery), but somehow saw no part for himself in *Letter*, nor, as it turned out, for Chris.

Chris's stage appearances in acts II and IV contrasted him to the play, broke through its emphatically rigid structure, not only because he had no share in the dialogue dominating the play but also because his idiosyncratic movements stood out against the tightly controlled choreography and the brief defined gestures of the performers proper, and his outgoing, relaxed good humor against their discipline. He did have a regular part, the same as everybody else's, in act III, and blended in somewhat: but Wilson made sure to restore the contrast by having him rise above the stage on his chair, — his deviation became noticeable. In acts II and IV he brought his tape recorder, sometimes recorded the others or things he said himself, sometimes replayed what he'd recorded. This did not give him the role of a recording awareness, but suggested alternatively a fragmented distorted double or a fragmentary intensely essential original of the play either of which would be free of its theatrical Structure. He thus, as in his appearances in front of the curtain, appeared as Wilson's alter ego.

Partly, at least, because the (Spoleto) sets were so awkward to put up and strike, and to keep the audience from walking out after the 3rd act under the misapprehension that the play was over, Wilson and Chris ended up covering the scene-changes in front of the curtain:

that her death was perhaps as reshaping an experience for Stalin as the death of his favorite grandson was for Freud. When in Sao Paulo in 1974 that wife died in Wilson's *Stalin* (which in deference to the military censors had been renamed after a West Coast assassin *The Life and Times of David Clark*), Wilson as Stalin comes in, followed by a double, just as she finally collapses on her bed all the way downstage, centerstage, seats himself, leaning forward, ›not believing his eyes‹, in one of the play's two emblematic armchairs, and then sits motionless, facing out toward the audience (his double seated in the other chair), head forward, hands slightly bent on the armrest of the sheeted chair. (Piano chords after a while.) White summer Stalin uniform, powdered hair, moustache. Suddenly, on two heavy chords from the piano, a big jump, arms flying up. White cloud of powder. He again sits immobile: staring at her. for a long time. Soft music (Paul Robeson singing *I love you*). He gets up after the first ›I love you‹, a little heavily, approaches the bed on which she lies on her back, dead, stands, arms hanging, watches her. He sits down on the edge of the bed, head bent, puts his hands on hers, folds her hands, slowly . . ., straightens (the Robeson tape has ended, Sheryl Sutton, another Stalin, is singing the same song now), very slowly gets up, turns away from the corpse, facing upstage, his (downstage) left hand goes behind his back (›sort of‹ helplessly). As a country-western, ›*I'm going down the road, feeling bad,*‹ starts, he goes off with bowed head, breaking into a loose-limbed dance as big Scotty Snyder comes on with her Iowa routine.

he and Chris between acts I and II, he by himself between acts II and III, Chris by himself between acts III and IV. These flexible appearances set off the clock-work organisedness of the play.

I habitually missed most of the number between II and III except its end which I saw through the curtain. It ends with a dialogue between Wilson and Chris done as dialogue between comedian and straightman, a repetition of Chris's ›and you sit on a bench and you wait for me till I come back.‹ They stand at a distance from one another, facing the audience, then alternately one or the other walks over and screams the line at the other who after a pause responds by a mild consent. The last time they quietly walk across together saying the line in unison.

Between II and III, Wilson as an absurd, gloved and hatted, elegantly cloddish figure, comes on stage-right, still there mimes at extreme length 2 poses of bewilderment, and then crosses, all angular crossing limbs, doing a non-verbal scream-monologue in the tone of wilful madness, empty obstreperousness, ending stage-left with 2 or 3 horrendous torrents of sound, topping one another, with short pauses between them, bent over, and then quickly leaves.

During the intermission between III and IV, Chris spins on what is otherwise throughout the play Andy DeGroat's spinning platform out front, stage left (Julia Busto throughout the play spinning on the corresponding platform stage right). Chris's spinning is a perpetually off-balance gyration not quite in place. While spinning he talks to the audience that's left or that is returning from the intermission, in a friendly conversational manner announcing act IV, telling them the number of minutes left before it's supposed to start.

When the audience is admitted, Mike Galasso is fiddling away and Queen Victoria (Alma Hamilton, Wilson's surviving grandmother) is in place in front of the curtain, stage-left. DeGroat and Julia Busto are turning. After prolonged fiddling by Mike, – Wilson is always late, at curtain time mostly because he has to take a few drags on his pipe first, – four personages, Wilson the last, at 14 second intervals at a run emerge from stage-right, envelope in hand, line up there, facing the audience, closely arrayed tear open the envelopes, take out the letter for the Queen, and simultaneously read it. The letter in a more 18th century than Victorian ornate style, exalts the illustrious personage to which it is addressed and declaims the author's nullity, but retracts both by proclaiming the grandiose infinity of all things finite. It heralds the disturbing (exhilarating) explosion of the Victorians' ordered universe of small things in their place. I wrote it during the time when in the 7th act of *Stalin* I was a typing clerk on a float to which a messenger delivered a ›letter for Queen Victoria.‹ The readers, possibly seeming representative of diverse types of intellect, all neatly dressed and extremely self-contained, pursue their solitary course in earnest, paying no attention to the queen or to the audience. Though the text is clearly intended to be closely followed, the readings cancel one another out. The audience can't make out the statement. The text's tone of an intellectual's circumspection and arrogant humility may variously pierce through the tones of the readers: Cation's briskly pleasant total non-committalness, Wilson's intermittent important announcements, colored by amazement, Chris's joyful or privately amused, sometimes earnest conquest of the words, my? –. Queen Victoria does not acknowledge the address but responds anecdotally, telling all how she needs 5 pills a day to keep her frail body going. Ending with the affirmation that she is still the monarch, she produces a prolonged frail scream, slowly lifting her arms. I think she wore dark glasses. (She reappears, homely and regal, at the end of act III, to repeat, down-stage, stage-left, her scream and gesture three times.) Her low, life-assertive wails astonishingly give an impression of force. Like the stronger screams of Sutton and Lubar they are inexpressive. Two of the readers, Wilson, personifying genius, and Knowles, personifying mental deficiency, speaking, alternatively, as one, have bridged the juxtaposition by a loudvoiced authoritative dismemberment of the play's title, a warning, probably instantly disregarded by the audience, not to look for meaning in the play. It's a respectful announcement of the play, torn up by the genius' hang-up on letters (›a,‹ ›b‹) and the idiot kid's concern with his sister's liking for TV: she likes to watch cartoons. After a formalised moment of indecision, the 4 file out on tiptoe.

The play starts out with screams from its two stars, Enigmatic Figures, alone on stage together as the curtain rises: stage-right down-stage, facing stage-left, a stocky dyke-like plain White girl-woman (Cynthia Lubar) draped in white, a white triangle extending behind her like a wing, upstage, stage-left a statuesque slim beautiful Black woman-girl (Sheryl Sutton) facing down-stage, very tall in black on a ladder-platform, her drape covering her and hiding the ladder, and laid out in a train toward the front of the stage ramp:

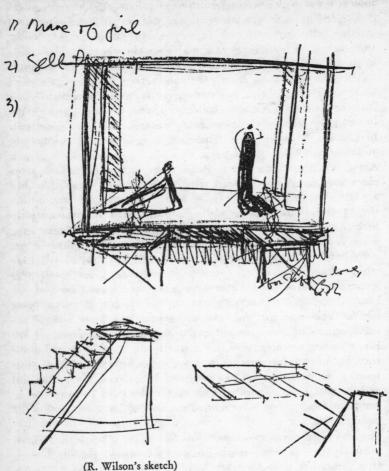

(R. Wilson's sketch)

The earthbound angel of light screams first, then, not in answer, the high-up likeness of the angel of darkness. The screams are drawn out, modulated. They are unemotional: the heavy figure's a brutal outpouring of power, the tall one's a cold eery melodious somewhat theatrical wail, both marked by control. The screams are repeated at the end of the play. The play, – speech, – arises out of and goes back into scream.

When both have screamed they reveal themselves as not only one another's but their own opposites. The tall one with a theatrical gesture ending arms up, the small one with a harsh gesture ending her arm behind her, open their capes, the black girl in black revealing an elegant white dress, the white girl in white a sober black one. Dropping her cape, the tall one slowly from her perch advances downstage, deliberately puts her foot in the jaws of a crocodile, which close on it. This is the end of the foreplay, the curtain falls (She repeats her action in the epilogue. The crocodile is smaller then. In the 3 times repeated text of act I, scene I, she at one point tells an invisible crocodile to ›get behind‹ her. The leviathan does not otherwise occur in the play.)

Act I, scene I, The curtain rises on the same two, in the same places, dressed in the costumes they had under their drapings. They are still imposing, by stances and delivery strong and cool, Sutton stately and refined, Lubar tough. They immediately start their dialogue, a ping pong of alternate short lines.

They are engaging in a personal verbal exchange, each contained within her own universe of pre-occupation, only instrumentally paying attention to the other, and though the exchange sometimes slips into the tone of social talk between two women (the text is social talk between two people[28]), they seem in conflict. There is tension between them, sometimes under the surface, sometimes emerging. The conflict seems grave, partly because there is talk of killing and threats to kill the other, partly because of their stances of watchfulness (Sutton) and controlled vehemence (Lubar), and because of the drive of their voices. The verbal exchange is quite inconclusive. (The spectator is quite confused about what they are talking about, it seems something else all the time, their tone and the references to many people by their given names suggest the relationship is personal.) The spectator sees *a* personal relationship and *an* antagonism. Sutton may seem the protagonist on the defensive, Lubar the antagonist on the offensive.

It is clearly theatre, they are both unnatural, the tall white one modulating her lines, the small black one repeating lines. It is clearly theatre, but the spectator can't get hisher teeth into it, can only look (listen) but not enter into the matter, doesn't know what it's about.

The same verbal exchange is repeated 3 times in somewhat differing

28 When Wilson started work with Sutton and Lubar on this scene, he mentioned to them they might imagine they had just, in different moods, stepped out for some fresh air from a party taking place behind a windowed wall stage-left. This wall was, for this scene, eventually done away with.

tones, Sutton discretely going from carefully saying her lines to saying them with expression, to saying them with emotion, the change probably registering as increasing vehemence: from matter-of-factness to emphasis and deliberation to engagement and strong address. There is no development, however: it's more as though the dialogue were being turned over for an exposition of its different emotional dimensions. But a spectator might come to feel that passion was at the heart of it.

The first time is separated from the second by a drop of the curtain (on which there was to have been but wasn't a picture of a ›Sequachee dam‹ mentioned in acts II and IV), the second from the third by a black-out, the third is ended by the entrance of a big woman (Scotty Snyder) saying ›hold it,‹ followed by the falling of a heavy metal grill which separates the rear of the stage from the front for the second scene of this act. The first time, they launch right into the dialogue and continue it through and past a minor intrusive parallel action (the pilots, cf. infra). The second time, there is an introductory encounter between them (›Hi Sheryl how are you?‹ ›OK‹ ›Do you want to go for a walk in the garden?‹ ›OK‹ – ›Hi Cindy how are your?‹ ›OK‹ ›Do you want to go for a walk in the garden?‹ ›OK‹), followed by a promenade, – they walk separately, each, on her half of the stage, along the curved legs of an x, the paths of a formal garden meeting in the center, – which ends with a joint held bow, during which there is a slide projection of an airplane (instead of an atomic explosion as originally intended). Then the dialogue is carried through again. The third time, they start right in again, omitting the encounter scene, but the dialogue ends at the point where the parallel action starts. The first two times the dialogue ends with the crocodile routine (which itself is slightly varied). With well-defined exceptions, each of the two for most of this scene stays in her initial place and says her lines from it.[29] The scene (and thus the act since this scene is by far its greater part) thus has a static visual definition. At the end of each of the first two sections, Sutton advances in a straight line downstage to the crocodile, and the second section has that introductory promenade, and when the dialogue gets to the part where Lubar, in response to an ›I don't believe you,‹ in a blackmailing way, getting back at Sutton, says ›oh, there is a smudge on your collar,‹ as though this were evidence against her, she goes up to her

29 As though he were painting, Wilson in all his plays tends to identify the different localities on stage by particular figures, assigning to each figure a locality of its own, a base, and some particular region or path of movement.

and puts a magnifying glass over her collar and they stand motionless while (while a slide of the smudge is projected onto the backdrop) Lubar looks around, smiles in a slow terrible way and says ›the still!:‹ but these movements are defined by those positions. In the latter part of the 3rd section, the dominant immobility of the scene dissolves: they advance and retreat from one another all across, all over the stage.[30]

In the first two sections, at a point in the dialogue when it suddenly and momentarily seems friendly talk about a movie, there is the line ›suppose there was a plane crash and everyone died but the pilot,‹ and two helmeted goggled figures in what might seem pilot's uniforms (airforce mechanic's zippered nylon jumpsuits) come on from each side downstage of the two women, and slowly, like zombies, advance toward one another, and stop, facing one another. The first time, both having slowly raised their arms sideways and placed their hands on their heads, they bow, rotate their heads on their necks, straighten up, raising one leg, pivot, and leave with steps as though walking in deep sand. The next time one of them stretches as he

[30] What Wilson gets from his performers is by no means always what he has had in mind or wants, – nor, of course, what *he* would do. (His stage-designs, when they are not geometric diagrams, are wild and dark, dramatic, highly emotional, quite unlike the quiet formal images he finally comes up with on stage. After *Letter* opened, he wondered, ›is it not too cute?‹) One reason he stayed out of *Letter* (and in the earlier spectacles confined himself to contrasting entries) is that he is afraid he's so strong he would wreck the composition, – as was the case with his vehement, aggressive, personal entrance in the 7th act of the Copenhagen *Stalin*: he seemed to want to wreck the quiet control of the play. When during the frantic period shortly before the real opening of *Letter* in Spoleto, he suddenly for the third time around of Lubar's and Sutton's act I, sc. I routine gave them a series of wildly acrobatic, madly aggressive, theatrical poses and runs, – demonstrating them, – to go with the more emotional tone, the movement came out flattened and inoffensive, subdued, the way Sutton and Lubar did it. What he had demonstrated was not Grotowskian bodylanguage of the passions, but a sub-text to it, illustrating not just the individual's inner conflict, but a dialectic of dependency and antagonism between it and relating-to-another, both perturbed: the inner life needing to express itself as relation to others, as life in a public space, but as unable to do so; an attempt at an inner integration by terrorised outwardness, remaining at all instants disequilibrated and frustrated. He would have had the two figures alternately approaching to make a pattern and receding as though chased till the whole stage separated them, throwing themselves on the floor, legs in the air, rise in approach, lie back down in sculpturalisations of solitary anguish. But when they tried it, he found ›the anger missing.‹ He then thought of going back to an earlier idea for this section; a discoordination of movement and speech, one fast while the other is slow, speeding up and slowing down independently, but there was no time to work this out. So he left it at their doing a pale, reduced, – stylised, – version of the approach/recession pattern: without emotion.

comes in (Wilson had seen him, waiting to go on for this routine, doing this during rehearsals: perhaps it went with the physical feel of it, it probably looked eery in the dim light), seems to discover the presence of the two women, exclaims ›excuse me!,‹ raising his hands turns abruptly, turning seems to bump into a glass wall,[31] and then hops off sideways, front to the audience, his hands still up as though supporting him on the invisible wall.

Act I, scene 2. The second time the cue for the pilots comes up, the lady imperiously saying ›hold it!‹ makes her appearance, the grill falls, and instead of the pilots two men in business suits, holding newspapers, one with a bulky briefcase, enter, oversize, electrified wooden armchairs with lights built into their fronts, – not unlike a metal chair of Robert Morris's that Wilson had liked, – being carried in just upstage of them,[32] and sit down center-stage facing one another, open their papers, and immediately, buried behind their papers, start conversing in a fake neutral tone.

They may seem engaged in a conspiracy. It is the image of a relationship, but an impersonal one, and one which is visibly secondary to the separateness of each. Since they seem to be making a secret of their communication, the spectator may feel their environment is hostile to them and their bond a conflict with it. While their words (not necessarily understandable) may initially convey disagreement, their speech soon makes it evident that they are, separately, of one mind.

Their secretive exchange develops into a stentorian declamation in 2 not too coordinate voices on the beauty of the Sundance Kid: one of them, his paper crumpled in his lap, is rocking forward and back quietly, the other, slowly in large arches and figure-eights moving his paper, held at arm's length, from side to side, diagonally up or down, may seem to be floating with it in space. Chris, the author of their peroration enters leading a bicycle and stands behind one of them valiantly doing his fumbling version of the letter to Queen Victoria. Wilson enters in his good black suit, stands behind the other.

31 This was Wilson's description of it when he directed this routine.
32 Wilson and Neu carried in the chairs, a simple stage-hand's job of which Wilson (not telling Neu to do anything with it) made a bit of acting, coming on real slow and as though he didn't know where he was. Wilson, I would say, thinks of the stage as a strange place, a different world, where anything can happen. One gets the impression he has to keep tight rein on his imagination or every little thing done in a production of his would proliferate into a more and more involved bizarre routine, adaptation in extremis to the involuted operation of mysterious forces.

In the rear, behind the grill, the stout ›hold it!‹ lady is carrying on an interrogation (as though a crime had happened, but this may not come across), notebook and ballpoint in hand, of the two figures of the previous scene: they act out their answers, a fourth reenactment, including the entrance of the pilots, in fragments and low voices, gestures and walks informally illustrative, of that scene. Toward the end of the Sundance paean, those behind the grill may, arms in the air, also seem to be floating off. All freeze as the lights go up and then the curtain comes down.[33]

Act II in dim light shows 4 people in bulky combat outfits caught, – holding out, left behind or left over, – in a house, indicated by a wall extending at a slight angle across most of the stage, at right angles meeting a shorter wall stage-left with a big window in it, in a combat situation: indicated by their uniforms, by sporadic shooting, explosions, keelings over, and by baled barbed wire beyond the window and smoke coming in through it. A projector outside the window throws the shadows of the combattants on the wall.

33 Snyder ends the first 3 or 4 sections of act II with her ›hold it!,‹ the performers freezing. The other sections of act II also end with freezes, the 5th, penultimate one with the lights going up. Acts III and IV end with freezes, but they are not total, one performer is doing something. After the freeze ending act IV, everyone floats off. The two pilots repeat their first routine at the beginning of the afterplay. The four performers in act II wear the same uniforms as the pilots in act I, and as in act I, they finally reappear in businessmen's suits. Stills are mentioned again in act II. The airplane is projected in each act. The talk in act I is sometimes (from *Birth of a Nation*, I believe) of the Civil War and its aftermath. Sutton in section 3 of act II and at one point in act IV, for a dialogue between two old men, appears in a Union soldier's uniform. A hidden mention of the Klan in act I (›And they would call Clanton Klux . . .‹) is echoed by one in act II. We hear no more of the ›smudge‹ of act I but it is again, during a brief appearance of Sutton's (caricatured by Lubar) projected in act II. Its possible implication of a crime done by Sutton has committed, and that the figure Lubar plays is on to, anticipates the relation of criminal to investigator between the figures enacted by Sutton and Lubar in act IV. There are half a dozen mentions, some referring to a divorce of hers, of a girl named »Manda« in act I, mostly by Lubar. In act II, one of Lubar's lines is ›You're in luck when you see what Manda saw.‹ In a wrapping-up speech in act IV, Lubar among other things tells the others, ›there Manda got a divorce.‹ In act I, one of Lubar's lines to Sutton is ›You killed my brother and what's between. I hate you.‹ In act II, she tells Cation, ›We killed your brother and feel real bad about it.‹ In the wrap-up speech in act IV she says, ›Jim didn't kill your brother.‹ –

Like slightly varied repetition, setting up audience anticipations and then only partially fulfilling them or fulfilling them with a twist, such anticipations/echoes, – formal visual or auditory rimes and reflections, teasing hints at a nexus of meaning (plot), setting the audience up for faint shocks of recognition and abortive intuitions of pattern, – are a major theatre device of Wilson's.

Though the repartee and the groupings suggest alliances and shifting personal relationships within the group, by its tone this act's talk is intra-group rather than interpersonal, the more or less idle or urgent practical talk within a team about what's happening and what should be done. The team-idea is supported by the similarity of the four, in the dim light, of roughly the same height (a consideration of Wilson's), wearing the same form-disguising uniforms.[34] The environment is hostile, they are in danger, they are reacting to it. The conflict is with an outside, not among them. Except that there is a high incidence of references to danger and to the need to take some action, what's said does not by its (mutually unrelated) meanings relate to this image. I think the tone was on the unemotional side, but this may have been naturalistically interpreted by the audience as expressing habituation to danger/war, and indeed I suppose we labored under some kindred fantasy.

The act as a whole may vaguely present the appearance of a dramatic action: more as a succession of moods or attitudes suggesting a sequence of situations, than as a succession of definite events. In section 1) (but again in sections 2) and 4): which would have obscured such an outline of a development) tension, antagonisms; an interval of hesitation; a moment of decision, of readiness for action, succeed one another. 3) shows a close group in a quandary 5), in a tone of approaching crisis, urgency, shows deliberation, discussion; euphoria of incipient action; the moment of crisis, things falling apart; 6), recollection in disintegration. Whatever the different tone in these sections, its variations, though perhaps sparked by individual lines, are nearly independent of the text, are conveyed by tone of voice and manner of movement and came about fortuitously (and without directions from Wilson) by the players' unconscious adjustment to one another's tones.

The act was a mechanical ballet in the space defined by the Wall and the Window. There are many changes of place (about 30 in just the first of the 6 sections), all the different combinations of 3 and 1 and

34 The anonymous performers: Ashley, Lubar, Kit Cation, myself. Sutton enters twice, Neu once. There is no discernible continuity of action or of characters between acts I and II,– or between any 2 acts of the play, nor, I would say, the air of any. I doubt that Ashley and I stood out as the same people that had read the newspapers in 1.2, or Lubar as one of the disputants of 1.1. But I suspect that the juxtaposition of Lubar and Sutton in the 2nd section of act II (like later their relations in act IV) at least faintly evoked their opposition in 1.1. And I suspect that both the general discontinuity and this negligible allusion were intended by Wilson.

of 2 and 2 (not so much of 1,1,1 and 1) from among the 4 figures: facing the wall or looking out the window or with the back to either looking at one or more of the others or not, or in the interior of the enclosed space, or withdrawn from the situation downstage or stage-right: those together talking to one another, talk going between two groups, talk between a momentary outsider and the grouped others. The changes of place – the changes in the spatial pattern of the team – are generally cued by the lines: each performer's generally by someone else's line: so that few of the lines are delivered in movement. It is these groupings that may have suggested different alliances and tensions, probably seeming due to different attitudes toward the situation.

For the first 5 out of the 6 sections of the act, the changes of position were generally brisk walks, the postures in place erect, arms at the side, there were almost no arm gestures, but Wilson had into this rigid minimalisation of normalcy interspersed some mysterious gestures, e.g. the first time one of the 4 lights a cigar in the half-dark, he uses a flash sheet; at a certain point, and this is repeated, another twice tugs with her right at the left shoulder of her uniform, and there are some contrived movements in unison, e.g. several times all slowly lift their lower right leg backwards and curve their right arms up above their heads, and, at other times, repeat slowly bringing their right hands behind their heads to their left ears while in a prone position.[35]

The dialogue for this act had been divided into 4 parts, the first of which was repeated twice (in the pattern 1-1a-2-1b-3-4). These 6 sections, not quite scenes, are terminated by the ›hold it!‹ lady and separated by brief blackouts. With the repetition-pattern of act I (dialogue, introductory dialogue plus dialogue, dialogue minus its last part, dialogue as background) still in mind, the audience, once in act II it sees 1 repeated by 1a is apt to expect another repetition of 1, but instead gets 2, and only then, no longer expecting it, gets another repetition of 1. Whereas the delivery of the repetition varied in tone

35 Wilson seeds all his plays with such signs that all is not normal, 1) making a performer do or say some little thing he/she is in the habit of doing or saying, something slightly idiosyncratic, that, exposed on stage, isolated and perhaps repeated acts as abrogation of standardised normalcy if not as intrusion of irreality, 2) contrived gestures or made-up words (e.g. ›Ipsick Dipsick‹ in act I). There are the address to the crocodile (and the crocodile), the pilots' routines, and the floating off in act I, a slow extension and retraction of the right hand in act III, 3 sudden upward swings of the arm by everyone (which Wilson spoke of as compelled by the sudden action of a force) at different points in act IV ...

systematically, the variation in act II, was mechanical: the first time it was done (the group stationary by the window, their backs to the audience), as a highspeed run-through, with ultrarapidity and without any gestures, the second time at a natural rapid rate, the third time at the same rate but with the pauses cut in half.

The 3 repetitions of the 1st segment of the dialogue (sections 1, 2, 4 of the act) each time started with nearly the same 5-part silent routine, a mimic abstract of an isolated social cell, a quick series of very briefly glimpsed positions by the rear wall, with very short blackouts between, starkly delineated by the slide-projector.[36] When the light first goes on, just after the curtain rises, the 4 players stand closely together in very slightly varied postures, flat up against the wall, their backs to the audience; the next time they are seen in the same positions, except that one has stepped back slightly and is leaning back, arms around the two on each side; the next time they have broken away from the wall, and stand in a rough parallelogram facing one another, not too far apart; the next time they are lying face down, toes by the wall, heads out toward the audience, parallel, their bodies straight out; finally, they are up, scattered, still not too far from the wall, one of them still up against it, facing it, one by the window, two half-facing the audience. After another, this time extended, stretch of silence in this position, during which there is some minor business, e.g. the lighting and smoking of a cigar by one of them, the dialogue starts. This routine is, again, slightly varied. The first time, instead of taking the fifth position, they all but one congregate by the window, the fourth behind them, the third time the first position is omitted. Wilson further elaborated this game of repetition and variation by having section 2 – intercaled between the second and third repetitions of section 1, – start with the fourth of the positions (prone on the floor)

(1)     a-b-c-d-e-dialogue 1
(1a)    a-b-c-d-f-dialogue 1
(2)          d-g-dialogue 2
(1b)   b-c-d-f-dialogue 1

This routine may have contributed to the impression of people caught in a situation, keeping being thrown back into it.

In section 1, one of the 4 to the sound of a gunshot collapses on the floor (and again in sections 2, 4), but after a while gets up. The

36 The Open Theatre is supposed to have originated this kind of mutational routine, the Living Theatre used it. But they did it improvisationally, and Wilson patterned it and rehearsed it.

preceding gunshot suggests it's a revival from a theatre death, but in accord with Wilson's directions the performer gets up ›dazed‹...[37] In section 5 the same performer collapses wounded and another of the 4 dies (and again comes to life). There are explosions, a verbal reference to the atom bomb may suggest they are nuclear. At one point someone asks ›where the planes are.‹

In section 3 (to the 2nd portion of the dialogue) at one point Sutton enters downstage from stage-right in a Union soldier's uniform, advances singing to center-stage, and crouched over, miaowing or sobbing delicately, and, leaves the way she came, all of which one of the 4 (Lubar) then imitates aggressively and exaggeratedly. There is a projection of the ›smudge‹ during this.[38] During much of this section Chris fools around on stage with his tape recorder, extended on his elbow downstage, stage-left on the floor, laughing much of the time, recording the ongoing dialogue and an occasional loud ›burrup‹ (his word for farts) from himself, and replaying what he has recorded.

Something like the semblance of a thrilling climactic crisis (as in an action movie) was apparently intended for near the end of the 5th section. The original stage directions read:

(men in uniforms, caps, etc. push boxes across stage (6 men) ... then someone steps out and says ›bring them in‹ – then we hear many clocks ticking very fast[39] and then we hear off-stage ›thank you‹)

The way it was eventually done, no six men, just Sutton in her Union uniform and Jim Neu, I doubt it came across that way. My back was turned, but I heard no ticking of a time bomb.

After Lubar collapses, section 5 was supposed to end:

(Soldier comes in and looks at person that fell. Loud sound – clocks ticking very fast.)
1. How much faster?
2. To withstand earthquakes.
(Christopher's tape of numbers, movie of Julie Weber's recording studio)

---

37 The 4 or 5 sections of act VII of *Stalin* taking place on a strange planet, end with everyone's collapsing: after a blackout the next section begins with everyone's getting up ›dazed.‹ In Wilson's mind, I suppose, the operation of a ›strange force‹ causes this, but it is not unlike him to superimpose on a simple nullification of a theatre death a hint that something else is involved, especially if this something else equates death and loss of consciousness.
38 The smudge and the caricature evoke the antagonistic relation of Lubar to Sutton in act I, sc. I. Lubar, in the play, is on to Sutton.
39 Originally, the ticking boxes were to reappear w/ the pilots in the after-play. I think this tie-in was dropped.

1. (Brings one box back on stage and opens it and slightly pulls out a metal container. Long pause.)
1. OK we have to go to the underground.[40]
2. I know I know it takes a lot.

It finally turned out, I believe, a little different, Wilson transforming the sentimental matter-of-factness of the ending of a War II movie about the anti-Nazi underground (which he may have been watching on TV) into a sustained sentimentally heroic tableau more like a take-off on a Broadway theatre transition. After ›OK we have to go to the underground,‹ with Lubar once again dead on the ground, another of the 4 crouched over her, a third one comes over with the line ›I know I know it takes a lot,‹ and kneels, profile to the audience, with his right consolingly/strengtheningly on the second one's shoulder, to the projection of a film of an oscillating curve and the playing of Chris's ›numbers tape.‹[41] The pose is held and the light comes up strong gradually.

When the lights go on for the last, 6th section, the 4 players have during the brief blackout rapidly gotten rid of their jump suits, and, in dark business suits, white shirt, tie, are on the floor on all fours. After a few lines, – the repliques are more fantastic in this section, sort of science fiction, – they shift into a circle, and, to a speech on the p.a. system about the chemical composition of protein, commence crawling, in a perhaps molecule-like ring, in a circle around on the floor as they speak their lines, gradually crouching down closer to the floor, finally, still in formation, on their sides in place, in foetus positions, some of them waving one arm and one leg in the air. Wilson had indicated that they had been reduced to protoplasmic primal slime in this section, but his only directions had been to pay attention to how we moved and to keep equal distances. Perhaps life as we know it had been ended by a nuclear holocaust. While they crawl, Chris flies across overhead in a harness, arms and legs ruddering insectlike, merrily shouting ›scarf.‹ After some more manoeuvres, perhaps, probably not, evoking structural changes in a molecule, they rise in turn, each moving rapidly backward (a reassembly as in

40 This line is obviously a distortion of ›ok we have to go underground.‹ The distortion is faintly comic, but is also the distortion of recall resulting from an overlay of different recalls. It sets up a faint disturbance for the ear. It is similar to Wilson's two other devices of hardly noticeable and of faintly varied repetition. The text of *Letter* contains many such minute lapses.
41 This tape records a rapidly, excitedly spoken series of numbers, over which he in subsequent recordings, while listening to the tape, and as though answering it, gleefully superimposed further numbers: a dense, jumpy tissue of numbers resulting.

a film of disintegration run backward) to sit in the window; one after the other again go into a prone position; each in turn sit up with his or her final line.

The regular dialogue in this section was compounded with a complementary dialogue of ›hap hath hat,‹ ›a o.k.‹ and ›infor informing very informing,‹ which was to be kept going as an improvised independent conversation with the other one. The section was to build rapidly in energy, speed and intensity to a climax at the end, speech and movement ending abruptly with the music.

The act III curtain goes up on 10 elegantly attired people (identical beige suits, grey turtle neck sweaters, white socks, the ladies with grey or beige hats), motionlessly slumped, hands on their legs, two and two, one male, one female, at five tables, each table with a rose in a vase, 2 spoons, two glasses. Downstage, stage-right there is a large mound of red cherries or other opulent fruit or vegetables. After a fixed small number of seconds they all sit up straight, after a few more raise their hands, after another seccond count start rapidly gesticulating with their hands,[42] after still another all start chirping ›chitter chatter‹ rapidly in high voices, and 2 seconds later one of the couples launches into a high-pitched high-speed mondaine conversation,[43] while the others keep up the ›chitter chatter.‹ Each couple has their turn at the pretentious, insincere, trivial, mocked high-society dishing. Each dialogue ends with the talkers rapping their glasses with their spoons. All this is very fast. The round of dialogues is at intervals punctuated by gestures made in unison, – an affected rubbing of the nose, a dainty patting of the lips with a napkin, polite tittering, a crossing of the legs. Occasionally shots ring out and one of the convivials collapses on the table, reviving some seconds after. During a mute pause cued by 3 ›well.‹'s and a collective ›oh ooo ah‹ the company, to loud bursts of gunfire on the p.a. system and to the moving slide projection, once again, of Santos Dumont's airplane of 1906 (substituted for the originally planned projection of the atomic mushroom), the company turns smiling faces to the audience, holding the smiles. At one point Chris, one of the elegants, rises up in the air on his chair, chitter chattering. At the end, the rapid music breaking off on an upbeat cadence, originally everybody suddenly jumped

---

42 Wilson wanted quasi-naturalistic conversational gestures placed in the framework of an imaginary small box in front of the chest, deployed as though an independent sign-language. The gesticulation ended up mechanically repetitive, rhythmed by the music, and not particularly naturalistic.

43 Lubar wrote the dialogues for and co-directed this ›Cafehouse dialogue‹ act.

up in the air in a seated position, smiling broadly, arms coming out and up, and the curtain fell, but for the Paris and New York runs, Wilson had his grandmother come in from stage-left at this point: the music ends, the party freezes, not smiling, Ms. Hamilton comes in as Queen Victoria with sun glasses and three times screams and raises her arms slowly.

Act III showed a formal group non-relating to the outside (the talkers ignore the war). The group was decomposed into sub-groups not relating to one another (no talk or attention between tables). Each sub-group (couple) communicates formally by a non-communicative exchange of conventional verbalisms and gestures, – the usual type of conversation here represented by a caricature species. Like the remainder of the play,[44] the act disassociates spatial (positional, gestural) from a verbal relating. As in act II, the conflict is with an outside, but is here refused.

Act IV was intended to be fairly explicitly a spoof, amusing the audience, slightly sardonic, but more tongue-in-cheek than either ironic or grotesque. Whether it came across this way I don't know. It is a camp about a criminal conflict, irrupting into robbery and murder, within a group of precariously and variously allied unsavory characters out of some Huston movie (Casablanca and To Have and Have Not provided lines for it), – as confusing as though by Dashiell Hammett. There is also a love element. While act I presented a relationship, II a situation, III a kind of people, and each a corresponding mode of talk, act IV represents action. Communication in it is means of treachery and deceit, oblique, half-revelation of secrets. While the verbal meaning of speech is rendered irrelevant in I by its function of expressing how people feel about one another, in II by its function of expressing how they feel about a situation, in III, by its function of expressing who people think they are, in IV it is rendered irrelevant by its function of expressing their relations within a group. The action takes place between a member of the group and an outsider, as though to emphasise the artificiality of theatrical plot and action.

For most of the act, the stage is apportioned between 5 performers

44 In act I, Sutton's gestures are so stylised, they no longer accord with her, according to theatrical conventions, more natural vocal delivery of the lines, Lubar stands like a block and moves by nervous approximations when she moves, but speaks with the dead assurance of a powerful automaton. The mechanical choreography. and paucity of gestures of sections 1-5 of act II parallels but does not relate to the speaking. The rooted positions of most of the speakers in act IV contrasts with the rapid verbal game.

(4 + the parroting alter ego of one of them): a self-possessed lead-ing-man and operator type (Jim Neu), — snazzy suit, lorgnette, cane, — a little ways in, stage-left about half way back; a large, strong, severely dry lady who is a little tense, perhaps a little threatening (Scotty Snyder) slightly downstage from him stage-right; her alter ego, myself, a seedy, middle-aged individual, in a seersucker suit, orange socks, orange string tie, dark glasses, right behind her, stage-right and upstage of her, between her and a palm tree; and the two principals of this act, a Chinese Investigator (Cindy Lubar), gotten up as Chinee, speaking in pseudo-Chinese accents, upstage, stage right, throughout the act half-invisible behind a very tall screen with Venetian blinds with moveable, mirrored slats, and enclosed up to her neck in a tall white egg-shaped container, and a smoothly dangerous, elegantly sexy adventuress (Sheryl Sutton) in an evening gown or ball dress, upstage, stage-left.

Until near the end of the act, the longest in the play, when we all congregate, backs to the audience, in front of the Chinaman's screen, these are our basic positions. They define the act's image. The big woman 2 or 3 times briefly exits, closely followed by her shady com-panion, turning and walking slowly into the stage-right wings right behind her. The dandified gent does the same (to get his cane) once, stage-left. The Chinaman leaves once or twice.

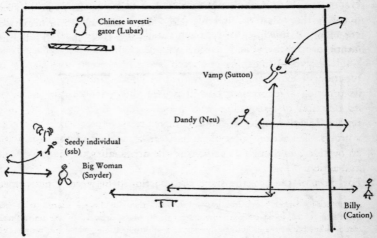

The slickly demure seductress, the active party of this act, is the only really mobile character, but even so definitely has the upstage, stage-left area for her home base, and moves in certain paths. She off and on retreats backwards offstage upstage. She has a long slow walk straight downstage; has a conversation there about old times with an additional, recurrently adventitious 6th character (Kit Cation as Billy, Billy having previously been incidentally mentioned by Kit in act II (›We want to help Billy‹). for this conversation dressed as a young boy with a long white beard; has a silent, beautiful love scene with Billy, now dressed as girl, in which she slaps her, on a bench center downstage; does a slow stylised parody walk, singing a burlesque love song, possibly addressed to Billy, from there over to the big woman and back, and then back up upstage; at one point advances to the screen and robs a jewel box from behind it (but then is held up by Billy, who, now dressed as a man, in a black suit, has reentered holding a gun and who is seconded by the dandy/operator: Billy shoots her, she bends sobbing, Billy gives her the gun, she puts the gun away); later slits the throat of Billy (now in a slinky burgundy gown, with heavy make-up) while Billy is extended on her back on the downstage bench, and then demonstratively extracts from the jewel box a translucent pink jewel-like lozenge which she sucks, smoking a cigarette; finally, from there, shoots the Chinaman . . .

The Chinaman most of the time seems to be addressing the whole group. The beauty seems to be speaking mostly with the dandy (who is courting her), and the big women (her alter ego in a parroty screech repeating the tail ends of her lines) also seems to be talking to him rather than to anybody else (she seems to get information from him). Billy doesn't say much. When she talks she talks to the beauty.

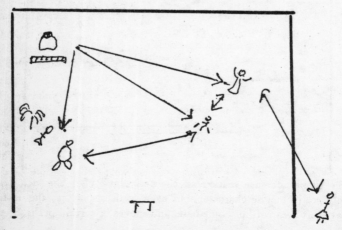

The big woman and her parrot toward the end exchange parts, her former alter ego then giving a speech to the audience indicating the group are desperate adventurers in a tropical clime, also croaking parts of hoagy Carmichael's *Hong Kong Blues* by way of informing the audience that what they are seeing is ›the story of an unfortunate colored man,‹ the hero of that opium ballad, and preaching Genesis i, 2 and 20 to the audience to remind them of the original origin of all this:

> And the earth was without form and void
> and darkness was upon the face of the deep
> and the spirit of God moved upon the face of the waters
> and God said, let the waters bring forth abundantly
> the MORNING CREATURES THAT HATH LIFE.

But the principal action is tall and beautiful Sheryl Sutton's, and though this *action* is chiefly between her and the Billy of the many metamorphoses, the principal *conflict*, by the cumulative impact of the act's talk and image, is between her and Lubar's Fu Manchu + Sidney Greenstreet + Mr. Moto Chinaman.[45] The Chinaman remains nearly invisible and immobile, but talks[46] a great deal, authoritatively and at length, mostly about himself, viz. his methods, often in a lecturing manner: his seems the power of the brain. One expects him to come out on top and is surprised when she does. In the end everybody except he lines up and floats away.

After a curtain, this act, a play in itself, is followed by a contrasting quick, impressively august, stately epilogue, a declamation of meaningless utterance (and eo ipso a summation), echoing the introductory scene and the whole play's beginning. The curtain goes up on Sutton, again black on her ladder upstage stage-left, and Lubar, white-winged, more downstage, stage-right. The 2 pilots enter as in act I, scene I, advance to center-stage, bow, in unison saying

> I don't know how to thank you (5 second pause) say (4 second pause) what (3 second pause) certainly,

exit. Sutton says, ›my knowledge about you is reduced to a handful of facts.‹ Sutton and Lubar alternately, in impassive voices, recite,

---

45 This almost imperceptible, undefinable conflict is Wilson's comment on the unity of action as *plot* in regular theatre. Cf. p. 291 re their conflict in act I, footnote 34, re their juxtaposition in act I, footnote 38 re the ›smudge‹ in acts I and II, p. 290 re their respective appearances as angels of darkness and light.
46 2 of his 3 speeches were written by Jim Neu.

Seem what
Seemed what
Seem
Seems the same
Seemed the same
Seems
Simultaneously o'city o'verst
Wheel what when now how
An alligator's span
Seem what
Seemed why
Seemed
Seemed
Seems
Screen tell a vision
Screened told a visions
Screen
Scream
A million dances,

and go into a rapid recitation compounded of ›a o,‹ ›hap hath hat,‹
›confor conforming very conforming‹ and ›a o.k.,‹ followed by

a bit
a little bit
the pilot tilting
a slanting pilot tiltings
a around a little bit
the angle of the thing angling,

and scream.

# The $-Value of Man.

A direct statement.

Starting in January 1975 Wilson ran workshops at the Spring St. Byrd building for which he asked contributions of a dollar or a dollar 50 cents, and to which more or less anyone was admitted. Tho never very disciplined or very focussed, they settled on certain themes, and resulted in a raggedy show entitled *The $-Value of Man* with about 5 dozen performers, about a fourth of them byrds (the two stars of *Qu. V.* absent), given in May (May 8-11, 15-18) in the Lepercq ›space‹ upstairs at the Brooklyn Academy of Music. For *Qu. V.*, he had used a selection of byrds, in this show they were swamped by non-byrds, mostly artists in their 20s; the structures of the endlessly rehearsed individual performances in *Qu. V.* had been very tight, in this piece, they were very loose, in fact timing and coordination were largely dispensed with (and the relative unity of the relaxed-intensive byrd style never achieved): the structure of the piece was an extrinsic composition, modular in the manner of Phil Glass' music,[47] a sequence of 9 elemental scenes of three sort (free dancing (F), vaudeville (V), casino (C)), one or more, separated by drops or partitions or not, done at a time in different parts of the 18' x 60' central playing area, the audience seated in two rows of chairs along one side and on high-rising bleachers at either end:

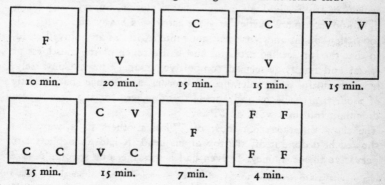

47 The wholeness of the art work, the crux, the pseudo-Aristotelean unities quite apart, of traditional drama and most other art, in modular art is formally, – not informally, as in art works representing themselves as parts or fragments of finite or infinite wholes, e.g. much of modern jazz, some of abstract expressionist paint-

For the C/V combination, the stage was divided by a high suspended (I believe black) curtain across its middle with a gate-shaped slit in it allowing glimpses of the spectacle at the other end. For the C/C combination, the stage at that end was divided by a suspended red cloth in the other direction. — Whether the V or C elements were the same each time, I could not say: they seemed basically but not exactly composed of the same units in their recurrence, the C element a spectacle composed of a few (4 or so) gestures that every one did and of various sentence fragments by Knowles and Wilson out of a sequence of 4-, 8- or 16-unit series of such (sold for a dollar in the lobby), the V element a variable collage of known jokes slightly developed into slight routines, all or most, sometimes the same one several times, done at a time.

One got the idea of permutations and combinations, something mathematical, and, as always from an abstract order imposed on life or on an activity, a feeling of proximate insanity: especially since the predominant impression was of disorder, even anarchy, — the crowds of people down there singly or in groups doing (and saying) a variety of things with different gestures, in unshaped ways, out of sync, without art, without discipline: and yet confined in blocks of time, squares of space (an attempt had even been made to have the overhead projectors project squares of light onto the floor for the dance areas). Thus one also observes in the wards of our insane asylums admirable varieties of extremely individualized conduct: geometrically confined and repetitive; and in our societies surging crowds of free individuals in reglemented motion. Superficially fresh, light and gay, more particularly the show was heavy and awkward: too little thought and work had gone into it, it was an unloved child, so that the fun seemed artificial and had a touch of the mustiness of jokes; and finally it seemed compulsive, insanely neat. Conversely, it was beautiful by its tolerance of disorder, a tolerance characteristic of *modern* art, science and administration, here for the first time a dominant trait of a work of Wilson's.

The show differed from most of Wilson's others in a way that showed he'd done it off the top of his head: it had an explicit and pervasive theme, money. It even had a message: one shouldn't have

ing, — relativized (reduced to an adventitious composition), although of course it can be reconstituted by such formal devices as e.g. pervasive symmetries, exhaustive permutation. $-Value is Wilson's only modular piece sofar: tho his repeated conjoining of several plays into one, — as e.g. the rhythm of endings/ beginnings, in *D G*, — indicates that wholeness is not an ideal of his, but bothers him.

to pay for things. Wilson feels this very strongly as for himself, but then all artists feel it. Price is the child's trauma. In practice, the resentment of it works out as elitism. Monetary economics are poor arrangements, but the show's protest, its shallowness unredeemed by exuberance, was childish.

The show's definitive statement of the theme was a beautiful, faintly but succulently ironic reading, several times interrupted at length by the continuous chorus of the collective performers' blandly elegant nonsense text, by George Ashley, a mellifluous man, of the source of it, the account, in a December 1974 issue of the New York Times, by a Long Island University professor of morality of a Socratic class room experiment, designed to demonstrate to his students their hypocrisy in denying putting a monetary value on the life of human individuals and/or in affirming their pricing to be independent of who or what those individuals are, – foolish liberal stuff.

Musicians provided more or less continuous (tho quantified) sound for the show from a high-up balcony, – the rectangular hall is perhaps 50' high, – at one end. It came in 4-, 6- or 8-minute, abruptly stopping sections, with silences in between that did not necessarily coincide with scene-changes: the composer, Mike Galasso's violin, the dominant instrument, madly filing away, another violin, viola, flute, clarinet and zarb. The sections for the Vaudeville scenes were more gay, those for the others, more trancy. I would say that this music was modular also.

The dance scenes (F) were De Groat's usual devotional anarchies of self-indulgently, smoothly gesturing people seeming to worship spirit.

In the Casino scenes and sub-scenes, the cast out of chest-high partitions, green on the inside, erected (and each time disassembled) a large rectangle, a gaming table, Joos' *Green Table*, looking like one, but hellish. It had no top: gelled strip lights on the inside of the walls reflected the green upward, creating the semblance of a green pool. After this recurrent work-activity, the performers – dressed in evening clothes, black, – the green light ghastly in their faces, – stood around it, shoulder to shoulder, extending and withdrawing their right arms over it as tho placing bets or perhaps putting down a card, occasionally making one of two other movements, a cigarette-handling gesture and another one.[48] They made these gestures, which were light, almost perfunctory, at different times, each player

48 Each performer did a gesture on every third line of his or hers. In the 6th scene they were 1) slow reaching gesture to front, 2) puff, turn head, blow smoke,

following his (or her) own rhythm, from time to time saying something, – »give you up,« »this is about the regular ones a,« »the badge ones of them,« »so it could be simple a« . . . .,[49] a gabble that was the texture of the show, gabble of impersonally personal talk among acquaintances, the surface texture of sociable life.

The Vaudeville scenes and sub-scenes were crowd scenes in which individual acts or numbers stood out more or less clearly, – chorus lines of business-men/gangsters/horse-players in hats and suits out of '30s Damon Runyon stories, everybody in men's suits, half-lines and whole lines advancing and retreating, saying (mostly inaudible) things, often with newspapers under their arms, hurried Groucho Marx walks in lines of 3 or 4, . . . – One number consisted of two such lines, arms extended, gleaming pistols in the hands, facing one another at some angle, after a long time both firing, all collapsing, – getting up, repeating the whole thing. Another, of one performer holding up another, the other sticking 'em up, disarming the mugger with a karate kick, holding him up in turn. Another in the deadpan telling of Jack Benny's story of the hold-up man and his victim, »Your money or your life!,« »Well! I said your money or your life!,« »I'm thinking.« Another (Abbot and Costello?) had one person reading a newspaper, the other comes up and reads over his shoulder, finally reaches, pointing, into the paper, reads some line there aloud, the other, enraged, turns on him, – »Slowly, slowly, I turn . . .« – to strangle him: this is repeated twice more, then the roles are exchanged. In the over-all hubbub/pandemonium, one rather beautiful, extended number, done by Jim Neu and the beautiful Julia Busto on home-made foot-elevations functioning as stilts, was a kind of very slow

3) fast arm directly in front, 4) putting down the cards. In the 7th scene, 1) push out chips, smoke, 2) nose scratch, push out chips, smoke.

49 Christopher Knowles writes poetry and typed letter shapes. His poetry, like Wilson's dialogue in *Qu.V.*, comes to him from tv, but more from rock lyrics than from late reruns. By their gentle lyricism, the Casino lines seemed to me more his than Wilson's. One of Knowles' poems:

HOW COULD I SEND YOUR MESSAGE TO YOU

If you know this thing is true. It would be very strange. If you know. If it to know.

On the suit for your kingdom for real ghost throat, if you know, if it is it.

If you say HI.

If I know that in since we off to the heat to hot too hot to keep us warm.

How could I send my message and your message to you in this how is done for this.

How could I send my of this.

How could I send your message.

dance of informal approaches and retreats, the man repeating, loudly, in an emphatic tone and with an emphatic arm gesture, but not acting out any villainy, »You must pay the rent,« the woman, – in alternation, – with a lifting up of arms, a leaning back and an uplifting of the face, also loudly, in a formally plaintive high voice and unemotional tone, »I can't pay the rent.« Galasso's square dance fiddling gave a nice background to this number.

Wilson and his protegé Knowles did their intermezzi duo act from *Qu. V.*, – but here, because of the context, seeming varying exemplars of the (organically, culturally) handicapped in a monetary society, – as non-functioning masters of ceremony: during most of the show standing at mikes positioned half-way down each side of the performance rectangle, opposite one another, talking to us, or, across the performance, bridging it, to one another. Chris, in his sometimes stammering delivery, the fresh friendly voice of an open kid, his shoulders hunched up, introduced the show (we should feel free to move about, have fun) and four times did his commercials, – slightly garbled renditions of tv commercials, – for eye glasses, for drinking coffee in the morning to stop your stomach from rumbling (»Is it embarassing or is it embarassing?!«), – each repeated continuously for a little while, Wilson, the night I was there, having to ask him for his last two performances of them. Wilson twice talked about the work on this show (he embarrassingly made it out as more serious than it had been): in a factual tone, unfinished sentences, hesitantly, modestly; said the Casino sentence fragments, letting them float; twice asked Chris to tell about the Self-Service in Paris, which Chris did: about how he ate there, – »maccaroni and so forth,« – found he had forgotten his money at the hotel, couldn't pay, was arrested; makes Chris tell about the exact time each thing happened (Chris remembers to the minute); asks him to tell what the play is about: Chris talks about buying things, – specific things, – at the grocery, paying for them.

The seating did not encourage moving about, but from the 4th scene, – the first composite one, – onward, an increasing number of spectators did move about, entering the performance space, the atmosphere increasingly that of *Paradise Now,* tho without its exuberance or channeled energy, more that of a fair, an approximation of what Marx has called the anarchy of the market place.

During the 7th scene, the Cs and Vs going everywhere, fog machines smoked up the room. The penultimate all-over dancing took place in this smoke, red and white projector shafts going down through it, –

a cheap mess, – and the smoke was still there when for the embarassing finale the performers entered in white, carrying ›evergreen boughs‹
and ›danced.‹

# Spaceman

RALPH HILTON and ROBERT WILSON
*Spaceman*, January 2-4, 1976
Video and live performance.

»The structural elements of this work fell into three categories: portrait, still-life and landscape .... »Spaceman,« located within a 12′ x 3½′ x 65′ tunnel of translucent plastic, represented Robert Wilson's first use of video as an integral part of the theatre experience. The images, portrait, still-life and landscape, were conveyed by performers, props, lights and pre-recorded videotapes. Eight different sets of color videotapes were played on over twenty monitors placed among the sets and actors. The abstract theme of the work was that of an unidentified »green thing« which had crawled up on the beach. Was it a threat or was it being ignored?.« (The Kitchen Center for Video and Music, 1975/76, yearly account.)

The categories in this notice to funders are insignificant. E.g. »portrait« does not apply to Sue Sheehy's sitting inside the tank fishing in some sand, or to Wilson's lying on his side, on the floor, looking at his watch and saying »There« into a microphone. And the green monster at one end of the tank, four performers heaped up in green snouty sheaths without openings (one of them inside her sateen reciting more or less the whole text of *Qu. V.* from memory) besides being just the opposite of an abstract theme, is not theme of the thing at all, but a joke. The idiocy of this official text (provided, I am sure, by Wilson's active erratic brain in an off-hand moment) reflects the indifference of the subsidisers of this »performance« (Stearns, ib.) or »intermedia art« (Peter Frank, ib.) at a point in time when »the heroic era of avant-garde art has ended« (Peter Frank, ib.). The sponsors seem to feel they don't have to worry. This is not only something for the sponsored to worry about, but creates an apparent social vacuum for them to create in.

The object was compressed like a junked car body. Nothing happened, there was no development: just small stirrings in the same condition, – a condition of containment, compression. This compressed space, – it was full of stuff, – was »space,« a confined condition of suspension in a void in which life consists in the reception and emission of information of a severely reduced nature. The spaceman himself in there is tied up, tied to a board, barely able to move his hands along two lifelines. But this object, the sound'ing box itself, object perceived, (as in this century Spaceship Earth has become perceived object), an overpowering tho reticent object, compact of references to message-transmission, quite loud at times, but even its loudness seeming to eat itself up, is not the dominant experience. What dominates is the contrast between the dense throng of in part seated, in part milling-about inspectors of the configuration, the visitors, – for whom not much space had been left either, but whose constriction accentuated the ›freedom to move‹ expressed by their recommended but, seeing as how the object did not change and could be completely inventoried in a couple of minutes, basically pointless peregrinations, – and the exposed objects within the not altogether cleanly transparent plastic, in a container, their activities on a physically minimal scale, and not engaging in observation, at least not observing directly, in particular not observing people, quiescent, passive: not observing, not relating to an object, but emitting and receiving information, integrated into an ongoing, internalised, UNCONTROLLED flow and interaction of information, dominating them, having taken them over, the mechanical synapses of an information-industry-cored culture, the cogs of an autonomous unconscious. The on-lookers were superfluous, superfluous even to themselves: old-fashioned PEOPLE, whose very freedom (detachment), expressed by their relating to an object (*the* object), negated them: they were not receiving any information, – other than that they were superfluous: detached in a void. The show thus was not so much the exposition of an object, as rather a museum, entering which the visitors found themselves behind glass, the museum's collectibles. (Superficially, this expressed itself by everybody's actual boredom (tho the exposition lasted only an hour and a half), and by the visitors' abortive attempt to turn the thing into a party, everybody was talking to somebody.) – I would surmise that Wilson's exposure to the tv coverage of the lunar expeditions inspired the show, and in particular its transmission of how the peculiar character of the astronauts' work of displacement, – so very different from that of the sea-faring discoverers of yore, – is that it consists in receiving and emitting information, their handling of the ship more than a mere analogy to a brain's activity, but of its nature, and above all requiring a continual close confinement, the pilot's steady reduction of himself to a mental process of transmission: his power not that of adaptation of sail and rudder to the vagaries of winds and currents, but a mathematical power of submission to the pull of gravity.

Chris Knowles was positioned at the other end from the monster using a kind of typewriter to produce patterns of numbers and letters on two video screens, one inside the box, one outside: next to him an architecture of tv sets showing identical images, not Chris patterns, but »real things,« on their screens, a seated man squeezed in between them: the repetition of images reenforced the indirection of perception formalized in a tv set, showing images of something else, but showing them as very much of its and its: the sign having become the thing.

It is hard to say whether communication at its most modern, such as the input-output nexus in a computer, or an astronaut's or airport controller's or taxi cab dispatcher's or U. N. translator's or a secretary's (typing out dictating-machine input) rule-governed semi-automatic transformations of machine-transmitted and -shaped informational input into an output of gestures operating a sign-producing machine, is to Wilson the acme-nadir of verbal communication (which he considers as crippling and as limited to trivialities) or a break-through into a higher mode of existence, an estimable mindlessness such as that of the user of a prayer-wheel. He once told me his mother enjoyed being a typist. – From the Paris *Overture* (the musicians' pit converted into the space ship control room), – or perhaps as far back as act VII of *Stalin*, The Planet, where, supposedly with a tree growing out of my head, I was, between fits of unconsciousness, busy typing away, space-visitor, so it seemed to an alien planet, – through *Spaceman* to *Einstein*'s final act, – the blinking console dominating the field-turned-spaceship, – Wilson has associated this automated emission of signals, – prayer, vain talk, or both, – with space travel: a verbal civilisation hurtling its last messages into the stone-studded void.

# Einstein on the Beach[50]

K 151
18:31
On the horizontal grey rectangle of the drop,[52] doubly framed in black, enormous, at the lower right a smaller, fatter, almost square rectangle, pasted to it, projector light that seems to spill over, a white rug, on the floor beneath the two women seated in front of it, a Caucasian (the dancer Lucinda Childs) and a Negro (Sheryl Sutton, a Wilsonian performer), the latter immobile, hands in lap, the former, within the maintained pose, shifting: contrast of self-contained quietude in concentration to tension imperfectly imposed on nervous agitation.[53] The image has marginally the aspect of a slide projection. *A sustained organ note, the space-filling sound of a present awareness, accompanies it (in the pit, by pale-green lights, the console*

18:32 *of an electric organ is visible). After a minute, the sound shifts down in pitch, holds there, an expressive, reassuring note now, with a hint*

18:34 *of power, fading into blankness, shifts up again, harmony has been created, a statement broached, back down.* The white girl is stiffly posed at the edge of her chair, hands on the desk, as tho to keep in touch or hold on, her left by its fingertips, fingers extended. Her

18:34 mouth has begun to move. We infer *the sound of counting from the vast grey drop* originates from her. She is counting time, — not in time with the music, which is so spaced out that it can't be counted

50 Open run throughs at the Video Exchange Theatre, Westbeth, the West Village, March 4th and 5th, 1976; excerpts shown at the Museum of Modern Art on March 31st; first performances at the Theatre Municipal, Avignon, July 27-29; performances at the Biennale, Sept. 13 (-15?), at the Theatre of Nations (BITEF), Belgrade, Yugoslavia, Sept 22 (and 23?), at the Theatre Royal de la Monnaie, Brussels, Belgium, Sept 28, 29, 30, at the Opera Comique, Paris, France, Oct. 4-13 (Festival d'automne), at the Deutsches Schauspielhaus, Hamburg, Oct. 17, 18, at the Rotterdamse Schouvburg, later in October (Oct. 22, 23, 24?); the (so far) last performances at the Metropolitan Opera, New York City, Nov. 21 and 28, 1976.

51 »K 1«: the first ›knee.‹ The marginal notations in the following refer to the time of day of Nov. 28th 1976, and to the parts of the play, and in the latter case either to ›knees‹ or to acts (Roman numerals) and scenes (parenthetical Arabic numerals), — ›train‹ (1) –, ›trial/bed‹ (2) –, or ›field/space machine‹ (3) -scenes.

52 American premiere of Robert Wilson's and Phil Glass' *Einstein on the Beach*: November 21, 1976, at the New York Metropolitan Opera. I am here describing the second performance, in the same place, the following Sunday, Nov. 28th, but include data re the first.

53 Wilson has maintained them in this contrast, analogous, relative to light, to that of black to white, through the play except for the concluding ›knee‹ (tho' act IV is such as to preclude its being in evidence). Self-contained black is to Wilson not negative. It is his own color.

to: sometimes she just names numbers, not in sequence, as tho stating some values occurring. It is *a calm self-possessed voice,* – that of a madwoman counting the non-existent. It evokes the world of numbers. The talk and rustle of the audience have subsided, and *the* 18:39 *sustained organ-notes have become louder. They are vibrations. The organ is creating an organisation out of sound (the held note), as tho the single sound, – some simple sound, – had an efficacious germinating capacity enabling sound to give form to itself, a void leaping chaos into the creation of a mathematical universe.* – Sometimes she is *talking,* telling something (».. . very fresh and clean«[54]), even explaining a little. *A few words* at long intervals at first, interspersed 18:42 in the counting, finally a *longer stretch of talk*: as tho the numbers gradually generated, – changed into, – speech. In front of the two women but below the stage, so that from the orchestra only their upper bodies are visible, there is a chorus assembly of a dozen or so young people in white blouses crossed by suspenders, looking like boy scouts, very clean. They have assembled gradually, one by one, each assuming a stately walking stance after stooping through a low entrance next to some glowing red lights. Their fists are oddly raised in front of their shirt fronts, and they look at us. There seems to be some variation in the way they hold their hands. The little group, 14 or so, finally, seems lost in the vast broad dark unmoving sea of spectators, – stuck over in that corner. *A single structure of sound*[55]

54 From Christopher Knowles' *These are the days of my friends*, a prose poem in several chapters.
55 »The Knee Plays are the short connecting pieces which appear throughout the work much as prelude, interludes and postlude. Taken together, they form a play in themselves. They can also be seen as the seeds which flower and take form in the larger scenes ... The musical structure of the Knee Plays can be seen in the following diagram:

| Knee Play 1 | Knee Play 2 | Knee Play 3 | Knee Play 4 | Knee Play 5 |
|---|---|---|---|---|
| $L + C_1$ | $A_1 - B - A_1$ | $A_2 - C_2 - A_2$ | $(A_1 + A_2) - C_3 - (A_1 + A_2)$ | $L + C_1 + C_3$ |
| | | (Bass Line) | (Bass Line) | |

The 2nd, 3rd and 4th Knee Plays share the same form – first theme, second theme and return to first theme. The »cadence« theme of the first train (Act 1, Scene 1) makes up the first theme in all of these Knee Plays, either expressed as violin arpeggios ($A_1$), in a chorale setting for voices ($A_2$), or, in the 4th knee play, as a combination of the two ($A_1 + A_2$). The middle theme (B) of the 2nd knee play, based on simple scale passages, reappears during the second dance and in the middle

*has defined itself, a downward progression of 3 notes, each holding*
*longer[56] than the preceding, 2 seconds, 3 seconds, 4 seconds, tho the*
*last seems longer, very long, the notes the same still, but growing*
*shorter: a minimal theme (oddly enough not seeming fortuitous, just*
*the opposite, in fact), a little tune, a statement in a serenely humorous*
*mood: »that, then, is how it is.« Very soon, the chorus begins to*
*count, their voices musical, in time with the music,[57] 1-2-3-4,*
*1-2-3-4-5-6, 1-2-3-4-5-6-7-8,[58] their attack and accentuation adding*
*a touch of sober determination, their timbre one of lightness, almost*
*gayety to the organ's amused contentment. The organ's segmental*
*piping and the choir's dotted lines of count form the landscape of*
18:50 *structure in which the white girl's chatter, now resumed and con-*
*tinuous, walks.* The brown girl has started counting calmly,[59] the
white girl is talking to herself with catatonic serenity (»... these are

section of the Spaceship music. The middle themes of the 3rd knee play ($C_2$) and
the 4th knee play ($C_3$) are different arrangements of the same material, easily
recognizable by its highly lyrical character. The root movement (implied bass line)
of this material is A-G-C. This becomes, in the pedal of an electric organ, the
opening descending bass line (L) of the 1st knee play. After a very extended beginning, during which the audience enters, the first vocal setting ($C_1$) of these harmonies appears. The descending bass line (L) reappears for the 5th knee play,
joined shortly thereafter by women's voices singing the vocal music of the 1st
knee play ($C_1$), and then by the violin, playing the middle theme of the 4th
knee play ($C_3$).« (Glass, *Notes on »Einstein on the Beach,«* part 1, Performing
Arts Journal, Winter 1978. Copyright Philip Glass.) – I.e., the opera starts with
what Glass calls the »root movement« of its »principal material.«
56 »They're all held for the same duration. Each time that they're held, they're
held for the same duration which gets shorter and shorter, but all three notes are
an equal duration. Well, let's put it this way ... each one is supposed to be the
same duration. I mean, whether it gets played that way every time or not is a
different story .... In the beginning Phillip would time each note with a stopwatch ... when to change ... he wouldn't count the beats ... just be watching
a stopwatch because he was holding them so long here. And then as they get
shorter and shorter you can count the beats and play it by ear.« – (Kurt Munkasci,
Interview, Feb. 18, 1977)
57 »The vocal texts used throughout the opera are based on numbers and solfege
syllables. When numbers are used, they represent the rhythmic structure of the
music. When solfege is used, the syllables represent the pitch structure of the music.
In either case, the text is not secondary or supplementary to the music but is a
description of the music itself.« – (Glass, *Notes*, part 1.)
58 I thought the chorus was adapting to the slight irregularity of the piped organ
notes by dropping some of the »1«s, but according to KM, it's a system for the
chorus to know which chord they are singing, – »when they are singing the »2«s,
they know they are on the second chord (KM).«
59 Sutton's lips are moving. Her voice is well-nigh inaudible. She may have
contributed some of the solo counting earlier.

the days my friends . . . It could be . . .«). The quiet jumble of words floats out, a *quick rolling dribble* above the *children's tune of the choir*. The two women sit sibilantly babbling away, retelling themselves some – their? – tale. Except for the white girl's restless hands, they don't move. The scene introduces us to image. After a while, *a sustained, wordlessly singing voice, – a high baritone?[60] – rises from the chorus, dropping and rising in seeming counterpoint,[61] lagging incrementally behind the pipe notes, a very ecclesiastic cover for the counting, the arching syllables with the natural numbers a protective foliage above the women's wandering voice, sprung from the single note 28 minutes earlier.[62]* The dark girl is, almost inaudibly, seconding the chant, *a mere shadow*. Lights and music out. A slide of a boy child, perhaps Einstein, briefly appears behind the two women. As it pales, the drop going up, *a quietly cheerful, but energetic, powerful rolling of the organ,[63] louder than before, sets in in full force, getting going as a bare ta$_{ta}$ta, a sunshiney speeding away, almost right away joined by a rattling ta$^{ta}$ta$^{ta}$tata, at least twice as fast as it; soon the two settling down into a dancing run ta$_{ta}$ta$^{ta}$, . . ., ta$^{ta}$ta$_{ta}$ ta$^{ta}$, . . ., ta$^{ta}$ta$_{ta}$, . . ., ta$^{ta}$ ta$_{ta}$ta$_{ta}$ ta, . . . etc.,[64] the rattle, roiling,*

18:59

18:59

1 (1)

19:00

---

60 According to KM, tenors, the male part of the chorus, accidentally dominated by one voice.

61 Glass' (Glass, *Notes*, part 1.) ›first vocal setting of these harmonies ($C_1$).‹

62 ». . . the opera is all around the key of E . . . like there are a lot of E's and A's in it, and some F's and some D's and not too many C's and G's. It's around E, the opera, is the best way to describe it. But it's modal . . . it doesn't really have a key. It's just sort of around E and notes that go along with E . . . it's very easy . . . to play Indian music around the key of E.« (KM, Interview.)

». . . the key . . . it's very hard to describe the key. It goes from E flat minor to F major in the knees mostly. They're E flat minor and F major. I've been actually trying to find out about the keys of all the pieces in the opera . . . I asked Phillip, I asked the horn players and I asked the singer . . . and everybody said the music's in a different key.« (KM, Interview.)

63 Actually organ, an alto sax and a soprano sax, soon joined by the other electric organ, an alto flute and 2 sopranos (Iris Hiskey and Connie Beckwith). No chorus. The stresses my underlining indicates were there, but were not supposed to be.

64 The first appearance of Glass' »first theme (based on the super-imposition of two shifting rhythmic patterns, one changing and one fixed) (Glass, *Notes*, part 1, p. 3)« of the first Train scene: »In a general way, the three main visual themes of the opera (Train/Trial/Field) are linked to three main musical themes.« . . . »The image of the train appears three times – first in Act I, Scene 1, then in Act II, Scene 2 (as the Night Train), and finally in Act IV, Scene 1, where it appears in the same perspective as the Night Train, but this time transformed into a building. The music for the first train is in three parts, or »themes«. The first theme (based on the super-imposition of two shifting rhythmic patterns, one changing and one

*churning coming in again, ...:* The white rectangle is still on the floor, a carpet, – the girls, their tables and chairs have disappeared. On the void of the stage, against the flat grey of a backdrop perhaps slightly darker than the front that just rose, stands a tall girder erection, an oilfield derrick or crane, or a railroad signal tower, the last inasmuch as it has a short horizontal extension, possibly like a signal arm, near its top. This tower, black, is on the left. The white girl of before has entered the empty, empty-looking right half of the stage. One notices the effective proportions of it all, a slightly bothersome perfection of taste. On the rigid structure's extension one spots a live

19:03 boy, standing. *The organ[63]'s cheerfully speeding toy train[64] – ta^tata ta – has been joined by a high chorus voice, bu^bubi bu, – which after a while bursts into song, – cloudy, cloudy, ... (actually do re mi) – to, now, ta^tatatata^ta, – and keeps following the shifting rhythm of the rolling wheels, dipping telegraph wires: the steam whistle, the calliope, the passengers. The speed is good, the trip is endless and fine. The rolling-along speeding joyous sound, tho it's a train chugging along in an animated cartoon, is powerful.* There is a string going across the rectangular opening of the stage, the missing wall, from

fixed) makes up most of the music of this scene. The second appearance of the train image, the Night Train, is a reworking of the first theme, this time with a larger complement of voices. The music for the Building is a development of the second theme, recognizable by its highly accented rhythmic profile, in which the repeated figures form simple arithmetic progressions. The third theme is a rhythmic expansion of a traditional cadential formula. This »cadence« theme forms the principal material of the opera, being used for the 2nd, 3rd and 4th Knee Plays, as well as almost the entire music for Act IV, Scene 3, the Spaceship.« (Glass *Notes*, p. 1 and 3)

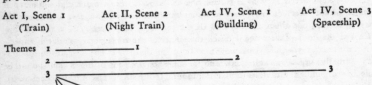

| Act I, Scene 1 (Train) | Act II, Scene 2 (Night Train) | Act IV, Scene 1 (Building) | Act IV, Scene 3 (Spaceship) |

Themes 1 ——————— 1
2 ——————————— 2
3 ——————————————————— 3

Knee Plays 2, 3 and 4

The first train scene's musical structure in terms of these themes is 1-2, 1-2-3, 1-2-3. 1 lasts about 5 minutes the first time, about 8-10 minutes the second, about the same the third. Munkasci thought of it as ›sort of in F major,‹ – whereas 2 and 3 for him were »sort of in E flat minor.«
According to Susan Flakes' article on the Avignon production of *Einstein* (the opera first opened July 25th, 1976 as part of the Festival d'Avignon) in the Dec. 76 issue of Kirby's Drama Review, »Glass wrote this music after Wilson gave him the image »train.« (Flakes, *Robert Wilson's Einstein on the Beach*, The Drama Review, Dec. 1976)

near the upper right-hand to near the lower left-hand corner, NE/SW. Other lines come down to the boy's cat walk, probably just support-wires. The girl, wan-faced,[65] hair down in her face, has begun a rectilinear walking dance on the right half of the stage, energising this area, dominating, striding backwards and forwards facing us, at a steady pressing pace along a short diagonal, her right hand, fingers extended, making some flicking movements, her left arm, out at an angle as tho permanently tossed there, moving in emptily declaratory, twisting, poking, energetic gestures, – there is something white, a piece of chalk,[66] in her left hand.[67] Her head is up challengingly with occasional jerks or tosses, she dances as much with the inclination of her face as with her body, her mouth pursed, her step bouncy. Forward and backward, – »because it pleases me.« She is acting, – projecting a character. Her exuberance and her sparse hand movements are nicely sustaining her against the roaring mirror of Glass' organ. She is, precisely, not dancing, not taking off, she is a pendulum, and all her energy goes into maintenance.[68] The picture of a locomotive, pale grey, large, almost life-size, yet definitely less than life-size, flat, in the simple lines of a cool recapitulation of a sentimental allusion, slowly slides, jerks, into our vision, hard up against the grey backdrop's towering vertical, coming out of the wings at its right edge, stopping and going. The slats of the cowcatcher and some of the engineer's cabin are now in view. One assumes it is

65 It is to her credit that Childs in the revolutionary fashion of lesbians does not use her beauty.

66 A pipe, according to Flakes, loc. cit., but she is describing one of the European performances preceding the NY one. Her description seems a little sloppy, but if we assume it roughly true, comparing mine with it would suggest a great many changes increasing the orderedness of the play.

67 The play does not as dramatic event dominate the stage actively, but is experienced as series of pictures placed on a stand for us to see. The spectator's orientation is therefore not from the view point of the making of it, which would be expressed in terms of stage-left and stage-right, but in terms of the seeing of it, i.e. in terms of right side, left side. But Childs and Sutton not only are strong but have been given leeway to come on strong, and so one tends to see as left the side of them that's left to them, as right the other.

68 When I first saw her do this dance, – her only one in the play, – at the March 5 (76) open rehearsal at Westbeth, it was a wild manic shook-up thing, now getting fatigued, now with renewed ferocity, spastic in Wilson's own manner almost. It is still not her own kind of dancing (as it was in her June 76 *Danspace* at St. Marks Church in the Bouwerie), a continuous modification of a geometrically defined space, arbitrarily chosen, in which she figures as the one in control, – but it had grown smooth, her feet had lost their independence, her arms their rebelliousness, it was like her monologue a portrayal of the individual as dynamo.

three-dimensional, but it doesn't look it. Its coming is moderately astonishing, nice, a reminder of an age of lesser speeds.[69] There are mild grey cloud puffs along the floor-boards and above the locomotive's childish funnel. The locomotive has settled into immobility.[70]

19:04 *Voice and organ are in a figure, ta*tatata*tata, of getting stuck or of an unjointed part's moving in place, a figure prepared 20 seconds or so earlier by overrepetition of the same itself repetitious sequence,* Childs

19:05 is moving on the right, the tower with the boy is starkly immobile on the left. The lights go out, *and the musical train, which has been rolling along safely and steadily again, tho momentarily sans its passengers*[71] *choral expression of their joy, breaks up*[72] *into increasingly insistent (accentuated) stationary flares, ta*ta ra ta ta*, . . ., ta*ta ta ta ta ta*, . . ., the fly-wheels are flying off, arrival of the moment of disaster! it's here! and, the breakdown by the addition of a shivery, shaky underneath rhythm subtly shifting into disintegration, the disaster! itself, everything has come apart!* a strip of strong white light grows downward over the backflat, cleaving it into a divided cloud-marbled night-sky[73] reducing tower and woman to silhouettes as abstract as

19:05 itself, a hint at the crack-up of the space we are looking into,[74] and Childs is heard loudly to say, repeating it dramatically three times, »1966.« *The organ,*[74] *with a single single-note final flare-up,*[75]

69 Our perception of it does not relate it to the music's image, tho they are out of the same drawer and it's the same thing: while the music elevates the cute to the grand, the visual image cools it. If we think of the association, however, it is a finely humorous contrast, and when in the sequel the mere not moving any further forward of the paper cut-out on the stage coincides with a music portraying a horrific break-down and disintegration, the contrast becomes grandiose, tho still not perceptually efficacious.

70 It's supposed to go a fourth of the way across the first time, half the next, 3/4s the third time it enters in this scene. Childs analogously dances her walking dance along 3 successively left-ward advanced obliques. Both in a good mood go backwards and forwards and don't make it anywhere: by the numbers.

71 Two sopranos. ». . . the singers have dropped out here . . . and it's just the alto and soprano sax and the flute and the two organs.« (KM, Interview.)

72 First appearance of theme 2 of the first train scene, – »recognizable by its highly accented rhythmic profile, in which the repeated figures form simple arithmetic progressions (Glass, *Notes*).« It only lasts about a minute each time.

73 Flakes, loc. cit., re the 1st train scene: »what look like cloud formations flash on the backdrop very briefly.«

74 The band comprised soprano sax and flute (2 of each) and a tenor sax and the violin: but one tended to hear the sound as construct of the many-voiced organ (played by Glass, Riesman, Andoniadis).

75 The crisis/disaster in the music took little more than a minute: break-up (passengers' awareness of its impendence), 20 seconds, disintegration, 45 seconds. Childs' evocation of a moment in time (1966) comes in during the last 15 seconds.

*changes tack to quiet serenity,*[75a] *ta ta*[ta] *ta, taa*[ta] *ta, and almost immediately (12 seconds) it's the merrily running-along train again, chorus
and all, (actually the sopranos (»do re mi sol«), the 2 organs, the two
saxes, the flute) nothing has happened,* the luminous split shrinks
away upward, it is dark on stage (*music going*), and when the lights
go on again after a few seconds, all is as before.

Childs, more toward the center of the stage now, is still going with
full energy, but the locomotive is no longer there, and another 19:07
slim, female mini-dancer (Dana Reitz) in light pants, short-sleeved
white shirt and suspenders, but pert-faced and her pants beige
(Childs' are grey), has been added in the lower, right-hand corner,
and is advancing unconcernedly in an Oriental-puppet or contrivedly
comic Frankenstein walk across the stage, jerky head-movements
switching her face right, left, forearms extended with hands droop-
ing, rabbit-fashion, then doing irregular flicking motions, bending her
legs at the knees as she lifts them for each step, and raising her feet
heels first, slowly, gradually, each time, her ups and downs as she
advances, in spite of the built-in jerks, a steady rhythm, contrasting
trivially with the briskness and freedom of Childs' pacing, – tho
otherwise the patterns of their movements are unrelated. They just
happen both to be on, a basic element, she an addendum.[76] Childs
may be moving more rapidly now, *the chorus,* chou[chou]pi*pi*, ..., 19:12
chou[chou]pi*pi ..., is with slight ambiguity alternating innocent exuberance and a possible excess of repetitive insistence, soon reverting to
carefree speed,* in discrete contrast to the slow advance of the locomotive, which is beginning to edge back in. The picture of a train, a
big Currier and Ives Train-in-Wintry-Landscape is lowered off-centre
down the backdrop, half as big as it. Its cosiness stands in a minor
confusing contrast to the cool lines of the stage-locomotive: they are
in the same mode of sentimental appeal, nostalgia. It rises again after
a moment. *The music is riding, now riding high, now pressing on, the* 19:13
*organ pipes swirling about the glad chorus.* The boy is up there,

75a Theme 1 again, – at first only the one organ and the two saxes. Beginning,
also, of the second section of the act's musical structure, – themes ›1-2-3.‹
76 Reitz' path, tho its over-all pattern never becomes clear, can be seen to be as
contrived as her walk. It's a 3-step stair-case line toward upstage stage right. Reitz
was not presented as a person, hence did not attract interest as a person, there
was no action for her to fit into, what she was doing was O.K., but uninteresting
and unlike Childs' thing did not represent energy. She was just a pictorial element
added to make the second ›movement‹ of the act different from the first, and so
was only disturbing. I assume that Wilson, this element meaning nothing to him,
did not know what to do with her.

seemingly unconcerned, lit by a spot. A white paper airplane drops into, through the scene. The boy, preoccupied, has launched it. A big blond mother-of-pearl conch is lying on the bare stage, not far from the tower. The static scene, including the two discordant dancers' repetitive movements, contrasts with *the intense movement onward of the music under its jubilant pipes*. The grey locomotive-smoke is an element by itself, figurates the backdrop into a vertical picture-sky.

19:13 The locomotive is about all the way on, the live, pipe-smoking driver, oddly illuminated from below, visible in his cabin, the plow nearly center-stage. Childs' arm-movements are wider now, opener, more abandoned, occasionally she slaps her thigh on the return from an outward fling of her arm. The other dancer has reached the backdrop, up ahead of the locomotive, on the left, is doing her movements in place, facing it, her back to us. As the locomotive stands, its tender partly in sight, a bland contrast to *the joyous swirls of the simulta-*
19:14 *neously climaxing music (sine chorus), the music breaks down (a flare-up into a grinding, sharper, piercing version of the preceding swirls),*
19:15 *disintegrates (insinuation of a jiggly rhythm, isolated flutish squeaks, ...), the organ goes queer (spout of revolving notes, up and down, over and over), spirals up[77] into an excited soprano's exclamatory song of woe, hadiredi, the organ underneath grinding to a halt, – in*
19:16 *a dirge, joining the soprano, once, twice, – but also briefly several times seeming to gather strength,* and 3 additional quasi-dancers enter in white, with strings, and execute an angularly geometric surveyors' mini-minuet, extending the string between them, gravely raising a triangle of string into an inclined plain contrasting with the flatness of the locomotive behind them. Lots of pretty smoke from the loco-motive. Childs has been carrying on quite vigorously more downstage, gyrating to the *strong singing voice,* her arms and hands moving with
19:17 violence, her walk momentarily disrupted. She loudly, in an emphatic, agitated voice again says »1966 ... 1966 ... 1966,« *and the organ, gone crazy, stops.* Lights out and the blinding white line comes down
19:17 the backdrop again, stays for a moment, shrinks back up, it's dark,

77 First appearance of theme 3 of the first Train scene, »a rhythmic expansion of a traditional cadential formula ... the principal material of the opera« (Glass, *Notes).* Glass (ib., part 2.) traces his music for *Einstein* back to *Another Look at Harmony* (spring of 1975), part 1 of which »became the basis of Act 1, scene 1 (Train): »In a general way, the three main visual themes of the opera (Train/Trial/Field) are linked to three main musical themes.« ... »Dramatically speaking, the violinist (dressed as Einstein, as are the performers on stage) appears as a soloist as well as a character in the opera. His playing position – midway between the orchestra and the stage performer – offers another clue to his role. We see

then the lights go on again,[78] *the train music starting all over again nicely, chorus and all, as before (the 1st theme and the scene's third sequence of themes).*

The surveyors are gone, and so is the locomotive, Reitz is downstage, stage-left, starting her ›funny‹ walk over, and a tall young fellow in a grey sweater (Richard Morrison) near her is standing with his back to us, rapidly writing what appear to be numbers and symbols, – equations? – way up on an imaginary blackboard in front of him, he has to stretch to reach,[79] in time to the *music*, – *a rather opulent music, little flutings sprightly jumping up and down in the foliage of deeper notes (which are progressively creating an aural aura),* – spotlights on them, on the pudgy boy on his tower, on the defiant waif, Childs, who is now over to the left of the stage a little, still doing her walk, – they are all, in their white shirts, bright disconcerting spots in the picture. A second additional performer, – the staging is such as to promote this counting, – a small dumpy female (Marie Rice) is standing leaning, one leg off the floor, next to the big conch shell on the left side of the stage, bent over a little, as tho listening very intensely, tho not to the music. Her feet are bare. There are several paper-planes on the floor by now. The writer is writing: a dance of hand which is really a dance of the working mind, creativity with a compulsive touch, the working mind nicely mimed by the very slight hesitations: giving an image of creative mathematical physics as a free flow, a rapid outpouring with no friction or resistance, the hesitations falling into it as elements of a spontaneous dancing. As the locomotive edges back on, a newspaper-reading black woman (Sheryl Sutton again) enters down-stage, him, then, perhaps as Einstein himself, or simply as a witness to the stage events; but, in any case, as a musical touchstone to the work as a whole.« I believe the musicians sometimes referred to this 3rd theme as the ›spaceship music.‹ Musically, then, from the composer's viewpoint, the opera is primarily a treatment of this 3rd ›cadential‹ theme – a »5-chord progression« – of the Train scenes, dominating the 3 Train-, as well as the spaceship scenes and the Knee plays (whose treatment of it strikes him as its major achievement): the music to the dance (Field) and Trial scenes is to him apparently wellnigh incidental. KM describes this: »it's like a big crescendo, sort of a grand finale kind of thing where the singers are holding sustained notes and the organs are going way down, playing very low notes. And the flute is sort of going crazy.« (KM, Interview.)

78 This is how I remember it from the first Met performance. From the second, I don't remember the light-line coming down at all at this point, but only a blackout, the music continuing, but only as a swirl of lower notes, which, when the lights go on again, shifts back to the onmoving drive of organ and chorus.

79 One of Wilson's personal images, the person writing in the air. S. K. Dunne did it in *Deafman Glance*.

stage-left, starts following Reitz who is pursuing the same path as before, ›covers‹ her. Sutton's presence, walking or standing, is at all times extraordinary, when she comes on, the stage suddenly acquires depth, power is felt, something seems to be going on: but only where she is. She is, as always, very straight, holding the paper spread all the way open in front of her as she walks, straight up and down, her dark arms, the elbows out, an elegantly angular frame, her head black against the print: it goes from side to side as tho she were reading rapidly. The smoothness of her displacement and her straight narrow back seem to place a straight vertical limit to her walk immediately in front of her, continuously displaced. Her motion is in her feet and knees, each foot rising slowly from the heel, held with only the toe touching, coming down only 2 or 3 inches in front of

19:25 the other. She is wearing blue sneakers. The writer, hand in the air, is immobile, – as tho reflecting. He has shed his sweater, is wearing a red shirt, the only color on the stage. Another plane off the tower (gliding prettily, very white, in several dips), then soon another. The moving figures on the vast dead stage seem refugees out of a single fantasy too weak to sustain them. *The music, – the flute above the*

19:25 *continuo has become steadier, more insistent, the continuo repetitive, stationary, – is sustaining*[80] what we see, Childs, steadily advancing and retreating, is the link between *music* and image, and also what's going on. Her movement's leftward displacement and the locomotive's (both advances sapped by retreat) are the development: a gradual and abortive extension of the mobile realm at the expense of the tower's space of stasis. Reitz, with Sutton at her back, has again reached the end of her path, they are up against the backdrop, crowded, visually, against the locomotive's incongruous flatness. The locomotive is now more than halfway across, stopped, part of its

19:26 coal-topped tender visible. *The organ, whirling in its upper registers, announcing a crisis and exulting in it, a conflagration of bright revo-*

19:27 *lutions, is disintegrating into over-fast agitation again*, Childs' dance, the more quietly, ditto, the man is figuring feverishly, the locomotive is puffing smoke, – but all this on the vast stage does not add up to any visual excitement, it is quite discrete, – and as a sturdy, bushy-haired male figure catatonically advances from left to right across

80 »... the band is warming up ... up until now they've been getting slowly into the music and towards this part of the music is where they're finally warmed up and they're playing, you know, they're playing all together and at their peak now.« ... »Even though it's really supposed to be the same all the way ...« ... »And also, at this point, is when the band is finally together and playing well, I started turning it up here and making it louder.« (KM, Interview.)

the stage, right hand lifted, (Reitz jabbing and jumping, Childs, half suffering child, half schizophrenic adult, now seeming to fight a non-existing opponent), *the music, a compulsive series of squeaks, spirals up in under the rising wordless song of a woman's voice, grinding on* 19:28 *more and more slowly underneath it, a rapidly twittering, agitated chorus*[81] *joining,* and the lights going out, the vertical light divider 19:29 grows down quickly behind the locomotive smoke stack, and the 19:30 tower in one movement[82] leans over, stands at an angle.[83]

Reitz and Childs are still moving quickly when *the voice suddenly ends, and the organ shifts into a high note, at first sustained,*[84] *by* 19:31 *itself, then in a series, then, again continuously sounded, accompanied by higher notes at long intervals, then sounded by itself, serially, again, etc.* The stage is dark except for the bright stripe, and as the performers, barely visible in silhouette, leave, the contrasts of this glaring band of light, first to the dark bulk of the locomotive (its driver no longer illuminated, the fire has gone out), then, the loco-motive gone, to the structure of the solid tower (again straight) 19:32 dominate the stage. *The upper register notes grow steadier, beginning to approximage a tune (KM, »the melody for the trial music.«) (tata tata) in a doubtful, sceptical, philosophic mood,* as an army of stage-hands rolls off the tower and brings in scenery for the next scene.[85] Stripe out. The stage is totally dark. *Isolated, very high and* 19:34 *lyrical, sorrowful pipe-notes, harmony notes, (KM, »one flute, two*

---

81 This is actually the first time in this act that the chorus, 5 singers, join in, counting »1-2-3-4:« in the 3rd theme end of the scene's 3rd repetition of themes.

82 At the first Met performance, the tower came over in a series of jerks, and the boy's platform, maintaining the horizontal, jerked up with it.

83 Cocteau so framed an action in *Blood of a Poet.* Wilson's tower does not collapse, it merely suffers in an instant what in Pisa took centuries, another manner of collapse. Note that the trick does not reduce a real tower to a piece of scenery. A picture tower remains a picture tower. It switches the perspective into the aspect of eternity in which towers do not endure even briefly but only an instant: ukiyo-e. To disturb in an instant a metaphysical solidity generated by a sustained exposure on stage is a recurrent compulsion of Wilson's art. Cf. e.g. the levitation of the pyramid's apex in *Deafman Glance,* of the movement of the Chinaman's cage in *Letter.* – But in the case of the tower in *Einstein,* the trick may not quite have worked: whether because too much, including the music, is going on for the tower's leaning to outbalance for us its prior standing, or because the tower is too unaffective for either its standing or its leaning to matter to us.

84 »... because the scenery was so difficult to work with we were never quite sure how long we would have to play this between scenes.« (KM, Interview.)

85 This post/pre-lude of stage-labor didn't work from the orchestra, was disruptive, but from the balconies it had a certain visual interest.

*flutes, —?«) have alternated with the gradual definition*[86] *of a strange* ›*haunting*‹ *delicate melody, a marginal evocation, stretches of* ti ti[taaa ba] *and of* ti ti[taaah] *in alternation.*[87] A broad horizontal rectangular band of light, shorter and wider than the vertical light-crack, and milky rather than glaring, is lowered into position center-stage, high off the floor. It is the sole presence there. Lights go up slowly.

I (2) Under the horizontal band of white light, crossing, on the back flat, a giant abstract black curtain, painted on, holding it together, the rectilinear grey planes of a raised oversize judge's seat (the high back of the wide bench behind the broad horizontal rectangle of the desk front). Two large light globes, floor lamps standing behind the desk, frame the seat, spheres in counterpoint to the straight lines. The ensemble adds up to an exquisite abstraction. A giant mattress-like slab, dully white, tho brightly illuminated from above, occupies the center of the stage,[88] extending from just below the court room dais to near the edge of the stage. From the orchestra one scarcely sees more than its front-edge, which is luminous, a wider parallel of the band of light above the judge's bench, too much, seen in a plane with the other brush-stroke of light and thus destroying the vertical harmony of the image, clumsy.[89] A scattering of furniture, — a very high stool to the right of the magistral bench, two short benches to the right, downstage, some standup stalls to the left and, downstage from these and in a little, two schoolroom-type desk-and-chair ensembles, one behind the other along the edge of the stage, the tops of the desks short and thick and rounded into consoles,

86 Glass is openly setting the stage as is Wilson, a nice touch, and one of the many close analogies between musical and visual development suggesting close cooperation between them and making one wonder who and which came first.

87 Glass in his *Notes* (part 1.), seems to characterise the music to the first 16 minutes or so of Act I, scene 2 as »opening« only: the *violin* after this long opening states what he considers the first of the 3 themes of the Trial scenes.

88 From the balconies, the big bed, perhaps 20 foot long, was just a piece of furniture and didn't fit in with the abstractness of the image, a stylistic incongruity perhaps intended to reinforce the incongruity of a bed in a court room, of such a private in such a public place. — The bed was non-sensically divided into an upper and a lower part by an upstage/downstage crack down its middle, a bolster at its right end defining its upper end, but failing to preserve its unity.

89 Wilson in *Einstein* tries to use light-emitting objects as abstract painterly elements: not, as e.g. in *Deafman Glance*, as illuminations of a personal vision. But since the images of *Einstein* do not appear personal visions, but are empty, these light-emitting objects appear as luxuries, and the images as glaring displays of command over money. — The idea may be the irruption of energy from material objects. But the dominance of elegant aesthetic form over these stage-images keeps this idea adventitious concept, it has no perceptual impact, — or only a weak one.

– little blue machines, – neither add to nor subtract from that dominant image.

As, *to that strange, extremely lovely tune from the organ,*[90] *the turning of a screw,* the lights go up a little more, performers are   19:37 entering from left and right, ceremoniously strolling, two young couples, – spectators? prisoners waiting to be arraigned? – seating themselves on the stage-left benches, three out of the four beginning to read newspapers, four or five persons, – the jury? – entering the stalls to the left, standing in two rows, pencils or ball points in hand, the tall writer in the red shirt among them, writing in the air, *their voices*[91] (they don't look as tho they were singing) *echoing the organ's notes as tho taking care of them.* Two young women in light green shirts, dark green pants, harmonising with powder-blue desks there, looking like dancers, enter from the left, walk to the school-desks, very slowly float their arses down into them, deposit their little brown paper lunch bags on the floor, in unison lift their enormous hand bags into the air, deposit them on their knees, and proceed to do various things that a court room stenographer might do while waiting for the court to go into session, dig for things in their bags, file their nails elaborately, hand extended with their fingers up ...   19:39 Sutton enters with a red book and a lunch bag downstage, stage-left, slowly, compelling as always, walks across, again very straight in a light tight vest, her straight arms (hands curving) in counterpoint to her water- or dream-walking long legs, an apparition as she crosses to *the magical music,*[92] past the vainglorious stenographers, turns up past the jury-stand and stands to the left of the judge's dais, between it and the jury-stand, but looking by herself.[93] The four spectators/ arraignees rising, the judges, two of them, in black robes and 18th century white wigs, one normal size (Samuel Johnson, an elderly black gentleman), one small (the little boy that was part of the signal

90 »Actually flute, organ, female voices,« (KM, Interview)
91 Female jurors only: »mi la mi la mi la.« Most of the ›trial music‹ is organ, female voices, flute, blending together.
92 If Wilson had been able (I don't know whether he wanted to) to make everyone enter and move as spiritually as she did, this peopling of the court room, aided by the music, would have given the court room and the following the aspect of a lovely midsummer night's vision, an air of unreality contrasting with the pomp and terror of the law as well as with the realism of the staging.
93 The place, across the stage from Childs', is her base-point during the trial scenes. – The program listed her as a witness, but she was more a lawyer, a (dispassionate) public prosecutor. Childs, also listed as witness, was clearly the defendant. I suspect Wilson of intentional obfuscation in these listings: retreat from the too-obvious of his own conception.

on the signal tower), enter and not too ceremoniously, their briskness a nice contrast to the formality of the preceding entrances, file along some Wilsonian path composed of cross-stage and straight up-stage-down-stage segments and right-angle turns up to the judges' double seat and sit, (the small judge now the taller, a little joke), bow to the court and to one another, and commence to arrange stuff on the

19:43 desk. The spectators/arraignees sit. Childs coming in quietly with a guardian, with a sudden violent wrench frees herself from his grip, – a splendidly sudden, *silent* violence,[94] – and followed by her guardian, who positions himself next to her walks to the high chair stage-left of the judge's seat: with an obstreperous air, a piece of acting, unpleasant in the general formal context, an individualisation, almost a heroisation of the indicted. She sits way up, hands in her lap, almost out of the picture, isolated, tho this effect is spoiled a little by her proximity to the judges and by the fairly strong figure of the guardian, right up against her. A light makes her face bluish, she is leaning stiffly to one side, – the defendant executed, a corpse.

The sequence 1 presentation of the staged image, 2 entrance and positioning of figurants has been very clear.[95] There is a little wheel on the diagonal Foremanian string across the stage.[96]

*The organ is doodling in steady swells, a spray of bells topping the sonorous formality of its wave's regular rise and fall, the bright procession of guardian voices filing past synchronously.* The judges, each each time first striking the desk three times with a gavel, the elevated small one thumping it, the bigger one giving it little taps, –

19:45 another little joke, – and each time afterwards giving three nods,

94 For the second Met performance, they spoiled the effect by rushing in like a couple of kids. And for this 2nd performance, she advanced *humbly* to her chair.

95 The stage is now crowded, the august splendor of the initial sparse image destroyed. The scattering of light-reflecting white shirts is irritating. It does not relate to the prominent luminous bodies, the two bands, the two globes. Their light is softer. – Wilson seems, quite inhabitually, to have given no consideration to the over-all choreography of the entrances. Perhaps he had in mind only its realism, i.e. its representation of the actual dribble into court rooms, spaces for public hearings, class rooms etc., the integration of divergently adventitious Individuals into a bureaucratic setting, their transformation into role-players. I suspect that generally his concern with the scenery and with coordinating the visual changes with changes in the music interfered with his organisation of entrances and placements.

96 »There's also a gyroscope that goes down a diagonal wire in the trial scene. It goes halfway in the first trial scene and the other half in the second trial. The trial is measured by the distance that the gyroscope travels on the wire. It's just a visual element representing the measurement of time: another clock. I just like the look of it!« (Wilson, Interview) .

330

alternatively intone, their words coming distantly over the p.a. system, »this court of common pleas is now in session.« Six times in all. *The ethereal spirit music stops.*[97] The humorous little ceremony has put a frame around the visual image, prevailing against *the music's attempt to negate its reality.*

*The music immediately starts up again, quietly affirmative do la s* [19:47] *from the chorus (male jurors), but the dancing organ*[98] *now dominated by the equitable sobriety of a violin,*[99] sawed by an Einstein-like womanish figure in make-up, elevated above the musicians' pit and lit up, visually linking *music* and image, *the fiddle's steady up-and-down*[100] announcing the image before us[101] will be on exhibition for

97 Flute drops out.
98 »sort of percussive, sort of vibrant, like a set of vibes.« (KM)
99 The violin is playing the first theme of the Trial scenes: »After the opening of the first trial we hear the violin, accompanied by men's voices, playing a simple, harmonically stable rhythmic pattern which, through an additive process, slowly expands and contracts. Later, the men's voices join in, producing a somewhat thicker texture. Towards the end of this scene, during the judge's speech, we hear the second theme, more chordal in nature, for solo electric organ. The Trial/Prison begins musically in the same way as the first Trial. After the stage divides, we hear the third theme . . . Towards the end of the scene, the witness remaining alone on the stage speaks, and, as the scenery is removed, we hear the second (chordal) theme – this time in soprano saxophone and bass clarinet.
The Bed scene begins with a cadenza for electric organ. As the bed lifts to a vertical position and flies up-wards, we hear the first theme again. Then, for the last time, we hear the second (chordal) theme, now accompanied by a solo singing voice.«

Theme 1 ─────────────── 1 ─────────────── 1
                    Theme 3
Theme 2 ─────────────── 2 ─────────────── 2

It is »based on one chord:« »The music based on one chord is first heard in the Trial (Act I, Scene 2) The violin, playing a figure in 7/8, outlines an $a^7$ harmony. A simple additive process begins as each successive figure adds a single eighth note, thereby changing its overall rhythmic character and causing the figure to gradually expand. The figure later contracts when the process is reversed, returning finally to its original form. The same process is heard later at the beginning of the Trial/Prison (Act III, Scene 1) and finally in the Bed (Act IV, Scene 2).« (Glass, *Notes,* part 2.)
100 »The violin is playing scales, or close to scales, – (KM)«
101 The visual image is not abstractly symbolic, nor merely pattern, but that of a court room, representational, and so perceptually unrelated to the *thin and strident tho sturdily energetic strokes of the violin and the chorus's slow bleating (»do-remi?«),* stridently discordant with them, a discordancy added to by the *occasional minor brouhaha of unintelligible voices over the loud speakers,* which to the spectator is part not of the music but of the visual image, – »Sutton reading

a stretch. *The two stenographers*, delectable modern maidens, clean, the secretaries in the vertically mobile salesman's dream, *are counting rapidly »1-2-3; 1-2-3-4,«* in pitch and time with the music, their hands, as for most of the 3 trial scenes, busily traveling as tho working a console in undulatory forward and backward pawing strokes over the rounded edge of their desks. From time to time, still counting, they do stylised versions of arranging their hair, gossiping (the front one leaning way back to do so, turning her head, then laughing at the other and giving a wink), etc. All their movements, humorous abstractions from observation, are smooth and highly stylised: their seated little ballet keeps going like a machine down in that corner. The jury is *accompanying the organ's doodling by pretty, patient-sounding genteel mooing*, taking notes[102] in the air at the same time. They don't move as tho they were singing. The tall calculator in the red shirt in the jury's front rank from time to time smacks an imaginary mosquito on his left cheek, from time to time just lifts his left hand to his face. The other jurors at corresponding times rub their left eye and do something else I forget, — distracted, almost distraught gestures, quite inobtrusive in the general picture. Sometimes they rub their hands a la Pontius Pilate. The four benched spectators or arraignees on the other side of the stage engage in their own ballet, a more angular, discontinuous and abrupt, — modern, non-

19:47
19:47

aloud, Childs talking, Mr. Bojangles counting with the stenographers (?), both judges at different times repeating ›Have you found it yet? No, I haven't found it yet. I'll just have to keep looking. We'll just have to keep on looking.‹ (KM)«

102 The jury's note-taking is part of the court-room image, but feeds into the play's preoccupation with writing, and — like the tall mathematician in the red shirt, the jury writes in time to the music, — with counting and calculating. Note-taking, counting and calculating is what the figures in this play do, and in conjunction with the mathematical structure and precision of the music, this effectively makes it a play about mathematical physics and about lives dominated by mathematical physics. This *subject matter* constitutes the opera's value and grandeur. It is neatly conveyed as form. That the writing when it's not calculating is note-taking defines the subject matter as mathematical *physics*. A second reason for the play's title not being fortuitous (if we take the »beach« of the title to refer not to Nature, but to the line dividing the ocean of cosmic energy from the more or less firm land of human reason) is that it is arranged to make the spectator centrally aware of the non-Newtonian time that man constructs by division, by seriation on the model of the natural number system. In complete departure from Wilson's earlier plays, the play deals with the discontinuous artificial time of the mathematical physicist. I don't know how clear this was in Wilson's mind, but in part it results from his having abandoned the continuous slow motion characterising his earlier plays. The insertion into *Einstein*'s divided artificial time of Sutton's walks brings out that it is about intellectual time, and does so better than the clocks and wristwatch-watchings-cum-freezes.

realistic, – one, punctuated by much more posturing sitting: a representation, could be, of existential despair, – sudden changes of posture, confrontations, separations. One of them (Reitz) is reading rapidly in a book she is holding up before her, her head going rapidly from side to side, an image uncomfortably close to the one of Sutton in the preceding scene, walking behind her.[103] *Sutton*, the public prosecutor up to the left *is reading aloud* to herself out of the book she brought along. Her manner suggests that in all modesty and with due respect for the court she thinks it proves a point. 19:47 Childs' voice, – it has been going since the beginning of the scene, – is *going along in an interior monologue*. Now and then, on her high chair, she extends a leg or an arm as tho she would make a break for it or cause a scene. Her guardian then extends his hand as tho to restrain her. – By and large these elements constitute the visual fabric of the entire scene,[104] its constant variables, except that a lot of stuff comes down from the fly-space.[105] Two enormous prints come down the backdrop side by side, both grey, dainty, vaguely architectural, 18th or 17th century book illustrations, unrelated to one another. They fill the background behind the judges, from the overhead light beam on down. One of them is sideways.[106] Their only virtue is that they throw vertical triangular shadows to both sides, turning the curtains into a beautiful giant pattern of interlocking grey and black cones. *In a clever struggling development, the violin, breaking out of its equitably indifferent presidency over life-as-usual, routine in process, during a momentary break in the*

103 The jurors' ballet does not relate visually to the stenographers': the disparity of conceptions and styles, and that each is executed with so much agression of definition, so competently, precludes even contrast. Since their clowning is merely a take-off on their presumed roles in the setting of a court room, unenriched by ambiguity or mystery, and is so professionally executed that we can't take interest in them as people, the unrelatedness rather than being striking is a deficiency. I imagine that Wilson directed the movements of the jury, but left the stenographers and spectator/arraignees do their own thing.

104 This second scene thus becomes a musical scene, what we see merely an incidental illustration. The scene has a lovely peacefulness, portrayal of court room ennui, interrupted only by minor incidents. But it is trivial.

105 The stuff seems mere objects, neither what it is specifically, nor symbols (of the relativity of time or of anything else). Mustily crowding in on the pale-faced prisoner, it may be intended for an effect of terror, but it clutters up the court room, the stage and the picture, and, a disgusting surfeit, as in a furniture emporium, both taste- and sense-less, it is hard to look at and impedes listening to Glass' ongoing beautiful chant of long summer.

106 According to Flakes, op. cit., they are a diagram of the interior of the palace at Versailles and a picture of its exterior.

*chorus' dumbly conformist-sounding do la, by a slight modification of*
*its doodling bends it into a Bachian fugue, elegant figure of with-*
*drawal, the do la s getting steadily shorter, turning into a solo, —*
*chorus and organ (and flute) fading, giving up,* — greeted, almost
immediately by an indignant »well!« from the spectator/arraignees,
but continuing for a little. The sudden and loud »well!« has been
accompanied by a left-arm fascist greeting. The two male spectator/
arraignees get up, consult, exchange seats. Sutton at the same time
19:53 goes up to consult with the judge(s), then stands taking notes, after
a while returns. *The chorus has reentered, its do la s even more*
*emphatic than before and speedier, gradually getting closer and closer*
*together, and the violin has imperceptibly but quite quickly shifted*
19:53 *back into its acquiescent see-saw enactment of life as it is.* Its recon-
19:54 version is countered by — or at any rate encounters — a strong bright
abrupt »No!« from the defendant, which during the sequel is from
time to time repeated by one of the jurors to a shaking of her head.
*The jurors' masculine do la s become so insistent, — fast now, the*
19:56 *violin going along agreeably, — that something like a break in the*
19:57 *action seems signalled, and as the organ flares up into (peaceful)*
*fanfares,* a big hand-less old-fashioned clockface,[107] 4 or 5 foot in
diameter, is lowered in over the prints, *and as the annunciatory*
*fanfares, covering the violin, quite take over, the do la s spacing*
19:58 *out, gradually crowded out by beatific feminine, quasi-angelic*
*la s,*[108] a gigantic lab beaker, 6 or 7 foot tall, or the picture of one,
comes down, hangs by the judges' table as tho standing on it, and two
smaller, half dark, half light clocks descend, hang in mid-air at both
ends of the bed, above it. Almost at the same time, Wilson in his
dark suit comes in, stands, his back to us, by the jury, downstage

---

107 »There's a clock in the trial scene which takes 20 minutes to go backward an
hour. We made it in Italy. In Milan we went to see this clock factory and Chris
said: »Can you make a clock that would go backwards?« And the man thought
that we were crazy! But then he did it and made the clock. I think Einstein would
have liked clocks that go backwards!« (Wilson, interv. in Interview, Feb. 1977) —
According to KM (interv.), the clock never worked at the Met. I saw no hands. —
Flakes, loc. cit., p. 75, re the avignon performance: »A scrim on which is a circular
figure resembling an ancient design of the sun,« — »lo ministro maggior della
natura / che del valor del ciel lo mondo imprenta / e col suo lume il tempo ne
misura.« (Dante, *Paradiso*).
108 Chorus of female jurors joining the chorus of male jurors. What I heard was a
»la« echoing the men's »do la s.« The »la« seemed by the organ stretched into a
»la be ma.« According to KM, the men continue their »do la s,« the women sing
»mi mi.««

from them, as tho inspecting them.[109] *The organ's heraldry and the* 19:59 *chorus' harmony of submission and benediction slow down and space out, as once more the elegantly detached Bachian fugueing of the violin, very much alive, emerges. Organ and chorus out (they don't make it back, so to speak). Violin only.* No movement on stage, 20:00 only the above-it-all violin. The two spectators/arraignees closest to us suddenly lean back and, arms and legs out, turn their faces to us, 20:01 make grimaces. *Organ and chorus resume as earlier (things are as* 20:02 *they are), the factual do la s, perhaps a little doleful by now, the feminine la s following them, transcendental blessings, as before,* the two stenos start their recording again, and[110] a big black disk very slowly on two strings moves in from the left (in the back), the same size and at the same elevation as the handless clock. As it approaches and then covers it, Sutton slowly, with a stationary vertical ondulation in each successive place, her whole straight and narrow body falling and rising, – she is walking behind the bed, so you can see 20:03 her only from the knees up, – walks across toward Childs, who is slowly raising her right, vaguely pointing toward the approaching Sutton, but continues the gesture (converting murder into suicide), till her index points to her temples, and then lowers her hand slowly when Sutton stops walking, stands near her. There is no interplay between them, each moves on her own like the hands of a clock. Her guardian, who is quietly mouthing notes, puts a restraining hand on her shoulder. *The firm strain of the do la s has speeded up and become even more emphatic* as Sutton approaches Childs and the black disk the clock, *the high la s above them fading out (the women singing do la along with the men) and the organ increasingly cheerful and more loud:* when the clock is blotted out, – the event seems ominous,[111] but the black face seems richer than the invalid white

109 The director's entrance makes the excess of things on stage seem monstrous.

110 A fake and trivial climax is after a momentary apparent return to normalcy followed by the real climax, equally minute, but seeming significance-laden. This is a recurrent device of Wilson's.

111 The extinction of the unregistering//hopeless clock, the analogously uncoordinated/out-of-it defendant being analogously at the same time put out by her darkly self-contained powerful accuser, comes as a four-minute climactic break, – a destruction of something (e.g. a person) in which the whole order of things falls apart, – after nearly half an hour (about 24 minutes) of quiet and orderly stasis, undisturbed by minor incidents. (I am leaving out something pertinent to Wilson's mind and mode of directing, viz. that the climactic break is itself the dramatic climax of a more extensive, – about 8-minute- climactic crisis.) I note first that the idea behind this directorial arrangement is a personal vision (a radical anxiety), necessary condition for its being art; next, that both the abstractness of the action,

one, all numbers and no movement, – *only the organ is still playing, a quietly content, perhaps a shade resigned do re* [laaah] *, a Glockenspiel theme, its timbre high, bell-like, accompanied by faint echoes of the la s, but rolling along like an accellerating, smooth and heavy wheel,* and everyone (the spectator/arraignees repeating the arm movement that accompanied their »well!«) reprovingly says »now, then!,« and two small lights go on on each side of the faceless clock;[112] and to *a bright melodic Glockenspiel of the organ's (do* [re] [laaah]*la), the voice* of reason (»there is nothing to be done«), which over the violin's *contentedly tinkling subordinate toy-Glockenspiel (da da* [da] [di]*da) over and over diminishes to a resignedly plaintive, fainting do re* [laaaaah], 20:05 *only to grow happy again, – an organ-violin duo,*[113] – everyone (only Childs remaining in her place, and Wilson walking off the stage) assembles down-stage in a strung-out group, lunch bags in their hands, the judges in the middle, a spot on the head-shaking Woman Who Reads a Book off, down-stage, stage-left. They stand and slowly open their bags and to *low-volume pretty high-register Glockenspiel, overlaid by the organ's repeated deep do re* [laaaaah] *s, the violin blending in,* eat and drink,[114] not talking to nor looking at one another (except the two stenos who are mimicking dishing and laughing), an 20:08 oddly quiet scattered gathering, their stance to *the dying music that*

– what goes on is undefined, we don't know what the specifics are, – and its restriction to the perceptual, – only what we see (and hear), without psychological or other, e.g. generically symbolic reference, is what happens and is to convey what is happening, – are intended and fine, and are of the essence of Wilson's art; and next, that the whole thing didn't work: partly because the stage-image didn't cohere, so that it became hard or impossible to get the development perceptually (as distinct from, as in this account, intellectually) or to be affected by it, partly because Wilson had overloaded the development with mechanical gimmickry, partly because the staging and acting misdirected one to realistic interpretations, viz. to thinking of everything in terms of court rooms, trials and of what happens at or leads to trials, and to an aesthetic approach, to merely appreciating the pictures. Personal vision furnished the idea, but did not control the execution.

112 »The black disk that covers the face of the clock with its two attached lights represents an eclipse of the sun in 1919. In this case one saw two stars next to the sun, that appeared on each side of it. You could only see the stars when you had the eclipse and for some reason this proved Einstein's theory that space was curved. He had talked about it before the eclipse.« (Wilson, interv. in Interview, Feb. 1977) 113 I understood KM to say that what I took to be the violin's high-tone, tinkling Glockenspiel, was carried by 3 flutes, – 2 of which then drop out, the third continuing in unison with the organ: the violin continuing throughout this, but very faint. 114 Everyone in the cast wears a wrist watch. Food and drink for the lunch break were real. This would have made a lovely contrast to the court session except for its being so cluttered with real things, props.

of waiting. *The organ (and the flute or flutes) cuts out,* and for ten
seconds or so *the violin accompanies the crinkling* of the paper bags
being folded up *with its playful, rather dry and even lame, tho
quite elegant theme. The violin stops, and in a ten-second silence* all
raise their wrists and look at their wristwatches, and freeze and
stand, *as from the organ there comes a new theme,*[115] *Bachian again,
but secular this time, very faint and fine, finely amused, out of the
18th century or another world, growing into the silence, over spaced
very deep notes.* The freeze dissolves, everyone ›wakes up,‹ ›dazed,‹
hands to their forehead, quietly resumes his or her place in the *quiet
of the lovely music, the bass notes getting sparser and sparser, volume
decreasing.*[116]

While, *to the ever fainter music,* the tall writer among the jurors,
out front at right angles to them, his back to us, does his rapid
voiceless calculations in the air, the older judge in pompous elocution,
gravely, sententiously,[117] immediately commences a stiffly disjointed 20:11
and by its tritenesses ridiculous[118] encomium to Paris, — a strictly

115 According to KM, actually organ, one flute, violin. The second theme of
this and of the 3rd Trial scenes, 3rd theme of the 2nd Trial scene, »more chordal
in nature.« (Glass, *Notes*) Glass characterises it as a 4-chord progression: »The
progression of 4 chords appears at the end of the Trial (Act I, Scene 2), Trial/
Prison (Act III, Scene 1) and Bed (Act IV, Scene 2). It is a rhythmic expansion of
the 4 chords:

$\underbrace{f - E^b - C - D}$    As indicated, the f and C harmonies are »paired« rhythmically, as
are the $E^b$ and D harmonies. Beginning with a simple pattern of
eighth notes, (f) ($E^b$) (C) (D), the phrase gradually expands, each new phrase being
played twice, until quite a long and elaborate final figure is produced. An example
of the rhythmic/harmonic expansion in its early stage is as follows:

|     | (f)           | ($E^b$)     | (C)           | (D)       |
|-----|---------------|-------------|---------------|-----------|
| (1) | 4 ——————————— | 3 ————————— | 4 ——————————— | 3         |
| (2) | (4 + 3) —————— | 4 ————————— | (4 + 3)—————— | 4         |
| (3) | (4 + 3) —————— | (4 + 3)———— | (4 + 3)—————— | (4 − 3)   |
| (4) | (4 + 3 + 2)——— | (4 + 3)———— | (4 − 3 − 2)——— | (4 + 3)   |

etc.

116 The 5-7 minute scene has been staged with exquisite sensitivity to the music or
else vice versa. Tho image and music in *Einstein* often don't relate in content/
feeling, their developments are marvellously coordinate, down to fine changes. Note
the music's comment on the action and note how Glass' music for the violin gives
the mathematical physicist an independent and only intermittently independent
attitude.

117 Johnson did this drily and without hamming, a clean job, but missed his
opportunity for an address from the bench.

118 A jocund moment in a pseudo-sophisticated guise. The judge's 2 speeches in the

337

idiotic speech, after oblique references to »beautiful men« »preferring
the darkness for their social activities« (laughter in the audience)
issuing into extensive praise of the very beautiful ladies of that city.
20:12 The (silent) jury are duly taking note of his points in the air. As he
finishes[119] on an »oh la la!« Childs' finger again going to her temples,
an extremely beautiful gauze drop with the voluptuous outline,
almost invisible, of a naked woman in a seated position, comes down
over the frozen scene, the judges white-wigged and black-robed central
behind (›within‹) it, showing through distantly, the others in darkness
and not seen,[120] and the two modern females, the stenographers, in
equally abstract outline, but solid, out in front of the drop, at its
edge. Almost immediately we hear the boy-judge saying something, –
»Would I . . .,« – in a raised neutral childlike voice,[121] – it hangs
in the air, – continuing, with similar dead intervals, »would I get
20:16 some . . . would I get some wind . . . would I get some wind for the . . .
would I get some wind for the sailboat.«[122] Lights out behind the
curtain, the scene there gone. Only the two great luminous bands are
left, outlining the figures of the two stenographers, who during the
drop-scene have provided the only movement, an extremely slowed-
down version, – with their right hands only – of their stenographer's
pawing dance of hands, and who now, having moved sideways in
their chairs, slowly lean over in the dark, and lean in two dark
arches on the floor, feet and fingertips touching. The (opaque) drop
20:17 comes down over them.

When the lights go on again,[123] the dark and the light woman, Sutton

play are grotesque: friendly ridicule of social order; provision of a hollow center
to the play's story-component (trial scenes); and part of the play's consistent
systematic devaluation of language: it cannot convey real experience. Neither can
the more, the only important type of language in this play, mathematics, language
of the intellect, but it is given the value of the power and danger of energy-control.
Johnson made up this speech himself according to KM: hoping to get laughs.

119 According to my notes re the 2nd Met performance. As I remember, at the
1st performance, the curtain descends after the boy-judge speaks and after the
stenos kneel.

120 I am not sure whether or not the defendant and her guardian were illuminated
also. – This concluding (like the opening) image of the scene was splendidly
beautiful: the only 2 moments of total aesthetic success (since Sutton's beautiful
walks were isolated elements of the stage-image only) in this scene, a mess.

121 The kid's silence-interspersed, – not halting, not interrogative, – voice over
the *clear tinkling of the old-timey sweet music and the rare deep notes* was rendered
repulsive by its babyish self-possession.

122 His minutely altered version of something in a text of Christopher Knowles'.

123 At both Met performances, a good many spectators left at this point, some,
considering the »knees« intermissions, only for the lobby. At the first performance,

and Childs, are in their original seats,[124] the rectangle of light again behind them as tho they were a slide projection, talking rapidly to *emotional fiddling*,[125] Childs talking to herself in the manner of one talking to an imaginary interlocutor, tensing against agitation, with shakes of her head, her hands contracting nervously on her thighs, Sutton talking to no one, not even herself, trick of an old Wilsonian performer, *their voices a sandy grit in the low-volume scrabble*[126] *of the violin*, Childs' the dominant one. Never stopping talking, they 20:19 get off their chairs and down on the ground, kneeling with their legs sideways, heads near the floor in a position of obeisance, echo of the last scene's finale, slowly get back up on their chairs, continue talking. They shift to rapid counting. Occasionally each repeats some gesture (visually irritating by its arbitrariness, a nervousness of the scene), Childs a slapping, Sutton a tapping: in time to *the violin*. Once or twice Sutton, to quiet »aaahh aaahh«s, looking like a good girl, raises her eyes alternately to the left and the right, not moving her head. They get down on the floor again (continuing to talk), get 20:21 back up, sit again, still talking. They bend over at an angle, feet off 20:22 the floor, arms in the air, and Sutton saying »Switzerland, 1905,« the 20:23 photo of a young man with a moustache, Einstein, is flashed on the rectangle behind them and briefly held. *Violin off*, lights off.[127] The drop rises on the lit stage on which a crowd of young people is running in various manners and at diverse speeds, – they are individuals, – in something like an oval pattern.[128] A young woman, solid, with long blond hair (Ritty Burchfield) is whirling about herself in the middle. Things don't change much during the next 18 minutes,

the audience was more from Soho and the upper westside, at the second more from the upper eastside and from around the park, but both times it was quite sociable, a lot of those in on the event known to one another.

124 At the second performance they entered after the rectangle lit up.

125 Glass: »The most important musical material appears in the knee plays and features the violin.« (Glass, *Notes*, part 1.) I quoted Glass on the musical structure of this knee play. Its first theme is the »cadence« theme, »rhythmic expansion of a traditional cadential formula« (Glass), the ›spaceship music‹ the »principal material of the opera« (Glass), here »expressed as violin arpeggios.« (Glass)

126 Possibly the second theme of this Knee play, »based on simple scale passages (Glass).« The violin then returns to the »cadence« theme.

127 The second knee was a variant of the first in the way one person's memory of something would vary from another's or that a single person's actual perception of something might be actually ambiguous. The ›knee‹-scenes don't so much link the other scenes (much less provide transitions), as they are cinematographic shifts of focus into close-ups, rhythmically lifting the pro-/an-tagonists into prominence.

128 As my notes have it, for the first Met program, Ritty came out or was on by herself first, was then joined by Reitz, the corps coming on only after this.

the principle of the thing is soft definition.[129] Definition is a no-no
and must not be reached, whether by an individual or by the group,
choreographically. In the main, in addition to a moderate amount of
intermittent turning about oneself in place, the dancing consists of
running, a steady shower of runs, with turns and bends, and, especially, leaps, arms and legs out, interspersed with just standing or
bouncing lightly in place. The oval pattern, more or less everyone
moving around in it, tends to reappear vaguely, also patterns of all,
perhaps in little teams, meeting in the middle of the floor and again
separating, or indistinct turbine patterns, or a chessboard pattern of
not quite stationary distribution. Sometimes individuals seem to meet
by prearrangement, encounters sometimes terminating in a brief loving holding on to one another, the men assuming the traditional
20:26 protective stance. Burchfield has a solo of whirling, Reitz standing in
one of her thoughtful not quite contorted positions on the down-stage,
stage-left white rug, the others having left. After a moment, Reitz
joins in, in her own angular, slightly jerky, free and easy manner.
The only powerful moment is Sutton's (she is not one of the dancers)
standing down-stage, stage-left, at the edges, for a moment, her stasis
a perfect foil to *the soughing, suctioning inhalations of the powerful
music accompanying the scene.*[130] At some point one notices a lit
ribbed flat disk, perhaps half a foot thick or less and two feet across,

129 Not e.g. insinuative definition (control of patterns to retain them perceptually
marginal), sabotage of definition (controlled frustration of imminent emergence of
definition as systematic element of definition), or ambiguity of definition.

130 According to KM, the music for both dance-scenes »is totally unrelated to all
the other music in the opera,« relates to Glass' *Music in 12 Parts.* – »The first
two appearances of the Field image are given over to dance and can be heard as
similar reflections of the same musical material. For me they are two pillars
equidistant from either end of the opera, sharing only superficial features with the
musical content of the other scenes.« (Glass *Notes,* part 1, p. 4) Glass describes the
music of the 2 dance-scenes as 2-chord progressions: »The material involving the
series of 3 chords makes up the music of the two dance sections (Act II, Scene 1
and Act III, Scene 2). The procedure here is quite different, setting three key centers
(A, $e^7$ and Bb) »around« a central key of d. At the beginning, each of the key
centers is associated with its own meter and all are played over a common rhythmic
pattern of 6/8. (This, incidentally, creates a secondary polymetric »flavor« throughout the music.) The key of A appears in dotted quarters, $e^7$ in eighth notes (a
substitute key of $C^7$ appears later) and Bb in half notes: After an excursion into
one of these key centers the music returns, always, to the central key of d. As the
music develops, the key centers begin to exchange metrical character. Later, these
form complex accumulations of meters in the same key before returning to the
central key, d. This accumulative process continues until the original key/meter
associations are lost in an overall texture of harmonies and meters.« (Glass, *Notes,*
part 2.)

suspended from 4 strings above the dancers, dangling, looking like an Art Deco chandelier. After a while one notices that it is changing position, now here, now there above the floor.[131] The precise diagonal line of the thin string across the stage-image is out of joint with the mild, floorbound turbulence. The relaxed, slightly clumsy folkdancing, animating the scene at low intensity, suggestive of silly play and of the futility of individual endeavour, exhibition of a life-style (how we feel about things below Houston St.), its choreography a little artfully simple, smacking a little of the sketchbook, is very pleasant to watch.[132] One thinks of leaves whirling in *the storm of Glass' organ*,[133] or perhaps, less pleasantly, because of the dancers' tan pants *of scum tossed on its untiring waves. The loud music, exciting, greatly exhilarating, a driving turbo-screw, rushing rivers, rivulets, ripples of sound, an aural helix growing by repetition, the vox humana (»Phaedra, Phaedra«) a high voice raised in exquisite song above its swirl, a cry of joyous drowning in its ocean, shouting to itself in expletive reiterations, carries the scene.*[134] — *The vox humana is going* »David, David, David, — peccavit, peccavit, peccavit,« the chandelier is wandering above the dancing: *suddenly the music ends.* Blackout. 20:42 Indistinct movement on the dark stage.

When the lights go on, very dimly, *the organ starting up again on* II (1)

131 The program identifies it as a spaceship. Tho I knew there was supposed to be an as yet distant spaceship hovering above this scene, I didn't see it as a spaceship. But people more used to seeing flying saucers might have.

132 Wilson gave this and the play's other dance to DeGroat. Tho the spaceships provide an artificial connection, the two dance scenes are not part of the play. Showing the figurants of the court room scenes, which, tho only ostensibly, by their semblance of content and action, make up the play proper, en masse and in a relaxed mood, they are the opposites of the ›knees:‹ telescopic shots. — The program calls them ›field-scenes, an appelation suggesting the straightforwardly Romantic idea, not inappropriate to these scenes, of young folk dancing in the meadow. The flying saucers accentuate the idea of a contrast of gay innocence or Nature to space-age technology, death and doom, a contrast somewhat analogous to that of the act I beach in *Freud* to the act II drawing room, or to that of the Forest to the Table-of-Judges component in *Deafman Glance*. Wilson may have figured that the wilful naiveté, one might almost say vapidity, the amorphousness and harmless friendliness of these scenes would mitigate the play's aura of cold calculation. The spectator is relieved by these scenes of inept playfulness in which for a moment to escape the director's total power and the humiliation of aesthetic coercion.

133 Instrumentation throughout this scene: 2 electric organs, a flute, 2 saxophones, 2 soprano singers.

134 Sound tho only the motion of material air is to perception energy whereas image the radiant energy is materiate form. Glass composes and instruments his music as energy, — in accord with its phenomenal mode.

*a quietly playful figure,*[135] *growing just quiet, quietly serious even, as a duet starts*, there is a train on stage, center-stage, down-stage, this time, the dark shape of a railroad car, off at an angle rearward, black in the night (deep blue sky, with a fat little butter-yellow moon), it's the last carriage on the train,[136] and in the two lit oval windows (one suspects oil-lamps inside) to both sides of the door onto the rear platform, photoframed in them like grandma and grandpa,

0:43 the two lovers (Sutton and Antoniadis) facing one another: in a *duet. Something like fasidobe (actually, »la si do si«) repeated, from her, laaam from him.*[137] *It's lovely.* The carriage looks lost — abandoned — in the effectively snowy expanse of the stage. The scene is an exquisite confection, superbly staged in the B'way style, nothing surreal about it, no irony, unless its perfection in the genre is itself the camp: a Romantic phantasy.[138] After a while, they stop outside,

20:44 he is in evening dress, Sutton is all in white, a headfitting little white soiré cap enclosing her head, d'Arcangelo has outdone himself in the ideal demureness of her perfume-ad gown. *They continue the sweet duet (she, vasedubibi, he, sisilaa and vasiii, then both lapalacidulci)*, executing a series of small manoeuvres, stand side by side, stand at angles to one another, move apart: Sutton turns this, by the refined delicacy of tiny movements, — the flowing curve of her upper body as she turns away, the placing of a gloved hand on the railing, the lifting of a forearm, fingers wiggling a little, — into a delightful, kinetically sophisticated ballet, the agressive stodginess of her partner (a performer given to acting, — with his chest) notwithstanding. Their

20:46 suddenly freezing for a moment, *silent*, while he checks the time on his wristwatch (the Now that splits open into infinity) does not cut

135 The music for this Night Train scene, according to Glass (*Notes*, part 1) is a »reworking of the first theme« of the first Train scene, »this time with a larger complement of voices.«

136 Some spectators may have made the photokinetic association that the train they had seen arrive in the earlier train-scene had travelled by and they were now seeing it from the rear, leaving, but to do so they would have had to assume a change in camera-angle changing the train from flat to three-dimensional. Others may have fancied they saw the then (thrice) arrested train from the rear during one of its stops.

137 »They were supported by another male and female voice from the pit, and one mostly heard these voices because they were miked better. When the couple have retired inside the train again (20:54), only the singers in the pit are singing.« (KM)

138 A graphic cliché from the public domain like the cast-uniform's allusion to Einstein in Life or whatever. Wilson uses the graphic images created by the media for their affective charge, a gesture of quotation leaving him uncommitted to the emotional effect, burdening the spectator with the shame of his response.

through the sacharine crap of the scene, as formally artificial as this gesture's infraction of it. Sutton's finesse, on the other hand, mars its vulgarity. *1-2-3 s are alternately repeated by both of them, then duce as they come and stand together (both, cim pa si, both alternately lapalaciduce. The wordlessness of their long-lasting song does not matter a bit:* the image is crap, but as it is, *the song conveys the feeling, — ›a perfect night,‹ — perfectly, the song's »it has no end«* complemented by the image's »would it would last forever.« *The organ behind the grand vocalisation of the joy of love is playing a joyous solo, a flowering in the sun, an (unaffected) Ode to Spring,* to the grandeur of which the image imparts a spurious nostalgia. Oddly, the instant exhaustibility of the image makes it *hard to listen to the music, one is not quite able to trust it either.* — He looks at his watch again, they freeze, *in silence, the duet continues, lapala-*   20:48 *cidulce, 1-2-3 s alternating with cibe ciba cibe (she), baaa baaa baaa (he): the duet is fast now, tho not hurried. 1-2-3-4, . . ., 1-2-3-4-5, . . ., 1-2-3-4-5-6, . . . s alternating with ha ha ha (she), vacidulce (he), — quite fast now. A stretch of fast and pretty lapalacidulce s.* The lovers retire inside their compartment, the door opening of itself for them, and the moon eclipsing: a black disk blots it out. The gag, a faintly ominous reminder of the first scene, gets applause. *The organ shifts into a new, slightly more emphatic mode,* small lights go on on both sides of the black full moon, *the duet[139] has recommenced on a more intense, almost frenetic accent, very rapid 1-2-3 s alternating with very rapid vowel sequences, the organ goes into its crisis mode.[140]*   20:55 Inside the carriage she is pointing pistol at him, the course of true love is never smooth, he raises his arms, *excited 1-2-3-4-5 s, 1-2-3-4 s on an ascending pitch, ultra-rapid lapalacidulce s, the song cuts out,* lights out. Train out in the dark. Strong applause.   20:58 *To a hammering organ backed by dry light percussion, a kind of*   20:59 *American Indian music,[141] high-tension, but calm,* the women-stand-

139 According to KM. this is actually the (full) chorus counting now. The chorus is in the pit: »In the past, the chorus used to be standing on a train platform on stage . . . but that would never work right. Whenever the train platform would come out on stage we could never mike the people on the train platform right either. So, finally, we just cut the train platform from the show.«
140 This recurrent both rhythmic and tonal effect of Glass', — prominent structuring device in the first train scene, — indicates an ending in the nature of a crisis, and coincides with like points in the visual ›action,‹ except that these visual terminations are minimal.
141 According to KM, this is the music for the 3rd train (the ›building‹) scene later on, an anticipation. Michael Riesman had taken over from Glass at the organ at this point. Only the organ is playing, — no percussion. (KM.)

20:59   ing-next-to-the-conch of the earlier train-scene appears in a white
circular spot holding the big pink conch to her ear and listening to
it, – in the same place and in the same posture as before, casting a
small shadow. The moon glows up again. On the other side of the
stage, to the right, there stands a small replica of the train-carriage,
its rear windows and door warmly lit: the train in the distance. The
mind supplies the train's motion away. The threesome of listening
woman, moon and traveling train, as lovely as the scene it is the
immediate recall of, but mystery rather than sentimental cliché has
21:00   the striking force of a vision.[142] Blackout.

K 3   The front-drop is down, and instead of[143] the rectangle of light on
its lower right-hand corner there is a large white board that seems
to have holes punched into it in the pattern of two overlapping
shooting-targets. As soon as Childs and Sutton have assumed positions
21:02   in front of the board, *the hammering organ cutting off, the un-
accompanied chorus,* visible in front of them, *starts a rapid musical*[144]
*1, 1-2, 1-2-3 with sudden stops,* and the two women, standing side by
side, their backs to us, in front of the two patterns, shifting lines of
21:05   yellow lights, – at first, for a long time, only two crosses, then other
lines, parallel or at right angles, finally concentric circles, beginning to
appear on the dash-board, do tracing motions with their raised hands,
at some moments the same motions, their bodies moving the same way,
mostly not. The movement of lights on the board, like that of an
animated electric billboard, evokes the discontinuous jumps of va-
lence-changing electrons, electronic motion. The two women are not
tracing these patterns, but related ones, not there, partly as tho in
response to the one there, by a touch-system or even merely by a
sign-language bringing about the succeeding one, partly in a dance
stylisation of the movements of telephone exchange operators. They

142 The person leaning on one leg listening is one of Wilson's personal images. In
earlier plays it was Busto or Neu listening to a wire, up on a ladder. The image
is a counterpiece to Richard Foreman's radio in the wall. Tapping the information
in the air.

143 Wilson by these substitutions approximating metamorphoses effects not only
continuity but ambiguity. The device has the potential of enriching perception by
charging each image with the co- and de-notations of the other, an enrichment
that if it occurs is apt to be greater than one might at first think, since without it
the perception may be purely aesthetic, lacking co- and de-notations entirely. In
the case at hand, a photostatic image has been changed into an image of electronic
motion. But the jump (from the images of K1 and K2 to that of K3) may have
been too great for the perceptual synthesis to have occurred in the audience.

144 The a capella chorus in this 3rd Knee play again starts from a version of the
»cadence« or »spaceship« music and at the end returns to it.

344

are stretching, bending, finally even crouching, but mostly it's a flutter of hands, Childs attempting a counter-point to the *hacking rhythm of the chorus,* Sutton going with it. Once or twice *(the chorus pausing in its counts (?)),* a projector light going on, they turn, raise their arms, show their teeth, turn back. *The twittering of the counting chorus has some of the anxiety of subjection to a necessity of instant response to change (a post-Bachian expressiveness,*[145] *occasionally, when the range of pitch becomes very narrow, a modernistic air of discord, contrasting with the pre-Bachian classicism of form).* The gesture dance on the board transmits this breathlessness to *the lovely two-voice harmony of doremis (female) and laba laba s (male) alternating with the counting. The chorus has for the second time switched into this latter mode,* and the movements of Childs and Sutton come to-  21:06
gether, each tracing the large circle now in front of her (the 2 circles overlapping) with parallel extended arms, down through a knee-bend and back up, – once, twice, and *the chorus cuts off,* they are standing still and the lights on the board flash on brilliantly. Applause. Blackout.

21:07

*Deep, spaced organ beeps in a single file.*[146] The drop rises on the  III
court room, a good clean image with its two light horizontals inset  21:08
as contrasting frame, the two yellowish light globes mediating between them and the non-luminous (and non-chromatic) other elements, cleansed of the clutter of the gear dropped into it when last we saw it and of people, the only persons there the two judges and 2 of the spectators/arraignees, quietly seated, As soon as the movement of the entering stenographers and (then) jurors, *the beeps turning into*  21:09
*drones,* turns the picture into non-picture, the image becomes messy. The drop-by-drop entrance-scheme is, again, pretentious, at best archly realist, portrayal of a drifting in. *A high organ pipe has joined*  21:09
*the single-note sequence for the entrances.* Childs, slick in white draped dress, white stockings, white shoes,[147] makes a deeply tragic entrance as tho with feet dragging, a to-the-gallows walk. Sudden tic gestures of hers and her guardian's, as they proceed to her place,

145 The middle theme of this Knee play is an »arrangement« of, it seems, the »harmonies« of an »implied bass line«, – the music that opened the first Knee play, »easily recognisable by its highly lyrical character« (Glass).
146 One-chord progressions as Glass describes them in his *Notes,* part 2.
147 Childs' change from the (ineffectually Einsteinian) pants/short-sleeved shirt/suspenders neutrality of her earlier appearances parallels Sutton's identical change in the preceeding scene, linking the 2 scenes, and instantly making of Childs the center of this scene, as Sutton was that of that scene. Childs' guardian in this scene evokes Sutton's paramour in the preceding by black pants.

are powerless against the solidly fake realist fabric, mere scratches, not cuts. The minute ballets of spectator/arraigness, jury and stenographers are in progress. Except that one of the spectators/arraignees has gotten up from his bench, nothing has yet happened when Sutton *to only the deep notes from the organ* repeats the upstage left-to-right walk over to Childs that a little over an hour ago climaxed the earlier trial scene, floating, this time, in a series of double bounces, – not projecting anything, just presenting that eery ghost-walk as a fact. *The organ starts piping regularly, the piping superimposed on the drones has become almost a tune,*[148] and Childs, her guardian walking off into the wings, descends from her high chair and stands facing Sutton, and the right half ot the court room slips off into the stage-left wings around them,[149] half of the judges' elevated chair-and-table, the defendant's high chair and its platform, the spectator/arraignees' benches, and, above all, half the giant bed, – the right half of the overhead light-band dimming as the right half of the one underneath it moves out with the bed-half. Childs crawls up on the smaller but still very big white bed.[150] A grille of vertical black bars

148 According to KM, the music for this trial scene has »the same theme with just minor variations« as the music for the first trial scene. Riesman is still at the organ. – The first theme of all the three Trial scenes, »a simple, harmonically stable rhythmic pattern which, through an additive process, slowly expands and contracts.« (Glass, *Notes*, part 1. – »based on one chord. (Glass, ib., part 2.) We here also have echoes of F. Lee Bailey's slicking up Patty for her trial.

149 The dissolving of half the court room echoes, – realises, – the repeated cracking apart of the train's landscape in the play's first scene. But it is perhaps rather seen as a scenically successful integration of scene-changing. It follows Sutton's walk over to the defendant, but I doubt that many spectators for that reason associated it with the blotting out of the clock that accompanied her previous walk across.

150 The court room has come apart, as the train's country came apart, and the person tried withdraws into the privacy of a bed as the person trying her withdrew into the privacy of her train compartment. This psycho-metaphysical story is conveyed by the affective charges of the imagery only: the feel of abortion, disintegration, retirement into self, and of the essential sameness of trying others and being tried; and the specificity of the imagery disavows the story in the presentation of it. But Childs' crawl into bed lacked the inexpressive formality requisite for this genre of story. It was in the petty contemporary vein of arbitrary action. It made no psychological point and none was in order. But it did not make the needed point: in the area of the phenomenology of the mind; via a cold yet affectively charged image. This was not her default only, but also Wilson's: as the coming apart of the court room was deprived of its perceptual impact by the messy specifics of the court room-routine image, so was Childs' retirement deprived of its perceptual impact by the nervous disorder of Wilson's staging of the rearrangement of the court room image. – The bed in the court room is really the

descends over the emptied right half of the scene. Sutton is still standing where she stopped in front of Childs, behind bars now. She is
looking off into the stage-left wings. A stage-hand enters to deposit
some stuff in front of the bars, a little black heap and a little white
one, walks out, and a plain back-drop with a large, island-shaped
rift in it comes down stage-left behind Sutton, half the width of the
stage, covering the half of the court-room curtain there and the
dimmed half of the overhead light-band. Sutton walks back to her
prosecutor's spot upstage, stage-right as two prisoners in green-striped
prison-garb with ditto prisoner's caps (2 of the 4 former spectator/
arraignees) enter and sit on the two benches that have reappeared
behind the bars.[151]

*The drone and then the piping have faded out, and as the organ goes*
*into a rapid cool twirling which gradually turns into almost-jazz*
*runs and boogie woogie figures,* the jury, unmoving, starts counting
(with their fingers also, their hands up in front of them vertically,
palms out), *1-2-3-4-5-6-7-8,...,* then in syncopated rhythms *6-6,*
*6-6,..., 6-1, 6-3, 6-4,..., 1-1, 2-2, 3-3, 4-4,..., 1-2-3-4, 1-1,*
*3-3,...,a complexly varied count,*[152] *and a single high abrupt hyster-*
*ical scream, immediately squelched,* shoots through their counting, and
Childs, sprawled abandonedly on her back, head toward us, her neck

court in the bed room, the trial an invasion of privacy. In the trial scene there's a
big bed in the centre of the stage. Einstein was the dreamer on the bed, who was
on trial. I always felt that the bed itself was on trial.

151 If this reads drily, that's how it looked. The bars coming down was effective
(tho not as effective by a long shot as the descent of the grille over the cave in
*Freud,* which clanged down metallically and was a shock), and so was Sutton's
standing there, but the minute or two after that had no visual or dramatic definition
and so were awkward.

152 The counting is on a new theme, the third of the 3 themes of the Trial scenes'
themes, first appearing here, and not appearing again: »— numbers sung by the
men and women in the jury box and lightly accompanied by harmonically shifting
arpeggios on electric organ.« (Glass, *Notes,* part 1.) – Glass describes this music
as 2-chord progressions: »The sequence of two chords is found in the Trial/Prison
music. The two harmonies, $a^7$ and $g^7$, are first heard as two alternating arpeggiated
figures in 6/8 (played on electric organ with voices chanting numbers representing
the rhythmic patterns). The music develops as each »half« of the figure undergoes
a process of rhythmic fragmentation (wherein small increments of the original
figure are added to itself. At first the process occurs equally in both halves (represented by the two harmonies) of the figure, thereby maintaining an exact overall
symmetry. Gradually, the two halves begin to differ rhythmically, reaching a point
where they are completely different and the figure is asymmetrical. At this point
two successive asymmetrical figures in the music begin to act as mirror images of
each other, thereby seeming to form one doubly-long symmetrical pattern.« (Glass,
*Notes,* part 2.)

off the bed so her face is showing upside down, a psychologically not bad nuance of rigidity, starts *chattering*[153] more or less continuously to herself in a schizophrenically reasonable tone, as tho explaining things in a justifying way while pretending there is nothing to justify: *it could also be the voice of someone overheard talking on the telephone except run together.* The jury's *arithmetical chorale makes a very cold calm background, its melody very serious: an extended, intelligent calculation, or rather the victoriously scientific recording of the Occurring Numerical Values, expression of the self-awareness of a Scientific Age: all is calmly noted, the pattern of strict predestination — the world's end not unlikely — is being registered. The clipped sober statements contrast beautifully with the only marginally grave/portentous Gay '90ies dips and ragtimey jiggle of the instrumental music.* Their backs to us, the 2 prisoners commence an angular seated dance, moving or sitting, chin in hand, backs to one another, in postures of dejection, an unemphatic but also uninteresting '60s ballet in tribute to Jerome Robbins re the difficulty-of-being-young, or perhaps a dance of interminable waiting, more likely, since their movements are tense, a dance of suspense and desperation.[154] The judge is writing, a hack into his job. Childs is immobile, white on white, the stenographers are quietly busy with their finger nails. Sutton takes another walk, the third, but, only half the court room being left, only half the way across this time, her left hand out in front of her, palm out as tho to halt someone or ward off something, floating up and down counter to the *music, — off-beat percussion behind the organ?* — stands center-stage, walks back again, stands in her official place, a darkness in it all, giving no sign anything around her exists, in no kind of agony, self-contained, a world, accusatory lacuna on a stage of vanities. Childs is shifting center-stage, flat out in luxurious minor agonies, *her voice a pleasant complement to the organ now running in a contained, introspective*

153 Her own text, not one of Knowles': »prematurely airconditioned supermarket and there were all these eyes, — And there were there bathing caps that you could buy and they had those kind of 4th of July . . .« This is not the way Childs would chatter. By its contrived simplemindedness, her text, unlike Mary Peers' in *Freud*, is literature.

154 Wilson may have intended us to equate subliminally the poor little rich girl's solitude with imprisonment. More probably, the whole prison-thing in this scene is simply the remnant of some fleeting plot-idea of Wilson's intended to make this 2nd trial scene seem temporal and causal sequel of the first (someone was found guilty!). It comes across merely as supplementation of the *general idea* of a court room. To my mind the challenge was to leave a void stage-left and make something of *that*.

*mood*. The stenos, very subdued in this second trial scene (itself 21:25
subdued), not writing, take a half turn toward us in their chairs,
then repeat that movement of bending over onto the ground on which
trial scene #1 finished, but come back up, recommence sitting. 21:28
Another *isolated scream*. Sutton *re-raises* her hand. Childs, — Patty,
— looks very lonely on her bed. The prison bars, soft, are moving.
Sutton, after a long minute, goes on another of her splendid sleep-
walks, this time in a more purely down motion, — presumably not
rising on her toes, deliberately bending in her knees, coming up discretely.[155] Stands centerstage, profiled, hand up. The judge is almost
not there, — *the jury's purely mathematical, hence pure enregistering
takes the heart out of any judgment a judge might render, seeing as
how the count is in touch with the law itself, viz. what's happening:
the Judgment is over us all.* His face is hidden under his white wig,
they are counting on their fingers, *the organ playful under their
steadiness.* Sutton quietly returns to her place: Childs is getting up 21:30
on her knees, still talking to herself like a loony, fourlegged, gets off
the canapé, self-assuredly[156] in her white gown walks down to
down-stage in front of the bars, stands, gay — or the ill-behaving
waif, back-talking, acting up, rebellious spirit, — her incarnation of
discordance with a regular world complementing the black person's
passive total refusal, — irrupts into a small set of movements in place,
comically appealing jumps, fingers spread, a dancer relaxing, *her
college-educated voice slipping along steadily.* From the white bundle
on the floor behind her she gets a pearl necklace, stands with it on,
the West Coast debutante before it all happened, takes it off and
puts it back, straightens up and walks over to meet a cavalier emerging from the wings (Frank Conversano?), stands hand in hand with
him looking at the audience. The smirks. They turn to one another,
her steadily continuing talk now seeming to him, he walks off. She
stands, bends down to the black bundle now behind her, and when 21:34
she turns back to us is Tanya as she was in the bank hold-up, in

155 The beauty of Sutton's movements is in their stillness: her body seems at one
with her mind, and her mind quiet. When in *Letter* she started to apply her technique of hightened or intensified natural movement (*Deafman Glance, Stalin*) to
acted gestures, vanity put them in quotation marks of affectation. Put in inferior
juxtaposition to Childs' big skilled ego in *Einstein*, she took the superior course of
negating herself, and now invests the contrived business given her to do in this
play with grand spiritual naturalness. Moment by moment, she stole the show from
Childs by her artistry.

156 I have seen her do this walk like a hurt dog also. Tho the way she does it is
moving, one suspects one is partly moved by pity for her as an actress over-acting
with the clumsiness characteristic of the professional performer.

black pants and a black jacket, open, gun held loosely in her hands, a spot-light on her, gay and relaxed. The stenographers are writing as tho she were telling all this from the witness stand. As she bends down once more, Sutton starts on her fifth walk across, in an ascending way this time, her finger slowly coming up, pointing in an admonishing way, but does not complete her walk, midway to center-stage in a smooth tigerish motion does a grand turn, 3/4s of the way around, her feet staying in place, coming up toward us her hand still out, now perhaps in a pistol-pointing gesture, but then untwists and finishes the walk to center-stage, stands there quietly with her finger still up. *The counting from the chorus has become simpler, clearer.* Childs has come up performer, Marlene Dietrich, piping on her tux, crushed black felt hat, wrists chained to one another, stands a mo-

ment, the star, walks off.[157] Sutton, otherwise immobile, has begun moving her upheld hand's fingers in a gesture of communication. The prisoners during all this have continued their occasional quiet antics, quasi-acrobatic mimicry, tho mostly doing dejected sitting. Now the male one lifts the female one by her feet, stands with her hanging against him while Sutton again briefly converses digitally, and walks

off with her as Sutton, who has also begun to talk to herself, à la Childs, really also a bad girl, briskly, by way of her upstage, stage-right base position (and down past the jury and back across to the right) walks to Childs' first place in front of the bars, stands talking, puts on the necklace, her movements smooth, she is not doing an imitation, she is the imitation, stands talking as her prince (a blond young fellow from among the singers this time) comes in (a small double image, smaller replicas of one of the prisoners' benches and of Childs' high chair, are lowered down the backdrop behind the bars), they seem to caress, he presents her to the public, flashes us a

smile, releases her hand, leaves. She gets into the Tanya outfit (part of it only, the pea jacket), and turns toward us in a more demonstrative stylised repetition of her upstage turn, the gun in her hands, sweeping with her, and *to swirls from the organ,*[158] *the choral counting cutting off,* picks up the hand cuffs and stands there, lengthily, it seems, still talking, the chain between her wrists, looking at us smiling, her head cocked ›meaningfully,‹ *the organ swirls becoming*

157 Childs' 7-minute down-stage show, – the life-story of Patty Hearst, and a psychological analysis of her, – is just a joke. Childs manages to make a sustained dance-number out of it. Its origin is the »Patty Album: an 8th-grader, at sister's debut, with Weed, as Tania, after arrest« in the February 16, 1976 issue of Time Magazine.

158 3 flutes and the other organ come in at this point.

*longer and more powerful, making of this a climax of the scene's action*, – a fine moment. As the other performers start leaving, the 21:42 stenographers first, then the jurors, one by one, their *resumed counting* stopping when only three of them are left, she turns to face into the stage-left wings, her chained hands lowered, in, again, her white shirt and pants. The little wheel on the diagonal string is pretty much all the way down now. The judge off inobtrusively. *The swift loud swirls from the organ now seem carried by two pipes, a sad tune. The climax apart, the music has not been pressing, more like present time, an indifferent medium*, – the action has not measured 21:43 out time. Sutton steps off into the wings in an unconcerned manner. 3 of the jurors are still there. The lights dim.

In that island-shaped rift in the right-hand backdrop, high above the stage, Childs has appeared, an apparition, quietly seated, hands in her lap, light on her, she's looking up into it, far away, the heavenly image of a fashion model, whispy contrast to the lone remaining solid juror (on whom there is also a spot, tho a dim one), standing a forefinger lifted in Sutton's earlier admonitory gesture, but not sharing the stage with him, seeming rather, the only one on it, all alone. It's a stunning image, sacharine crap. Apotheosis of – ? – the victim?[159] *The grand Bachianly fugueing organ is still continuing (in the dark, the violinist is assuming his place)*, the courtroom's two horizontal bands of light are there, a faint cone of light is spilling onto the stage floor from the opening through which Childs is appearing. *The loud organ is cut off*, – bands of light off, spot on 21:48 juror out, juror off, – *and to spaced, slowly drawn, deep notes from the violin (actually: a bass clarinet), and then a slow lugubrious even tragic solo[160] (a soprano sax playing the ›Einstein theme‹)*, the image, working its fingers in its lap, has a speech, »I feel the earth move... I feel the tumbling down tumbling down...« etc.,[161] turning into repeated alternating telling when various disk jockeys are on. Childs with arguing head movements gives the piece as chitchat, very rapidly

159 Wilson in *Einstein* uses Childs, as he used Sutton in *Deafman Glance* and *Queen Victoria*, where *she* was the criminal, to contrast the human world of passion/crime/guilt to the world of the mind (Freud in *Freud*, the Chinaman in *Queen Victoria*), with the suggestion that the latter is piffling or wrong in the context.
160 The second of the Trial Scenes' themes, ending each of them, – what Glass calls the »chordal« theme, a »progression of four chords,« – in soprano saxophone and bass clarinet.
161 A text of Christopher Knowles'. It has reference to Carol King's song *I feel the earth move*.

and smoothly, in a friendly, not too emphatic tone, and continuously as though she meant it. The compulsive flow is a tour de force. After 21:50 a while which seems long but is not tedious, the backdrop in front of her goes up, and you see her as only now in the flesh, on her high stool which is on its pedestal, in her court room setting, but all alone now (still talking), a child steeped in the media-time. The change-over, a revelation of levels of illusion, is a neat trick of Wilson's. She is a fine performer, but the choice of tone and perfection of execution flattened the number to an aesthetic event, devoid of meaning and affective reverberation, pleasant, pretty and surprising, just a little disagreeable because of its aura of pretentious sentimentality. The 21:51 spot on her dims, voice out, *sax*[162] *out (the sax resumes for just a* III (3) *moment after its first cut off, a fine effect of suspending a transition),* 21:52 spot out, blackout and *to a tremendous blast* (the stage is brightly lit) *from Glass' organ,*[163] *turbulent and pressing, in conflagration, the vox humana or chorus singing viva viva viva, a scraping gipsy-violin* (violinist lit up) *running within the organ's excitement, — a next-to-jubilant presage of doom, — »the fat is in the fire!«* — the dancers are out dancing, lightly, sparse on the big stage, without much fire, their shirts the colors Tudor composed for Cunningham, a beauty of good taste. The motion is subdued, the mood generated tho not the manner almost depressed, what they do roughly the same as before, tho there seems more standing around at distances from one another, thinking, and more solo posturing in the manner of making a sign of oneself.[164] Sometimes the men swing a female round and round, but, perhaps a question of muscle, more as a gesture of what they would like to do. Still, against the warm tan of the brightly lit but dull plain backdrop and the cool irregular grey of the floor, the commotion by its slightness makes a pleasing contrast to the *power of the music, raging like a great fire.* Sutton, in demonic black, perhaps on a mission of espionage from the space ship (it's her costume inside it later), makes several entrances, an actress dancing,[165] re-

162 And clarinet. The clarinet has played up to now, but less audibly than the sax. I didn't hear it.
163 According to KM, the music for this scene, quite unrelated to the other dance music, starts off with an 8-note soprano solo, »re-mi re-mi . . .,« and then the organ (Riesman, not Glass), the violin and 5 other singers (2 female, 3 male) enter.
164 According to Wilson 7 minutes have been allocated to improvisation in this scene, whereas the other was »all written down.«
165 Always graceful, she is not a dancer. It is as tho when she tries to think move-ment, she thinks stances instead: one sees her aiming at them, thinks of her thinking of them. Whereas when she moves on her own time, slowly, the moments fuse into pattern.

presenting the *agitation of the musical jet* coolly. The chandelier- 22:02
spaceship, a most identifiable foreign object, moves in, much bigger
than last time, perhaps 4 feet across, quietly hangs here and there
above the dancers, stopped as tho for observation, its tubular
shadows moving with it on the floor: a designedly ineffective representation, looking entirely harmless, somewhat ridiculous. Its warm, 22:05
yellow-pink light goes out for a moment, goes back on. *The music is
a dynamo generating power out of its own revolutions, its mini-
tunes, enhanced by repetition.*[166] Only Ritty Burchfield in her long 22:13
blonde hair, nicely rotating and Reitz doing angular abstractions are
left out there now, *the organ gyrates above its tense hunting cries*,
and a gauze curtain, a hazy grey-white starred with white snow-
flakes, drops, *the organ revolving in isolated notes. To a violin solo,
repeating the organ's last theme,* Burchfield whirls behind the scrim
(Reitz, her off-set, sculptural out front.) Blackout, *the violin solo*
*continuing,* lights up. The gauze curtain is gone, the solid grey drop is   22:14
down, the light and the dark woman (Childs in white shirt and grey     K 4
pants, Sutton in white shirt and white pants) are down-stage stage-   22:15
left, on their backs on the thin glass tops of high narrow chrome
tables, writing,[167] Childs in a perhaps unintended representation of
sexual arousal, Sutton doing a langorous number with vining arms
*to the shivering, writhing sawing of the violin, an insanely decorative
music, changing direction all the time,*[168] *suddenly breaking off,*  22:16
*shifting into a sentimental solo, the infinitely hurting accompaniment
to the chorus' (a half dozen strong, out front) church-choir, unctu-
ously sorrowful smooth and sad chant of fasidomi,* – the two women
going into a slower, more soulful twisting and turning, – *then in an
aberation of distortion turning discordantly crazy again to a weirdly
Gregorian doremifasol from the chorus, shifting back* (the tossing Ss
of the bodies on the table following) *into the sweet sadness of the
fasidomi, and again back into the madness of the do(re?)mifasol: the*  22:20

166 According to KM, this is the theme of the ›space ship scene's‹ and the opera's
›grand finale,‹ ›one of the Einstein themes.‹
167 »you see two characters lying on plexiglass tables: they are supposed to be
floating in water. In 1900, there was a 25 ft. diameter barrel of water that had
mercury in it. They shot two beams of light through this to measure the speed of
light.« (Wilson, interv. Interview.)
168 Glass describes the music for this knee as again three-partite, and again
beginning and ending with the »cadence« or »spaceship« 3rd theme of act 1, scene 1,
– the first and last parts this time conjunctions of the treatments of this theme
characterising the 2nd and 3rd Knee plays, i.e. violin arpeggios *and* choral setting
for voices, – the middle theme, as in the previous Knee play, a »lyrical« »arrangement« of the same material.

*violin slow, the voices ultrarapid, both suddenly breaking off,* the girls freezing a leg in the air to the projection of a slide of a page from a mathematical manuscript, pale, the writing spindly. Blackout *and the onset of slow trumpetings from the organ.*

v (1)  Lights on. A silo or the like, an industrial building, an electrical plant perhaps, — actually the air shaft, one of four according to Wilson, of the Holland Tunnel,[169] — a painting on a drop, back a ways from the stage-edge. Way up there (actually perhaps about 20 foot up), behind one of the two windows, a man writing rapidly. The building could be the Institute for Advanced Research or one man's jail. This is all that happens for a while. A grand image, the power of the

desperately writing solitary man equal to that of the *music, the waves of which are now swelling higher:*[170] a kid scoots in on a skate board. He stops and looks up at the window. A little cute this, — the genius and the little kid,[171] suffer them to come unto me, — but Wilson has been tempted into a further accessibilisation of the image: a whole lot of people stroll in gradually, the whole court room gang, including the Woman Reading a Book placed down-stage, stage-left, off

by herself, a painterly element of no interest placed with perfect taste, and gather in a crowd gazing up at the writer, — the little people and the thinker, humanity in admiration of the Intellect to whose depradations it is helplessly exposed... The gathering has been staged perfectly so as to yield a giant Saturday Evening Post cover, a heart-warming lie that things are that way: directed into a representation of reality, an actual gathering of unrelated undistinguished people out for a stroll happening onto this great man at work. *The sound is now trumpets and horns, raw and grandly blaring open horns mixing in with the baying of hounds, and the yelp of the fox, squeaks and a jangle of bells and a jiggly pulse underneath, — a little Ravel at times. Its growing volume (Glass uses volume, electronically adjusted, as 4th musical dimension) makes this splendidly vibrant, triumphant outpouring not only a celebration of Einstein, the lone worker, but chronique of a development, — whichever,*

169 The silhouette of the building is like that of the train in the last train scene, the train »becomes the building (Wilson):« but I did not make this association, perhaps because the mood of the two scenes is so utterly different.

170 The music for this scene according to Glass is a »development of the second« of the three first Train scene themes, »recognizable by its highly accented rhythmic profile, in which the repeated figures form simple arithmetic progressions« (Glass).

171 The Lone Writer and The Old Man Writing (or Reading) are in Wilson's stock of images, and the genius-with-child schema may have seemed applicable to his appearances with Christopher Knowles between the acts of *Queen Victoria.*

– of his *oeuvre and efforts, and the ornamentation of hunting sounds etc. brings in a wildness hinting at a lack of control.* The crowd drifts off (Conversano acting this out!), the kid on his skate-board and the Woman Reading a Book last, the writer still writing, *the music strong as ever, speeding, flowering, flourishing on all registers and with Bolero blarings, but then begins to turn a little manic: repetitionsly repetitive, insistent, stuck,* the writer stops writing, his fist raised, the image of him rides up behind the window, for a moment you see only his legs and the lower part of his body,[172] then he moves down past the window, still standing, and out of sight, and the lights suddenly go out, and the building drop rises in the dark to an *organ prelude that starts up instantly, after a cut-off, but is instantly squelched by a continuous sustained organ note in an agonised mood,* as on the dark stage is revealed nothing but the broad luminous band that we earlier on saw as the foot of the bed, separated from the stage by a strip of black shadow, and above it only the darkness. *The note is held* as we stare at the radiant monolith or it at us, *but then shifts into the piping of a Bachian prelude with all the serenity and feeling of Bach.*[173] The rectangular beam of light, a glowing rock (2001!) lies there self-sufficiently, a flat rectangle, faintly patterned by cross-figures of stronger light, actively radiating as tho musicating. *The piping is turning[174] into a duet of two pipes or intercourse between two notes, a planetary pattern sometimes, over its underground of deeper, closely repeated notes faintly figuring a more elaborate dance also,* and the beam, solid or surface, starts shifting, rising at one end, levitating (you can faintly see the ropes, they don't matter), and keeps rising as tho with an impossible slowness getting ready for flight. (Rapt attention from the whole audience throughout this ›scene,‹ the spectacle is fascinating.) The beam is of the order of magnitude of big things, yet has the power of a geometric element and its successive illusorily discrete positions seem respective *signs. The organ's drone is the event's engine, the dance of pipes its calculatory process, and over the inobtrusive continuo, the high register process is bogging down into static repetition at increasing intervals, with only occasional ›mirroring‹ ›revolving‹ or ›dance‹ effects, quickly abandoned, like echoes only:* the block

172 This incident may have been due to a malfunctioning at the 1st Met performance. I don't remember what happened at the 2nd performance.
173 According to Glass, a »cadenza for electric organ,« not yet one of the »themes.«
174 Glass' ›first theme‹ »based on one chord,« of the Trial scenes.

is at about a 45° angle, its lower (right) end not quite hovering above the floor, but neither seeming to rest on it. *The dying effect from the organ continues* as the beam continues to straighten up, faster now, it seems. It is almost straight up and down. It slips into place, its bottom sliding a little to the left, a slightly awkward detail, in the center of the stage, i.e. of the darkness in which it is rising. It is straight up and down, a little off the ground and swinging a little, hangs, *and the organ changes into a different kind of music, a beautiful Romantic melody in a thoughtful mood,*[175] *as a soprano starts singing a song of vain regrets, sadness, resignation,* and the beam starts rising very slowly vertically upward, swinging slightly, a little like a cigarette ad, its ascension very moving, a grandiosely simple effect, creating something like a religious (and perfectly vaccuous) awe,[176] *the lyrical, lost, lonely chant, regretting not the departing light nor the growing darkness, but some unrelated universally personal fate, soaring over the organ's spinet or clavichord notes, setting off* the coldness of the vertical rising line, *in flight through the darkness,* as it is in suspension. *The voice is immaterially sound, being wordless,* as the beam is immaterially light. We see both an intact rising column and, the upper end disappearing behind the dark of the overhead drop, an upward shrinking column. The former is a space age image, relating to those elements of the play, tying in, perhaps, with the flying saucers and the coming scene,[177] the latter reminds us of the vertical cleaving of the space of the first scene by the descending stripe or crack of light, and thence of the halving of the court room. The column becomes very short, a peculiar drama, an anxiety, attaching to its last moments. Then only its shadow remains, a light purple shower on a screen. The stage is dark now, *voice and organ still on,* indistinct workmen are moving on the stage.

IV (3)  The drop rises *(voice still on).* In the dim stage-light, a spotlight,

---

175 3rd and last repetition of the second of the Trial scene themes, »— the »chordal« theme, a »progression of 4 chords.««

176 That the effect's being obviously contrived and, it being so grandiose and lovely that one doesn't think of it as contrived to affect one, seemingly contrived for its own sake only, is inoffensive is a considerable achievement of Wilson's. The scene is *pure art,* the sensory elements relating directly to the emotions, with ideas utterly irrelevant.

172 The *E/B*-film-outline suggests that Wilson thought of the scene as metaphor for Einstein-the-mathematical-dreamer's mind: »The bed . . . disappears up into space, leading us into . . . the interior of the spaceship.« The flight into space, — detachment from the mundane, — installs the Space Age.

visible in the air, is picking out two poles next to a square hole in
the floor, upstage, stage-left, there is a light in one of the two small plexiglass hemispheres set on the floor downstage, stage-right, and as the light grows a little less dim on scaffolding going all the way up on the backdrop wall at the rear, a glass coffin rises, perhaps a little late, up out of the square hole, and rows of identical red lights, horizontal and vertical, go on on the board beyond the scaffolding, their glow outlining the dark shape of a figure passing up on it.[178] *The soprano stops and the organ twists into slightly ominous chords, dire pitch ascensions ornamented by a harmonious tinkling next door to a fugue.*[179] A black acrobatic figure (De Groat in tights) flashes through the air in a spidery motion hither and yon, landing and bouncing back up. Tho it's not the 0-gravity motion one has read about, it may make one think of it, more likely of Superboy. »Oh shit!« about covers the scene. You are having a pinball machine, a jukebox and a cash register thrown at your eye ball, and as the pages of the comic book turn quickly, – »Wham!!!,« »Bang!!!!,« »Slam!!!!!« – stars explode like amusement parks. $E = \frac{1}{2} mc^2$, and so $m = (2/c^2) E$, but the revelation of the modest patent office clerk as electronic space wizard is garish in proportion to the dearth of suggestion. People are mounting onto the scaffolding, compartmentalised by its girders into a three-tiered board of perhaps 15 squares, – among them, on the uppermost catwalk, the third from the right, Glass in front of a console, the only one standing in profile, – there are perhaps as many as 20 dark shapes up there now, distributed into groups, some by themselves, their backs are to us, they are up there rather quietly. No jumping about, no contortions. The drama is in the computer. The pattern of glowing dots, lines at right angles to one another, is growing more extensive, a somewhat irregular but repetitive pattern. The clock-case, – there is a clock in the glass coffin – and someone prone, – hangs there horizontally, swings at half-height, moves off, past the board, up-stage, stage right. The little kid is out on the stage, facing us hands up, steering. There is a woman seeming to peer through a tele-scope. *A sudden ultrarapid chorus of 1-2-3s and of* ha haaaa<sub>hehaheee</sub> s

178 This scene has been related to Fritz Lang's *Metropolis*.
179 At the first Met performance, the organ crashed brutally into what relative to it and initially seemed a delicate visual construct. Perhaps KM had set the volume too high. The ›cadential‹ 3rd theme of the first Train scene, »progression of 5 chords,« twice repeated in it, developed in the Knee plays, the »principal material of the opera,« furnishes »almost the entire music« for this (except for the post-ludial final Knee) final scene of the opera.

*in the mode of a conclusion, but it lasts, presumably from the people operating the board, but you can't tell, and the sound is coming from up above the front of the stage, over to the left:* Sutton in something like a black jump suit, shades, a female Super Dude, a rapid fox, has come out with two flashlights in her hands, dances with them (»is like calling signals (Wilson)«) in a stage-left area of three overlapping spotlight circles, as a second glass coffin sinks out of sight beside her, moves backwards and forwards (in an exaggerated version of Childs' movements at the beginning of the play) flashing *to the blare of the chorus' overbearing chant of peremptory consecration (the lit up violinist out front sawing away).*[180] The coffin, it seems larger than the other, is coming back up; the first coffin has come back in, is floating (horizontally) up-stage, stage-right, moving along in invisible track. It's Childs inside it. The dark figures by the light-board are going quietly about their business in the hectic scene, rendered hectic by the *wild music* and by the moving gimmickry and the lights, dark

2:58   repetitions of the board's verticals, the alchemist's lab assistants. *The chorus stops.* Sutton is going ape cooly to *dramatic swirls, runs of the organ,* the elevators are passing, *there is a rapid, excited babble on the air,* – as tho something were going wrong in the governing

3:02   mathematical machines, – *intercom interchange, circuitry chatter,*[181] *and a lone voice scat-singing, wop-e-wop, once, twice, the organ is howling, now Childs' voice, superfast, is loud on the p.a. system,* a toy plane of supersonic configuration slips upward on a diagonal wire, a

3:03   black figure is sitting on the floor in front of Sutton as tho admiring her dance, *and the organ, joined by the chorus, is shifting back to its praise of the Lord again,* – *Childs' voice out,* Sutton out, – and the other black figure (Wilson in a black wig and what might as well be a black leather jacket but seems satin) has taken over the flashlights and is doing his spastic number, very tall and angular, arms and legs going out, crouching, a very dramatic Elvis Presley street-fighter act, by its theatricality totally out of the scene's sci fi flatness, holding his flash lights like knives. Untoward events aboard, Hal is going berserk, the old Adam coming out in him. Multiple concentric light circles are appearing on the board, a multiple zeroing in. The tough-guy

23:05   dancer in black is playing his lights threateningly or conjuringly on the two little plexi-glass domes stage-right out front, twisting, stalk-

---

180 According to KM. the violin is here playing the ›real Einstein theme.‹

181 In the Paris *Overture*, Wilson used the plexiglass-covered orchestra pit as space ship control room to produce similar chatter by simultaneous miked readings from diverse texts.

ing, *the music, — it is tremendously loud now, — is disintegrating, a trying to get going, starting over and over again, an irritated, static rather than, as previously, dramatic music, Glass' crisis music,* and two figures, Childs and Sutton crawl out of the holes underneath the domes accompanied by smoke, — survivors saved, it would seem, rather than captives, — Wilson watching and dancing *and the music up full volume, dying a mighty death*, — and crawl down-stage, a gauze-cover with the print of a plane streaking over the top of the earth and some text, — half a page out of some technical manual, — coming down over the scene behind them as they crouch quasi-foetally down-stage. Behind the curtain, Andy De Groat is flying through and the now fully patterned board is pulsating to *the mighty organ's upbeat swirls of agony. The music snaps off* and the lights go out behind the drop.

23:08

*The music immediately resuming, — single, spaced-out notes at a much lower volume*,[182] — stage-hands enter behind the two genuflecting women and clear away the plexiglass covers. The curtain with its image is held for a moment, then Wilson, still in his black costume enters from stage-right to bring in a bench and places it behind the women, stands, acting out something like dejection, leaves, and a drop comes down behind them, covering the gauze-curtain, the same drop, for this after-play, as in the train scenes, the faint long cloud-streaks on it blue now, against a dark-blue sky. There is a spotlight on the 2 girls, *and a very light harmonious 1-2-3-4-5-6, 1-2-3-4-5-6-7-8 starts* as they slowly rise and assume seats on the bench. The blunt nose of a night-time vehicle, not much like a bus, its driver inside lit up dramatically from below, edges in at the opposite side of the stage. The girls, watching it, *start*, with slight held gestures, *intermittently talking and counting with the sweetly sad and gentle organ music and the gentle, serene Hosannah of the choral counting behind,* as the bus driver, Mr. Johnson, his voice not too loud but dominating, starts telling what seems a romantic story but is a gradually building moderately funny joke. All sound off, as the enormous yellow plush house curtains come down.

23:10

K 5

23:11

23:12

23:13

23:15

*Einstein on the Beach*[183] was as seductive as any of Wilson's previous pieces, but differed from them

182 The »descending bass line« that started the opera, »root movement« of its principal »5 chord,« »cadential« theme's »material.«

183 For a fashionable and brilliant analysis of *Einstein*, I refer the reader to the

by its vaccuity: tho in fact not without content, it took one in as pure surface, aesthetically;

by being composed but not developing: its content divorced from its form, an actual structuration may be inferred, but its apparent structure is a mere formality;

by the dilution of Wilson's earlier august presentation of personal visions to Cute Realism (style of the Broadway musical comedy): ingratiating humor has replaced whimsey, abstraction from real life the juxtaposition of personal data, the exploitation of cliché its use;

by a resolution of the tension between imagery and dreamlike movement in favor of the images: Wilson not only cut out the slow motion defining his earlier theatre (so that his second star's, Sheryl Sutton's fine solitary walks are static images), but virtually eliminated displacements other than off-hand serial entrances, assigning performers places in the images and on stage: and so, foregoing development, made of the now predominant imagery a serial exposition of flat pictures, – the stage in *Einstein* has lost the depth Wilson gave it in his earlier pieces, and the stage sets are now just that, – and stunning, – instead of being, as earlier, mental environments;

by replacing the epiphany of personalities by the exhibitions of applied skills: it's a cast of performers, not of people;

and by a change from duration to measured time: *Einstein* comes in sub-divided pieces, is marked by cuts instead of by beginnings and terminations.

This left the splendid rudiments of a conventional New York musical, a shuffle of painted scenes and engineering works, their awesome scale mitigated by their appeal: for each of these immensely costly constructs (in the sparse mathematical baroque of the contemporary Westphalian engravings) was homey too. And Wilson's genius for spectacle was undiminished: it was all beautiful.

The music and the spectacle were unrelated. One heard one piece and saw another, and noted that they divided time the same way: as tho Wilson and Glass had referred to the same ur-piece, a purely temporal structure. The cooperation[184] between music and spectacle worked this way: the energy deployed by Glass sustained the admiration of

characteristically dimwitted essay by Craig Owens in the Fall 1977 issue of *October* (# 4).

184 »*Einstein on the Beach* is the first opera that Bob Wilson and I have done together. It was jointly conceived. We began working over two years ago when we decided to do this piece together, chose the subject and made the outline. We chose Einstein as a subject for a couple of reasons: I was originally interested

one's eyes, and the steady circus of minor visible events so splintered the music that undisturbed by its defined variety one could give oneself to the scenery's painterly bravura. An occasional concordance of statement was less important than the semblance of a general concordance of subject matter. The styles were disparate: cumulative repetition enriched by mutations, a progressive structure that seems itself the work-process of its creation (Glass) vs. sustained exposure of major themes subjected to minute fractures, extrinsic structuration of anxiety (Wilson): a naively exuberant vs. an insidiously elegant style. A Beaumarchais spectacle scored by Wagner.[185]

in doing something to do with science fiction. Although Bob was at first not so interested in this, about a week later he came back and said: »Look! What about Einstein?.« This fit in perfectly with what I wanted to do.« (Phillip Glass interview by Maxime de la Falaise, Interview, Feb. '77)

»The music for »Einstein on the Beach« was written in the spring, summer and fall of 1975. Bob Wilson and I worked directly from a series of his drawings which eventually formed the designs for the sets. Prior to that period, we had reached agreement on the overall length of the work, its divisions into 4 acts, 9 scenes and 5 knee plays, and the general thematic content. We also determined the makeup of the company – 4 principal actors, 12 singers doubling when possible as dancers and actors, a solo violinist, and the amplified ensemble of keyboards, winds and voices with which my music is usually associated.

The company came together for the first time during the major rehearsal period which began in December, 1975 and lasted for three months. I worked with the singers and rehearsed the dance sections with Andy DeGroat and the dancers. Bob Wilson, working with the company, set the action to the music. The sets were built by Broggi Brothers, Milan, under his supervision, in May and June of 1976. At the same time, in New York City, a highly flexible sound system, capable of mixing and balancing speaking voices, singing voices and amplified instruments, was designed and built by Kurt Munkacsi with Gregory Shriver. The company reassembled in Avignon, France in early July for a final three-week rehearsal period, and the opera was premiered at the Avignon Festival on July 25, 1976.

In a general way, the three main visual themes of the opera (Train/Trial/Field) are linked to three main musical themes.« (Glass, Notes, part 1.)

»For Einstein, when I was setting these actions Phil would tell me about the music and what the counts were and how many sections there were and I would map out something along those lines and they fit together with his music. Sometimes I worked against the music, sometimes with it. Before that we made overall decisions about the length of the piece and the number of sections. When we decided to do an opera together we would meet once a week and just talk about it. We would talk about the length, what sort of space we wanted to work in, and how to treat the subject matter and what subject. We made the decision to work on Einstein and that it would be about five hours long. Then when we worked separately, I worked on the settings.« (Einstein at the Met (an operatic interview), Bob Wilson talks to Maxime de la Falaise, Interview, Feb. '77)

185 »Philip Glass was born on January 31, 1937, in Baltimore, Maryland, received a BA degree from the University of Chicago in 1956 and an MS degree from the

Wilson's earlier pieces had no evident structure.[186] One suspected there had been a work-scaffolding and that it had been dismantled, or else was buried in the piece. It didn't matter, was not even relevant: he'd

Juilliard School of Music in 1962. Between 1964 and 1966 he lived in Paris, returning to New York in 1967. By 1968 he had formed an ensemble of amplified instruments which is currently the main medium of his music. Some of the original members of the group – Dickie Landry (saxophone, flute, piccolo), Jon Gibson (saxophone, electric organ), Arthur Murphy (electric piano) – still play with the ensemble. More recent members are Robert Prado (electric piano, trumpet), Richard Peck (saxophone), and Rusty Gilder (trumpet). Kurt Munkasci is responsible for the design and fabrication of the channel sound system and also assists at concerts.«
(Avalanche, Summer 1972, p. 27) –

I thought Glass' music was the grandest music by a 20th century white man I have heard. By its development and defined variety it seemed to me a breakthrough in his development. Its expressiveness seemed astonishing to me, given its formality. It seems to me to express a joyous nihilism suiting me. Not understanding music, the only response to it I can verbalise is in terms of visual images. E.g. the music, – I believe it was *Music with Changing Parts* (1970), – Glass' Ensemble played at the 4th of their concerts inaugurating the Institute of Art and Urban Resources' Idea Warehouse at the Clocktower at 108 Leonard Street below Soho (Feb. 2, 9, 16 and 23, 1975) evoked in me the image of »an icebreaker/the Titanic/an old big cargo hull, rearing up over a float of ice or ice shelf or hill of ice, all blue white around, but bearing down or going over and down or sinking also; in that act, forever in that act, or at the moment of this uprearing-and-over-and-down reaching motion (which repeats its linear shape), during an instant of this act, or repeating it in a series over and over again, a perspective of such beak-like inverted ›Ls,‹ curving rising line sharply joined to curving, barely convex down-hanging, -tending, -falling line: the black lines in my mind, the color of ice in the ice; and perhaps this ship is rather a slowly shifting iceberg itself, or the large motion of a paw of air thermodynamically up-and-over-floating: whether there are many nervous hearts inside and cries in the unstewarded corridors, foolish heads, opening and closing eyes, failing affections, moments in lives, or a black untenanted space (volume) merely is unclear: all this could also be a balloon steadily rising slowly, some pastel color, in humorous grey city air: but that repeated cutting motion of descent, disappearance, that vanishing in a last vestige of forward motion, joining of solid to water by immersion, dying out of motion, self-giving-over of impulse and direction into a self-ending curlicue seemed my upmost inner pictorial event/content exposed to the sustained warm bath of the music's cumbersome post-Gregorian adumbration, all single sustainments in sheaves of white radii, lines of fog, blueprint imprints in hair-thin candle-wax, sheaves in several curving planes, rectilines, scatter-pointed, single notes of the clarity of simplicity over an earth of unqualitative, marrowed-out neo-sound, not rhythm, but repetition of pulse movement as of a tiny tricky heart under foetal breastskin in an animal family scene or a gleaming laboratory, gotten going, keeping on happening: but its continuo suspect. The in-between layering levels of single-noted sound arising shivering between mathematical positions multi-defined by notes played or produced curved through the vast light-colored low-ceilinged, 6th floor downtown loft, hill-scape outlines in mauve or unemphatic muddled purple, reaching down and through the seated frozen audience persons over the floor. The continuo itself shifted itself

found a way to have his pieces *develop* (as dreams develop) – had substituted the internal temporal structuration of development for traditional whole/parts (internal and/or external) structure.[187] His

constantly minutely, series of micro-themes gear-shifted one into another/the-same, the rug's figure of figures over which in a small-seasonal succession rose the inceptions never more than sheer beginning indices of possible melodies from individual wind instruments or possibly the keys of other consoles: momento of 16th or 17th century Roman Catholic indoor celebrations (services), beggarly in their aggregate beauty, – open to the charge of prettiness.«

In Glass' music, the elements of music have been rudimentified, it seems, to an extreme: a minimum of notes, the octave and conservatory practice runs in dominant positions, repetition of note-changes, simple note-patterns, few rhythmical counter-points ... Abrupt transitions (e.g. from Glass' electric organ to the chorus, or from counting chants to fa-sol chants) and very gradual shifts within the scads of notes issuing from Glass' keyboard, a note not there before substituted for another so that in the package, still issuing, everything really is a quantum up or a quantum down because the one note is a new note, up or down. Glass to an extent here is presenting music as music the way modern American painters represent painting as painting: the conventions and elements of the art/craft/medium are not just made explicit, they are explicitly, ostensibly, formally elements, form-elements of the music: the reduction of art to the simplest (with which Glass here builds up a good deal of variety and – I would think – some nice complexities shows the structure, incorporates into the music the tools of music making. Plus the music has a grandly devilish feeling to it, the pure hosiannas of artistic (or other) elation (which transcends and loses its object/cause/occasion), as tho it vented the pride of music-making. These two aspects of it perhaps are mostly what impress me.

It shares them with Michael Snow's *Central Region* which works out to possibly the first grand work of film as art (in its own right): tho' its focus on camera motion makes it possibly a little more special than Glass' *Einstein*. It has the same post-religious elation and the same modernity of making the medium formally explicit, – the art work as process before your eyes (or coming to your ears) of constructing it: according to some explicit rules, posed *within* this process as artificial if not arbitrary, as set up, instituted, chosen rules of making, out of similarly artificial elements. Both also make a royal *extension* (in time) – built up from repetition (variation within repetition, but the repetition key-device) – important, essential, explicit: the art-work not apologising for itself by brevity, not humbly ingratiating itself (e.g. by a 2-hr duration, by a mereness of time) into adventitious consumers' making-a-living or getting-by schedules. They share a certain savagery and/or brutality: not molded for the eye-ear of the status-upholder. They have disco-drive, are not efforts of feeding mini-structures to individuals who withhold themselves while seeing and listening. They are not for dope-addicts either, tho: not religious, but contained within their perceptual media, – seeing, hearing: you are invited on a ride, to a swinging feast (of that sort, so delimited, self-defining).

R. Foreman's statement in the $10.- »work-book« (?) sold at the Met performance formulated things I believe I sensed myself, but could not have put even w/ his statement's deficient clarity: »Philip Glass' compositions are all based upon the premise of a performing group of five to eight musicians. All amplified instruments

363

slow motion, the mental-environment imagery were the means for this effect: that, his images being personal, he was able to make them metamorphose out of a compelling inner necessity, was the essence of

(electric organs, viola, cello, soprano saxophones) play in unison throughout each piece. The method is constant in Phil Glass's music: simple addition allowing for the expansion and contraction of musical phrases, and simultaneous playing. I would relate the ›additive‹ nature of Glass's structure to his own growing vision of his music as primarily a kind of ›performance piece‹ rather than a disembodied sound phenomenon which stands by itself. The compositional exploration of addition and unison playing leads directly to a consciousness that the performers themselves are cellular units who maintain their identity, just as the musical phrase is added to but never manipulated and reshuffled. Unison playing reveals each player as a unit ›added‹ to the next, contrary to the normal situation where performers intertwine their musical lines in such a way that they lose their identity in the service of a composition that exists as a kind of transcendental structure.

This method of composition then is a total rejection of serial method, for process here is the subject rather than the source of the music. The web of lucidly clear, reiterated yet slightly ›shifting‹ sound created by Glass is not to be understood as a disembodied ›force‹ of sound, snatched by the artist out of some normally ›unheard‹ level of sound ›elsewhere.‹ The commentators who have up to now written of Glass's music err in linking it to Eastern music (which might indeed be thought of as a sound continuum snatched from elsewhere). Though there is a certain similarity in the texture of shifting sound, Glass's compositions are rather to be understood as performance situations in which musicians (and spectators) put themselves in a certain ›place,‹ located through the coordinates of the specific phrase. Then this place – which is not an evocative composed ›elsewhere‹ but rather the here-and-now of a chosen method of procedure – slowly opens, becomes slowly filled and informed with the shared ›space‹ of consciousness which is founded at each moment as the spectator ›allows‹ the piece to exist.

The capacity which the work's process of ›being-present‹ brings to consciousness is not the capacity to ›feel,‹ to experience a variation of an internal ›yes‹ or ›no;‹ but rather a capacity of attention in which the internal ›noticing‹ seems cleansed of the need to constantly check whether or not it is pleasure or pain. The noticing of process itself becomes exhilarating.« (R. Foreman, *EB* »workbook.«)

What Foreman says of the immanence of structure to sound in Glass' music seems true to me, tho I think he confuses (speaking of having seen them perform, not about listening to their records) the makers and the making of sound-elements with those sound-elements: the Glassian performer (sound-maker, not structure-maker) is as irrelevant to Glass' music as the Foremanian performer (Kate Manheim excepted) to Foreman's theatre. His next-to-the-last sentence is true: the Glass- or Snow-accurately, structural harmony. What is sought for here is a new solution to the has done: but in part, I suspect, because both men in fact do aim to please, and bring it off. – Cf. e.g. the to me displeasing theatricality of the singing on the over-dubbed, »space-rock« *North Star*, and cf., infra, Glass' reference to »moment-to-moment content and »flavor«« and his emphasis on »sound« as distinct from »structure.«

– Glass traces the music as follows: »Einstein on the Beach« is part of an ongoing musical project begun with »Another Look at Harmony« in Spring, 1975. This is, in turn, based on »Music in 12 Parts« (completed in 1974), which developed a

it. The superficially unconnected images on view at any one time cohered for the same reason.

Ostensibly an alternation of graphic themes generates the structure

vocabulary of techniques to apply to problems of harmonic structure, or, more accurately, structural harmony. What is sought for here is a new solution to the problems of harmonic usage, where the evolution of the harmonic material can become the basis of an overall formal structure intrinsic to the music itself (and without the harmonic language giving up its moment-to-moment content and »flavor«).

Parts 1 and 2 of »Another Look at Harmony« became the basis of Act I, Scene 1 (Train) and Act II, Scene 1 (Field) of the opera and were the starting points from which additional material and devices were developed.« (Glass, *Notes*, part 2, p. 1) –

I note that following a premiere (?) of *Music in 12 parts* at the Whitney Museum in May 1971, – the Ensemble gave a first *complete* performance of it at Town Hall in July of 1974, – Glass was reported in the fall-of-1971 issue of Avalanche as feeling that his »latest work, while retaining the additive process and rhythmic unison, treats the instruments polyphonically, which makes for very gradual changes in rhythmic content and overall texture:« this may relate to the 1977 remark cited supra re »structural harmony.«

An interview of Glass' of June 1972 gives a splendid over-view of his enterprise till then, – note, as to the change from »structure« to »sound« around 1970:

»PG: In the late sixties some people, including myself, were working in a structural way, a very reduced way. For example, in my ensemble we were playing pieces in unison – actually playing only one line of music – and there were other musicians working along equally formal lines.

Yvonne (Rainer) and I were talking about dancers and she said that was also true of people working in dance at that time. In the last two years there's been a real change of sensibility, in the content of the experience that we're interested in. In my work, it's taken the form of becoming interested in other aspects of music. Let's put it this way, my earlier pieces *Two Pages, Music in Fifths* were very clear structures. I thought that I was making structures in sound and that's what interested me most about those pieces. When that problem was no longer urgent, I began listening to the »sound« of the music and I found that had become more interesting than the structure. It didn't mean that I had to abandon the structures. In fact I needed them. However, I had become less interested in purity of form than in the kind of almost psycho-acoustical experiences that happened while listening to the music.

I wasn't listening to the piece in terms of some kind of architecture anymore. I think audiences may have been ahead of me in that respect – when I was still superconscious of structure and purity of form my audiences were already picking up on the sound. I had to get over my preoccupation with formalism before I began noticing what I was doing. And in the last two years this has become the real thrust of my work.

Interviewer: When specifically did you become aware of this?

In the Spring of 1970. We were playing in a theatre-in-the-round made of wood in Minneapolis. It was like playing inside a Stradivarius. It was the most beautiful sound I ever dreamed of. We were playing then the piece we're going to play at L'Attico tonight called *Music in Similar Motion*, a piece I wrote in '69. We were

of *Einstein,* each graphic theme not a specific image, but imagery associated with a word. Trains (1), a court room (2), the field (3) alternate 1-2-3-1-2-3-1-2-3. Each occurrence of a theme is a scene.

rehearsing in the hall and when we go into the end of the piece, I thought I heard someone singing. I *did* hear someone singing, in fact, and I stopped, thinking Arthur, one of the guys who likes to horse around, was improvising and I said, come on, who's singing, and we looked around because we thought someone was there. It was that real an experience. It wasn't us playing. But there was no one in the room; as I said, it was a rehearsal. So we started playing again and the sound came back, and of course then we realized that the sound happened because of the accoustical properties of that room and because of the texture of the music. I talked to Jon about it the other day and he too remembered it very clearly.

. . . . that was the first time I actually began to think about music in this way, although I had been writing this kind of music since '66 . . . In terms of the phenomenon of sound. And a composer who really thinks about the phenomenon of sound is La Monte. I don't think that's true of Terry or of Steve; Steve is very committed to structure.

Formal structure lost its importance, it was no longer an urgent problem. That's how I work, certain things seem urgent to me and they have to be done at that time; they become my obsessions. I had worked out a very broad vocabulary that would allow me to make different kinds of musical structures, and I didn't see the point of repeating it endlessly in all its variations. I had achieved it very clearly in some earlier pieces. *Music in Fifths* was beautiful in that way; it was structurally self-revealing. We haven't played it in two or three years, but I heard a tape of it the other day. I thought it was a good piece, but . . .« (Avalanche, 1912)

186 Musically, according to his account, Glass' opera leaves out or separates as incidental the dance (Field) and Trial Scenes. We might say it consists of the Knee plays, Train scenes and the Spaceship scene. ». . . one can say that, in a general way, the opera begins with a 19th-century train and ends with a 20th-century spaceship. Events occur en route – trials, prison, dances – and throughout the continuity of the Knee Plays.« (Glass, *Notes,* part 1.) The knee-plays »form a play in themselves (Glass, Notes, part 1.).« They relate to the scenes »as the seeds which flower and take form (ib.)« in the scenes. Glass here in fact rejects Wilson's play as an arbitrary composite: and rightly so: the musically incidental scenes are intrusive in the Wilson-work, e.g. the trial scenes a separate play. The reason for this failure of Wilson's is that the play's real content, cf. infra, is present in it only as setting and ambiance, not as theme; and that Wilson failed to find themes appropriate to it. Of course, he would never, like Glass, want to make Einstein a central figure or explicit theme.

187 Consider e.g.: »*Stalin* was designed so that the first act (The Beach) was parallel to the seventh act (The Planet), the second act (The Victorian Drawing-room) paralleled the sixth act (The Victorian Bedroom), the third act (The Cave) paralleled the fifth act (The Temple). The fourth act (The Forest) was in the middle, and the scene of the death of Stalin's first wife was the center of the fourth act and of the entire piece.

The parallels between the various acts were based on similarities in the type of space and on the repetition of certain patterns of movement, images, activities, gestures, and signs. For example, in both the first and the seventh acts, the stage design emphasized open space with one painted drop. In both acts, movement

Each scene, except the first two field scenes, which are amorphous dances, has something of a climax; each scene, other than those 2 and other than the 3rd train and trial scenes, either by repetition or as stages of a presentation divides into 3 or 4 parts. The sequence is segmented and framed by short tableaux (called ›knees‹) in front of the curtain, each a close-up in the same place of the two main figures in the play together: k 1 2 k 3 1 k 2 3 k 1 2 3 k. The program calls these segments ›acts,‹ but inasmuch as they have neither evident internal unity nor are evidently stages of a development, they are not acts. The segmentation is ineffective, does not enrich the perceived structure: the ›knees‹ only produce a secondary rhythm of alternation. (Nor are they joints: they do not link what they separate.) A device of scenic after-images, not quite consistently used, rhythmically differentiates the apparent structure: k 1 1′ 2 2′ k 3 1 1′ k 2 2′ 3 k 1 2 3 3′ k, or more precisely, since the first two field scenes are not part of the apparent structure: k 1 1′ 2 2′ k (3) 1 1′ 2 2′ (3) k 1 2 3 3′ k. The alternation of graphic themes (secondarily that of groups of those with ›knees‹) provides an effective SURFACE STRUCTURE, even tho each of the themes is progressively subverted. The theme of trains turns into that of the solitary mathematical physicist (mental power in our age), that of a court room into that of lying on one's bed (privacy), then into a levitating pillar of light (energy), the theme of the field into the interior of a space vessel (space age technology). Alternation remained effective because the alterations are camouflaged, a constancy is maintained in some dimension: the bed is part of the court room to begin with, as is the space ship of the field and the pillar of light of the bed, and the mathematician's building has the outline of the train. It remained effective even tho the camouflage was not wholly effective, e.g. one was apt not to make the association of the rising pillar of light with the luminous foot of the bed (nor to see it as the bed itself rising[188]), the sameness of shape of the train

occurred on horizontal planes. In both acts, performers carried out a particular seven-part sequence of movements, a runner passed with a letter, a girl played in the sand, a dance was performed by a padded figure, and a man appeared with a bird. A »Mammy« dance at the end of the first act was paralleled by an »Ostrich« dance at the beginning of the seventh act. At the beginning of the first act, a Stalin poster and Ivan the Terrible were juxtaposed; the same juxtaposition of Stalin and Ivan the Terrible occurred in the last scene of the seventh act.« (Frantisek Deak, *The Byrd Hoffman School of Byrds/Robert Wilson*, The Drama Review, T 62, June 1974, p. 68).

188 »in the fourth act ... all that remains is the bed. It is alone in this visual space and rises up and flies away.« (Wilson, interview, Interview, Feb. 77)

and the building may not have penetrated, the association of the interior of the space ship with the flying saucers over the field was only a thought. And it was effective even tho the first two field scenes did not come across as parts of the play at all, but as relaxing dance interludes. But tho this alternation (with the help of the program) structured experience of the play, this structure was felt to be a merely external, arbitrary ordering, a composition: for the three graphic themes have no evident relation to one another.

Being unrelated, their alternation is specifically surface structure. They are genuinely unrelated: I don't think they related in any way in Wilson's mind.[189] Nor does their use in this play suggest they separately had any importance to him: unlike e.g. the burial tomb pyramid, the old man reading, the ice man coming, the dark lady, they don't matter to him. He used them as insignificant chance motifs: without hope that their occurrence to him or the access of the energy to decide to use them would certify their significance.

This is why the play is vaccuous. Wilson's imagination in fact failed him, e.g. the way it didn't fail him when the graphic themes of beach, drawing room, cave occurred to him before *Freud*. And it similarly, – and necessarily, since these insignificant point-of-departure themes meant nothing to him, – failed him when it came to their elaboration:[190] the track signal post (elaboration #1 of the train theme) lacks the psychic energy charge of the haystack-in-the-drawing-room in *Freud*. Etc. Not being able to think of any concretisations charged, for one, with one's psychic energy, – the incapacity for reification, – is the non-artist's definition: also it is the artist's recurrent desperate

189 »As for the trial and prison, I just thought about the dramas of our time: courtroom dramas, Watergate, people even in Brazil rushing home to watch their TVs in an effort to follow these dramas.« (Wilson, interview, Interview, Feb. 77)

190 »The different kinds of precious stones – as they occur, as they are encountered – are by no means good, fresh and green; the desirable, the coveted, the longed-for, the wanted. For there is the so-called mother. It is only a common stone, an ordinary stone; one not honored nor desirable; not regarded. Wherever it is, it is passed by; it is bypassed or just cast aside where one dwells.

But this, the so-called mother of the precious stone, is not the whole thing. It is only where it is placed: perhaps well within, or on its side; not all, only a little, a bit, a small part, a fragment there wherever it is sprinkled, located.

And those of experience, the advised, these look for it. In this manner (they see,) they know where it is: they can see that it is breathing, (smoking,) giving off vapor. Early, at early dawn, when (the sun) comes up, they find where to place themselves, where to stand; they face the sun. And when the sun has already come up, they are truly very attentive in looking. They look with diligence; they no longer blink; they look well« (Br. B. de Sahagún, *General History*, bk. 11, *Earthly Things*, 8th chapter.)

situation. But Wilson went ahead without materials: an act of desperation.

The irrelevance of the play's themes and the desperate situation it puts the artist in are formalised by the play. The train is shown as unable to go anywhere; its arrests and restartings structure its (initial!) appearance and are paralleled musically and by that scene's chief parallel action (Childs' dance); its landscape comes apart[191] each time it gets stuck; the collapse of the train signal ends the scene, its climax: the train neither can nor can't go. The (unmoving but divided) time of the trial is symbolically destroyed as climax of the court room's first appearance: in its second appearance the court room comes apart as did the landscape. The field as defined, – plain for horizontal motion, – is destroyed by the arrival of a space vehicle and/or by the end of the world in nuclear fission. Each of the themes is supplanted: trains by the mathematical physicist's building, the court room by the invasion of a bed; the open field by the interior of a space ship. These supplantings would in Wilson's earlier plays have appeared as metamorphoses: but here they are discardings of the given themes which we see dropped. By its treatment of its themes, the spectacle thus presents itself as the product of exhaustion, of the normal person's neurotic condition. The themes one can think of don't work.

That none of the themes gets anywhere (that of trains no more than the train, that of a courtroom no more than the trial in progress, that of fields, no more than the dance danced on them), and that instead each is destroyed (both by a graphically literal disintegration and by supplantation by another theme) is a parallel development of each of the themes, is one of the play's generic themes, and provides a SECONDARY SURFACE STRUCTURE to the play and to our experience of it, a negative structure (compared either to conventional plots or to Wilson's earlier plays' development) more subtle than the alternation schema, – more subtle because of the camouflage of the supplantations (providing an appearance of continuity) and because the disintegrations are partly metaphoric, e.g. the trial theme's abortion

191 That Wilson may have thought of the vertical stripe of light as an atomic explosion obliterating a landscape by the old-fashioned train defined as 19th century is suggested by the description of the corresponding scene in the outline of a film based on E/B: »It's an old fashion locomotive, emitting a steady stream of smoke while blasts of steam surround the wheels. Suddenly the screen is divided by a vertical light, so strong it obliterates all the other images. Just as quickly it's gone, and we see the train, further along, still crossing the field.« (Film-outline, RW and PG)

by the blotting out of the court room clock, the train trip's by the leaning over of the track signal, and partly generic, e.g. the splitting apart of the train landscape, the disappearance of half the court room, a scrim's hint at the field's destruction by a picture's suggestion of a nuclear holocaust.[192] It is a modern structure to the extent that it shows the artist at work, a modernity the music also hints at. But the pattern is formalised. One doesn't see the artist, one sees pictures that refuse to become stories. The music conversely shows sound that does succeed in becoming music: it similarly substituted formalism for a show of the artist at work by making the development seem autonomously that of the sound.

A figure of fun, a black man, and a cute kid apart, the play has two central characters and a set piece: the other performers are singers and dancers and part of the scenery. The set piece, a man doing calculations in the air, variously reoccurs throughout the play[193] and has a scene (the train-theme's third appearance, as building) of its own. The play's title draws attention to him by helping to define him for us.[194]

192 This SECONDARY STRUCTURE emerges very clearly in the series of dark drawings in which Wilson has sketched the play as tho for a cartoon movie, a somber comic book contrasting illuminatingly with the play's musical-comedy surface. (»Robert Wilson/ drawings,« Paula Cooper Gallery, NYC, Nov. 30- Dec. 24, 1976.)

The lighting effects that *make* this picture sequence were absent in the stage production, sacrificed to its luxuries. If the spectacle had had the musical tension they provide to the stasis of the picture sequences, the spectacle's secondary surface structure would have been primary. The play would then have been about this black landscape of frustration or anxiety.

193 . . . »sort of measures the time span of Einstein's life: when he was a young man there were steam engines and when he died a few years ago we were flying in space machines. It's a graphic way of illustrating the time span.« (RW, interview, Interview)

194 »En fait, le titre de mes productions est un substitut à la partie narrative absente, si bien qu'en donnant ce fil narratif dans le titre, je n'ai plus besoin de raconter vraiment l'histoire, elle est déjà connue. *Einstein*, par exemple, c'est toute une histoire et nous la connaissons bien. Tout ce que nous voyons dans ce contexte va lui être alors associé, dans la mesure même ou nous apprenons à voir les choses à partir de ce qu'il a pensé . . .« (Wilson, interview, Tel Quel, #s 71/73, autumn 1977). »I always thought the opera was about Einstein. I got the title from Ambassador Hoveyda, who's always encouraged me and given me ideas. He said, »You've done Freud, Stalin and Queen Victoria. Why not Einstein?« I worked also from a photo of Einstein which was a gift from Paul Walter who collects photos. He gave it to me after I'd started on the opera. I started looking at it and I looked at other photos and I noticed the wrist watch, starched white shirts and baggy grey pants held up by his suspenders. He wore black sneakers. Everyone on stage was dressed as Einstein. He seemed a sort of Everyman. He was easy to identify by his clothes. He represented himself that way. He always said, »I'm not

The two central figures are the only performers cast as persons, they are opposites (black and white, calm and nervous, inward and show-off, prosecutor and defendant), and the spectacle relates them to one another (both by their roles and by their placements on stage). The equation of these opposite and opposing figures, – by a graphic metaphor that is part of the climax of the first court room scene, and by a parallel (the parallel underscored by identical costuming) withdrawal (the black woman's into romantic fantasy in the second train scene, the white woman's into day dreaming in the second court room scene), – so that in the end (the third field scene and the fifth ›knee‹) they are the same,[195] – contributes a further element of APPARENT STRUCTURE, something like an ACTION, and the three figures give the spectacle a SURFACE UNITY.

In the actual watching of the play, the alternation of trivial themes predominates, the obscurely related heroines provide a kind of continuity, the Einstein-representative and they some kind of unity, and between the non-story of the heroines and the pointless leapfrog of those overdefined visually overwhelming themes, a somber PATTERN of stasis-followed-by-the-appearance-of-a-crack peeps out. By way of content, structure and definition, that seems about all there is to the spectacle, except for a certain AMBIANCE. This AMBIANCE is relative to its figures in fact the play's CONTENT. But one is apt to take in this AMBIANCE as a SETTING for the aforementioned, light-heartedly inspired in the director by his apparently no less light-hearted pick of a title; a contemporary predilection in his choice of elements of presentation.

These elements provide a setting in which Mind qua Intellect[196] is engaged in the control of Energy qua Substance, specifically, is by mathematical physics creating space age technology:

extraordinary. I'm just an ordinary man!« I thought of him as a dreamer. He differed from other nineteenth century scientists who wouldn't dare be mystical, they were all so intellectual.« (Wilson, interview, Interview, Feb. 77)

195 Childs is central to the 1st train- and the 2nd trial- scenes, Sutton to the 2nd train-scene, they both are, in opposition, central to the 1st trial-scene, and, to a lesser extent (and not in opposition) to the 3rd field-scene. The first 4 ›knees‹ present them in close-up doing the same things in different ways relating to their opposite-ness. In the fifth ›knee,‹ they do the same thing the same way, at peace.

196 Glass conceived of Einstein as the opera's central figure, and thought of him as represented by the violin-playing Einstein: as outside the action, a »Witness;« and may have thought of the »cadential,« »5-chord« music attending the train-to-spaceship progress as defining this to him innocent on-looker's – a mathematical and Jewish technician-scientist like himself, – view of this progress, a negative view.

The last page of calculations made by Einstein.
From Banesh Hoffman, *Albert Einstein Creator and Rebel*, —
one of Wilson's sources (© New American Library).

The effort is presented as lethal, along the lines of the idea that since mathematical physics has understood matter as energy, its logical employment is the general transformation of matter into energy. We get blown up. Whether this is good or bad does not become clear: from a Buddhist view it would not be so bad, — annihilation is salvation. Nor is the ambiance of this setting necessarily anti-intellectual:

intellect appears to swing with cosmic energy, energy seems essentially Pythagorean.

The man developing equations in the air is not the exclusive or even main carrier of the TOPIC (appearing as SETTING) of mathematical physics, i.e. the dissection by numbers of ultimate reality, of the flow of energy as registration of its necessities. The music, product of as well as an actual piece of mathematical physics,[197] energy in its mathematical form; the chorus counting,[198] a modern form of the Greek chorus' statement of fate; the incessant note-taking by everyone, including the two heroines (it's the main activity of the play); and the pervasive reference to clock time, provide the setting of mathematical physics. The underground of energy emerges not only as musical form, but as luminosity, partly through Wilson's innovative use of luminous bodies as parts of the stage setting, – the third trial scene is entirely devoted to the levitation of a luminous body, – partly (in the first train scene) when the world splits apart and reveals just light. The link of mind to energy, electronic technology, is the topic of the third field scene, the play's last scene, prepared by the third ›knee:‹ mental (computer-operated) control of motion by means of electronic feed-back.[199] – Trains, trials, frolicking on meadows screen this SETTING as well as anything else in our lives the corresponding reality.

The spectator is apt to relate the spectacle's formal pattern (SECONDARY SURFACE-STRUCTURE) of stasis/disintegration to this SETT-

---

197 »Einstein was also a scientist involved in all the imagery of modern science that we are accustomed to. My music is something that I subjectively associate to modern machinery, engines and motors and that kind of thing. The idea of doing a piece that combined all these aspects was very appealing to me, it came close enough to the theme of science that interested me that we could arrive at the subject matter together.« (Glass, Interview).

198 The *E/B*-film-outline suggests Wilson intended a marginal evocation of geometry. In the film-equivalent of the first dance (Field) scene, the dancers are »making geometric patterns almost like moving points,« in the second, their »movements make visible geometries.« – The eclipse of the sun, itself to Wilson reference to a scientific confirmation of the theory of relativity, in the first Trial scene is accompanied by a blotting out of the 18th century (film-script!) courtroom by »various instruments clearly associated with scientific experiments,« which (the bed!) Wilson seems to associate with the dreams of physicists.

199 The outline of a film-treatment of *E/B* suggests Wilson thought of the scene of this Knee play as the interior of a space-ship: »Once again we are in the white room. This time part of a large control room. The two women operate switches on a large board. This is the interior of a spaceship. A chorus sings, quickly repeating a series of numbers. The movement of the switches sets off patterns of light on the board.« (Film-outline, p. 4)

ING as the setting's catastrophic potential. Train landscape and court room appear subject to fission, the field-scenes are not only relaxing dance interludes but distribute the approach of the end (as signified by the space-ship's arrival) throughout the play. It's a jolly space-ship as it comes, and when we get to look inside, things are as usual, partly routine, partly people are carrying on. Our annihilation is merely hinted at by an alarming pattern of lights on a board, by a picture on a transparent screen. The vessel seems to save the heroines. This ambiguity may be a welcome to our demise. It also serves to keep the setting incidental.

We are less apt to relate the heroines to the setting. They perform as formal elements, create images, – Childs' dance (1st train scene) and monologues (2nd trial scene), Sutton's walks (1st and second trial scenes). Their parts deviate into anecdotal story-telling, – Childs' Patty (2nd trial scene), Sutton's Romantic phantasy (2nd train scene). They relate to one another as identifying opposites. Their stance is withdrawal followed by detachment. But if one does relate them to the setting, they figure as The (non-intellectual) Individual, private and guilty, material body disposed to dramatic fantasy, whose survival is at stake: collaborator and victim, possibly survivor: refusing to relate to such a setting.

Relating them to it, viewing the play as succession of PERCEPTUAL POTENTIALS, fraught images, but THINKING about it a little, a BASE-STRUCTURATION, the auto-structuration of a development, paralleling but not coinciding with its division into ›acts,‹ emerges:

Act I, scene 1 (train) and 2 (trial). The individual in the world, caught up in activity. The activity is abortive progress, the individual's participation in it frenesy or suffering in place. The involvement seems to end in the individual's destruction, but perhaps only in withdrawal. Act II, scene 1 (field). Interlude. Approach of the end of the world and/or of salvation.

Act II, scene 2 (train), act III, scene 1 (trial). The individual withdraws into private phantasy.

Act III, scene 2 (field). Interlude. Approach of the end of the world and/or salvation.

Act IV, scene 1 (train), scene 2 (trial). The forces governing the individual's life: mind and energy.

Act IV, scene 3 (field). The space age, electronic computation in command, mind's control over energy; and the destruction/salvation of the individual and of the world.

But in the watching of the play, the elements of the setting emerge only as formal and incidental elements. They are not perceived as subject matter, nor in their own nature, nor do their relations to one another or, especially, to the play's persons, inform one's experience of the play. Instead the three graphic themes and their alternation preoccupy one, surface elements irrelevant to Wilson and to oneself. One watches appearances and enjoys them aesthetically. The play's content remains contingent on interpretation.

Wilson failed to find images for what was on his mind. The themes he hit on do not relate to the content. He changed his style to divorce the spectacle from its content. Watching it, we see the meaningless alternation of meaningless themes, and perhaps the theme of failure.

*Nov., '76 – March '77.*

# I was sitting on my patio.

*I was sitting on my patio this guy appeared I thought I·was hal-
lucinating* (a non-Actors' Equity production of Richard Barr's at the
swish little West Village Cherry Lane Theatre (199 seats?), produced
(Soho Weekly News, v/19/77), including the 5-6 week tour preceding
the N.Y. run, at a cost of $30.000.–,[200] started its run on May 10th[201]
1977, didn't catch on, closed May 30th, a flop. Wilson wrote, and he
and Lucinda Childs supposedly co-directed it, they were the only
performers, Beverly Emmons did the universally praised lighting
design, – »down stage area in front of the performers bright and
well-defined, the upstage area (behind them) dim and vacant (Will.
Harris),« – that made it appear two-dimensional.

There was a small movie-screen fed from a back stage projector
suspended in the upper left of the proscenium, that from time to time
had home-movies of ducks, dogs, penguins on it, and occasional
language off a tape, and a ringing telephone, but essentially the play
consisted simply of Wilson's, then Childs' TALKING in a room, each
for 40 minutes and going through the same text,[202] imaginary or
day-dream dialogues,[203] paranoid in his case, schizophrenic in hers, –
in continually switching tonalities of sociability, mostly bland or
whimsically mad, but on the whole melodramatic in content, e.g.
the repeated »ready, aim, fire« (that Wilson tho not Childs rather
bore down on and dramatised, and that echoed a shot heard early
on, and a »don't shoot« in response to it.[204])[205]

200 $5.000.– of which went for the three pieces of furniture designed by Wilson,
a rectilinear reclining brushed aluminum chair upstage, stage-right, a wall glass
shelf with a long-stemmed glass on it, upstage, stage-left, and a little aluminum
telephone table, downstage, stage-left.

201 It has opened at Eastern Michigan University on April 5th.

202 The text of course didn't sound the same, and not only because Wilson has a
hard time remembering lines, but chiefly because they emphasised different things
and varied in the emotional and situational implications of their tonal gestures.

203 Tho the interlocutors were imaginary and one heard only one side of the
dialogue, the text was spoken as participation in dialogue, and dialogue was what
one heard: a succession, for each of them, of dialogues, because the situations
implied by the speech and the language continually – tho discontinuously –
differed or seemed to differ: evocation of quite different, unrelated situations
(relationships, events, histories) succeeding one another.

204 Several of my friends thought the dialogue was between a queer and a pick-up
who attacks him, a literally and metaphorically traumatic event for cruising
homosexuals addicted to real or make-belief heterosexuals as partners for the
scenarios of brief encounters or one-night stands. This may have been an esoteric

To me, this mirror-form talkie was about loneliness. The old men and women (of the lowest class) talking to themselves on the sidewalks of our big cities are the clear images of loneliness: they are always talking to imaginary others, by the invention of an interested listener creating their opportunity to express themselves forcefully and so to make an impression, – unlike the ragged solitary ranters, whose screaming not only serves self-affirmation, – they are continually fading away in their own eyes, – but expresses a craving for justice, and unlike those that talk to *themselves* while going about some task in their homes, by their mutterings, in the guise of mnemonic devices, doubling themselves into company.

Each would come on, the back, as the lights went up, a series of three tall blank white windows between black rectangles of wall, silently hold an image for a prolonged moment, – he angular, clean-cut, – his black shoes the only soft thing on the stage, – tensely, uncomfortably, lying-seated in an artificial pose on the linear abstraction of a couch for one, she standing in her black slacks and short little white pull-over,[206] with her back half toward the audience, just a woman, – then there would be a black-out, the lights would go on again, – the back wall now three book cases framed by the black verticals, filled with the serried backs of grey ledgers,[207] – and the talking would start: he making full use of the couch (doing most of his performance from there), the glass (fiddling with it much of the

reference of Wilson's, but an unimportant one: all his plays have references to murder in them, partly because it's on his mind, partly because it peps up interest.

205 Because of the nature of the text and the acting, especially Childs' acting, then also because of the elegant decor, the (approximate) verbal identity of the two texts became irrelevant, one focussed rather on the different characterisations by the two performers of a character that one fancied involved in some generalized situation of tension, anxiety, danger and decision-making in a multi-faceted way *denoted by* the text, semi-defined by it: one suppositionally inferred such a situation from the text, i.e.: one attributed a *meaning* to the text.

206 The script specifies: rayon pants and silk blouse.

207 Wilson's original image, in December 76, according to R. Kostelanetz (NY Times, May 8, 1977): »I've had the idea for a long time of a room with a lot of books, all placed neatly on shelves, and something slicing through the shelves. There is a telephone, and a telephone wire. There is a scrim or gauze over the front of the stage, and images are sometimes projected on it.« He was at this time thinking of it as a solo performance for himself, Kostelanetz says, and writing down lines as they came to him. By January, he described his ideas to Kostelanetz by drawing »a stage set that had three tall windows through which ... the audience could see the ocean,« but »several minutes after the play's opening ... the stage would suddenly change, and the windows completely fill with books.« He was now also thinking about a second performer, probably a woman.

time from some point on), and the telephone (picking up the receiver, putting it down on the floor, – the telephone would keep on ringing), she not using any of the props much, – at the end of her act standing up on the chaise longue (glass in hand?), with the back wall all the way up, revealing a brightly lit recess, all dead light. – The moment of voiceless introduction for each of them counterposed *them* to their talking selves.

The stage was gray (the carpeting), black and white, with touches of silver from the crystal wine glass and the straight-lined chair. The performers were dressed in black and white, – Bob got expensive clothes. The predominant impression was not that of minimality but one of elegance, – shitty elegance: the elegance of an early black-and-white Vogue fashion drawing perhaps, a picture-elegance.[208] From the 20th row, he looked like a 1920s movie hero, i.e. romantic lover, pale, – hair parted in the middle and slicked down. From the first row, he had the face of a cat, – a dead cat, and one saw the heavy face powder, the eye lashes sticky with black, the glistening eyes, the line eye brows. His black house coat, his stance, were elegant. The same was true of her because of her dancer's posture and poses, her bone structure, the erotically anodyne beauty of her body, and the simplicity of her clothing.[209] The talk, tho it had other – sinister – aspects, was light and social. There was, then, the surface of a

208 After the open run throughs before the tour, she progressively made herself look older and uglier, – red on her cheeks, staring eyes outlined in red, the mouth a dull glistening dark red, furled brow, lank, dry hair, – until she looked like a victim out of a Hoppe horror movie. The idea may have been characterisation, or perhaps only artificiality and a contrast to Wilson's matinee idol.

209 – The script's directions give an idea of the eventual dandyism: »Prologue. The stage is set but dark except for a spotlighted telephone on a small aluminum table downstage left. The telephone begins ringing continuously 10 minutes before the curtain. After 10 minutes, as the houselights dim in a count of ten seconds, the light on the phone grows brighter.

Blackout.

The lights come up in one second to reveal a room as the phone stops ringing. The backdrop is a black wall with 3 open arches. Behind the arches very bright lighting suggests an open space. Against the black wall there is an illuminated glass shelf, on which is a spotlighted wine glass. Upstage right a man wearing a white silk shirt, a black silk robe, black silk hose and black slippers is lying on a brushed aluminum chaise lounge. He ignores his surroundings and moves in a totally self-absorbed manner following his own thoughts in silence for 4 minutes.

Blackout.

When the lights come up the arches have been blocked from top to bottom with grey filing books, and a small movie screen hangs just under the proscenium arch down stage right. The man leans forward and speaks his words punctuated by music played on an offstage piano.«

drawing room comedy, – or of an ageing Bel Air queen's sitting room seen through the eyes of a Union Square pick up, a novice at the game, a poor boy.[210]

210 The reductionist elegance that betrayed what I thought was the intended abstractness or essentialism of *Patio* was similar to that of Scott Burton's *Pair Behaviour Tableaux, 1975-76* shown February-April 1976 in the Guggenheim Museum basement in which two for all practical purposes identical young men on a brightly white-walled elevated stage, set into the wall, lit at even intensity and empty except for two chairs at the extreme right and left and a low bench in the middle, all against the rear wall, without facial expressions, each of them thin and in 3, the same 3, quasi-colors, the darkness of their short hair and elevator shoes, the lightness of their tight T-shirts, the light brown of their khaki pants, go through a sequence, perhaps a progression, of gestures, i.e. poses and transversal movements relative to one another: approaches turning into passings-by, partial confrontations, movements of the one in the direction of the other, the 4 dozen or so (47?) tableaux, punctuated by near-total black-outs, in the course of an hour all in all perhaps going through the story of the inception of a relationship and of its waning, or of the abandonment of the attempt. Each rests his hand on the other's shoulder once. Tho Burton's theme seemed inhibition, or perhaps fear of exposure, – each seeming to have to overcome pride and self-love, a liking for his own purity, – as in *Patio* a high tragedy of isolation emerged. Tho the Museum's description seemed more wishful than anything else, – »investigates different patterns of behaviour ... demonstrates possible relations ... expressed ... through body language and personal space behaviour« – the suggestion of story sequence seemed involuntary: as in *Patio* the suggestion of story. Whereas the minimalist visual elegance of Burton's piece seemed to serve his theme, that of behaviour stunted by aesthetics, it seemed to go neither with *Patio*'s more lushly dramatic references, nor with what I took to be its original concern, the critique of language. Burton's development, – he was born in 1939, in Alabama, – setting aside his street-performed *Street Works* of 1969, hardly parallels Wilson's, tho an excellent account in the Winter '75 issue (#8) of Art-Rite suggests some similarity of sensibility in the *Furniture Landscape* of 1970: »*Furniture Landscape*, set up in Iowa in the summer of '70, was a suite of furniture moved into a forest, with natural clearings for rooms. The furniture, which Scott selected from what he found locally, was of natural wood and floral patterned fabric, to blend into the forest as if it lived there. The furnishings had an antique air, heightened by their placement in the woods. The human time furniture signals contrasted strongly with the time signaled by nature. Identifying with the conceptualized language of the '60's, Scott once described the piece as a »transference« (trans-forest), a psychologyless mix-up of contexts. In light of subsequent work, this piece seems more personified, the furniture anthropomorphic, with its own kind of imaginary sentience. A chest of drawers, transformed through the agency of man, here visits the ancient home of its forbears, the trees, in a mythified before and after. The »Furniture Landscape« was in many ways akin to earthworks, but had more overt romanticism, a coy old-fashioned homeliness, and less marshalling of the construction industry.
*18 Tableaux* at Finch College, March, '71, all brief, with and without props, aided by numerous Finch students, a keen and clean bunch. Scott defines »tableau« as a frozen moment full of significance, adventure, and usually drama; a focused moment which happens to be looked at in the proper frame, and then draws your

Wilson's performance built up a powerful image of a lone individual, of the autism in all of us, of someone beset by encroaching shadows, or simply by too many concerns, harassed to the edge of disintegra-

entire attention. When successful, or genuine for the spectator, the tableau really freezes time and self while the mind races wildly. In the tableaux, people and furniture assume the same beingness as humanized props (the first duet between a woman and a couch). The furniture was adequate to match meaning with the performers because of the »period« and »class« signs it carried. The performers, like choreographed mannikins, defined simple roles rather than characters, roles that were mock cultural icons. There are billions of these; some of Scott's came from cheesy graduation photos, pinups (»girls in decorative postures«), classical statuary, and the vectorized energy of the idealized poses in socialist realism.

*Behavior Tableaux*, at the Whitney Museum in the spring of '72, consisted of almost 80 brief, silent tableaux vivant, separated by blackouts and performed by five tall, similarly dressed men in an »institutional« set of stark furniture. An extremely complex work, it dealt with hierarchies of offices, businesses, and formal inter-actions, and with »proxemic and kinesic behavior.« Psychological push and pull was implied by stage position, grouping, and minute head and arm movements of the figures; the scenes were ominously silent with no theatrical flourishes. The actions signified sets of relationships that were ultimately antagonistic and paranoid; definitely a prenarrative art piece, but less blithe and more agonized in its content.

The angst-ridden meaning is built upon a tight conceptual schema, one that recalls certain game theories: in a group of five, power is never static, for the even divi-sion will always allow the weakest member to multiply his/her strength by tipping the balance one way or the other. But this method of analysis demands logical choices all around, inconceivable in the tense psychology of the tableaux. They encapsulate social conflicts: the pragmatics of eye contact, lack of acknowledgement, ignoring and rejecting, challenges accepted and met, estrangements, rebuffings, surrender. »There's one tableau where the lights go up and it is simply a guy sitting there with his head back and four others grouped around him. It only lasted 90 seconds and I thought it was electrifying (laughs). I thought it was incredibly violent.«

The audience sat 40 feet from the stage, so the performers lost any personal charisma and became stark human symbols. The performance seemed to last beyond comfort, the curtailed action agonizingly slow. One had to strain all senses to perceive, and through this remove, the performance shifted from being simply the outcry of a petty loiterer in a hierarchic world to the surreal statement of the post-existential who knows what he is up to. »How curious it is, how very bi-zarre.«

The logical exit from this Kafkaesque nightmare of faceless antagonisms was a renewed definition of a personal self image. In a sort of King Kong self-bravado, he presented himself to the public as The Artist in *Lecture on Myself* at the Museum of Fine Arts in Boston in April, 1973. With his performance a year later, called *Self-Portrait as a Modern American Artist with Cothurni and Ithyphallus*, he moved from a real life portrait of himself to a generalized, mythified image of the »free-thinking,« creative individual (the so-called Artist).

Pieces currently in production:

*Light Box Narrative*, or *Photonovella*, is a series of color transparencies mounted with backlighting – a sort of extended subway lightbox. The novella is overtly

tion, or, rather, not of any individual, but of that state. Before the tour, his many instant sure vocal shifts from one situation, relative to one interlocutor, to another, relative to another, each definitely engaged in, his voice NEVER AN ACTOR'S VOICE[211] (Mr. Barr, the producer, Albee-partner and president of the incorporated League of N.Y. Theatres and Producers, said of him »he'll never be an actor«), were amazing, amazingly natural: a month and a half later, he had filed his delivery down to a low key monotone (Andringa: like a silent movie), in which that expressiveness, sublimated

narrative, telling a simple story about a woman and her dream, such that the dream sequence echoes the larger narrative with subliminal alterations. The photonovella is a study in a series of images – how much can you leave out and yet retain continuity. The composition of events is linear, but control of direction and speed of time flow belong to the ambulatory viewer. The story in itself is surreal and banal, and its charm comes from the evolution of detail, and methods of punctuation and accent. Scott is a homegrown director of his own work, and shirks from laboring in a studio. He has a 9 to 5 job, and uses the money to have professionals execute the work for him; in this case a photo retouching lab, and in the case of the furniture, a craftsman works under his direction.

*Table Series* is a set of pairs of tables in a group of 10, varying in size (from coffee to banquet) and in materials and workmanship (from raw wood to polychromed wood to glass and metal). Beyond this group, he hopes to make a majestic table of galvanized tin and mother of pearl. Scott loves furniture; he looks at a table like a mother would look at a son. Would he ever love people so uncritically? (Why did Cezanne paint so many apples?) These tables, two of which will be in the Whitney Biennial, are the first real furniture design on his part, and appear influenced by an odd combination of Bauhaus and art deco. They are the most severe and austere of his work, for the psychological transference is extremely muted.

The *Pastoral Chair Tableau*, a finished piece which only needs funding for installation, consists of six chairs arranged on a long strip of artificial grass, with blue gauze hung behind to simulate sky. Another of his exercises in furniture typology, the piece consists of two chrome and naugahyde chairs (in love: face to face), three slightly face-lifted wooden art deco kitchen chairs at the other end (having a chat), and a single chair, in the middle (rejected by both groups).

An untitled street armchair brings him full circle from his street performance beginnings. This chair, to be cast in bronze and placed outside on the sidewalk, was left in Scott's apartment by the previous tenant, one Ernest Cardinale. This man had lived there in Little Italy for ages, and had »signed« his entire apartment by scratching his name into a windowsill. The bronze chair will be a monument to this anonymous proletarian, an empty chair which symbolizes death. This monument is a rarity in its category, for it is exactly »lifesize.« It is designed to be indistinguishable from any chair left outside, hence it is both utilitarian and garbage (according to NY slum habits).« (Art-Rite, #8, p. 9-10)

211 He spoke in a very low voice, – can't project, – used a contact-mike (it sat like an insect by his tie) that badly, especially when he was prone, distorted his voice.

but still there, had become secondary to the presentation of an image.

Childs, on the other hand, – I suspect each of them directed him/ herself, – started out (as for her part in *Einstein*) acting out a dominant psychosis by twitches and ticks, a foolish dance, but progressively shed them, – leaving merely somatic traces of neurosis in a general cool, her shoulders too far back, a suppressed jerk to her head, the slight shivers of a rigid neck, – trivial tricks of a cerebral but shallow professional actor, – and instead went all out to be variedly naturalistic in an impersonative way, with many facial expressions for every line, and even worked for laughs. She was continually impressive, her portrayal of a mask for madness a compendium of peeking-out hysterias that would go down well on Broadway. And tho miked also, she knows how to project. Mr. Barr said of her, »She's a very, very good actress ... extraordinary, absolutely spellbinding onstage.« She did not come up with a real person, let alone a state of man, but with a sharp glitter of suppositious identities. Her jittery artifices shattered the show: broke the tension established by Wilson's show of solitude, of the finitude of a man's mind, made it meaningless.

Of course, this show of Wilson's wasn't that much to begin with. The foolishness of the texts, – far from far out, cute, rather, – not to mention his showman's flair for a bit of melodrama, and the swish decor, absolutely precluded the show from going very far, – anywhere.

First the idea of a guy in a library. Surrounded by all that silent speech. Changed to the idea of him first in a room with an ocean view, exposed to infinity, this vista, – contact and openness, – then blotted out by language.[212] Either idea probably accompanied, possibly followed by, the idea of having him talk: sentences that lodge in a head, – coming out of the air. This interior occupation made manifest. Or else: a guy talking. This is very pure sofar, – minimal, conceptual, essential (-ist). Now Wilson collected the text.[213] Not his actual thoughts, nor everyday talk, – snappy, smooth, whimsical, dramatic lines of dialogue, – the imaginary talk of movies, tv dramas, tough guy novels. Charged with connotative resonance, implying

212 In practice, the scenechange worked out differently: the windows were white blanks, the books covers of ledgers, both interior decoration, the change a change of mood from zero to grey.

213 Kostelanetz, loc. cit.: this two took weeks, Wilson carrying a 9″ by 12″ note book.

situations, – relationships, events, personal histories, – and all phony. (Also some social small talk, – host to guest, – tinted by the foregoing.) The idea now had become: verbal evocation of so many situations and relationships they cancel out one another: verbation as a mind's abstract sociability. Communication without an interlocutor: like a ringing telephone. Wilson's tho not Childs' final style of delivery was adequate to this idea. But the patter wasn't: it attracted attention to itself: a *text*; and to its meanings, – relationships, events, personal histories. By intention, the idea at this point may have been: a show of language as social obfuscation of individuality, – or as irrelevant incursion, powerless to add or detract from it. But in practice, because the imaginary fragments of dialogue were neither general, natural nor arbitrary, the idea had come down to: theatre with negative means, – all the conventional effects, but language violated. To this then was added the idea of a doubling of the talker,[214] – bringing home the point that what was said, the meaning of it, wasn't important, but only who said it.

The challenge was to the writer: to find the language for speech demonstrating its own inadequacy for communication[215] not through semantic inadequacy (such as disconnected meaning), for that would be begging the question, but in spite of being semantically perfectly adequate; and so natural, the point would be general, and so plain, the point would be clear, attracting attention neither to what was said, nor to what was meant. But someone intent on making this point would be unlikely to have the liking for language requisite for making it.

214 At the time this was reported to have as objective only to make the venture commercially more viable. Wilson's debts from *Einstein* were considerable, a bankruptcy, endangering future funding, threatened.
215 Unlike Becket, Wilson's concern is with the inadequacy of language for communication, not for life.

# Epilogue

We see in these pieces of 74-77, not a man worn out, not the one-shot artist having nothing more to show, not a man corrupted by hunger for success, but a man of integrity and daring, and a genius, desperately, – perhaps a little anxiously, he can't stop working for immediate results, keeps working, has no time to build that wall in the Texas plains, that retreat in the mountains of British Columbia, – attempting to transcend the limitations of his achievements.[216]

216 »It is only in man, in the peripheral segments of the nuclear zones of the analyzers and of the motor cortex, that structural and functional differentiation into highly specialized, distinct areas, concerned with the analysis and integration of stimuli of especial importance to the various aspects of speech, took place. For instance, a special area in the posterior segment of the peripheral field of the auditory cortex (Wernicke's »center«) is concerned with the analysis and integration of the receptive elements of spoken language or phonemes, and an area in the peripheral fields of the visual cortex is concerned with the analysis and integration of the visual elements of receptive language. In areas of the inferior segments of the parietal region, situated next to the cutaneokinesthetic zone and in direct contact with the sensory »centers« of the arm, lips, tongue, and larynx, the analysis and integration of cutaneokinesthetic reception fundamental to articulation takes place. A certain portion of the periphery of the motor cortex, the inferior segments of the premotor zone (Broca's »center«), is the seat of the neurodynamic processes involved in the synthesis of the individual sounds of spoken speech into complex, successive units. In another portion of the premotor zone, adjoining the motor »centers« of the upper limb (in the posterior segment of the mid-frontal gyrus), are located the cortical mechanisms for the programming and performance of the complex systems of successive movements and motor skills.

As a result of the segregation of specialized speech areas of the cortex in the peripheral fields of the nuclear zones, the neuronal structures of the central fields of these zones become perfected and capable of perceiving the elements of speech and of differentiating their sensory and motor components with a high degree of precision. This process is particularly conspicuous in the central auditory field. The work of Blinkov (1955) has shown that in man this field is much more extensive than in the monkey, both absolutely and relatively, and has undergone further differentiation into a series of subsidiary fields. These progressive structural changes reflect the fundamental role of spoken language in the entire system of verbal communication.

The upshot of the qualitative transformation undergone by the overlapping zones of the analyzers in the frontal portion of the cortex following the formation of the secondary signal system is that all of man's conscious mental processes, governing his actions, involve the participation of the system of verbal communication and, indeed, are under its domination.« (G. I. Polyakov, *Modern Data on the Structural Organization of the Cerebral Cortex*. In: A.R. Luria, *Higher Cortical Functions in Man*.)

# III. Appendices

# 1. Robert Wilson on *The King of Spain.*[1]

Wilson had the vision that *The King of Spain* (1969) was based on while resting in a barn at Grailville: »(Missing section in which Wilson speaks, inter alia, of his inspiration for the *King of Spain* in a barn in Ohio, – I believe he was doing an ›environmental‹ piece there in a field, with telegraph poles.) . . . overlays of thinking, and part of what I was thinking at the same time was – when I was I was I was in second grade the teacher had – she said – but – and she was asking everyone what they wanted to be when they were big – I don't know what, just somehow it came out, I said I wanted to be the king of Spain – I don't know where that came from or what it, but it's – and I remember she didn't like it and I was and I just I was somehow very confident even in saying it (She thought you were satirical) Yeah, and and I was, I don't know I can remember like being very sincere at the same time (Question as to how this related to the other givens, the drawing room, etc.) At the time, at the time I didn't connect it with the room or somehow, but it was like – later when I looked at it, more with a perspective eye, I looked at all that information – also I kept thinking about these giant cat legs I even like was thinking of being there in the barn. Later when I was looking I was thinking about and then doing the *King of Spain* uh I, it was – the images that I had that night at that it was it was a very short time that they all came – they were so clear, they were just crystal clear – they had such a clarity – and somehow I couldn't explain it but it (Was it a room or?) The images of the room, the idea of the king of Spain and the idea of the cat legs I think that all of that, all those images somehow together seemed to be right. (Could you say a little bit more, about the quality, of life in that room . . .) Yes, it – yeah it was very peaceful, it was hum, it was almost the evening or tea time – there was almost that quality about it and it was – as if no one had to talk – there was that quality – it was like it was still like a communication – or connection between people – at the same time that – I think the best phrase that I said was that it was very much like a pasture, it had that feeling. And uh, also I think, I made that whole piece from that one, one night. Because I was in a barn and there was hay in the barn and somehow then the hay ended up in the *King of Spain* and it was like – and all of that image seemed so right together at that time – that time of thinking about it. And later I tried to do other things – I tried to introduce other ideas and they didn't seem right. It seemed that that information that I got that night was right, all the parts were right together and even now I – I've always had trouble, like I think well maybe it's just me – that it's right to me that, but they – like I learned to trust that, but I felt . . . What I realized was happening is that – what interested me was that – well one

1 From my interv. w/Wilson, 1970.

thing say that I'm trying to do in the theatre, I think that I'm not interested in, like it's very it's very difficult to say now, well – I – I went to Mr. Brecht's study and I talked with him – it's like you can say that on one level but on one level, I mean, it just doesn't mean anything – cause like, I'm thinking about maybe something I did this morning or something, or the time I had in Ohio three years ago or uh you know that I have to be somewhere tonight or I don't know, it's like all sorts of things are going on. And that's what was going on that night, at that moment, like I was also thinking about when I was in second grade, I was also thinking about that drawing room, I was also thinking about the hay in the barn, and they were all overlays of images. And it seemed that at that one moment, too they all seemed so clear somehow together. (What were you thinking about in second grade that time? – when she asked you what you wanted to be? – She probably asked the other kids that too?) Yes she asked other kids that and – and they (What was your feeling about that?) I-I was wondering, I guess like where that came from – why did I say the king of Spain and what did that mean and had I ever – (Can you remember the teacher not being pleased?) I remember the teacher not being pleased and I remember – also I – I was trying to remember what, was in my head – like did I really imagine myself being a king, or was it – I didn't think it was that, so much, you know – I mean, I thought it was another thing – and then, also – a thing I hap- left out. The thing also that happened, at that time I saw this picture of my head, again, of this figure, of a big – of this beast was a – and for the first time like I saw like with when I thought of the king of Spain like I saw the figure – and, I had never (Was it you?) It wasn't me, no, it was just a figure – a character, like. And what I did was model – that was the first time I'd ever done that – I think when I was painting I would always like paint from nature or paint from something – I was always painting from something – and it was like – but, the first time like I had something inside me that I was trying to make – that one image – and that was the – I did pretty much the whole piece that way, but, what was interesting is that the-the king of Spain – the figure with the big head – was pretty much exactly like I saw it that time – like I still can see – seeing that image the first time. (What did he look like) Well, he had white pants (laugh) and he had black boots and he had uh red hair and uh he was friendly, he was almost grotesque, an enormous head and he had, had this gesture of it was – and uh he was it was almost as if he was smiling, was happy but it – I mean it was right, there seems to be a lot of things – (But there, in the barn, you associated it with the figure – with the king of Spain?) I did, I thought I thought of Henderson (?), when I was in the second grade, I thought of saying that and I thought – and I saw the figure. (At that time when you said it, – when you were in second grade?) No, no, I didn't see it at that time, only-only at this moment – and I'd never seen an image with it before, I had just said it … and uh and then-then somehow he just seemed right sitting in that room. I mean that-that there was nothing-nothing strange about it – I mean it was like this beast in the center of that room – just sat there and it was just (Now, in the *King of Spain* – he sits in the armchair, and the armchair has its back toward the audience?) Yes. (You don't see him, or hardly see him?) You don't see him until the very end, yeah. (Now what was it he does in the end?) He-he merely stands and faces the audience. It's like, it's almost like I guess in the play like he's not seen – like you don't know that he's there, then suddenly he's been there the whole time in the center of the stage. (What does he do?) Just merely that he appeared, I think. And then he just did the one gesture of raising his hand (Now, this was like three or four years ago that) I did, that, that that happened, yeah. And then about a year later I hum that was very much in my head like, it was just very clear in my head and I did other work – and I was doing a lot of other things but that somehow stayed in my head very clearly – so I said, I just did it, I said I that's – I would like to do a play like this. (Did you ever take notes on it, write down anything?) No, I never did. It just like, I couldn't get it out. (The mask of the king of Spain, you made that yourself?) I did ... No I did that myself, the time I was making it I thought – I could see the image in my head and I thought – I didn't work with a sketch, I just had it in my head and I kept – it's amazing, the whole time I was making it I thought this is the first time I've made something that I – like I see something and I'm really making what I'm seeing. It was-it was very – I don't even like to say it so much, but it was very strange, at the time, all the time I was making it with the papier-mache I knew that it was happening.

... what I call *The King of Spain* it's a play by itself and uh then I expanded it ... There's no script ... I started making the piece ... about a year later.[2] I made the mask, I made the head ... Well then I started I uh uh – – – – I'm trying to remember, I just started, I just somehow I got the Anderson Theatre and knew I wanted this drawing room and uh I I just I didn't even think I was – yeah I was consciously aware of it – where I'd gotten the information and that it all fit together. And I sat down and I made like a draft for it, a plan, like I I knew I wanted the runner outside, I wanted that action in the drawing and I wanted uh I wanted the piles of hay and the pile of people and I wanted this other crazy figure that somehow I'd made up too – the mammy, that black mammy, that came up – that, that was almost like a, I don't know – I always thought a lot of things about that. At that time I was working uh with-with this boy who was catatonic and I-I had an image that was associated with him, it was almost like – it was almost like a heavy thing around him like a-a black – he-he gave me – it was a very strange thing, he gave me a doll – it was a black, black doll – and I always thought it meant like I could see a lot in him doing that to (?) me. It was almost – I always thought of that figure, I've

2 After, while making *Poles* (1967), he had the vision realized by *The King of Spain*. Cf. the footn. citing Wilson concerning this vision in my *Introduction*.

never told anyone this – I don't know, but – I always thought like that figure was, had something to do with like a heaviness like that that child couldn't get out – couldn't get through, you know what I mean? – it was like, it was like a heavy thing around him that he, and it – it was almost black but, he wanted to so desperately to get through but there was like a heavy thing around him that prevented him from getting through and the mammy at that time almost reminded me of that (She didn't seem heavy to me, but she did seem black, something black about her ...) Heavy, but it was almost too that what happened structurally in terms of the whole piece is that every-everyone sitting in the rooms was – was almost, they were presenting themselves as they are or uh there was a certain naturalness about all of that, and this – this was something totally unreal, it was a guy doing a woman and it was you know a white person doing a black person – it was theatrical, it was – so that it was articulated as such – you know like and suddenly it had uh it had theatrical lighting, it had you know obviously colored light and it was like it had a whole other sort of – it was like a fantasy. (You acted her?) Yes, yes I did, so it – it was almost like a spirit or something had just passed through the room – that was unnoticed too, I mean or or noticed but not visibly noticed. ( – I talked to this man Lichtenstein[3] the other day. He wasn't sure you'd acted the Big Mammy.) Did he like it? (Very much) Did he? (Oh yes) Oh good, because I wasn't sure of that, I didn't know, he never said anything to me so I didn't know whether – I felt maybe there was – from one of the departments anyway, there was, they weren't all that supportive but – I don't know, I've never had a lot to say to him – and we (This black mammy now, she was not one of the things that came into your mind in that barn in Ohio that time?) No, I think it was more of an added thing – and uh (inaudible) Yeah, it wasn't uh, no it wasn't so much like that – Aunt Jemima figure, but it was uh uh black and I thought – and I can even see how in the piece it's almost like attached or opposed to the other activities which are very – of another kind of nature. (Did you play anything else in the *King of Spain*?) No, I did the runner a couple times when I did it at the Anderson Theatre, I did it just a couple of times, but I – I did it only as the as the runner would do it, I mean, *and* I didn't do anything special. (All that time you were in New Jersey or in New York and working with people, doing classes and also young people and then you started talking to them about your idea of putting this on the stage) But I went to uh I went to several places to try to raise money and uh hum it it was very difficult for me to talk about the work and I didn't have the script and I said well it's somehow different from the other work – cause the other work had no scenery it was a very, very simple sort of exercise – it was like the Bleeker Street one[4] and then I hadn't – I didn't (What other work was this that you were –) Say like the Bleeker Street or I'd also done

3 At that time director of the Brooklyn Academy of Music.
4 »Theatre Activity.« Bleeker Street Cinema, 1967.

several other pieces (Several other pieces?) Yeah, and I had never gotten very much support for that work although what was interesting is that some people were coming back to see it – I never publicized it very much so there wasn't – and I hadn't invited the press or anything like that too I had always done the other things so there was nothing written about it – (What work did you do with people?) For rehearsing it? (Rehearsing or exercises or –) Well, what I did – say with *Freud* – is well almost never rehearsed it – (Well, the *King of Spain* first) What I did is, we never rehearsed so much until the very end the specific activity as that I gave them exercises which I felt would hum would-would make-make the performance possible – I mean, I didn't – somehow I sensed that it wouldn't be a good idea say to rehearse the material a long time because hum a certain freshness or life would be missing so we would almost go into performance and like they were doing it for the first time, but they have all the information before they get there so they have that security (what kind of exercises?) We did hum sitting sometimes – an exercise where we would sit on chairs and the people could get up and they could do one activity, one, – something with their body uh and it might be for an hour like say an hour period. I had – when I did the *King of Spain* we had 30 people in the show – 40 or something – and I remember on three rehearsals – and a lot of people dropped out because they didn't feel anything was happening or they felt they couldn't do it hum – but three rehearsals, I think they were on Wednesday nights, they were a couple of hours long, two and a half hours long – and half the time, say an hour, we were – we sort of had a line of chairs and we sat we said within this hour period you can do one activity, you'd get up and do it and then come back and sit down (You said people thought they couldn't do it) Couldn't, could not do it, they couldn't sit that long, they were – they were bored or they you know – they didn't want to do it – so, that was OK, they left. But then some people didn't and then – it was amazing we never touched each other, we never had sort of a relationship that way, but we came very close as a group, just sitting there – and I did, I'd we'd go through a warm-up, before we I'd do that so we'd spend 45 minutes doing-doing a warm-up uh I do also, I did exercises like uh – it was more in trying to get-get inside like I'd take, uh, I'd say take three minutes to take your arms from here to here sort of a – ya know and then-then back down, take your head around left from this shoulder to left shoulder or something in a long period of time so that it's more inside that it's happening and then I'd I'd play records, rock and roll records, or I'd play uh Bach – and we'd move always with our eyes shut in rooms with very little light so that you didn't feel like someone was watching you – you feel or something and uh then I'd try to say get get the movement uh I'd notice that like it was very outside, so then I'd try slow it down so they still had the had the energy going, still moving, but it was like it had gone to the inside, you were suddenly still but you were still moving, inside – and then we did concentration exercises where we we'd just look ahead like we would just increase maybe the space between things we'd see ahead of us. Or just, we'd start listening with say listening to this sound, listening to that sound, and then the sound beyond that until like you're hearing anoth-er-another body of sound or something. I don't know. It was like – some of the exercises (inaudible question) – Yeah – the trouble I had always was that – and then I would have them go outside of the room and then walk in and sit down and that was the most difficult – cause the, people had the idea that they would have to show a skill or that they'd have to perform or – they'd want to walk on their toes to show that something special, ya know that – like you're interesting just like you are, that's what really interests me – so just just walk in and sit down, and that was very difficult for people to do because suddenly all their crutches – they were like so stiff now that it was hard for them to do that to walk in and just-just sit down, they wanted to always do something to show – show-off – so then when we tried to eliminate that – and try to get them to be confident and just be themselves and walk in and sit down and not – and all of that happened through I guess a six week period or something like that before, and some of the people I did – had been working with much longer in classes, some of the people had never worked with me before, so – and they were – all the exercises were-were very simple anyone could do them – like I had children to old people and they were all-all able to fit in, to do them, almost. And And (Some of the exercises that the lady does near the piano there are not that easy –) No, no she is extraordinary.[5] *That* woman is the one who had arthritis and couldn't move at all and she-she's just extra-ordinary (laughs) I mean she's really, she's almost 70 now – amazing, (laughs) it's – she's really an amazing woman, and she's never performed, or, she's never done anything – a very intelligent lady – she, she's always had trouble, she's uh uh a woman of some some wealth and she lives in Short Hills, New Jersey and it was always difficult for her to-to sort fit in with that society – people in-in the community and this has been an enor-mous outlet for her to be able to do this (Can I ask you – now what you saw there originally, – it's just a picture, now this question of time se-quence, – how did you get into that, I mean did that develop naturally from the picture or –) It did, it developed naturally from the picture, also from from the way I'd been working before – in that, one thing that was happening, say, more than a few years ago, that, I remember when I'd go to the theatre, and I've never been to the theatre so much, unfortunately my background is very limited but, – is that I always felt too much was hap-pening – like I couldn't focus on everything that was happening, I felt I was – and that – that was interesting as one approach for working but I felt I was being bombarded with so many, sort of things happening at one time and I could'nt get – I could only hear the surface of it uh and-and that's interesting, but, I was interested in uh in getting more beneath the surface – so the way I think I constructed it was that – was like they

5 Mary Peer.

were moving pictures and like I felt for you to be be able to-to get inside of it – you know once you could register or have experience of that material then the picture would change – so that you could experience the next picture – see the next picture, see the inside of it.

(Could you tell me the contents of the *King of Spain*, what was done first, second, third –) Well, I did, you mean what actually happened on the stage? (Yeah) (R. W. sighs) The first thing that happened is that you saw the room empty with the runner, going in the very beginning cause he's always there, and that structure was – also in *Freud* – At first I didn't consciously do it and then later I looked at it and like I just sort of sensed it and I went back and looked at it and I could see the structure seemed to make some sense, that you would have that static figure, say in the *King of Spain* you have the king of Spain sitting there and you have the runner and he's like the fastest, always going and then you have the other one that doesn't move at all, – and say in *Freud*, you have the Bird Woman in the first act and the runner in the second act and in the last act you have them both sitting together, the Bird Woman and the King of Spain and then you have the runner still going – Then, the king of Spain is there but you don't see him – and then you have uh people that slowly begin to fill that – that area (Can you tell what comes first?) Who comes first? What comes first? Yes, there was a game table that uh and uh uh ah well people playing at the game table. (Those men came in first?) Yes. I always felt, the reason one reason that happened first I think is that I always felt that that was like uh uh a miniature play or that was like a tiny sort of capsule of what was happening. (What was happening?) Yeah, it was like a, like just that happening, that's sort of like what's happening in the larger stage picture. So, that's like setting up the nucleus for the larger thing. And uh so that happens and uh then the candles were lit on the shelf – that was another thing that I'd seen too, that was, – a row of candles – and uh then other people come in and they make drinks, they talk – some, they sit down you hear chairs squeak – and what happened is that slowly in-in an additive process you begin to fill these layers, these horizontal layers *around* that area on the stage – the stage-zones, that one area sort of became in its fullest focus or fullest register all the way across and that-that room looked like every – it was complete – what was happening with that picture so that then the next sort of picture happened in front of that and that was it (In front of that – you filled it up from the rear?) Hm, Hm. You had the runner, and then you had the drawing room and then you had in front of that you had the two piles of people and hay and – That almost like made almost a visual block too that made the others sort of seem further back – but it was always there (People come in, make themselves a drink) They would sit down and uh they made conversation (They made conversation? You could hear them?) Some, not much, just small – yeah, just small conversation. And then, Mary Peer came in, and with a mike on her and that uh and and she is – she was telling stories – one thing that was amazing about her – those stories – taking her with me, you know, to classes – to other classes – and it, just uh – in teaching, – the thing that was always most impressive to me is that, is that she was able to talk to almost any kind of person, she could connect with them – she'd find a way (inaudible question) She talks about herself, Yeah and, but the whole structure for the way she talks and the language is – is very interesting, it's like she sort of gets one thing going and then she starts another thing and then she'll start the third thing and then she goes back to the first thing and then she starts a fourth and a fifth and she's back to the second and the first and she keeps going back to all of them and she is connected – it's like, it's very interesting on that level, just her talk but more important – like she had uh – I have to go – I'm sorry . . . .« (Interv. w/Wilson, 1970)

## 2. Robert Wilson on *Freud*.[6]

»(We were talking about the *King of Spain* and how at some point you felt that this was really about Sigmund Freud) Oh and about the time I did it – I had a funny feeling that, at that time, it's like, if you have an idea then it just keeps growing bigger uh my original idea had now expanded into like another thing it was like uh (inaudible) and I felt that that was what had happened – I felt in order to really keep working at it I should like do these other ideas but we were already in the theatre (inaudible) but at that time I was already thinking of-of (How did that piece by itself make you think of Freud – what relation did you –) I don't know – I – at that time – well one of the ideas I had about that time was inserting Freud in the drawing room –, again, like a picture without focus, and suddenly, click, it went into focus and then it just seemed to be right, I could see Freud on the beach and then – in the drawing room and then in the cave, with the animals – and that came pretty quick like I just thought it through. And then I do it. I – I sort of go to work and scratch my head and start working in classes (?) on exercises which that I see are leading to, the production.

(In your own mind, there must have been some kind of a guiding thing, some objective at some point, – what did you want? What did you head for? About Freud, – or, as a total effect on people?) I think I said for the – the guiding thing about Freud – I didn't know quite so much at the time, as just something I-I sensed – it, it was something I would have liked, you know – I could get into something – just sort of not to do it uh when then – later when I was actually working on the piece I was very clear and I could say you know what that was – and I had gone through that process – that I knew that I wanted to say – I-I felt, I never talked like this – that there were very definite times in his life and I and I don't like to say so much what they were but they were like general times in his life I felt that somehow they conveyed that one layer – was like a time in Freud's life, and I didn't care what people saw – I realized – but I felt that that information also was was large enough that it could tell a very raw thing – outside of just Freud's life – it was – Also then, I felt there was another thread and I even told it like it weren't Freud and the different times in the play and then they're together at the end of the table and the whole – one little scene – setting up that picture there was very specifically then that moment that I wanted to, like, underline about Freud – this is a very important point and about Freud and so, that-that scene is like most literal – it's like the only real – to me it was in the whole piece – that thread – (But at some point there must have gone through your head – say, for instance, a relation between the image of the king of Spain and Freud

6 From my interviews of him, 1970.

or ... or ... whatever the larger piece would be about – there must have been a change, an expansion or something) Not direct connections that way so much, sometimes I did like uh not-not specifically. In the *King of Spain* there-there was one moment – Kenneth King when he did it in December and I asked him to do it again and somehow he didn't want to so I – didn't want to pursue it – but he wore a black hood – and he comes out and he's moving very fast and Freud's walking across and I always loved that – but to me I'm sure like I'd have, it was a very personal reference is what that meant – that was almost – like Freud never – there were mystical references – but Freud never went into that, at least, in fact, that's where he, he was, one of the big differences when he was young and he said when he was very old if he had to relive his life that he would go – and I always felt like when Kenneth came up with that black hood over his head that was like this thing that was passing by – but it was a heavy – it was like he felt – (inaudible) – you knew he spent his time in other areas – mystical references – (What uh ...) Well I felt like when the apple came out of the turtle's mouth (I didn't notice that) Oh, you didn't see that? (No) Well, there are little things like that happen with like almost – like no one sees that apple coming out of the turtle's mouth because it was very slowly – it took hours to rig – the turtle's going across the beach there's a red apple that comes out of his mouth and he keeps traveling up and goes diagonally off into the wing – and uh I always loved that (laughs) (But what is a mystical reference?) I don't know what a mystical reference is (laughs). (Would you say that children have a sense of mystery?) Oh sure. (I'ld say they have a sense of wonder but not of mystery)

(Let me ask you for a favor – it may be sort of painful, but – would you mind saying what was in the play – go through the contents for me, tell me like the individual things that happened) I-I can tell you and it will be like a very mechanical thing (That's all I want) But I can tell you what happens. Uh, what happens is – first of all I know that I'm in an opera house, I'm not in a law firm or anything like that – and I know that. I'm using an opera house, – And, – I know that I want to keep the audience attracted so – so – I want – wanted to be viewed at a distance (That struck me as strange relative to your wanting to expose people – the individuals –) I felt – I felt that you could still look at the people and also the larger stage picture was always very important – everything happened together – and if you got too close, if you got in one area then you missed the overall and that – I-I went in the theatre and I sat down and that's what happened and – I went to the performances there to – to see what, I kept looking and that bothered me about-about my piece, and I felt that it was most important in seeing all of them – and all the stuff together – so – also I liked the idea of not, – of having little things and being far away from them – I thought just, structurally, that that would bring you closer into the little things, – I mean, really, I think that worked. Then, I've had for a a long time, even when I was doing plays with children – I-I usually

396

have a prince, that comes in and sits and watches, – watches it – I did a play in a garage oh 15 years ago, with children – they came into the audience and as the last person was seated – and all the lights went down – and this, and this – and sometimes there are funny characters that come in and are seated. And uh then I had the ring suspended over the audience and and uh it was almost like a marker hum and I mean I've had that for as an element for a long time – for at least ten years – almost in every piece I've had – the rings, and they are moved, during the piece. (Like in a pool parlour) Right. This, And I'll probably even have it in the next piece –.

Then I come out standing while the speech is being given – about my experiences – but I'm not as myself – there's like another layer over me – another man, standing there – but yet it's like obvious that –, it's like a kid, you know – you know it's, it's like theatrical makeup – it's like the overlay, costumes on – and uh then I announce the piece – it' very dead and – it's sort of like starting out (clicks his tongue?) – it's like another sort of thing that we started out with – and then the curtain goes up, there's another reality – and I'll always walk – it was like walking into my piece – I walked on – into this, this space – and sitting on the stage, the stage is empty – we've been now from a dark theatre – and suddenly it's bright lights and we are on a beach and it's very, very bright – it's vacant and there's one seated figure, in black – a woman in black, a black victorian dress holding a black bird and uh – a girl who was dressed in khaki – – – – – and the (inaudible) up stage – the runner's returned – and I had – this time I had as the curtain went up, I had – this – we – I just raked all the sand and had a blower so it was like sand all in the air and like a dust storm – just as the curtain was going up the whole stage was filled with that and I had uh 14 tumbleweeds and it blew up – and just as like the curtain was going up there was like a couple – a pair (inaudible) and the runner continues all the way through and he's all the way up stage, and he's about the only color – all the rest are natural colors (inaudible) and-then-a girl comes out, up stage – doing a seven part movement – and hum that's repeated all the way across – it is back and forth – she's doing that sort of (inaudible) and then another girl comes out doing it and then a third and then a fourth and the boy – this last time we did it (garbled) and it was – oh, it was almost beautiful what happened, the last time. And, they continue, and then, a guy comes out uh with a fan, and he's uh he drags himself along through these three people moving and then he later becomes the walrus – in the second act he's got a walrus head on and then in the third act he's got a complete walrus costume on – he saw this little fan – I liked that, it was – in uh the cave in the – last act he comes and it-it's very sort of – I always thought – this didn't happen in December, it happened later and like – somehow this piece was so heavy that – I thought that-that this was – it was just too heavy, I felt and somehow I needed – and so what happens if the walrus walks in through the opening in the cave and he has a little fan and he's making some gestures like that and – and in the third act it flipped – it suddenly it – it became like, I don't know – it cancelled the heaviness in the right way, it for me at that moment – it it was like Charlie Chaplin inside the Marx Brothers inside of a walrus or something you know (laughs) – this piece – it's so – it had – I don't know it was like a nice thing that happened there – but anyway he – you see him in the first act just walking all the way up stage – sort of dragging himself – and then, – I think I come out and I have a bird on my shoulder and I do a movement in striped pants, backwards – as I'm coming out, a black bear is coming towards me – go away, the black bear goes off and I come in – and as I leave the stage four black bears come in and then they go off – and-and I've never seen the bears – and then an old woman[7] comes out, an 87 year old woman comes out but she does uh a movement that's in four parts and it's sort of like this – in this space – this first – it was – we worked on it together in class, it was mostly her movement – in the first part she was a young girl and uh in the second part she's a middle-aged woman and in the third part she's an old woman – and it had a lot of meaning for her – it-it was very symbolic – she's Russian, she's an incredible woman – and then she thought – I had her in class teach her movement then to-to a young girl in the class, so what happened in space was this sort of thing was that uh – Hope, the older woman started out here as the young girl and Kit[8] started out from this side of the stage as the young girl doing the old woman – she ends up being the young girl – she *is* a young girl – so you had like this sort of thing happening, this cross – and the women would meet here, they are like doing the same thing, the same age. That wasn't seen so much but the symbolism, the feeling would seem to be right. Yeah I was just – Well, well let's see what happened after that the – there's a a boy – a little boy comes out dressed up as an old woman and uh it's obvious that it's a k-k child and in some ways – it's not so obvious that it-it's a boy doing a girl I mean there's there's like a strange sort of thing an old – a lot of figures that just – and and and then a guy comes out – this was in May, we – and – with a snake, and as he comes out with the snake, from one side of the stage, hum the grandson comes out from the other side of the stage and then he goes off and the guy with the snake, – a rope is being lowered as he came out and he came to the rope and he stepped up on the rope and we flew him out – and as we flew him out a pink angel came down and uh the pink angel stayed for a while and then after a while it flew out and then hum – the piece is very un it-it's in space, there were layers (garbled) and you have the turtle moving, oh the turtle comes out in the very beginning and very slowly goes all the way across the stage and it takes the turtle the 30 some odd minutes the act is long to make that cross to the static figure that's here – so there are like very different time things happening all the way through it seems, it's – and then, – but the overall picture seems to be – the dynamics of

7 Hope Kondrat.
8 Kit Cation.

398

the piece seems to be pretty static – until – and then Freud comes out – and he walks on the beach with Anna but somehow too the air – like the air of the piece gets a little – because Kenneth[9] came out with this very fast movement and it's almost a twister in the sand – the sand suddenly starts moving – and suddenly it's like a twister blowing across the stage with Freud's going across and at the same time too that a lot of the people didn't see it because of where they were sitting and there was nothing I could do about it in the theatre, unfortunately but there's a boy that's across the stage and he came down from – from the sky and they walk across and – And uh the heavy man is going here with a black hood across and Freud is walking across very slowly hum I think that's on this side too, and hum I think the angel flew off again and a boy with crutches who was in one of my classes appears a couple of times in the piece – he just comes out – and then – then I, I come out as the mammy and I do that one – and suddenly like – everyone has been presented himself – it's had a sort of like (what do you do as the mammy?) I did, I do uh – well the mammy was like uh well let's see in the larger sense I can think uh it's like a, it's like an an artist's fake theatrical thing and uh and it was like – the other people almost didn't have that quality and also it's – it was like a fantasy of something that suddenly happened or another sort of air that was like – suddenly the piece just took another-another-another air or something – (Could you say what air it took?) Well, in – in – it was – yeah. I – it was like uh – well, I don't know – I always sort of like – it was totally unreal – sort of thing. (When I wrote about it, I used words like the ›eerie,‹ the ›weird‹ and ›verging on the sinister but not quite getting there.‹) It does, it gets – that whole black figure that black course – it's almost like uh I don't know, it seemed, I don't – I just don't like to talk about it because I say something and I think well there were so many other things that it means too – to say one thing maybe puts weight where it shouldn't be but, it seemed right (laughter) I sensed that uh like maybe – later, you know – a couple of months from now I'm more able to easily say what it means, but I sensed and I believe, like I trust that – like I believe my body doesn't lie and it's easy you know to rely very much on that – that sense that it's ok – I'll say ok and I can say oh, yeah that was one, two, three and I didn't realize it, that way at the time – that if I can just can trust myself – that usually that's true with so much that the body just hum seldom lies – lies, it seems to be you can trust. (inaudible) But like if I find that I really have to make a decision about something I'm not sure – like I sort of shut my eyes and think – usually I can get a clearer sense or something but if I listen to myself I guess, no I really shouldn't do this I should stay – like . . .

. . . like I sensed the other day when the pictures were taken that I shouldn't have done it and I did it anyway – and then afterwards I knew I shouldn't have – I said I should have like – really stayed with what my

9 Kenneth King.

intuition was – but – just – but I didn't like the pictures anyway – they took Freud – but – I rented a lion, because I, somehow I wanted a lion to walk the beach and I thought that would be nice – that was difficult because the costume almost was comical or something (inaudible question) But I – no I even thought of a real lion, in fact we checked into renting a lion – and I had all sorts of ways of doing it and then I even rented a stuffed one, a real one – but – that had been stuffed, for the photographs this past week, and they had Freud sitting on the lion and uh well the little mammy is on the lion – I kept saying but no (laughter) that isn't right – it's not that sort of thing – not at all, it's going to look like a freak show or something (laughter) in a way it's like there was another feeling for Freud and uh (laughter) he had, we had a pile full of lemons cause I had lemons in the sand and hum and he had Freud like holding a lemon up on his head looking up to it like this and a lot of lemons poured all – and I said no, wait you know, like that's that's not at all what happens (fairly lengthy pause) there was like no respect too – it was like I talked with him and he was interesting as a person uh he was very honest, in some ways, like I wanted a group-photo – I wanted a shot of all this together somehow and Freud, and I had arranged compositions and I thought that I could get in all the information cause I thought how you do it in a time thing – like it – like when I think about Freud like it's all these elements together that are important so like, you just show one scene, you see – you just – one of the girls doing that movement and that doesn't – that was just one part there – was there any way to like get an overall – so I made like it was almost a collage or again it was like all sorts of layers of things – it was a very rich thing, but he wouldn't do it, he wouldn't photograph that – he said – and I said well why – and he said, he said well, if you want someone to do that go to someone like uh so and so he said, he, you know, the photographer said – he said, I can't do that either he said, like go to Avedon – but he said, what I can do and what I know best is this, and he was very clear about that – so I respected, I said, fine. He said, I can do one, two, three figures in a space and I can get you uh uh what he thought was a good photograph. And he was a big photographer and I respected that he had that perspective about himself and uh knew himself that well so I said fine – and so okay well maybe we could have like instead of having one big photograph you know something like that – we could have like a series – lots of little ones that would get in all the information. He said fine but – so I was – I thought it was going to work but hum when he finally got hold of the material – it was – he just tore it apart – he did all sorts of things with it – there was like a nothing I could do to – I kept saying, but, no, wait (laughs) – and all the people there – my people, they kept thinking, what is happening (laughs) and they stopped, and – well – but, but maybe maybe something else will turn out with the photographs – but I don't think so (pause) I'm sorry – I was telling what happened, ok – so, Freud walks out, I come out as the mammy, I go to the seated woman, the bird woman and stop, the runner is still going and the turtle is just about off and these people are clearing the stage – and then a little girl comes out as a man, and she's a black girl, in identical costume, and then one lion steps out here and then another lion steps out – and the Blue Danube's been playing, it stops – it's like we're starting again – it's like suddenly this ridiculous thing that's happened has just been blown out of proportion and even becomes even more ridiculous because, we've got another lion that comes out and then you realize the whole – that there are black people doing them and then there are white people doing them and that there are men doing them and there are children doing them and it's like all – very old people doing them – there's, it's like every (laughs) – and then another lion comes out and then another lion comes out – so it just keeps getting more and more ridiculous and then then the next one and the next one and the next one and then they go across – and uh as they are clearing – just as they're clearing and all the dust from the sand is is up in the air – the back-drop which is setting up the next picture, it's sort of come in, – it is the drawing room – that is being pulled up very slowly and the whole lighting eh is changed and then we see the runner out the slit in the drawing room – this is like the skeleton now of the next act – none-none of the furniture is there and it's like this picture is dissolving into the next and then she goes to the table which is – oh, I'm sorry, I bring out the table at the very beginning too – Freud's table – and that's like a picture that's going into focus that whole time – it's in front of the whole piece – cause the chair is being lowered also during this act – it's going – the third act is going to end at the table – the grandson is walked walks away uh and she goes over to the table and places, at the end of that act uh an Egyptian figure (an Egyptian figure?) Yeah. Which Freud, like I-I got that from the pictures of his study – he had those things around him – also on this table – now, so – in the second act – is uh hum so the curtain – in the curtain – she puts the figure on the table the curtain falls – in the second act – this time – this time I had a deaf, this deaf child sing – what's interesting (garble) are the graphic or parallel – structures – of the whole piece turn – just – like you get – always these layers of sort of things happening and all say – that's the first act – the second act there's not – these layers of things too – it's almost like what happened in this – say in the dynamics or graphics, dynamics is that it's everything is moving fairly even except for this one little interruption where Freud maybe comes in and then Kenneth coming out the movement finally was twisted and faster and there was like – at that time there was like – there was like a little more activity happening on stage than had ever happened before, just at that one moment so there's like a swell in the piece in the – but in the end when the mammies come out suddenly there's music and there's a lot of lots of people and everything is sort of – the dynamics is a whole another reality – suddenly the whole reality is just the-the dynamics is changed so that it has that sort of graphic structure and then for this act the same thing happens — it seems almost to (In terms of that thing then the line, so to speak, of energy of the act is upward, — or?) Upward, or but-but it's not say not always going up and down, up and down — it's very even too — if it's going up it's very even or uh it's a very — it's a very — the dynamics are not like-like — this thing happens and that thing happens (No) It's not that kind of dynamics because it's more like (raps out a steady beat on the table) and that sort of dynamics that — which does have like uh momentum after a while (— building up after awhile?) Yeah, it happens, but it's almost like if I take this and go (knocking in a steady slow beat) after awhile what begins to happen is another thing and yet I'm still just doing that uh you know what I mean? — it's like another thing begins happening after awhile — and that's interesting, it seems by the third act that-that we've got that established — that — to cope with — then hum — you see like what happens here is that the dynamics again are very even except there is another swell here when Freud comes out it seems even more so this time is that — because everyone is moving a little bit sort of doing small movements like this or whatever and maybe not even that much — but when he comes out — it's like for a minute no one moves — it's like suddenly like the little movement is even — and he just stands in the doorway of the drawing room — so it's like — and it's like the frame of the picture just froze and then — and then it goes back to what it is like — he goes out — but it seemed like the dynamics have changed there too — and then at the end when the mammy comes out again — the single mammy comes out — and then the cat legs — it's like that's — suddenly like the scale of the activity and it's like suddenly — it seems like that — and then the king stands out too — it's like those are strong punches in the piece — so the dynamics is somewhat similar to the first act it seems (I get it. My image of an increasing energy, ascending line is not right. It is really rather as though at the end there is an act transcending or negating or framing the whole thing) It also, this one ends with the king standing, and this one begins with the king sitting on the stage and this one sort of ends with the drawing room going up and it's like this is setting up this one, this is sort of setting up this one this is a revealing of this area and it is an unfolding and then also what happens is that the table Freud has is — when he stands up he's got a Chinese figure, that went — on Freud's table — so this is like bringing this picture more into focus too which is the final picture that we end up with — so it's like — it's like oh a collage it's a — bringing it into focus — and what happens in addition too is that on this table we had an additional figure that came in during the intermission and then we have this — like we had like a vase — of flowers or something just for the — (What I saw was oriental objects) Yes, it's just becoming more and more like a setting that — then the chair is going in — also the boy is — we see him once again — the guy — there's this snake uh — and what happens in this piece is you know the runner, going, and you have this king of Spain sitting here — I think, I might have gone over this — and then you have the drawing room fits in here and those people

and then you have, out here occasionally you have other things that happen
– a big black bird, six foot black bird, goes by – this time I had uh uh
one of the animals went by or something – it's like – and one of the runners, or one of the girls that's in this last act here is doing some of these
movements – it was. (Intermission between acts I and II, Raymond
Andrews singing.) – He's just *barely* – picking up on this, and he's he's
just beginning to have a little experience – with his – voice. It's *al*most
like he's crying too. It's like that. – and he's black, he's a black boy.
(inaudible) But that's going on during intermission, so, again, you're not so
focussed watching, it's like people are *talk*ing, you know, smoking, and – so
they can hear inside, and some people are standing (inaudible) so it's somewhat *can*celled by – the distraction – of various –. Uhum ah during *this*
intermission – (What happens during act II?) There's a game table *here* –.
And – that's the first thing that happens. Then people come in – the runner
is going outside –. The king of Spain is already seated, but we don't see so
much of him, he's just, – maybe a piece of his *hair* or something. Uhum,
there's a *game* table started here, – and, – that game is played throughout,
it's like *nuc*leus, of the piece, and that, – coming out in *here* –. Uhum
someone comes and makes a drink, and sits on a chair here, – someone
mixes a drink, there's a chair here, –. This chair is miked. There are *all*
sorts of little things like, – that we like see it – you can *hear* the sound. –
But, a lot, *all* people didn't realise it. It's like, – maybe, maybe you *sen*sed
it, – like something is a little *strange* (short laugh) but I didn't want 'em to
say ›*oh* they've got that chair miked,‹ it wasn't that; but – the reality was
– s-*slightly* off, was like, – sort of *ba*rely, you know, and it was just that
I didn't want it to (?) – and also I had a mike on the *ice* cubes here,
too, – but it was off just a little bit so that, – the loud sound carries
a *little* – little louder than natural, but not – and then I had – I don't
know, on the *tea* cart I had a-a string, and a couple of times, after people
made a drink and put the *ice* cubes in, and and they were just sort of leaving, the tea cart would make a sound so that it was like, – their their time-
thing was like a little off (inaudible), and it was a whole –. One time that
someone *didn*'t come in and make a drink, we'd just shake the or make the
cart just rattle a little bit – (How did you shake the – –?) We had a *string*
tied to it, so we pulled it. But. Also, then I, – a girl came in and she walked
to a chair. She sat down and the chair moved. As she, as she was walking
towards it the chair just moved back, and then she'd sit it would stop and
she sat down. Uhum. A woman[10] comes in – telling this, telling s-stories,
and again that's, – it's like the stories are, – I don't know, the way she
tells them, I mean that whole thing is, – it seemed very important, and she
is miked. – And then, she does a, she has this amazing ability to talk to
people, too, like, I always felt, she, – that was one of the things I'd noticed
*about* her that – and then (inaudible) she'd come to a class I had of say six
graders and she was able to *talk* to them. I mean she really could con*nect*

10 Mary Peer.

with them some way she's she's –. An amazing (inaudible) about it, so –. And then also, in another sense, it seemed very right for *Freud* (short laugh), that, like somewhere under that, there was, you know, –. A *wal*rus came out with her. – And. I think this is a guy just with a walrus' *head* on, – in costume. And he just – he's like, – he's in*side* of her, in a very, – there is a very strange relationship between the two. But he's like another *side* of her, – that's, that you see (inaudible). There's a *man* that comes out in a *bur*gundy smoking jacket here, – a very *formal* (?) sort of attire. And there is a woman[11] in a in a burgundy ah-gown here, a Turkish wedding gown. And one time she comes over and sort of stands with her back to me (inaudible) but like they never *touch*, I mean (inaudible) but it was like a –. But and when *he* comes in he leaves a *rose* in the chair for her. And when she comes in later, she picks up the rose and holds it. There's like that, there's lots, – and there is like another relationship over here between a couple, but it's very, – it's like, – it's *so low*, the key of it, that, that you, that you, *most* people don't see it. And *that*'s o.k. Like, – like I said, one, last time, it would be like needlepoint (inaudible), it's all *wo*ven together, but, it's like when you look at it from the distance, you are ‹o far from it, you almost sense it, you know it's like, you just see the larger picture. Then when you, if you get really *close* to it, you s-see these other things happening. Like there's a *pipe* in the wall, with *smoke* that comes out just a, – like from inside a (inaudible) or something, a drop here, and there's a pipe, and it's just a trail of smoke that comes out every once in a – there's a, – but, –. There's a *lot* of things (?), like the visual things are mi- –, I don't – a *lot* of re*lat*ionships among the *peo*ple, too, that- there's one between two women that's that's some kind of uh – like we, – all the movements they've been (inaudible) designed and planned ahead of time (inaudible) most of it (inaudible). – But we do other things, but there are certain moments there like, it was, it was very beautiful, I don't think people saw it, they are sitting with their two heads like this and suddenly they would come – down, and then one would get up and then another'ld get up and then they'd sit down. – So it's, at times some of those things were planned and structured, – but the way they appear is al-, they appear *al*most as if they're happening, – and then a lot of, – *most* of the things *are* just happening.[12] But there *are* *are* *times* that that we very carefully'd been going through. But what we've tried to do then, in rehearsal, is *not* – as if they they the seemed very natural (short laugh). And *that* seemed, –

11 Liba Bayrak.

12 »the »activities« (the play) were all set as a general kind of framework to guide the people in it, even though probably most of the audience wouldn't see, or consider it to exist. And this in turn set up a series of theatrical contradictions that didn't seem arbitrary, say, but that arose spontaneously *and* visually in the performing situation . . . . the activities weren't arbitrary, but the encounters of the people within were flexible and immediate in relationship to the being of each person and to the group – sort of like an incalculable margin, a kind of human

like there was a *feeling* that I always had about that drawing room that – that ah – I saw a lot of lot of things about it but, again, I, that that – I didn't think it was about that *fee*ling that I wanted to create in that drawing room among those people. Anyway, ah- (you mentioned that, but a feeling among them wasn't particularly clear to *us* –) – as a group of people sitting together in that room. (inaudible) And, – and it's interesting, a *lot* of people saw that – *diff*erently from the way *I* saw it. And it didn't bother me so much. I-I saw it as a very uh, it was almost like a pasture or something, it was very pastural, it was almost like, – *cows* grazing, so it, it was *hea*ven, eh, it was very *peace*ful to me, some people didn't *see* that, that I always, I always thought, I thought and there were other sides to it too, I didn't think it was only that. There's a very relaxed thing about a cow, just sort of . . . . . (But also isolated) yes, and (pause), in fact (laugh) at one time (pause) ah, I wasn't going to do the cat legs – – – – – again because it was *so* difficult, and, we couldn't, that-a in December we had trouble finding *tracks*, there was *no* place where we could rent tracks, to-to operate them, because of – the places that had them were had rented them out and we couldn't get them from anyone -f-, anywhere, and we had to have two oneway tracks and they'ld have to be very *long* and . . . We had a lot of *problems*, and we, whether we'd have one made it'd be very expensive so (short pause) I was gonna have *cows* walk on it there, there were like twenty cows, – very slowly, just fill that room, as if people (?) and then I thought of *sheep* – too, – but, it-alm-it almost, the cows seemed right too like the room had filled with cows because, – it was like, – to me, it was like, the same thing, but a-another another thing too, it's like, you know, repeating it but in another way (short pause) (inaudible) (There's

consideration that usually never has a chance to erupt in most traditional theatre.« (Wilson, *Production Notes* on *The King of Spain*, p. 250.)
Wilson is here speaking of the *action* (not quite a *plot*) of the play. He doesn't like to specify it, not that he wants to *hide* from us what he conceived, not that he feels he doesn't *know*, but because it *is* to be an esoteric frame for the spectator's non-discursive intuition of an atmosphere compounded of the *essentials* of the relationships and interactions of *these* people: so that divulgation would distort the effective nature of the play intended. – Compare this with his withholding, in the speech introducing *Freud* (appendix III), the nature of the ›2 levels of reality:‹ »They are obvious and opposed in nature and . . . .«. Here, I would say, he was, unsure of what they were, – how to put it: he feels he doesn't quite know, and the secretiveness relates to a fear of seeming foolish or trite. Compare both with Wilson's reticence as regards the candlelighting boy's being at the *bottom* of the pile of people forming down-stage in *King* and in act II of *Freud* (cf. appendix II); and with his reticence as to why when he was in second grade he said he wanted to become king of Spain (App. I) – »I don't know where that came from or what it . . .« and »I – I was wondering, I guess like where that came from . . . I mean, I thought it was another thing – and then, also – a thing I hap- left out.«). In these two matters, the secret seems something to be *hidden*: the role of the candle-lighting boy and of the king who is Wilson himself.

a boy lighting candles?) Oh, yes, a boy that lights candles and (inaudible)
Yes, and he lights them, and that was sort of – the bringing *in*, – later on
other people piled on top of him, that was the beginning of the pile that –
that one beginning element that happened way before the others start –
start and – ah (pause), what happens I think is the grandson, or, he comes
in here, appears through the slit, there's a dog that runs across a couple of
times too with the runner, than there's a camel, ther-ah-the woman[13] who
comes in the burgundy gown, she has a whole *air* about her that, she always,
her head, ah, it's almost, she always reminded me of a camel, when I saw
a camel, – ah, she looks so much like a camel (laughter), 'cause the-the way
that sort of thing they have with their eyes and their head it's like Liba, so,
I, – just before she came out I had – I had a a camel that slipped out, and
it's out, and it went off, it was out ... (It sort of peered in?) it peered in, in
profile and it goes off and then she comes in – and then she went over to
her seat, but, I don't know, it-even some people didn't see the camel, but,
that was okay. And, (pause) there's also, the the animals coming in, it's
almost bringing it, *this* and more-more into focus *too* with *these* elements,
like, suddenly it became more together in this act, yes, I think so, – But
you seen them in all the other acts. And they always have a, a natural
quality, it's like one thing I liked is that we did have like *real* animals. And
– a sheep or a dog or, – And then, – like one thing. – I remember when
I went to see a play, or, on Broadway, ah, you know, several years ago, it'd
look so tricky seeing people (laughter) with that, because the animals were
so natural – somehow. I mean they were, – and then then suddenly the
those people doing all of that, that (laughs) – it was interesting, I didn't,
but, I just thought one interesting thing about the work we are doing is
that, that *didn't* happen. It seemed like that, ah, that the people, they
seemed natural being toge*the*r. I thought that was, that was int*e*resting, I
liked that. Even the fact that that beast, uh, Chris, was sitting there with
a real lamb, with someone who is a *fake* bear, someone who's a *fake* mammy,
or someone who is very *real*, I mean it was, like, – it all seemed *na*tural
together, I yah, yah, I liked that. And even like, this time, I had, I think
there was a bal*let* dancer, (inaudible), I – Like one thing I can say about
the *Living Theater*, I always want to take a Madison Avenue businessman
or something – and put him right in the middle because, the-a group, – a
group becomes just *one* thing, it's like (Flat.). Yeah, and that's like, – it's
really, it's really difficult to do when you start *work*ing cause suddenly, like
you-you start *form*ing ideas and then you get people that are sympathetic
around you and then it's like, – it's all *over* somehow, it's like –. One of
the rich things, like I *still* like, – I'm interested in keeping *all* these, if I
can, – because there're lots of different minds in work and different *kinds*
of people with different *es*thetics and different *abil*ities and different fantasies about what they're doing and who they *are* and ... I think that's one
of the *rich* things in the group, all the different *ages* and it's-it's-it's the

13 Liba Bayrak.

*most*, to me, the *most* important thing of the work, – and it's also the most difficult, – to keep going (laughter), by far, by far, yes, – Because, to somehow get all those people together that's, – well, but that's the *rich* thing, that, uh – But, – I get, I felt, someways bad about it this time, doing-doing a piece, you know, say with Cambodia and Kent *State* and all that, it's like, – I thought, well wow, you know, – here I am here-ere I am in the opera house doing this *big*, – yah, – pro*duc*tion, and then, – but somehow I liked seeing the piece at this time, and – what-what I guess I'm saying is that it's im*por*tant, it seems, while you're *wor*king, to, wh-what we were saying before, to always have an awareness of what's happening *now*, I don't think you should, you can can, – you can't for*get* that.

(Could you describe Act Three of *Freud* for me – it would help me to write about it.) – Yah, if I can help you. Ah, Act Three, what – what I did, see, Stefan, a lot of the ideas that I had for December, didn't appear because there wasn't time, I still, like the work was still – in the process, you know – so more things happened this time and I still didn't have, I still had ideas you know didn't get in cause I didn't have the time to – – cause there is a time problem of being in that particular space for a very, very long length of time, having all the elements together, lights, scenery, costumes, people, like, I could never get them together except first a very few hours before the performance, so you have a lot of ideas, but there's no time to set up everything and get everyone in place (pause) So, one-one of the things that did happen before the house curtain, was that one of the mammies in white came out this time riding on a bull all over the place (?) – and this almost paralleled Raymond, the deaf child, who sang between One and Two, this last time (Yah) I did the mammy and someone else did another mammy and then we were all in white with silver glasses and a green scarf, and, (pause) I don't know, it was-it was, it had to happen (?) during the intermission some people were sort of walking and talking and not completely focussed on it, somehow, I've-you sensed I think an air of something that only brings the curtain – – – – – it was like a cry and it was like, seemed to, it was almost painful, and there was a lot of things sort of in it I thought, in it, that happened, and there was a, friend of mine involved who's a concert pianist – – – – – and it was over and over and over again – – – – – and that's before the house curtain, and then the Prince and Princess come out and sit in the balcony, and the curtain goes up and the stage is dark, and we see floating in the air a baby, a live baby, and the baby is crying, and then another piece of music – that's been composed – (?) is played – and you see an old woman, doing, sort of a gesture, sitting at the entrance of the cave, she's sort of, she's outside the cave and it's all dark, except the baby boy, and the woman then goes inside the cave an old, old woman – the gate keeper goes to light a candle and he lights a (inaudible) to the entrance of the cave and suddenly we see all the – – – – – and then the the picture outside the cave, there's fog and there's smoke coming inside, here it's dark, and then we ss . . . so that picture dissolved

and we went to the picture outside, the cave — — — — so it's like the
start of the Third Act without focussing, we went into focus, then we
registered that image that it like a continuum or something that's constant — — — — we still see the runner outside on the beach running — And
then we see girls and boys and the man was painted (?) with gold, in the
sunlight, and they are doing exercises, a ritual, and, (inaudible) again the
we're all — — — — and there're zones — — — — outside the cave, about
eleven zones? in which different activity happens — from the audience, you
didn't see it so much, but there was, it's like different horizontal zones of
layers of activity (How much space did you have?) I had twenty-one feet,
I think — It's very deep, I think, and the cave was brought in (?) like a
Freudian symbol very deep in the stage so it was about midway, I'd got a
lot of depth back there — but I had, ah, this time s-it was like much richer
so that outside the cave there were again, like layers of activity happening,
you begin seeing all sorts of things? and the child is Freud's grandson, . . .
(What kind of activities?) Ah, well, the one who was the furthest away
from the audience is the runner so he's always running constantly and in
front of that was, sort of, a movement that got made up and in front of
that was another movement (What kind of movement was that?) Ah, it-
it was hard to say, but I know like, anyway, the two in front of the runner
were very opposed to each other, or something, and that kept happening
all the time, they were always sort of very opposed in nature, sort of, like
two halves of something, you know, never somehow complete together, and,
then there was another chorus of people who came in that-that have, that-
that they bring in was a-a- the-the man with the snake, someone holding
the lamb, the child dissolves, the child is floating in the-in the air 'cause
there is an opening, a hole in the cave wall you see the child through, so
just the baby is beginning to seem distant, it disappears and then we see the
lamb and afterwards the man holding the snake comes –, Freud's grandson
comes in (outside the cave?) Yah, outside the cave, And we see a woman
inside the cave lighting a-a black lamp (?) – she does a whole ritual with
it, from the East to the West, now something – and the king of Spain's
sitting on stage (pause) (He is elevated?) Yes, he's sitting on on top of
(inaudible) and there's straw on the floor (?) of the cave, and, then, the bird
woman comes in and sits with him and then, what happened in the First
Act, she sits all the way through the First Act, in the end she gets up and
places the figure on the table, he sits all the way through the Second Act, in
the end he gets up and puts a figure on the table – and, in this Third Act,
they both sit together – and she comes in, she sits down and the people
outside the cave bring the grandson, the little boy, and, almost the lamb
becomes the child (whisper), the child goes and (inaudible) to the table in
the last act, and it's almost as if that picture is beginning to come in focus
too — — — — on stage with Freud's table, there are now more objects on
the table – the figure from the *King of Spain* appears – figure of the bird
woman, and now flowers and other — — — — some things that Freud

would have around him, on this table, or on the table — and the chair is getting closer to the table now, it's being lowered all the way down to the table, so that picture is also coming into focus — ah, and then, — the people outside the cave continue what they're doing, animals begin to come in, and there are all kinds of animals we see here — We see a cow, we see an ape, we see a lion, you see a tiger, you see all-all kinds of animals — And they come in at — they lie down, almost on top of each other, it's very peaceful ————— there are bears on top on cows and on top of tigers and — a walrus, and the animals — animals, throughout the last act come down around Freud's table — they almost make a-a hover — around it — Freud's table, until that-that picture and then — the chair comes all the way down to the table. This time I had a — a halo for the king of Spain a triangle halo and it came on just for a second, or so, a couple of times during the last act (It came on?) Yes, it was a neon tube that (Oh? Mostly they're not free floating, they're attached ——) Yah, well I just suspended it ————— with a sort of switch that'd go click-click (laugh) ————— a triangle halo that came on . . . And we, and I also had a swa- a girl doing a dying swan outside the cave — and also there was a bird, and that I had had in the Second Act, and also briefly for a moment in the First Act — it was a big, black bird — costume — it was a big, black bird — this big, black bird comes in and the swan, the girl doing the dying swan, but, very, very beautiful — girl and all. I liked it for a lot of reasons. Like particularly the girl that did it — I thought she was — like things are always — you like them visually for what it is ————— also, just the fact that — that girl was a ballet dancer, she's like a principal dancer and dances with ballet companies and she was able to come down and work with this group and take direction — instantly — and work under the most difficult conditions (laugh) with a ground cloth on the floor, lots of sand ————— and it's very difficult to move — and never once complained and m- just be there too, in terms of a problem — I thought that I didn't know anything about ballet, as far as giving her (whisper) (inaudible) ballet's and stuff so our communication was another sort of thing and yet the movement was im-possible, I don't know somehow I don't know those movements — it was a very interesting way to work — we had to communicate in another sort of way — She had been tuned in to what was happening, it was another sort of sensitivity happening there — I th-thought that was very, very remarkable for her — that — cause I've been watching rehearsals of ballet dancers and I just don't think many of — of those dancers could have done that — to-to they wouldn't have done it — it just couldn't — they wouldn't (What effect did you look for in working with her . . . .?) Well, she just saw what was happening somehow — what was happening outside there — and I explained to her — and she did it once, in a rehearsal and I think ————— three times a swan — I just talked to her and she was sort of sensing what was right — and there was a guy that she worked with — the guy who was holding this drink — and he, had never of course worked with a dancer like that — then suddenly there he was picking her up and putting her down – and they were working very much together – there was a certain sort of life there – or she had never had to–––––I told her this afternoon – I think it meant a lot to her too – to have this performing experience. – It was ineresting too 'cause she liked it very much, – she wanted to do, quote, »Avant Guard Art,« you know, – she wants to (inaudible) . . . »So you just do your ballet, because you are so extraordinary to me, and the, and for a ballet dancer to do what you did, you know – it's very, very much« (laugh) –––––that's a remarkable thing – and that's her knowledge, that's what she knows and she's extraordinary doing it, I mean that's, I mean, she's been like a principal dancer but, like, you know, most of the companies seem –, she's, I think, a dancer really, she shouldn't throw that acclamation away – she thinks now if she goes out and does like a whole thing it's gonna look like doing like, quote, what the avant guard dancer would do, – »no, just do the ballet, I-I think that that's – they'll see (?) a remarkable thing« – outside the cave, ah, outside the cave is bright sunshine, we still see the beach, look at the runner, and that picture almost dissolves until a period, a time thing, it's been on, timeless – the people, khaki clothes, without props, and, there's no reference, specific reference to time. And suddenly it begins, it goes to a 19th century time – and suddenly we see people in 19th century clothes and they're running, or, doing something, some movement – and then a banner comes in, and the king of Spain's head is painted on it, just his head is painted on it, and it's carried across. All outside the cave, wreaths of flowers are brought in – the music is still playing and they're, they're singing–––––music outside the cave–––––But anyway, finally in that picture, finally, it's almost as if it's happening outside – the cave has become, its fullest register and then suddenly, and the pace of what's happening is more like that and you feel like it's reached a point that inside the cave are – what happens is that Freud comes out – then he sits at the table – the-that picture is almost registered at its fullest thing, so what happens is that something else takes over now – and, you see, Freud and his grandson, ah, and the child's crying. The idea was not to, like like the little boy who cried, he said, ah, what am I supposed to think about? am I dying? I said no, just do it you know like you're gonna cry thirteen times – and I want it to come really from inside, way down deep, and I want it to be loud, but you don't have to think about any of this, just do it, just do it thirteen times and count, do it, wait, and do it, and wait – and-he- I liked the way he did it 'cause it wasn't like expressing – it was more like, more functional – 'cause at that time everything is so loaded, we have all the information, we don't need the expression, the expression wasn't necessary – he's overloaded – I thought that, thought like in *Freud*, there were a lot of things happened that – that was very (inaudible) 'cause I was worried about that, there's -s so many things happening that, – everything had to be very economical – I wanted – It was enough that he was crying thirteen times, just, just AHHHH! that was enough, we got the idea, and it's all I wanted, so ever-there's a control-on- I went to see Ethel Merman on Broadway last week and I liked her very much She's a great performer. She's got that ... I liked her because .... When it came to the »Hello Dolly« number and everyone is really going, I mean like, like the chorus (! ! ! ! !) really sockin it to 'em and she's really sockin' it to 'em too, but like she's watching herself do it, I mean she's like, she sort of does that and they are all going (! ! !) and, it wasn't her age, it was like, it was all that was necessary, she, she's right in in the center of that-that music, I mean right at the core of it, and she, she just how much – is – it's, it's, it's this sensibility thing and everyone sees it differently but (laugh) I sure liked it – I-I liked the whole, the whole approach to the role, I mean this – I I felt that never extraneous, never – there was a very fine sensibility there, what was right and what was necessary and (short pause) a very powerful performance – I can tell like that sometimes she's really good and sometimes she wasn't and something and I just went and I -er-there was no need for her to be extraordinary – but, I liked her, she was very detached in this play and very much in-into the material – sh-she had-, she had, she had that, she could s – I don't know, a perspective of herself – a very intelligent performer – yeah – very intelligent, s-s-so intense and yet s-s-so contained – she-l-l, she lets you, she lets you get into the material too, like she gets with a super-high gear and then she holds on to it, so it's not like she lets it all go, so like, you-you-you have a chance to, go into it, like in *Freud*, like the first act, no one faces the audience, no one ever confronts the audience except for the woman who puts the figure on the table (Yah) and she-she goes to the table and she puts it on the table, she's like, that's the only time anyone ever faces the audience – and this, this second act, it's almost the same thing, like the *King of Spain* in look – – – – – a confrontation – but, of, what happens, is, in the process, part of this is the audience has a chance then, to like go into it – – So many times, it seems that the theatre is so anxious to *go* (makes noise) (laugh) seems like, you know (Right) and the audience (laugh) sometimes that's interesting, tho – Then what happened in the last act was – Freud sits at his table and the lights are down, the people outside the cave – all the bars have fallen, at that time, over the entrance to the cave and they separate that activity from the inside of the cave, show the picture down front, closer, larger, layered, and, and (pause) just as the child cries for the last time, Anna Freud comes out too, and it's almost like you see her doing – I don't know, a lot of things happen – at first I didn't have her – a – like in my head I'd always seen Freud with a grandson, 'cause that's what happened – in reality when the child dies there, and suddenly, when I saw it in the theater it seemed so like a female figure was so important there, to being her out there – it seemed we needed that – to me – it made it – – – – – statement – – – – – much larger sense then ... (What does she do?) She runs out and – as the child is crying we've suspended a piece of glass in the orchestra pit ... and there's a white banner, just slowly coming up to shield the glass (Uhum) and the child cries for the thirteenth time, the banner has reached its – – – – – then she runs out – – – – – Anna Freud – it's a picture that suddenly just goes into focus very quickly -sh-sh she slips in at the very end it's like the sun's out and then she's stopped – she's frozen just as the last cry happens and the pane of glass falls – a gesture like this ... almost again parallel to the king of Spain sitting there for a very long time and just as he gets gets up to face the audience the curtain comes down – just as soon as she got that registered, she very quickly disappears and (pause) so – you see a lot of –

there are all sorts of things that come back in like – you've seen some animals in the first act and you see a few more in the second act and you even see people making animal sounds in the second act – like there's some of the people in the drawing room – some people didn't even notice it but like there's a woman at one time who moos like a cow and another woman going Bah-haah, like a sheep, while she's just sitting there because I think I said we are almost (inaudible) of pastures but she's – the people almost – they are making animal sounds and you see the walrus (inaudible) them – following that animal (?) with a (?) microphone – and then in the last act you see more animals that are coming in – it's very silent – in the first act you heard birds – you hear one bird and you hear more birds and more and more birds and in the second act there was a hum like a – almost like a refrigerator hum, like there's almost a hum in this room, – then- then you hear the cows and the sheep, sometimes you hear birds and in the last act you hear the ocean – it's like the sound score was going to its fullest register in the last act because on the beach we didn't have the sound of the waves and we didn't have – and in the last- (You didn't have – at both performances you had the rope that slapped) -and I think it happened the same way this time too – one performance the rope slapped – I let someone do that, and uh I told them if you want to you can do that and if you don't want to – and I think that one time the guy hit it on the floor, the next it just moved away (?) but uh, you hear the action of the waves, you hear, – the hum comes back in in the last act – you hear the birds from the first act and you hear the other animal sounds. It's almost like all the sounds from all the animals are coming into their fullest register in the last act, you've seen mammies in the first act, we've seen more mammies in the first act, well that time – like that element was almost in its fullest register, we'd say, just say mammy-element, you know. There – there were themes (?) like that – like there are tying elements too, like – at the same time there's always a very specific sort of time reference to the time of Freud's life. There – there are also other time references so that it's it's not only that time but sometimes it seems that it even goes back further – and sometimes it goes ahead – time references. (In terms of the sound you described, there was a linear build-up throughout the piece, but in the second act it actually, really; went down, – it seemed to me it relaxed –?) Yeah, it does, – no it doesn't – I didn't mean it varied – it's like hum once I explained it like in Chinese checkers – like if you have all the marbles in the pegs, some of the time – and then like the next time maybe you just have less of the marbles, and the next time you have all of the marbles and that's like – that's what I meant by registers like – sometimes you have like like the whole pattern filled and sometimes it's partially full, less full and sometimes it's completely full – and like, it doesn't mean that they are all in their fullest register in the last act – it doesn't progress necessarily that way – although it is something that does happen just in watching things happens – just in the experience after having been that long through all this information, all this material, you build it up to a certain point, but sometimes just looking at the individual elements and specific things in the piece I found that like sometimes they're at their fullest point in the first act, sometimes they were at their fullest point in the second act and sometimes in the third act. As far as structuring all that information, working it out and putting it together – that – I keep finding that there are all sorts of parallels in all three acts – that – that's how I keep it together – like, – I find that materials repeat hum a performer repeats or a character or an animal or a sound or something – there are all sorts of things like that tie it together – like you see uh – like you see uh you see a hay stack in the thing and you see like hay all in the last act – it's just like the hay is just – sort of just suddenly coming in – because it comes in at the end of the second act – and suddenly you see it all over the space – that – in the last act – and suddenly, it's like the king of Spain you see only – sort sort at the end of the last[14] act and then you see him already – you see him there when the curtain goes up in the last act – it's like he appears, and then the curtain opens up for the last act you see him there too. (Who joins him in the third act?) The bird woman – the woman in the first act (And she doesn't relate to him at all, of course, in the first act). She doesn't, she relates only sort of structurally in that – they're both seated figures – she's seated in the chair the whole time and she never moved until the end of act three – he does the same thing – he's seated in his chair the whole time and – that's also, like, as far as different time things, like, they're the stillest in the whole – she – she's – sits in the first act and the runner's going and he sits in the second act and the runner is going – so it's like in between those those two different times things or all other kinds of time, (Let me ask you one thing, – you would, I assume, see some continuity between the *King of Spain* and *Freud* and then the next thing that you have in mind doing – and it's different from most other theatre around. What kind of quality would you mention or how is it different?) One way, like the first thing that came to my head is that – and this is where I get the most criticism too – I'm not convinced it's a positive you know or a good thing but maybe it is – it's a very personal – It's very much out of my experience and very much from the inside of me, it seems – like it very much came from like something inside, you know, so – I mean it happens that I uh sense that it's right or I mean that's what I trust, that's what I rely on, instead of like say

14 Wilson probably meant »the first act« (of *Freud*).

studying – a way of doing it like say a school or theatre or school of thought – it might encompass those ideas I mean I guess – (One of the things you mentioned was that people didn't face the audience except at some point – I mean one difference–) I can tell you why, part of that, I mean you know some of the things I realize later after I do them why I did them and I found for the most part that the thing that I just I just shudder (laughs) when I go to the theatre – especially seeing dance, they are always going Huuuu (aggressive, scaring noise), – and got out to the audience and I found that so repulsive (both speak at once) it's like – ME! – I always thought – I couldn't look at them because they're very – I just (coughs) – to me I couldn't get interested – I – I wasn't allowed to get into them or – to them – I couldn't be sensitive – it was like – I don't know – for a lot of reasons – that – it was easier for me to see what was happening – and they weren't coming at us – I could participate as a viewer or audience – so that was one – and then the king of Spain – this is in the second act – it is true that most people are sort of turned outward but their focus is almost always down – it's never like this – so – I always felt like the first act was almost in profile cause everyone was focussed into the wing – and the second act they almost focussed – in the first act they're always passing from one side to the other always – and in the second act they're collecting and they keep facing out (pause) but at the same time they are never like, not so much at the audience, it's more a 45 degree angle (mumble and pause) (The communication between you and the audience seems to relate to this thing of body awareness – offering up something – the only thing is, you require an outgoing gesture from the audience really – doing that) Exactly (YOU let them in at most so to speak – you offer up a present to them) Also what happens is that, yeah, it's almost that the audience is needed then to – for support, and it's almost like – instead of going out so much like that – it's almost like like they have to come into it to help make the other happen – it seems to me – like it feels – like I felt the other night when I saw *Dolly* – or when I see most theatre – that almost the audience is not needed to be there – that they're so into the material that there's no room for the audience – you know, it's like – like if – like they've completed a circle – it's interesting, but what happens then is that your experience is so limited – it seems to me, now I don't know – this is – I may be completely wrong but, say – like that's what I don't like about the ballet – visually it's very beautiful and like I look at it and I saw wow that's, you know, visually, ok – I can't get that far – it's extraordinary that they do that – but, at the same time, I feel that – I always leave the ballet with my head empty and I feel like it never stimulated my head – I never was allowed to sort of experience, that sort of thing, with my head – and then this may be my freakiness, but – what I always thought would be more interesting if say, they let me participate, with my own mind and I could go – if they held back so that I could go into it, sort of like we were making it – just (?) like that sort of exchange of working together, feeling that sort of thing happening and I feel that that does happen, with my work cause the performer is very much really listening to the audience and they're very much in one sort of way – they're very much, not at the same time, but I think – I don't know there's another sort of awareness at[14a] (You tend to think in terms of horizontal layers of the

[14a] Detachment such as Ethel Merman's in *Dolly* according to this speech to Wilson figures as a kind of (I suppose to him unacceptable) alternative to the withholding he wanted. – I do not suppose, incidentally, that he would agree to my term »withhold.« Richard Schechner's notes on audience conduct during *Stalin* may perhaps suggest one dimension of the audience-»connection« to the theatre achieved by Wilson: »At the December 1973 performances of Robert Wilson's *The Life and Times of Joseph* – Such detachment on the part of a performer thus to Wilson figured as a kind of (I suppose to him unacceptable) alternative to the witholding he wanted. – I do not suppose, incidentally, that he would agree to my term »withhold.« Richard Schechner's notes on audience conduct during *Stalin* may perhaps suggest one dimension of the audience-»connection« to the theatre achieved by Wilson: »At the December 1973 performances of Robert Wilson's *The Life and Times of Joseph Stalin* at the Brooklyn Academy of Music's Opera House, the LePerq space – a room of about 150 feet by 80 feet – was set up with tables, chairs, refreshments: a place where people went not only during the six 15 minute intermissions but also during many of the acts of Wilson's seven act opera. The opera began at 7:00 p.m. and ran more than 12 hours. I remember coming back to Manhattan at about 8:30 a.m., stopping at Dave's Corner at Broadway and Canal, and having an early morning egg-cream: a re-entry ritual into New York ordinary life. Each of *Stalin*'s seven acts had been performed before, either as part of Wilson's earlier work or as independent pieces. Thus, the 12 hour performance in the opera house was a retrospective. Most of the people in the audience had seen at least some of Wilson's work before (this is an assumption I can't prove, but think true). They assembled for *Stalin* not only as a thing in itself (accidental audience) but as a ritual experience (integral audience).

The behavior in the LePerq space was not the same throughout the night. During the first three acts the space was generally empty except for intermission. But, increasingly as the night went on people came to the space and stayed there speaking to friends taking a break from the performance, to loop out of the opera, later to re-enter. About half the audience left BAM before the performance was over; but those who remained, like repeated siftings of flour, were finer and finer examples of Wilson fans: the audience sorted itself out until those of us who stayed for the whole opera shared not only the experience of Wilson's work but the experience of experiencing it. The opera was advertised and tickets sold publicly. But the accidental audience aspect of the performance was winnowed away by the long hours, the LePerq space, and the fact that the performance was a retrospective.

A loop developed between the LePerq space and the opera house. The house was a place of silence, attention on the performance, and – as the night went on -a more and more spatially scattered audience, until at the end less than $1/2$ of the 2200 seats were occupied. The LePerq space started out being used only during intermission. But, as the evening went on the tables and chairs were rearranged according to the size of the parties using them, and the space was used continuously

performance space and building them up from the rear, from the point remotest from the audience?) Sometimes it doesn't, sometimes they start in the middle or something (But why these layers, I mean it's an unusual way to think of the stage?) Cause – first of all I just did that and then then it seemed right and then I tried to analyze it and say why have I done it and why does it – why does it seem right – what makes it seem right – and one of the things that makes it – makes it seem right – it's like – I think something we talked about last time – when you think of your experience of the thing or – you go back, the mind goes into many different things at one time – it goes through many different realities or – time – like while I'm talking to you now like I'm thinking about when you're talking to Mary or talking to Sarah or having dinner, oh we are going through lots of different things are going through my mind while I'm still talking to you so – that was one way of arranging different – different activities (Different, but do you build it up like that so these zones are significant? From what you said about the zones outside the cave, it wasn't apparent that there was a plan or systematic variation or different levels of reality, – that was mentioned in the introductory speech, – not levels of awareness, but of reality, – layers of reality ... It wasn't apparent from what I saw in the theatre or from what you've said that there were layers of reality, or a build-up, really ...?) It doesn't – it doesn't necessarily build up I don't think – in that – say – take the first act (too softly spoken to be audible) say – the runner is running, like in – now he doesn't at all, say – in any outward way relate to the three people that are doing the movement – in this layer – and that they're doing the same movement and it's uh all the way across and they don't outwardly relate to the runner there and they just – this is one area designated for that and they don't relate to the bird woman that's here and that's like another – but yet when we see them all stacked on top of each other – then we see these different layers of reality – maybe that's not the right term – we see – these – these different things happening – we see hum – we see Freud – he walks out and we see the heavy man who goes across – we see the man with the bird on his shoulder – it's like – they all – it's not this sort of like exchange that we're having here – they're all unhappy but in their own layer or zone

until, at around dawn, there were about $^1/_2$ as many people in LePerq as in the opera house.
What happened during *Stalin* was unusual for orthodox American theatre but common in many parts of the world. People selected for themselves what parts of Wilson's opera to pay attention to, and what parts to absent themselves from. When they went into the LePerq space to rest, socialize, have a refreshment, prepare for a return to the opera house, or whatever, the spectators were not ignoring the performance, they were adding a dimension to it. The social end of the loop was as important to *Stalin* as the aesthetic end. In Madras in 1971 I was impressed by the behavior of the audience at a concert .... The festival lasted more than a week ...« (R. Schechner, *Selective Inattention*, Performing Arts Journal, Spring 1976, vol. 1, no. 1).

– that – that's their own reality – that they make they're – the old woman who comes out, doing her movement, with the young girl, It's – it's not important that you think of it that way I think but what – what happens is a conglomeration of all those things that are on top of each other (But what I was asking really was, is there a more or less systematic change as you approach the audience from the back of the stage – is there more relating to the audience or are things more pertinent or more dramatic or anything of that sort?) No. (There is no formula covering this . . .?) No. – There's no formula – no – what I did – the only thing I did do is think of the whole piece, all three acts – it was like – say – different pictures – they were moving pictures or a collage of moving pictures and this one image – this attached in front, and it's a boy – there is this table, the chair, the-the objects on the table and the dancer, so, throughout the three acts that does get richer and more full – we get more information about that scene (Uhum) and that's down front, it's like, taking that and putting this on it, or, another image on top – Picasso painting on top of it (short pause) And like, if I was gonna do a Picasso painting, I would take, first, you know, one element, in the picture, another element – another – and another – I don't know – like I always think, in some ways as long as I talk it doesn't, – it doesn't mean very much, it's like, it's mostly what you experience when you see it – and then (Yah) Sometimes you, like, you can sit, like sometimes I think I can sit home, and you think of things like that and they don't work, you know (laugh) you know it's like (laugh) – It scares me 'cause lots of times I feel like I do too much work just lying in bed and thinking (laugh) so – (pause)« (Interv. w/Wilson, 1970.)

# 3. Robert Wilson's speech introducing *Freud*.[15]

The Byrd Hoffman Foundation, Inc. with the Byrd Hoffman School of Byrds is currently working on two projects. One is this year's production of THE LIFE AND TIMES OF SIGMUND FREUD, and the other project is a summer art program. The summer art program is being organized so that a group of young people of various capabilities can travel to Texas next summer to purchase ranch land and begin build-

15 »Bob tells me he wrote (the speech) for Mary Peer to read, wearing the black dress with feathers (which later came to be known as the »Audrey Monk dress«), very dignified – in contrast to her rolling summer saulting monologue. Bob wanted to do the »And now in saying something, something« section (at the end of this speech (Brecht)), but he was unable to memorize it in time so they read it together. Then in the 2nd production of *Freud* Audrey Monk read the speech and Bob was able to recite the last section. In Nancy the blonde lady who did the role translated the intro into French, but Bob did the last section in English. In Paris the Intro was dropped except for Bob doing the last section in English.« (George Ashley, letter of VII/18/75.)

»Then – before the house curtain, as the audience is coming in, there is the speech about the play – and that never did work like like I wanted because somehow we never were ready backstage to bring the curtain up so we all always have to wait and people would have to sit down and listen to the speech – but the idea was that they were having this, the play was being explained to them as they were walking in – so you could sort of get it, but at the same time you didn't have to sit and listen to the speech – a lot of people ended up sitting down and listening – and I always felt that there were a lot of overlays to that situation because those were my experiences and some people would realize that – or some people might realize it would be strange for the person giving the speech and the person giving the speech was saying the speech in my language which had its crazy sensibility and somehow unlike seeing a performer doing or someone giving – cause it was strange seeing that person somehow going through these experiences but I liked that – whether people realized it, I just thought it made it interesting in terms of dealing with the material (I didn't know if it was a spoof or) There are lots of those things going because, suddenly when she is doing it (laughs) it became crazy – like, you didn't know what was going on, like – there were lots of realities within it – it she looks almost like someone from (laughs) the women's auxiliary board or something and then, you think that's not real and yet underneath all this there's – it's a very sincere thing and a very valid – I'm saying pretty much how I structured the piece and how the things that I'd like to do – it's – but somehow you think it's all crazy – but I liked that too because then it – then it didn't become quite so serious – cause I'm – it's a pretty serious thing (laughs) to tell the people what you're gonna do. I talked to – there were lots of things sort of working against which I was for – I never was that – people, everyone told me not to do that – all my friends – just don't do that – but I did it anyway – and I was never that sure. Then I come out standing while the speech is being given – about my experiences – but I'm not as myself –« (Wilson, interv., 1970)

418

ing a wall – a core structure – from which, eventually other structures may radiate, to give us a permanent site for our school enabling us to further our work by reaching a new community. And we're hoping that this play will serve as a kick-off for the summer ranch project. THE LIFE AND TIMES OF SIGMUND FREUD is a three-act dance play. The structure of each act is very similiar. And the people, characters, materials, activities and sounds parallel and repeat throughout the entire play. Each has a full register. This means that at any one point an element may be in full focus with all its parts together and later less or more of the parts are together. Like Chinese Checkers with all the marbles in pegs some of the time, other times, less or more. There are two main levels of reality that we are attempting to maintain through out the play. They are obvious and opposed in nature and through out the three acts they change until the final scene they are seen to have completely reversed themselves. Perhaps it's more like making an »X« in that one level starts low and the other high; the other the opposite, that's thinking of it though in graphic terms. If you think of it in terms of color one starts out black and ends up white and the other starts out white and ends up being black. Most of each act is very self-contained, or stripped down until the end, which is very open, rich and (purposely) theatrical. But the end of each act, which in-itself is very short in time balances the preceding time – or »contained duration.« Compare it to a long line with a block at one end, and the block (necessary for) balancing the line. The same basic quasi-structure is repeated throughout each act though that happening may not (upon first viewing) be apparent. And that same hidden structural skeleton is latently apparent for all three acts taken together. All three acts are contained (unto themselves) compared to the ending which is the biggest opening – in the sense of release (and relief). And that's the scene with Freud and his grandchild. I guess almost anyone setting out to do a play about Sigmund Freud the man would have become overly (and overtly?) concerned about the role of his studies and intellectual life – his mind, and what I was thinking about was that those things are popularly familiar – everyone knows them. The things that impressed me most though about Freud as a person being and having these ideas which seemed to have influenced just about everything when reading about him was the fact that he was very human – intensely ordinary and very sort of bourgeoise in one sense – and that was precisely part of his enigmatic brilliance. Yet while we know that attention is hardly ever given to that side of him. History has recorded

him as someone who was particularly motivated by having theories –
theories which, by the way, structurally and systematically seem to
defy just what we mean by the words structure and system and logic.
This piece though, as a kind of hybrid »dance play« doesn't deal
with any big ideas – it just pays inordinate attention to small, *detail*
things. Although we do see him plotting and making charts, notes
undoubtedly the most moving event in his life was when his prized
grandchild, Heinerlie, died – he never got over that – something
within him was smothered for the rest of his life. He said that. A
very simple emotional experience. A death. And suddenly all of his
ideas about living and theorizing about feeling were suspended,
rendered meaningless.

There are a lot of reversals in this piece, such as the ending, a tableau
in a cover with all those animals. It's like going back. Going back to
some indefinable time or memory too hazy to specify in exact particulars. That is, in another sense though, I suppose, the same as moving
continually ahead. Isn't that called *retroactive?* No, not actually. I
mean it's going back as well as in the same time forward. That is,
Freud is plotting and scheming up these charts and yet what we *see*
happening – the stage activity, is very human-like – someone runnig
and someone sitting, another making small talk, someone pouring a
drink, someone dancing, people doing ritualistic exercises. The activities are just very mundane and thus in that way pointedly
human.

Another thing that happens is that the stage is divided into zones –
stratified zones one behind another that extend from one side of the
stage horizontally to the other. And in each of these zones there's a
different »reality« – a different activity defining the space so that
from the audience's point of view one sees through these different
layers, and as each occurs it appears as if there's no realization that
anything other than itself is happening outside that particularly
designated area. People might associate this with Freud and the layers
of consciousness – different levels of understanding but that kind of
obvious intention has been erased or eradicated from this production.
I see it more simply as a collage of different realities occuring simultaneous like being aware of several visual factors and how they
combine into a picture before your eyes at any given moment.
Awareness in that way occurs mostly through the course of experience
of each layer rendering the others transparent. And this might, at
first of course, confuse some people, because we are so being used to
going to the theater and having the play explicitly narrated to us in

verbal direct(ed)ness. Like Shakespeare. Like Shaw. Like Tennessee Williams. Those kinds of plays are primarily constructed *with* words, although other elements are included. On the other hand in dance people as diverse as Jerome Robbins, Merce Cunningham and Yvonne Rainer focus the intention of their work on the formal presentation of movement. The focus here is neither verbal nor concerned with specifying the physicality of people in virtual space. It's simply more visual. And people are just beginning to return again to discerning visual significances as a primary mode – or method – of communicating in a context where more than one form, or »level« exists. In that sense of overlays of visual correspondences we can speak of multi-dimensional realities.

And another thing – everytime The Byrd School does something it seems people mistake it. They think it's a »Put-On.« Well it's certainly *not* a Put-On and that's why we're here having to explain explicitly all these things. Why, after our last production, THE KING OF SPAIN last year at the Anderson Theater one of the financial directors of the Ford Foundation himself told me it was a Put-on – a Joke – *he* was certain of it. Well, it wasn't a joke. That man, he just had a *very* limited way of seeing things – or, maybe he had a hard time seeing – or maybe, maybe there was nothing to see. More likely all possibilities. That is, the broader your experience the more to see, or the less. And it's interesting too the mixture of people, all ages, all kinds of peoples being together. When I go to the Living Theater, or the Polish Lab Theater I wonder why they don't also include a Madison Avenue guy – an egregious PR representative right there in the middle of the stage, since he's as much a necessary figure, or »agent« in getting it on, isn't he? See, we're not particularly interested in literary ideas, because having a focus that encompasses in a panoramic visual glance all the hidden slices ongoing that appear in clear awareness as encoded fragments seems to indicate theater has so much more to do than be concerned with words in a dried out, flat, one-dimensional literary structure. I mean The Modern World has forced us to outgrow that *mode* of seeing. We're interested in *another* thing – another *kind* of experience that happens when encoded fragments and hidden detail become without words suddenly transparent. Unfortunately, the usual bill of theater – like all those year-in-year-out tired Broadway productions mounted (and, destroyed) each season is that they are dealing with all those stories, and those are the same old stories over and over. The same stories Shake-.

speare told. The same stories that the soap operas tell on television. The same stories that Tennessee Williams is telling. And they're o.k.; they're interesting, but like, you get that – you know that instantly you're just being handed the same thing over and over differently disguised and I always say, well so what? You see we're interested here in a theater that deals totally with another sort of thing, even though we're not sure exactly what that is. I feel that when theatre really connects with an audience or when a group of people really connect with one another that there are a lot of things involved. It's always a mystery, isn't it, when you have to stop to analyze it? I am now remembering something a little girl said to me about 4 years ago when I was her teacher. This child had a speech impediment and had a very difficult time speaking at every stage of learning to say a word. I was tongue-tied myself, and, so I was sympathic with her. I could understand part of the problem though in an instant. She wanted desperately to sing but she couldn't get into the school choir, cause of course she couldn't say the words and she couldn't make those sounds. You know, like that. So I said, well, that doesn't make any difference you know, you can, you *can* sing. She said, well I can't carry a tune. She said, »I know I'd *like* to sing.« So I said, well just go ahead and, you know – *sing*. So then she did and then after a couple of years of working with it she really developed an incredible thing with her voice and it was very moving to hear her sing. And eventually by gaining confidence in herself this way she learned in the same manner to talk. Two obstacles were removed. And then one day I heard her working with another child – and this child was singing along with a Bob Dylan recording or something like that. And that little girl, who originally had the speech impediment said emphatically OH NO! SHE SAYS, WHY DO YOU WANT TO SING THOSE SONGS? YOU KNOW, WHY DO YOU WANT TO LEARN MUSIC THAT WAY? You know she continued enthusiastically you can sing your own way. No; don't sing like the Beatles you know. Don't sing like Frank Sinatra. Don't sing like, you know. Sing your *own* way. And that's what interests me because last year when I was teaching in New Jersey at a private school and the director in charge was rehearsing a Shakespearean play that she insisted was the only proper kind of culture she kept demanding that this one child repeat one of the lines over and over again – so as to say it *her* particular way. Bum te bum te bum te bum bum bumm. And the child said, I know. But then the child would say her lines and she would go bum bum bum bum bum bummm. And the director getting more and more infuriated. It was some scene, believe me the director a messenger of culture saying no, no, no, can't you *see*, Shakespeare 's trying to say *this*, and he's trying to say that the lines must be said the way I am saying them so that the audience will understand, so say the words dear bum te bum te bum te bum bum bumm. And the child tried but every time the words would come out they came out bum bum bum bum bum bumm. And finally the director got so very mad and losing control of her temper said you *can* learn it, you know you just have to, to, to D-I-S-C-I-P-L-I-N-E yourself dear to say bum te bum te bum te bum bum bumm. And the child she did she tried but finally after all this hassle the Director said, NOW SAY IT DEAR and the poor child, thoroughly intimidated, frightened and cringing tried desperately once again but what came out was – you guessed it – bum bum bum bum bumm. Now the Director was beside herself; livid and shouted no nO NO NO NO NO NO. That's *not* right. You just *can't* understand. And just when *I* thought the child would break down or freak out something else happened. Sure enough she finally got very strong, stood there firmly and very definitely said, »Well, I don't care,« she said, »I like it my way,« and I sitting in the back of the room yelled »BRAVO!« and I yelled out for that kid and the director of the school of course was even more furious then. I thought though that that was extremely remarkable for a child in the 8th Grade to know that much about herself and sure enough the child went right ahead and she played the part by uttering in her distinctive though thoroughly monotonous rhythm bum bum bum bum bum bummmm but it worked it really worked because she connected with the audience in a way the other children couldn't imagine and it was because of knowing something special about herself something curiously distinctive and *that* was more important than the old story or more important than Shakespeare. After all. The child being suddenly more comfortable with herself made it possible therefore for the audience to respond authentically.

And now in saying something, something introductory to get something settled or someone adjustered there is going on and getting started. ON WITH THE SHOW! as they used to say in the days that I like to remember driving through tunnels when people used to waltz. And when they square-danced. And when they sat in drawing rooms and played pianos gently to themselves. Then it all changed. Some one got an idea. Things were – no, no I won't say it but, then I see pictures and in the flood of encoding of the detail the voices of beasts the power coming over the walls through them memory as they do slicing the onion the man into (his) particulars and appearing as they do on the trail of a voce singing a void asserting a beach dissolving through his ears of the cave.

# 4. Richard Foreman's review of *Freud*.[16]

Unfortunately not too many people made the long trip to the Brooklyn Academy of Music to see the Byrd Hoffman Foundation's production of Robert Wilson's »The Life and Times of Sigmund Freud.« Unfortunate – because Wilson has created one of the major stage works of the decade, based on an aesthetic quite different from the one that underlies most of the current work of the theatrical avant-garde.

Up until now, leading theoreticians and practitioners of theatre have seen its procedure as a series of strategies designed to manipulate audiences in various predetermined, aimed-at-ways (to translate an idea into »stage terms,« to evoke a specific emotion in response to a specific object, etc.). Wilson is one of a small number of artists who seem to have applied a very different aesthetic to theatre – one current among advanced painters, musicians, dancers, and film-makers – a non-manipulative aesthetic which would see art create a »field« situation within which the spectator can examine himself (as perceptor) in relation to the »discoveries« the artist has made within his medium, then presented to the spectator with maximum lucidity (the specific »aesthetic« emotion of lucidity replacing the more melodramatic emotions of both daily life and most theatre).

Wilson also seems to transcend the popular notion of theatre as universally centered upon the talents of the specially trained and developed performer, and returns us to a healthier »compositional« theatre in which the directorial effort is not a straining after more and more intense »expression« of predetermined material, but is a sweet and powerful »placing« of various found and invented stage objects and actions – so placed and interwoven as to »show« at each moment as many of the implications and multi-level relations between objects and effects as possible.

The play itself proceeds as a series of »tableaux vivants,« in silence or against occasional sound backgrounds. Act one is a sort of beach scene with real sand covering the vast Brooklyn Academy stage, a cloud-flecked sky behind. Performers start slowly crossing the stage, performing simple activities like sowing seed, running, crawling over the sand, as if the »cells,« the building blocks of life (simple bodily resources), are laid out for us. A big turtle is slowly pulled across the

16 Village Voice, 1/1/70. Copyright by Richard Foreman.

stage. Freud and his wife walk across the sand, and what is slowly developed is a profound sense of the *true* rhythm of life, which builds not through the exercising of the will in moments of crisis and decision, but in the slow accretions that are spun around the human animal as his body and mind chew and re-chew on the materials of his mental and physical space. (And Freud walks through, musing on this slow accretion!) The act ends with one of the performance's many fantastic images: as performers start whirling and kicking up sand, we see Wilson himself as an over-stuffed black mammy – suddenly, fantastic! – joined by a chorus of 20 or 30 over-stuffed mammies (they look like birds with puffed-out bosoms and asses), and they all shuffle over the sand as the sky darkens.

Act two, a vast drawing room with an up-center entrance through which, at long intervals, people enter – I mean people! not *performers*! A collection of all shapes, sizes, ages. They really *walk* across the stage, and *plop* down into chairs, and one realizes that few directors have ever before composed their stage time-space so that bodies and persons emerged as the impenetrable (holy) objects they really are, rather than the usual virtuoso tools used to project some play's predetermined energies and meanings. Then more impenetrable objects and acts – 30 foot-high hairy animal legs stride across the stage and the assembled guests solemnly file out after the beast. I relate this presentation of the impenetrable (self-sufficient) body and act to Heidegger's profound observations on art: »The earth appears openly illuminated as itself only when it is perceived and preserved as that which is essentially undisclosable.« I think Wilson demonstrates what might be deduced from Heidegger (and Gertrude Stein too) – that profundity and holiness re-enter the theatre through the proper articulation of the landscape aspect of the drama, filling the stage-space with real (i.e., impenetrable) objects in such a way that they *are* impenetrable, and that very *impenetrability* as what satisfies as it produces awe and delight. This is the goal of drama, rather than working on the audience's head and gut with mere »pretend« objects and acts that are little more than stimulants to our habitual, conditioned, emotional patterns and brain-sets.

For me the last act was most powerful of all. Wild animals (15 or so) slowly enter a cave one by one, and lie down in the straw. Beyond the mouth of the cave, in the sunlight, half-naked boys and girls run, exercise, and play. As the animals enter, iron bars slowly fall over the cave opening, separating animals from the world outside.

426

Finally Freud enters, and sits at a little table amidst the resting wild beasts, and a small boy cries at his feet. This takes half an hour or so, and it is slow and gigantic and wonderful, and the emotion that arises in viewing this 20th-century nativity scene is not the emotion that the theatre usually evokes (those emotions that bind us ever more firmly to what we have been conditioned to be) – it rather evokes the whole spectrum of feeling tone that is our biological and spiritual given – and having that whole *spectrum* of feeling awakened in us is the freedom-bestowing aim of art on the highest level.

Wilson's spectacle is one of the masterpieces of the »artist's theatre« which exists almost in secret in this country, and readers of The Voice had better keep their fingers crossed that the Byrd Hoffman Foundation will somehow be able to find the backing to mount another of these gigantic performances. And then they had better make sure they attend – because in this new Aquarian Age, or in the 1970s, or in whatever new era we're coming upon, this is the kind of theatre we need.

## 5. Robert Wilson on his work with Raymond Andrews on *Deafman Glance*, and on getting the play financed.[17]

»Like I'm very, very involved with a child now, he's never been to school – he's 13 years old, he's a black boy and he's totally deaf and uh the same problem again is that there's no way to test this child because uh uh he grew up on farms in Alabama and he uh he has no academic background uh he can not read lips he doesn't hear sound uh so it's very very difficult to to test him and it's also a problem then to educate him cause the schools are so structured when you have to put him in a class – we can't put him in first grade cause he's much more advanced on many levels than a first grader and we can't put him in a seventh grade because he doesn't have the academic information. It's difficult to find a teacher who can work with him and But the interesting thing about that child is that, again, it where he's highly developed – is that his body is so sensitive. I did a piece this weekend in Pennsylvania at the school (George School, New Hope, Pennsylvania) and – he he sang in the, he did several things – but at one time uh there was something to happen on the stage and uh it was important that it happen at that moment – and he was in the back of the auditorium doing something and right away he saw it and I saw him go down to the stage and he went over to the stage and made it happen but he he's so conscious like the body is so conscious – like he knows what's happening behind him all around him – it's – ya know – it it's amazing to watch him dance to – with a record when he doesn't hear the sound and yet he's right with it – the body perceives the sound – you know. (That's strange). It's very strange, the beautiful thing that's happening with him and he sang in *Freud* this last time too. Finally, and it's happening just now in the last six weeks mostly that he's found a release with sound – the sound energy in him that he's expressed himself with sound, just with a voice. And I don't know whether you know much about deaf deaf people but usually the sound is monotone – it's almost all in one range ahhhhhh you know it never varies – and now he's finding sounds all over and it doesn't even sound like a deaf person making sound. And yet, six weeks ago – he's now in school and there's a problem because he's in a school, in a class for handicapped children and they are children ... the teacher is not qualified for hard of hearing or for deaf children, she's her background is for any child that has a handi – is handicapped – well and she finally said well she just couldn't work with him – she felt ... he's, it's a very difficult problem to work with him. And I went to the school, this is in New Jersey, I was

17 From my interviews of him, 1970. – Cf. also the reference to the child that threw a brick through a window in appendix VII: the beginning of Wilson's relation to Andrews.

talking with her and the director of the school and I told them about his singing, what was happening, there was no way for them to – they said, well what does it mean and then – and the director of the school came to a class I have in New Jersey and Raymond sang to the class and the director of the school said, »what is this going to do for him?« There's no way for them somehow to understand and I was I was so amazed that – I mean I don't I can't know what direction it's going in – but in just the fact that he can communicate with his voice, with sound song and and this is the one area cause we, we were told that he would never be able to talk. And that's a fact! I mean because he just started too late in life to learn, he'll never, even if he'd started as an infant his chances of learning words would be very, very slim – but what's happening now is that he's able to express himself, he's able to communicate – with sound, with his voice. (In other words, he doesn't sing words). He doesn't sing words, he just makes sounds and he's now working with a radio, a record-player and I turn it very loud so that he, he feels this vibration and he puts his voice with what he feels here with his ear. But the fact that he's gained confidence, you know, that way, seems to be a break-through.

... he's so amazing to me, his paintings, his drawings are so amazing to me – cause he doesn't talk, he's never been to school, he doesn't hear sound, he hasn't learned to read lips – he – so his way of communicating is a whole other way – the drawings are amazing, and the feelings, the colors that he associates with people – the way the light that's with people – it's very revealing – there's nothing – it's very perceptive – it's a very perceptive way of seeing things and the – the symbols that he associates with people are amazing and where he's found the symbols – and where he even got that information, I don't – I can't understand because it's hard to see it in his environment or in his background. He lived on farms in Louisiana and he was sort of sent from family to family and no one realized that his problem was just a hearing problem – they thought the child was a freak or an idiot – I don't know, it's amazing the wealth of knowledge that he has (How – how does he know?) He developed another sense of seeing-hearing that, that's very amazing – his association with color or light with people is – just amazing, amazing – and he always, if he wants to – if he wants to tell me about someone he doesn't know how to write their name or spell their name he can draw some symbol or some meaning, that you know who that person is or what it is – I mean you, he's got the information there. He's I don't know in that child there's a – there's a great knowledge of a mystical – there is – I don't know it seems to me that – but I don't think that-that, you know – there's a child who is handicapped – I mean –

Throughout, it-a- sort of notes that I've made from, a just thir-fourteen, thirteen year old boy, deaf, that I'm working on, it's about him, images that he's had, I think I talked to you last time about his drawings and the colors – colors, the whole, a lot of his imagery, it sort of, I don't think he understands so much now that we are making them into a theatre thing (?), but like we, there's some sort of exchange of communication about the material and he knows like I'm collecting certain bits of information, which very much come from him, and it's – it's been good for me, because suddenly it's, it's almost like his material and it's not so much mine, and I mean, it is somewhat mine, it's interesting, it's like, it's almost in some ways like, I tried to explain that to him, so maybe he'd understand, it's almost like a script, you know, I feel like I'm almost dealing with say this, it's not mine because it's almost like, I almost think, well is that really Raymond, you know, or something like that (Yah) and it's a respect to him, in-in his sensibility, and his way of seeing and trying not to, like, you know say, this is, I mean it's not like my idea so, I mean, it is in a way, I like that, it's (Uhum) I almost find that I have another sort of freedom, (laugh) (Yah) You know, because it's almost like, it's his material almost – to me – I'm-I'm helping him – arrange (?), I don't know, it's this is a crazy way to work with (Yah) it's given, I think, the-the most positive thing is, it's given me a perspective of the material too, I'm sort of detached, I mean in a funny way, more so than say when I did the *King of Spain*, when I thought that it was all coming from inside of me, that sort of thing, with this I feel like I'm working with that child, it's also, I'm very excited too, because he doesn't yet understand, I haven't explained to him so much that, that I'm working on a theater thing, but he knows that we're working on an idea (Uhum) and he talks to me about it and he brings me information about it, and it's amazing to me. I-I keep thinking what's, what-what image does he have in his head, or what idea, or maybe he doesn't have any – about why we're gathering this information or what it's about, but it's, it's a beautiful, ah, thing, that's happening because he's in the spirit of it, and he knows it's happening, he feels already the generating points of this thing being made, and that he brings information to me about it, it's, it's a very interesting kind of work (Are you working towards something?) Towards performance, and-and it's like, I mean, very clear, but it's, and we almost, a lot of it is me because, first of all I'm very close with him so like, whenever, like when I was working on *Freud* suddenly he was making drawings of animals, and he was building things about animals, and, or he would do a – – – – – in the imagery of the piece he was-he was into, it was like his image was so, it was very close, and sort of tied there, but so-a-a lot of his images are very close to me I guess that's why – – – – – but, it's, it's like a collaboration, yah, very strange, (What, I mean, what would you be thinking of there, a certain mood, or a certain effect, or, idea or?) Well, again, it's, I think the reason that I've sort of worked with him is that it's very visual, his communication is very visual, if he wants to tell me something he'll draw a picture of it, if he has a feeling about someone he does it sort of in color, and he sees things very, there's a lot of a person in that, you can understand a person from – say like a color or a light or, I don't know, something is very very revealing about them, but – – – – – so, that's how we're sort of making the piece, like I've taken things that he's done and I'm sort of now structuring, arranging images and characters (Ah, structuring now, what do you mean?) Yah, well, I guess that is again very very personal like, most times people don't see it, but like I'm very interested in the way things fit together, you know, what they seem like next to each other or against each other or with each other or what happens in time, like all of that is my work, like he's given me the information and I'm sort of arranging it now – putting it together – finally, th-th-that's my sensibility or that's my (pause) Also, I think too, once it's done, it's going like to do something for him or in some way, like, I think I almost – – – – – see the possibilities of, of I don't know, or maybe like, I don't know – Almost I want to tell him too, like I, 'cause I could, I could explain to him about it, I'm always waiting for him to say, oh – – – – – maybe he won't (Do these things relate to one another, I mean do they relate, between you and him, as they come up?) They relate to things we've done together, ah, they relate to things that we've done in other theater work, they relate to things that are very personal to me, but the interesting thing is, and now of course, I'm doing a lot of eliminating, they seem to be of one air, of one family, one nature (That's what I was wondering, I mean, if you ask him something, would he feel that it related to something else you've mentioned?) Well, somehow, it all started, Stefan I had – I've a file and, ah, I had Raymond's drawings or something, in a cabinet, he knew that there's that file, he liked to put things in that, and he knew that also I was selective about what I put in it (Uhum) but he would always give me paintings or drawings or and some of them I would put elsewhere, some of them I'd throw away, ah, but some of them I would put in that folder, and he knew 'cause one day like he, like I knew that was going through his head, why, why these (Yah) and then I think maybe he even realized it, like that there was something about that selection, and I wasn't even so aware of it at the time, it was like of one nature or of one quality or something, and then he would give me things to put in that file, like, you know, like this one is gonna go in that file, that I would like it for that file (laugh) and then, I started making drawings, I made some, I was, I went to California and New Mexico, I wrote him letters and also I made some drawings, and when I came back I put those, and he'd save some of those things and I'd put some of those things I'd written to him in the file and then I had done some things on my own that I put in the file and he saw them, and then he saw, saw my ideas with his ideas and, ah, and now almost every time he comes he's like, I know he's been thinking about it, 'cause I can see like, he's almost like developing information that's there (Yah) (Can you say what constitutes the unity of that file?) I don't know, I-I it's hard to say because it's (pause) well we (pause) a lot of things. He's very involved with an ox, for some reason. It's almost like, – he's drawn an ox, and something about this image that keeps coming back, he almost for-for a time, he almost used it like a signature, he almost signed things with an ox, ───── it's like other things were happening, with this ox, and people or characters or other things, but somehow always the ox was there, so suddenly there's, that was one of the key elements in the story, and we almost like to have this, like that's almost a symbol, for like this information, this material that we exchange, this ox, and I don't know where he got that or how that came at all . . .

(What does the loft thing hinge on?) On money, if I can get it ───── and pay for it ───── someone wanted, a producer called me, wanted to, it's a very freaky thing that happened, to-to do, say this new piece, like off Broadway theater or something, but he didn't seem right and it's like I couldn't talk to him like I'm talking to you about how I'm working with this child, you know, and I thought, suddenly it's like a whole other sort of element interfering, maybe, I don't know, maybe I'm wrong, I was afraid that, maybe it was interfering with what I was trying to do with that child, like that is, means more to me than, having a show on, you know, like ───── I knew that, a, suddenly I realized that I couldn't talk to him and that there was, it was gonna suddenly put all sorts of pressures that are not there (?) and, that, they shouldn't be my instincts told me this and ───── something else was . . . more important. So I-I don't know. It was interesting, too, to think about that kid, maybe showing all, – I mean, they're not interested in these things – they're like he wants – he wants like to make money and it like – this whole thing and it's – – I-I-I don't know people like that, so – I haven't had that experience yet, eh, I just said, I tried to like, talk to him – I just said look here, this is what I'm really interested in – and like I'm working this way and like, it doesn't mean anything to you – or – and, this is what's happening and that there's sort of . . . information – I think an artist to start working – and that I do want to work and about this piece, and (pause) I could tell, he listened but he wasn't at all sensitive, yah, it was like another sort of thing happening, – and that, – maybe it's not possible to show the work, I don't know, there's, there's (pause)« (Interv. w/Wilson, 1970)

## 6. Louis Aragon on the Paris production of *Deafman Glance*.[18]

## Lettre ouverte à André Breton
*sur Le Regard du Sourd l'art, la science et la liberté*

Mon cher André,
il y avait peu de chance que je t'écrive plus jamais une lettre. Voilà
près de quarante ans que cela ne m'est pas arrivé. Je ne l'ai pas fait
*toi vivant,* et après . . . Je me souviens de ma colère dans un pays
lointain, et socialiste par-dessus le marché, quand un inconnu m'ap-
porta une lettre pour Eluard mort, me suppliant de la déposer sur son
tombeau. Ce n'est pas ce que je fais avec toi maintenant. Je t'écris
parce que je ne t'ai pas écrit *avant,* bien que tous les signes étaient
qu'à l'automne de 1965 nous aurions pu nous retrouver, au moins une
fois, quelque part, dans un de ces lieux d'autrefois qui furent mar-
qués du miracle, un café par chance demeuré lui-même (*Tout va
bien* n'existait déjà plus et *La Régence,* où Nadja t'avait vainement
attendu, avait tant changé que l'ombre de Diderot l'a fuie), ou au
*Palais des Miracles* qui existe encore au Musée Grévin, ou sur la place
Maubert d'où Etienne Dolet s'envola, ou sur le Pont des Suicides aux
Buttes-Chaumont . . . Cela ne s'est pas fait, mais le miracle s'est
produit, celui que nous attendions, dont nous parlions (te souviens-tu
de cette promenade le long des Tuileries où tu m'as dit: *Si jamais
nous cessions de croire au miracle . . .*), le miracle s'est produit quand
depuis longtemps j'avais cessé d'y croire. Ces jours-ci. Dans un théâtre
qui fut l'ancienne Gaîté-Lyrique, et te rappelles-tu ce long séjour
dans le square, devant la Gaîté, un jour de mai 1918 avant qu'on
nous sépare?
Ce devait être un dimanche, le silence était alors absolu. Pas une
voiture à cheval, pas un taxi qui tousse. Tu me dis: »Ecoute le silence,«
et nous avons ri pour tous les chevaux absents de hennir à cette idée
d'écouter le silence . . . soudain, avec le plus grand sérieux, tu m'as
dit encore: »C'est que nous sommes devenus sourds pour croire ainsi
Paris muet . . .« Eh bien, c'est là précisément que s'est passé le miracle.

18 Les Lettres Francaises. June 2-8, 1971. Copyright 1971, L. Aragon.

433

Le silence. La pièce qu'on jouait, mais était-ce une pièce, et la jouait-on? qui? s'appelait *Le Regard du Sourd*, mon ami. On y arrivait de l'enfer de Paris, du vacarme du boulevard Sébastopol, et tout d'un coup on n'avait plus, ou peu, besoin de ses oreilles. Le monde d'un enfant sourd s'ouvrait à nous comme une bouche muette. Plus de quatre heures, nous allions habiter cet univers où, en l'absence des mots, des sons, soixante personnages n'auront de parole que bouger. Je veux te le dire tout de suite, André, parce que même si ceux-là qui ont inventé ce spectacle n'en savent rien, c'est pour toi qu'ils le jouent, pour toi qui l'aurais aimé comme moi, à la folie. Car j'en suis fou. Ecoute ce que je dis à ceux-là qui ont des oreilles, semble-t-il, pour ne pas entendre: *Je n'ai jamais rien vu de plus beau en ce monde depuis que j'y suis né, jamais jamais aucun spectacle n'est arrivé à la cheville de celui-ci, parce qu'il est à la fois la vie éveillée et la vie aux yeux clos, la confusion qui se fait entre le monde de tous les jours et le monde de chaque nuit, la réalité mêlée au rêve, l'inexplicable de tout dans le regard du sourd.*

Il y a des gens qui disent de ce grand Jeu du Silence, de ce miracle des hommes et non des dieux, que c'est là du surréalisme de pacotille, du surréalisme de vitrine, est-ce que je sais! Parce qu'à l'heure qu'il est le surréalisme est sur toutes les langues, on dit d'une baraque un peu baroque que c'est une maison surréaliste, tout le monde veut, les vieux de notre temps, et d'autres qui ont surgi plus tard du terreau que nous avions laissé, tout le monde veut être, se dit surréaliste, et Dieu merci! les sourds ne les entendent pas. Le spectacle de Bob Wilson (qu'il me pardonne de préférer le diminutif à son prénom), le spectacle de Bob Wilson qui nous vient d'Iowa n'est pas du tout du surréalisme, comme il est aux gens commode de dire, mais il est ce que nous autres, de qui le surréalisme est né, nous avons rêvé qu'il surgisse après nous, au-delà de nous, et j'imagine l'exaltation que tu aurais montrée à presque chaque instant de ce chef-d'œuvre de la surprise, où l'art de l'homme dépasse à chaque respiration du silence l'art supposé du Créateur. Peut-être aurais-tu dit de ce produit de l'avenir comme tu le fis des magiciens passés, des *Nuits* d'Young, de Swift, de Sade, de Chateaubriand, de Constant, de Hugo, de Desbordes-Valmore, d'Aloysius Bertrand, d'Alphonse Rabbe, etc., qu'ils étaient non point surréalistes, mais surréalistes dans quelque chose, aussi bien Edgar Allan Poe que Baudelaire ou Rimbaud, Mallarmé, Jarry... et tiens, le plus beau, le plus proche après tout de ce spectacle, c'est ce que tu as trouvé pour Germain Nouveau, disant qu'il était *surréaliste dans le baiser*, et tous les peintres mis en note de

Seurat à André Masson ... mais je veux trop dire pour en venir à jurer Dieu que tu aurais écrit que Bob Wilson est, serait, sera (il aurait fallu le futur) surréaliste par le silence, bien qu'on puisse aussi le prétendre de tous les peintres, mais Wilson c'est le mariage du geste et du silence, du mouvement et de l'inouï.

Il n'est pas possible que tu ne voies pas cela, André, pas possible que tu n'entendes pas cette prodigieuse absence du bruit que très tard dans le spectacle vient encore souligner une musique souvent au loin, faible et sans rapport avec ce parler du corps qui n'a nul besoin de l'oreille. Ah, je pense à ce moment, on est dans un pays de mines, avec un terril à l'horizon, mille choses qui se passent, ici même aboutit comme si nous étions chez William Blake une sorte de bouche de l'enfer, mais dans un coin sans aucun souci de la foule qui s'agite autour de lui, pour lui seul, un garçon demi-nu danse à contre-temps des autres, pas à contre-temps, puis-qu'il n'en tient simplement pas compte, et ne s'occupe ni de la place où il est sur la scène, ni de ceux qui passent, pour une danse de son propre plaisir, une improvisation continuelle là-bas, à droite, une sorte de satisfaction prise de lui-même, comme un rire qu'on entendrait pas.

Imagine-toi qu'il y a aussi le problème du temps, avec l'être humain pour horloge: ces garçons-là et ces filles qui passent à la limite profonde de la scène et de l'inconnu, est-ce une plage, un champ de courses ... comme de simples coureurs de gauche à droite, de droite à gauche, et perpétuel retour, et qui sont l'horloge du temps humain; ou bien ces hommes-poissons rampant sur le ventre à l'avant-scène, les coudes pour nageoires, d'un côté à l'autre du théâtre, et recommencer; ou encore le temps-objet marqué par une chaise qui met plus de quatre heures à descendre des cintres au bout d'une corde. Eh bien, non ce n'est pas, Messieurs, *du* surréalisme, c'est-à-dire pour vous une chose classée, un objet de thèse, d'enseignement, de Sorbonne, non, non et non! Mais c'est le rêve de ceux que nous fûmes, c'est *l'avenir* que nous prédisions.

Si je voulais, comment le faire, c'est impossible, même appelant à l'aide Raymond Roussel et Lewis Carroll, pour donner idée, si je voulais absolument trouver un précédent à ce spectacle, il me faudrait transcrire un texte, André, dont tu t'es une fois servi.[19] Il s'agit d'un passage de *Ma vie*, de Jérôme Cardan, où ce grand mathématicien raconte les rêves de son enfance, quand son père lui imposait de rester au lit *jusqu'à la troisième heure du jour*, et qu'il apercevait se

19 Dans ce Cahier consacré au rêve (Cahiers G.L.M.) de 1938 *dont les documents sont dits assemblés par André Breton.*

mouvant de tout petits anneaux d'airain montant en demicercle de l'angle droit du lit pour disparaître vers la gauche. Mais, dit Cardan, *j'avais le temps d'apercevoir, des citadelles, des maisons, des animaux, des chevaux avec leurs cavaliers, des herbes, des arbres, des instruments de musique, des théâtres, des individus de différents aspects habillés d'étranges vêtements, mais je voyais surtout des sonneurs de trompettes; les trompettes paraissaient résonner, pourtant je n'entendais rien. J'apercevais aussi des soldats, des foules, des formes que je n'avais jamais vues, des prairies, des monts, des forêts et beaucoup d'autres choses dont je ne me souviens plus maintenant ...*

Même si ce sont sur tout autres objets que se pose *Le Regard du Sourd*, rien n'y ressemble plus que ce catalogue des rêves qui sont *les carrés négatifs des réalités*. Tu m'excuseras de chercher référence à nouveau chez Cardan, parlant de toi, parlant du ... mais je suis bête: tu nous avais déjà quitté, tu n'as pas connu ce texte écrit en 1966. J'y prenais l'image du *Poisson soluble* qui est tienne pour l'exemple même du carré négatif en poésie. Eh bien, dans le spectacle du *Théâtre de la Musique*, tout est »poisson soluble« jusqu'à ces mesureurs du temps à qui un personnage de pêcheur à la ligne jette sans jamais les prendre l'hameçon. Sauf qu'ils sont hommes de chaïr, et la différence est là, que les termes de la métaphore sont plus encore que décors et costumes des personnages vivants.

Aussi bien n'en suis-je revenu demander autorité à Jérôme Cardan que pour une raison bien différente d'il y a cinq ans, comme *l'occasion* en est differente. Je disais alors, parlant du roman pour ma part, et je défendais à la fois le réalisme et le surréalisme, leur donnant pour avenir *l'inimaginable*, mais autant te citer ce que n'ont pas lu tes yeux:

*Peut-être (disais-je) sommes-nous arrivés à l'heure où le roman doit sauter le fleuve infernal et pénétrer dans le domaine de l'inimaginable, se faire conjecture afin de contribuer au progrès de l'esprit humain, hâter la transformation de l'homme et de la nature. Peut-être sommes-nous à l'heure d'un grand défi, où le roman osera ce que ne peut encore qu'apercevoir la science la plus évoluée, la plus avancée. Peut-être que c'est lui qui va sonner dans l'avenir les trompettes qui font s'écrouler les murs, les limites, et que, par lui, nous allons pénétrer dans l'homme, cet imprenable Jéricho, plus loin que l'homme n'ira jamais dans les astres ...*

Je parlais pour mon saint, dans les murs encore debout du sanctuaire. Voici qu'accès nous est *ailleurs* donné dans la citadelle, sans un mot, dans le monde sourd de Bob Wilson et d'un petit enfant. Le spectacle, car comment le nommer? ce n'est ni le ballet, ni le mimodrame, ni l'opéra (encore que ce soit peut-être cette étrange chose, un *opéra sourd*, comme si nous étions à un moment du monde analogue à ce seizième siècle italien qui avait vu Cardan et voyait naître, de Caccini à Monteverde, *l'opera serio*, le baroque de l'oreille, passant du contrepoint vocal des chants religieux à cet art nouveau, profane en son essence) … le spectacle fait appel aux moyens nouveaux de la lumière et de l'ombre, aux machines réinventées d'avant le jansénisme des yeux, si bien que la chaisehorloge qui mesure verticalement la durée du spectacle est comme une mécanique à remplacer le balancier, fait humain, des coureurs dans le fond de la scène. Tout semble être critique de ce à quoi nous avons habitüde. Tout est expérience. Jusqu'au jeu laissé libre à ceux que je n'appellerais ni danseurs ni acteurs, car ils sont cela et autre chose: expérimentateurs d'une science encore sans nom. Celle du corps et de sa liberté. Le *spectacle* raconte ici l'histoire d'un enfant déficient, et par cela devance en ce domaine où elle piétine la science médicale, il *écrit* sur l'espace avec ces caractères mouvants, hommes et-femmes, et la couleur y joue, les noirs au milieu des blancs et des monstres, y ont part prépondérante. Le *spectacle* est celui d'une guérison, la nôtre, de »l'art figé,« de »l'art appris,« de »l'art dicté.« Il relève d'une science particulière, celle des probabilités (j'ai l'envie de dire et *des improbabilités*). Il nous guérit, nous dans les loges, le parterre, d'être comme tout le monde, de ne pas avoir les dons divins du sourd, il nous fait sourds par le silence et, magnanime, de temps en temps nous rend l'oreille pour la musique, on cette voix soufflée des coulisses qui rythme une étrange et merveilleuse valse (ainsi) de Strauss en comptant les temps: one – two – three – one – two – three – one – two – three – one – two – three … peut-être un quart d'heure à la fin de l'acte premier.

Et j'ai l'envie d'écrire, ô tentation bleue du papier blanc! que le voisinage étrange (un baroque de l'avenir) de la science et de l'art est la clef même de cette liberté que Robert Wilson réclame pour son art. Il y a (j'entendais cela ces derniers jours à propos de l'émission de Nicolas Schöffer à la télévision, Nicolas Schöffer en un certain sens qui est une sorte de de Bob Wilson en son domaine du merveilleux futur) bien des gens, et pas nécessairement des sots ou des monstres, qui redoutent la substitution de la science à l'art, la »robotisation« de l'humanité dans ce qui est sa particularité sublime, et d'une certaine façon, je les comprends de redouter que change ce qu'ils aiment. Comme tous ceux-là qui pleurent que la lune a, ces derniers temps, perdu son mystère. Je les comprends, mais je ne les approuve pas.

Toute conquête de la science est un triomphe de l'humain, de l'homme. Sa liberté s'exerce au-delà du champ qui était jusqu'alors le sien: comme les canalisations le relèvent de la nécessité d'aller au puits, et ne regrettons pas la beauté du geste des femmes quil faisaient remonter le seau du fond de la terre. L'homme chaque jour commence au-delà de lui-même, au delà de son passé, de ses erreurs et de ses découvertes. Je dis cela, et pour la cybernétique, et les ordinateurs, et la matrise de l'atome, et cette chose encore sans nom, la beauté nouvelle, dont sans aucun doute pour moi le spectacle dont je parle est la première aube. L'homme part de ce qu'il invente. Et ce n'est pas la perversion qui peut être faite de *l'usage* des machines, qui doit nous détourner d'elles ou comme, au temps de la première révolution scientifique, entraîner les plus malheureux des hommes à briser les machines qui ne sont pas leurs ennemies, mais le point de départ de leur liberté. Un spectacle comme *Le Regard du Sourd* est une extraordinaire machine de la liberté. C'est comme tel que je supplie d'y aller tous ceux qui voient et entendent, tous ceux dont le cœur bat au seul nom de la liberté.

Jamais comme ici, d'un trou noir de la salle, je n'avais éprouvé, comme devant le spectacle de Robert Wilson, que si jamais le monde enfin change et cesse d'être cet enfer qu'on voit au bout de près de quatre heures sur la scène, et c'est l'enfer ou c'est la mine du terril des Intermèdes, si jamais le monde change et les hommes deviennent comme ce danseur dont je parlais, libres, libres, libres . . . c'est par la liberté qu'il aura changé. La liberté, l'éblouissante liberté de l'âme et du corps.

*Aragon*

P.S. – Tout ceci, André, à toi s'adresse, peut-être à toi seul, et c'est peut-être de ma part utopie que j'en fasse une lettre *ouverte* et pourtant voilà: je l'ouvre.

(L. Aragon, Les Lettres Francaises, June 2-8, 1971.
Copyright L. Aragon 1971.)

## 7. Wilson's program notes to the first production of *Deafman Glance*.[20]

»AND THE FOURTH, THE DIMENSION OF STILINESS
AND THE POWER OVER WILD BEASTS . . .«
Ezra Pound

»IOWA CITY NOTES: DECEMBER 1970

It was two years ago September. The child threw a brick thru a window as I was going to an ART class in Summit on my way I saw the judge about to hit him as the mother pressed her hand against his head I crawl on his back to relieve the pain he was ten years old September. The line out my window leads to the Sun, the ox, the child and to all of us becoming worms. At Pratt I wrote my thesis on designing an imaginary cathedral or a fewture city perhaps. Then there was a murder, a murder in the eyes at the top of the cathedral two years ago September as the red dog howled into the moon light son notta wink! Only the bones can tell.

Running together. we caught each other falling standing still still we fell into each other falling into the wall walling again and again and again again I talked of Isadora Duncan.

»WHERE A HUNDRED LITTLE GIRLS SHALL BE TRAINED IN MY ART, WHICH THEY IN TURN WILL BETTER. IN THIS SCHOOL I SHALL NOT TEACH THE CHILDREN TO IMITATE MY MOVEMENTS, BUT SHALL TEACH THEM TO MAKE THEIR OWN . . . I SHALL HELP THEM TO DEVELOP THOSE MOVE-MENTS WHICH ARE NATURAL TO THEM. AND SO I SAY IT IS THE DUTY OF THE DANCE OF THE FUTURE TO GIVE FIRST TO THE YOUNG ARTISTS WHO COME TO ITS DOOR FOR INSTRUCTION FREER AND (MORE) BEAUTIFUL BODIES-AND TO INSTRUCT THEM IN MOVEMENTS THAT ARE IN FULL HARMONY WITH NATURE . . . THE DANCER OF THE FUTURE WILL BE ONE WHOSE BODY AND SOUL HAVE GROWN SO HARMONIOUSLY TOGETHER THAT THE NATURAL LANGUAGE OF THAT SOUL WILL HAVE BECOME THE MOVEMENT OF THE BODY . . . HER DANCE WILL BELONG TO NO NATION-ALITY BUT TO ALL HUMANITY.«

Then I read Stein to class then gave a reading list:

Gurdjioff
Stein

20 »Performed by the Byrd Hoffmann School of Byrds in association with the Center for New Performing Arts, University of Iowa. December 15 and 16, 1970, Iowa City, Iowa.«

Duncan
Jill Johnston
Angela Davis
Langer
National Enquirer
Cassirer
Houdini
Edgar Cayce

And how it hurt seeing the dance program wishing the fishing the kids kidding could for a minute read the list knowing that we all cannot being kidded liking like Sheryl take taking five minutes to put on the glove only her fingers moved waiting motionless for ten minutes waiting to begin the film. Geeze, she's a star!

And Andy just brought the Requiem by chance he said, knowing all along he would add the final peace Art then said he would follow following few fewer futures. HOPE has a vision. There's a boy in the East seven tonight midnight that will lead the world for a few times. It's in the stars an old woman wrote on the wall at the bus station not by chance fewture following few fews fuses. S. K. moved six hours continuously while we sold Art Cindy wrote of her piece in the Orange state they were walking hands, turned upheld, held in Circles for seven hours thru the night Terry writes he's getting a piece of his too and may make a presentation in the spring, he's not only 14. No doubt about it, he's a star! There are 14 cows out my window. Only their heads move. Jerry wrote me of a beautiful dream. The lion's leader leads to the Sun, the East, the son, the child. The broken arched windowed woman's house sinks as the deaf child sings an onion sliced in two (his) particulars. a don't a men.

Byrd hoffMAN
(ten years ago woooooooooooooo)

The original theatre of the City of New York.
From the mid-60s to the mid-70s.

Book 1. The theatre of visions: Robert Wilson.
Book 2. Queer theatre.
Book 3. Richard Foreman's diary theatre. Theatre as personal phenomenology of mind.
Book 4. Morality plays. Peter Schumann's Bread and Puppet theatre.
Book 5. Theatre as psycho-therapy for performers.
    A. Joe Chaikin's Open Theatre. The Becks' Living Theatre.
    B. Richard Schechner's Performance Group. Andre Gregory's Manhattan Repertory Company. With notes on Grotowski and Andre Serban.
Book 6. The 1970s hermetic theatre of the performing director. Jared Bark. Stuart Sherman. John Zorn. Melvin Andringa. With appendices on Ann Wilson, Robert Whitman and Wilford Leach.
Book 7. Theatre as collective improvisation. The Mabou Mines.
Book 8. Black theatre and music. With notes on the Duo Theatre and M. van Peebles.
Book 9. Dance. Merce Cunningham, Yvonne Rainer, Meredith Monk, Douglas Dunn. With a note on Ping Chong.